INTRODUCTION TO

CRIMINAL JUSTICE

Kendall Hunt
publishing company

GARY WILL

Cover © Shutterstock.com

Kendall Hunt
publishing company

www.kendallhunt.com
Send all inquiries to:
4050 Westmark Drive
Dubuque, IA 52004-1840

ISBN: 978-1-5249-5079-8

Published in the United States of America

CONTENTS

© Guido Vrola, 2011. Used under license from Shutterstock, Inc.

CHAPTER 1

Introduction to the Justice System

KEY TERMS

Crime Control Model
Corrections
Due Process Model
Herbert L. Packer
Justice
Jails
Law Enforcement
Police
Prisons
Social Justice
Social Contract
Society

CHAPTER OBJECTIVES

After reading this chapter you will be able to:

1. Understand the concept of justice as it applies to the criminal justice system in America.
2. Explain the notion of social justice and how it varies within the different societies in which we live.
3. Explain what the social contract is.
4. Compare and contrast the due process model and the crime control model.
5. List the basic components of the criminal justice system.

Chapter Overview

The criminal justice system in the United States is built upon the concept of justice. The notion of justice will be looked at from several different perspectives. This chapter will discuss justice in terms of the traditional way that it is applied to our overall justice system. We will also look at the concept of social justice and how it affects the different societies that we all live in. The principle of the social contract will also be discussed in this chapter.

There are two models that help explain the differences in ideologies within the criminal justice process in the United States. These models, which were developed in 1964 by Herbert L. Packer,[1] are the due process model and the crime control model. We will see that there are strong advocates and opponents for both of these models and we will look at the positions of both. The chapter will also give a brief overview of the three components of the criminal justice system: the police, corrections, and the courts.

The Concept of Justice

Justice While the term justice can have a variety of meanings, for criminal justice it is best described as fundamental fairness.

A discussion about the criminal justice system must start with a basic understanding of the term **justice**. Justice has come to have different meanings depending on how it is used and what it is associated with. The New Oxford American Dictionary[2] defines justice as "the quality of being fair and reasonable." Justice can also be described as fundamental fairness. Aristotle said that justice is equality for equals and wrote that: "Injustice arises when equals are treated unequally and also when unequals are treated equally."[3] President Theodore Roosevelt gave a very good summary of the term justice when he said:

Theodore Roosevelt

> "No man is above the law and no man is below it; nor do we ask any man's permission when we require him to obey it."
>
> PRESIDENT THEODORE ROOSEVELT—1903[4]

What President Roosevelt was saying was that all persons, regardless of their status in society, are expected to obey all of the laws within our society. In order to have true justice, it must be administered fairly and equally to everyone.

Social justice is more of a concept than an actual occurrence. Social justice varies from society to society depending on the perception of what constitutes right from wrong within that society. Social justice can also change over time within the same society as the mores and moral values change. Since social justice deals with the fundamental notion of right and wrong as defined by a society, it can also vary within a society.

Social Justice The concept of social justice varies from society to society and deals with the perception of what constitutes right from wrong within that society.

Society A society is a structured group of people with similar traits (traditions, culture, nationality, moral values). We all live in several different societies at the same time.

We all live in several different societies simultaneously, each with their own set of values. We all live in the global society of the world where the most basic values of right and wrong are universal. This would include such things as murder and the stealing of property that belongs to others. We also live in the society of the United States, which is one of the most multi-cultural societies in the world. Since our country is represented by so many different cultural and ethnic backgrounds, it can arguably be said that we cannot come to a consensus on very many important issues. The federal government, through our legislative branch (the House of Representatives and the Senate), makes the criminal laws that affect everyone in the country. These laws, at least theoretically, reflect a consensus of the moral values of all of our citizens because they are written by elected officials who represent the populace. The moral values of the country change over time and are reflected by changes in our laws. It should be noted that the values of individual political parties have a direct influence on the types of laws that are passed, but again, the party in power changes as the values of the country change and new representatives are elected.

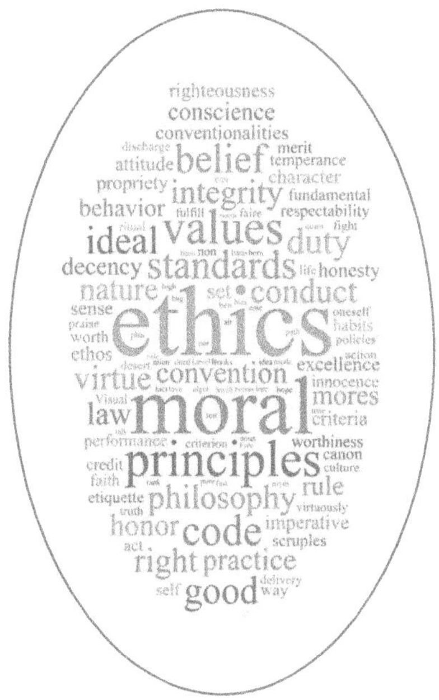

We also live within the society of the individual State that we reside in. Although the overall moral values of each state generally reflect the values of the United States as a whole, there are distinctive differences that can be found. What may be legal in one state may be illegal in another. Marijuana laws are one example of

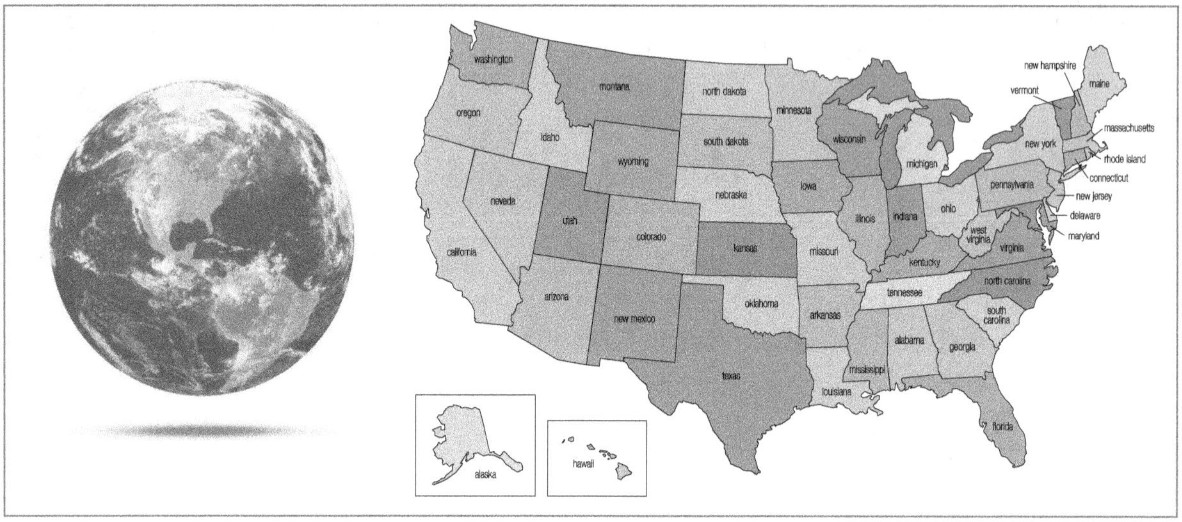

Globe © Alex Staroseltsev, map © jamie cross, 2011. Used under license from Shutterstock, Inc.

this concept because they vary tremendously in different parts of the country. Recreational use of marijuana has been legislated as legal in several states, a citation offense in some, a misdemeanor in others, and is still a felony in several. The consensus of the citizens within each state is what motivates differences in the laws. Another example of how moral values can vary from state to state would be the State of Nevada. Nevada is the only state that allows for legalized prostitution in the form of brothels in some parts of the state. All of the other forty-nine states have laws making all forms of prostitution illegal.

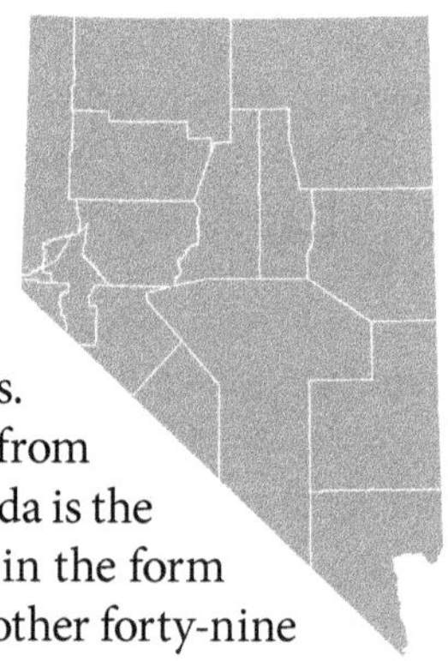

© jamie cross, 2011. Used under license from Shutterstock, Inc.

The smaller the society that we are a part of, the more agreement there is in relation to our moral values. The society of our local community is more harmonized as to our moral values than the larger societies, and local laws reflect this consistency. The smallest society that we are a part of is the most influential and generally the most cohesive when it comes to our moral values. This is the society of our family. The family is where we shape our individual values and they are influenced by the way we are raised. Our overall perception of what constitutes right and wrong is fashioned and reinforced by our parents or guardians as we grow up. While these values can change over time, they influence the decisions we make throughout our lives and ultimately become an integral part of the larger societies that we become a component of.

© Liv friis-larsen, 2011. Used under license from Shutterstock, Inc.

To summarize, we can see that the notion of justice in the United States is greatly influenced by the diverse ideals that make up the social justice concepts within the various societies that we live. It is therefore critical that our criminal justice system remain fluid and adaptable to keep up with the changes that take place within the different levels of the societies in which we all live.

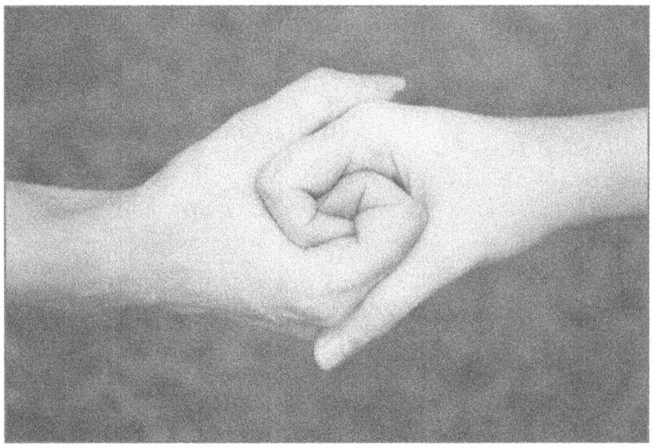

© Losevsky Pavel, 2011. Used under license from Shutterstock, Inc.

Social Contract

The term social contract refers to an implied agreement between citizens and their government as a way of maintaining social order. The people make a trade-off by giving up some of their rights to a government in return for being able to benefit from a greater social order. The concept of the social contract provides the rationale behind the historically important notion that legitimate state authority must be derived from the consent of the governed.[5] To put this in simple terms, the concept of social justice means that all of the citizens of a society agree to allow the government to represent them and to make the laws of that society. In return, each citizen is expected to obey those laws in order to obtain the benefits provided by the formation of social structures.

Social Contract The social contract is an implied agreement between citizens and their government as a way of maintaining social order.

The government establishes laws that represent the norms of the society, and any person who violates any of these laws violates the social contract and must be punished in order to restore order.

Due Process vs. Crime Control

© Onur ERSIN, 2011. Used under license from Shutterstock, Inc.

VERSUS

© Scott Rothstein, 2011. Used under license from Shutterstock, Inc.

Herbert L. Packer Herbert L. Packer (1925–1972) was a Professor of Law at Stanford University who wrote the paper "Two Models of the Criminal Process" in 1964.

In 1964, Herbert L. Packer published a paper entitled "Two Models of the Criminal Process."[6] This paper has become a standard among criminal justice scholars and students in the debate over the best way to control crime and criminals within our society. The two models are called the "crime control

Crime Control Model This model is based on the proposition that crime must be controlled at all cost in order to have a safe society. In this model the rights of the many (society) outweigh the rights of the few (those who are accused of crime).

Due Process Model This model is designed to protect the rights of the individual who is accused of a crime and make sure that all legal resources and protections are available and utilized. In this model the rights of the accused outweigh the rights of the many (society).

model" and the "due process model." The **crime control model** is based on the proposition that crime must be controlled at all costs in order to have a safe society. Packer says of this model that: "The failure of law enforcement to bring criminal conduct under tight control is viewed as leading to the breakdown of public order and thence to the disappearance of an important condition of human freedom."[7] The **due process model** is designed to protect the rights of the individual who is accused of a crime and make sure that all legal resources and protections are available and utilized. These rights and protections are designed to present a formidable obstacle to the government and the criminal justice system when trying to prosecute those charged with a criminal act.

The basic premise of the crime control model is speed and efficiency. This model says that it is more important to protect society as a whole against the injury caused by criminals than to protect the single person who committed that injury. Society must be able to live in safety and in order to do this we must effectively and efficiently rid the country of those who commit crimes. Packer said that in the crime control model, "all of the components of the criminal justice system must work together to increase the capacity to apprehend, try, convict, and dispose of a high proportion of criminal offenders whose offenses become known."[8]

© Rainer Plendl, 2011. Used under license from Shutterstock, Inc.

The crime control model suggests that our system of justice can be sped up, and therefore become more efficient, by determining early in the process who is probably guilty and who is not. If an accused person is determined to be innocent, they can be weeded out of the system early. Those that appear to be guilty can then be pushed through the system with a limited amount of procedural delays. The ultimate goal is to obtain the adjudication of guilt as quickly as possible so that the proper form of punishment can be implemented and society can be made safer.

The crime control model is likened to an assembly line because speed and efficiency are the key components of this model. The due process model is compared more to an obstacle course because the system is designed to present formidable impediments at every stage of the process. This model says that the individual is more important than the many. It is more important to protect the rights of the accused than to protect the interests of society as a whole. The criminal justice system is a system of man and man is not perfect, mistakes can and are made in the process of justice and the accused must be protected against these mistakes. This model is based on the premise that the constitution guarantees all citizens the right to due process9 and this and all of the rights enumerated in the Bill of Rights will be fully complied with in every instance.

The due process model says that even if a person appears to be guilty, the system is designed to safeguard the integrity of the justice process. To give explanation to this premise let us look at the following hypothetical scenario. The police are dispatched to a location where shots have been fired. The first officer on the scene sees a body on the ground lying in a pool of blood. There is a man standing over the body with a gun in his hand and several witnesses shouting that the man with the gun had just shot the victim. The man puts down the gun and tells the officer that he just shot the victim. The officer places the man in handcuffs and arrests him for murder. Witness statements are taken and the man is taken to jail and booked.

© Kenneth William Caleno, 2011. Used under license from Shutterstock, Inc.

The above hypothetical situation could make a reasonable person come to the conclusion that there would be a strong presumption that the man arrested is guilty of the crime of murder. Proponents of the crime control model would say that this is a perfect case for bypassing many of the procedural requirements of the criminal justice system and swiftly adjudicate the accused and apply the appropriate criminal sanctions without any unnecessary delay. Proponents of the due process model, however, would say wait a minute, we need to slow down. The appearance of guilt is not sufficient to speed up the process; there are too many legal variables that have to be considered. Only an impartial tribunal can be trusted to make determinations of legal as opposed to factual guilt. Herbert Packer stated it best when he explained that: "the tribunal that convicts him must have the power to deal with his kind of case ("jurisdiction") and must be geographically appropriate ("venue"); too long a time must not have elapsed since the offense was committed ("statute of limitations"); he must not have been previously convicted or acquitted of the same or a substantially similar offense ("double jeopardy"); he must not fall within a category of persons, such as children or the insane, who are legally immune to conviction ("criminal responsibility"); and so on. None of these requirements has anything to do with the factual question of whether the person did or did not engage in the conduct that is charged as the offense against him; yet favorable answers to any of them will mean that he is legally innocent."[10]

The due process model protects the criminally accused against the overwhelming power of the government that is charged with prosecuting the cases. Due process insures all citizens that this immense power is neutralized so that they can compete fairly within the justice system. The crime control model wants to streamline the system so that those who deviate from society's norms and values are dealt with swiftly in order to protect those that are law abiding.

It would appear that these two models of justice, each with their seemingly competing ideologies, could never come together to form a consensus system of justice. The reality of this is that they actually do. Our criminal justice system is in a constant state of change, and components of each system manage to influence the philosophy that guides justice within our society.

The Components of the Criminal Justice System

The criminal justice system of the United States consists of three major components or functions: the police, corrections, and the courts (judicial). There are numerous subcomponents of the system, each of which falls under one of the three main categories. These subcomponents include such things as parole, probation, juvenile justice, and others that will be addressed separately later.

The system also works on three different governmental levels. We have one federal system, fifty different state systems, and thousands of county and municipal systems. Local governments spent more on criminal justice direct expenditures than the states or the federal government. Direct expenditures for each of the three major criminal justice functions have increased steadily since 1982. In fiscal year 2012, federal, state, and local governments spent an estimated $264 billion for police protection, corrections, and judicial and legal activities. Local governments account for a majority of the cost of the criminal justice system with expenditures of $132 billion of the $264 billion spent. State government spending accounted for $81 billion, while the federal government spent $52 billion in the same year.[11]

Nationally, there were approximately 2.1 million people employed in the justice system working at the federal, state, and local levels in 2012. The overall growth in the criminal justice system remained relatively stable during the decade between 1997 and 2006. The economy since 2008 has had a slightly negative impact on employment in the justice system, but there has been a significant increase in criminal justice employment over the last decade. Overall, employment in the criminal justice system has remained stable even during tough economic times.

Police Police departments (at all levels) are the largest and most visible component of the Criminal Justice System and operate under the Executive Branch of government. Police are tasked with the job of enforcing the criminal laws within their jurisdiction.

Law Enforcement Law enforcement is a term that describes the individuals and agencies responsible for enforcing laws and maintaining public order and public safety.

Police

The largest component of the criminal justice system, both in terms of employment and overall expenditures, is that of the **police**. The United States Department of Justice estimated that there were 891,289 full time law enforcement employees in the United States in 2012.[14] Approximately 76 percent of these employees, which includes both civilian and sworn positions, work for police protection at the local level. The federal government accounts for about 14 percent of the employees and the remaining 9.2 percent work for state police protection agencies.

"**Law enforcement**" is the term that describes the individuals and agencies responsible for enforcing laws and maintaining public order and public safety. Law enforcement includes the prevention, detection, and investigation of crime; and the apprehension and detention of individuals suspected of law violation.[16]

© Anton Prado PHOTO, 2011. Used under license from Shutterstock, Inc.

There are over 18,000 different law enforcement agencies in the United States. Most of these agencies operate at the local level, which includes cities and counties. There are a wide variety of specialized police agencies which include: school police, campus police, park police, transit police, bailiffs, marshals, and sheriffs, just to name a few. A detailed discussion about law enforcement and the specialties associated with them will be presented in Chapter 4 of this text.

Corrections The correctional component of the criminal justice system is responsible for overseeing those individuals who have been arrested and are awaiting trial, as well as those who have been convicted of a crime and are sentenced to serve time. Corrections include both jails and prisons.

Jails Jails are usually local facilities that serve several different functions including housing people who have been arrested and awaiting trial and those who are serving time for misdemeanor crimes.

Prisons Prisons are long term facilities that are operated by state and federal governments and hold prisoners who have been convicted of felony crimes.

Corrections

The correctional component of the criminal justice system is responsible for overseeing those individuals who have been arrested and are awaiting trial, as well as those who have been convicted of a crime and are sentenced to serve time. **Corrections** include both jails and prisons. **Jails** are usually local facilities that serve several different functions. When a person is arrested for a crime, they are taken to a jail facility to be processed (booked) and held until they can make bail or see a judge or magistrate. These people have not been convicted of a crime and therefore are presumed innocent; however, they can be held in the jail facility until they are tried for the crime they are accused of. Jails are also used to house those persons who have been found guilty of lesser crimes (misdemeanors and ordinance charges) and have been sentenced to a term of incarceration.

Prisons differ from jails in several respects. Prisons are operated by the various states or by the federal government, not by local governments.[17] Prisons are used to house persons who have been convicted of felonies and are serving a sentence of incarceration of over one year.

The jail population changes constantly as prisoners are released, make bail, or are convicted and transferred to prisons to serve their sentence. New offenders are also arrested and booked and enter the system. Jail facilities in the United States admit and process about thirteen million people a year with almost 800,000 offenders in our jail facilities at any given time. Our state and federal prisons house approximately 1.6 million offenders at any given time.[18] A detailed discussion of the correctional system will be presented in Chapters 8, 9, and 10 of this text.

© WilleeCole, 2011. Used under license from Shutterstock, Inc.

Courts

Court The court system in the United States (part of the judicial system), is comprised of many different types of courts: criminal, civil, administrative, and a variety of specialized courts, as well as our appellate courts.

The judicial component of the criminal justice system is comprised of the courts. Like the other parts of the system, the courts operate on the federal, state, and local levels. The **court** system in the United States is comprised of many different types of courts: criminal, civil, administrative, and a variety of specialized courts. The court system also includes all of the various appellate courts that function on both the federal and state levels.[21]

The criminal courts in the United States handle the most cases within the judicial system, with over 86.2 million criminal cases handled in 2015.[22]

Caseload Composition, Total by Tier, 2015

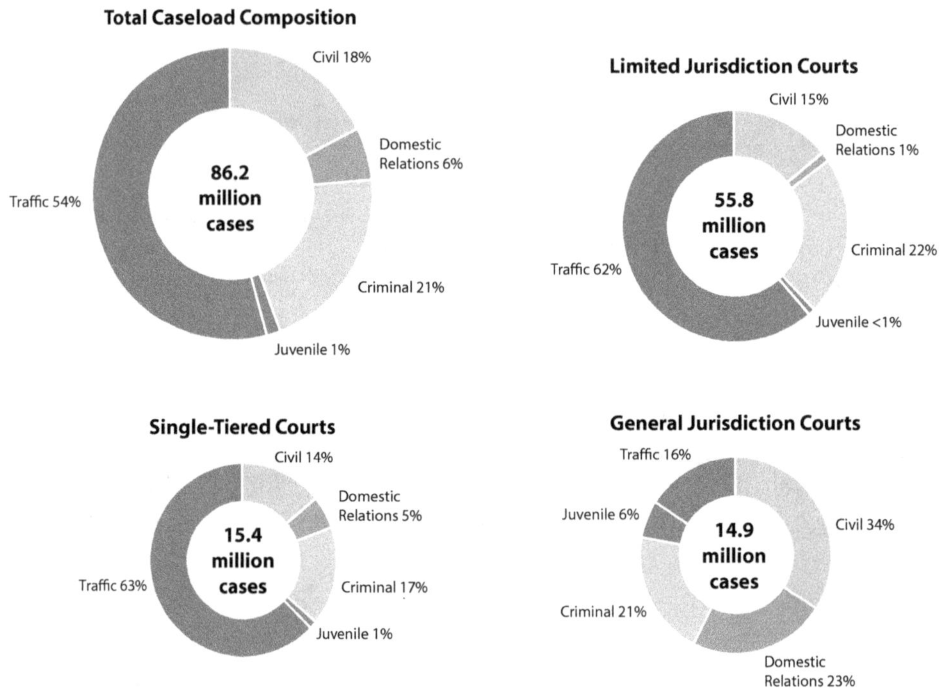

Source: Court Statistics Project, National Center for State Courts, *Examining the Work of State Courts: An Overview of 2015 State Court Caseloads.*

Review Questions

1. ____________ can be referred to as fundamental fairness.
2. The concept of ____________ ____________ changes over time as the moral values of a society change.
3. The implied agreement between citizens and their government as a way of maintaining social order is called the ____________ ____________.
4. "Two Models of the Criminal Justice Process" was written by ____________ ____________.

5. The basic premise of the ___________ ___________ model is speed and efficiency.
6. The ___________ ___________ model has been compared to an obstacle course.
7. There are ___________ main components of the criminal justice system.
8. The ___________ component of the criminal justice system has the largest yearly expenditure.
9. Persons housed in a ___________ have been convicted of a felony and are serving a sentence of incarceration of over one year.
10. When a person is arrested, they are taken to a ___________ to be processed and booked.

Critical Thinking Questions

1. How have the moral values in the United States changed over the past two hundred years and how have these changes affected our laws?
2. Discuss how the laws in your local community may be different from those in other communities around the state or the country.
3. Select either the Due Process Model or the Crime Control Model and give the reasons why you think that model should be adopted as the sole basis of the criminal justice system in the United States.
4. Discuss why there are over 86 million court cases processed in the United States every year. Why is this number so high? What can we do to reduce this massive caseload?

Endnotes

1 113 U. PA. L. Rev. 1, 1964.

2 2nd Edition (New York: Oxford University Press, Inc., 2005).

3 Connie Ireland and George E. Rush, *The Dictionary of Criminal Justice With Summaries of Supreme Court Cases Affecting Criminal Justice,* 7th Edition (New York: McGraw Hill, 2011).

4 *Quotations of Theodore Roosevelt* (Bedford, MA: Applewood Books, 2004).

5 New World Encyclopedia contributors, *New World Encyclopedia,* "Social contract," accessed on February/2011 at http://www.newworldencyclopedia.org/entry/Social_contract?oldid=901448.

6 U. PA. L. Rev. Op cit.

7 Ibid.

8 Ibid.

9 As stated in the Fifth, Sixth, and Fourteenth Amendments.

10 U. Pa. L. Rev. Op cit.

11 Bureau of Justice Statistics, accessed on January 12, 2017 at https://www.bjs.gov/index.cfm?ty=qa&iid=416

12 Bureau of Justice Statistics, accessed on July/2011 at http://bjs.ojp.usdoj.gov/index.cfm?ty=tp&tid=5.

13 Ibid.

14 U.S. Department of Justice, Office of Justice Programs, Bureau of Justice Statistics, *National Sources of Law Enforcement Employment Data*, April 2016.

15 Bureau of Justice Statistics accessed on January/2011 at http://bjs.ojp.usdoj.gov

16 It should be noted that there are prisons that are operated under contract with the various states and the federal government. Chapter 10 will discuss private prisons in more detail.

17 United States Department of Labor, Bureau of Labor Statistics, accessed on February/2011 at http://www.bls.gov/oco/ocos156.htm.

18 Bureau of Justice Statistics, accessed on February/2011 at http://bjs.ojp.usdoj.gov.

19 United States Department of Labor, Bureau of Labor Statistics, accessed on February/2011 at http://www.bls.gov/oco/ocos156.htm.

20 The court system will be discussed in detail in Chapter 8 of this text.

21 National Center for State Courts, "Court Statistics Project," accessed on January/2017 at http://www.courtstatistics.org/~/media/Microsites/Files/CSP/EWSC%202015.ashx.

22 Ibid.

23 Ibid.

© carl ballou/Shutterstock.com

CHAPTER 2

Theories of Crime and Behavior

KEY TERMS

Atavistic man
Biological theories
Chicago School
Classical school
Compurgation
Conflict theory
Crime index
Criminal behavior
Dark figure of crime
Deterrence theory
Developmental pathways
Deviance
Differential association theory
Feminist theories
General deterrence
General strain theory
General theory of crime
Integrated theories
Labeling theory
Left realism
Life course theories
National Incident-Based Reporting System (NIBRS)
National Crime Victimization Survey (NCVS)
Peacemaking criminology
Personality theories
Positivist school
Pre-classical school
Reintegrative shaming
Routine activities theory
Self-report survey
Social control theory
Social disorganization theory
Specific deterrence
Strain theory
Trial by battle
Trial by ordeal
Uniform Crime Reports (UCR)

CHAPTER OBJECTIVES

1. Differentiate between the concepts of criminal behavior and deviance.
2. Report how much crime there is in the United States and crime trends.
3. Define and discuss the various methods of gathering crime data.
4. Demonstrate an understanding of the causes of crime.
5. Analyze the various theoretical perspectives explaining the causes of crime and their application to behaviors.

Case Study: Gang Violence

Luis Sanchez was born in Chelsea, Massachusetts, and exposed to the perils and temptations of a gang lifestyle at an early age. His mother had systematically kicked out his older siblings as teenagers, and Sanchez too was nearly legally disowned by his mother, but at age 13 he was considered too young by the court. After being mugged for the first time, Sanchez decided he needed a different means of protection due to his lack of family support. He soon joined a gang and became involved in a variety of criminal activities, including selling illegal drugs such as cocaine and marijuana. Sanchez, fortunately, was able to escape his criminal lifestyle by joining a youth program in Boston in 2004, breaking his gang connections, and becoming a student at Boston College.[1]

Sanchez's case is not at all uncommon: many other young people are in similar situations. Sadly, in many cases, these individuals are unable to escape a life of crime and deviance as Sanchez did. A perennial concern for the criminal justice system in the United States is gang-related crime and violence. Much of the worry consists of trying to determine precisely what events, factors, environment, and inherited traits combine to produce a gang member inclined to commit crime.

Understanding the causes of crime is instrumental in our ability not only to predict future offending, but also to determine the appropriate responses to the crime and the offender. The example of Luis Sanchez illustrates that the causes of crime may be the product of multiple underlying factors (poverty, gang allegiance, drugs, personal quarrels, alcohol). Why do some people in Sanchez's situation join gangs while others do not? This chapter will review the extent to which crime occurs and the various theoretical propositions used to explain the behavior.

What Is Criminal Behavior?

The concept of crime and its subsequent causes has been debated for centuries. Many theories about the causes and reasons for criminal behavior have been presented. These include the classical perspective, in which offenders are considered to be free will thinkers, and the positivist perspective that looks to the individual or their environment for causes or influences toward crime. Despite these categorical explanations for crime, debate still exists among practitioners, lawmakers, criminologists, and the general public as to what constitutes criminal behavior. More specifically, within this context and framework, one must differentiate between deviance and criminal activity.

The concept of **deviance** is usually defined as behaviors considered outside of or inconsistent with normal behavior for that community or group.[2] Therefore, deviance may differ depending on where you live and the accepted norms, ethics, and morals of the community. Broadly speaking, deviance can be understood from either a positivist or a constructionist point of view. *Positivism* basically asserts that things have distinct, real "essences," and therefore deviant behavior is wrong because it is inconsistent with what is objectively right. In the context of positivist criminology, deviance is thought to be caused by internal and external factors beyond the criminal's control.[3] Related to positivism is *rational choice theory*, which posits that criminals make a cost/benefit analysis to determine whether or not to commit crime.[4] *Constructionist* interpretations of deviance believe that categories of right and wrong, and therefore deviance from them, are social constructs that depend greatly on the perspective of the individual observer.[5] In sociology, deviance refers to actions (or behaviors) that contravene either social norms or written legal codes.

Deviance Behaviors considered outside of or inconsistent with normal behavior for a community or group.

Criminal behavior, appropriately, is defined by legislation, statutes, and codes. There are two classifications of these behaviors. The first classification, *mala in se* crimes, covers acts that are deemed illegal because they so violate the norms and moral code of society that they are wrong in and of themselves. Such offenses—murder, for example—are almost universally prohibited. The other classification is behaviors that are deemed illegal not so much due to inherent immorality, but because they are defined as such by those living within that particular society. Essentially, they are crimes because society has enacted laws and statutes that say they are crimes. These are known as *mala prohibitum* crimes. Such crimes are likely to vary from culture to culture (e.g., sex crimes, gambling restrictions, drug and alcohol laws, and so forth).

Criminal behavior Behavior defined by legislation, statutes, and codes.

These two definitions are both incorporated into a legal system based on an understanding of crime that is, to some extent, socially constructed. To be sure, crime can be understood as a codification of deviance: violating social norms, taboos, and laws is often legally criminal. Crime has been succinctly described by Morrison (2006) as "an act or omission that is defined by the

© Iakov Filimonov/Shutterstock.com

Mala in se crimes, such as robbery, are almost universally prohibited.

validly passed laws of the nation state in which it occurred so that punishment should follow from the behavior."[6] It is within this framework and context that the criminal justice system operates and functions. Therefore, what constitutes criminal behavior and the appropriate punishments ascribed to those violations of law may change over time.

Measuring Crime

To understand how much crime there is in the United States, it is important to assess not only the different types of measures that are used but their origins, strengths, and weaknesses. The most frequently used means of data collection are the Uniform Crime Reports (UCR), the National Incident-Based Reporting System (NIBRS), the National Crime Victimization Survey (NCVS), and self-report surveys.

Uniform Crime Reports (UCR)

Prior to 1930, no centralized program for gathering crime statistics existed. Data that were collected were deemed unreliable because of legislative differences in criminal codes and enforcement practices. Because of the diversity of techniques and procedures, it was nearly impossible to compare crime data in any meaningful way between jurisdictions, let alone states. Law enforcement officers and legislators needed a better way to assemble data to assist with allocation of resources and manpower. This desire to improve data collection efforts was best demonstrated in 1927 by the International Association of Chiefs of Police (IACP). The IACP formed the Committee on Uniform Crime Records to assess the possibility of developing a standardized, centrally located mechanism for gathering crime statistics.[7] Most important was the creation of standardized definitions of crimes. These efforts resulted in the 1929 publication of the first standardized collection of statistics on crimes reported to the police and crimes cleared by arrest.

Uniform Crime Reports (UCR) An official data-reporting tool created in 1930 to provide uniform definitions for crime data so that results could be compared by month, year, state, and jurisdiction.

Crime index An index reported by the Uniform Crime Reports. Crimes are divided into Part I and Part II index offenses. The Part I index consists of a total of eight offenses divided into the violent crime index and the property crime index. The Part II index comprises a total of 21 categories of less-serious crimes.

Beginning in 1930, this tool, known as the **Uniform Crime Reports (UCR)**, was officially implemented on a large-scale basis, with law enforcement agencies volunteering for participation in data collection and reporting to the FBI. The primary purpose of the UCR was to provide uniform definitions for gathering crime data so that results could be compared by month, year, state, and jurisdiction. Since its inception, the UCR has added information on law enforcement officers killed and assaulted on duty as well as hate crime statistics.[8] Today the UCR, which is still a voluntary program, includes approximately 18,000 reporting law enforcement agencies nationally, representing more than 97% of the entire U.S. population.

UCR data are divided into two categories: Part I index offenses and Part II offenses. The Part I **Crime Index** includes a total of eight offenses divided into a violent crime index and a property crime index. Part II covers the less serious offenses. (See Figure 2.1 for an overview of the included index offenses.)

In order for an offense to be included in the UCR,[9] it must follow the counting rule, which states that only the most serious offense committed in a single incident is included in the UCR data, although the offender may be charged with more crimes. Additionally, the UCR follows what is known as the hierarchy rule. Offenses are placed in the specific order in which they are supposed to be recorded, beginning with criminal homicide and ranging through runaways in the Part II Offense category. The UCR further distinguishes between time and place. If a criminal event that occurs is a continuation of another event, then the UCR counts those as one single incident. If the criminal events are related but not a single incident, then law enforcement officers must record those as separate incidents.

Data are reported in one of three ways: (1) crimes reported to the police (reported in raw numbers), which includes any offenses that have been reported to the police and have been verified as possible crimes by law enforcement; (2) rates per 100,000 residents, calculated as Total Number of Crimes Reported ÷ Total U.S. Population × 100,000 = Rate per 100,000 Residents; and (3) rate of crime over time or trends. Finally, crimes cleared by arrest are included in the final report. These data include the number of reported offenses where either an arrest was made or at least one person was charged in the incident.[10] Data are further aggregated by community type. These divisions include Standard Statistical Metropolitan Areas (SMSAs); other cities, most of which are not incorporated; and rural counties.[11] Although the data do not allow for individual comparisons by the victim or specific characteristics of crimes, they do allow for comparisons by these types of jurisdictions. Despite every effort to account for all criminal offending, there still exist a number of offenses that go unreported to the police. This category of crime is known as the **dark figure of crime**.

Dark figure of crime
Offenses that go unreported to the police.

FIGURE 2.1 UCR OFFENSES

Part I Offenses

Part I offense classifications include:

Violent Offenses	**Property Offenses**
Murder	***Burglary***
The willful (non-negligent) killing of one human being by another.	The unlawful entry of a structure to commit a felony or theft.

Forcible Rape

The carnal knowledge of a female forcibly and against her will. Attempts or assaults to commit rape by force or threat of force are also included; however, statutory rape (without force) and other sex offenses are excluded.

Robbery

The taking or attempting to take anything of value from the care, custody, or control of a person or persons by force or threat of force or violence and/or by putting the victim in fear.

Aggravated Assault

Unlawful attack by one person upon another for the purpose of inflicting severe or aggravated bodily injury.

Larceny-Theft

The unlawful taking, carrying, leading, or riding away of property from the possession or constructive possession of another.

Motor Vehicle Theft

The theft or attempted theft of a motor vehicle. In the UCR Program, a motor vehicle is a self-propelled vehicle that runs on land surfaces and not on rails.

Arson

Any willful or malicious burning or attempting to burn, with or without intent to defraud, a dwelling house, public building, motor vehicle or aircraft, personal property of another, etc.

Information from FBI: http://www2.fbi.gov/ucr/cius2009/index.html

Part II Offenses

Part II offenses encompass all other reportable classifications outside those defined as Part I. Law enforcement agencies report to the FBI only arrest data involving the Part II crimes:

1. Other Assaults
2. Forgery and Counterfeiting
3. Fraud
4. Embezzlement
5. Stolen Property: Buying, Receiving, Possessing
6. Vandalism
7. Weapons: Carrying, Possessing, etc.
8. Prostitution and Commercialized Vice
9. Sex Offenses
10. Drug Abuse Violations
11. Gambling
12. Offenses Against the Family and Children
13. Driving Under the Influence
14. Liquor Laws
15. Drunkenness
16. Disorderly Conduct

17. Vagrancy
18. All Other Offenses
19. Suspicion
20. Curfew and Loitering Laws—(Persons under 18)
21. Runaways—(Persons under 18)

From Uniform Crime Reporting Program Staff. (2004). Uniform Crime Reporting Handbook. Clarksburg, WV: Federal Bureau of Investigation, p. 8.

Although the UCR does provide a mechanism for comparison between jurisdictions and states, there still are some data that are excluded from these efforts. For example, demographic characteristics of the offender are excluded from crimes reported to the police and in most instances with crimes cleared by arrest. The reason for this exclusion is because the witnesses may not be able to accurately account for the offender characteristics or data may not be available in any consistent manner even when crimes are cleared by arrest. Second, law enforcement officers are not required to collect and submit data on crime victims. Third, because data are collected on an aggregate level, individual cases are not followed throughout the system. Therefore, it is impossible to determine whether the offenders were charged in a particular event and/or whether conviction was obtained; UCR data only include whether an arrest has been made or a confirmed suspect has been identified. Finally, the UCR excludes some offense categories, such as the federal offense of kidnapping, that are deemed important. This limits the ability to compare and track data over time.[12]

There are a variety of factors that affect the reporting of crimes from both a law enforcement and an individual perspective. For example, when assessing criminal events, responses to crime by law enforcement are often in reaction to citizen complaints as opposed to the officer witnessing the event themselves. Likewise, many non-serious crimes go unreported. Therefore, inclusion of the most serious criminal offenses makes sense, given the ability to compare across jurisdiction and offense categories. This also includes the difficulty with the type of crime, even if serious. For example, the crime of rape, although serious by nature, often goes unreported because of the sensitive nature of the event, embarrassment, and fear of reprisal.

Because most crime comes to the attention of law enforcement through the efforts of the victims or witnesses, it is important to consider why a victim may not report a criminal event. Research has suggested that many victims report they believe nothing can be done. Lack of faith in the system to either detect or prosecute may preclude many of them from going through the "hassle" of reporting the event. Some victims report they believe their victimization is not important enough to occupy the law enforcement community's time and they do not want to bother the police with such trivial matters. Other victims report that the incident is a personal or private matter that should be handled within the family or between friends, while others fear reprisal. In some cases, the relationship between the victim and offender is such that the victim does not want harm to come to the offender. Crimes that occur between strangers are most likely to be reported. Finally, victims indicate that they report their victimization to others such as family members or social services for assistance with the event.[13]

Law enforcement officials report that there are a variety of factors that affect whether an offense is recorded. Influences such as funding decisions may dictate whether an agency wishes to participate in the UCR at all. Most federal and state funding initiatives require that law enforcement participate in either the UCR or NIBRS (see the next section for a more detailed explanation of NIBRS). While in theory the UCR is a voluntary program, these funding requirements all but force an agency to participate.

Community desires or needs will also influence whether an agency processes a crime officially or unofficially, particularly for less serious offenses. Communities that have seen an increase in certain types of offense categories (e.g., drug usage), may choose to "crack down" on these offenses and formally prosecute violators. Communities may also face political pressures to reduce crime.

Other extralegal factors may play a role, such as the sex, age, and race of the offender and whether the dispatcher names the offense when notifying law enforcement officers.[14]

One of the key benefits of participating in the UCR program is the ability to examine crime trends within a single jurisdiction. These data may be particularly important to a chamber of commerce or tourism bureau that uses the information to market a community.[15] Data may also be used to examine homicide trends across jurisdictions. These trend data can be very beneficial in determining or making staffing decisions or informing legislators to craft new anti-crime policies.[16] Further data may be used to inform the public about crime trends and to encourage appropriate support and response to crime prevention techniques. Finally, researchers use UCR data to test theories and to identify causes of crime.[17]

National Incident-Based Reporting System (NIBRS)

Because of changes in the nature and complexity of crime since the UCR's inception, the law enforcement community during the 1970s began studying the benefits and limitations of the UCR program. The result of this study was the creation of the **National Incident-Based Reporting System (NIBRS)**. The goal of the NIBRS program was to enhance the quantity and quality of the information provided and to enhance the methodology for collecting, analyzing, and publishing crime data.[18] In the most recent *Crime in the United States* report, the FBI stated that for 2012 a total of 6,115 law enforcement agencies reported their UCR crime statistics via NIBRS out of 18,290 total police agencies participating in the UCR program. Although participation is more limited than the UCR reporting program, many state and local agencies are in

National Incident-Based Reporting System (NIBRS) A national crime data collection program created and implemented during the 1980s in an effort to enhance the methodology for collecting, analyzing, and publishing crime data.

various stages of transitioning from the UCR to NIBRS. One impediment to this transition is the limited resources available for technology upgrades and training. Data for the NIBRS are not currently reported as separate categories. Instead they are incorporated into the UCR reports and included in the annual *Crime in the United States* publication.

There are a significant number of key differences between the UCR and the NIBRS systems. The NIBRS system includes an expanded offense reporting tool.[19] The program includes a total of 22 offense categories made up of 46 crimes. An additional 11 offenses are included in a group B category (see Figure 2.2 for a list of the offenses in Groups A and B). This expanded list of NIBRS offenses does not follow a hierarchy rule. The NIBRS is an incident-based system.[20] Information is collected on all individual incidents and arrests. Prescribed data allow for the researcher to collect information on each individual offense such as the type, age, sex, race, ethnicity, and residence status of the victim as well as the type of offense and injury sustained. The same type of information is included on the offender, along with the elements of the crime.

The NIBRS uses new and revised definitions from the UCR, such as the definition of rape. The NIBRS also includes new definitions of offense categories that are not represented by the UCR. The NIBRS system provides an opportunity for more specificity in the criminal acts. This includes the ability to compare offenses by individual characteristics as well as business crimes, residency status, weapons used, injuries incurred, etc. The NIBRS system includes a category representing crimes against society, which are *mala prohibitum* categories of crime such as drug offenses, gambling, prostitution, etc. Unlike the UCR, which only records the distinction between attempted and completed crimes in cases of forcible rape and murder, the NIBRS system distinguishes between attempted and completed for each offense category.

In addition, the NIBRS gives the ability to conduct correlations between the offense categories, property, victims, offenders, and arrestees. These linkages are both explicit and implicit. There are implied linkages between the victim and the offender within the offense category and explicit linkages to the crimes committed against the victim. The NIBRS includes the victim-offender relationship. Unlike the UCR, which only records this information for homicides, the NIBRS reporting system records victim-offender relationships for all crimes against persons and robbery.

Another key difference between the two systems is that the NIBRS reports more of the circumstances surrounding the event. In the UCR, information about the circumstances of the event is only included for homicides. NIBRS has expanded this system to include circumstantial information on assaults as well as homicides.

Both the UCR and NIBRS include circumstantial information on homicides.

The NIBRS incorporates the hotel rule in a different way. For the UCR, the general hotel rule relates to the number of dwellings and how burglaries are reported. If there are a number of burglaries in one complex and they are likely to be reported by the manager, then they are counted as one offense. With the NIBRS, these data are expanded to include rental storage units and to include the number of rooms, units, or storage compartments that were victimized.

Lastly, the NIBRS and UCR report data to the FBI in different ways. For the UCR program, local agencies are permitted to use manual forms to submit data. State agencies must record their data on magnetic tapes. For the NIBRS system, all reporting agencies must record their data on magnetic strips.[21]

National Crime Victimization Survey (NCVS) A survey conducted on households in the United States that includes detailed descriptions of criminal events, including the victim, potential precipitating factors, consequences of the event, and the offender.

National Crime Victimization Survey (NCVS)

Victimization surveys give researchers and policymakers the opportunity to delve further into a criminal incident from the perspective of the victim. Although a variety of different victimization surveys have been developed, the most widely used ongoing effort is known as the **National Crime Victimization Survey (NCVS)**. First administered in 1973 and originally known as the National Crime Survey (NCS), the NCVS is conducted on

FIGURE 2.2 NATIONAL INCIDENT-BASED REPORTING SYSTEM (NIBRS) OFFENSE CATEGORIES

Group A Offense Categories

1. Arson
2. Assault Offenses
3. Bribery
4. Burglary/Breaking & Entering
5. Counterfeiting/Forgery
6. Destruction/Damage/Vandalism
7. Drug/Narcotic Offenses
8. Embezzlement
9. Extortion/Blackmail
10. Fraud Offenses
11. Gambling Offenses
12. Homicide Offenses
13. Kidnapping/Abduction
14. Larceny/Theft Offenses
15. Motor Vehicle Theft
16. Pornography/Obscene Material
17. Prostitution Offenses

18. Robbery
19. Sex Offenses, Forcible
20. Sex Offenses, Non Forcible
21. Stolen Property Offenses
22. Weapon Law Violations

Group B Offense Categories

1. Bad Checks
2. Curfew/Loitering/Vagrancy Violations
3. Disorderly Conduct
4. Driving Under the Influence
5. Drunkenness
6. Family Offenses, Nonviolent
7. Liquor Law Violations
8. Peeping Tom
9. Runaway
10. Trespass of Real Property
11. All Other Offenses

For more information on NIBRS see National Incident Based Reporting System, Volume 1: Data Collection Guidelines (2000) at http://www.fbi.gov/about-us/cjis/ucr/nibrs/nibrs_dcguide.pdf (p. 11)

households in the United States by the U.S. Census Bureau on behalf of the Bureau of Justice Statistics. The NCVS may be used to accomplish a variety of different goals from a crime prevention perspective. Most importantly, it is used to tap into the dark figure of crime, enhance the ability to compare victimizations by types of areas and over time, provide uniform definitions of crime, and include detailed descriptions of the criminal event, including the victim, potential precipitating factors, consequences of the event, and offender.[22] Each year, data are obtained from a nationally representative sample of about 90,000 households, comprising nearly 160,000 persons, on the frequency, characteristics, and consequences of criminal victimization in the United States.[23]

The key to the NCVS is that the study population is the household as opposed to the individuals. Should the individuals move, the address/house will remain in the study for a maximum of three years. Each member of the household age 14 and older is interviewed directly and asked to report the frequency and details of individual victimization(s), including characteristics of the victims and crimes both reported and not reported to law enforcement. Children ages 12 and 13, or individuals who are older and physically unable to participate, are interviewed via a proxy. The proxy also reports household victimizations.[24]

© Brian A Jackson/Shutterstock.com

The NCVS records data on property victimizations, such as burglary, as well as personal victimizations.

There are two types of counts that are collected from the NCVS: incidents of crime and victimizations. Incidents of crime correspond with the UCR categories, while victimizations include the number of victimizations the individual experiences[25]; the relationship between the offender and the victim; the month, date, and location; self-protective actions; losses incurred; the consequences of victimization; whether the offense is reported and why or why not; the presence of weapons, drugs, and alcohol; and the demographic information of both the victim and the offender.[26]

The advantages of the NCVS include the ability to record data on the individual level for personal crimes and the household level for household crimes.[27] Because the NCVS data are only recorded for a sample of households, not all victimizations are included in the data set or the data collection instrument. Likewise, not all cities are represented in the sample; therefore, you cannot estimate crime rates for most of the United States, nor can you estimate crimes for most cities.

As with any data collection effort, there are various problems associated with the NCVS. First, one of the most common problems associated with any form of interview data collection effort is the *interviewer effect*. There is always the potential for the interviewee to become bored or resistant to the interview process. There is also a possibility that the interviewer has very little to give the participant in terms of rewards for participating in the study. One of the ways to verify the information provided in the study is to conduct reverse records checks for those offenses that were reported to the police.

A second problem associated with the NCVS is telescoping.[28] *Telescoping* refers to remembering events as occurring more recently (forward telescoping) or further in the past (backward telescoping) than when they actually occurred. Time bounding the survey instruments is one way to minimize this shortcoming of the data collection effort.

Household movement, also known as *mover-stayer*, is a third problem with the NCVS. Because the NCVS tracks household crime, if the residents at the current address move away, the study does not follow them. Instead, the new residents will be included in the study. This is of particular concern for time bounding as well as differences in lifestyle. Time bounding is an issue because the survey is ongoing and the first interview with the new residents will not be time bounded, so telescoping is a real concern. Likewise, lifestyle differences may skew data for increases or decreases in reported victimization. For example, should the original study group be elderly, the research demonstrates that these individuals are among the least likely to be victimized, particularly by personal crimes. Should a young college-age couple with no children move into the residence, because of their lifestyle difference (out later, access to entertainment, etc.), they are more likely to be victimized than the previous residents.

A fourth problem is sampling error. Although the sample includes 90,000 households in the United States, these households may not represent all demographics and regions, such as rural areas. To account for differences, researchers must use very high confidence intervals (meaning the range for margin of error is quite large) to obtain significance.

A final problem arises with the proxy interviews themselves or response bias. For example, if there is only one person over the age of 14 in a household, that person is responsible for reporting all crime committed within the household. If the representative for the household is the perpetrator, such as in domestic offenses, these crimes are not likely to be reported, thus resulting in response bias.

Career Connections: Survey Researcher

Survey researchers, along with market researchers, are primarily responsible for finding out what people think. In general, they collect statistical data about people and their opinions; as a result, they spend the balance of their time designing and implementing surveys. This requires precision, diligence, and attention to detail, since data analysis is an important part of their job. Additionally, they must be able to work well as part of a research team, and be able to communicate effectively when reporting their findings.[29]

Survey researchers come from diverse backgrounds; there is no specific academic or professional path they must travel. Typically, researchers will have at minimum a bachelor's degree in order to enter the field. Advancement or a more technical position might necessitate a master's degree or doctorate.[30] A background in the social sciences is common, as well as some exposure to business, psychology, marketing, and sociology. Due to the central role of statistical data gathering and analysis in their work, survey researchers must possess a strong background in quantitative analysis. Math and science courses, with sampling theory and survey design as part of the curriculum, will be helpful in acquiring the necessary analytical and mathematical skills, especially in statistics and data analysis.

Survey researchers use questionnaires and surveys to collect information about people, including their beliefs, behaviors, thoughts, and personal data. They should therefore be adept at interacting with people, interviewing, and writing reports to present and summarize their findings.[31] Students interested in careers as survey researchers should investigate the possibility of an internship with a consulting firm, nonprofit organization, or government agency to gain practical experience with conducting surveys and gathering data.

Professional survey researcher.

There are many employment opportunities for survey researchers in both the government and the private sector. Survey researchers can find work as consultants for management, scientific, and technical companies. They work in market research, public opinion polling, and data gathering. Many work in academia, at colleges or universities.[32] Given the pace of globalization and the demographic shift in the U.S. toward a more diverse population, it is vitally important to have accurate information on foreign populations and how they affect the 21st-century economy. According to the Bureau of Labor Statistics, employment in survey (and market) research is likely to grow 28% from 2008 to 2018, making its growth far bigger than most other fields.[33]

Self-Report Measures

Self-report survey A data collection effort asking participants to report the number of criminal offenses or activities they have committed.

Another method of collecting data is the **self-report survey**. There is no one standard method for collecting data using the self-report method. However, this technique was developed and began being used more frequently during the 1950s. Probably the most frequently recognized historical study was conducted by Short and Nye (1957, 1958) and the National Youth Survey. More recently, the Office of Juvenile Justice and Delinquency Prevention (OJJDP) has supported a multi-site, multi-year study to follow youth throughout their childhood and into adulthood in three specific locations: Denver, Colorado; Rochester, New York; and Pittsburgh, Pennsylvania.[34] Another study funded by OJJDP in Maricopa County, Arizona, has explored possible ways to stop youth offending.[35] Results from these recent studies have been used to inform policy and establish best practices in the juvenile justice field.

As stated, there is no one standardized technique for collecting or counting self-report data. Typically, convenience samples are drawn from school-aged populations. These populations are either given a survey instrument or are interviewed to determine the prevalence and incidence of delinquent or criminal offending. *Prevalence* refers to one or more persons reporting the same offense or behavior during the reference period, while *incidence* refers to the reporting of one delinquent or criminal behavior during the reference period.[36] Advantages of using a self-report survey include tapping into the dark figure of crime, collecting more detailed information on the participants/delinquents, and collecting information on the causes or motivations behind the offending.

Although self-report studies provide another tool for tapping into offenses that are not known to the police, there are still a number of weaknesses that must be taken into consideration when using self-report studies or measures. First, because the majority of self-report studies include a convenience sample of school-aged youth, it is possible that these data do not reflect the larger community and cannot be generalized to all youth. Second, there exists the possibility for overreporting or underreporting delinquent or criminal activity. One way to validate the responses is to include a random records check; this technique gives researchers an opportunity to verify the accuracy of results, or at least establish confidence intervals

Ethics and Professionalism: Honest Reporting

You are a police chief in a large U.S. city. One of the biggest problems in your city is an increase in the occurrence of hate crimes. Recently, the Attorney General of the United States has called for more comprehensive and accurate reporting of hate crimes. You are especially afraid of sensationalist coverage by the mainstream media; specifically, you worry that this will lead to negative perceptions of your department that will, in effect, penalize you. It may also lead to charges of departmental incompetence or insensitivity. For example, if an individual reports the murder of a black man in an Asian community, your desk officer may not have thought to investigate whether the murder was racially motivated.[37] Should you report your embarrassing statistics in their entirety? Or should you not report the hate-driven motivation of such crimes?

to draw conclusions. Third, many self-report studies have been criticized for low response rates and usability of returned surveys. Fourth, there is some debate about which type of methodology should be used to collect data (e.g., surveys versus interviews). This is most important when you are asking participants to report their delinquent or criminal behaviors. For participants, this may be a concern when they have actually violated the law and fear that researchers will report their behavior. From a research standpoint, an ethical dilemma may arise between protecting the confidentiality of the participants and having an implied and sometimes stated duty to report criminal behavior. One final weakness of self-report studies is that because there is no one single technique, it is nearly impossible to compare results across studies.

Crime Statistics

Given the various data collection efforts, it is important to understand the various crime trends from both officially reported offense data and victimization data. This section of the chapter reviews the crime data recorded in the Uniform Crime Reports (UCR) and the National Crime Victimization Survey (NCVS).

According to the UCR, in 2015 there were more than 9.1 million Part I index offenses committed. Of those, approximately 87% were property offenses while 13% were violent offenses. Larceny-theft accounted for 71.4% of all property offenses, while aggravated assault accounted for 63.8% of all violent crime.

More than 10.7 million arrests were made in 2015. Drug abuse violations accounted for the largest number of arrests (1,488,707), while larceny-theft (1,160,390) and driving under the influence (1,089,171) followed. The five-year property crime trends (see Figure 2.3) revealed an 13% decrease, while violent offenses (see Figure 2.4) declined 0.7% during that same time period and 16.5% during a 10-year time period. Males accounted for nearly 73.1% of all persons arrested, while "69.7 percent of all persons arrested were white, 26.6 percent were black, and the remaining 3.6 percent were of other races."[38]

FIGURE 2.3 PROPERTY CRIME TRENDS, 2011-2015

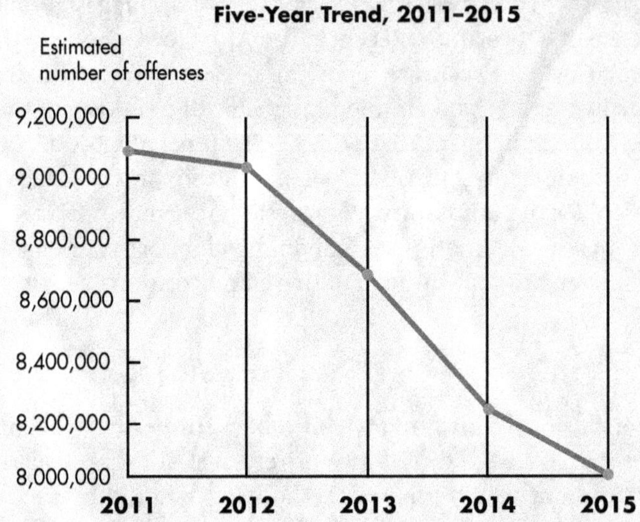

Source: https://ucr.fbi.gov/crime-in-the-u.s/2015/crime-in-the-u.s.-2015/offenses-known-to-law-enforcement/property-crime

FIGURE 2.4 VIOLENT CRIME TRENDS, 2011-2015

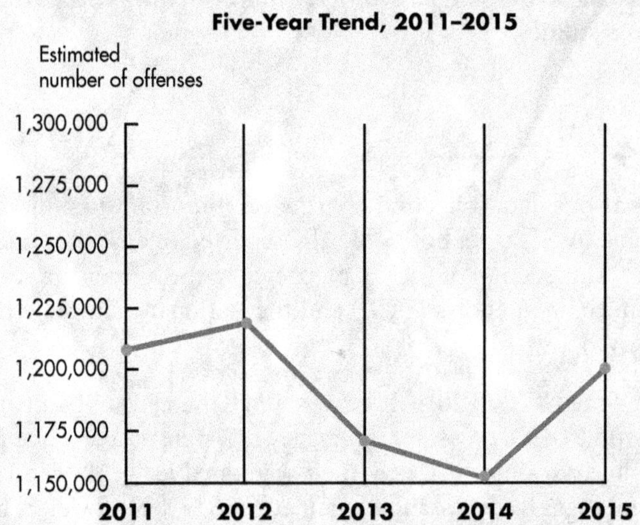

Source: https://ucr.fbi.gov/crime-in-the-u.s/2015/crime-in-the-u.s.-2015/offenses-known-to-law-enforcement/violent-crime/violentcrimemain_final

According to the NCVS, there were an estimated 14.6 million violent and property victimizations in the United States in 2015.[39] The reported victimizations included an estimated total of 5 million violent victimizations and 14.6 million property crimes. Similar to the UCR data, the NCVS indicated a 6.6% decrease in violent crimes and a 4.4% decrease in property offenses between 2014 and 2015 (see Figure 2.5 for criminal victimization trends).

Critical Thinking

How might data collected from the UCR and NCVS shape policy?

FIGURE 2.5 VIOLENT CRIMINAL VICTIMIZATION

Type of violent crime	Number		Rate per 1,000 persons age 12 or older	
	2014*	2015	2014*	2015
Violent crime[3]	5,359,570	5,006,620	20.1	18.6
Rape/sexual assaultb	284,350	431,840‡	1.1	1.6‡
Robbery	664,210	578,580	2.5	2.1
Assault	4,411,010	3,996,200	16.5	14.8
Aggravated assault	1,092,090	816,760‡	4.1	3.0‡
Simple assault	3,318,920	3,179,440	12.4	11.8
Domestic violence[c]	1,109,880	1,094,660	4.2	4.1
Intimate partner violence[d]	634,610	806,050‡	2.4	3.0
Stranger violence	2,166,130	1,821,310	8.1	6.8
Violent crime involving injury	1,375,950	1,303,290	5.2	4.8
Serious violent crime[e]	2,040,650	1,827,170	7.7	6.8
Serious domestic violence[c]	400,030	460,450	1.5	1.7
Serious intimate partner violence[d]	265,890	333,210	1.0	1.2
Serious stranger violence	930,690	690,550‡	3.5	2.6
Serious violent crime involving weapons	1,306,900	977,840†	4.9	3.6‡
Serious violent crime involving injury	692,470	658,040	2.6	2.4

Note: Detail may not sum to total because of rounding. Total population age 12 or older was 252,242,520 in 2008 and 254,105,610 in 2009. Total number of households was 121,141,060 in 2008 and 122,327,660 in 2009.

~Not applicable.

*Difference is significant at the 95%-confidence level. Differences are described as higher, lower, or different in text.

**Difference is significant at the 90%-confidence level. Differences are described as somewhat, slightly. marginally, or some other indication in text.

[a]Victimization rates are per 1,000 persons age 12 or older per 1,000 households.

[b]Percent change calculated based on unrounded estimates.

[c]Excludes murder because the NCVS is based on interviews with victims and therefore cannot measure murder.

[d]Includes rape/sexual assault, robbery, and aggravated assault.

[e]See *Methodology* for discussion on changes in the rate of rape/sexual assault between 2008 and 2009.

[f]Includes pocket picking, completed purse snatching, and attempted purse snatching.

Source: Truman, J. L. & Rand, M. R. (2010). *Criminal victimization, 2009. National Crime Victimization Survey* (NCJ 231327). Washington, DC: U.S. Department of Justice, Bureau of Justice Statistics.

Drop in Crime Rates

The data cited above demonstrate that there has been a general drop in the overall crime rate in recent years. This is unusual at first glance, as logically a poor economy would seem to correlate with an increase in crime, but the recent statistics are consistent with the overall trend toward a decrease in crime since the 1990s.[40] Explaining this drop in crime rates is a challenge, with no clear consensus as to an explanation. Tufts University sociology professor John Conklin, in his book *Why Crime Rates Fell*, asserts that the drop is due to the fact that more Americans are incarcerated than ever before.[41] For Conklin, the simple drop in the number of criminals on the street means fewer of them are able to commit crime. A more controversial theory, espoused by economist Stephen Levitt, is that the legalization of abortion in the early 1970s was one of the main causative factors in the decrease in crime.[42] In short, he argued that fewer unwanted children in the 1970s and 1980s led to fewer criminals from the 1990s until today.

Correlates of Crime

Sociologists, and criminologists in particular, are especially interested in the study of the causes and correlates of crime. *Causes* are the factors that directly precipitate criminal offense. *Correlates* are factors that are mutually related, but are not necessarily causal. The important distinction is that correlation does not necessarily imply causation. The most prominent correlates for criminal offending that are of interest to researchers are age, race, socioeconomic status, education, and previous exposure to violence. Each of these correlates/causes has differing levels of empirical support.[43]

Age

Crime is most common in the second and third decades of the life of the offender.[44] This is a long-accepted tenet of criminology. The aggregate number of arrests in a society may change over a period of time, but the basic breakdown of the relative magnitudes of age groups remains fairly consistent. The 25–29 age group continues to have the highest arrest rate with 1,379,975 arrests in 2015.[45] Moreover, according to Hirschi and Gottfredson, the relationship between age and crime is consistent across both race and sex,[46] which would tend to suggest that it is almost a constant (it does not vary across different categories).

Race

Race is one of the most studied correlates of crime in the U.S. There are many theories about the relationship between race and crime, most of which are concerned with environmental and social factors. Relatively few researchers advocate for biological reasons to explain race as a cause of crime.[47] The disproportionately large representation of minorities in both arrest and victimization reports is generally accepted,[48] while the root causes of that disparity are hotly debated. Generally speaking, areas that are racially diverse tend to experience higher crime rates.[49] While the majority of arrests are white offenders, African-Americans are represented at a rate two to three times their presence in the general population.[50]

Socioeconomic/Education Status

Generally speaking, higher socioeconomic status (affluence, education, health, etc.) correlates with lower rates of criminal offense.[51] Criminality correlates highly with unemployment and high frequency of career change. However, it should be borne in mind that so-called "white-collar" crime is a poignant reality, in addition to violent crime and petty theft. The effects of such crime can be equally devastating: doctors cheat on Medicare, lawyers misappropriate funds, business owners run Ponzi schemes, and industrialists dispose of hazardous waste in illegal and unsafe ways.[52] Therefore, explaining criminality solely by reference to the socioeconomic status of the offender is insufficient (although not without merit).

Previous Exposure to Violence

A final potential correlate for deviance is previous exposure to violence. Children who are exposed to violence at a young age are especially vulnerable to offending as adults.[53] The trauma of witnessing violence at a young age may cause mental stress that leads to delinquency or violent behavior.[54]

Theories of Crime

Each of us brings to the world our own unique ideological viewpoints, based upon traditions or what we inherently "know" to be true. How do these ideological foundations affect criminological theory? As Lilly, Cullen, and Ball (2007) note, why is it that crime is higher in some communities?[55] Why is it that some people break the law and others do not? Why is it that people, regardless of economic status, commit crimes? From a criminological viewpoint, it is important that we delve into this behavior to capture answers and offer solutions. Criminological theory should guide efforts to react to deviant and/or criminal behavior and prevent it from occurring. Most importantly, theory should inform policy.

Understanding theory is critical in exploring every facet of the criminal justice system, from prevention to crime detection, enforcement, prosecution, sentencing, punishment, incarceration, and re-entry. Theory should help establish the consequences for criminal offending and deviant behavior. Historically, criminological theory can be categorized into three different schools of thought: the pre-classical school, the classical school, and the positivist school.

Pre-Classical School

Prior to modern-day naturalistic explanations of crime and criminal behavior, crime was understood as a concept of spiritualism and retribution. It was believed that crime was caused by supernatural forces as opposed to natural forces. This was the **pre-classical school** of thought. During the Middle Ages in Europe, the old adage "the devil made me do it" was the guiding philosophy for determining what was considered a crime. Individuals turned to religion and the Bible to determine what constituted violations of law. Crimes that today are not considered illegal—possibly just deviant, or not enforced at all—were worthy of retributive responses, including death or excruciating pain. Likewise, crime and offenses were considered to be private matters, and the responses to these private matters were handled by the individuals and their families.

Pre-classical school A school of thought that held that crime was caused by supernatural forces as opposed to natural forces.

Trial by battle A mechanism for privately resolving disputes during the pre-classical time period, in which the victim or a chosen member of the victim's family would battle with the offender or a chosen member of the offender's family to determine guilt.

Trial by ordeal A method of handling conflict privately during the pre-classical time period, in which proving innocence involved the use of extremely painful or life-threatening methods of punishment.

Compurgation A method of handling offenses during the pre-classical time period, in which individuals who could find a reputable person in their community to speak on their behalf would be found innocent.

One response to criminal offenses and punishment was the **trial by battle**. Trials by battle were handled by the victim and the offender. Since it was a private matter, the victim or a chosen member of the victim's family would battle with the offender or a chosen member of the offender's family to determine guilt. The belief was that if offenders were innocent, they would win or not be harmed, therefore proving their innocence.

Another variation of handling the matter privately was the **trial by ordeal**. The trial by ordeal method for proving innocence involved the use of extremely painful or life-threatening methods for punishment. The belief was that if you were innocent, then God would protect you. Examples of punishments included dunking individuals or burying them in heavy stones.

The final example of punishment as a private matter was **compurgation**. In this method of handling offenses, individuals who could find a reputable person in their community to speak on their behalf would be found innocent. This practice led to distinctions by class and in some instances the truly guilty never being held accountable. It should be obvious to a modern observer that the cure did not always logically follow from the cause.

The primary shortcoming of any spiritualistic explanation of crime is that it cannot be scientifically proven. Naturalistic explanations, on the other hand, rely on science to explain the causes of crime. Evidence suggests that as early as 460 B.C., Hippocrates was pointing to the brain as an "independent organ of the mind."[56] Since naturalistic explanations could be used to explain behavior, they could also be used to scientifically study criminal offending. Naturalistic explanations were used to scientifically advance the understanding of behavior during the 16th and 17th centuries in Europe with the development of the classical school of thought.

Classical School of Thought

The Enlightenment brought an end to the use of brutal and arbitrary punishments. In his 1764 publication, *On Crimes and Punishments,* Cesare Beccaria, known as the father of classical criminology, proposed the removal of harsh punishments and a focus on deterrence principles, in which the offense was punished rather than the offender. The Enlightenment philosophers argued that individuals were free-will thinkers who had the ability to weigh the costs of the punishment with the benefits of the offense. Known also as the *pleasure-pain principle*, this placed the responsibility for behavior on the offender. Further, these philosophers believed that the creation and enforcement of laws should be equal and follow the utilitarian principle of the greatest good for the greatest number. Beccaria and his fellow philosophers further contended that each person in a society agreed implicitly to adhere to the social contract, in which they forfeited certain rights to those in charge in exchange for protection. There was the belief that the government had a right to punish, and that failure to do so was a violation of the social contract.

One of the most important tenets put forth by Beccaria was the idea that punishments should be just, and no greater than the harm caused to society. This tenet called for an end to brutal responses to seemingly minor offenses. More specifically, Beccaria was opposed to the use of the death penalty as a punishment. Instead, he advocated for what we now know as deterrence. **Deterrence theory** is based upon the premise that for any punishment to be effective, it must be swift, severe, and certain. If these three conditions are met, the argument goes, then crime will diminish. There are two forms of deterrence: general and specific. The goal of **general deterrence** is to deter the public from committing future criminal acts by ensuring that punishment is focused on potential criminals as opposed to the individual. The goal of **specific deterrence** is to deter a particular individual from committing future criminal acts by focusing the punishment on that individual.[57]

Deterrence theory
A theory of punishment based upon the premise that in order for any punishment to be effective it must be swift, severe, and certain. There are two forms of deterrence: general and specific.

General deterrence
A form of deterrence used to deter the populace from committing future criminal acts by ensuring that the principles of punishment are focused on potential criminals as opposed to the individual.

Specific deterrence
A form of deterrence used to deter an individual from committing future criminal acts by focusing the punishment on that individual.

Classical school
A philosophy of crime that placed the responsibility for behavior on the offender.

Jeremy Bentham, in his work, *Introduction to the Principles of Morals and Legislation,* extended the work of Beccaria to include the concept of utility or utilitarianism. "Bentham further specified the idea of utility, or utilitarianism, which emphasizes maximization of pleasure and minimization of pain. This can be viewed on both the individual and aggregate level. On the individual level, this means that an individual will engage (or not engage) in activity that maximizes pleasure and minimizes pain, as perceived by the individual prior to the act. On the aggregate scale utilitarianism argues that the state or government will implement laws that benefit the 'greatest good for the greatest number.'"[58]

Although the **classical school** was an advancement from the spiritualistic view of crime and punishment, it still often resulted in harsh punishments. As scientific exploration and knowledge grew, so too did the pursuit of science to explain criminal behavior. Despite losing favor in recognition of what is now known as the positivist school, the views of the classical school have been revitalized in theories such as routine activities theory.

© ID1974/Shutterstock.com

Archaic methods of punishment and deterrence involved extremely painful or life-threatening acts.

Routine activities theory A theory of criminal offending positing that crime is a function of opportunity—the convergence of a motivated offender, a suitable target, and a lack of guardianship.

Routine activities theory posits that crime is a function of opportunity. More specifically, as Lawrence Cohen and Marcus Felson (1979) contend, crime occurs when a motivated offender, a suitable target, and a lack of guardianship all converge.[59] Crime as a function of everyday life becomes most prevalent when an individual's routine, either the mundane or the normal, creates a circumstance where these elements converge. Using elements of crime prevention through environmental design allows potential victims to address the issues of routine and mundane behavior.

The *theory of rational choice* contends that traditional theories fail to recognize the merit of choice in criminal acts. Rational choice theorists believe that acts made by offenders are sequenced and purposeful. Under this theory, the criminal act is the result of a rational choice made in the course of a cost/benefit analysis; if the potential gains exceed the punishment, the perpetrator will commit the crime. This perspective advocates for situational crime prevention to reduce opportunities for crime and victimization.[60]

Positivist School

The classical school, though popular, still came under attack by scientists who argued that not all behavior is reflective of free-will thinking or rational decision-making. Rather, some behavior occurs as a result of factors outside of the control of individuals. This idea led to the formation of the **positivist school** of thought, a philosophy based on biological, psychological, and sociological theories of crime.

Positivist school A school of thought on crime arguing that some behavior occurs as a result of factors outside the control of individuals.

Biological theories Theoretical propositions that look to the body to identify individuals who are predisposed to criminal offending.

Biological Theories of Crime

The first **biological theories** of criminal offending were geared toward the elimination of certain groups or classes of individuals. Most notable was the development of *eugenics*, which focused on monitoring and controlling the deviant population through sterilization. Many of the techniques used in such monitoring were essentially pseudoscience, such as craniometry and phrenology.

One example of using biological explanations was the development of craniometry as a field of exploration. Scientists studying craniometry believed they could identify superior versus inferior groups by the size of the skull, and applied this belief to racialized propaganda.[61] The belief was that the skull mirrored the shape of the brain and therefore predicted superiority. Most studies by craniometrists found that white western Europeans were most likely to have the largest skulls and therefore to be superior. This proposition held true until one key researcher, K.F. Gauss, died and an autopsy revealed that his skull and brain were smaller than average. Scientists have subsequently tended to emphasize factors other than the size of the skull or brain, such as the complexity of its development.[62]

Eventually the study of craniometry waned and gave way to phrenology, the study of the bumps on an individual's head. Borrowing from craniometry, phrenologists believed that the skull mirrored the shape of the brain; therefore, skulls that did not conform to the norm were deemed inferior and predictive of criminal offending. Although phrenology as a predictor of criminal offending was not supported by scientific research, more recent studies have revealed a connection between trauma to the left temporal lobe above the ear and violent offending.

Another example of early biological propositions was physiognomy, the study of facial and other features that led to the development of problem behaviors such as criminal offending. The study of facial and body features led to the argument that certain races and ethnicities were superior to others. Such arguments were often made implicitly; for example, James Redfield in *Comparative Physiognomy* (1852) compared the features of different races with different animals, in terms of both appearance and character.[63]

The final proposition that set the framework for the study of biology and crime was the work of Charles Darwin in *The Origin of Species*. In this work, Darwin argued that man evolved from earlier primitive species, and that certain individuals within the species would thrive while others would fail to thrive. This led to the conclusion that there were certain ethnic groups that were essentially throwbacks to an earlier time and therefore inferior. Although Darwin did not specifically study criminality, he did lay the groundwork for the study and application of these principles to understanding the causes of crime.

Cesare Lombroso conducted the first major scientific study of crime, incorporating tenets of all the previously mentioned biological theories. Lombroso first presented his ideas in 1876 and argued that criminal behavior could be differentiated from what one considers to be normal behavior. He contended that individuals who participated in criminal offending were throwbacks from a primitive time, also known as the **atavistic man**. He argued that individuals most likely to be criminals could be identified through recognition of at least five *stigmata* or characteristics, including both physical and extraphysical abnormalities such as "ears of unusual size, sloping foreheads, excessively long arms, receding chins, and twisted noses."[64] He also contended that individuals who displayed tattoos and had a family history of epilepsy and other disorders were more likely to be criminal.[65] Further, Lombroso argued that offenders could be classified into four major categories: "(a) born criminal or people with atavistic characteristics; (b) insane criminals including idiots, imbeciles, and paranoiacs as well as epileptics and alcoholics; (c) occasional criminals or criminaloids, whose crimes are explained primarily by opportunity, although they too have innate traits that predispose them to criminality; and (d) criminals of passion, who commit crimes because of anger, love, or honor and are characterized by being compelled to crime by an 'irresistible force.'"[66, 67]

Atavistic man
An identification of individuals participating in criminal activity as throwbacks from a primitive time.

Although Lombroso's theory did not withstand the test of time, his ideas continued to guide researchers. For example, the ideas put forth by Lombroso were further expanded by Raffaele Garofalo. Garofalo shared the belief that certain physical characteristics indicated a criminal nature: for instance,

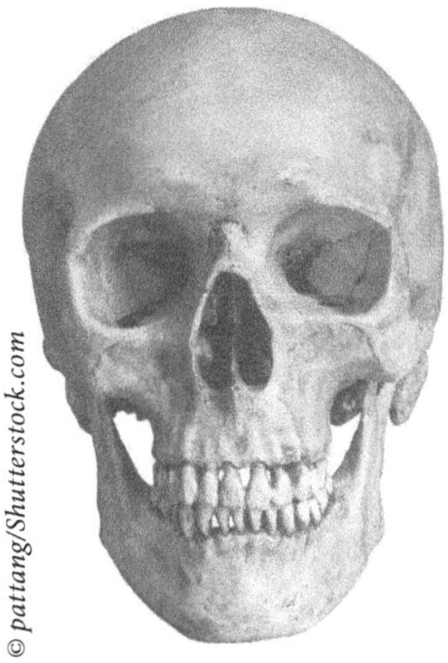

© pattang/Shutterstock.com

Scientists studying craniometry believed they could identify superior versus inferior groups by the size of the skull.

he thought criminals had less sensitivity to physical pain, demonstrated by the fact that prisoners frequently received tattoos while in prison. Enrico Ferri continued these ideas but included a sociological and psychological component, stating that a combination of many biological, social, and organic factors caused delinquency.[68]

More recent research explored the connection between criminality and inherited traits. One widely cited study was conducted by Richard Dugdale.[69] Dugdale identified a family of individuals, the Jukes (not their real name), who were known to participate in criminal activity. He studied these individuals to determine whether there were specific traits that were inherited by families. He concluded that the poor environment in which the Jukes lived was responsible for their criminality, and that "environment tends to produce habits which may become hereditary."[70]

Another biological explanation for crime was put forth by William Sheldon.[71] Sheldon argued that criminals could be distinguished from the normal population based upon physical characteristics that made them more prone to criminality. He identified three specific body types, known as *somotypes*, that he used to classify the general population. The first body type classification was the *endomorph*: these individuals were characterized as having heavier builds and moving slower. The second type of body classification was the *ectomorph*, tall and slim. The final body type, *mesomorphs*, were best characterized by their overall athletic appearance and build. These individuals were very strong and tended to be aggressive. Sheldon argued that most criminal offenders would be classified as mesomorphs. Further studies and research revealed little or no empirical support for these propositions. Therefore, this theory lost intellectual credibility (though it remains present in ingrained cultural stereotypes).

Researchers have also explored the influence of genetics on criminal offending, questioning whether crime is a function of nature (genetics) or nurture (environment). One way this phenomenon has been studied has been through twin studies. Early studies of twin behavior revealed a significant relationship between identical twins (monozygotic, or MZ) and crime, whereas the relationship between criminal associations and fraternal twins (dizygotic, or DZ) was not significant. A review of relevant studies conducted between 1929 and 1961 found that 60% of MZ twins shared criminal behavior patterns compared to only 30% of DZ twins. Karl Christiansen studied 3,586 male twin pairs and found a 52% concordance for MZ pairs and 22% for DZ twins.[72]

Another way to explore these connections between nature and nurture is through adoption studies. The most frequently cited study on adopted children was conducted by Hutchings and Mednick.[73] They analyzed 1,145 adopted male children born in Copenhagen, Denmark, between 1927 and 1941. They were most interested in looking at the connection between biological or adoptive parents. A total of 143 criminal adoptees (that is, children whose biological fathers had criminal records) were matched with 143 non-criminal adoptees. Results revealed that adopted youth whose biological fathers had criminal records were 24.5% more likely to have a criminal conviction.

Critical Thinking
What policy/policies to prevent crime would a biological theorist most likely support?

Psychological Theories of Crime

Psychological theories, in general, deal with individual traits that manifest themselves in criminal behavior. For the purposes of this chapter, psychoanalytical and personality theories will be reviewed. More recent expansions of psychological concepts combine these propositions with biological and sociological theories.

© Lightspring/Shutterstock.com

Sigmund Freud correlated crime to the interplay between the id, ego, and superego.

Psychoanalytical perspectives have their roots in the works of Sigmund Freud. Freud argued that all behavior is motivated by wishes and desires found within our unconscious (or subconscious) minds. It is the interplay between the id, ego, and superego that dictates which unconscious desires will be fulfilled.[74] In Freudian terms, the id includes the unconscious wishes developed in the early stages of life. The superego includes the unconscious wishes developed from watching others around us, such as our parents. The ego serves as the mediator between the id and the superego, translating complex wishes and desires with realistic expectations on a daily basis.[75]

A frequently cited example of Freud's work in practice is August Aichhorn's 1925 book *Wayward Youth* (translated into English in 1935). Aichhorn described how he utilized Freud's work to resolve chronic delinquent behaviors in youth in both conventional and individual settings. He recognized the interplay between the ego and the superego, arguing that an ill-developed superego led to delinquent activity. For Aichhorn, the key to addressing delinquent activity was moral education. His techniques could be used in a training school setting in small groups. Long-term follow-up studies of youth who worked with Aichhorn revealed changes in behavior after only one session.[76]

Personality theory is another way that psychological perspectives have been used in a criminal justice setting. Unlike psychoanalytical theories that explore the involvement of unconscious wishes and desires, **personality theories** look to explain criminal behavior as expressions of impulsiveness, aggression, or sensation-seeking. A variety of tools have been used in criminal justice settings to identify problems and disorders associated

Personality theories
Theories of crime that look to explain criminal behavior as an expression of impulsiveness, aggression, or sensation-seeking.

with personality. These include the Minnesota Multiphasic Personality Inventory (MMPI), the California Psychological Inventory (CPI), and the Hare Psychopathy Checklist (PCL-R).

Another psychological theory is behavioral and/or learning theory using operant conditioning. This therapeutic approach uses reinforcers (both positive and negative) to encourage individuals to perform desired social behaviors.[77]

Critical Thinking

What policy/policies to prevent crime would a psychological theorist most likely support?

Sociological Theories of Crime

By the early 1900s the city of Chicago, Illinois, had experienced unprecedented growth that ultimately would change the face of the United States. Immigrants from all over the world were flocking to the city in the hope of a better life. This cultural and structural shift prompted faculty members and students from the University of Chicago to explore and study the impact of growth on the city during the 1920s. The result was a specialized body of work in urban sociology that has come to be known as the **Chicago School**,[78] which made use of the city to study "alcoholism, homelessness, suicide, psychoses and poverty." Robert Park, a journalist and sociologist by training, played a significant role in reviewing and covering how the city developed. He focused specifically on the assimilation of immigrants into the general population of the United States, seeing Chicago as a crucible for the process of civilization and a way to view it "under a microscope."[79]

Chicago School
A specialized body of work in urban sociology that made use of the city of Chicago to study alcoholism, homelessness, suicide, psychoses, and poverty.

Ernest Burgess, a colleague of Robert Park, sought to graphically depict the outward growth of the city of Chicago. Unlike previous researchers, Burgess contended that there was a distinct pattern to the city's growth.[80] According to Burgess's **concentric zone theory**, the development of the city of Chicago could be divided into five distinct zones or rings. Zone I was the Loop, or the business district. This zone was the heart of the industrial complex. There was a great deal of transportation in and out of the city, including rail and waterways. Zone II, known as the zone in transition, was located just adjacent to the business district. This zone was best defined by deteriorated housing, tenement conditions, continual displacement of residents, and a high rate of turnover by the immigrant population, and was the least desirable place to live in the city.[81] Zone III, working men's homes and multiple-family dwellings, was an area where apartment buildings and modest homes were found. Zone IV, known as the residential zone (single-family homes), consisted of nicer apartments and higher-priced homes. Zone V, known as the commuter zone, was a suburban area.[82]

Park and Burgess's descriptions of the development and growth of Chicago led Clifford Shaw and Henry McKay, sociologists employed by the state of Illinois, to explore the effect of the city's growth patterns on juvenile delinquency. Shaw and McKay[83] proposed that communities with higher rates of social ills—including a breakdown in family composition, dilapidated buildings, unsupervised teenagers, high rates of poverty, high rates of residential mobility, and ethnic heterogeneity—were most likely to experience high rates of crime and delinquency. They postulated that the controls or bonds that would keep youth from committing delinquent acts would be diminished because of these social ills, therefore resulting in increases in delinquent and criminal activity. Communities characterized by intact homes and neighborhoods were known to be more socially organized. Known as **social disorganization theory**, this theory laid the foundation for looking at the causes of crime in the environment, not just at the individual level.

Social disorganization theory A theoretical proposition stating that communities with higher rates of social ills, such as breakdown in family composition, dilapidated buildings, unsupervised teenagers, high rates of poverty, high rates of residential mobility, and ethnic heterogeneity, are most likely to experience high rates of crime and delinquency.

To test their theory, Shaw and McKay[84] reviewed juvenile court records, commitments to correctional schools, alleged delinquency handled by police or probation, and juvenile arrests and commitments. Using census data, juvenile court records, and housing and welfare records, they confirmed that crime flourished in zones I and II of Chicago. The highest rates of delinquency were found in communities with the highest rates of social ills that failed to regulate behavior and had the most unsupervised teens. This theoretical premise became the foundation for many advancements in understanding crime and behavior.

© Stepan Bessmelnitsin/ Shutterstock.com

In Burgess's concentric zone theory, Chicago's Zone II was characterized by deteriorated and abandoned buildings.

In 1930, Edwin Sutherland joined the faculty of the University of Chicago. Rejecting the individual explanation of crime, Sutherland argued that crime was a product of the social environment in which individuals gained their values from those around them.[85] Sutherland proposed that criminal behavior was learned like all other conventional behavior. In his **differential association theory**, Sutherland identified nine different propositions to explain learning:

Differential association theory A sociological theory positing that crime is a product of the social environment whereby values are gained from those around individuals.

1. "Criminal behavior is learned.
2. Criminal behavior is learned in interaction with other persons in a process of communication.
3. The principal part of the learning of criminal behavior occurs within intimate personal groups.
4. When criminal behavior is learned, the learning includes (a) techniques of committing the crime, which sometimes are very complicated, sometimes are very simple; [and] (b) the specific direction of motives, drives, rationalizations, and attitudes.
5. The specific direction of motives and drives is learned from definitions of legal codes as favorable and unfavorable.

6. A person becomes delinquent because of an excess of definitions favorable to violation of law over definitions unfavorable to violation of law. This is the principle of differential association.
7. Differential associations may vary in frequency, duration, priority, and intensity.
8. The process of learning criminal behavior by association with criminal and anti-criminal patterns involves all the mechanisms that are involved in any other learning.
9. While criminal behavior is an expression of general needs and values, it is not explained by those general needs and values since noncriminal behavior is an expression of the same needs and values."[86]

During the 1930s, the Chicago School dominated thought and explanations for crime and criminal behavior. Robert K. Merton, however, rejected these ideas. He was influenced by an understanding of the breakdown of norms and values (normlessness) that was termed "anomie" by Emile Durkheim.[87] Merton expanded upon this, and proposed that when individuals failed to conform to cultural values or achieve financial success, they turned to crime and deviance. In other words, society puts pressure on individuals to live up to certain cultural norms, which can frustrate and put strain on those who are unable to meet those norms. Merton's theory was known as **strain theory**.

Strain theory A theoretical proposition contending that crime rates are produced by an individual's inability to conform to cultural values or achieve monetary success through accepted norms.

Strain theory was further expanded in Lloyd Ohlin's study of delinquent boys. As a student of Merton, he contended that delinquent youth banded together by abandoning middle-class values and creating their own separate sets of values.[88] Richard Cloward (also a student of Merton's) later joined with Ohlin to extend this notion, arguing that the social environment generated pressure for deviance. They argued that the high level of strain experienced by lower-class youth permitted them to adopt illegitimate means for obtaining their goals. In organized slums, younger members of the slums modeled older youth and formed a separate subculture. Similarly, some drug-involved youth further separated themselves as a distinct subculture.[89]

During the 1990s, strain theory was further expanded by Robert Agnew in his **general strain theory**.[90] According to Agnew, Merton did not include all of the strains that existed in an individual's life. Agnew argued that strain could be categorized into three distinct types: 1) "strain as the failure to achieve positively valued goals (traditional strain)"[91]; 2) "strain as the removal of positive stimuli from the individual"; and 3) "strain as the presentation of negative stimuli."[92] The more strain individuals were exposed to, the more likely they were to participate in delinquent or criminal activity.

General strain theory An expansion of strain theory stating that the more strain individuals are exposed to, the more likely they are to participate in delinquent or criminal activity. Types of strain include the failure to achieve positive goals, the removal of positive stimuli, and the presentation of negative stimuli.

Control theories seek to add a component of motivation. Like strain theory, social control theory has its roots in the work of Emile Durkheim. Durkheim contended that crime is a normal function of society that serves to unite individuals against a common threat. He further argued that a society without crime is by definition abnormal. Crime and deviance, therefore, serve to establish the moral boundaries for those living within the community.

There are a number of variations of control theories. One of the most significant is Travis Hirschi's **social control theory**. Unlike other theories that sought to explain why individuals committed crimes, Hirschi's theory sought to understand why individuals chose *not* to participate in delinquent or criminal activity. Hirschi characterized the social bond as having four elements. The first, *attachment*, involved identification, emotional bond, concern, and respect for peers or parents, as well as engagement in activities with peers, supervision and intimate communications by parents, attitudes toward school, and concern and sensitivity for the opinions of parents, peers, and teachers. The second element, *involvement*, involved time-consuming activities such as work, sports, recreation, hobbies, and homework, as well as nonactive leisure time, lack of boredom, and time spent interacting with friends. The third element, *commitment*, involved investment in education, career, family, and society, as well as academic and educational competence, aspirations, and expectations, achievement orientation, expected occupation, and importance of reputation. The fourth element, *belief*, involved respect for authorities and law, and the absence of neutralizations. Many have argued that social control theory may be best for explaining less serious forms of delinquency.[93]

Social control theory
A theoretical proposition that contends that the more strongly individuals are bonded to their community, the less likely they are to participate in delinquent activity.

© Andrey_Popov/Shutterstock.com

Social disorganization theory holds that communities with higher rates of social ills—including high rates of poverty—are most likely to experience high rates of crime and delinquency.

In 1990, Travis Hirschi diverged from his original theory of social control and bonding when he, along with Michael Gottfredson, proposed the **general theory of crime**. Departing from Hirschi's original theoretical premise, they argued that crime was not controlled by bonds to society, but rather by an individual's inability to demonstrate self-control. Crime and other analogous behaviors such as smoking, drinking, driving fast, having multiple sexual partners, etc., provide short-term gratification for those with low self-control. These behaviors begin in early childhood and continue on into later adulthood. Individuals with low self-control are more impulsive, participate in risk-taking behavior, are self-centered, have extreme tempers, and are more physically active.[94] These individuals typically fail at life events that require delayed gratification, such as marriage, education, employment, or other activities that require planning. Crime in general is a not a planned event; rather, offenders act on impulse as a mechanism for gratifying their needs. Gottfredson and Hirschi (1990) contended that there were 10 elements of social control that kept individuals from committing and participating in criminal activity. Those elements of self-control are as follows:[95]

General theory of crime
A theoretical proposition that crime is not controlled by bonds to society, but rather by an individual's ability to demonstrate self-control. Under this theory, crime in general is not a planned event; rather, offenders act on impulse as a mechanism for gratifying their needs.

10 Elements of Social Control

1. Criminal acts provide immediate gratification of desires.
2. Criminal acts provide easy or simple gratification of desires.
3. Criminal acts are exciting, risky, or thrilling.
4. Crimes provide few or meager long-term benefits.
5. Crimes require little skill or planning.
6. Crimes often result in pain or discomfort for the victim.
7. Crimes require the interaction of an offender with people or their property.
8. The major benefit of many crimes is not pleasure but relief from momentary irritation.
9. Crimes involve the risk of violence and physical injury of pain and suffering on the part of the offender.
10. The risk of criminal penalty for any given criminal act is small but this depends in part on the circumstances of the offense.

Opponents of the general theory of crime have argued that many of the theoretical principles involve circular reasoning. For example, how do we know whether an individual is impulsive or just acting out? This theory further fails to account for personality disorders, racial and gender issues, moral beliefs, and ecological or individual differences. Similarly, this theory purports that behavior does not change over time, and that once an individual demonstrates low self-control, this behavior will continue throughout his or her lifetime. However, other theoretical propositions, such as life course theory, have demonstrated that criminal propensity can change.

Some criminological theories focus on the criminal self as it develops through its relation to others. In 1902, Charles Horton Cooley proposed the idea of the "looking-glass self," which postulated that the self was determined by the perception of others and society's interpersonal interactions.[96] Cooley was a direct influence on George Herbert Mead, a sociologist commonly associated with the Chicago School. Mead saw the self in symbolic terms, specifically as a symbol that can be understood only in its relationship to society as a whole.[97] For Mead, the self is, in some sense, disintegrated by its encounter with society, and then reconstituted as a response to it.[98] Cooley's and Mead's ideas directly influenced labeling theory.

Labeling theory
A theoretical tradition in which criminals become set in their roles as criminals as a result of their stigmatized status.

Labeling theory was developed by Edwin Lemert. He argued that when an individual is labeled by society as deviant or criminal, the individual is likely to accept the label as true and begin to self-identify as an offender. These individuals are more likely to continue this form of behavior.

Howard Becker further advanced the concept of labeling, arguing that there are four distinct categories of individuals: conformists, pure deviants, falsely accused, and secret deviants.[99] The *conformist* abides by all of the rules and laws of society. The *pure deviant* commits criminal acts and is caught.

The *falsely accused* individual does not commit criminal acts, but instead is falsely accused of crimes, typically as a result of factors such as socioeconomic status, sex, age, race, etc. The *secret deviant* commits acts but is not formally caught and processed; there are a significant number of individuals who fall within this category.[100]

Edwin Lemert's labeling theory contends that when an individual is labeled by society as deviant, the individual is likelier to self-identify as an offender.

Another variation of labeling theory, known as *radical nonintervention,* was put forth by Edwin Schur, who argued that juveniles who violated delinquency laws should receive no punishment or intervention. Schur contended that any intervention would label an individual as delinquent and would therefore make him or her more likely to commit delinquent behavior—a sort of self-fulfilling prophecy.

More recently, the concept of labeling has been extended into John Braithwaite's theory of **reintegrative shaming**. In *Crime, Shame and Reintegration* (1989), Braithwaite contends that punishments designed to stigmatize the offender are counterproductive.[101] Instead of reducing crime, these efforts may in fact further encourage delinquent or criminal offending. Publicly shaming offenders may lead them to be alienated from society and make it difficult, if not impossible, for them to reintegrate. With this in mind, Braithwaite argues that societies should use reintegrative shaming, whereby offenders are punished—therefore repaying their debt to society—and then forgiven for their transgressions and reintegrated back into society. This reintegrative shaming technique has been shown to reduce criminal activity in other countries.[102]

Reintegrative shaming A process whereby offenders are punished, therefore repaying their debt to society, and then forgiven for their transgressions and reintegrated back into society.

Conflict theory emphasizes how power is used to create conflict in society.[103] This theory builds off the works of Karl Marx and Friedrich Engels, who argued that capitalist societies create power structures that produce struggles for more money and wealth. This power struggle results in conflict and crime.[104] Power is typically associated with wealth and resources; therefore, those with the most wealth in society are more likely to create the laws, maintain control, and have power over the lower classes.[105]

Conflict theory A theory concerned with how power is maintained in a society rather than how individuals function within that continuum. Conflict theory holds that those with the most wealth in society are more likely to create the laws, maintain control, and have power over the lower classes.

As Reiman and Leighton (2010) contend, the "repressive" nature of law helps maintain the current criminal justice system. In the Marxist tradition, those in power establish a system that fills the needs of the "haves" at the expense of the "have-nots."[106] A variety of different forms of conflict theory exist. More recent versions of conflict theory include peacemaking criminology and left realism.

Critical Thinking

What policy/policies to prevent crime would a conflict theorist most likely support?

Peacemaking criminology A theory proposing the use of mediation, love, respect, and forgiveness to resolve societal conflicts and reduce recidivism and crime.

Peacemaking criminology utilizes the concepts of religion, spiritualism, and forgiveness to resolve the conflict that exists within society. Richard Quinney and Harold Pepinsky[107] argued that the keys to reducing recidivism and crime were mediation, love, respect, and forgiveness. They recognized that conflict would continue to exist in any society, but advocated that responses should come from a place of forgiveness.[108]

Left realism A philosophical approach advocating for more minimal responses or sanctions for street-level crimes and less serious offenses, and more stringent responses and social control for white-collar crimes and crimes against society.

Another modern-day variation of conflict theory is known as **left realism**. Developed in Britain in the 1980s, left realism branched off from the traditional focus on understanding crime as a class issue and focused on what it deemed the "real aspects of crime."[109] Left realists sought to understand the etiology of everyday crimes that were being committed by the working classes. They advocated for more minimal responses or sanctions for less serious offenses—such as drug use, prostitution, minor property offenses, and victimless crimes—and more stringent responses and social control for white-collar crimes and crimes against society.[110] According to Akers and Sellers (2009), left realism is a philosophical approach that in essence calls for the dismantling of the entire criminal justice system.[111] This approach has been criticized for a variety of reasons. Most notably, the lack of empirical research classifies this approach as philosophical rather than theoretical. Also, this approach calls for punishment responses to offenses rather than rehabilitation or forgiveness, which does not hold to the values of other types of conflict theory.[112]

Feminist theories Theoretical explanations of crime, justice, and the entire criminal justice system from an androgynous perspective.

Feminist theories of criminal justice seek to extend the understanding of criminal justice from an androgynous perspective. Many traditional criminological theories fail to take into account that women commit crimes for different reasons than men and they respond to treatment differently as well. No one single feminist perspective exists, but for the purposes of this chapter, a general description of feminist theory will be provided. Feminist theorists argue that the disparities in treatment of men and women in the criminal justice system are as important, if not more important, than the disparities in race and class. Traditional theories of crime have focused on patriarchal explanations.

The *chivalry hypothesis* states that women and girls are treated more leniently in the criminal justice system. This is dismissed by most feminists, though, who instead argue that there is a paternalistic approach in which women are treated on the opposite ends of the continuum—either very leniently or very harshly as a mechanism of control.

Daly and Chesney-Lind (1988)[113] contended that women's roles in society differ fundamentally from those of men, and that these differences in how men and women are viewed in society greatly impact both our understanding of behavior and responses to it.

Another area of feminist literature that has gained recent attention is the *gendering of crime*. This is the exploration of how gender and the roles ascribed to both men and women influence the types of offenses committed.

As Messerschmidt contends, boys and men are raised to be masculine. A sense of being a "man" is defined by "toughness" or assertion. Women, unlike men, take on socially ascribed roles of being the "nurturer" or homemaker. Therefore, if these roles are fulfilled, men should be committing more violent acts as opposed to women, who would be responsible for more property-related offenses.[114]

Integrated theories stem from the idea that there are many different theories about crime. Many of these theories fall short because they lack empirical support or because they do not thoroughly explain the causes of crime. One way to address these shortcomings is to combine the most powerful components of each theory into a new theoretical proposition, known as an integrated theory.[115] Theory integration seeks to combine elements of two or more theories into one explanation.

Integrated theories
Theories that identify the most powerful elements of other theories and combine two or more of them into one explanation.

Theory integration may combine elements such as control and social learning theories to explain why gangs are formed, or combine strain with social learning theories to explore the impact of the weakening of the social bonds on conventional society.[116]

Wilson and Herrnstein (1985),[117] in their book, *Crime and Human Nature*, proposed an integrated biosocial theory that combined biology with psychology. These authors proposed that biology affects how an individual reacts to their social environment. More specifically, they contended that parents play a crucial role in how children respond to their environment. Individuals seek approval from those closest to them (peers, friends, family) as a mechanism to support acceptable behavior. Wilson and Herrnstein further believed that for punishment to be effective, it must begin with parents and be state-reinforced as a deterrent.

A second variation of integrated theory is the integrated strain-control paradigm developed by Elliott et al. (1985).[118] Elliott and his colleagues proposed that theories of strain, control, and learning could be combined to create a more robust explanation of juvenile offending. For example, they proposed that "(1) strain (in the family and school) weakens (2) social bonds to conventional society, which in turn promotes (3) strong bonds to delinquent peers. It is these strong bonds to delinquent peers, therefore, that are principal factors in (4) the commission of delinquent behavior."[119] They further contended that strong attachments to conventional activities such as school or church reduced the propensity toward crime and delinquency.

© Odua Images/Shutterstock.com

Women commit crimes for different reasons than men and respond to treatment differently.

In general, integrated theories have been criticized for a variety of reasons. One of the biggest concerns is that combining two different theories may violate their own assumptions: for instance, control theories seek to explain why individuals do not commit crime, while learning theories seek to explain why they do.[120]

The study of criminal behavior has traditionally focused on the causes of offending among youth or young adults. Theories fail to follow the paths of offending from birth through death. One exception to this rule has arisen in the development of **life course theories**. The life course theorists contend that criminal offending is influenced by two specific patterns of behavior. First, crime is dependent upon the state of the perpetrator: that is, it is malleable based upon previous experiences that influence the individual. Second, crime and behavior are governed by traits that are not changeable, such as impulsivity, age, etc.[121] Individuals establish patterns of behavior in infancy through attachments and reinforcements with parents or caregivers. These attachments or the ability to bond with positive influences continue on into adulthood.

Life course theories The contention that criminal offending is influenced by an individual's previous experiences as well as traits or characteristics that are not changeable, such as impulsivity, age, etc.

One of the most influential studies of the life course perspective was developed by Robert Sampson and John Laub.[122] They found that criminal or delinquent offending does not occur in a vacuum. Rather, this behavior is influenced by one's environment and structural characteristics such as poverty, residential mobility, family size, and other factors. The family serves as the strongest instrument of control in a child's life through monitoring and attachments. Children reared in unstable homes with few bonds are more likely to grow into adults who have few stable bonds such as employment or marriage. Despite these deficits, research demonstrates that it is not impossible for individuals to overcome these barriers. If individuals are able to establish meaningful bonds in adulthood, these elements may function as "turning points" in their lives to keep them from continuing down a path of crime and delinquency. As noted by Sampson and Laub, it is these informal social controls and bonds that are most important in reducing or preventing crime throughout an individual's lifetime.

Critical Thinking

What policy/policies to prevent crime would a life course theorist most likely support?

In 1986, the Office of Juvenile Justice and Delinquency Prevention commissioned a study on the causes of delinquency. As part of this study, researchers from the University of Colorado, the University of Pittsburgh, the University of Albany, and the State University of New York interviewed over 4,000 youth at regular intervals, collecting information on their characteristics and behaviors. Information gathered from the study of all-male youth conducted by the team at the University of Pittsburgh helped identify three distinct pathways to crime: the authority conflict pathway, the covert pathway, and the overt pathway.[123] These **developmental pathways** were characterized by differences between these youths and normal offenders.

Developmental pathways A description of the various paths a youth may take into delinquent or criminal offending. These pathways include the authority conflict pathway, the covert pathway, and the overt pathway.

Damaging property is a characteristic of the covert pathway of juvenile crime.

FIGURE 2.6 THREE PATHWAYS TO BOYS' DISRUPTIVE BEHAVIOR AND DELINQUENCY

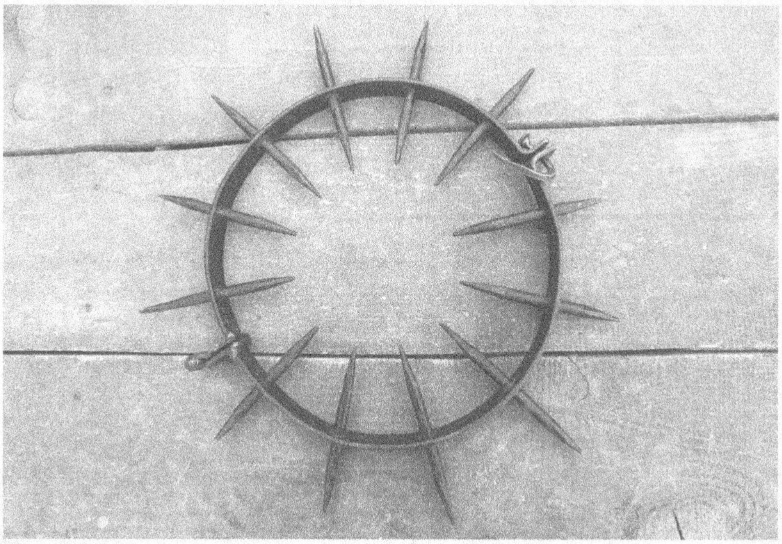

Source: Kelley, B. T., Loeber, R., Keenan, K. & DeLamatre, M. (1997). Developmental pathways in boys' disruptive and delinquent behavior (NCJ 165692). Juvenile Justice Bulletin. Washington, DC: Office of Juvenile Justice and Delinquency Prevention, p. 9.

For certain youth, disruptive behavior would manifest itself early in life and continue throughout their lifetime. Research revealed that for stubborn behavior, the median age was nine, with some displaying these characteristics as early as the age of three.

Figure 2.6 illustrates the distinct pathways to crime. The first pathway, the *authority conflict pathway*, begins when a child displays stubborn behavior at an early age. This leads to defiance (such as doing things one's own way and disobedience) and then to an avoidance of authority (such as staying out late or running away). The second pathway, the *covert pathway*, begins with minor dishonest or deceitful behavior (such as lying, shoplifting, or damaging property). This behavior then escalates to more serious crimes, ranging from joyriding, pocket picking, and larceny to using stolen credit cards, breaking and entering, dealing drugs, and stealing cars. The third pathway, the *overt pathway*, includes aggressive acts such as annoying others and bullying, and eventually leads to physical fighting and violent crimes (attacking someone, robbery).[124]

As further noted by the study, of most concern were the issues related to those whose offending persisted over time. Youth who experienced both family dysfunction and neurological problems were most likely to continue down these paths.[125]

Chapter Summary

- Society differentiates between the concepts of deviance and criminal behavior. Deviance is defined as behaviors considered outside of or inconsistent with normal behavior for a community or group, while criminal behavior is defined by legislation, statutes, and codes. It is important to understand these differences in terms of how society and the criminal justice system respond to illicit activities and behaviors.
- In 1930, the Federal Bureau of Investigation began collecting data on crimes reported to the police and crimes cleared by arrest on a voluntary wide-scale basis. This information is collected in the Uniform Crime Reports (UCR), and divided into Part I and Part II offenses. Part I index offenses are the most serious crimes committed in the United States.
- During the 1980s, the FBI sought to rectify some of the problems encountered with the UCR. The result was the creation of the National Incident-Based Reporting System (NIBRS). There are 13 key differences between the UCR and the NIBRS systems. Unlike the UCR, the NIBRS system includes a total of 22 offense categories made up of 46 crimes. This is an incident-based system that allows for the inclusion of both completed and attempted offenses. Although this is an enhanced version of the UCR, to date it has not been implemented widely. All data collected by the NIBRS system are collapsed into the UCR categories for reporting.
- The National Crime Victimization Survey (NCVS), first administered in 1973 and originally known as the National Crime Survey (NCS), is conducted by the U.S. Census Bureau on behalf of the Bureau of Justice Statistics on households in the United States. The most important functions of NCVS are to tap into the dark figure of crime, enhance the ability to compare victimizations by type of area and over time, provide uniform definitions of crime, and include detailed

descriptions of the criminal event, including the victim, potential precipitation, consequences of the event, and the offender.

- Another method for collecting data is the self-report survey. There is no one standard method for collecting data using the self-report method. However, this technique was developed and began being used more frequently during the 1950s. Data from self-report surveys are used to identify the number of crimes not reported to the police.
- Understanding theory is critical for exploring every facet of the criminal justice system, ranging from prevention to crime detection, enforcement, prosecution, sentencing, punishment, incarceration, and re-entry. Theory should establish the context in which consequences are developed for criminal offending and deviant behavior.
- Prior to the modern-day naturalistic explanations of crime and criminal behavior, crime was understood as a concept of spiritualism and retribution. This school of thought is known as the pre-classical school. At that time, it was believed that crime was caused by supernatural forces as opposed to natural forces. Therefore, punishments were considered a private matter and handled as such.
- The Enlightenment brought an end to the use of brutal and arbitrary punishments. Cesare Beccaria set forth a series of propositions advocating the removal of harsh punishments and a focus on deterrence principles whereby the offense was punished versus the offender. The Enlightenment philosophers argued that individuals were free-will thinkers who had the ability to weigh the costs of the punishment with the benefits of the offense. This "pleasure-pain principle" placed the responsibility for behavior on the offender.
- With the development and use of scientific principles, a new realm of theoretical understanding developed known as the positivist school of thought. These theories are best understood in terms of the following categories: biological, psychological, sociological, critical, feminist, peacemaking, and left realist. In all of these explanations, theorists contend that criminal behavior can be explained by forces either inherent within the individual or as a response to societal conditions.

Critical Thinking?

1. As noted in the beginning of the chapter, distinct differences exist between behaviors that are considered deviant and those considered criminal. Historically, behaviors such as drug use or prostitution were once legal but considered deviant. What factors do you believe should be taken into consideration when deciding whether behavior is illegal? What are some of the unintended/intended consequences of criminalizing behavior?

2. As noted in the statistics presented from both the UCR and the NCVS, crime rates have declined since 2008. What do these statistics reveal to us about crime reduction strategies? How might these data be used on a local and state level to respond to crime?
3. You have just been elected mayor in your community. You ran on a platform of reducing both spending and crime in your community. Given what you know about crime and its causes, how might you accomplish this task?
4. In the case study example provided at the beginning of the chapter, how might biological theory explain the shooting? Create a policy using biological theory that would prevent this crime from occurring in the future.
5. In the case study example provided at the beginning of the chapter, how might psychoanalytical theory explain the shooting? Create a policy using psychoanalytical theory that would prevent this crime from occurring in the future.
6. In the case study example provided at the beginning of the chapter, how might social disorganization theory explain the shooting? Create a policy using social disorganization theory that would prevent this crime from occurring in the future.
7. In the case study example provided at the beginning of the chapter, how might life course theory explain the shooting? Create a policy using life course theory that would prevent this crime from occurring in the future.
8. In the case study example provided at the beginning of the chapter, how might the general theory of crime explain the shooting? Create a policy using the general theory of crime that would prevent this crime from occurring in the future.
9. In the case study example provided at the beginning of the chapter, how might conflict theory explain the shooting? Create a policy using conflict theory that would prevent this crime from occurring in the future.

Media

Bureau of Justice Statistics: http://www.ojp.usdoj.gov/bjs
The Department of Justice website discusses the methodology of crime statistics and provides archived results from the past.

The National Center for Victims of Crime: http://www.ncvc.org/ncvc/Main.aspx
The NCVC is a resource and advocacy organization for victims. This website has useful information for both researchers and victims.

National Crime Victimization Survey: http://bjs.ojp.usdoj.gov/index.cfm?ty=dcdetail&iid=245

The NCVS is the crime victims' survey favored by victimologists. It allows researchers to track trends in victimization.

National Criminal Justice Reference Service: http://www.ncjrs.gov
The NCJRS is a federally funded, comprehensive website run by the Office of Justice Programs. It contains information relating to the Justice Department for research and public policy.

National Institute of Justice: http://www.ojp.usdoj.gov/nij/
The National Institute of Justice is dedicated to using science to help understand and reduce crime.

Occupational Outlook Handbook, 2010–11 Edition: http://www.bls.gov/oco/
This government-run site, published by the Bureau of Labor Statistics, details careers and their future outlook.

U.S. Department of Justice: http://www.usdoj.gov
The official website of the Department of Justice includes information about the roles of the department and the attorney general.

Uniform Crime Reports: http://www.fbi.gov/ucr/ucr.htm
The UCR, published by the FBI, are the most comprehensive statistical reports on reported crime in the United States.

Endnotes

1 McCaffrey, F. (2011). "Panel Examines Youth Gang Violence." The Gavel Online. Retrieved from http://bcgavel.com/2011/03/20/gang-violence-examined-presidential-scholars-program-hosts-panel-of-speakers/

2 Clinard, M. B. (1968). *Sociology of Deviant Behavior* (3rd ed.). New York, NY: Holt, Rinehart, and Winston, 28.

3 Lombroso, C. (1876). *L'Uomo Delinquente.*

4 Cornish, D., & Clarke, R. V. (1986). "Introduction." In D. Cornish & R. Clarke (Eds.), *The Reasoning Criminal* (pp. 1–16). New York, NY: Springer-Verlag.

5 Goode, E. (2001). *Deviant Behavior* (8th ed.). Upper Saddle River, NJ: Prentice Hall.

6 *Morrison, W. (2006). Criminology, Civilisation and the New World Order. London: Routledge.*

7 Uniform Crime Reporting Program Staff. (2004). *Uniform Crime Reporting Handbook.* Clarksburg, WV: Federal Bureau of Investigation, 2.

8 Ibid.

9 See the Uniform Crime Reporting Handbook at http://www.fbi.gov/about-us/cjis/ucr/additional-ucr- publications/ucr_handbook.pdf for more information on how data are collected and reported to the FBI.

10 O'Brien, R. M. (1985). *Crime and Victimization Data.* Thousand Oaks, CA: Sage.

11 Ibid., 22.

12 Federal Bureau of Investigation (FBI). (2011). *Uniform Crime Reporting Statistics: Their Proper Use*. Retrieved from http://www.fbi.gov/about-us/cjis/ucr/ucr-statistics-their-proper-use

13 Ibid.

14 O'Brien, 1985.

15 FBI, 2011.

16 Ibid.

17 Ibid.

18 FBI. (2000). *National Incident-Based Reporting System, Volume 1: Data Collection Guidelines*. Clarksburg, WV: Federal Bureau of Investigation, 1.

19 FBI, 2000, 9.

20 FBI, 2000.

21 Ibid., 9.

22 National Archive of Criminal Justice Data (NACJD). (2011). *National Crime Victimization Survey Resource Guide*.

23 Bureau of Justice Statistics. (2015) Data Collection: *National Crime Victimization Survey (NCVS)* Retrieved from http://www.bjs.gov/index.cfm?ty=dcdetail&iid=245.

24 NACJD, 2011, 1.

25 O'Brien, 1985.

26 NACJD, 2011.

27 O'Brien, 1985, 47.

28 NACJD, 2011.

29 U.S. Department of Labor, Bureau of Labor Statistics. (2009a). "Market and Survey Researchers." *Occupational Outlook Handbook, 2010–11 Edition*. Retrieved from http://www.bls.gov/oco/ocos013.htm#addinfo

30 Council of American Survey Research Organizations (CASRO). (n.d.). "What Qualifications/Education Do I Need?" *CASRO Careers*. Retrieved from http://www.casro.org/careers/page1.html

31 U.S. Department of Labor, Bureau of Labor Statistics, 2009a.

32 CASRO. (n.d.). "Employment Outlook." *CASRO Careers*. http://www.casro.org/careers/page4.html

33 U.S. Department of Labor, Bureau of Labor Statistics. (2009b). "Occupational Information Included in the Handbook: Job Outlook." *Occupational Outlook Handbook, 2010–11 Edition*. Retrieved from http://www.bls.gov/oco/oco2001.htm#outlook

34 Thornberry, T. P., Huizinga, D., & Loeber, R. (2004). "The Causes and Correlates Studies: Findings and Policy Implications." *Juvenile Justice Journal, IX(1), 3–19.*

35 Mulvey, E. P. (2011). *Highlights from Pathways to Desistance: A Longitudinal Study of Serious Adolescent Offenders* (NCJ 230971). Washington, DC: Office of Juvenile Justice and Delinquency Prevention.

36 O'Brien, 1985.

37 CNN U.S. (2000, October 5). "Reporting Hate Crimes Presents Dilemma for Many Officials." Retrieved from http://articles.cnn.com/2000-10-05/us/justice.hate.crime_1_crimes-ethnicity-or-national-origin-incidents?_s=PM:US

38 FBI, 2001, 1.

39 Truman, J. L., & Rand, M. R. (2010). *Criminal Victimization*, 2015.October 2016, NCJ 250180. Bureau of Justice Statistics. Retrieved from http://www.bjs.gov/content/pub/pdf/cv15.pdf.

40 FBI. (2006). "Crime in the US, by Volume and Rate per 100,000 Inhabitants, 1986–2005." *Crime in the United States 2005.* Retrieved from http://www2.fbi.gov/ucr/05cius/data/table_01.html

41 Conklin, J. (2003). *Why Crime Rates Fell.* New York, NY: Allyn and Bacon.

42 Levitt, S. D. (2004). "Understanding Why Crime Fell in the 1990s: Four Factors That Explain the Decline and Six That Do Not." *Journal of Economic Perspectives, 18*(1), 163–190.

43 Ellis, L., Beaver, K. M., & Wright, J. (2009). *Handbook of Crime Correlates.* San Diego, CA: Academic Press.

44 Ibid.

45 FBI. (2015) "Arrests by Age" *Crime in the United States 2015.* Retrieved from https://ucr.fbi.gov/crime-in-the-u.s/2015/crime-in-the-u.s.-2015/tables/table-38

46 Gottfredson, M. R., & Hirschi, T. (1990). *A General Theory of Crime.* Stanford, CA: Stanford University Press, 126.

47 For a critical overview of the latter, see Tubman-Carbone, 2009, 50–54.

48 Gabbidon & Greene, 2005a, 31–33; Walsh, 2004, 19–36; Wright, 2009, 143–144.

49 Ellis, Beaver, & Wright, 2009.

50 Gabbidon & Greene, 2005a, 31–33; Walsh, 2004, 22–23, 37–51.

51 Ellis et al., 2009.

52 Gottfredson & Hirschi, 1990, 184.

53 Lauritsen, J. L., Sampson, R. J., & Laub, J. H. (1991). "The Link between Offending and Victimization among Adolescents." *Criminology, 29,* 265–292.

54 Mazerolle, P., Burton, V. S., Cullen, F. T., Evans, T. D., & Payne, G. L. (2000). "Strain, Anger, and Delinquent Adaptations: Specifying General Strain Theory." *Journal of Criminal Justice, 28*(2), 89–102.

55 Lilly, J. R., Cullen, F. T., & Ball, R. A. (2007). *Criminological Theory: Context and Consequences* (4th ed.). Thousand Oaks, CA: Sage.

56 Ibid., 14.

57 Ferris, T. (2005). *Sentencing: Practical Approaches.* Toronto: Lexis-Nexis, 357.

58 Tibbetts, S. G., & Hemmens, C. (2010). *Criminological Theory: A Text/Reader.* Thousand Oaks, CA: Sage, 90.

59 Cohen, L. E., & Felson, M. (1979). "Social Change and Crime Rate Trends: A Routine Activities Approach." *American Sociological Review, 44,* 588–608.

60 Cornish, D. B., & Clarke, R. V. (Eds.). (1986). *The Reasoning Criminal: Rational Choice Perspectives on Offending.* New York, NY: Springer.

61 Thomas, D. H. (2001). *Skull Wars: Kennewick Man, Archaeology, and the Battle for Native American Identity.* New York, NY: Basic Books, 38–41.

62 Cosgrove, K. P., Mazure, C. M., & Staley, J. K. (2007). "Evolving Knowledge of Sex Differences in Brain Structure, Function, and Chemistry." *Biological Psychiatry, 62*(8), 847–855.

63 Redfield, J. W. "Comparative Physiognomy or Resemblances between Men and Animals: Illustrated."

64 Lombroso, 1896.

65 Ibid.

66 Wolfgang, M. E. (1973). "Cesare Lombroso." In H. Mannheim (Ed.), *Pioneers in Criminology* (2nd ed., pp. 232–291). Montclair, NJ: Patterson Smith.

67 Lilly et al., 2007, 19.

68 Ferri, E. (1897/1917). *Criminal Sociology.* Boston, MA: Little, Brown.

69 Dugdale, R. L. (1910). *The Jukes: A Study in Crime, Pauperism, Disease and Heredity.* New York, NY: G.P. Putnam's Sons.

70 Ibid., 66.

71 Sheldon, W. H. (1940). *The Varieties of Human Physique: An Introduction to Constitutional Psychology.* New York, NY: Harper & Brothers.

72 Moffitt, T. E., Ross, S., & Raine, A. (2011). "Crime and Biology." In J. Q. Wilson & J. Petersilia (Eds.), *Crime and Public Policy* (pp. 53–87). New York, NY: Oxford University Press.

73 Mednick, S. A., Gabrielli, W. F., & Hutchings, B. (1984). "Genetic Influences in Criminal Convictions: Evidence from an Adoption Cohort." *Science, 224*, 891–894. doi:10.1126/science.6719119

74 Lester, D., & Van Voorhis, P. (2000). "Psychoanalytic Therapy." In P. Van Voorhis, M. Braswell, & D. Lester (Eds.), *Correctional Counseling & Rehabilitation* (4th ed., pp. 111–128). Cincinnati, OH: Anderson.

75 Ibid.

76 Barton-Bellessa, S. M. (2010). "August Aichhorn: Wayward Youth." In F. Cullen & P. Wilcox (Eds.), *Encyclopedia of Criminological Theory.* Thousand Oaks, CA: Sage.

77 Ibid.

78 Cavan, R. S. (1983). "The Chicago School of Sociology, 1918–1933." *Urban Life, 11*, 415.

79 Park, R. E. (1928). "Human Migration and the Marginal Man." *American Journal of Sociology, 33*(6), 890.

80 McKenzie, R. D., Park, R. E., & Burgess, E. W. (1967). *The City.* Chicago, IL: University of Chicago Press.

81 Ibid.

82 Lilly et al., 2007.

83 Shaw, C. R., & McKay, H. D. (1942). *Juvenile Delinquency in Urban Areas.* Chicago, IL: University of Chicago Press.

84 Ibid.

85 Sutherland, E. (1934). *Principles of Criminology.* Chicago, IL: J.B. Lippincott.

86 Sutherland, E. H., & Cressey, D. R. (1970). *Criminology* (8th ed.). Philadelphia, PA: Lippincott, 75–76.

87 Durkheim, E. (1951). *Suicide: A Study in Sociology.* New York, NY: The Free Press.

88 Ohlin, L. (1956). *Sociology and the Field of Corrections.* New York, NY: Russell Sage Foundation.

89 Cloward, R., & Ohlin, L. (1960). *Delinquency and Opportunity.* New York, NY: The Free Press.

90 Agnew, R. (1992). "Foundation for a General Strain Theory of Crime and Delinquency." *Criminology, 30*(1), 47–87.

91 Ibid., 50.

92 Ibid., 57.

93 Hirschi, T. (1969). *Causes of Delinquency.* Berkeley, CA: University of California Press.

94 Brown, S. E., Esbensen, F., & Geis, G. (2004). *Criminology: Explaining Crime and Its Context* (5th ed.). Cincinnati, OH: Lexis-Nexis.

95 Gottfredson, M. R., & Hirschi, T. (1990). *A General Theory of Crime.* Stanford, CA: Stanford University Press, 89–90.

96 Cooley, C. H. (1902). *Human Nature and the Social Order.* New York, NY: Scribner's.

97 Mead, G. H. (1913). "The Social Self." *Journal of Philosophy, Psychology and Scientific Methods, 10*, 374–380.

98 Ibid., 379.

99 (1963). *Outsiders: Studies in the Sociology of Deviance.* New York, NY: The Free Press.

100 Brown, Esbensen, & Geis, 2004.

101 Braithwaite, J. (1989). *Crime, Shame, and Reintegration.* Melbourne, Australia: Cambridge University Press.

102 Braithwaite, J. (2000). "Shame and Criminal Justice." *Canadian Journal of Criminology, 42*(3), 281–298.

103 Akers, R. L., & Sellers, C. S. (2009). *Criminological Theories: Introduction, Evaluation, and Application* (5th ed.). New York, NY: Oxford University Press.

104 Lilly, J. R., Cullen, F. T., & Ball, R. A. (2011). *Criminological Theory: Context and Consequences* (5th ed.). Thousand Oaks, CA: Sage.

105 Williams, F. P., & McShane, M. D. (2004). *Criminological Theory* (4th ed.) Upper Saddle River, NJ: Prentice Hall.

106 Reiman, J., & Leighton, P. (2010). *The Rich Get Richer and the Poor Get Prison: Ideology, Class, and Criminal Justice* (9th ed.). Boston, MA: Allyn & Bacon.

107 Pepinsky, H., & Quinney, R. (Eds.). (1991). *Criminology as Peacemaking.* Bloomington, IN: Indiana University Press.

108 Pepinsky, H. (1999). "Peacemaking Primer." In B. A. Arrigo (Ed.), *Social Justice: Criminal Justice* (pp. 52–70). Belmont, CA: Wadsworth.

109 Lilly et al., 2011, 208.

110 Ibid.

111 Akers & Sellers, 2009.

112 Lilly et al., 2011.

113 Daly, K., & Chesney-Lind, M. (1988). "Feminism and Criminology." *Justice Quarterly, 5*, 497–538.

114 Lilly et al., 2011.

115 Barak, G. (1998). *Integrating Criminologies.* Boston, MA: Allyn and Bacon.

116 Ibid.

117 Wilson, J. Q., & Herrnstein, R. J. (1985). *Crime and Human Nature.* New York, NY: Simon & Schuster.

118 Elliot, D. S., Ageton, S. S., & Huizinga, D. (1985). *Explaining Delinquency and Drug Use. Beverly Hills*, CA: Sage.

119 Ibid., 94, 146.

120 Akers & Sellers, 2009.

121 Wright, J. P., Tibbetts, S. G., & Daigle, L. E. (2008). *Criminals in the Making: Criminality across the Life-Course.* Thousand Oaks, CA: Sage, 6.

122 Sampson, R. J., & Laub, J. H. (1993). *Crime in the Making: Pathways and Turning Points Through Life.* Cambridge, MA: Harvard University Press.

123 Kelley, B. T., Loeber, R., Keenan, K., & DeLamatre, M. (1997). "Developmental Pathways in Boys' Disruptive and Delinquent Behavior" (NCJ 165692). *Juvenile Justice Bulletin.* Washington, DC: Office of Juvenile Justice and Delinquency Prevention, 8–9.

124 Ibid.

125 Ibid.

CHAPTER 3

History of Policing

KEY TERMS

- Bow Street Runners
- Brigade de Surete
- Common Law
- Gendarmerie Nationale
- Marechaussee
- Metropolitan Police Act of 1829
- Night Watchmen
- Politia
- Scotland Yard
- Scirgerefa
- Sheriff
- Shire-Reeve
- Vigilante

CHAPTER OBJECTIVES

1. Differentiate and explain the history of policing before 1829 and after 1829.

2. Explain how the Metropolitan Police Act of 1829 has influenced U.S. policing.

3. Define and discuss the various methods of gathering crime data.

Providing or requiring a body of citizens to take responsibility for protecting each other and their property is recorded in the earliest records of human activities. That is not to say or suggest that in history there were police forces as we understand them today. In most instances, policing was fragmentary and comprised of local men often unwillingly conscripted into a role that they performed under duress. Those in power often created the position of bodyguard to make sure they were personally protected. Today we usually consider this a paid position, but it was certainly not the case for those providing protection to ancient kings, pharaohs and Caesars. Additionally, many males were employed or forced into door keeping roles to protect valuables, not just the leader or temples but also food and supplies for the citizenry. **Night watchmen** and guards were also either military personnel or, in remote rural communities, men and boys from the village who took turns watching the perimeters of the village to ensure that others in the community could sleep safely at night. There are records from ancient Egypt of an organized force of men providing security to tombs and living souls, and these men appeared to receive a salary for their work from the pharaoh's treasury. Exactly when in history this transformed into 'policing' is not clear. The word itself has origins in the Greek '**politia**', but this had a far broader application than we now apply to many of the law enforcement responses in countries such as the UK and the US. As we shall see soon, in many continental European countries the police undertake a considerably larger number of civic activities than seen in the **Common Law** countries, such as Canada, the US, the UK, India and Australia. And in many respects, the original *politia* with its connotations of civic administration is one model of policing still applied today; and a different model, the non-military with more limited responsibilities is a different model used in those countries that are not following their roots back to Greece so closely. The word 'police' first appeared in use in France, probably as a derivation of policy, and the UK during the 16th century, although Chaucer alluded to a *policie* in his *Canterbury Tales.*

Night Watchmen A group of men organized to deter crime and perform other services such as detect fires, light street lights and recover stolen property

Politia A Greek word meaning civil administration and later used to mean maintaining order, preventing and detecting crime and enforcing laws

Common Law A body of law that comes from past judicial decisions. Common Law Countries are those countries that abide by prior court decisions.

It is not my intention to cover the extensive history of policing from Hammurabi through Greece and Rome. That said, it is important to recognize that many of the police forces of the world today owe their origins to either the Greek and Romano based Civil Law policing systems or the Common Law derivation. They are fundamentally different. Those nations that adhere to Civil Law principles tend towards a military or quasi-military form of policing with armed officers who look and feel like military personnel. These police are normally highly centralized and may answer to a Ministry of the Interior or a Ministry of Defense. Frequently the officers live in barracks and have a rigid, hierarchical rank structure. Police officers under the Common Law model tend to be local and de-centralized; they may or may not carry a weapon and they are answerable to a combination of local interest and a minister. They rarely if ever live in barracks, and the value of this model is believed to be that the people serving are part of the community they serve. It is important to recognize these differences from the outset as there is no one model of policing and what it means to be a police officer can and does vary greatly in different jurisdictions.

In this chapter, I am going to talk about the origins of the police under the Common Law. These are the **sheriffs** and helpers and night watchmen and beadles, the **Bow Street Runners** and eventually full-time uniformed police officers providing a local service to the citizens of cities and towns. Let us look at the history of policing in England and how this informed policing in a number of other countries, including the US.

Sheriff The sheriff is the legal official responsible for the English Shire or the American County. Originally the Shire Reeve

Bow Street Runners London's first police force who worked for the magistrate serving writs and arresting suspects on warrants issued by the magistrate.

There is a widely held view that is authored in a number of US criminal justice textbooks that the overwhelmingly major influences upon policing in America have been Robert Peel and the **Metropolitan Police Act of 1829**. In this chapter, I will explore this position and suggest that the influence of Peel is important but represents only one part of a far more complex policing history for the US that draws in part from 17th century Paris and evolved in England around 1720 with adoption of the word 'police', more by accident than by choice. Over the course of the following 100 years, and frequently to the chagrin of the British political elite, England subsumed a number of European policing models alongside the work of uniquely English marine insurance detectives. Thus, by the end of the 18th century the Fieldings, Colquhoun and eventually Peel all recognized that elements of the French policing model were advantageous and applicable to England and eventually to the US. The product of these modern developments, alongside the public and private law enforcement responses of greater antiquity, was transported in stages and absorbed into the policing landscape of the US. In effect, 21st century policing in America is the result of a complex and multi-faceted policing history influenced by an English metropolitan police, a French gendarmerie, a Roman **vigilante**, a contemporary 12th century Norman tax collector (who acted as a part-time peace officer) and private detectives from French prisons.

Metropolitan Police Act of 1829 An Act of Parliament that was introduced by Sir Robert Peel the Home Secretary to create a police force for London.

Vigilante A member of a group of citizens who conduct law enforcement without any legal authority to do so. Sometimes organized groups and at other times persons present who wish to take matters into their own hands.

Influences upon policing in the US are as diverse[1] as the pattern of policing within the country. It was perhaps inevitable that given the swaying power of Britain upon the early development of the USA there would be an adoption of established criminal justice practices from Britain, especially those from England and the Common Law. Consequently, the English criminal justice lexicon—sheriff, constable, 'Hue and Cry', magistrates, justices of the peace, circuit judges and a concept of what it means to 'police'—are all largely, but not exclusively, informed by England. However, a closer inspection of the informing factors reveals that much of what occurred in policing in England throughout the Middle Ages and into the 18th century was not exclusively a domestic creation. Subsequently, what transferred to the US as an English system was in fact a concomitant of Anglo-Saxon[2] and Nordic customs with influence from France in the 11th century and then again, significantly, in the 18th century.

Shire-Reeve Shire is a government unit formed in the middle ages in England. The Reeve is the person responsible for enforcing the Kings laws and collect taxes. the Shire-Reeve became the Sheriff meaning Chief of the County

Scirgerefa Scirgerefa the chief officer of a shire. Later shortened to Reeve

"The office of sheriff is the one secular dignity generally known in English-speaking lands which for more than nine centuries has maintained a continuous existence and preserved its distinguishing features."[3] Variously known as the **shire-reeve**, sheriff or ***scirgerefa***,[4] and eventually elevated to the title of vice-count or viscount[5] in some instances, the sheriff[6] is a well-known feature of the Common Law criminal justice landscape that has a history that can be traced back to at least the reign of Ine[7] as a royal appointee with local administrative functions.[8] Over time the responsibilities of the shire-reeve increased and his role developed into, *inter alia*, those of tax collector, jailer and court administrator.[9] The task of securing felons and then holding them until the arrival of a court was a responsibility assigned to the sheriff from the period of Alfred the Great.[10] "Moreover he was a royal steward and was associated with the king's *tun* by the fact that he fed the king's prisoners there."[11] Securing the attendance of suspects before a trial court remains a primary function of the office of sheriff today. In his role as the chief law officer for a shire the sheriff held authority to demand assistance from local village people. Over time various appointments were made to provide a level of local rudimentary protective services that from modest beginnings as watchmen and vigilantes[12] would eventually form the basis of a professional police force for England. In London, we have specific references to the official powers of the sheriff in the laws of King Athelstan.[13] "For this district the reeve has apparently been holding a folkmote, within it he takes pledges for the observance of the peace, and in London region its men are to be led by him in pursuit of the thief."[14]

William the Bastard,[15] Conqueror and first Norman king of England, significantly increased the responsibilities of the sheriff. Within the first few years of his reign he appointed numerous fellow countrymen to the county shire-reeves position to ensure that there was a close watch upon the fiscal as well as local feudal responsibilities.[16] Importantly though, local and new French sheriffs did not lose any of the previous responsibilities of the office. "Among these may be named his powers connected with peace and with police."[17] Whereas in the pre-Norman period the sheriff had authority to preside over a hundred court hearings, to uphold the king's peace and to apprehend suspected criminals, under William these functions were formalized and positively encouraged.

The office of constable also existed prior to the arrival of the conqueror. At the time of the invasion, sheriffs were ordered by Harold of England to ". . . appoint constables in the hundreds, townships and neighbourhoods." All were to obey the head constable of the shire in matters 'ad defensionem regni et pacis conservacionem contra alienigenas, vel contra quoscunque alios pacis perturbatores'.[18] Aside from his famous dispute with Thomas Beckett, Henry II was responsible for many legal innovations. The Assize of Clarendon, 1166, has frequent references to the sheriff[19] in their policing and custodial roles:

"And when a robber or murderer or thief, or harbourers of them, shall be taken on the aforesaid oath, if the Justices shall not be about to come quickly enough into that county where they have been taken, the sheriffs shall send word to the nearest justice through some intelligent man, that they have taken such men; and the Justices shall send back word to the sheriffs where they wish those men to be brought before them: and the sheriffs shall bring them before the Justices."[20] King John reluctantly signed the Magna Carta in 1215, one year before his death. This famous document contains 63 clauses, 27 of which relate to the role and functions of the sheriff. Clause 47 states that "We will not make men justices, constables, sheriffs, or bailiffs, unless they are such as know the law of the realm, and are minded to observe it rightly."[21]

By the time of Henry III,[22] roving felons were a significant problem and constables were regularly assisting sheriffs in providing patrols within villages and across the countryside to ensure safe passage between villages and to market towns.[23] Henry III also increased the remit of his peace officers to take responsibility for patrolling the English coastline and vulnerable fortifications.[24] Towards the end of Henry's reign, the sheriffs and their assistants, the constable, had accumulated significant powers, including the provision of protection to inland castles. To counteract this encroachment upon their 'bailiwick',[25] the barons collaborated and managed to reaffirm themselves as the primary custodians of the shire. This marked the end of shrieval dominance in county peacekeeping, albeit a number of the newly appointed shire and region keepers were themselves former sheriffs.[26] Under the new system sheriffs were still responsible for apprehending and securing the attendance of felons, and in real terms the new shire keepers often served under the sheriff when he exercised policing powers and functions. It was not the case, however, that the shire keepers would answer to the constable, who remained a lower level 'peace keeper' answerable to the authority of the sheriff. By the close of this century, the 'shire keepers' role had developed into a regional responsibility,[27] which in some respects had the effect of restoring the primary policing function within the bailiwick back with the sheriffs[28] and constables. The elevated office of shire keeper remained and gained in stature to become the primary administrative functionary of a county. It still exists in England today as the, largely ceremonial, Lord Lieutenant[29] who is served by his assistant the High Sheriff.[30] As Professor Raymond Moley of Columbia University once stated, "Today in England the sheriff is a dignified and gentlemanly non-entity who guarantees for one year the proper performance of work in which he plays no part. An under-sheriff performs legal routine chiefly in relation to civil proceedings such as the summoning of jurors, the execution of civil judgments, and the returns of the results of parliamentary elections."[31] The first person to hold the office of sheriff in America was William Stone in 1634 in the County of Accomack, Virginia.[32] One visible policing aspect of being sheriff was the ability to require that local citizens assist in the apprehension of offenders. This right to demand help existed in medieval England as well as in colonial America. The formation of a posse[33] gained greater actual, as well as fictional, notoriety during westward expansion in the US. It has also been attributed to the development of vigilantism and private policing during the 18th and 19th centuries.[34] In terms of policing models, the sheriff is one of the only examples of centralized policing ever to occur in England. Its transposition to the US alongside decentralized city forces gives the US uniqueness lost to England centuries ago.

Marechaussee A French local guard force commanded by a marshal providing protection

In England, the night watchmen, beadle and constable limped through protecting citizens and apprehending criminals for the next 500 years. In France, the king had created a policing presence, the ***Maréchaussée***, as far back as the early 1100s. This was followed by a larger military police response from 1337[35] onwards. Between 1536 and 1544, King Francis I implemented a range of measures to formalize policing across the nation. The 'Sun King' Louis XIV reigned in France from 1643 to 1715. He was renowned for his work on legal reform largely instituted and executed by his minister Jean Baptiste Colbert.[36] In October 1666, Louis ordered Colbert to design a plan for a Paris police force. By March of the following year, Louis authorized the creation of the office of Prefect of Police for Paris,[37] followed in 1699 by a royal decree that authorized the establishment of Prefecture of Police for each major city in France.[38] The range of policing responsibilities was very broad and went extensively beyond the activities associated with contemporary policing in the US.[39] Over the period of the next 150 years, the role and function of the city police of France expanded. This occurred particularly with the Prefecture of Police and his officers, who assumed judicial responsibilities unfamiliar to sheriffs and constables in England. In one instance, the 'police court' at *Le Châtelet,* Paris, heard 200 cases in a three-hour period. Forty-five women and 16 men were sentenced that day, May 25, 1759.[40] The sentencing powers of the police court were also extensive. Benjamin Dechauflour was tried for sodomy on May 24, 1726. He was convicted the same day and sentenced to death by burning. The punishment was carried out the following morning.[41] As the pending revolution gained momentum in France, so too did the anxiety of the monarchy, and Paris slid into a period of sinister policing where spying became the main thrust of police work within the capital. Often quoted but never verified, Gabriel de Sartines, Lieutenant-General of Police from 1759 to 1774, reportedly told the king that wherever three persons speak to one another on the street, one of them would be one of his police spies.[42] Undoubtedly, the pre-Revolution Paris police[43] represent a well-organized body of law enforcement personnel that had specialist skills and responsibilities far beyond those represented in England during the same period. The cities of France had a formal civilian police presence and the smaller towns and villages had the protections provided by a military police. By 1788, there was one police officer for every 193 residents of Paris.[44]

Gendarmerie Nationale One of two national police forces in France. It is part of the armed forces with responsibility to both the Ministry of the Interior and to the Ministry of Defense for law enforcement activities in smaller towns, rural and suburban areas of France.

After the tumultuous events of the revolution, the *Maréchaussée* managed to remain in form but were renamed the ***Gendarmerie Nationale***.[45] "The accession of Napoléon Bonaparte as first consul in 1799 reinvigorated the trend towards the centralization of the police."[46] The Napoleonic Codes brought order to the legislation of previous regimes and provided a comprehensive body of all applicable law to all citizens. Application of the new codes rested with the existing civilian police forces and a re-designed and higher profile military police force to be called the *Gendarmerie Nationale.* Drawn from the ranks of serving military personnel, the *Gendarmerie Nationale* consisted of well trained, well resourced, well paid military men who lived in barracks[47] and provide police services to the citizens and the highways of rural France. As 'the man who would restore order to a society plagued by crime, violence and uncertainty',[48] Napoléon created a military police force that was copied throughout continental Europe. His less famous civilian police continued to employ dubious spying methods under the directorship of Joseph Fouché;[49] but combined, the military country police and the civilian city police provided a comprehensive and effective policing response for France that was superior to every other nation state in the world at the time. All that remained was to ensure effective supervision within those towns of smaller populations and this was achieved through the creation of the *Commissaire de Police.* The commissaire reported to the Prefect of the Département but with the ability to circumvent this line of authority if needed. "This made the *commissaire* a very powerful and influential figure locally. Thanks to his 'direct-line' to powerful figures like Fouché and Savary,[50] he was often able to outflank not only the prefects[51] and mayors of his department, but even the judiciary and the gendarmerie, when it came to identifying common criminals, political subversives or wayward, allegedly corrupt local officials." In 1829, the same year that Robert Peel finally managed to convince the British parliament to authorize a police force for London,[52] France re-established the *sergent de ville.* A uniformed civilian appointment that had been present in a variety of forms across Europe for more than 200 years,[53] the Renaissance version was charged with providing a police presence in the smaller towns of France that would supplement the work of the *Commissaire de Police.*[54] Much like Dickens' ridicule of the beadle and watchman of London,[55] the *sergent de ville* did not escape the critical tones of Victor Hugo in the role of Javert[56] in *Les Misérables.* The comedy of policing the combination of a military gendarmerie and a civilian police force across all of France positioned the country to be at the forefront of policing in the later years of the 18th and the early years of the 19th centuries. "Perhaps the highest compliment ever paid to the Napoleonic Gendarmerie came from Britain, the arch-enemy of Napoleonic France, when in the 1820s, the secretary for Ireland, Sir Robert Peel, chose it as his model for the new Royal Irish Constabulary. Even Napoléon's bitterest enemies came quickly to acknowledge the usefulness of this particular institution."[57]

In 18th century England, the word police was virtually unknown.[58] When the word was introduced ". . . it was regarded with the utmost suspicion as a portent of the sinister force which held France in its grip."[59] As Edward Burt wrote in 1720, ". . . Soon after his arrival in London, he had observed a good deal of Dirt and disorder in the Streets, and asking about the *Police,* but finding none that understood the Term, he cried out, Good lord! How can one expect Order among these people, who have not such heard a Word as Police in their Language."[60] London was reeling under a crime wave and the local watch and beadle system was woefully incapable of dealing with the organized serial felon. The constable system was still a reflection of medieval England and the night watchmen were old, inept and frequently asleep or drunk on duty.[61] In 1792, the Middlesex Justices Act created the establishment of a police office within London. In reality, much had been achieved before passage of this legislation and a recognizable police force had been in existence in a number of manifestations for the City of Westminster and the River Thames for many years. "In fact, there were a number of police offices, all rather similar to the Bow Street police office which had been functioning for 30 years."[62] In the early years of the 18th century, Thomas de Veil was appointed as magistrate to the City of Westminster. Over the course of the next 17 years he established his Bow Street office as one of the most efficient within the metropolis. In 1748, the novelist Henry Fielding and his half-brother John Fielding succeeded De Veil.[63] Henry soon authored *An Enquiry into the Cause of the Late Increase of Robbers* and, to the surprise of some of his contemporaries, Fielding immersed himself into writing about[64] and working towards the establishment of a police force for the City of Westminster and Middlesex County from the Bow Street residence. Over time, the mixed bag of assistants that Fielding managed to employ proved themselves to be reliable thief catchers with an in-depth knowledge of the criminals within the immediate vicinity of Bow Street.[65] His associates were soon nicknamed the Bow Street Runners,[66] and their official title was Principal Officer of Bow Street.[67] The Bow Street Police Office was far from an ideal solution to the London crime problem. What it represented was a practical move towards a permanent police force for the metropolis. Regency England was still plagued with reward systems and general mistrust of a permanent force that might in any way appear to represent a standing army. Sir Leon Radzinowicz described the Bow Street Office as "The headquarters of a closely knit caste of speculators in the detection of crime, self-seeking and unscrupulous, but also daring and efficient when daring and efficiency coincided with their private interest."[68]

The combined efforts of De Veil, the Fieldings and Patrick Colquhoun all amount to a significant influence upon policing London. Armed officers patrolled the main streets of London during the nighttime;[69] the highways into and out of the metropolis were 'policed' by 68 patrols;[70] and on the eve of the 1829 Act, uniformed officers patrolled the central streets during daylight hours.[71] In 1792, a Scottish born merchant who had spent a number of years in Virginia was one of the first appointees under the new legislation that created stipendiary magistrates.[72] Patrick Colquhoun[73] immediately took up the issue of providing London with a regular, paid, full-time police force. He anonymously published *A Treatise on the Police of the Metropolis* in 1795 in which he estimated that the indigent population of London was so great that there was in existence a class of habitual criminals, 50,000 in number, who had no alternative but to engage in crime.[74] He even suggested that the French police[75] were a suitable model[76] for adoption in England.[77] Needless to say, these views won him no friends in the British parliament and his strenuous attempts to bring about the adoption of legislation that would establish a London police force were repeatedly defeated.[78] Undaunted by the intransigence of the British ruling elite, Colquhoun persisted. and he can certainly be credited with playing a significant role in the establishment of a full time police force for the River Thames.[79]

By the late 18th century, more than 13,500 vessels were competing daily for space on the River Thames.[80] Crime was rampant and the merchants of London united in supporting the establishment of a permanent protection force.[81] In June 1798, the merchants of London established a Marine Police Establishment[82] with a permanent staff of 80[83] and a reserve of more than one thousand. By the end of the year, *The Times* reported that, "It is astonishing the effects the institution has already achieved in the preventing of piracies and robberies. . . ."[84] In 1800, the British government endorsed the private policing enterprise and a Police Bill[85] was passed to formalize and make public policing of the River Thames. The main proponents of the bill[86] were John Harriot,[87] Patrick Colquhoun[88] and Jeremy Bentham.[89] There can be no doubt that London now had a permanent, uniformed police force that operated as a "public institution, regulated by statute and designed to safeguard commercial and other property on the river."[90]

Views about the impact of the Fieldings and Colquhoun are varied. Emsley refers to them as a "veritable holy trinity" in the eyes of Whig historians,[91] whereas Critchley considered their achievements meager.[92] In a sense, both opinions are correct. The Fieldings undoubtedly moved the policing agenda forward to the point at which, small though it was, London had a group of paid, permanent 'police' officers. Colquhoun, although personally frustrated by the lack of recognition he received for his attempts to change the hearts and minds of the British parliament, also raised the level of awareness and the volume of discussion, as well as achieving the personal satisfaction of ensuring that a marine police force was established that still exists within the Metropolitan Police today. If we attribute the introduction of the word 'police' to the Fieldings, then it is to Colquhoun that we owe thanks for its absorption into the English lexicon. What the "holy trinity" did not achieve was to convince the British public that a permanent police force would be anything other than a foreign invasion. This sleight of hand was left to a politician, Robert Peel, and another round of crime waves in the early 1800s.[93] However, one of the great achievements of this trio, whether by design or default, was that they managed to change the negative perception of foreign policing to a uniquely English entity that focused exclusively upon maintenance of the peace and the prevention and detection of crime.[94]

Opposition against a fulltime land force for London was still strong in the early years of the 19th century. Britain was at war with France and the populous, the press and the parliament repeatedly rejected anything that had the slightest resemblance to a *Gendarmerie.*[95] "The necessities of time, emphasized by the crime wave and frequent riots, created the stage for London police reform; however, little could have been accomplished without the political skills of Sir Robert Peel."[96] Peel[97] was promoted to Chief Secretary for Ireland in September 1812. His responsibilities included the maintenance of law and order in the country, and to this effect he was responsible for the Peace Preservation Act 1814,[98] which established the Irish Peace Preservation Force,[99] a forerunner to the Royal Irish Constabulary of 1822.[100] Public disturbances had become a regular feature of life throughout Ireland and the government frequently faced the task of quelling public disorder. "Peel's arrival coincided with a lull in banditti activity, but it was his job to muster the forces of authority in anticipation of the inevitable trouble to come."[101] Peel was much impressed by Napoléon's *Gendarmerie;* he approved of the military rigor and the utilization of a barrack system to house members of the force. And whereas he might not have been as enamored as Colquhoun, who had referred to the French police as having "The greatest degree of professionalism,"[102] he certainly recognized the value of having a countrywide paramilitary policing response that was answerable to a central authority. Peel was pleased with his creation and wrote somewhat prematurely, "Although the police bill has been but a few weeks in operation, the effect is already such as to justify the most sanguine expectation of its ultimate success."[103] Peel retired from his post as Chief Secretary for Ireland in 1817 and returned to England. His departure from Ireland was lamented in many quarters,[104] and it has been said, perhaps generously, that he may have intentionally created the Peace Preservation Force to help alleviate the "pitiable condition of Ireland"[105] by providing a source of employment. Peel left Ireland with the blueprint for a Common Law Gendarmerie that was to be exported around the globe to almost every former British colony. Some considered it as, "Being without parallel in its semi-military organisation, with exception, perhaps, of the French gendarmerie. . . ."[106] In 1822, Peel was elevated to the position of Home Secretary where he would now have the opportunity to grapple with the police issue back in England.[107]

"Coloring the entire discussion was the example of an efficient and repressive system of police in France, where extensive intelligence networks caught ordinary criminals as well as those who spoke and acted in ways that undermined the stability of the regime. . . ."[108] Peel had become an astute and cautious politician. He recognized that to move forward he would need to advocate a moderate approach that emphasized preventative measures and crime detection provided for by a uniformed but distinctly civilian force.[109] A compromise was inevitable. One significant factor for Peel was the strong opposition voiced by the financial 'City of London'.[110] He decided not to attempt to bring the 'Square Mile' into his new plans,[111] and on Tuesday September 29, 1829,[112] the first uniformed officers of the London Metropolitan Police commenced evening patrol across the metropolis, save the City.[113] Their uniforms were carefully chosen to reflect civilian fashion of the day, top hat and blue tunic tails,[114] and they carried no more than a truncheon to protect themselves against the criminal underworld of the metropolis. Within eight months the initial intake of one thousand men[115] had risen to more than three thousand.[116] Two commissioners led the new police force, both of Irish descent, one a lawyer, Richard Mayne,[117] and the other a former military officer, Lt. Colonel Charles Rowan.[118] Despite initial criticism of Peel and his influential supporter the Duke of Wellington, London's 'Raw Lobsters'[119] slowly turned the hearts and minds of its skeptics and the more endearing terms 'Peelers' and 'Bobby'[120] began to enter the 'new policing' language. As one commentator noted, "And yet a couple of years later these same vestries agreed the unfavourable impression and jealousy formerly existing against the new police is rapidly diminishing . . . and it has fully answered the purpose for which it was formed. . . ."[121] Every recruit to the new London Metropolitan Police was issued with a handbook of *General Instructions* compiled by Sir Robert Peel. It stated: "It should be understood at the outset that the object to be attained is the prevention of crime . . . The absence of crime will be considered the best proof of the complete efficiency of the police."[122] These words have endured and are still viewed as the fundamental basis for policing in many parts of the world today. By 1856, the County and Borough Police Act required every county and borough in England and Wales to establish a police force.[123] The following year similar legislation was passed in Scotland.

One of the dilemmas Peel faced was whether to establish a uniformed or a plain clothed police force. Either way he was likely to be criticized.[124] If uniformed, they would be a *Gendarmerie,* and if plain clothed, they would be Paris police 'spies'.[125] As we know, he opted for uniforms. A detective unit was not established in London until 1842. During the interim period, Principal Officers[126] from the disbanded Bow Street Police Office served as a detective agency available for hire to individuals as well as to the Metropolitan Police. In France, a significant detective police department, much maligned by the English as 'sinister', had been operational for more than one hundred years. Then under Fouche, this unit gained greater notoriety and the name ***brigade de sûreté***. But it was not until the arrival of a former criminal, Eugène Vidocq, in 1812 that the *Sûreté* became synonymous with sleuths and undercover work associated with contemporary police detection.[127] Vidocq was variously described as, "A lower type of man, yet still a great name in the history of French police . . . who began his career as a thief"[128] and "From unpromising origins as a two-bit thief, army deserter, grafter and convict, he rose in fame to become the celebrated chief of the Paris Sûreté police and an internationally renowned private detective."[129] The 'poacher turned gamekeeper',[130] Vidocq was apparently a larger-than-life character who captured the friendship and imagination of Dumas and Balzac. He was "Known to embellish his tales, and historians have difficulty separating fact from fiction in his accounts."[131] Regardless of the criticism and colorful nature of his character, Vidocq was a pioneer in detective techniques. Not only did he utilize handwriting, paper, and ink analyses to solve cases, but he also foresaw the day when fingerprints would be used to identify suspects'.[132] After his departure, the *Sûreté* continued to rise in stature as the preeminent detective police agency until the arrival of '**Scotland Yard**'. Notwithstanding the rise of the 'Yard', Vidocq's impact traversed the Atlantic and he is credited with inspiring Allan Pinkerton[133] and J. Edgar Hoover.[134] The quality and effectiveness of the *Sûreté* did not go unnoticed in London either and a number of years after Vidocq's[135] resignation, a London Metropolitan Police officer implemented a version of his model. There are two dates associated with the introduction of plain clothed detectives in London, 1842 and then 1878.[136] The first attempts to run an effective detective unit were plagued by allegations of corruption and scandal[137] culminating in the "Trial of the Detectives" in 1877.[138] The following year Charles Howard Vincent,[139] a lawyer, police officer and politician, was given the

Brigade de Surete
Created by Eugene Francois Vidocq made up of ex-convicts who worked undercover in Paris to catch criminals.

Scotland Yard
Scotland Yard is the name given to the Metropolitan Police Service (MPS) of the greater London area. It comes from the original entrance to the first police station.

opportunity to re-organize the detective branch and form the modern C.I.D. Over time, Scotland Yard detectives became synonymous with criminal investigation excellence[140] and surpassed the *Sûreté* in stature.

Between 1605 and 1905 policing in America was influenced by a multitude of European forces. There is a collective agreement among a number of authors[141] that early policing methods were drawn from the established roles of the sheriffs, constables,[142] Hue and Cry, night watchmen, vigilantes and 'watch and ward', along with the wide and varied assortment of criminal justice law enforcement officials that had developed over the previous sixteen hundred years, mostly from England.[143] Attractive as this simplistic and often very brief approach may be, these accounts rarely, if ever, pay any attention to the role of France and the influences made upon English policing by the French. In reality, much of the old world systems were either irrelevant or rejected by the new settlers and the utilization of an established system of policing was adopted due to familiarity until a better system was created that would be uniquely American. For the time that colonies were forced to operate under the English crown, adoption of English law, and its policing style, was inevitable. But once the opportunity arose to forge a new body of policing and laws the colonists moved forward swiftly, modifying the familiar and substituting the irrelevant.[144]

Although few formal policing systems were in place in 17th century America,[145] informal ancient and familiar vestiges of a manorial system were prevalent, especially in the Northern states. In England, bringing a prosecution for a criminal matter was still an individual affair. The private citizen bore the entire cost of the prosecution until legislation partially relieved this burden in 1752. In an effort to encourage the participation of the public in curbing the 18th century crime wave, the crown offered increasingly large rewards[146] to those who gave evidence against felons.[147] Due to the high cost of taking a case before the courts, it became common practice for merchants, farmers and civic groups to form associations to help defray the cost of bringing a criminal prosecution.[148] A version of the English associations manifest as a more forceful 'crime-control vigilantism'[149] was the preferred adoption in America, where a relationship between the sheriff and the posse, of which a number grew into vigilantes, was not an uncommon feature of the American frontier.[150] A crucial distinction should be drawn, however. The English societies never operated outside of the law whereas the American development into vigilante groups[151] frequently did.[152] Nevertheless, the similarities are clear; both developments were in response to inadequacies in established policing provision and failures of the criminal justice system to protect the interests of the individual. The similarities between the extra-legal methods employed by the American frontier vigilantes and the emergence of private policing groups that used strong arm tactics on behalf of railroad and mining companies should not be understated.[153]

By the close of the 18th century, much of England was struggling to make sense of its own crime problems, especially those in the capitol. America too needed to apply a diversity[154] of police responses to the wide variety of challenges facing Southern business entrepreneurs, Northern biblical refugees and Westward bound migrants. Critics of this view may seek to take refuge in terminology and explain the history of individual entities such as sheriffs as being distinctly different from those of the police. Yet we have seen that the term police was unfamiliar in England during much of the colonial years and, once adopted, had a broad and varied application. Narrowing the parameters of the word to Peel's application may indeed have been for the English a way of circumventing something overtly French, but the early role of the police constable in America carried a very broad portfolio of responsibilities far more closely resembling a *sergeant de ville* than a 'Bobby'. As Inciardi reminds us, "But while the powers of the English sheriff diminished over time, those of the American sheriff expanded to include not only the apprehension of criminals, but also the conducting of elections, the collection of taxes, and the custody of public funds."[155]

Alongside appointed local and municipal law enforcement officials, America also adopted private policing.[156] This was due in part to the slow development of city and statewide policing responses, as well to the expansion of railroads, industry and commerce that sought to protect its own interests often in the face of worker unrest and labor disputes. Familiar names like Wells Fargo,[157] Brinks,[158] The Pinkerton Agency[159] and The Burns Detective Agency[160] identified a lacuna in the protection of goods and property that public entities were unable to fill. At the same time, population growth, industrialization and the development of cities drew much of American society closer to contemporary European standards. Consequently, the policing needs of the burgeoning East Coast cities were very different from the needs of the rural communities and the pioneers. Social unrest, unemployment and vagrancy needed a policing response in accordance with contemporary European models. Pioneers attempting to conquer 'the Elephant'[161] made do with self-help, vigilantes, posses and the sheriff.[162] There is mixed evidence with regard to the proactive nature of these 'self-help' organizations, but it is clear that these groups were ". . . appendages to the institutionalized legal system with intention to circumvent it."[163]

By the end of the 19th century, Alan Pinkerton, "The Vidocq of the West,"[164] and other private police agencies found it opportune to transition from personal protection to property protection. By the close of the 19th century, unemployment was at 20 percent in America's declining employment market, 600 banks had closed and unions had become a significant force in US employment,[165] which meant that American industry increasingly needed to have a body of 'Cossacks'[166] or hoodlums to break strikes.[167] In 1902, the Great Anthracite Coal Strike devastated Pennsylvania. Coal prices soared[168] and the national and state governments were at a loss how to deal with the private labor dispute. Municipal police officers were either incapable or unprepared to arrest striking miners, and the private police responses provided by the Coal and Iron Police[169] under the supervision of Pinkerton's Detective Agency were heavy handed and frequently accused of brutality by the miners.[170] It was clear to many observers that these groups ". . . owed a duty to no one but their employers, and these in turn hired for their private police force the most irresponsible toughs and rough-necks obtainable."[171]

In 1905, the Pennsylvania state governor, Samuel Pennypacker, signed Senate Bill 278 into law. This legislation created the first statewide police agency in America, The Pennsylvania State Constabulary. Captain John Groome,[172] formerly of the Philadelphia City Cavalry, was tasked with creating and supervising a working statewide police force. During a subsequent Congressional investigation[173] into alleged reprisals against striking miners by the new force, Major Groome stated, "Of course there were no rules, no regulations, and nothing to go by; and these men were divided into four troops.[174] They were sent to barracks. I designed the uniforms, decided how they should be armed, and decided that it would be necessary for each man to be mounted; and purchased the horses and drilled men and gave them as much instruction."[175] When questioned about the inspiration for the force, he replied, ". . . I got the Italians, the Germans and Royal Northwestern police, and the Irish police; and from going over their reports I came to the conclusion that the conditions in Ireland were more similar to those in Pennsylvania, so far as the industrial and agricultural conditions and the character of the population were concerned."[176] Major Groome then reported to the Committee that he had paid a three week visit to the R.I.C. to fully investigate its organization and operations.[177] Advocates and opponents of the Pennsylvania State Police[178] are agreed; the statewide force copied the Royal Irish Constabulary.[179]

By 1845, New York had abandoned its previous system of watchmen and adopted a London-style municipal police force. It was the first outside of the British Empire.[180] The new force appeared very different from the London model. Officers did not wear a uniform,[181] simply a copper badge, and very soon they exchanged truncheons for firearms.[182] But it was not the external appearance of the officers that denoted fundamental differences; it was the exercise of power.[183] The London force had been created to be politically neutral and institutionally controlled.[184] The New York officer's authority was limited by the ballot box.[185] Interestingly, in New York there was a general concern that the London 'Bobby' was too centralized and accountable to the government, and yet the London force was considered de-centralized and independent within England. By 1857,[186] the municipal force was abolished and a metropolitan force was created that would be commanded by state-appointed commissioners.[187] The New York police,[188] although allegedly modeled on the English police, were soon undertaking a range of tasks far closer in practice to the Paris police than to their London brothers. For example, New York officers provided babysitting services at the police station, helped people find employment, fought fires, fed the homeless and provided basic medical care.[189] They ". . . returned lost children by the thousands, shot stray dogs, enforced sanitation laws, inspected boilers, took annual censuses, and performed myriad other small tasks."[190] "Arrests were of little importance, the primary mission of the police was to provide services to citizens and garner votes for politicians."[191] In Paris, the police were tasked with controlling begging, issuing licenses to wine shops and food stores, firefighting and flood control, as well as providing care for abandoned children and pursuing unfaithful wives, inspecting the jails and having oversight of the public drainage system and sewers.[192] The London Bobby was maintaining the peace and preventing and detecting crime. Not only was there a remarkably different political and social setting for policing New York, there was a remarkably different job specification.[193] In reality, adapting the London police model to New York meant discarding political neutrality and increasing individual discretion.[194] This looks very much like a different force altogether, one that more closely resembles the French police who, like America, were born out of political instability resulting in a broad palate of responsibilities. As Monkkonen noted, "At best, one could say that the creation of the police force reflected a growing intolerance for riots and disorder, rather than a response to an increase in crime."[195] It was not until after the impact of initial formation settled that the city forces of America became practitioners of the narrow term police[196] and "urban reformers took over the welfare functions of the police."[197]

Sheriffs from Anglo-Saxon England whose powers were enhanced by a Frenchman, Hue and Cry vigilantes[198] in "rural areas and small towns across the nation,"[199] uniformed officers patrolling Paris in the 17th century and military police, policing civilians in rural France and Ireland,[200] a convict turned sleuth who inspired the establishment of private policing in America and city police officers responsible for political policing and the provision of welfare services—all were part of the development of American policing. We have credited Robert Peel with being the 'father' of American policing. But perhaps it is time to adopt a contemporary view and consider him more of a 'Significant Other' than the exclusive patriarch.

Chapter Summary

What is termed policing today began centuries ago. Different countries adopted various forms of laws and ways to enforce them. The United Kindom developed a system that changed with the times. In 1829 Sir Robert Peele created the Metropolitan Police Act. This was the beginning of what is modern policing today in much of the world.

Critical Thinking?

1. How has the evolution of British policing impacted policing in the United States?
2. Has other countries policing systems had an impact on policing in the United States? If so how? If not, why not?
3. Is American policing today similar to the vision of Sir Robert Peel or is it different? If it is different, how different? If it is the same, why do you think it is still the way he originally intended policing to be?

4. What influence did the military have on policing in the United States? Does it still have any influence on American policing? If so in what ways? If not, should it?
5. In most states, the sheriff is elected while police chiefs are generally appointed. What are the issues with electing the sheriff or chief of police? Which system do you believe we should use, electing our chief law enforcement officers by popular vote or appointed people based on their qualifications? Why?

Endnotes

1 It is believed that there are in the region of 20,000 assorted law enforcement agencies in the US. Many of these are very small in size and comprise of as few as one to six sworn officers. For the purposes of this paper, my discussion will focus upon the development of state and local forces. Each of the large number of federal agencies in the US has produced a version of its history that can be viewed on the agency website. Also c.f. the following article that discusses the history of the reorganization of federal agencies: Grafton, C. The reorganization of federal agencies administration & society. February 1979; 10: 437–464, doi:10.1177/009539977901000403

2 Comprehensive coverage of the entire period is contained within the influential works of, *inter alia*, William Maitland's History of the English law, William Holdsworth's History of English law and, more recently, Leon Radzinowicz's
A history of the English criminal law. These works are voluminous and remarkable reading.

3 Morris, W. The office of sheriff in the Anglo-Saxon period. The English historical review. Jan. 1916; 31(121); 20–40 at 20

4 Late O. E. scirgerefa "representative of royal authority in a shire," from scir (see shire) + gerefa "chief, official, reeve" (see reeve). In Anglo-Saxon England, the representative of royal authority in a shire. As an American county official, attested from 1662; sheriff's sale first recorded 1798. http://www.etymonline.com/index.php?term=sheriff

5 First recorded usage is in the 12th century to denote the deputy count or holder of a shire. Shire having replaced the Anglo-Saxon term scir. C.f. http://www.etymonline.com/index.php?search=count&searchmode=none

6 For a thorough discussion, see: Irene Gladwin, The sheriff: The man and his office. London: McCartney; 1984.

7 King of Wessx 688 to 726. Known for formulation of legal codes, Ines laws, 694 and later subsumed into the legal code of Alfred the Great. Ine abdicated in 726 to pilgrimage to Rome.

8 Supra, Morris, p. 20.

9 During the later part of the Anglo-Saxon period, the alderman was the chief judicial officer within the shire and the sheriff served as the second.

10 Alfred the Great reigned from 849–899. He was responsible for the division of lands into boroughs and a number of boroughs together were designated as a shire. Consequently, many cities in Britain are named as boroughs, such

as Edinburgh, Peterborough and Wellingborough and numerous counties are shires, e.g. Cambridgeshire, Worcestershire, Leicestershire. In the late 880s or perhaps the early 890s, Alfred issued his legal codes known as the *domboc.*

11 Supra, Morris, p. 21 and footnote 5

12 We take the term from the 3rd century Roman firewatchers, Vigiles. The term has commonly come to mean legal, or extra-legal, citizen participation in law enforcement.

13 The first king of England. Ruled from 924–939.

14 Supra, Morris, pp. 21–22 citing 5. Athelstan, 1.5 and 6 Athelstan, 10.

15 His mother never married his father, hence he was referred to as 'William the Bastard'. He invaded and conquered England in 1066. He already held the title William of Normandy from 1035.

16 William also retained the services of a number of English sheriffs, such as Marloswein, Freeman, Robert fitz Wymarc, Round, Touid, Davis, Edric, Edwin and Elfwine. Source: Morris, supra, p. 26, note 52

17 Supra, Morris, p. 30.

18 Harding, A. The origins and early history of the keeper of the peace. Transaction of the Royal Historical Society (Fifth Series). 1960: 10: 85–109 at 87. ". . . for the preservation of the peace of the kingdom and against foreign invaders or against others acting against the peace of the realm."

19 Clause 1. Referring to the harboring of robbers, murderers and thieves, "And the Justices shall make this inquest by themselves, and the sheriffs by themselves." Cited in Ernest Henderson, Select historical documents of the Middle Ages. London: George Bell and Sons; 1896, 16 (Taken from Stubbs, Charters. P. 142).

20 Ibid., p. 17.

21 Op. cit., Henderson, p. 147.

22 Henry III of England 1207–1272.

23 Harding, supra, cites an example form the Public Record Office J. I. 1/734 where in Shropshire 1256 "there were . . . 186 cases of homicide presented, but only 19 felons executed . . . Crime after crime was presented as committed by *malefactores ignoti* [persons unknown]. The system was incapable of dealing with the hardened criminal who wandered from shire to shire." At p. 86

24 Harding, supra, p. 89.

25 Bailiwick is an interesting term that is a combination of French and English, *balli* a French administrative official and *wick* an Anglo-Saxon village. The Oxford English Dictionary Second Edition apparently implies that the term originates from the 15th century. Harding, supra, p. 92 has sourced this term to the 13th century with his specific reference p. 92 note 5 to C.P.R. 1258–66 at p. 283. C.f. http://www.wordorigins.org/index.php/bailiwick/

26 E.g. Fitzpeter, Clifford, Lestrange, Nevill, Gesemuth, Montalt and Eustace de Balliol. Source: Harding, supra, note 6, p. 92.

27 Perhaps an early example of auxiliary policing, to support the local police in cases of civil disobedience, is found within the Harding, supra, p. 99 where "Edmund of Cornwall was appointed general 'keeper of the peace' in

the English counties with power to appoint deputies to deal with improper assemblies beyond the sheriffs' control" citing Calendar of Chancery Rolls, various, pp. 271–218. Footnote 5.

28 E.g. In 1236 we see the sheriff continuing to have responsibility for forming a jury. C.P.R. 1232–47, p. 65 cited in Harding, supra, p. 103 at note 9. This function remained with the sheriff until 1857. (In 1856 all policing functions were transferred to local police constabularies, and all prison functions were transferred, in 1857, to the prison service.) The other previous primary role, tax collection, had already been handed to the Exchequer under Henry I. For further discussion see: Carpenter, D. A. The decline of the curial sheriff in England 1194–1258. The English historical review. Jan. 1976: 91(358); 1–32.

29 The Lord Lieutenant is the monarch's personal representative in a county.

30 The High Sheriff is the sovereign's judicial representative in a county.

31 Moley, R. The sheriff and the constable. *The annals of the American Academy of Political and Social Science*. 1929: (146); 27–33 at 27.

32 See: Harry C. Buffardi. The History of the Office of Sheriff, Schenedachy County Sheriff, 1998. Not paginated. The appointment was soon followed by numerous other counties and states across colonial America and the sheriff became the *de facto* ranking police officer and chief tax collector for many counties. In 1679, the sheriff of Middlesex County appointed a jailer to run the county prison. Ibid. Accomac [sic] County Records 1640–1645, p. 150 in Karracker, CH. The seventeenth century sheriff. Chapel Hill: University of North Carolina Press; 1930.

33 *Posse comitatus*, meaning "the power of the county," was the legal basis for sheriffs to recruit assistance from any male over the age of 15 years to assist in the pursuit and capture of felons.

34 infra

35 This *connetablie*, or military unit, was directed by a Constable of France.

36 In association with his legal colleague Guillame de Lamoigen, Colbert drafted more than 150 pieces of legislation, including the 1670 Ordinance on Criminal Law and Criminal Procedure.

37 The office was first held by Nicholas Gabriel de la Reynie.

38 Jones, M. and Johnstone, P. History of criminal justice. 5th ed. Boston: Anderson; 2011; 220–221.

39 E.g. supervising markets, repairing municipal drains, inspecting food and wine, surveillance of foreigners, arresting sorcerers and directing firefighting. C.f. Jones, supra, p. 219.

40 Jones, supra, p. 220.

41 Ibid.

42 Ibid.

43 By 1716, the police wore a blue uniform, walked a defined beta and were the only citizens of Paris permitted to carry a firearm. Jones, supra, p. 221.

44 Ibid.

45 Germinal 28, Year VI of the French Revolution. April 17, 1798.

46 Jones, supra, p. 222.

47 Typically in brigades of six to ten men. Preference was for single men but married men were permitted to serve. It was intentional that the officers were recruited from an area different from where they would be policing. However, the Gendarmerie was eventually close to the people and held in higher regard than the despised Administrative Police of Fouche. Notwithstanding this, the period between 1789 and 1799 placed France under enormous internal conflict and upheaval and the Gendarmerie was often interpreted as a pro-revolutionary faction that was caught between supporters of the old regime and those who were forging a new. C.f. Broers, supra, p. 28.

48 Broers, M. The Napoleonic police and their legacy. History today. 1999; 49(5); 27–33 at 27.

49 Minister of Police 1799–1810 and 1815–1816

50 General Anne Jean Marie Rene Savary. *Aid-de-camp* to Napoléon and then succeeded Joeseph Fouche as Minister of Police until Napoléon's abdication.

51 Broers, supra, p. 29.

52 infra

53 For a comprehensive discussion see: Catherine Denys, The development of police forces in urban Europe in the 18th century. Journal of urban history. 2010; 36(3); 332–344.

54 The *sergents* were designated specific beats or areas of a town to patrol rather than to replicate the previous model of walking around without specific purpose. The result rarely led to arrest and supplied ample material for ridicule.

55 E.g. Little Dorrit, Oliver Twist, The Old Curiosity Shop, The Detective Police.

56 Believed to be based upon the real life criminal-turned police detective Eugene Francois Vidocq. infra

57 Broers, supra, p. 33.

58 Emsley, CFC. The great British bobby: A history of British policing from the 18th century to the present century. London: Quercus, 2009. Radzinowicz refers to the influence of Henry Fielding in bringing the term 'policing' into popular use. He cites Maitland's definition as "such part of social organisation as is concerned immediately with the maintenance of good order, or the prevention or detection of offences." Radzinowicz, supra, p. 4 and footnote 18.

59 Radzinowicz, L. A history of the English criminal law. London: Stevens; 1956. Vol. 3; p. 1.

60 Cited by Radzinowicz, supra, p. 1.

61 Jones, supra, Chapter 10.

62 Supra, p. 227

63 Blinded at the age of 19 years Sir John Fielding could recognize criminals by their voices. It is reputed he knew 3,000 London criminals by their voices alone.

64 Henry Fielding was well known for his work of fiction A history of Tom Jones. He also authored 15 plays and a novel based upon the life of London criminal Jonathan Wild. He also wrote the weekly law digest the Covent

Garden Journal as well as the Police Gazette (which remains in publication today as a source of information for serving police officers).

65 Contrary to some incorrect reports (a 'Google' search of this term shows five incorrect entries on the first page), this group did not wear uniforms and were never referred to as "Robin Redbreasts." They did, however, carry a truncheon as a weapon and this instrument frequently bore a crown or other insignia denoting authority. Dodsworth, F. Civic police and the condition of liberty: The rationality of governance in eighteenth century England. Social History. May 2004; 29(2); 199–216 at 212.

66 For a full account of the establishment of the Bow Street Runners, see: David Cox, A certain share of low cunning: An analysis of the work of Bow Street Principal Officers 1792–1839. London: Whillan; 2010. The somewhat disparaging term "Runners" may have been first used during a criminal trial at The Old Bailey in 1755. Cited by Emsley, supra, in Cox at pp. 2–3.

67 Six were initially appointed. This grew to eight by the early 19th century. All were 'sworn constables' of the City of Westminster.

68 Radzinowicz, supra, p. 263 cited in Jones, supra, p. 229.

69 In 1792, policing for London was divided into seven districts.

70 Emsley, supra, p. 22.

71 This later group wore blue trousers and red waistcoats. They were soon dubbed the "Robin Redbreasts." C.f. "The Police of London," London Quarterly Review. July 1870; 129; 50.

72 The Middlesex Justices Act 1972.

73 He established himself at Worship Street and then moved to Queen Square where he remained until 1818. Source: Radzinowicz, supra, p. 212.

74 Jones, supra, p. 229.

75 "In his opinion the French police were worthy of careful and impartial consideration." Radzinowicz, supra, p. 249.

76 For further discussion about the impact of Colquhoun, see: David Barrie, Patrick Colquhoun. The Scottish enlightenment and police reform in Glasgow in the late eighteenth century. Crime History and Society. 2008; 12(2); 57–79.

77 His *Treatise* appeared in French in 1807. Radzinowicz, supra, p. 221, note 3.

78 He was alone in attempting to introduce legislation. William Pitt introduced a Police Bill in 1785 and four Police Bills were introduced in 1799. All were defeated.

79 Colquhoun was closely associated with the Thames Marine Police and at one time held an official position with the office as its Receiver.

80 Patterson, D. The Thames Police history. Article compiled by PC 128A Richard Paterson 1974–2001. Thames Division available at Thames River Police Museum, Wapping, London. pp. 1–8 at p. 2. For a comprehensive discussion see: Leon Radzinowicz, A history of the English criminal law and its administration from 1750. London: Macmillan; 1957. Vol. 2. Part IV. New Departures, Chapters 12 and 13.

81 By the end of the 18th century, nearly four-fifths of all imports into England came through the Port of London. Source: Radzinowicz, supra, Vol. 2, p. 350.

82 Located at No. 259, Wapping New Stairs. Source: Radzinowicz, supra, Vol. 2, p. 363; and Patterson, supra, p. 4.

83 The force had written "General Instructions" pertaining to roles, responsibilities, conduct, rates of pay and the entire range of standing orders that are associated with a police force. Radzinowicz, supra, Vol. 2, p. 365. In addition to the 80 permanent staff, a further 1,120 were available and utilized as needed on a part-time basis. Radzinowicz, supra, Vol. 2, p. 372.

84 Quoted in Patterson, supra, p. 5.

85 It was also in 1800 that Colquhoun authored Treatise on the commerce and police of the River Thames London, Baldwin, 1800, a work that included specific costs associated with the level of crime being committed on the river estimated by Colquhoun to be at least £232,000 in 1798.

86 The final version was significantly different from the previous draft supplied by Colquhoun and Bentham. The bill passed into law on 28 July 1800. 39&40 Geo 3. C. 87

87 Master mariner and friend of Colquhoun's who later served with Colquhoun in the Wapping Police Office. John Harriot was himself a justice of the peace and is credited with being the author of the first written plan for the river police. "I have lost no time in transmitting your very sensible paper to Mr. Dundas, which contains a very excellent plan for the protection of shipping in the River Thames . . ." cited in Radzinowicz, supra, Vol. 2, p. 373 and note 65. Reprinted in Harriot's memoirs Struggles through life, Exemplified in the various travels and adventures in Europe, Asia and America, etc. (3rd ed. 1815)
3 vols. Vol. 3, pp. 112–113. Radzinowicz also supplies evidence of Harriot having first submitted his plan to the Duke of Portland in 1797 in Radzinowicz, supra, Vol. 2, p. 373 and at footnote 66.

88 By this time Colquhoun was already deeply involved with the Marine Police Establishment as noted in the Lloyd's Evening Post and British Chronicle June 27–29, 1978, A new office sitting at Wapping New Stairs, to be under the direction of Patrick Colquhoun, Esq. cited in Radzinowicz, supra, Vol. 2,
pp. 371–372

89 In an earlier version of the attempts to gain support for the establishment of a government funded river police, Colquhoun, May 1, 1799, refers to assistance from ". . . a friend of great legal knowledge." This legal friend was Jeremy Bentham. Radzinowicz, supra, p. 385 and note 19. Bentham later reports on this involvement in his own memoirs and works, "Memoirs . . . including autobiographical conversations and correspondence" (Bowring's ed. 1843) Vol. 10, pp. 330–333. Ibid.

90 Radzinowicz, supra, Vol. 2, p. 389

91 Emsley, C. The English police; a unique development? in Ideology, Crime and Criminal Justice: A Symposium in Honour of Sir Leon Radzinowicz. Bottoms, A. and Tonry, M., editors. Cullompton, UK: Whillan; 2002. Chapter 4, p. 75.

92 Critchley, TA. A history of the police in England and Wales 900–1966. London: Constable; 1967 cited by Mark Neocleous, "Policing and pin making: Adam Smith, police and the state of prosperity." Policing and Society. 1998; 8; 425–449 at 426.

93 Jones, supra, p. 231 and also, in particular, the Ratcliffe murders of 1811. Reported variously e.g. Radzinowicz, supra, p. 315.

94 The new 'Police science'. Neocleous, supra, p. 440.

95 For example, the MacDonald Bill had failed in 1785 for these reasons and little had changed as the fervor of war and jingoism increased at the end of this century. See: Neocleous, supra, p. 209.

96 Jones, supra, p. 230

97 Robert Peel served as British Prime Minister from 10 December 1834 to 8 April 1835 and again 30 August 1841 to 29 June 1846. He went to Harrow boys school and then read classics, physics and mathematics at Christ's College Oxford where he took a double first. He trained as a lawyer, Lincoln's Inn, and then entered politics in 1809. He made his maiden speech in the Commons in January 1810. Throughout his career Peel was supported by the Duke of Wellington.

98 Act, 54 George III, c. 131, July 25, 1814. "To provide for the better execution of the Laws in Ireland, by appointing Superintending magistrates and additional Constables in Counties in certain cases," Herlihy, infra, p. 29. This act created a permanent police force for rural Ireland. It did not include policing for the city of Dublin that had established a city force under the Dublin Police Act 1786 comprising 10 officers, a chief constable and a night watch. The force wore a uniform dress and carried muskets. Herlihy, J. The Royal Irish Constabulary: A short history and genealogical guide. Dublin: Four Courts Press; 1997. P. 27. The force was short-lived. It was abolished in 1795. Dublin maintained a separate force until merger in 1836 when one combined constabulary was established for all of Ireland.

99 John Brewer, Max Weber and the Royal Irish Constabulary: A Note on Class and Status. The British Journal of Sociology. Mar. 1989: 40(1); 82–96 at p. 82.

100 Bestowal of the title 'Royal' upon a police force was unique at the time. ". . . a circumstance unparalleled and unprecedented in any police force in the world." Brophy, M. Sketches of the Royal Irish Constabulary. London: Burns and Oates; 1886. P. 17.

101 Broeker, G. Robert Peel and the Peace Preservation Force. The Journal of Modern History. Dec. 1961; XXXIII(4); 363–373 at 363.

102 Barrie, supra, p. 5 citing Critchley, TA. A history of police in England and Wales 900–1966. London: Constable; 1967.

103 Herlihy, supra, p. 31. Shortly after this statement there were intense disturbances in Ireland and the army was called in to assist the new force in establishing order.

104 Fifty-seven Irish Protestants in the House of Commons signed a petition requesting he not leave.

105 Brophy, supra, p. 3. "One could almost believe that Sir Robert Peel, inspired by Mr. Drummond, seeing the pitiable condition of Ireland, and feeling that the powerful sister-country had a hand in bringing that condition about, determined on making some small restitution by creating employment of some useful kind, one branch of which assumed the shape of a police force twelve thousand strong." Ibid. There is some degree of support for this if consideration is given to the number of Irish aristocracy who joined

the R.I.C. "Serving in the ranks are to be found the sons and heirs of the embarrassed or utterly ruined landed gentry." Ibid.

106 Brophy, supra, p. 14.

107 For comprehensive discussion see: Elaine Reynolds, Before the bobbies: The night watch and police reform in metropolitan London 1720–1830. London: Macmillan; 1998.

108 Jones, supra, p. 231

109 The Royal Irish Constabulary required all officers to wear a uniform but to have available a suit of civilian clothing to perform duties that required a civilian presence. Brophy, supra, p. 18. This was likely to be interpreted as far too similar to the Paris police 'spies' in London, and therefore the metropolis did not have a detective plain clothes presence until 1842. Jones, supra, p. 232. Initial detective work was provided for by the Bow Street Principal Officers. Cox, supra.

110 "Even had the City authorities been anxious to co-operate with the metropolitan force, either in action or in the exchange of information, their very multiplicity would have made it impracticable." Radzinowicz, supra, Vol. 4, p. 171

111 The 'Square Mile' established its own police force under the City of London Police Act 1839. Daniel Whittle Harvey was the first Commissioner of a force of 500 men. The City of London Police continue to operate today across the "Square Mile." There are currently 850 officers and 450 support staff of London Police that were formed. For further comprehensive discussion see: Andrew Harris, Policing the city: Crime and legal authority in London, 1780–1840. Columbus. OH: The Ohio State University Press; 1968.

112 Ten years later, the 1839 Metropolitan Police Act extended the initial ten-mile zone from Charing Cross to 15 miles. This Act also increased the force size to 4,300 officers.

113 Officers were required to walk a beat at a regular and steady pace. Initially set at three miles per hour this was soon reduced to two and a half miles per hour. Infra, Emsley.

114 For those opposed to a full-time police presence even the uniform was criticized as "The chief offence of the new police in the eyes of these patriots was the similarity of their dress to that of French gendarmes. Any coats would have been forgiven but blue coats." Hayden, BR. Correspondence and table-talk. London: Chatto and Windus; 1897. 2 Volumes. Vol. 2, p. 340.

115 Eight Superintendents, 20 Inspectors, 88 Sergeants and nearly 900 constables. Radzinowicz, L. A history of the English criminal law. Grappling for control. London: Stevens; 1968. Vol. 4, p. 161.

116 Emsley, C. The great British bobby: A History of British Policing from the 18th Century to the Present. London: Quercus; 2009. P. 39

117 Mayne was born in Dublin and after attending Trinity College was called to the bar at Lincoln's Inn. He served as the first joint commissioner and then second joint commissioner after the retirement of Colonel Rowan. Mayne finally became sole the first sole Commissioner of the force in 1855. And remained in this post until his death in 1868. He served a total of 39 years with the London Metropolitan Police and remains the longest serving commissioner to date.

118 One source of criticism even suggested that, "The appointment of a military officer, Colonel Rowan, of the Irish Constabulary, betrayed the intention of creating a 'veritable gendarmerie'." Major Arthur Griffiths, Mysteries of police and crime: A general survey of wrongdoing and its pursuit. London: Casell and Co; 1899. Vol. 1, p. 85. Charles Rowan served in the British army and then as a magistrate in Ireland, his country of birth, before accepting the position as Commissioner of the London Metropolitan Police in 1829. Rowan was not Peel's first choice, which was Col. James Shaw, but he refused and Rowan was offered the position.

119 Ibid.

120 Numerous sources trace the introduction of the term 'Peeler' to describe a 'new' police officer. It is specifically mentioned in the press: "The 'Peelers' withstand riots in London." The Guardian. Friday, 12 November 1830.

121 Griffiths, supra, p. 87

122 Reith, Charles. 1948. A short history of the British police. London: Oxford University Press. P. 62 also cited by Radzinowicz, supra, Vol. 4, p. 163. There are a number of variations upon the actual number of "Principles" that Peel developed. Some sources cite 9, others 12. E.g. Reith, ibid. and Jones, supra.

123 This Act established the system of HM Inspectors of Constabulary who conducted inspections of each force annually. Every force needs to achieve an 'efficient' grade if they were to receive one quarter of their budget from the Treasury.

124 Radzinowicz makes numerous references to the obstacles facing Peel especially, supra, Vol. 3. His treatment of the subject is discussed by Emsley in Ideology, crime and criminal justice, supra. There is also discussion of these matters in Philip Stead, The Police of Britain. New York: Macmillan; 1985, and Eric Monkkonen, Police in urban America, 1860–1920. New York: Cambridge University Press; 1981. An overview of these contributions is available in Wilbur R. Miller, Police and the state: A comparative perspective (review essay). American Bar Foundation Research Journal. Spring, 1986; 11(2); 339–348 at 343.

125 A discussion about the concern over police spies and the Popay affair, infra, is found in Emsley, supra, The great British bobby, pp. 56–64.

126 The Principal Officer was disbanded in 1839 after 90 years of service. It was replaced by the Metropolitan Police Detective Branch in 1842. Jones, supra, pp. 232–233.

127 For a colorful description of policing from the eyes of an early 20th century magazine, see: Richard Kemp, The evolution of the Police. Munseys Magazine. April 1910 to September 1910 at July 1910; XLIII(4); pp. 439–450.

128 Kemp, supra, p. 446

129 Walz, R. Vidocq, rogue cop. In: Francois Eugene Vidocq memoirs of Vidocq: Master of crime. London: AK Press; 2003: xi.

130 Emsley, supra, p. 89

131 Jones, supra, p. 223

132 Ibid.

133 See also: Morris and Vila, supra, pp. 40–42

134 Vidocq memoirs, supra, p. ix

135 1829. He opened a paper mill, lost all his assets and returned to working for the police, but after a scandal involving theft he was dismissed. Francois Eugene Vidocq died in Brussels in 1857. As was stated about him, "He has two valid claims for inclusion in the rolls of fame—as the Legendary Detective and as The Father of the Detective Story." Translator's notes form the 1935 original edition of Vidocq, supra, 1935 Edition translated by Edwin Gile Rich, p. 367.

136 Another plausible reason for the delay in establishing the detective unit is that Richard Mayne 'distrusted' the existing detective police and therefore was not motivated to increase the size or sphere of its responsibility. Miller, supra, p. 92

137 The Sergeant Popay affair of 1833, the Mazzini mail scandal of 1844, both cited by Emsley, supra, p. 90

138 Also known as the Turf Fraud Scandal, it was prosecuted at The Central Criminal Court (The Old Bailey), 22 October 1877. R v Clarke and Others. The case involved a horse racing fraud perpetrated by a number of senior Metropolitan Police detectives. Inspector Meiklejohn, and Chief Inspectors Clarke, Druscovich and Palmer, all stood trial for corruption. D.C.I. Clarke was acquitted; the other three were convicted and given two year terms of imprisonment.

139 He was placed in an unusual situation in this role in that he reported not to the Commissioner of the Metropolitan Police but directly to the Home Secretary. His rank was equivalent to assistant Commissioner, but he never held the formal title. His familiarity with the French Surete came about during his time studying law at the *Faculte de Droit*, Paris (now Pantheon-Assas II). He resigned from the force to enter politics in 1884. His title in the police was Director of the Criminal Investigation Department, C.I.D.

140 "The detective branch of the (French) civil police, aided by broad powers in investigation and evidence gathering arising from the state's concern for security developed a reputation for being the best in the world during the nineteenth century." Miller, supra, p. 344

141 E.g. John Fuller, Criminal justice: Mainstream and crosscurrents. Upper Saddle River, NJ: Pearson; 2006; 146–152; Robert Bohm and Keith Haley, Introduction to criminal justice. 5th ed. Boston: McGrawHill; 2008; 139–142; James Inciardi, Criminal justice. 5th ed. New York: Harcourt Brace; 1996; 163–167; Roy Roberg et al, Police & society. 5th ed. New York: Oxford University Press; 2012; 30–36; Gene Scaramella et al. Introduction to policing. Los Angeles: Sage; 2011; 6–7; Kenneth Peak, Policing America: Challenges and best practices. 7th ed. Boston: Prentice Hall; 2012; 4–18.

142 Also referred to as 'Schouts' in the Dutch settlements. See: Brian Vila and Cynthia Morris The Role of police in American society: A documentary history. Westport, CT: Greenwood Press; 1999; 8.

143 E.g. Fuller, Bohm and Haley, etc., supra. "Every cunstable . . . hath, by virtue of his office, full powr to make, signe, & put forth pursuits, or hues and cries, after murthrers, manslayrs, peace breaks . . ." Taken from Massachusetts statute 1646 reprinted in Inciardi, supra, p. 167.

144 Jones, supra, pp. 112–132.

145 Boston introduced paid night watchmen in 1648 and the Dutch copied this model for New York in 1663, but the expense of running these systems

proved too great and both were disbanded due to cost. Jones, supra, p. 233. See also The Boston night watch. Vila and Morris, supra, pp. 6–8.

146 Of course the reward concept has never left either the UK or the US where it operates nationally and internationally today. One manifestation of the 'reward' that is enshrined in legendary views is that of the reward for the capture of a frontier outlaw. See further: "One feature of the early police system in England that was generally accepted and profoundly affected American law enforcement practices in the eighteenth and nineteenth century was the offer of a reward for the return of stolen property and the arrest and conviction of criminals." Traub, SH. Bounty hunting, and criminal justice in the West: 1865–1900. The Western Historical Quarterly; 19(3); August, 1988; 287–301 at 288.

147 E.g. 5 Anne, c. 31 (1706) that created a reward of £40 for prosecuting burglars. For a comprehensive discussion, see; J. M. Beattie, Policing and punishment in London 1660–1750. Oxford: Oxford University Press; 2004; and also Frank McLynn, Crime and punishment in eighteenth century England. London: Routledge; 1989.

148 "Emerging evidence suggest that 'associations' found in this region (Halifax, Yorkshire) are very similar to the numerous others that spread throughout the rest of the country during this period," Little, CB and Sheffield, C. Frontiers and criminal justice: English private prosecution societies and American vigilantism in the eighteenth and nineteenth centuries. American Sociological Review. Dec., 1983; 48(6); 796–808 at 798. At least 450 associations were formed between 1744 and 1846. Ibid.

149 Ibid.

150 As Little and Sheffield comment though, "It would be wrong to infer that vigilantism arose on the American frontier solely in response to a tidal wave of lawlessness. To the contrary, in many cases the *lack* (original emphasis) of crime posed no need of a regular, full-time system of law enforcement . . .", supra, p. 804. Note 18.

151 See further: C.C. Rister, Outlaws and vigilantes of the southern plains, 1865–1885. The Mississippi Valley Historical Review. March, 1933; 9(4); 537–554; J.W. Smurr, Afterthoughts on the vigilantes. The magazine of western history. Spring 1958; 8(2); 8–20. Published by the Montana Historical Society.

152 A limited number of English style societies did exist in America, in particular, anti-horse theft societies, some of which were incorporated into state law and achieved constabulary powers. Ibid.

153 "The big 'establishment' security companies, Pinkerton and Burns, abandoned labor espionage and union-busting services completely by the 1930's in favor of the burgeoning areas of industrial espionage and counterespionage, corporate embezzlement and fraud, and residential and commercial security policing." Weiss, RP. From cowboy detectives to soldiers of fortune: Private security contracting and its contradictions on the new frontiers of ccapitalist expansion. Social Justice. 2007–2008; 34(3–4); 1–19 at 6.

154 Boston had a 'warden' as early as 1749 and day watches were prevalent in most major cities by the middle of the century: Philadelphia, 1833; Boston, 1838; New York, 1844; San Francisco, 1850; and Los Angeles, 1851. By the

end of the decade these cities had combined the day Constables with the Night Watch to provide comprehensive municipal police cover.

155 Inciardi, supra, p. 168. In some states the sheriff had authority to direct and control the police and in some cases order the call out of the state constabulary. Milton, C. Legislative notes and reviews. Edited by W. F. Wood. The American Political Science Review. Feb. 1921; 15(1); 82–93.

156 England was very familiar with private policing as this had been the model within the City of London for 700 years. The Bow Street Runners, though publically funded, also provided private policing services and the Principal Officers of the Bow Street Police Office hired out their services to private and public entities. Supra.

157 Established in Buffalo, New York, March 18, 1852, by Henry Wells and William G. Fargo

158 Established as a parcel company by Washington Perry Brink in Chicago, 1859.

159 Famous for allegedly providing personal security to President Abraham Lincoln, the agency was started by a Scotsman, Allan Pinkerton, and a Chicago lawyer, Edward Rucker. Originally named the North-Western Police Agency, they changed the name to The Pinkerton National Detective Agency in part to secure federal contracts. By 1871, the newly formed Department of Justice had hired Pinkerton's to detect and prosecute those committing federal crimes. The relationship lasted until enactment of the Anti-Pinkerton Act of 1893, which no longer allowed private agencies to be employed by the government.

160 This agency was established by William J. Burns in 1909. Prior to starting the William J. Burns National Detective Agency, he had worked as a Secret Service agent. He returned to federal employment in 1921 to become head of the Justice Department's Bureau of Investigation, which on retirement he handed over to J. Edgar Hoover as Director of the FBI.

161 See John Reid, Dividing the elephant; The separation of mess and joint stock property on the overland trail. Hastings Law Journal. 1977; 28(3). Jones, supra. The continent was sometimes referred to as the Elephant by pioneers.

162 Written in 1922. Frederic F. Van de Water, author of Grey Riders: The story of the New York State Troopers, New York: Putnam's Sons; 1922. Page 16 stated, "In America to-day, the countryside for the most part still turns for protection against marauders to the constable and the sheriff's posse that came into being under English law in 1295, as part of the militia system. These no longer carry the long bow or go about jingling in chain mail. Otherwise there is little to distinguish them from the keepers of the King's law in Merrie England of the Thirteenth century." The American militia system that Van de Water refers to ". . . grew out of the English Assize of Arms which, dating from the reign of Henry II, required all free men to provide arms and submit to training." Robert Reinders, Militia and public order in nineteenth-century America. Journal of American Studies. April 1977; 11(1); 81–101 at 82.

163 Little and Sheffield, supra, p. 806.

164 Jones, supra, p. 245.

165 Ibid.

166 Ray, GW. From cossack to trooper: Manliness, police reform, and the state. Journal of Social History. Spring 1995; 28(3); 565–586. Weiss, RP. Private detective agencies and labour discipline in the United States 1855–1946. The Historical Journal. 1 March 1986; 29(1); 87–107.

167 The Replies to Representative Maurer's Questions Reveal Distressing Conditions in Nearly Every Locality Where the Cossacks Were Located. Madison (Darrah P.O.), Pa., Feb. 22, 1911. Hon. James H. Maurer, House of Representatives, Harrisburg, Pa. 1911. It appears that the terms, 'Cossacks', 'Yellow Dogs' and Hoodlums' were in use against the Coal and Iron police as well as the Pennsylvania State Constabulary.

168 $20 per ton. The equivalent of paying $12 per gallon for gasoline today.

169 "It was a grime joke. The Coal and Iron Police were actually the mercenaries of the great industries." Van de Water, supra, p. 24.

170 E.g. The Lattimer Massacre that occurred near Hazelton, PA on 10 September 1897.

171 A history of the Michigan state constabulary. Detroit, Michigan State Con. stabulary Association; 1919. Chapter 2, p. 31.

172 Captain Groome was apparently promoted to the rank of Major once he took responsibility for the Pennsylvania State Constabulary. There are also a number of later references to Groome as Superintendent and also to Commander Groome. The congressional hearing, supra, consistently refers to him as Major Groome.

173 May 6, 1915. The Commission on Industrial Relations created by the act of Congress on 23 August 1912, held at the Shoreham Hotel, Washington DC.

174 Groome took responsibility for a broad range of functions associated with the new force, including setting standards for recruits. During the Industrial Relations Committee Hearings, James Maurer, President of the Pennsylvania State Federation of Labor, was asked, "From what forces are the State constabulary recruited?" to which he replied, "The men are recruited from the ranks of ex-United States soldiers, and again many of them are recruited from the ranks or from the degenerate descendants of the middle classes, young men who are educated, but never amount to anything and no good for anything and generally hunt a job in the State police force." Final Report and Testimony Submitted to Congress by the Commission on Industrial Relations. 6 May 1915. Vol. XI. Document No. 415, p. 10932.

175 Williams, D. State police and the Irish "Black and Tans" in The Bridgemen's Magazine. January 1921; XXI(1); 77.

176 Ibid.

177 An interesting lack of geographical knowledge is displayed by Chairman Walsh, who at one point asked, "Does the constabulary in Ireland have authority in the large cities like Glasgow and Dublin?" Williams, supra, p. 78. A more pertinent question followed: "You spent, you say, three weeks at the barracks?" Major Groome. "Yes, and got their ideas and their rules and regulations." Ibid.

178 It is variously described as the Pennsylvania State Police and the Pennsylvania State Constabulary. Williams, supra, Munsey's Magazine, supra, Van de Water, supra.

179 Describing the officers employed by the new constabulary, Major Groome stated, "My instruction to each trooper leaves a great deal to his discretion. If he starts out to get his man, he must get him, even if he has to butt into the middle of a mob to find him. The troopers are advised not to use their guns unless they have to." Munsey's Magazine, supra, p. 448. This makes an interesting contrast with Peel's policing principles.

180 Jones, supra, p. 234.

181 When introduced the police were mocked. See Monkkonen, supra, p. 551.

182 See further: Vila and Morris, supra, pp. 36–39.

183 Miller, supra, pp. 345, 346, 347.

184 Miller, WR. Police authority in London and New York City 1830–1870. Journal of Social History. Winter 1975; 8(2); 81–101. This posits that the fundamental difference between the two jobs is that the authority each officer possessed was different. The London "Bobby' had impersonal authority and the New York 'Cop' had far greater discretion. He cites the example of carrying firearms and how the American officer took to taking a firearm to work and as such became a more powerful presence than his London colleague.

185 "Throughout most of the 19th and into the 20th century, the basic qualification for becoming a police officer was a political connection, rather than demonstrated ability." Scaramella, supra, p. 9.

186 This relationship lasted until 1870 when a second municipal force was created. In the same year, 1857, Boston, having rejected a London police model in 1832, decided to move forward with the creation of an amalgamation of night watch and day police to form a full-time police force.

187 Jones, supra, pp. 234–5.

188 See: Vila and Morris, supra, pp. 35–37.

189 Scaramella, supra, p. 9.

190 Monkkonen, supra, p. 554.

191 Ibid.

192 Jones, supra, p. 108 and 219.

193 It can be further suggested that the London police were a centralized force due to the sole reporting line directly to the Home Secretary. This is true also of the Paris police, but not so of the New York police who were decentralized by the Municipal Police Act. It is recognized that local town policing in England became de-centralized by the formation of countrywide forces in the 1856 Act, supra.

194 Monkkonen, supra. Notes four important innovative features of the new police in the US. The second of these is that the US police located the police under the executive rather than the judicial branch. This differed from London where the police ran courts for many years. "This shift also sent the American police down a different developmental path from the English police, who long remained much more active and involved in preparing and prosecuting criminal cases than did their American counterparts." P. 550.

195 Monkkonen, supra, p. 553.

196 By the early 1900s, most major cities in America had established police forces that prioritized crime fighting as a primary role. The issue of political

influence remained prevalent, however, until the 1920s. Commentary on this and upon the impact of August Volmer as a voice in establishing policing priorities supra, note 134.

197 Miller, supra, p. 347.

198 C.f. Roberg et al, pp. 36–37 and Jones, supra, pp. 242–243.

199 Fuller, supra, pp. 151–152.

200 Brophy, supra, relates a fascinating event when two R.I.C. officers were on vacation in Paris at a military parade. They both wore their green R.I.C. uniforms at the time. Apparently Napoléon III saw the officers and questioned their origins. He then invited them to join in the parade and later referred to them as "Officers de la gendarmerie Irlandaise." Pp. 22–23.

CHAPTER

4

© GERARD BOTTINO/Shutterstock.com

Policing: Roles, Functions, and Challenges

KEY TERMS

Aggressive patrol
Bias-based profiling
Blue code of silence
Broken windows theory
COMPSTAT
Crime analysis
Crime mapping
Criminal investigation
Deep cover
Directed patrol
Discretion
Excessive force
Field interrogation
Follow-up investigation
Intelligence-led policing
Light cover
Operational styles
Order maintenance
Preliminary investigation
Preventive patrol
Problem-oriented policing
Role
Role conflict
Role expectation
Selective enforcement
Social contract
Symbolic assailant
Thin blue line

CHAPTER OBJECTIVES

1. Define the various roles and duties that police officers have in enforcing law and maintaining order in society.
2. Distinguish among the different styles of policing used by police officers.
3. Identify the various functions of police departments in America.
4. Explain the components of the police subculture, including issues related to discretion, stress, ethics, and corruption.

Case Study: Less Lethal or Deadly Force?

Police work can be a dangerous profession, and sometimes the police are required to use physical force to subdue criminals. Historically, the police have carried batons or nightsticks and firearms. In more recent years, new, less lethal technologies have been developed so the police do not have to resort to deadly force. Stun gun technology sends electroshocks into the suspect's body that cause a loss of neuromuscular control and contract the muscles in the body. The most commonly known stun gun used by police departments across the country was developed by TASER International nearly two decades ago. Proponents of the use of the TASER have found it to be a useful tool that has prevented police from having to use deadly force. While these proponents view the use of stun gun technology as preventing deaths of suspects, an alarming number of suspects have died after being "tased." Numerous civil lawsuits have been filed against police departments and stun gun manufacturers, including TASER International, but at present, the courts have ruled against the plaintiffs and found that the deaths were not a direct result of the electroshock weapon.

On September 22, 2005, the Nashville Police Department was called to the Mercy Lounge, a Nashville nightclub, to remove 21-year-old Patrick Lee. When police arrived, Lee was already outside the club and could be observed undressed and rambling incoherently. Earlier in the evening, Lee had reportedly ingested the hallucinogen LSD. In an attempt to control him, police deployed their TASERs and jolted Lee 19 times. Paramedics were called to the scene when Lee was unresponsive, and he died in police custody 39 hours later. When an autopsy was conducted, the medical examiner ruled that Lee's death was caused by a "drug-induced excited delirium." Lee's parents filed a wrongful death lawsuit against the Nashville Police Department, the police officers involved, and TASER International. Eventually, a federal jury cleared all defendants in the lawsuit.

Do you believe the shocking of Patrick Lee 19 times was an excessive use of police force? With the number of deaths that have occurred following the use of electroshock, even though the courts have yet to find its users responsible, should the police still continue to employ this form of less lethal weapon?

Roles of the Police Officer

Seneviratne (2002) described the role of police officers as being the gatekeepers to the criminal justice system.[1] It is their sworn duty to investigate crimes and arrest the offenders. Their arrests lead offenders through the gates into the criminal justice system. In addition to arresting offenders, police officers have a variety of functions and roles they are expected to perform. Performing these functions and roles does not come without a cost. The nature of police work leads to unique challenges as a result of the powers that police have, the dangers they face, and the temptations all around them. This chapter discusses the roles, functions, and challenges for the police officer in American society.

When citizens think of the police, they most likely envision a uniformed officer who is operating a vehicle marked with emblems and striping and emergency lights mounted on the roof. This description is of the officer who is patrolling a beat and responding to calls for service in the community. Although there are many different law enforcement agencies on the federal, state, and local levels of government, each with its own geographic or criminal responsibility, the patrol officer is the face of law enforcement in America.

The relationship between the public and the government is commonly referred to as the **social contract**. This contract is the agreement into which the public enters with its government allowing it to provide for public safety and security. One form of protection that the public seeks is that of the law enforcement agencies that police America. The police represent a formal state control that is necessary and embodies what Hunter (1985) referred to as public social control.[2] Without the police, the public would be left to its own devices, and crime and victimization would undoubtedly result. The police are said to be a **thin blue line**, named for the color of most police uniforms, between the lawful and the lawless on our streets. Klockars (1985) defined police as "institutions or individuals given the general right to use coercive force by the state within the state's domestic territory."[3]

Social contract An agreement between the public and government in which the public allows the government to provide safety and security.

Thin blue line The line between the lawful and the lawless and between social order and chaos on the streets.

A **role** is defined as the position one holds within a social structure. The role police officers assume when policing a community can be vague and ambiguous. Take, for example, a community that has an ordinance against doing vehicle repairs on the street. Community residents in an upper-class neighborhood who do not want to see cars sitting on cement blocks and motor oil spills on their streets may call the police department demanding action against a violator. In contrast, residents in a poorer neighborhood may overlook this violation because they know the neighbor doing his own repair work cannot afford to take the car to an automobile repair shop. This example refers to what is termed as **role expectation**. While the residents

Role The position one holds within a social structure.

Role expectation The behaviors and activities that people expect from a person in a particular role.

of the upper-class neighborhood expect the police to issue a citation for the ordinance violation, the residents in the poorer neighborhood do not. Role expectation is the behavior that is expected of someone in a particular role.

Dunham and Alpert (2010) saw the role of the police officer becoming increasingly more complex and citizens' expectations of the police continually expanding.[4] The expectations of the police officer's role not only reflect the wishes of community residents; the officer must also deal with the expectations of police administrators, political leaders in the community, and sometimes the state legislature. In our example involving vehicle repairs on the street, although residents in the poorer neighborhood do not want violators cited, the police chief may expect officers to cite any violator of the ordinance regardless of where they reside in the community. The mayor of the community may insist that the police department escort funeral processions to the local cemetery as a service to the public, while the officers may not see this role as one that law enforcement should assume. State legislatures have enacted laws restricting police officers' use of discretion when dealing with domestic violence cases: police officers may prefer to mediate a domestic dispute, but they may be required by law to make an arrest in the case.

© Ivan Kokoulin/Shutterstock.com

Role conflict is the conflict between what police officers may prefer to do and what they are expected to do.

Role conflict can result from the opposing expectations that police officers receive from different sources. Role conflict is the conflict between what police officers may prefer to do and what they are expected to do. While police officers may view themselves as crime fighters, the public may see them as peacekeepers or even "social workers" whose role is to control social problems. They may be expected to serve as social workers and intervene in a domestic dispute, but then have to arrest one of the parties involved because they are legally bound to do so even if they believe arrest may be unwarranted. The police may want to pursue a traffic violator who did not stop after they activated their emergency lights and siren, but not be able to because agency policy prohibits vehicle pursuits of vehicle operators wanted only for a traffic violation. The community and the police department largely base the police officer's role on the social contract that has been agreed upon.

Role conflict The conflict between what a person may prefer to do and what the person is expected to do.

Controversial Police Roles

The police are expected to ensure that the rights of citizens are not violated and they are afforded their due process. If police engage in unethical or coercive practices, they are only serving to endanger the public and subject citizens to the very risks the police were given power to prevent. Reiman (1985) argued that the police must be accountable to the public they serve for their use of public power.[5]

Police searches, use of force, vehicle pursuits, and citizen encounters can cause controversy among the public if not performed ethically and within the legal boundaries of the law. For example, in the case of *Mapp v. Ohio* (1961), the United States Supreme Court ruled that evidence obtained illegally by the police must be excluded in state prosecutions.[6] Stuntz (1997) found this exclusionary rule, as it is known, to be useful in that it allows the courts to serve as watchdogs for police misconduct regarding the collection of evidence against a suspect. Stuntz called the exclusionary rule the best legal tool available for regulating the police. While critics of the exclusionary rule might focus on a suspect walking out of a court as a result of a legal technicality due to police misconduct, Stuntz stated that the rule is important because the courts see the consequences of the constitutional rules they create for the police.[7]

In contrast, Keenan (1998) noted that another Supreme Court decision of the 1960s involving police searches was widely criticized for being too pro-police.[8] In *Terry v. Ohio* (1968), the court ruled that police have the authority to detain or "stop" a person briefly for questioning and "frisk" the person for weapons if the officer has a reasonable suspicion the person may be armed and dangerous. The court found the "*Terry Rule*" to be necessary for the safety of police officers when dealing with suspicious persons. However, police must have a legitimate reason for conducting a "stop and frisk" so as not to violate an individual's rights against unreasonable search and seizure.[9]

The authority to use force in the line of duty is a second controversial aspect of police work. The videotaped beating of Rodney King in 1991 by several police officers from the Los Angeles Police Department provided the nation with an example of the possible consequences of police use of force. More controversial is the use of deadly force by police. In the landmark *Tennessee v. Garner* (1985) case, the Supreme Court ruled that a police officer may not use deadly force to prevent the escape of a suspect unless probable cause exists that the suspect poses a threat of serious physical injury or death to the officer or other persons present.10 As a result of the *Garner* decision, police departments began to make changes in agency policies regarding the use of deadly force.[11]

Deadly force must be the last resort for the police officer. Unfortunately, police are usually unable to choose the time, place, or circumstances of a potentially deadly encounter. Fyfe (1986) described the split-second syndrome police officers face when they encounter violence, during which time they must diagnose a problem, perform under stress and time constraints, and make an assessment of the justifiability of their actions.[12]

Another controversial role of the police officer involves vehicle pursuits. Alpert (1993) observed that pursuit driving on public streets at excessive speeds is a dangerous police tactic that presents risks to all involved, including the officer, the suspect, and any innocent motorists or pedestrians who may be nearby. Alpert stated that police must balance the need to immediately apprehend a suspect with the likelihood that an accident or injury may occur.[13]

Hicks (2006) warned that police officers are charged with protecting the public, and exposing these members of the public to unnecessary risk is counter to this primary police responsibility. As a result of the danger posed by high-speed police chases, Hicks recommended that police officers be provided with written guidelines regarding the procedures that should be followed when considering the initiation of a vehicle pursuit.[14] The police may argue that policy restrictions imposed on pursuits inhibit their ability to apprehend serious offenders. Many police pursuits initiated for simple traffic violations lead to the apprehension of suspects wanted on felony charges. In a study of police pursuits in the state of Michigan, one-third of pursuits—most of which were initiated for traffic offenses—were found to lead to a felony arrest.[15]

Bias-based profiling Selection of individuals based solely on a common trait of a group such as race, ethnicity, gender, sexual orientation, or economic status.

© Anne Kitzman/Shutterstock.com

African-Americans are more likely than whites to view police traffic stops as unjustified.

A fourth issue of controversy involves police-citizen encounters and particularly the issue of **bias-based profiling**. Bias-based profiling, previously referred to as racial profiling, is defined as the selection of individuals based solely on a common trait of a group such as race, ethnicity, gender, sexual orientation, or economic status. Race is a significant factor influencing individual attitudes about police, with African-Americans having the most negative attitudes toward police while whites hold the most positive attitudes toward police.[16]

The most common site for a police-citizen encounter is the traffic stop,[17] and the most controversial aspect of those is the phenomenon known as "driving while black."[18] Research has indicated that blacks stopped by the police are more likely than whites to view the stop as unjustified.[19] Brown (2005) wrote that many public surveys have shown that a great number of American citizens believe the police treat African-Americans more harshly than white Americans. In Brown's study of police-suspect encounters in Cincinnati, Ohio, the findings suggest that police base arrest decisions on strict legal criteria when encountering white suspects, but are influenced by demeanor, age, and gender when encountering black suspects.[20]

Critical Thinking

Should police officers be permitted to engage in vehicle pursuits for traffic violators who are not suspected of having committed a more serious offense?

Duties of the Police Officer

In the broadest sense, the role of the police officer is multidimensional. The influence that the community has on the role of police officers requires them to perform a variety of duties. The police are expected to be crime fighters, security guards, peacemakers, lawyers, judges, investigators, social workers, clergymen, psychologists, and medical first responders.

Generally, the role of the police officer falls into four categories of duties:

- Law Enforcement
- Order Maintenance
- Crime Prevention
- Service Provider

These duties that police officers are required to perform are based in large part on the size of the police department and the expectations of the community. Police officers may view themselves as law enforcers, but actually spend most of their time maintaining order in the community. For example, in a large urban police department, the police may deal with a major crime problem that would preclude them from responding to scenes of minor traffic accidents. On the other hand, in a small rural police department, the crime problem may be minimal, so officers are expected to investigate every traffic accident, regardless of how minor it may be. The large urban police department might be exerting most of its efforts maintaining order and enforcing the law, while the smaller rural department is providing services to the community and preventing crime from occurring.

Additionally, the duties police officers perform often overlap. For example, a police officer might be dispatched to the scene of a dispute between two neighbors over the boundary line between their properties. The officer may expect to reach a peaceful resolution to the dispute to maintain order in the neighborhood, but when one neighbor decides to punch the other, the officer may now have to perform a law enforcement duty and arrest the aggressive neighbor. While each category of duties is discussed below, the reality is that the police officer's role includes many overlapping and sometimes conflicting responsibilities.

Law Enforcement

Enforcing the law is traditionally considered to be the primary responsibility of police officers. Police officers have the power to investigate crimes and arrest offenders. Within these two broad powers are numerous duties, including enforcing traffic laws, interviewing victims of and witnesses to crimes, interrogating persons suspected of committing crimes, collecting physical evidence at crime scenes, conducting undercover and covert operations, and assisting in the prosecution of individuals charged with crimes. When performing these duties, police officers must always be mindful of the legal rights of any accused persons under the United States Constitution to ensure that they have been safeguarded against violations such as unreasonable searches and seizures and notified of their right against self-incrimination and right to counsel.

Selective enforcement The decision made by police as to which laws they wish to enforce and when they choose to enforce them.

Police officers are sworn to uphold and enforce *all* laws, but this can be unrealistic or unwanted. Most police departments practice **selective enforcement** of the law, in which they decide which laws they wish to enforce and when they choose to enforce them. Police departments must allocate manpower and budgetary resources where they can do the most good and deal with the more serious offenses and offenders. Police officer discretion also plays a role in law enforcement. Traffic enforcement efforts usually permit police officers to decide whether to issue a warning or a citation to traffic violators. But at times, the police department may choose to set up a "speed trap" and selectively enforce excessive speed violations, issuing citations to all violators on a particular roadway in the community where they have observed an increase in fatal traffic accidents.

The fact that the public often refers to police officers as "law enforcement officers" suggests that they see this duty as the primary function of the police. In reality, law enforcement takes up a small percentage of time spent by police officers when they are on duty.

Order Maintenance

The duty of the police officer to act as a peacekeeper and maintain order in the community dates back to the early English watchman with his lantern and baton. Police officers may engage in **order maintenance** more than any other duty that they perform.

Order maintenance
A method of policing whereby officers interpret the law and decide on a course of action based on each individual situation when assigning blame and choosing whether or not to arrest.

Order maintenance situations may or may not involve criminal activity. For example, crowd control may be necessary at a public event such as the state fair. In this case, it is unlikely that criminal activity will occur, because these events are typically family-oriented. The police presence is usually meant to ensure that the flow of pedestrian and vehicular traffic remains orderly, though of course unruly persons at the fair would be dealt with and arrested when necessary. In contrast, order maintenance at the site of a political rally involving a hotly debated issue will most likely involve citizens who have a different agenda than those seeking a fun day at the state fair. Arresting drunk or unruly people at the fair is a very different use of state power than arresting protestors engaging in the political process.

One of the duties of police is maintaining order, such as at a protest, concert, or other gathering.

Police officers are often dispatched to domestic disputes between individuals such as family members, neighbors, or landlords and tenants. In domestic disputes, police officers intervene and attempt to resolve the situation to the satisfaction of all parties involved. If the problem is unresolved, or one of the parties involved has violated criminal law, then the police may choose to make an arrest. Even loud music complaints or dog barking calls can be resolved by simply issuing warnings to the responsible parties. If the music is turned down and the dog is kept from barking by its owner, then order is maintained. If not, then it might be necessary for police to make an arrest.

Police officers prefer to deal with order maintenance issues without having to arrest a citizen. Generally, the public favors this approach. But there are times when what began for police as an order maintenance duty becomes a law enforcement duty.

Crime Prevention

Crime prevention is another duty that the community expects the police to perform. When police officers are on routine patrol in marked patrol vehicles, they are looking for criminal activity that may be in progress. Their mere presence may also deter crime. The public views the high visibility of police as one of the most important ways to prevent crime. It is also common for the police department to increase its visibility in high-crime areas or areas of the community where the public congregates. This is done by use of a variety of patrol techniques. For example, the police may utilize foot patrols and mounted horse patrols on a Saturday night in the nightclub section of the community. These increased patrols can have the effect of inhibiting bar patrons from engaging in criminal activity they may otherwise have attempted if police had not made their presence so evident.

In addition to the use of routine patrols and increased visibility, the police department may engage in activities specifically designed for crime prevention. For example, police units will often conduct speed traps using radar devices to apprehend speeding violators. These traps also serve as a deterrent by discouraging motorists from exceeding the speed limit on roadways known to be locations that police frequently monitor. DUI checkpoints, which are often previously announced in the local newspaper, are meant to prevent vehicle operators from driving while drunk. Even visible foot and vehicle patrols in areas of the community known to be frequented by prostitutes and their potential customers have been useful in dealing with this crime problem.

Finally, many police departments implement organized crime prevention programs. Neighborhood watch programs are designed to encourage neighborhood residents to collaborate with the police department and maintain security in the community. A program for juveniles such as the Police Athletic League (PAL) is another example of crime prevention that targets at-risk youths.

Visher and Weisburd (1998) argued that for decades there was very little positive evidence that police crime prevention strategies worked. These authors reported that in more recent years, there has been reason for optimism, as police departments have begun to focus more on high rate offenders and "hot spots" of crime.[21] Still, even with these newer strategies that target specific offenders and crime areas, the sight of a patrol car passing by a resident's home can provide a sense of security for community residents.

The mere presence of a police car may help prevent crime from occurring in a particular area.

Service Provider

The services provided by the police department typically depend on the size of the department and the amount of time officers can devote to providing service. Kennedy (2002) stated that, as 24/7 agencies, police departments are always available. As such, agencies must prioritize calls and make decisions regarding which calls will be answered and which ones will not. It is expected that the public will seek the assistance of the police when they have been a victim of or witness to a crime, or have been in some other emergency situation. In some communities, it is also expected that the police will perform services for their residents and respond to non-emergency situations. Large police departments may not be able to provide the community with the more personal attention that small departments can.[22] While busier police departments that must respond to numerous emergency calls might offer no assistance to non-emergency callers, a small local police department may respond to both emergency and non-emergency calls.

Police officers act as service providers, performing such tasks as giving directions.

Quite often, the non-emergency service calls to which a police department responds reflect the wishes and expectations of the community. For example, the police department may be expected to assist stranded motorists, provide directions to lost motorists, escort funeral processions, and unlock car doors. A large police department may not have the time to remove cats from trees or provide parenting advice to a distraught parent with a troubled teenager, but the public may expect these types of services from a small-town police department.

Operational Styles of Policing

Several researchers have studied the police officer position in an attempt to determine how officers approach their jobs. These approaches to performing police duties are referred to as **operational styles**. These operational styles can reflect community expectations for police officers, the expectations of police administrators for their departments, and individual police officers' own philosophies on how they should perform their duties. In police departments that do not have a formal agreement on how the community should be policed, individual officers may adopt their own styles.

Operational styles The approaches police officers use to perform their duties.

For example, the community may expect its police officers to adopt a watchman style. This style may be adopted in a very small community where the officers in the police department are familiar with members of the community. The community and the police may agree on informal controls instead of strict enforcement of laws. *Informal social control* refers to a willingness of local residents to actively participate in crime prevention in their neighborhoods.[23] Reisig and Parks (2004) believed the movement toward community policing, which is discussed in further detail later in this chapter, emphasized the positive contribution of police-citizen partnerships that could control crime and build informal social control.[24] Silver and Miller (2004) found that when residents believe police are successful in addressing their crime problems and represent a legitimate institution of public social control, they feel more empowered to partner with police and to engage in their own informal social control.[25] The community and the police department may agree that it is preferable to warn traffic code violators for minor violations instead of issuing citations. The community may prefer that juveniles who are caught in the act of underage drinking should be escorted home to their parents instead of charged with a violation. The community and the police will most likely agree that in serious cases, criminal law must be enforced and offenders charged.

It should be noted that the public's perception of the police department or an individual officer is often determined by the style of policing officers are practicing as a result of the police-citizen contact. The traffic violator who receives a citation may believe that the officer's style is that of an enforcer. This may or may not be valid. Often, the officer is acting in the role of enforcer because strict enforcement of traffic violators at a particular intersection has been ordered due to the high volume of traffic accidents at the location. While an officer would typically practice a watchman style, orders from the police chief have required the use of an enforcer style.

Wilson's Styles of Policing

Wilson (1968) developed one of the earliest studies of the operational styles of police officers. Wilson found three distinct styles that he termed the watchman style, legalistic style, and service style.

In the *watchman* style, the police officer emphasizes a more informal way of handling disputes within the community. The watchman is most interested in keeping the peace and chooses to arrest only as a last resort to resolve a dispute. This style of policing would be best suited for poorer, economically deprived communities and small towns where informal control is practiced.

Wilson's second style of policing is the *legalistic* style. As the name implies, this style of policing emphasizes strict enforcement of the law and the use of arrests to resolve disputes in the community. Communities with higher crime rates, which are more common within our larger metropolitan areas, would more likely practice the legalistic style of policing, believing that the community will become safer if more offenders are removed from the streets.

The third operational style is Wilson's *service* style. Affluent communities may be more likely to emphasize this style of policing where the police are asked to serve the public's needs. The emphasis of the service style is to assist the community rather than arrest offenders. The use of social service agencies, diversionary programs, and community treatment programs is preferable to the use of the criminal justice system.[26]

Broderick's Styles of Policing

A second approach to the operational styles of police officers was developed by Broderick (1987). Broderick labeled his officer styles as enforcers, idealists, realists, and optimists.

The *enforcer* has more concern for maintaining the social order and puts little emphasis on the individual rights of citizens or due process. The *idealist* emphasizes social order as well, but unlike the enforcer, places a high value on individual rights and due process. The *realist* places little value on social order or due process and seems to accept society as it is. Finally, the *optimist* values individual rights and due process and is mainly concerned with acting as a public servant, giving a lower value to social control.[27]

Muir's Styles of Policing

A third classification by Muir (1977) studied the methods by which police officers used their authority on the streets. Muir saw police officers as using *passion*, which was defined as the ability to use force to resolve conflict, or *perspective*, which was described as using force ethically and dealing empathetically with those who are less fortunate. Muir's styles of police officers included the enforcer, reciprocator, avoider, and professional.

The *enforcer* is the police officer who possesses the passion for enforcing laws and has a comfort level with using force to deal with problems. The *reciprocator* lacks any passion for the job, takes little action enforcing law or making arrests, and has a difficult time using force when it is warranted. The *avoider* is the officer who has neither passion nor perspective and takes little action. The *professional* combines the judicious use of passion and the perspective necessary to successfully perform the job.[28]

Critical Thinking

Among the various styles of policing discussed in the chapter, which type of police officer would you like policing your community?

Functions of Police

The functions that are carried out by the police are determined based on the size of the police department, the makeup of the community, and the crime problems that the community faces. The following are some of the major functions of a police department.

Patrol

Patrol is considered to be the backbone of policing. The uniformed police officer in the marked police vehicle patrols the streets of the community and serves as the first responder to calls for service and citizen complaints. In a small police department, it would not be uncommon for all officers, including the police chief, to engage in patrol. In larger police departments that have a variety of specialized functions, patrol officers comprise the largest unit in the department.

The patrol officer is the first police officer dispatched to calls for service. Patrol officers respond to family disputes, neighborhood disputes, traffic accidents, burglar alarms, and any other kind of call that is made to the police department by the residents of the community. In addition to responding to calls for service, the patrol officer is expected to look for criminal activity that might be occurring in the community. The patrol officer's duties can involve investigating crimes such as traffic law violations, driving under the influence, disorderly conduct, domestic violence, burglary, and theft.

Preventive Patrol

Adams (2006) identified a number of methods that the police employ to patrol the community. The most common method is preventive patrol, which is sometimes referred to as routine or random patrol. **Preventive patrol** involves patrolling the police officer's sector or district in the community on an unpredictable, random basis. The amount of time spent by police officers on preventive patrol is often dependent on the number of calls for service to which they respond. The more time the patrol officer spends answering calls, the less time he or she can spend patrolling the community to prevent crime or look for crimes that may be in progress.[29]

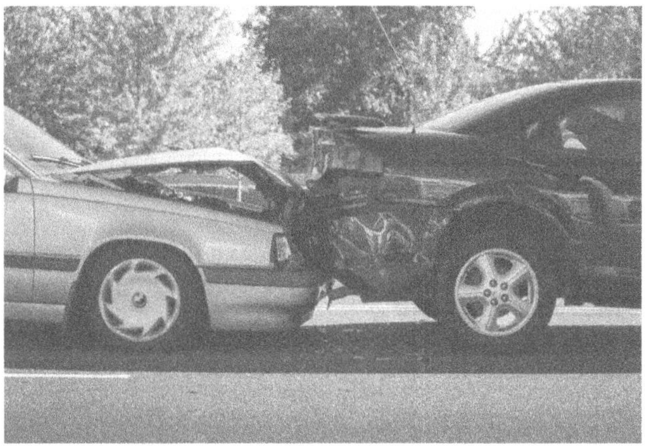

© Robert Crum/Shutterstock.com

Patrol officers are dispatched to calls for service, including traffic accidents.

Preventive patrol
Patrolling the community on an unpredictable and routine or random basis.

Although preventive patrol has been used for centuries, its effectiveness was not studied until 1972 in the well-known Kansas City Preventive Patrol Experiment.[30] This study is still considered to be the most comprehensive look at preventive patrol. The experiment divided the patrol districts in Kansas City, Missouri, into 15 beats, with five beats in each of three different groups. Each of the three groups was similar in demographics and calls for service. The first group of five beats were "proactive beats," in which two to three times the normal level of preventive patrol was conducted. The second group of five beats were "reactive beats," in which no preventive patrol was used, and officers only entered the beats when responding to a call.

Finally, the third group of five beats were the "control beats." Control beats maintained the usual level of preventive patrol that had historically been conducted.

Following the year-long study, the surprising results indicated that neither increasing nor decreasing patrols impacted crime rates in the community. Furthermore, the citizens of Kansas City were unaware that any changes to the way the community was being patrolled had occurred. Citizens' fear of crime, attitudes toward the police, and even their review of police response time to their calls for service remained unchanged. In more recent studies involving police patrol, researchers have found that instead of using a generalized preventive patrol, the focus should be on specific places or "hot spots" where crime is most concentrated.[31,32,33]

The results of the Kansas City Preventive Patrol Experiment caused many police administrators to rethink their positions on the effectiveness of routine patrol. Yet, years after the study, preventive patrol remains the most widely used method for patrolling our communities. As a result of the study, however, alternatives to preventive patrol are being practiced when particular problems in the community warrant their use.

Directed Patrol

Directed patrol Spending an allotted amount of time patrolling a specific area of the community that is considered to be a high-crime area.

A **directed patrol** requires that patrol officers spend an amount of their patrol time in a specified area of the community.[34] These may be known high-crime areas or areas where there has been a noticeable increase in one type of criminal activity. For example, the police department may be aware as a result of crime analysis information that during the three weeks prior to Christmas, the parking lot at the local mall has had an increase in vehicle burglaries and muggings of shoppers. As time permits during the shift, police officers may be ordered to direct frequent patrols through the mall parking lot in order to prevent these crimes from occurring or possibly catch suspects in the act of committing these crimes.

Foot Patrol

Prior to the use of motorized patrol vehicles, police officers patrolled on foot. Adams (2006) stated that although foot patrol confines police to small areas, it is among the most effective types of patrol.[35] The motorized patrol vehicle has permitted patrol officers to cover more ground and respond more quickly to calls for service. Unfortunately, a negative effect of the use of the patrol vehicle was that police officers began to become more distant and aloof from the community. Foot patrols allow police officers to have more personal contact with the community and move more quietly into areas of the community where the sound of an approaching vehicle may alarm a suspect.

FIGURE 4.1 SCHEMATIC OF 15 BEATS IN KANSAS CITY PATROL EXPERIMENT

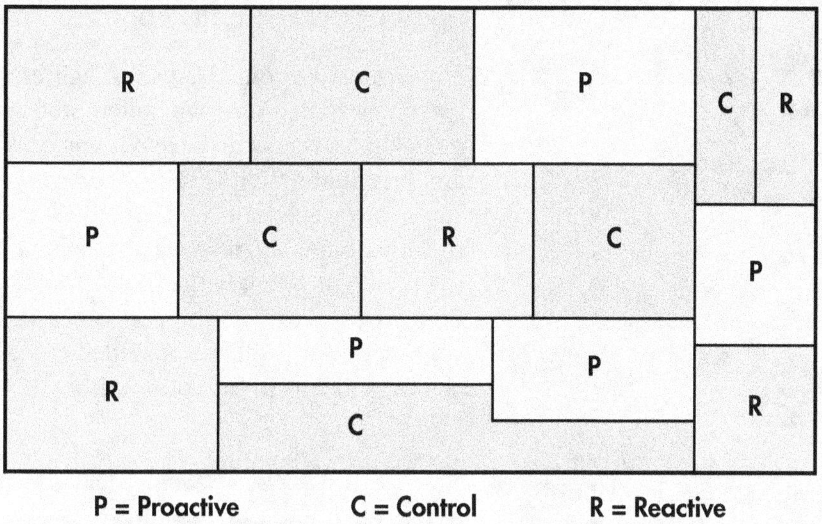

© Kendall Hunt Publishing Company

Two important studies were conducted in an attempt to determine the possible benefits of the use of foot patrol. The Newark, New Jersey Foot Patrol Experiment found that foot patrols did not affect crime rates, but had a positive impact on citizen satisfaction with foot patrol officers.[36] In a similar study conducted by Trojanowicz (1982) in Flint, Michigan, it was found that citizens also showed an increase in satisfaction with police services and a decrease in fear of crime.[37] Whether or not foot patrol reduces crime is uncertain, but it has led to a more positive relationship between the police and the public.

Aggressive Patrol

Aggressive patrol strategies require patrol officers to maintain a more active or "aggressive" style of policing. Gaines (1996) recommended the use of aggressive patrol because it maximizes police effectiveness in crime reduction.[38] When conducting aggressive patrols, officers are expected to make frequent traffic stops and inquiries of suspicious persons on the streets of the community. The intent of an aggressive patrol is to potentially uncover criminal activity that might otherwise have been missed had officers not stopped the motorist or the pedestrian. For example, stopping a motorist who has not made a complete stop at a stop sign may seem to be an unnecessary and inconvenient action to some residents of the community, but if the stop results in a drunk driving arrest, the residents may feel otherwise. A stop by a patrol officer who conducts a **field interrogation**, which is a temporary detention in order to question

Aggressive patrol
Patrolling the community by making frequent and numerous traffic stops and field interrogations of suspicious persons.

Field interrogation
A temporary detention of an individual in order to question the individual about a suspicious circumstance.

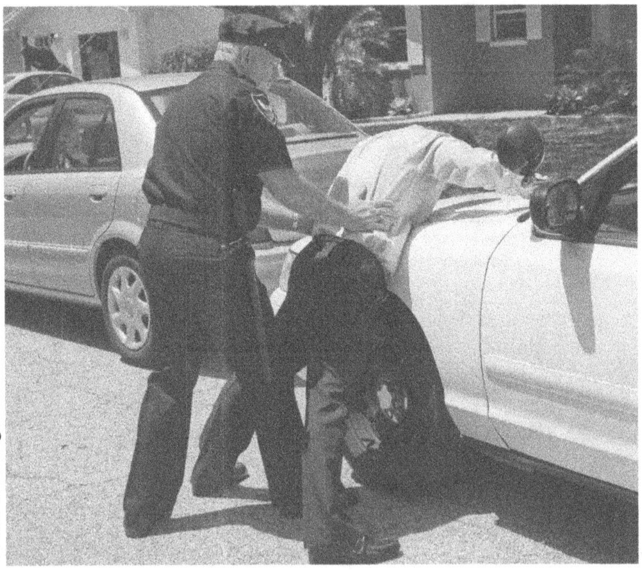

© Lisa F. Young/Shutterstock.com

Aggressive patrol can lead to arrests of lawbreakers, such as drunk drivers, who otherwise might not have been caught.

a suspicious person, may lead to the arrest of a person who is wanted by the police. Gaines called field interrogation an indispensable part of police efforts to control street crime and disorder.[39]

One concern about the use of aggressive patrols is that police will often stop and question citizens who have not engaged in any criminal activity. These inconvenient stops may anger law-abiding citizens. On the other hand, aggressive patrols that lead to arrests for offenses that might not have been discovered had the police not acted aggressively are often applauded by law-abiding citizens in the community.

Saturation Patrol

It is sometimes necessary for the police department to increase patrol activity in a particular area of the community. Crime analysis information may indicate an unusual increase in a certain type of crime in that area. It might also be evident that on Friday and Saturday nights, the increased population of patrons in the bar and club areas of the community requires increased police presence. In these instances, the police department may employ saturation patrols, in which they utilize a variety of patrol methods such as routine preventive patrol, directed patrol, and foot patrols to "saturate" the area. Fritsch, Caeti, and Taylor (1999) found that saturation patrols work provided they are directed toward a particular offender, place, victim, or offense. In their study, these researchers found that aggressive curfew and truancy enforcement resulted in significantly reduced gang violence in Dallas, Texas.[40] Saturation patrols can have a crime reduction effect similar to that of aggressive patrols because police visibility may inhibit possible offenders, while the additional police presence may lead to quick apprehension of those persons choosing to commit crime.

Career Connections: Uniformed Police Officer

Uniformed police officers from municipal, county, or state law enforcement agencies perform a variety of tasks for the community. In general, the duties of a police officer include enforcing the law, assisting the public, investigating crime, and preventing crime. They also maintain order by directing traffic, issuing traffic citations, making arrests, responding to maintenance of public order incidents, and preparing police reports. Each day can be a new challenge and a new adventure. One day, the police officer may conduct traffic stops at a busy intersection, counsel a distressed mother who is dealing with her adolescent son, and conduct an investigation at a residence that has been burglarized. The next day, this same officer may have completely different duties to perform.

In order to become a police officer, a candidate should be a U.S. citizen, be at least 21 years of age, have at least a high school diploma, and be able to pass a criminal history and background check, physical abilities test, and psychological examination. The specific requirements for employment vary from state to state and within each police department. Candidates must also graduate from a state-approved police academy where they are taught the basic requirements for performing the duties of the police officer position.

The ideal police officer candidate should possess strong interpersonal skills, critical thinking and analytical skills, and problem-solving ability. Because police work can be dangerous and very stressful, a successful police officer should also possess excellent physical conditioning and emotional stability. A career as a police officer can be very rewarding. It takes an individual with a strong commitment and a special mix of knowledge, skills, and abilities to choose to become a police officer. The challenges of police work are extraordinary, but the satisfaction that one receives from serving the public can more than compensate.

Traffic

Vehicular traffic direction is a second function performed by police officers. The police have been given the responsibility for the enforcement of traffic laws, the direction and control of traffic, the investigation of traffic accidents, and the assistance of motorists on the roadways.

Traffic enforcement involves the issuance of citations or warnings for moving and non-moving traffic violations, driver and vehicle licensing violations, and vehicle equipment violations.

© Paolo Bona/Shutterstock.com

Traffic direction is a function of the patrol officer.

The enforcement of traffic laws is usually the responsibility of the patrol officer. When the patrol officer is on routine preventive patrol and not responding to a call for service, observing motorists obeying traffic laws should be of high priority. Many police departments also create organized traffic units with the specific responsibility of traffic law enforcement.

Police officers are responsible for the direction and control of the flow of traffic at busy intersections, at scenes of emergencies such as traffic accidents, or during special community events when an increased number of vehicles can be expected. Parking enforcement is also a responsibility of many police departments that do not have a designated civilian parking enforcement unit.

The responsibility for the investigation of traffic accidents also belongs with the police officer. The police officer's role in accident investigation and reconstruction can affect both criminal and civil liability. A traffic accident may be due to negligence on the part of a motor vehicle operator, which can result in violations of traffic laws or more serious criminal charges such as drunk driving or even vehicular homicide. A police investigation of a traffic accident can also be used by automobile insurance companies to determine the operator who may have been at fault for the accident and affect the civil settlement for any losses as a result of the accident.

Police officers are sometimes called upon to assist motorists when they are on traffic patrol. This assistance may include providing directions to lost motorists, assisting stranded motorists whose vehicles have broken down on the roadway, or changing a flat tire for a motorist.

Criminal investigation A lawful investigation to reconstruct the circumstances of an illegal act, determine or apprehend the guilty party, and assist with the state's prosecution.

Preliminary investigation Evidence-gathering activities performed at the scene of a crime immediately after the crime was reported to or discovered by the police.

Follow-up investigation Continuation of the preliminary investigation in an attempt to reconstruct the circumstances of a crime.

Investigations

A third function of the police is to investigate criminal activity. The term *criminal investigation* usually conjures up a vision of a plainclothes detective. In reality, all police officers conduct investigations. Uniformed police officers who are called to domestic disputes investigate to determine if an arrest is warranted. At scenes of traffic accidents, these same officers investigate to determine if any traffic citations should be issued or other more serious charges filed.

Criminal Investigation

Criminal investigation is defined as a lawful investigation to reconstruct the circumstances of an illegal act, determine or apprehend the guilty party, and assist the state's prosecution.

Generally, a criminal investigation process is divided into two separate parts. The **preliminary investigation** consists of evidence-gathering activities that are performed at the scene of a crime immediately after the crime was reported to or discovered by the police. The patrol officer is usually the first responder to a crime scene. This officer is responsible for assessing the situation; determining if a crime has, in fact, been committed; securing the scene; interviewing complainants, witnesses, and victims; making an arrest, if appropriate; arranging for crime scene assistance; and documenting the incident in a report.

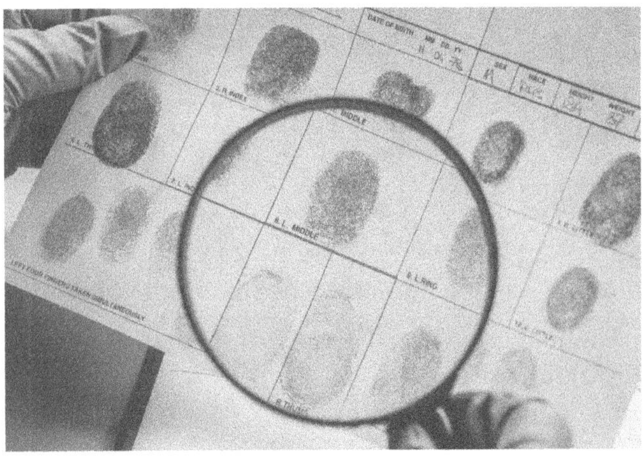

As part of the criminal investigation process, a police officer may take and analyze fingerprints from suspects.

If the police department in which the responding officer works does not have a detective unit, the officer will also be responsible for the second part of the criminal investigation. This is referred to as the **follow-up investigation**. The follow-up investigation is the continuation of the preliminary investigation in an attempt to reconstruct the circumstances of the crime. The results of the preliminary investigation are reviewed; crime scene evidence is analyzed; complainants, witnesses, or victims are re-interviewed; suspects are apprehended; and the prosecutor is assisted with the court case. In a police department that has a detective unit, the follow-up investigation is assigned to one of its detectives.

Major Case Investigations

Undercover Investigations

One of the most common forms of criminal investigation conducted by police departments is the undercover or covert investigation. Undercover operations involve the police while a criminal activity is in progress or prior to the crime actually being committed. These operations typically involve crimes such as drug trafficking, gambling, prostitution, and the buying and selling of stolen property.

Police investigators may operate undercover for short periods of time, referred to as **light cover**. A light cover investigation might involve using a male undercover officer to act as a "john" in an attempt to solicit prostitutes in the red light district of the community. In contrast, a **deep cover** operation may involve undercover investigators who infiltrate a criminal organization, gain their confidence, and spend a lengthy period of time gathering intelligence while preparing for major arrests within the organization.

Light cover Undercover police operations for a short period of time.

Deep cover Undercover police operations for a lengthy period of time.

Undercover operations can be extremely dangerous for police officers. Undercover investigators are often without any communication with fellow police officers, and if their true identity is discovered, it may lead to safety concerns for the officer. Miller (1987) found undercover police work to be extremely emotionally draining for officers and the risks to be greater as the undercover officer penetrates more deeply into an illicit activity. Miller also indicated a concern that undercover officers could be tempted to engage in entrapment, in which an otherwise innocent citizen is coaxed by police to commit a crime they had no intention of committing.[41]

Terrorism Investigations

Following the September 11, 2001 attacks on the World Trade Center and the Pentagon, the prevention of terrorism has become an important focus of law enforcement in America. The primary responsibility for the war on terrorism has been given to federal law enforcement agencies. The creation of the Department of Homeland Security brought together several federal enforcement agencies to collaborate and share information and intelligence necessary to keep America safe.

The role of most state and local police departments is to assist in this effort by being better trained and equipped to respond to suspicious activity that might uncover a possible terrorist plot. Lyons (2002) wrote that the war on terrorism would place powerful pressure on local police to expand collaborative efforts with state and federal law enforcement agencies. Lyons stated that these efforts require increased information sharing, use of crime analysis, and the development of paramilitary task forces.[42] In addition, community-police partnerships should be encouraged in order to build trust within the community and gain their cooperation. O'Connell (2008) stated that the military and intelligence communities would not be able to succeed in our defense without active cooperation from local police departments that are well informed and well prepared, which requires training and financial support.[43]

Tools of the Investigator

There have been a number of advances over recent decades that have assisted criminal investigators in bringing criminals to justice. The following are a few of these newer tools of the investigator.

FIGURE 4.2 ADVANCES IN POLICE TECHNOLOGY IN THE 20TH CENTURY

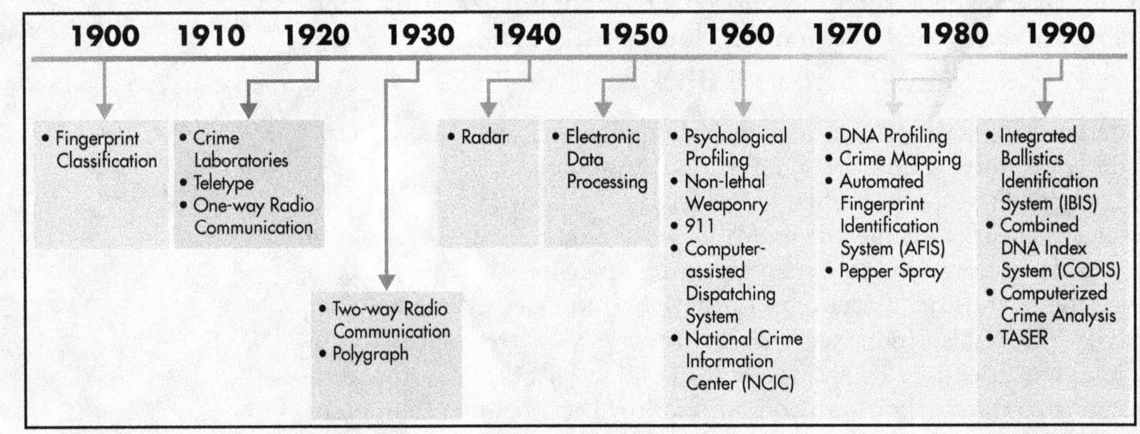

DNA Profiling

The use of DNA profiling has revolutionized crime fighting and has led to both the conviction and exoneration of criminal defendants. The genetic profile that can be derived from blood, semen, hair, or other bodily substances collected at a crime scene can be matched with DNA samples taken from suspects, giving a high probability of guilt or innocence. DNA profiles can be used at murder scenes where a suspect's blood or tissue may have been left, or at rape scenes where a suspect's semen has been found.

The Combined DNA Index System (CODIS) is a DNA database maintained by the Federal Bureau of Investigation (FBI) that has a collection of samples from biological evidence found at crime scenes and samples from individuals who have been convicted of crimes in states throughout the country. DNA samples have typically been collected from convicted murderers and rapists, but more recently samples have also been taken from convicted burglars. In time, it is believed that DNA samples may be collected from all persons convicted of crimes. Some proponents of the use of the CODIS database would like samples to be taken from all individuals who have been charged with crimes. Just as "mug shots" and fingerprints are taken of arrestees during the booking process, proponents believe that DNA samples should also be collected. Berson (2009) reported that about 20 states and the federal government have already passed legislation requiring DNA collection upon arrest.[44]

Critical Thinking

Should DNA samples be collected from all arrestees, regardless of the criminal charges, for submission to the CODIS database during the booking process just as fingerprints and photographs are taken today?

Crime Analysis and Mapping

Crime analysis involves a systematic collection and analysis of crime data used to support a police department's efforts in crime and disorder reduction and crime prevention. The study of police activities can provide data to analyze current crime trends, patterns, and series.

Crime analysis A systematic collection and analysis of crime data used to support police efforts in crime and disorder reduction and crime prevention.

A related technological advancement to crime analysis is **crime mapping**. Crime mapping involves using geographic information systems to conduct spatial analysis and investigation of crime. Prior to the use of computers, police investigators identified a crime pattern by putting push pins on a map to indicate where crime was occurring. Crime mapping acts as a computerized "push pin" method of tracking crime. Geographic information system (GIS) software tools allow crime analysts to map crime in various ways, such as a simple point map or a three-dimensional visualization.

Crime mapping A process of using geographic information systems to conduct spatial analysis and investigation of crime.

The more sophisticated computerized crime analysis and mapping systems can identify crime patterns much more rapidly. Many police departments have computerized report writing systems that give the crime analyst instantaneous access to the reports. If a crime pattern is occurring, it becomes apparent much sooner, allowing investigators to compare the evidence that they have gathered in each individual case to look for similarities that may tie the crimes to one offender or group of offenders.

Investigative and patrol units can both benefit from the use of crime analysis and mapping. For example, if it has been determined that a series of convenience store robberies are occurring and it is apparent that they are being committed by the same offender, both units can be positioned at a certain time of day or day of the week as well as a location where the offender is most likely to strike next.

Crime analysis also has other applications. It is being used as a tool to evaluate police department efficiency and effectiveness, crime clearance rates, and tracking of registered sexual offenders.

Electronic Surveillance

Newer advances in electronic surveillance have greatly enhanced the abilities of police investigators to gather intelligence related to criminal activity. Law enforcement agencies are increasingly using surveillance technologies such as thermal imaging technology, closed circuit television, miniature voice transmitters and video cameras, voice and retinal scanning devices, and more. Still, the wiretap that is used to listen to conversations between persons suspected of crime is the most common electronic surveillance technique for the investigator.

With all of the sophisticated surveillance devices that are available, it is important that procedural safeguards are in place to ensure that citizens' rights against unreasonable searches and seizures are not violated and that a reasonable expectation of privacy is ensured. In *Kyllo v. United States* (2001), the United States Supreme Court addressed the issue of the use of thermal imaging devices by law enforcement. In this case, a federal agent used a thermal imaging device to scan the home of Danny Lee Kyllo, whom they suspected of harvesting marijuana, to determine whether heat emanating from the residence indicated the use of heat intensity lamps. When several relatively high levels of heat were found in areas of the home, agents secured a search warrant and found over 100 marijuana plants. Kyllo was arrested as a result of the use of the thermal imaging device as well as other evidence, and was subsequently convicted. His conviction was appealed based on the evidence gathered by use of the device. The Supreme Court sided with Kyllo, ruling that the warrantless use of thermal imaging technology aimed at a private home to detect the amount of heat within the home constituted an unlawful search and a violation of a citizen's expectation of privacy.[45]

The use of thermal imaging can help build evidence in a case.

Psychological Profiling

Psychological profiling has become a tool used by criminal investigators when they suspect that a series of similar crimes are occurring and the pattern seems to indicate the same offender is committing the crimes. Profiling uses major personality and behavioral characteristics of an individual determined by analyzing the series of crimes that have been committed.[46] Psychological profiling is most often used in unsolved cases involving serial murderers or serial rapists, and aids in the investigation by providing investigators with a profile of the characteristics of the probable offender that may be matched to a suspect in the case.

Automated Fingerprint Identification System

The Automated Fingerprint Identification System (AFIS) is a computerized database system that stores thousands of sets of fingerprints and is used to match and identify latent prints found at crime scenes. This automated system has replaced the older method that required fingerprint examiners to sort through fingerprint cards by hand, which could take several months to review. The FBI has the largest AFIS database, with over 60 million prints on file. Many states have their own AFIS-like systems as well.

Integrated Ballistics Identification System

The Integrated Ballistics Identification System (IBIS) is a computerized method to digitally compare images of ballistic evidence stored in a large database. When bullets are fired, unique marks can remain on the projectile and on the shell casing. Forensic firearms examiners can then link the projectile and the shell casing with a particular firearm and crime. The IBIS technology allows police investigators to match over 30,000 pieces of firearms evidence currently stored in the database.

Special Police Functions

All police departments, regardless of size, employ patrol, traffic, and investigations functions. In a small department where it is necessary for all police officers to patrol the community, officers will be required to perform each function.

Other special police functions may include a canine unit, marine unit, aircraft unit, mounted unit, or SWAT team. *Canine units* are used for search and rescue efforts, drug enforcement, and building searches. Police officers may be assigned a canine that is trained to sniff out drugs, follow the trail of a missing or wanted person, or go into buildings or other structures in search of suspects. Marine units are employed by police departments that border lakes, rivers, and other waterways. *Marine unit* officers will enforce vessel safety regulations and investigate cases of drunk operation of vessels. Police departments deploy *aircraft units* for traffic enforcement and searches for missing

Mounted patrol units are often used for crowd control at community events.

and wanted persons. Aircraft units are very expensive to maintain, but can prove invaluable as air support for police officers on the ground. *Mounted units* can be used for crowd control. Mounted patrols are also useful for conducting search and rescue missions in undeveloped areas and natural terrain.

The SWAT team is specially trained to perform in high-risk situations such as barricaded suspect incidents, hostage rescues, and counterterrorism operations. As a result of the Posse Comitatus Act of 1878, the four branches of the military—with the exception of the United States Coast Guard and National Guard units—are not permitted to participate in domestic law enforcement. The military services have served as an auxiliary to law enforcement in drug interdiction and illegal immigration activities and, more recently, to combat domestic terrorism, but the responsibility for dealing with police issues that require a paramilitary presence has been left to SWAT teams.

Changing Philosophy of Policing

During most of the 20th century, in a period known as the Reform Era, policing in America adopted a professional model that closely resembled the philosophy popular in business and the military. In a historical study of the evolution of policing, Kelling and Moore (1988) viewed it through the framework of a corporate strategy. The authors wrote that the organizational form adopted by police reformers reflected the scientific theory of administration developed by Frederick W. Taylor.[47] This professional model of policing encouraged efficiency, task specialization, chain of command, and written orders and directives. Police officers were expected to respond to calls for service in a timely manner, handle their calls for service as quickly as possible, and return to patrolling the community. Any interaction between the police and the public beyond addressing the reason for the call to police was discouraged because it was assumed that any relationship that might develop could lead to favoritism and corruption.

The turmoil in the 1960s as a result of the Civil Rights Movement and opposition to the Vietnam War led to increased disorder in America. The public viewed nightly news reports depicting the police attempting to quell protests and riots by use of shields and batons. As the crime rate rose steadily over the next two decades, the relationship between the police and the public continued to decline. The public lost trust in the police to solve the crime problem and were angered by what they perceived as an increased use of physical force. Ponsaers (2002) stated the public no longer felt confident that the police could solve their problems. This led many, particularly minority groups, to feel alienated from the police.[48]

Police departments began to implement police-community relations programs in an attempt to heal the strained relationship. Unfortunately, these programs were viewed as little more than "window dressing" and failed to satisfy the community. Kreps and Weller (1973) wrote that the most important factor that led to the expansion of existing community relations programs and the rapid adoption of new programs was the series of urban civil disturbances in the late 1960s. The authors cited a study conducted at Michigan State University in 1967 that found community relations objectives were both ambitious and ambiguous and program goals were too abstract to put into concrete practice. The study also found the public to be suspicious of the conveniently timed adoption of those programs and questioned police motives and sincerity.[49] It began to become apparent that the professional model of policing might have outlived its usefulness. A newer philosophy of policing the community that would foster a partnership between the police and the public was needed to create a safe and secure environment in order to achieve a higher quality of life.[50] The time was right for the implementation of community policing.

Community Policing

Community policing encourages a partnership between the public and the police for the purpose of working together to identify, prioritize, and solve problems within the community.[51] It is the intent of community policing to deal with the problems of crime and disorder, community decay, and the fear of crime in order to improve the quality of life for community residents.

Broken windows theory
A theory involving crime and disorder that states that if a community is allowed to physically deteriorate, an impression will be given that no one cares, causing crime to occur.

The foundation for the implementation of the community policing philosophy was influenced by the **broken windows theory** introduced by James Q. Wilson and George Kelling (1982). Wilson and Kelling argued that when a window is broken in a building and it is not quickly repaired, more windows will likely be broken. The authors theorized that if the community is apathetic toward the destruction occurring within their neighborhoods, they are sending a message to criminals that they can assume control over the neighborhood. In time, as one broken window leads to another, the neighborhood will succumb to physical decay and disorder. Wilson and Kelling believed that police should consider dealing with both minor and major crimes instead of just the more serious crime problems. Concentrated efforts on minor crimes such as vandalism, public drunkenness, and panhandling will help the public begin to feel safer in their neighborhoods. With a reduced fear of crime, citizens begin to develop a feeling of pride and eventually retake ownership of their neighborhoods.[52]

The broken windows theory holds that when a community is apathetic toward destruction in their neighborhoods, they are sending a message to criminals that they can assume control over the neighborhood.

Gaines and Kappeler (2009) suggested that one of the two major components of community policing was to develop a relationship with the residents of the community.[53] The police understood that for community policing to truly succeed, cooperation with community residents was imperative. In order to achieve this success, community policing officers were assigned to each neighborhood to forge these partnerships and then work together with residents to address their concerns.

One important result of a partnership between the police and the public is the trust that can develop. The police cannot succeed without the assistance of the public, especially when it comes to solving crime. The public can be the eyes and ears of the police in the community. Police need the public to come forward when they are aware of crimes occurring and who may be committing them. Unfortunately, some community residents pressure other residents not to inform or "snitch" on lawbreakers. This "stop snitching" movement has even found its way into pop culture. Masten (2009) wrote that as a result of a cultural campaign spawned by rap music and clothing, many teens and young adults were refusing to speak to the police even when they had witnessed violent crimes. Masten saw this "stop snitching" phenomenon as part of a deeply rooted distrust toward the police, posing a potential hindrance to America's criminal justice system. The author suggested that police must repair the decades of mistrust built up between the public and the police in order to make the "stop snitching" code less attractive to follow.[54]

The second major component of community policing, as defined by Gaines and Kappeler (2009), is problem solving.[55] Traditionally, when police have responded to calls for service, they have dealt with the incident, but not necessarily with the underlying problem that led to the call. Herman Goldstein (1979) first proposed **problem-oriented policing** to address the concerns of the public. A problem-oriented or problem-solving approach emphasizes identifying a problem, exploring alternatives to deal with the problem, weighing the merits of each alternative, and, finally, implementing the best alternative to solve the problem.[56]

Problem-oriented policing An approach to policing in which the underlying causes of crime are identified and addressed.

A problem-solving approach to dealing with community concerns requires both creativity and commitment on the part of the police department. The police and the public must be in agreement regarding the problems in the neighborhood that should be addressed. Cooperation may also be required from other stakeholders in the community, such as business leaders, elected officials, and other public and private agencies that serve the community.

Although some police administrators may claim otherwise, the practice of community policing seems to be waning. Federal funding for community policing efforts, which was once in abundance, has all but dried up. In 2010, the Office of Community Oriented Policing Services (COPS) allocated approximately $600 million to assist law enforcement agencies in their community policing initiatives. That amount of funding is a far cry from the $11 billion that had been allocated at the height of the trend, and thus the decline of the practice may be due more to the funding drying up than to the failure of the philosophy. A study by Zhao, Scheider, and Thurman (2002) found that funding community policing had a positive effect.

The authors examined COPS Office grants awarded between 1994 and 1998 and their effects on crime rates in 6,100 cities in the United States, and their results indicated that funding to medium and large cities had been effective at reducing violent and property crime. Additionally, innovative programs that targeted special crime problems or locations were found to be a most effective contributor to crime reduction.[57]

Still, because federal funding has decreased, many police departments that once displayed an agency-wide commitment to community policing have now resorted to smaller units that operate on an as-needed basis, while some departments have totally abandoned the philosophy, returning to the more traditional incident-based policing.

Intelligence-Led Policing

The latest movement in policing is the use of crime data analysis to influence decision making. **Intelligence-led policing** uses a business model in which data analysis and criminal intelligence are used to facilitate crime reduction, crime prevention, and enforcement strategies that target the most serious offenders.[58]

Intelligence-led policing A business model in which data analysis and criminal intelligence are used to facilitate crime reduction, crime prevention, and enforcement strategies that target the most serious offenders.

The move toward an intelligence-led policing model may be a natural progression in policing from the community policing and problem-oriented models. Both community policing and problem-oriented policing require data collection and crime analysis in order to solve crime problems, although not nearly to the extent that intelligence-led policing utilizes data.

One of the first examples of the use of a data-driven method for determining crime problems took place in the 1990s in New York City.[59] The New York City Police Department became known for the implementation of the COMPSTAT program. **COMPSTAT** is a managerial system that uses criminal intelligence that identifies crime problems and then determines a crime reduction strategy. The system provided timely and accurate intelligence that indicated "hot spots" of crime that police officers were expected to eliminate. Police administrators were then held accountable for the implementation of the reduction strategy and a subsequent reduction in crime. Crime was reduced dramatically in the city, although arguments persist over whether the COMPSTAT program was the primary reason for the reduction. Zimring (2011) credited the COMPSTAT program in New York City with being instrumental in the compilation of data on serious crime that led to police emphasis on "hot spots," drug interdiction, and an aggressive program of street stops and misdemeanor arrests. Zimring also praised the city of New York for choosing not to implement a "broken windows" strategy, which he believed would have concentrated precious resources in marginal neighborhoods rather than neighborhoods with the highest crime rates.[60]

COMPSTAT A managerial system that uses criminal intelligence to identify crime problems and determine a crime reduction strategy.

The intelligence-led policing model and its use of crime analysis can provide the foundation for crime prevention and reduction and decisions for directing police resources.

Critical Thinking

Should police departments adopt a zero tolerance policy for all crimes, regardless of how minor, or should police concentrate their efforts on the most serious offenses and offenders?

Challenges for Police Officers

The nature of police work can place great demands on the police officer. Police officers are often called upon to make split-second decisions that sometimes involve use of physical force or even deadly force. The ever present dangers that police officers face can come from many different sources. Every day, police officers risk being killed in the line of duty while serving warrants, conducting traffic stops, responding to domestic violence calls, or interviewing suspicious persons.

Besides the dangers that the job brings, police officers are required to witness the worst that society can offer. The police must investigate the most gruesome suicide or homicide scenes, respond to abuse cases where children may have been physically or sexually assaulted, and reconstruct traffic accidents in which several members of a family may have been killed.

The challenges that police officers face play a part in how they come to view themselves, the public, and their jobs. This can lead to a unique subculture within the police profession, a stress level that is often greater than what is found in other professions, and a temptation toward corruption if they stray from expected ethical and professional boundaries.

The Police Subculture

Every profession has its own set of values and behavioral patterns that are unique to members of the profession. The police subculture is a product of the responsibilities of the job along with the effects that can result from having carried out these responsibilities. Common attitudes in the police subculture include authoritarianism, cynicism, and solidarity.

Authoritarianism

Police officers possess a unique power that is not afforded to most professions. The police have the right to arrest individuals, search persons or their belongings, and seize evidence from people. In order to perform these authoritarian duties, police officers are guided by both legal guidelines and their departmental policies. For example, under case law, a police officer who stops a suspicious person may not conduct a warrantless search of the suspect without probable cause to do so.

Additionally, police have the right to use physical force, including deadly force. The police are permitted to utilize physical force when necessary to effect an arrest, although a police officer may be held criminally or civilly liable if the amount of force used is considered to be excessive. Probably the most awesome power that the police officer has is to use deadly force. Of course, this power to use deadly force also comes with responsibility. Deadly force must be the last resort for the police officer.

In the past, police officers only had the baton and the handgun to subdue suspects. In more recent years, new weapons technology has led to the development of nonlethal weapons. Weapons such as rubber bullets and beanbag projectiles have allowed officers to neutralize potentially deadly situations without having to resort to deadly force. The most common type of nonlethal weapon used today by police officers is the Taser technology that sends an incapacitating electric shock to the individual that it strikes.

An important concern regarding police authoritarianism is the abuse of this power. The police must ensure that the rights of citizens are not violated when they engage in arrests, searches, or seizures. They must not use **excessive force**, but only a level of force necessary to effect an arrest or to protect themselves or others from bodily harm. Bohrer and Chaney (2010) wrote that the public's perceptions of police officers involved in shootings are wide and diverse. They point out that while some members of the public believe that if the police shoot someone, the individual probably gave police no choice, many members of the public are quick to assume the police acted inappropriately.[61] Police officers who exceed the authority they have been granted can jeopardize the community's perception of their police department as well as the entire police profession.

Excessive force
An amount of physical force beyond that which is necessary to control a suspect.

Cynicism

Symbolic assailant
An individual whose dress, behavior, and gestures indicate suspicion and possible danger to a police officer.

Cynicism is a mistrust of human nature and motives. The nature of police work requires that officers view citizens with suspicion. The police interview individuals who will often lie to them. They approach individuals who may be dangerous. Police officers are trained on how to cautiously approach the public on the streets, during traffic stops, or when entering a residence. They are trained to uncover a suspect's lies in order to reach the truth. Through their experience, they can often sense that a suspicious person fits a particular type of individual who may be dangerous. This **symbolic assailant** is an individual whose dress and gestures indicate to the experienced police officer that this person is up to no good.

© somsak suwanput/Shutterstock.com

Police officers may have to use physical force to arrest uncooperative suspects or to protect themselves or others from bodily harm.

Neiderhoffer (1969) conducted a classic study of police cynicism in the New York City Police Department. The study found that cynicism among police officers developed as early as the police academy, when recruits were taught about the ignorance of the public and the superiority of the police. Cynicism initially increased sharply and then at a slower rate between years two and six of the police officer's career. After year six, cynicism decreased and leveled off over the remainder of a career.[62]

The unfortunate consequence of police cynicism is that it can cross over into an officer's personal relationships with family and friends. The suspicions that police officers have about people's behaviors and actions may lead them to believe that all people, including those closest to them, should be viewed with suspicion and not be trusted.

Solidarity

The third component of the police subculture is solidarity. Police officers develop a strong connection with other members of the profession. Officers must depend upon their partners for backup and protection. Along with their cynicism and mistrust of the public, this solidarity within the ranks causes an "us versus them" mentality. Police officers close their ranks and insulate themselves from others. Just as cynicism can lead to mistrust of family and friends, police solidarity can lead police officers to become isolated from their relationships outside of the profession.

Blue code of silence The unwritten code of protection among police officers.

One unfortunate result of police solidarity is known as the **blue code of silence**. This is a code of protection among police officers in which they do not report activities of fellow officers that could violate department policy or the law. Police solidarity may be so ingrained within the profession that police officers may be more likely to protect corruption within their ranks—jeopardizing their own careers—than to report corrupt fellow officers.

Critical Thinking

How can the blue code of silence be eliminated so honest police officers are willing to report dishonest officers?

Police Discretion

Discretion The autonomy a police officer has to choose from a variety of courses of action in various situations.

Discretion is defined as a police officer's autonomy to choose from a variety of courses of action in various situations. Alpert, MacDonald, and Dunham (2005) stated that an officer's discretion to choose a course of action such as stopping a citizen usually begins when the officer observes the person appearing suspicious or violating the law.[63] Probably the most common example of the use of police discretion involves traffic stops. Police officers use their discretionary power to determine if a motorist who has been stopped for a traffic violation should be given a warning or issued a citation.

The patrol officer may exercise the greatest discretionary power in the police department. Officers who are on patrol are usually out of the sight of their supervisors. Walker (1993) wrote that most police-citizen encounters occur without outside supervision, which gives the police officer a great deal of discretion.[64] They have the discretion to stop a vehicle operator for a traffic violation in the first place. They have the discretion to stop a suspicious person on the street to conduct a field interrogation. When dispatched to a loud music call, the patrol officer may have the discretion to charge the resident with the appropriate offense or simply order them to turn the music down.

In some instances, police discretion can be controlled and limited. The National Research Council (2003) found that the most important factors associated with police officers' decisions to use their legal authority included the influence of the police organization, legal factors related to the severity of the crime, and the strength of the evidence.[65] The police department may influence the level of discretion that officers have. For example, as discussed earlier in this chapter, the department may have developed a written policy that limits vehicle pursuits. Department-written policies and procedures are often used to control police officers' behavior. At times, special orders may also temporarily limit police discretion. The police chief may have learned that the number of traffic accidents at a particular intersection has increased, and may order all patrol officers to issue citations to any vehicle operator who is observed committing any traffic violation at the intersection, no matter how minor. Even peer pressure among officers within the department may affect police discretion: veteran officers may chastise the newest officer in the department who is giving too many traffic citations to community residents. Alpert, MacDonald, and Dunham (2005) found that officers employed in a police department that emphasized a service approach were less likely to arrest offenders for low-level crimes than officers from a department practicing a legalistic style of policing.[66]

Legislatures can also limit police discretion. State legislatures and local municipalities enact statutes or ordinances. A local community may pass an ordinance that makes it illegal to panhandle on the roadways. The police department may have previously turned a blind eye to the panhandlers, even though they were well aware that many of them were homeless and could be charged with a vagrancy statute violation, but now their discretion will be influenced by this new ordinance.

An example of legislation influencing police discretion occurred as a result of the Minneapolis Domestic Violence Experiment.[67] Historically, the police have used three methods to resolve domestic violence calls: mediate the dispute and leave the partners together, separate the partners by asking one of them to leave the residence for a "cooling off" period, or arrest one of the partners. In the experiment, police were told to either arrest, separate, or mediate incidents on the basis of a random selection. The results of the experiment indicated that those persons who were arrested in the incident were half as likely to reoffend against the victim. These results led many state legislatures across the country to enact mandatory arrest policies for domestic violence perpetrators when an injury to the victim was observed by the police. These new domestic violence laws greatly inhibited police officers' discretion in responding to domestic violence calls. An interesting side note to the results of this landmark experiment was that when similar studies were later conducted, the results did not confirm that arrest was the most effective way to handle domestic violence interventions.

Finally, our courts can also limit police discretion. Decisions made by courts can take away options that police officers may have to deal with criminals on the streets. For example, patrol officers have a limited number of options when they want to conduct warrantless searches of persons, property, and vehicles because the courts have restricted their actions in order to protect the constitutional rights of citizens.

Additional Factors Affecting Police Discretion

There are a number of factors that can affect a police officer's use of discretion. The seriousness of the crime determines if the police will pursue a case more or less vigorously. Homicide cases are usually investigated with vigor, while a minor neighborhood dispute may not be. The strength of evidence in a case may also affect the extent to which police investigate a crime. Initially, the homicide case will receive strict attention, but once the trail of the killer goes cold, police may have no choice but to move on to other cases.

The nature of the individuals involved in a police encounter may factor into police discretion. The relationship between an offender and the victim may affect the decisions that the police officer makes. For example, in a reported theft case involving two ex-lovers who had lived together, in which the accused was removing some items from the residence that he believed were his property, police officers might choose not to make an arrest. Conversely, a victim who is intent on the offender being arrested may exert influence on police to make the arrest against their better judgment. Police may use the demeanor of an individual as a factor to determine the course of action. A polite and respectful traffic violator may be less likely to receive a citation than an angry and verbally abusive motorist. Sometimes, race, gender, or the income of an individual can play a role in a police officer's decision making. This behavior may be inappropriate, but unfortunately it does sometimes occur. A young male motorist might be more likely to be cited than a young female. An African-American male walking on the streets of a community at 3:00 in the morning may be more likely to be stopped and questioned than a white male, and an affluent resident who complains about juveniles running through his upscale neighborhood may receive more appropriate police action than a long-haired and tattooed trailer park resident making a similar complaint. The National Research Council (2003) found that individual variables such as age, race, social class, or demeanor of a suspect play a minor role in a police officer's decision making.[68] In contrast, Sun and Payne (2004) reported that race is the most important individual factor in police-citizen interactions.[69] Although the research may be mixed, it is important to consider the possible influence of individual variables on the police officer's use of discretion.

Police Job Stress

Stress can be found to some extent within every vocation and in people's everyday lives. However, Dantzer (1987) stated that law enforcement ranks among the top five most stressful occupations in the world.[70] Police stress is somewhat unique as a result of the nature of the police officer's job. The danger that officers can face, along with the horrors of society that they often witness, can take a great toll on their emotional and physical well-being.

Sources of Police Stress

For the police officer, there are a number of different sources of stress. One is the physical danger that officers face as an inherent part of the job.[71] It is understandable that one major stressful event can affect a police officer. For example, a use of deadly force situation involving police officers can cause great stress. Shootings in which police officers may see a fellow officer killed or be wounded themselves are very stressful events that can leave lasting emotional scars. When a police officer must use deadly force against a suspect, the officer may find it difficult to deal with afterwards.

However, most police officers will not be involved in events like those just described during their careers. Most stress for the typical officer comes from the continued response to daily calls for service. Responding to calls where they see physical injuries as a result of domestic or child abuse or deadly motor vehicle crashes can leave lasting impressions on a police officer. Even the most routine calls can produce low-grade stressors that, over time, can cause stress for the police officer.

© Prath/Shutterstock.com

Police stress is sometimes caused by grisly or horrible crime scenes that officers must investigate.

The police organization is a second source of stress for police officers. Anderson, Litzenberger, and Plecas (2002) found that within the organizational structure, issues such as lack of group cohesiveness, lack of support from supervisors, and lack of opportunities for promotion make law enforcement an especially stressful job.[72] Police officers usually work in a quasi-military bureaucracy where they have little input into the decision making. They sometimes observe a lack of administrative support and petty department politics. Police officers often view their job as one with inadequate pay and benefits, work schedules that include shift work, weekends, and most holidays, and sometimes periods of monotony and boredom.

A third source of stress for police officers can result from their own personal behaviors. Police officers often develop poor eating habits while on duty as a result of the emergency nature of their job. It can be easy to stop by a fast-food drive-through for a quick lunch between calls for service. Shift work can also affect proper eating habits and lead to fatigue. If the police officer does not eat properly and exercise regularly, poor health can result.

Effects of Police Stress

The effects of police stress can be both psychological and physical.[73,74] Stress has been linked to physical disorders such as high blood pressure, ulcers, and heart disease. More common for some police officers is the emotional toll of police stress. The police profession has a high rate of alcoholism, drug abuse, marital problems, and suicide. More police officers commit suicide each year than are killed in the line of duty.

Stress can also affect a police officer's productivity on the job. An officer who has withdrawn from his or her work can become complacent, have lower morale, and feel indifferent toward the job and fellow officers. Post-traumatic stress disorder (PTSD), which is most associated with military personnel, also affects some police officers who have witnessed combat-like situations such as shootings. PTSD can manifest itself in memory loss, loss of concentration, bouts of depression, impulsivity, or anxiety, and can cause recurring nightmares and flashbacks.

Management of Police Stress

Police organizations and each individual police officer within the profession can find ways to manage and reduce stress. Atkinson (2004) stated that stress can be managed by identifying specific strategies in the areas of nutrition, exercise, sleep, and relaxation.[75] Every police officer should be aware of the sources of stress and the effects stress can have. By maintaining a healthy diet and engaging in regular exercise, police officers can do their part to reduce their stress. Family and spiritual support has also been found to be helpful.

Each police department must address police stress by emphasizing stress awareness. Frequent stress reduction training courses should be offered. Support systems such as mental health programs and critical incident stress debriefing teams should also be implemented to assist officers in need of professional assistance.

Police Ethics

Ethics involves the moral choices that individuals must make regarding good and bad conduct. The social contract that the public has with its government to provide for its safety and security comes with the expectation that those who are asked to provide that protection maintain high standards of ethics, professionalism, and integrity. Generally, the public expects police officers to exhibit even higher standards of behavior than the general population. A lack of ethical behavior on the part of a police officer can lead to corruption. Whenever officers misuse the authority they have been given, they are engaging in some form of corruption.

FIGURE 4.3 OFFICERS KILLED IN THE LINE OF DUTY, 2000-2010

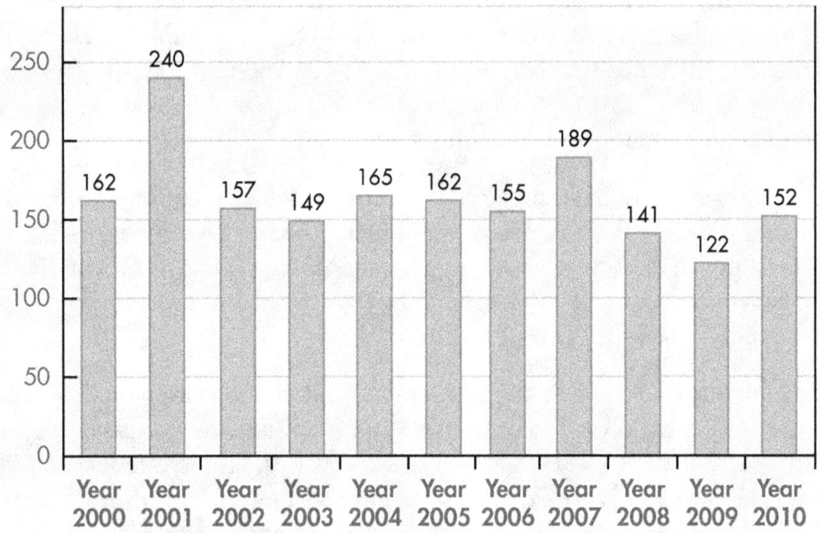

Source: National Law Enforcement Officers Memorial Fund www.nleomf.org

Forms of Police Corruption

Police corruption may involve unethical acts that violate department policy or illegal acts that violate the law. Corruption within policing may be department-wide, where all members are engaged in corrupt acts or at least aware that they are occurring and turning a blind eye to them. On the other hand, it is more common that individual officers may be engaged in corrupt acts unbeknownst to others in the police department except the corrupt officers' closest confidants. The more common examples of police corruption include the following.

- **Bribery or Extortion**—Accepting offers of cash or gifts from citizens in the form of a bribe for not enforcing laws against them, or demanding remuneration in the form of cash or gifts as a form of extortion for not enforcing the law against citizens.
- **Theft**—Planning burglaries and thefts on or off duty, or taking items of value from scenes of crimes that officers are called to investigate.
- **Alcohol or Drug Abuse**—Consuming alcoholic beverages or taking illegal drugs while on duty or off duty in violation of department policy or the law.
- **Goldbricking**—Avoiding work when on duty by not responding to calls for service, engaging in private business, or sleeping on duty.
- **Gratuities**—Accepting or demanding free or discounted items such as coffee, meals, or entertainment tickets, which may or may not be in return for favorable treatment for the giver at a future time.
- **Sexual Misconduct**—Engaging in sexual acts while on duty, exchanging favors for sex, or sexually harassing coworkers.

Control of Police Corruption

There is nothing that shakes the public's confidence in police more than learning that the police have engaged in acts of corruption. Weitzer (2002) found that incidents of police misconduct have a pronounced effect on public opinion, particularly when they involve highly publicized events.[76] Walker (1992) stated that corruption can be controlled with effort from law enforcement, but this requires each police department to take a proactive approach to reducing and controlling it.[77]

Several researchers have suggested ways in which corruption can be controlled.[78,79,80] First, it is important that during the recruitment and selection process, police departments set high standards for police officer candidates and have methods in place to determine the ethical and professional values of the individuals they choose to hire.

Additionally, each police department should have written policies that define what constitutes corrupt acts and a disciplinary apparatus that spells out the actions that will be taken against officers violating established policies. Each police department should require periodic ethics training classes for all officers. A police officers' code of ethics should be prominently placed in the department as a constant reminder to all officers that they have sworn an oath to perform their duties both ethically and professionally.

Exhibit: Law Enforcement Code of Ethics from International Chiefs of Police[81]

Ethics and Professionalism: Blue Code of Silence

On August 9, 1997, a 30-year-old Haitian immigrant by the name of Abner Louima was arrested by New York City Police Department officers following a disturbance outside a Brooklyn nightclub. While being held at the 70th Precinct stationhouse, Louima was brutalized in the precinct bathroom. He was held down by one officer while the other officer shoved a wooden toilet plunger handle into his rectum and then thrust it into his face. The police officer who assaulted Louima mistakenly believed that he had punched the officer in the head during a street brawl outside the club.

It was reported that several NYPD officers either participated in the assault or witnessed it. After hearing of the incident, then Mayor Rudy Giuliani and Police Commissioner Howard Safir insisted the case would prove that the "blue code of silence" did not exist. The case included allegations of perjury and ultimately resulted in convictions of four police officers—three of which were later overturned on appeal.

Does the "blue code of silence" still exist in policing, all these years after the Louima case? What would cause a police officer to engage in such violent behavior against a suspect? How could other officers look on and allow this to happen without stepping in to stop it? Why would these officers all choose to lie and cover up the incident?

Police departments should also have an internal affairs unit that investigates alleged unethical or illegal activities involving police officers. External investigations or reviews by citizen review boards, special investigators or prosecutors, and the courts should be used to ferret out police misconduct when necessary.

Finally, the responsibility for ending police corruption belongs with each individual police officer. One way that can be accomplished is for officers to resist the pressure to adhere to the blue code of silence. Instead, honest police officers should see it as their duty to rid the law enforcement profession of corrupt officers by reporting any unethical or illegal behaviors that they observe.

Chapter Summary

- The roles police officers assume are based on the issues and problems that are unique to each community. The police officer's role can be vague and ambiguous because the expectations of police administrators, local political leaders, the public, and police officers themselves can conflict. Role conflict results from what police may prefer to do versus what they are expected to do.
- The duties performed by police officers are multidimensional and dependent on community needs. Generally, these duties include law enforcement, order maintenance, crime prevention, and providing service. Enforcing the law is considered to be the primary responsibility of police. Police often act as peacekeepers and maintain order in the community, which may or may not involve dealing with criminal activity. The mere presence of police in the community serves as an important way to prevent crime from occurring in the first place.
- The most common functions performed by police departments include patrol, traffic, and investigations. Routine preventive patrol is the most common form of patrol, but police departments will also use special patrol methods such as directed patrols, foot patrols, aggressive patrols, and saturation patrols. The traffic function includes traffic enforcement, control and direction, accident investigation, and assistance to motorists. Types of police investigations include preliminary investigations, follow-up investigations, and undercover investigations. Advances in technology have provided criminal investigators with a variety of new tools to fight crime. Larger police departments may employ more specialized functions such as canine, marine, aircraft, mounted, and SWAT units.
- The community policing philosophy attempted to encourage a partnership between the public and the police for the purpose of working together to identify, prioritize, and solve community problems. As community policing began to fall out of favor, it was replaced by movement toward an intelligence-led policing philosophy, which emphasizes the use of data analysis and criminal intelligence to facilitate crime reduction, crime prevention, and enforcement strategies that target the most serious offenders.

- The nature of police work puts great demands on the police officer. While every profession has its own set of values and behavioral patterns among its members, the police subculture is quite unique with a composition that includes authoritarianism, cynicism, and solidarity.
- Police officers can suffer from job stress that can come from a variety of sources. Many police officers experience stress resulting from continued responses to daily calls for service. Police stress can also result from the police organization and from an officer's own personal behaviors. Police stress can lead to both psychological and physical problems. Police departments can assist officers in dealing with the problem of stress by offering programs that help to manage stress.
- Police ethics involves the moral choices that police officers make regarding good and bad conduct. Corruption within the police profession occurs when police officers misuse their authority for personal gain. Police corruption can be controlled by use of high selection standards, written policies regarding corruption, internal and external investigation of alleged corruption, ethics training classes, and a code of ethics, as well as dismantling the blue code of silence.

Critical Thinking?

1. Should electronic devices known as "red light cameras" be used to catch traffic violators running red lights at intersections?
2. Should police officers be permitted to accept gratuities such as a free cup of coffee or a half-price meal when on duty?
3. Among the various methods of patrol, which do you believe works the best to prevent crime and apprehend criminals?
4. What can be done to keep police officers safe on the streets and reduce the number of officers killed in the line of duty?
5. How might police departments eliminate corruption within the ranks of the police?
6. Can you imagine a situation in which it would be acceptable to repeal the Posse Comitatus Act?
7. Explain why you would be in favor of or against giving up some of your individual rights under the Constitution to allow law enforcement to conduct searches and seizures of your personal property without probable cause.
8. Based on the results of the Kansas City Preventive Patrol Experiment, do you believe that police should still conduct routine random patrols throughout the community?
9. Is it a good idea for police officers to be allowed to use discretion in the performance of their duties? Why or why not?

10. When the police conduct an undercover operation in which female police officers are placed in an area known to be frequented by prostitutes and their customers, are they actually encouraging criminal behavior?

Media

Law Enforcement News: www.officer.com
This website provides information on current events in policing and police officer news around the United States.

Bureau of Justice Statistics: http://bjs.ojp.usdoj.gov/
The Bureau of Justice Statistics provides comprehensive data on reported criminal activity throughout the country, including frequency of crime and criminal characteristics.

Franklin Zimring Interview: http://www.youtube.com/watch?v=EXZgSnKfN5U
In this interview, criminologist Franklin Zimring discusses how New York City dramatically reduced its crime rate.

Endnotes

1 Seneviratne, M. (2002). "Ombudsmen and Police Complaints." *The Journal of Social Welfare & Family Law*, 24(2), 195–215.

2 Hunter, A. (1985). "Private, Parochial, and Public Social Orders: The Problem of Crime and Incivility in Urban Communities." In G. Suttles & M. Zald (Eds.), *The Challenge of Social Control*. Norwood, NJ: Ablex.

3 Klockars, C. B. (1985). *The Idea of Police. Beverly Hills*, CA: Sage.

4 Dunham, R. G., & Alpert, G. P. (2010). *Critical Issues in Policing*. Prospect Heights, IL: Waveland Press.

5 Reiman, J. (1985). "The Social Contract and the Police Use of Deadly Force." In F. A. Ellison & M. Feldberg (Eds.), *Moral Issues in Police Work*. Savage, MD: Rowman & Littlefield.

6 *Mapp v. Ohio*, 367 U.S. 643, 655 (1961).

7 Stuntz, W. J. (1997). "The Virtues and Vices of the Exclusionary Rule." *Harvard Journal of Law and Public Policy, 20*(2), 443–455.

8 Keenan, J. F. (1998). "The Proper Balance: Exclusion of Evidence or Expulsion of Police Officers." *St. John's Law Review, 72*(3/4), 1376–1384.

9 *Terry v. Ohio*, 392 U.S. 1 (1968).

10 *Tennessee v. Garner*, 471 U.S. 1 (1985).

11 Walker, S., & Fridell, L. (1992). "Forces of Change in Police Policy: The Impact of *Tennessee v. Garner*." *American Journal of Police, 11*(3), 97–112.

12 Fyfe, J. J. (1986). "The Split-Second Syndrome and Other Determinants of Police Violence." In A. Campbell & J. Gibbs (Eds.), *Violent Transactions*. New York, NY: Blackwell.

13 G. P. (1993). "The Management of Police Pursuit Driving." In W. G. Bailey (Ed.), *The Encyclopedia of Police Science*. New York, NY: Garland.

14 Hicks, W. L. (2006). "Police Vehicular Pursuits: A Descriptive Analysis of the State Agencies' Written Policy." *Policing, 29*(1), 106–124.

15 Payne, D. M. (1997). "Michigan Emergency Response Study—Phase III. Implications of the Failure to Report Pursuits and Inaccurate Accident Reporting: A Research Note." *Policing, 20*(2), 256–269.

16 Weitzer, R., & Tuch, S. A. (2005). "Racially Biased Policing: Determinants of Citizen Perceptions." *Social Forces, 83*(3), 1009–1030.

17 Bureau of Justice Statistics. (2001). *Contacts Between Police and the Public: Findings From the 1999 National Survey*. Washington, DC: U.S. Department of Justice.

18 Harris, D. (1997). "Driving While Black and Other Traffic Offenses: The Supreme Court and Pretextual Traffic Stops." *Journal of Criminal Law and Criminology, 87*, 544–582.

19 Bureau of Justice Statistics, 2001.

20 Brown, R. A. (2005). "Black, White and Unequal: Examining Situational Determinants of Arrest Decisions from Police-Suspect Encounters." *Criminal Justice Studies, 18*(1), 151–168.

21 Visher, C. A., & Weisburd, D. (1998). "Identifying What Works: Recent Trends in Crime Prevention Strategies." *Crime, Law & Social Change, 28*, 223–242.

22 Kennedy, L. W. (2002). "Issues in Managing Citizens' Calls to the Police." *Criminology & Public Policy, 2*(1), 125–128.

23 Silver, E. E., & Miller, L. L. (2004). "Sources of Informal Social Control in Chicago Neighborhoods." *Criminology, 42*(3), 551–583.

24 Reisig, M. D., & Parks, R. B. (2004). "Can Community Policing Help the Truly Disadvantaged?" *Crime & Delinquency, 50*(2), 139–167.

25 Silver & Miller, 2004.

26 Wilson, J. (1968). *Varieties of Police Behavior*. Cambridge, MA: Harvard University Press.

27 Broderick, J. J. (1987). *Police in a Time of Change*. Prospect Heights, IL: Waveland Press.

28 Muir, W. K. (1977). *Police: Street Corner Politicians*. Chicago, IL: University of Chicago Press.

29 Adams, T. F. (2006). *Police Field Operations*. Upper Saddle River, NJ: Prentice Hall.

30 Kelling, G. L. (1974). *The Kansas City Preventive Patrol Experiment: A Summary Report*. Washington, DC: Police Foundation.

31 Weisburd, D., Maher, L., & Sherman, L. (1992). "Contrasting Crime General and Crime Specific Theory: The Case of Hot-Spots of Crime." *Advances in Criminological Theory, 4*, 45–70.

32 Sherman, L., & Weisburd, D. (1995). "General Deterrent Effects of Police Patrol in Crime 'Hot-Spots': A Randomized Controlled Trial." *Justice Quarterly, 12*, 626–648.

33 Weisburd, D., & Green, L. (1995). "Policing Drug Hot-Spots: The Jersey City Drug Market Analysis Experiment." *Justice Quarterly, 12*, 711–735.

34 Gaines, L. K. (1996). "Specialized Patrol." In G. W. Cordner, L. K. Gaines, & V. E. Kappeler (Eds.), *Police Operations: Analysis and Evaluation*. Cincinnati, OH: Anderson.

35 Adams, 2006.

36 Pate, A. M., & Skogan, W. G. (1985). *Reducing the Signs of Crime: The Newark Experiment.* Washington, DC: Police Foundation.

37 Trojanowicz, R. (1982). *An Evaluation of the Neighborhood Foot Patrol Study in Flint, Michigan.* East Lansing, MI: Michigan State University.

38 Gaines, 1996.

39 Ibid.

40 Fritsch, E. J., Caeti, T. J., & Taylor, R. W. (1999). "Gang Suppression Through Saturation Patrol, Aggressive Curfew, and Truancy Enforcement: A Quasi-Experimental Test of the Dallas Anti-gang Initiative." *Crime & Delinquency*, 45(1), 122–139.

41 Miller, G. I. (1987). "Observations on Police Undercover Work." *Criminology, 25*(1), 27–46.

42 Lyons, W. "Partnerships, Information and Public Safety: Community Policing in a Time of Terror." *Policing, 25*(3), 530–542.

43 O'Connell, P. E. (2008). "The Chess Master's Game: A Model for Incorporating Local Police Agencies in the Fight Against Global Terrorism." *Policing, 31*(3), 456–465.

44 Berson, S. B. (2009). "Debating DNA Collection." *National Institute of Justice Journal, 264*, 9–13.

45 *Kyllo v. United States*, 533 U.S. 27, 150 L. Ed. 2nd 94, 121 S. Ct. 2038.

46 Douglas, J., Ressler, R. K., Burgess, A. W., & Hartman, C. R. (1986). "Criminal Profiling from Crime Scene Analysis." *Behavioral Sciences and the Law, 4*, 401–421.

47 Kelling, G. L., & Moore, M. H. (1988). "The Evolving Strategy of Policing." *Perspectives on Policing* (NCJ 114213). Washington, DC: National Institute of Justice.

48 Ponsaers, P. (2002). "Reading about 'Community (Oriented) Policing' and Police Models." *Policing, 24*(4), 470–496.

49 Kreps, G. A., & Weller, J. M. (1973). "The Police-Community Relations Movement: Conciliatory Responses to Violence." *The American Behavioral Scientist, 16*(3), 402–412.

50 Ibid.

51 Gaines, L. K., & Kappeler, V. E. (2009). *Community Policing: A Contemporary Perspective.* Cincinnati, OH: Anderson.

52 Wilson, J. Q., & Kelling, G. L. (1982, March). "Broken Windows." *Atlantic Monthly.*

53 Gaines & Kappeler, 2009.

54 Masten, J. (2009). "'Ain't No Snitches Ridin' Wit' Us': How Deception in the Fourth Amendment Triggered the Stop Snitching Movement." *Ohio State Law Journal, 70*(3), 701–753.

55 Ibid.

56 Goldstein, H. (1979). "Improving Policing: A Problem-Oriented Approach." *Crime and Delinquency, 25*, 236–258.

57 Zhao, J., Scheider, M. C., & Thurman, Q. (2002). "Funding Community Policing to Reduce Crime: Have COPS Grants Made a Difference?" *Criminology & Public Policy, 2*(1), 7–32.

58 Ratcliffe, J. H. (2008). *Intelligence-Led Policing.* Cullompton, UK: Willan.

59 Henry, V. E. (2003). *The COMPSTAT Paradigm: Management Accountability in Policing, Business and the Public Sector.* New York, NY: Looseleaf Law Publications.

60 Zimring, F. E. (2011). "How New York Beat Crime." *Scientific American Magazine, 305*(2), 74–75, 79.

61 Bohrer, S., & Chaney, R. (2010). "Police Investigations of the Use of Deadly Force Can Influence Perceptions and Outcomes." *FBI Law Enforcement Bulletin, 79*(1), 1–7.

62 Neiderhoffer, A. (1969). *Behind the Shield.* Garden City, NJ: Doubleday.

63 Alpert, G. P., MacDonald, J. M., & Dunham, R. G. (2005). "Police Suspicion and Discretionary Decision Making During Traffic Stops." *Criminology, 43*(2), 407–434.

64 Walker, S. (1993). Taming the System: *The Control of Discretion in Criminal Justice, 1950–1990.* Oxford: Oxford University Press.

65 National Research Council. (2003). *Fairness and Effectiveness in Policing: The Evidence.* Washington, DC: The National Academies Press.

66 Alpert et al., 2005.

67 Sherman, L. W., & Berk, R. A. (1984). *The Minneapolis Domestic Violence Experiment.* Washington, DC: Police Foundation.

68 National Research Council, 2003.

69 Sun, I., & Payne, B. (2004). "Racial Differences in Resolving Conflicts: A Comparison Between Black and White Police Officers." *Crime & Delinquency, 50*, 516–541.

70 Dantzer, M. L. (1987). "Police-related Stress: A Critique for Future Research." *Journal of Police Criminal Psychology, 3*, 43–48.

71 Anderson, W., Swenson, D., & Clay, D. (1995). *Stress Management for Law Enforcement Officers.* Upper Saddle River, NJ: Prentice Hall.

72 Anderson, G. S., Litzenberger, R., & Plecas, D. (2002). "Physical Evidence of Police Officer Stress." *Policing, 25*(2), 399–420.

73 Rizzolo, D., & Sedrak, M. (2010). "Stress Management: Helping Patients to Find Effective Coping Strategies." *Journal of American Academy of Physician Assistants, 23*(9), 20–24.

74 Atkinson, W. (2004). "Stress: Risk Management's Most Serious Challenge?" *Risk Management*, 51(6), 20–24.

75 Ibid.

76 Weitzer, R. (2002). "Incidents of Police Misconduct and Public Opinion." *Journal of Criminal Justice, 30*(5), 397–408.

77 Walker, S. (1992). *Police in America*. New York, NY: McGraw-Hill.

78 Ivkovic, S. K. (2005). *Fallen Blue Knights: Controlling Police Corruption*. New York, NY: Oxford University Press.

79 Arrigo, B. A., & Claussen, N. (2003). "Police Corruption and Psychological Testing: A Strategy for Preemployment Screening." *International Journal of Offender Therapy and Comparative Criminology, 47*(3), 272–290.

80 Jones, T. R., Owens, C., & Smith, M. (1995). "Police Ethics Training: A Three-Tiered Approach." *FBI Law Enforcement Bulletin, 64*(6), 22–26.

81 http://www.theiacp.org/PoliceServices/ExecutiveServices/ProfessionalAssistance/Ethics/FocusOnEthicsTheLawEnforcementOathofHonor/tabid/167/Default.aspx

Richard Thornton/Shutterstock.com

CHAPTER 5

Police Officers: Hiring and Training Guardians

KEY TERMS

Occupational stress

Police cynicism

Peace Officer Standards and Training

Police subculture

Symbolic assailants

LEARNING OBJECTIVES

After reading this chapter, students should be able to:

1. Describe which personal qualities and characteristics make good officers.
2. Explain why hiring diverse officers is important for police-community relations.
3. Define police subculture and explain how it impacts officers and the profession.
4. Describe the state of education in policing.
5. List the sources of occupational stress in policing.

Successful democratic policing requires additional attention to the recruitment, selection, and training process. The need is for diverse men and women who can deal effectively with the realities of the job as a guardian of democracy rather than as a warrior in some kind of "war" on crime. This means recruiting individuals who are smart, reasoned, and service-oriented. The selection of the right individuals, combined with the proper training and enculturation process can be the difference between a department that garners a high degree of public trust and legitimacy, and one that lacks public confidence and spends a lot of time defending itself and its officers against allegations of impropriety and abuse of power.

In the review questions for the previous chapter, we asked you to take a look at official agency Web sites, in part to see whether the imagery presented by these agencies matched their stated missions. If you took up this challenge, your textbook authors are willing to bet that you saw some pretty interesting things as you surfed around—everything ranging from departments with elaborately produced recruitment videos that highlight SWAT team members being inserted by helicopters and "pie-ing" the entryway of a building with laser-sighted automatic weapons, to departments using the images of smiling actors in police uniforms posing on a city sidewalk with diverse and happy members of some fictitious community. Reality lies somewhere between these extremes. Do you think that this kind of imagery has any relationship to the pool of potential recruits that a department tends to attract, the subsequent quality of enforcement, and/or the legitimacy of the police in the eyes of the public?

In this chapter, we explore the recruitment, selection, and training process. We also look at the personal qualities and characteristics that make good officers, why the hiring of diverse and educated officers is important, and how diversity and education have impacted policing. In addition, we examine how officers change between recruitment and retirement and look at the impact that occupational stress has on officers and their families.

The Job of Police Officer: Fact versus Fiction

A time-persistent "problem" for the police has been dealing with the myth of the crime fighter—the idea that the police are first and foremost crime fighters who, were it not for their constant vigilance, prevent society from rapidly devolving into a chaotic world ruled by crafty, murderous criminals. The police are the "thin blue line" between order and chaos. These crime fighter police spend their entire shifts spotting crimes in progress, chasing and arresting criminals, as well as stopping crimes before they actually occur. All other activities are incidental. If they stop for lunch, they will drop their sandwich and coffee on the ground as soon as a call comes over the radio so they can get back into the fray. They do not have lives outside of their crime fighting role and their only off-duty activity is sleeping in preparation for another day of crime fighting. The lines between patrol officer and detective are blurred; forensic evidence of some type is utilized in every situation, but is still no match for physical crime fighting in the form of dramatic foot or car chases, gun play, and danger at every turn.

We put "problem" in quotes because at various times this crime fighter image has actually been quite useful for the police. For example, the crime fighter image serves the police quite well when they need to argue for additional resources. Recall also from the chapters on police history that there was a time that the police actively sought to portray themselves as crime fighters in order to help burnish their public image as detached, professional law enforcers. The police and popular media have occasionally managed to align their interests, with the police department seeing a public relations benefit and the media seeking increased viewership (and/or readership). The old television show, *Dragnet*, popular in the 1950s and again in the late 1960s, is a classic example of such cooperation.

Who doesn't like a good television police drama? The fact that there are so many police dramas being supplied by television producers tells you that there is a substantial public demand for them. *Hawaii Five-O, Hill Street Blues, NYPD Blue, COPS, Law and Order, CSI, The Wire*, just to name a few. Some of these shows are more realistic than others, but certainly all of them must emphasize the dramatic aspects of policing. Who would want to watch police officers fill out paperwork for an hour (or 2 hours, split into two exciting episodes)? Would it be any more interesting if in the second episode you got to see them standing around, talking to some people on the street? Maybe seeing them negotiate with and ultimately assist a mentally ill, homeless person to find a safer place to sleep and then connect them with available services? How about watching them clean the vomit out of the back of their patrol car after transporting an intoxicated person to the precinct?

The reality is that most of what the police do all day is not "crime fighting," but more of the order maintenance and service function. As such, while it is certainly important that potential recruits be suited for, and trained and equipped to handle potentially violent situations, make arrests, and "catch bad guys," it is arguably more important that they be suited for, and trained and equipped for *service*. The more a potential recruit understands about the reality of policing, the more likely they are to successfully self-select into the profession. When there is a substantial disconnect between the image and the reality of policing, the potential exists for an unsuccessful recruitment and training process, as well as subsequent poor performance and negative behavior on the street. But the burden does not fall entirely on the potential recruit; much of the burden falls on the police themselves who bear some responsibility for "truth in advertising" in their recruitment process, as well as in the design of academy training.

Police cynicism an attitude that develops among officers that they must be skeptical of all people and can trust no one.

While police officers perform a variety of duties, their ability to provide service is possibly most important.

In his classic study of **police cynicism**, Arthur Niederhoffer (1967) sought to explain why some officers "go wrong" during the course of their careers, especially in light of the increased standards for selection, better training, and high performance standards that came with the police professionalism movement. He proposed what is essentially a strain theory to explain the generation of cynical attitudes among police officers: police officers experience frustration and disillusionment when faced with this disconnect between the "ideal" expectations they pick up in the academy and the "reality" of police work on the street (where they are told to forget the academy and rapidly learn how policing is really "done"), which generates cynicism and, without return to professional commitment, eventual apathy and alienation, or anomie. He argued that this process occurs over the course of officer careers, beginning with the contrast between academy training and initial field experience, and later as an effect of continued exposure to a police administration perceived as out of touch with street-level policing, the perceived failures of the criminal justice system, as well as contagion effects from other cynical officers (Neiderhoffer, 1967). In its worst form, an advanced stage of "aggressive cynicism" may develop; this is marked by overt hostility toward the sources of frustration and rejection of the goals or objectives that cannot be attained. Cynical attitudes will manifest in problem behavior as officers "act out" their frustrations in the course of their daily interactions with citizens and other officers (Niederhofffer, 1967). This cynicism, along with other ramifications of the selection process and the disjuncture between the myth and the reality of the job, help explain the existence and perpetuation of a distinctive police subculture—an issue that is discussed later in this chapter.

Patrol Officer Job Description

Individuals are often drawn to police work because of the variability of the job. This variety makes the job of patrol officer very difficult to conceptualize and describe, more so than possibly any other occupation. Baehr and colleagues (1968) conducted comprehensive field observations and developed a behavioral analysis of a patrol officer's job and a list of the most important attributes required for success in the field. Although the behavioral analysis is more than 40 years old, it is still applicable today.

1. Endure long periods of monotony in routine patrol, yet react quickly and effectively to problem situations observed on the street or to instructions issued by the dispatcher.
2. Know the assigned patrol area, not only its physical characteristics but also of its normal routine events and behavior patterns of its residents.
3. Exhibit initiative, problem-solving capacity, effective judgment, and imagination in coping with the many complex situations he or she is called to face, such as a family disturbance, a potential suicide, a robbery in progress, an accident, or a disaster.
4. Make prompt and effective decisions, sometimes in life-and-death situations, and be able to size up a situation quickly and take appropriate action.
5. Demonstrate mature judgment, as in deciding whether an arrest is warranted by the circumstances or when facing a situation in which the use of force may be needed.
6. Demonstrate critical awareness in discerning signs of out-of-the-ordinary conditions or circumstances that indicate trouble or a crime in progress.
7. Exhibit a number of complex psychomotor skills, such as driving a vehicle in emergency situations, firing a weapon accurately under extremely varied conditions, maintaining agility, endurance, and strength; and showing competence in self-defense and apprehension.
8. Perform the communication and record-keeping functions of the job, including oral reports, formal case reports, and departmental and court forms.
9. Endure verbal and physical abuse from citizens and offenders while using only necessary force in the performance of his or her job.
10. Exhibit a self-assured professional presence and a self-confident manner when dealing with offenders, the public, and the courts.
11. Be capable of restoring equilibrium to social groups (e.g., when restoring order in a family fight, in a disagreement between neighbors, or in a clash between rival gangs).
12. Tolerate stress in a multitude of forms, such as meeting the violent behavior of a mob, coping with the pressure of a high speed chase or a weapon being fired, or assisting a woman bearing a child.
13. Maintain objectivity while dealing with a host of special-interest groups, ranging from relatives of offenders to members of the press.
14. Maintain a balanced perspective in the face of constant exposure to the worst side of human nature.
15. Exhibit a high level of personal integrity and ethical conduct.

Adapted from Baehr, M.E., Furcon, J.E., & Froemel, E.C. (1968). Psychological assessment of patrolman qualifications in relation to field performance. Department of Justice, pp. 11.3–11.5. Washington DC: U.S. Government Printing Office.

The Importance of Recruitment and Selection

> *Law enforcement officers should have the wisdom of Solomon, the courage of David, the patience of Job, and the leadership of Moses, the kindness of the Good Samaritan, the diplomacy of Lincoln, the tolerance of the Carpenter of Nazareth, and finally, an intimate knowledge of every branch of the natural, biological, and social sciences.*
>
> —August Vollmer

Washington Stateis using some innovative training at thier centralized training acadmey that incorporates the idea of democractic policing. This shift in their training model seeks to emphasize core democratic values and transition the police culture away from the warrior mentality (i.e., police as urban warriors equipped and trained for battle) and toward the idea of police officers as protectors and guardians of democracy (i.e., police as community guardians with a strong focus on procedural justice) (Rahr & Rice, 2015). As this guardian model of policing continues to accumulate national support, what kinds of characteristics are police leaders seeking in police recruits? Consistent with the broader emphasis on procedural justice, police leaders tend to emphasize critical thinking and independent decision-making skills, as well as the ability to socially engage with humans in a respectful manner, and to be effective at de-escalating conflict.

Critical thinking refers to the ability to objectively analyze a particular issue and independently form a conclusion or judgment about the issue. It is best thought of as a general way of thinking, not as a tool that can be applied to solve particular problems. Your professors are probably somewhat obsessed with critical thinking, since we are often evaluated on our ability to stimulate critical thinking in the classroom. We tend to approach critical thinking by encouraging students not to take things at face value; not to presume that something is so, simply because someone has said so or because it appears in a book; to dig deeper, try to free yourself from any preconceptions, do your own research, and come to an informed decision on your own. This is important in policing for a number of reasons. While police culture tends to emphasize adherence to policy and procedure, most would agree that memorizing the policies and procedures manual and attempting to follow it to the letter and apply it in every situation is a recipe for disaster. We need officers who can think on their feet and are comfortable with the exercise of discretion in unique and dynamic environments; if we wanted strict application of the policies and procedures manual, we could replace the officer with a robot—there would be no need for a reasoning human. In addition, officers who are good critical thinkers are open minded and empathetic, and as such they actively seek out different perspectives, different sources of information, and creative approaches to problems. When faced with a problem, good critical thinkers aren't looking for the "easy" answer, nor are they necessarily looking for the "right" answer—they seek the "best" decision given the information that is available to them.

© John Roman Images/Shutterstock.com

Officers who are good critical thinkers are able to creatively approach problems.

Good critical thinking is essential to the guardian model of policing because of the increased importance placed on officer discretion, as well as the increased amount of discretion, necessary to fulfill the focus on procedural justice. Ultimately, the behavior of the police and the legitimacy of the police as an institution in the eyes of the public will be contingent on the perception of fundamental fairness in their use of coercive authority. The intelligent use of coercion is the key; we need to ensure that the police are adequately trained to intelligently exercise discretion in their use of coercion, and seek to minimize unnecessary physical coercion. In addition to improved interactions with the public, as well as improvements in perceived legitimacy, there is also a benefit to officers in terms of increased safety. As Rahr and Rice (2015:5) note,

> *... much recruit training focuses on physical control tactics and weapons, with less attention given to communication and de-escalation skills. The reasoning for this approach is the sacred mantra of officer safety. We train relentlessly—as we should—in physical tactics for the high-risk, low-frequency attacks. Less instructional attention is focused on human behavioral science. Yet seasoned cops and statistics tell us that the officer's intellect and social dexterity are often the most effective officer safety tools. For the sake of safety, voluntary compliance should be the primary goal in resolving conflict, with physical control reserved for those who present an immediate threat and cannot be managed any other way.*

The Recruitment and Selection Process

Law enforcement agencies invest a considerable amount of time, money, and effort in selecting and hiring the highest quality candidates possible. The process to become a police officer is more extensive than almost every other job out there. There are stringent age, physical, and medical requirements as well as a battery of tests that reveal an applicant's suitability for the job and which may predict the applicant's likelihood of success.

Eligibility Requirements

Because of the physically demanding nature of the job, police departments are generally looking for physically fit candidates between the ages of 21 and 38. Although there is not usually a stipulated maximum age, the minimum age is usually between 19 and 21 (depending on the state and the agency). Even though someone may meet the minimum age requirement, that is often not enough. Law enforcement agencies are looking for mature individuals with life experience, something than many candidates in their early twenties lack.

Peace Officer Standards and Training organizations (usually state-level) that set eligibility and training standards for peace officers.

Beyond age, recruits must have good vision which is defined by each agency and is sometimes stipulated by the state **Peace Officer Standards and Training** office (POST). Departments also require candidates to meet minimum physical fitness standards which usually, though not always, involves meeting a specified height/weight ratio (or Body Mass Index), passing a medical test, and/or passing a physical agility test. Some departments require recruits to possess a 2-year or 4-year college degree but these are the exception rather than the rule. Most agencies only require candidates to have a high school diploma or equivalent (more on this). Finally, some departments have residency requirements which means that officers must reside in a specified geographical area for a defined period of time (possibly, the person's entire career); some departments extend this rule to recruits and only accept applications from individuals who live within the specified boundary.

Testing and Screening

© pio3/Shutterstock.com

There are a variety of tests that an applicant must undergo to determine whether that person will be suitable for the job of police officer.

The selection process also involves multiple stages of testing and screening, which serve as a weeding out process so that only the most mentally stable, morally upright, and qualified candidates become officers. In addition to a personal interview, criminal records check, drug test, and driving history check, which almost every recruit in America must pass, many recruits are also subjected to a psychological evaluation, a written aptitude test, and/or a drug test. Credit history checks and personality inventories are also common. Surprisingly, only about a quarter of agencies require candidates to pass a polygraph exam (Burch, 2012; Reaves, 2010). Each of these screening devices gives the agency unique information about the candidate. For example, the driving history check tells the department whether the applicant is a safe driver who can be trusted with agency equipment (multiple tickets can indicate an unsafe and immature driver who places others' lives at risk unnecessarily and could be a liability for the department). The credit history

FIGURE 5.1 APPLICANT SCREENING TOOLS

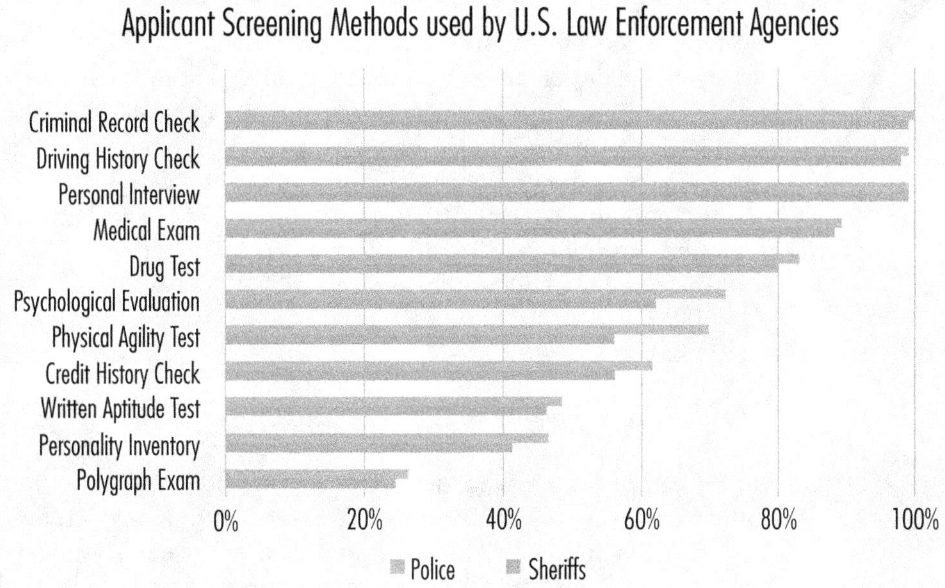

Adapted from Reaves, B. (2010, December). Local police departments, 2007. Bureau of Justice Statistics, p. 35–36. Washington DC: U.S. Government Printing Office. And Burch, A.M. (2012, December). Sheriffs' offices, 2007-Statistical tables. Bureau of Justice Statistics, p. 8–9. Washington DC: U.S. Government Printing Office.

check, on the other hand, tells the agency how well the applicant manages her money—whether she lives within her means and pays her debts. This not only provides information about the applicant's character but also indicates whether she might be tempted to steal evidence or take bribes on the job. The larger the agency, the more likely it utilizes most or all of these screening devices. Figure 5.1 shows which screening tools are most popular in the United States.

Other than the physical agility test and written aptitude test which are performed prior to any personal interview, the other tests are generally conducted as part of the background investigation process which happens after the agency has decided they are interested in hiring the applicant. These specialty tests are designed to predict whether a candidate will become a successful officer or whether they are likely to fail out of the grueling training program or become a liability for the department. Intelligence tests, in particular, are controversial because minority candidates tend to score more poorly than white candidates and there is much debate about whether or not they actually identify better qualified candidates. Even though many question the utility of personality tests and criticize their high false positive rate, the strongest predictor of job performance has been found to be the California Personality Inventory test.

Another important part of the process is the personal interview. These interviews are often panel interviews in which two to four officers of varying ranks question the job candidate. The point of the interview is to assess applicant qualities that are not easily evaluated through other means, such as an applicant's poise and demeanor, self-confidence, and interpersonal skills. Interviewers also assess a candidate's ability to communicate and think in a high-pressure environment, and whether he/she is easily provoked to anger. It is common for candidates to be given scenarios and asked how they would respond to the situation. Whether an interview is indicative of future job performance is up for discussion but interviews do help agencies determine which qualified candidates are good fits for the department.

The final stage of the process, the background investigation, happens after agency representatives have decided they want to hire a candidate. It involves an extremely thorough search into a candidate's background to assess their character. Family members, past and present roommates and friends, current and previous employers, military colleagues and supervisors, and sometimes even instructors are contacted to verify the candidate's reputation, level of maturity, and integrity. This is the final check of trustworthiness and it takes months to complete.

Training New Recruits

The Bureau of Justice Statistics conducted its first national study of law enforcement training academies in 2002, and updated the study in 2006 (Hickman, 2005; Reaves, 2009). The landscape of law enforcement training, much like the landscape of law enforcement in general, reflects the history and tradition of State's rights and local control. As such, law enforcement training across the states is done a little bit differently, depending on where you live. While there are no national standards for law enforcement training, there is a major professional association for those who are involved in establishing State-level training standards and administering law enforcement academies, the International Association of Directors of Law Enforcement Standards and Training, or IADLEST, www.iadlest.org. These individuals are generally associated with the many state POST agencies, boards, and/or commissions that determine the training standards for their states.

In the 2006 study, BJS identified 648 law enforcement training academies across the country providing basic training to entry-level recruits. In some states, all basic law enforcement training is conducted at a centralized state academy. Washington State is an example, where all basic law enforcement training is conducted at the Washington State Criminal Justice Training Commission facility, which is also the state POST agency (the exception is the Washington State Patrol, which operates their own basic academy). In other states, training is decentralized to the county-level, regional areas (including multiple counties), or to college, university, or technical school programs. Some larger municipal law enforcement agencies and sheriff's offices operate their own academies, and there are about 200 of these.

Excluding any field training component of academy curricula, the average length of basic recruits training programs was about 760 hours, or roughly 19 weeks. About a third of academies included a field training component, and this added about 450 hours on average to the total training time. Recruits typically had large instructional blocks related to learning firearms skills (the median instruction time is 60 hours) and self-defense skills (about 50 hours) (see Table 5.1). The next largest instructional block was health and fitness training

TABLE 5.1 TOPICS INCLUDED IN BASIC TRAINING OF STATE AND LOCAL LAW ENFORCEMENT TRAINING ACADEMIES (2006)

Topics	Percent of Academies with Training	Median Number of Hours of Instruction
Operations		
Report writing	100%	20
Patrol	99%	40
Investigations	99%	40
Emergency vehicle operations	99%	40
Basic first aid/CPR	97%	24
Computers/information systems	58%	8
Weapons/self-defense		
Self-defense	99%	51
Firearms skills	98%	60
Non-lethal weapons	98%	12
Legal		
Criminal law	100%	36
Constitutional law	98%	12
History of law enforcement	84%	4
Self-improvement		
Ethics and integrity	100%	8
Health and fitness	96%	46
Stress prevention/management	87%	5
Basic foreign language	36%	16
Community policing		
Cultural diversity/human relations	98%	11
Basic strategies	92%	8
Mediation skills/conflict management	88%	8
Special topics		
Domestic violence	99%	14
Juveniles	99%	8
Domestic preparedness	88%	8
Hate crimes/bias crimes	87%	4

Adapted from Reaves, B. (2009). State and local law enforcement training academies, 2006. Bureau of Justice Statistics. Washington DC: U.S. Government Printing Office.

(46 hours). Also common to all academies was training related to patrol procedures, investigations, and emergency vehicle operations (typically 40 hours each). You can see the wide variety of instructional areas and median instructional time listed in Table 5.1; consider these in light of Rahr and Rice's (2015) concerns regarding the lesser attention given to training in communication and de-escalation skills. It will be important to incorporate better measures of training in these areas in future iterations of the BJS training academy study.

More than 90% of academies also provided basic training on community policing topics in 2006. Very common topics included identifying community problems (provided in 85% of academies), and the history of community policing (83%) (Reaves, 2009). More than half of academies provided training on the environmental causes of crime (62%), prioritizing crime problems (62%), using problem-solving models (60%), and organizing/mobilizing the community (54%) (Reaves, 2009).

During 2006, an estimated 57,000 recruits started basic training in academies across the country. About 1 in 6 recruits that year were female, and in terms of race/ethnicity categories about 70% were white, 13% black, 13% Hispanic, and 4% in other categories. About 49,000 of the recruits who started basic training, or 86%, completed training and graduated from the academy (Reaves, 2009).

A New York City Police Officer graduate takes his oath.

Completion rates varied by type of academy, with state police academies having lower completion rates on average as compared to other types of academies. Some of this may be explained by the academy training environment. Academy training environments can generally be characterized as falling along a continuum ranging from "stress-based," military boot-camp style academies, to "non-stress based" academies that may be more like academic campuses. According to the BJS study (Reaves, 2009:10),

> *The more traditional stress-based model of training is based on the military model and typically includes paramilitary drills, intensive physical demands, public disciplinary measures, immediate reaction to infractions, daily inspections, value inculcation, and withholding of privileges. Proponents of this approach believe it promotes self-discipline in recruits resulting in a commitment to follow departmental policies, better time management, and completion of duties even when undesirable.*
>
> *The non-stress model emphasizes academic achievement, physical training, administrative disciplinary procedures, and an instructor-trainee relationship that is more relaxed and supportive. Proponents of this approach believe it produces officers better able to interact in a cooperative manner with citizens and community*

organizations, and therefore more suited to the problem-solving approaches of community-oriented policing.

The BJS data show that state police academies are more likely than other types of academies to fall into the stress-based end of the continuum, and this may contribute to the lower completion rates observed among recruits in those academies. Figure 5.2 below shows the distribution of training academies in terms of their training environment: 15% indicated a predominately stress-based environment, 38% more stress than non-stress based, 38% more non-stress than stress based, and 9% predominately non-stress based.

Academy completion rates in 2006 also varied by the race and gender of recruit. Males had higher completion rates (87%) than females (80%), and Whites had higher completion rates (87%) than Hispanics (82%) and Blacks (81%). In terms of race and gender interactions, white males had the highest average completion rate (about 95%), followed by white females and black males (about 88% each); Hispanic females had the lowest completion rates (see Figure 5.3). A related implication for stress-based training models is that there does appear to be a gender effect in completion rates. The BJS study found that in academies having a "predominantly non-stress" training environment, male and female recruits had an equivalent completion rate (89%). As the academy training environment moved toward an increasingly stress-based model, academy completion rates declined for both genders but at an accelerated rate for female recruits (see Figure 5.4). In academies having a "predominately stress" training environment, male recruits had a completion rate of 81% while female recruits had only a 68% completion rate.

FIGURE 5.2 TRAINING ENVIRONMENT OF STATE AND LOCAL LAW ENFORCEMENT TRAINING ACADEMIES, 2006

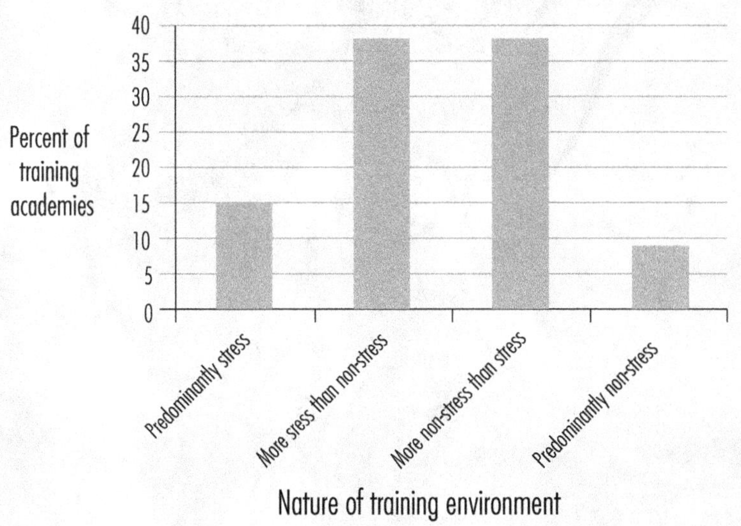

Adapted from Reaves, B. (2009). State and local law enforcement training academies, 2006. Bureau of Justice Statistics. Washington DC: U.S. Government Printing Office.

FIGURE 5.3 COMPLETION RATES FOR RECRUITS IN STATE AND LOCAL LAW ENFORCEMENT TRAINING ACADEMIES, BY RACE AND GENDER, 2005-2006.

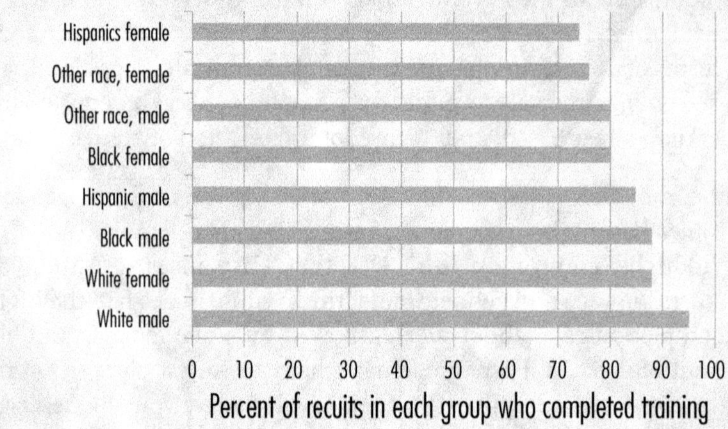

Adapted from Reaves, B. (2009). State and local law enforcement training academies, 2006. Bureau of Justice Statistics. Washington DC: U.S. Government Printing Office.

FIGURE 5.4 COMPLETION RATES FOR MALE AND FEMALE RECRUITS IN STATE AND LOCAL LAW ENFORCEMENT TRAINING ACADEMIES, BY TYPE OF TRAINING ENVIRONMENT, 2005-2006

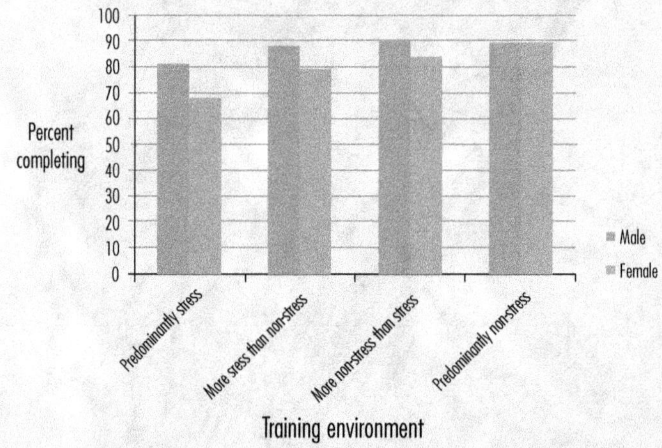

Adapted from Reaves, B. (2009). State and local law enforcement training academies, 2006. Bureau of Justice Statistics. Washington DC: U.S. Government Printing Office.

Think about it

Recall from earlier in this chapter that some of the innovative changes going on at the Washington State Criminal Justice Training Commission to support the Warriors to Guardians transition are aimed at reducing some of the militarization of the training environment, for example, eliminating "bracing," replacing the "tune-up" day with coaching, and generally moving away from the boot camp model. What do you think is the optimal training environment to support democratic policing?

The Extent and Impact of Diversity in Law Enforcement

As should be evident by now, becoming a police officer is a difficult process and not everyone makes the cut. It takes strength of character, integrity, sound judgment, and a variety of other traits to be selected for the job. Once selected, it takes commitment, tenacity, and about 12–24 months to make it through the background investigation, academy training, and field training before a new officer patrols the streets on her own. Who makes it through? Do the successful applicants and academy graduates who become law enforcement officers reflect the population at large? The answer is: it depends on where you live, but probably not.

Today, 1 in 8 officers (12.2%) are women. This represents an approximately 160% increase since 1987 when only 1 in 13 officers (7.6%) were women (Reaves, 2015). In fact, the proportion of female officers has grown every year since BJS began tracking this information (see Figure 5.5). As indicated in Table 5.2, the percentage of female officers is greatest in our largest police departments, where more than 16% of officers are female (that's 1 in every 6). While this is encouraging, women comprise almost 50% of the workforce, reminding us that women are still very much underrepresented as sworn officers. Females are also underrepresented as supervisors and chiefs. In 2013, only 9.5% of first-line supervisors and 3% of chiefs were women even though they comprised 12.2% of officers (Reaves, 2015).

The number of female officers continues to grow each year.

As indicated in Table 5.3, the proportion of racial and ethnic minority officers has grown at a similar pace as female officers. In 1987, about one in seven officers (14.6%) identified as a racial/ethnic minority, today more than one in four officers (27.3%) identify as a racial/ethnic minority (Reaves, 2015). Black/African-American officers represent the largest minority-status

FIGURE 5.5 FEMALE REPRESENTATION AMONG FULL-TIME SWORN PERSONNEL IN LOCAL POLICE DEPARTMENTS, 1987–2013

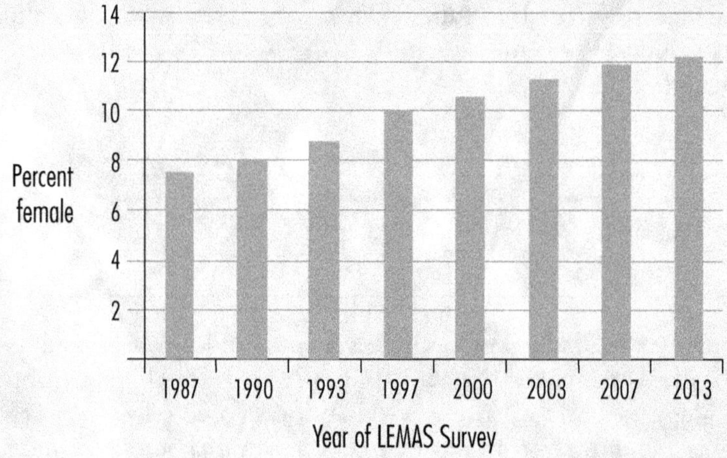

Adapted from Reaves, B. (2015, May). Local police departments, 2013: Personnel, Policies, & Practices. Bureau of Justice Statistics, p. 4. Washington DC: U.S. Government Printing Office.

TABLE 5.2 SEX OF FULL-TIME SWORN PERSONNEL IN THE UNITED STATES

Population served	Male		Female	
	Police	**Sheriffs**	**Police**	**Sheriffs**
1,000,000 or more	82%	85%	18%	15%
500,000–999,999	84%	86%	16%	14%
250,000–499,999	85%	86%	15%	14%
100,000–249,999	88%	88%	12%	12%
50,000–99,999	90%	90%	10%	10%
25,000–49,999	91%	91%	9%	9%
10,000–24,999	92%	92%	8%	8%
2,500–9,999[a] Under 10,000[b]	93%	94%	8%	6%
Under 2,500	94%		6%	
ALL SIZES	88%	88%	12%	12%

[a]–police departments, [b]–sheriffs' departments *may not equal 100% due to rounding

Adapted from Reaves, B. (2015, May). Local police departments, 2013: Personnel, Policies, & Practices. Bureau of Justice Statistics, p. 4. Washington DC: U.S. Government Printing Office. And Burch, A.M. (2012, December). Sheriffs' offices, 2007-Statistical tables. Bureau of Justice Statistics, p. 11. Washington DC: U.S. Government Printing Office.

TABLE 5.3 RACE AND ETHNICITY OF FULL-TIME SWORN PERSONNEL IN THE UNITED STATES

Population served	White		Black/African American		Hispanic/ Latino		Asian/Other Pacific Islander		American Indian/Alaskan Native		Two or more races	
	Police	Sheriffs	Police	Sheriffs	Police	Sheriffs	Police	Sheriffs	Police	Sheriffs	Police	Sheriffs
1,000,000 or more	564	66%	17%	12%	25%	19%	4%	3%	<1%	<1%	<1%	<1%
500,000–999,999	60%	77%	23%	11%	10%	11%	5%	1%	<1%	1%	2%	<1%
250,000–499,999	67%	83%	19%	10%	11%	6%	2%	1%	<1%	<1%	<1%	<1%
100,000–249,999	74%	88%	12%	8%	11%	3%	3%	<1%	<1%	<1%	<1%	1%
50,000–99,999	80%	91%	8%	6%	9%	3%	2%	<1%	<1%	<1%	<1%	<1%
25,000–49,999	86%	88%	6%	8%	6%	4%	1%	<1%	<1%	1%	<1%	<1%
10,000–24,999	88%	88%	5%	9%	6%	2%	<1%	<1%	<1%	1%	<1%	<1%
2,500–9,999[a] Under 10,000[b]	89%	91%	4%	3%	4%	5%	<1%	–%	1%	1%	<1%	<1%
Under 2,500	85%		6%		5%		<1%		3%		<1%	
All Sizes	73%	81%	12%	9%	12%	8%	2%	1%	<1%	<1%	<1%	<1%

[a]–police departments, [b]–sheriffs' departments

* may not equal 100 % due to rounding

Adapted from Reaves, B(2015, May). Local police departments, 2013: Personnel, Policies, & Practices. Bureau of Justice Statistics, p. 4. Washington DC: U.S. Government Printing Office. And Burch, A.M. (2012, December). Sheriffs' offices, 2007-Statistical tables. Bureau of Justice Statistics, p. 10. Washington DC: U.S. Government Printing Office.

group with 58,000 officers (12.2%). Hispanic/Latino officers are next with 55,000 (11.6% of all officers). The percentage of African-American officers has grown slowly from 9% to 12.2% over the past 26 years while the percentage of Hispanic/Latino officers has more than doubled (from 4.5% to 11.6%) in the same time frame. Members of other minority groups account for approximately 3% of all officers today, which is about a 400% increase since 1987 when they accounted for 0.8% of all officers (Reaves, 2015).

Does it matter that women and minorities are underrepresented in policing? Remember, police officers are not just people paid to enforce the law and keep the peace; they are visual symbols of the criminal justice system and of government. In poor, disadvantaged communities of color, that means that police officers are "the tangible target for grievances against shortcomings throughout [the criminal justice] system: Against assembly-line justice in teeming lower courts; against wide disparities in sentences; against antiquated correctional facilities; against the basic inequities imposed by the system on the poor—to whom, for example, the option of bail means only jail" (Kerner Commission Report, 1968 as cited in Vila, 1999, p. 190). For this reason, it is important that officers are able to relate to the community, not only to encourage law-abidingness but also so that community members will trust and support the police in their endeavors to protect the public's safety. Insofar as minorities are able to generate higher levels of trust among community members than white male officers, improving diversity is beneficial to departments.

There was deep-seated distrust and hostility between police and "ghetto communities" in the 1960s. This hostility resulted in numerous civil disturbances and riots during the decade. At this time, police officers were almost all white men. Both the President's Commission on Law Enforcement and the Administration of Justice and the Kerner Commission addressed the low number of minority law enforcement officers in their reports. The Kerner commission discovered that, in those cities that experienced significant civil unrest and disorder, the percentage of minority officers in the police department was dramatically lower than the percentage of minority community members. In spite of the importance of hiring minorities, The President's Commission recognized that "inducing qualified young men from minority groups to enter police work" was going to be a difficult task "in view of the distrust for the police felt by members of minority groups, especially by young men" (1967, p.102). Toward this end, the National Advisory Commission on Criminal Justice Standards and Goals (1973) set criteria to help agencies achieve increased minority and female recruitment to mirror the makeup of their surrounding community.

All else being equal, research consistently demonstrates that cities with a large minority population have more minority police officers than cities with a small minority population. Interestingly, research from public administration also shows that having a black or Latino mayor or city council members generally increases minority representation in the police force (Gustafson, 2013; Sharp, 2014; Zhao et al., 2005). Having a minority police chief and being the subject of a consent decree are also associated with greater police diversity (Gustafson, 2013). Agencies that want to increase department diversity must take affirmative steps to recruit women and minorities. This means developing recruitment materials that appeal to these groups as well as advertising in places that are likely to draw these groups.

The Effectiveness of FEMALE AND Minority Officers

Are women effective officers? Yes. Two major studies, and several smaller studies, have shown women to be just as effective on patrol as men (Bloch & Anderson, 1974; David, 1984; Morash & Greene, 1986; Rabe-Hemp & Schuck, 2007; Schuck & Rabe-Hemp, 2005; Sichel et al., 1978; Stalans & Finn, 2000). For example, research has found no differences in arrest rates or conviction rates between male and female patrol officers, but has found that women receive fewer citizen complaints, are charged with improper conduct less often, and are seen by the community as more pleasant, respectful, and competent than men, which might explain why women are more likely than men to receive community support. A study of New York police officers found that men and women react very similarly to violent confrontations but that women are more emotionally stable and better able to deescalate potentially violent situations. Women are also less likely than their male counterparts to use a firearm, cause physical injury, or become physically injured on the job. In terms of improper behavior, women are significantly underrepresented in complaints, sustained use-of-force allegations, and agency civil litigation payouts. A review of LAPD civil litigation costs from 1990 to 1999 revealed that payouts for excessive force for male officers surpassed payouts for female officers by a ratio of 23:1 even though male officers outnumbered female officers by only 4:1 (National Center for Women & Policing, 2002).

Unlike the plethora of studies that have examined women as police officers, there is very little research on the performance of minorities as police officers. A recent study examined whether minority representation in government and in police agencies translates to police practice and found that black political representation reduces black order maintenance arrests but black representation on the police force does not (Sharp, 2014).

© Rob Byron/Shutterstock.com

Cities with a larger minority population tend to have more minority officers.

Additionally, a few studies have examined differences in attitudes between white and non-white officers and found some dissimilarities. For example, black officers are generally more supportive than white officers of community policing, citizen oversight, and police innovation in general. It has also been found that black officers take quality of life policing issues more seriously and place more importance on neighborhood conditions and fear of crime than their white counterparts (Boyd, 2010). One of the issues that affect black male officers more than any other demographic is the threat of being killed on the job by friendly fire. In particular, when African-American officers work plain clothes undercover assignments, they are at increased risk of being mistaken for a criminal and killed by a uniformed officer unfamiliar with the undercover officer.

The Push for College-Educated Officers

Although August Vollmer introduced the idea that education could improve policing in the 1920s, it was not really until the 1960s–1970s that the issue was debated in earnest in the United States. The increasing crime rate and urban riots of the 1960s pushed the issue to the forefront (Roberg & Bonn, 2004). The President's Commission on Law Enforcement and the Administration of Justice (1967) advocated for college-educated officers as a solution to the growing crisis of confidence in policing. In response, Congress passed the Omnibus Crime Control and Safe Streets Act (OCCSSA) of 1968.

OCCSSA created the Law Enforcement Assistance Administration (LEAA) (and within it the Law Enforcement Education Program) and provided money for education, research, and equipment. As a result of newly available federal funding, the number of colleges offering police science or criminal justice degree programs increased exponentially. Unfortunately, the quality of the programs was not uniform and many programs were nonrigorous extensions of police academies (Roberg & Bonn, 2004; Sherman & the National Advisory Commission on Higher Education for Police Officers, 1978). This hurt attempts to increase education standards for entry-level officers. While poor quality instruction is no longer a pervasive issue, research on police education has yet to produce the clear, unequivocal results that many U.S. police leaders desire in order to change policy. Still, the value of a college-degree for officers holds much appeal; especially in light of the varied and complex tasks that today's police officers are expected to perform (tasks that were not expected of officers 30 years ago).

Does a College Degree Make a Difference?

Research evidence on the value of a bachelor's degree for police officers is somewhat mixed; some studies find positive benefits but other studies find no correlation. On the whole, more research indicates positive effects than no correlation or negative consequences. Even though they typically receive higher salaries, research suggests that college-educated officers (those with a bachelor's degree or higher) save departments money. This is because research has found that college-educated officers take fewer sick days, have fewer on-the-job injuries and accidents, and have fewer individual liability cases filed against them (Carter & Sapp, 1989; Cascio, 1977; Cohen & Chaiken, 1972). They also may be better employees; college-educated officers are better report writers, more innovative, more reliable, more committed to the agency, more likely to take on leadership roles within the department, and more likely to be promoted than officers without a college degree (Carlan &Lewis, 2009; Cohen & Chaiken, 1972; Krimmel, 1996; Trojanowicz & Nicholson, 1976; Whetstone, 2000; Worden, 1990). If degree-holding officers are truly better report writers, that could translate into better investigations, higher court case filings, fewer evidentiary constitutional challenges, fewer false confessions or wrongful convictions, and/or more successful prosecutions.

It also has been found that college-educated officers are less resistant to change and more likely to embrace new methods of policing (Roberg & Bonn, 2004). They also have fewer citizen complaints filed against them, have fewer disciplinary actions taken against them, use force less often, and use less force than officers without a college degree (Chapman, 2012; Cohen & Chaiken, 1972; Fyfe, 1988; Kappeler et al., 1992; Lersch & Kunzman, 2001; Manis, Archbold, & Hassell, 2008; Roberg & Bonn, 2004; Rydberg & Terrill, 2010; Wilson, 1999). These last benefits may be particularly valuable for agencies which serve majority–minority communities where police-public relations are often strained. There are also benefits for agencies committed to community policing, problem solving, intelligence-led policing, as well as other newer policing strategies.

Balanced against these benefits are research findings that suggest that college-educated patrol officers may be less satisfied with their jobs, hold less favorable views toward management, and are less public service-oriented than their non-college educated peers (Paoline et al., 2015). Furthermore, college-educated officers are more likely to see police work as a "job," instead of a "calling" like their non-college-educated colleagues (Carlan & Lewis, 2009). Whether, or how, this impacts their service delivery is unknown.

Minimum Education Requirements

Despite these known benefits, only the state of Minnesota and a handful of agencies in other states require applicants to possess more than a high school diploma. As Table 5.3 shows, only 1% of police departments and no sheriffs' departments in the United States require a 4-year college degree for employment as a police officer (Burch, 2012; Reaves, 2010). Fully 82% of police and 89% of sheriffs' agencies across the nation only require a high school diploma (or equivalent). Interestingly, higher education requirements are more popular among state police agencies than local agencies. In fact, 19 of the 50 primary state police agencies require at least some college (of those, four require a B.A. and five require an A.A.; the rest have a "units completed" requirement) (Burriesci & Melley, 2001). LEMAS (Law Enforcement Management and Administrative Statistics Survey) data tell us that larger agencies often have more stringent education qualification requirements than do smaller agencies. For example, 36% of police departments and 22% of sheriffs' departments that serve a population size of 1,000,000 or

TABLE 5.4 EDUCATION REQUIREMENT FOR NEW HIRES IN THE UNITED STATES

Population served	High School Diploma		Some College		2-year College Degree		4-year College Degree	
	Police	Sheriffs	Police	Sheriffs	Police	Sheriffs	Police	Sheriffs
1,000,000 or more	64%	78%	7%	15%	29%	4%	0%	–%
500,000–999,999	70%	83%	19%	8%	7%	6%	4%	4%
250,000–499,999	70%	90%	15%	2%	9%	6%	7%	2%
100,000–249,999	78%	81%	8%	5%	10%	13%	3%	–%
50,000–99,999	75%	85%	8%	3%	12%	10%	4%	–%
25,000–49,999	75%	89%	4%	2%	18%	7%	2%	–%
10,000–24,999	81%	89%	6%	3%	12%	6%	–%	–%
2,500–9,999[a] Under 10,000[b]	86%	94%	2%	2%	9%	4%	1%	–%
Under 2,500	86%		3%		9%		–%	
All Sizes	84%	89%	4%	3%	10%	7%	1%	–%

[a] – police departments, [b] – sheriffs' departments

Adapted from Reaves, B. (2015, May). Local police departments, 2013: Personnel, Policies, & Practices. Bureau of Justice Statistics, p. 7. Washington DC: U.S. Government Printing Office. And Burch, A.M. (2012, December). Sheriffs' offices, 2007-Statistical tables. Bureau of Justice Statistics, p. 8. Washington DC: U.S. Government Printing Office.

more require at least some college (Burch, 2012; Reaves, 2015).While a college degree is usually not required to become a police officer, it is required to promote through the ranks. A recent study of California law enforcement agencies found that merely one-third of agencies would promote an officer with only a high school diploma to sergeant and most agencies in the study required a 4-year degree to promote to lieutenant (Gardiner, 2015).

Why do so few agencies require a college degree to get hired? There are several reasons. One reason is because agencies generally have to pay a higher salary to attract college-educated officers and some agencies are unable to offer the competitive salaries necessary to recruit college graduates. Agencies with a small tax base (residential areas that serve predominately poor communities) have an especially difficult time offering competitive salaries. Another reason is because agencies do not think it is necessary to require a 4-year degree to recruit high quality candidates. Some think it would unnecessarily limit their ability to hire high quality candidates without degrees (e.g., individuals turning to policing as a second career or after military service).

Finally, some agencies are concerned about being able to recruit qualified minority or female candidates (Gardiner, 2015). The latter concern is unwarranted, as two recent studies have found that agencies with higher education requirements employ higher percentages of female officers than do agencies which only require a high school diploma (Gardiner, 2015; Schuck, 2014).

How Many Cops Have a College Degree?

Fifty years ago, in 1960, only 3% of officers held a 4-year degree (in comparison, 7.7% of U.S. residents 25 and older did) (Rydberg & Terrill, 2010; U.S. Census, 2006). By 1988, 22.6% of sworn officers in the nation were college graduates and for the first time, the percentage of officers with degrees was higher than the general population, which was at 20.3% (Carter & Sapp, 1990; U.S. Census, 1989). Unfortunately, we do not have a current, nationally-representative dataset that can tell us what percentage of officers nationwide have a college degree. We do, however, have several small studies that are informative and reveal two things about the state of education in policing: (1) the percentage of college-educated officers is increasing, and (2) there is great variability between departments. Of the departments which have been recently studied, the percentage of college-educated officers ranges from 11.6% in three medium-sized, majority/minority communities in New Jersey to 65.2% in a medium-sized mid-west police department which requires at least some college to get hired and serves a 97% white population (Gardiner, 2015).

© Matt Benoit/Shutterstock.com

Less than half of officers across the nation have a college degree.

On average, it appears that between 25% and 45% of officers across the nation have a college degree. However, it is important to keep in mind that the percent of college-educated officers in a department is dependent on several factors, including:

1. The agency's minimum education requirements—agencies which require some college or an AA have a much higher percentage of officers with a BA;
2. Geography and demographics—in California, agencies located in urban areas with a high cost of living and an educated populous had more than twice as many officers with a college degree than did rural areas with a low cost of living and non-educated populous;
3. The size of the agency—larger agencies employ a higher percentage of college-educated officers than do smaller agencies;
4. Starting salary—though not a perfect relationship, the percentage of officers with a college diploma increases with starting salary (of course, starting salary is dependent on cost of living, type of county, surplus/ deficit of qualified job candidates, and many other factors), and

5. Promotion requirements—departments that require a bachelor's degree to promote to lieutenant employ a higher percentage of college-educated officers than do agencies without this requirement (Gardiner, 2015).

Policing: Blue collar or white collar?

In the early days, policing was considered a blue-collar job. Depending on where you live in the country, this may no longer be true. Today there are many college-educated police officers earning high salaries and great benefits.

In California, many entry-level police officers make more money than college professors! What do you think—white collar or blue collar? Does knowing that you could make a good living change how you feel about possibly pursuing a career as a police officer? Should officers get paid more than professors? Why? Why not?

Police Subculture

Is there a distinct police "subculture?" Are police officers somehow different than people in the general population? Do they see the world differently than the average citizen? Do they behave or interact with other members of society differently than if they were teachers, engineers, or store clerks? Many scholars think so and research supports this view.

Police subculture the accepted norms, values, attitudes, and practices shared by law enforcement offices.

The term **police subculture** refers to the accepted norms, values, attitudes, and practices that are shared by officers. William Westley was the first scholar to propose a distinct police subculture in 1970. Based on his observations of police officers in Gary (IN), he suggested that the police subculture was defined by loyalty, secrecy, and a strong desire to help others in need. Since then, many scholars have studied and elaborated on the components that comprise the police subculture. As a result, we now consider a desire for adventure and excitement, a strong sense of mission, a macho attitude, political and ideological conservatism, authoritarianism, cynicism, and bravery to be among the traits shared by officers throughout the western world (Reiner, 1992; Waddington, 2008).

Symbolic assailants an individual whose dress, behavior, and gestures indicate suspicion and possible danger to a police officer.

One of the most famous police scholars to write on this issue is Jerome Skolnick, who argued that the police subculture is shaped by three defining features of a police officer's job that are not found in the same combination in other jobs: *danger, authority*, and *efficiency*. According to Skolnick, these three occupational traits explain how officers develop a "working personality." First, recruits are taught the importance of being suspicious and developing a "sixth sense" to identify **symbolic assailants**—people who are unusual or look out of place, people who could cause harm to the officer—so that they (officers) may remain safe in a potentially dangerous job. The other defining aspect of the job, authority to enforce laws, puts officers at odds with many members of the society and exposes them to allegations of hypocrisy. According to Skolnick, officers become cynical and develop a "we vs. they" mentality because, by virtue of their job, they must be skeptical of all people, trusting no one except their fellow officers (*after* they have been vetted and passed the test). A situation made worse by a conceptualized "war on drugs" and "war on crime," which causes officers to see themselves as fighting against a specific enemy, further solidifies the cynical "us vs. them" mentality. This cynicism makes officers isolate themselves from others and increases group social solidarity, which is manifest in the police subculture. In addition to the cynicism and suspiciousness, officers feel a constant need to be efficient—to clear a call quickly so they can be available for the dispatcher and any other officer or member of the public who might need them at a moment's notice. Together, these three elements of the job push officers closer together and cause them to isolate themselves from the general public who, in their perception, "doesn't understand" the things they see and deal with every day.

While individuals who apply to become police officers are not much different than the rest of us, by the time they hit the streets in uniform they have begun to transform into the "thin blue line." Several studies have confirmed that a change in values takes place during academy training. Van Maanen (1973) and Harris (1973), for example, found that solidarity emerges during academy as recruits are taught the shared norms and values of the subculture, socialized into the depersonalized and defensive atmosphere of the job, and trained to take this interpersonal style to the streets (recall the discussion in this chapter about changes made to Washington State's academy to transform the academy atmosphere from one that produced warriors to one that now produces guardians). The change in values happens through both enculturation (learning the system) and socialization (learning the rules of the game) not only during academy and field training especially, but also throughout one's career (Ruess-Ianni & Ianni, 2008). Researchers have documented that officers become more cynical after academy as the reality of the streets hits and they start to lose friends due to shift work and the nature of their chosen career. Their cynicism continues to grow during their first several years on the job but begins to decline in their mid-career years, possibly due to promotion or salary increase and as they begin to look toward retirement (Neiderhoffer, 1967). War stories are one of the main socialization tools used by veteran officers to teach recruits and newer officers about potential sources of danger, citizen complaints, and administrative difficulties (Waddington, 2008).

It used to be thought that police culture was homogeneous and stable but that view is no longer held, as research has affirmed that police culture has indeed changed as the workforce has become increasingly diverse and found that some agencies and specialty units develop their own unique subcultures (Waddington, 2008). While the "cop's code" that gives such pieces of advice as to not trust a new guy until you're sure about him, don't make waves, be aggressive but not too eager, and don't give up another cop (Ruess-Ianni & Ianni, 2008) still exists, it does so with more nuances and less conformity. For example, researchers have found distinct police cultures in rural and urban agencies, between routine patrol officers and community police officers, police paramilitary unit officers, and detectives. Research also indicates that subculture varies between officers of different races, different sexes, and different educational levels (Waddington, 2008). Additionally, there are unique subcultures for middle managers and command staff, who arguably have different concerns than patrol officers (Ruess-Ianni & Ianni, 2008). It has been proposed that individual officers, rather than assume the entire police subculture as their own, now select the features they agree with from a pseudo-list of subculture characteristics and adopt only those elements that are congruent with their views and goals (Waddington, 2008).

The police subculture, which is sometimes viewed as negative, is functional and necessary in a job that is always unpredictable, often alienating, and sometimes dangerous (Chan, 2008). It gives meaning to officers' experiences and provides occupational self-esteem in a job that is largely invisible and autonomous (Waddington, 2008). It is also important because culture determines action and helps explain why officers support some policies and practices while ignoring or subverting other policies or innovations. How an officer sees herself (guardian or warrior; conflict negotiator or crime fighter) impacts how she approaches the job and interacts with her fellow officers and members of the community, both law-breaking and law-abiding. The warrior mentality is ingrained in the traditional police subculture and ethos which means that it may be quite difficult to shift officers who identify completely with this subculture toward a guardian, or community-oriented, philosophy. This suggests that in order to move away from a warrior/crime-fighter mentality toward a guardian mentality (or any other innovative practice that is not aligned with the traditional police subculture), police executives may need to first change the subculture. Besides orienting job performance, subculture can be a source of occupational stress for the growing number of officers who view themselves as "outside" of the subculture—an issue that will be discussed in the next section (Rose & Unnithan, 2015).

Police Stress

Occupational stress mental or emotional strain that results from circumstances that develop in or are related to a person's workplace or occupation.

There is little doubt that police officers experience occupational stress. The CareerCast.com annual jobs report usually ranks "police officer" among the top 10 stress-producing jobs in America. In addition to the typical personal stress that most individuals experience, as well as the standard organizational and administrative stressors that many working adults experience, officers are exposed to unique operational stressors by the nature of their job. But is this stress significantly greater than the level of stress experienced in most other jobs? And what effect does it have on officers and their families?

Oxford dictionary defines stress as "a state of mental or emotional strain or tension resulting from adverse or very demanding circumstances." There are five types of occupational (or workplace) stress—organizational structure/climate, interpersonal work relationships, career development, role in the organization, and factors unique to the job (Murphy, 1995).

- *Organizational structure/climate stress* results from the quasi-military, hierarchal structure of police agencies, and police work. In particular, the irregular working hours associated with shift work, having to work holidays, not having control over ones schedule (i.e., not being able to count on ending a shift on time) and inability of officers to participate in major decision-making or having influence over their general work activities contribute to officers' occupational stress.
- *Interpersonal work relationship stress* arises from problematic relationships and interactions with coworkers, administrators, or subordinates in the workplace. For example, antagonistic relationships between various work groups (such as command and line staff, separate specialty units, or officers on different shifts) but also work environments that include harassment, discrimination, bullying (from superiors or colleagues), threatened violence, rumoring, and intentional humiliation by others.
- *Career development stress* occurs when one feels "stuck" in their job. It can result from, among other things, job insecurity, being passed over for a promotion, being in a position with little potential for promotion, and lack of career development opportunities.
- *Role in the organization stress* occurs when one must perform multiple job duties due to short staffing or other issues and from role ambiguity. Employees feel particularly stressed when there are excessive work demands placed upon them or they are unclear about their job, their responsibilities, or how to satisfy their supervisor(s).
- *The factors unique to the job stress* category includes some of the job dimensions described above—unpredictability, the potential for danger, having to use force, perceived lack of support, the routinely negative interactions with the public, mediating other people's disputes, and needing to show courage in dangerous situations and to always be observant and attentive to evolving situations. It also includes the stress that results from the unique demands and constraints of the criminal justice system and its various actors.

Which factors cause officers the most stress? It turns out that it is a difficult question to answer. New York officers ranked killing someone in the line of duty, experiencing the death of a fellow officer, and being physically attacked at the top of their list of police stressors (Violanti & Aron, 1995) (see Table 5.5). Officers in Illinois, however, identified organizational factors (including interpersonal work relationships) as the most stress-inducing and concerns over occupational danger less stress-inducing

Many different circumstances in the job cause stress for police officers.

TABLE 5.5 HIGHEST RANKED POLICE STRESSORS

Stressor	Mean Score	Stressor	Mean Score
Killing someone in the line of duty	79.4	Insufficient personnel	58.5
Fellow officer killed	76.7	Aggressive crowds	56.7
Physical attack	71.0	Felony in progress	55.3
Battered child	69.2	Excessive discipline	53.3
High speed chases	63.7	Plea bargaining	52.8
Shift work	61.2	Death notifications	52.6
Use of force	61.0	Inadequate support (Supervisor)	52.4
Inadequate department support	61.0	Inadequate equipment	52.4
Incompatible partner	60.4	Family disputes	52.0
Accident in patrol car	59.9	Negative press coverage	51.9
		Overall mean score of 60 stressors	44.8

Adapted from Violanti, J. & Aron, F. (1995). Police stressors: Variations in percent among police personnel. Journal of Criminal Justice, 23(3), 287-294.

(Crank & Caldero, 1991). Other studies have similarly found that officers report that organizational factors are more aggravating than job/task-related stressors (Buker & Wiecko, 2007; Gershon et al., 2009; Morash et al., 2006; Shane, 2010).

Why do these, and other, studies report divergent findings? One reason is different samples. The New York officers in Violanti and Aron's study worked for a large police department, and large departments are often located in urban cities with higher-than-average violent crime rates and higher perceived dangerousness. The Illinois officers, on the other hand, all worked for medium-sized departments which may have been perceived as less dangerous. Timing is another factor to consider—gang violence was near its height in the early 1990s when Violanti and Aron conducted their research and may have influenced their findings.

Another main reason the findings from multiple studies may differ is research methods—how a study is conducted. Most studies on police stress use a self-report survey approach that asks officers to rank order a variety of possible stressors according to the degree of stress the officer thinks each causes. There is very little direct measurement of stress in real-world settings (Hickman et al., 2011). This is important because stress induces psychological and physiological responses in the body. Acute stress, for example, activates the body's fight-or-flight response which triggers a complex set of physiological responses, including increased heart rate, elevated blood pressure, increased blood flow to the muscles, increased production of glucose, and elevated cortisol levels. Some of the physiological responses that indicate the body is under stress, especially those that continue for a prolonged period after the "danger" has subsided or those can be caused by other factors (such as headache, fatigue, inability to concentrate, muscle aches, etc.), go undetected by or are dismissed by the officer as not stress-related. Chronic stress can have some of the same effects on the body and is even more likely to go undetected or ignored. Thus, an officer's actual stress triggers may differ from her perceived stress triggers.

To date, it appears that only one study has used heart rate monitoring to directly and systematically measure police stress during a regular work shift. Anderson and colleagues (2002) studied 76 Canadian officers from 12 municipal police departments during their 12-hour shifts. They found that officers' heart rates were higher during their shift than before or after their shift. They further found that officers' average "above-resting" heart rates were highest at the beginning of their shift and lowest at the end of their shift (validating the idea that police work, in and of itself is stressful). Additionally, above-resting heart rates were highest when officers were wrestling with or handcuffing a suspect and elevated when an officer placed a hand on his gun, responded to a call to back up another officer, or drove "code 3" to an emergency call. Moreover, the researchers found that although officers' heart rates dropped after "critical incidents," their heart rates continued to be elevated for 30–60 minutes after the incident which indicates that officers remained in a hyper-vigilant mode long after the immediate threat subsided.

Hickman et al. (2011) expanded on this study by adding a GPS component to the real-time measurement of officer heart rates. One of the goals of the study was to be able to place the measurement of police stress in a space-time context so they could understand both when and where officers were likely to experience stress. Using monitoring units that simultaneously record heart rate as well as latitude and longitude enabled mapping of the stress data, and on a theoretical level, it would be possible to generate valid "hot-spot" style maps, although such maps would depict average officer heart rates (in density terms) instead of crimes. Figure 5.6 shows the heart rate trace of a test officer during his shift. The major "peak" in the chart corresponds to a particularly stressful incident. The initial call was for a "hit-and-run" by a pick-up truck that had hit several vehicles and stop signs. The test officer located the vehicle and pursued, but the driver did not respond to lights and siren. After some distance, the driver finally stopped his vehicle by means of hitting a curb. The test officer issued repeated commands over the PA system to the driver to turn off the ignition and throw his keys on to the pavement. The driver was non-responsive. The test participant exited the cruiser and drew and pointed his service weapon at the suspect vehicle's driver compartment; at this point, his heart rate peaked at 165 bpm as depicted in the trace. The test

FIGURE 5.6 HEART RATE RECORDING OF TEST OFFICER

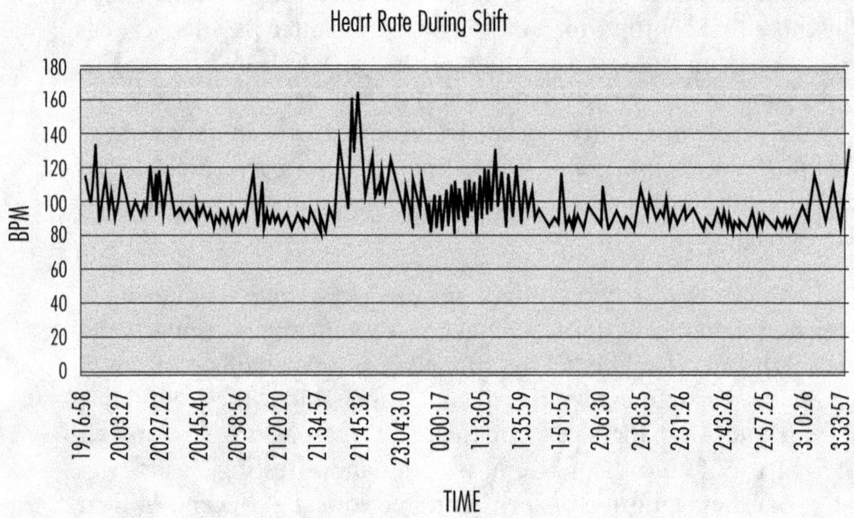

Adapted from Hickman, M., Fricas, J., Strom, K., & Pope, M. (2011). Mapping police stress. Police Quarterly, 14(3), 227–250.

officer advanced on the driver's vehicle, repeatedly issuing commands to the driver to put his hands out of the window. When the test officer arrived at the driver's window, he issued a command to unlock and open the door. The driver was again nonresponsive. Finally, the test officer opened the door and assisted the driver out of the vehicle, at which point the driver—obviously intoxicated—simply collapsed onto the ground. The test officer then rolled the driver onto his stomach and handcuffed him.

Figure 5.7 shows the mapped heart rate data from the officer's shift. As noted, the ellipse drawn within the map identifies the conclusion of this hit/run call that evolved into a DUI arrest at gunpoint. As the officer chased the vehicle through the city and began to realize that he was dealing with a non-compliant, potentially intoxicated and dangerous subject, his heart rate steadily increases. After the vehicle was stopped and several opportunities for compliance were offered, the officer's heart rate maximized at the exact moment that he decided it was necessary to draw his sidearm and began advancing on the vehicle. This is depicted in the map by the largest graduated point marker to the right side of the ellipse. Other notable incidents from the officer's shift included a call to assist a repo-man confronted by an angry car owner wielding a baseball bat (due East of the DUI incident described above), and a call reporting screaming and a possible knife within a Seattle Housing Authority apartment building (Northwest of the DUI incident).

FIGURE 5.7 MAP OF POINT DATA COLLECTED VIA GPS-ENABLED HEART RATE MONITOR

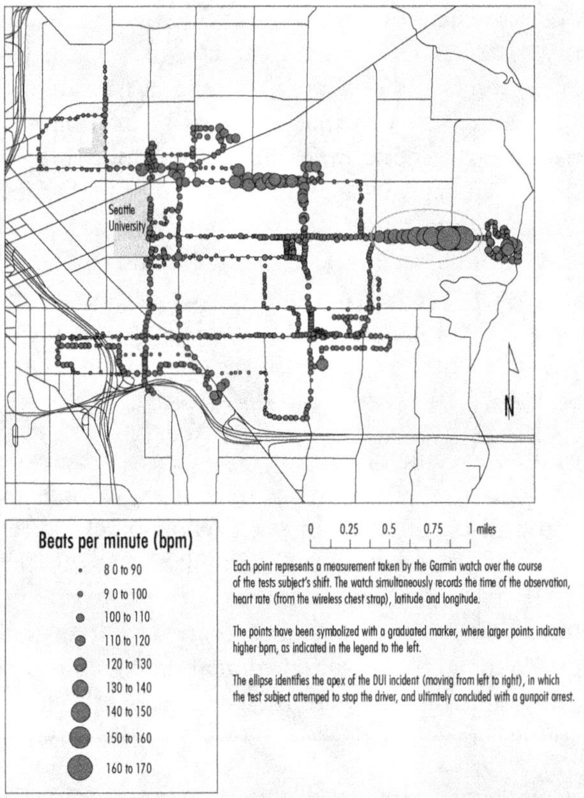

Adapted from Hickman, M., Fricas, J., Strom, K., & Pope, M. (2011). Mapping police stress. Police Quarterly, 14(3), 227–250.

Stress mapping on a more systematic basis may enable hot-spot style analyses that could inform beat/district modification, with an eye toward balancing stress, and could assist departments in thinking about how officers are deployed in order to minimize repeated exposure to highly stressful situations. It could also inform stress inoculation training (SIT). Much like the inoculations delivered in the medical field to prevent the onset of more serious forms of disease, the idea here is that by exposing an individual to mild forms of stress you can improve their ability to cope with more severe forms of stress (e.g., Meichenbaum & Novaco, 1978; Novaco, 1977). Police training is designed to some extent with this process in mind; simulated stressful conditions are a common part of academy training that prepares recruits for real-world stressful condition (often referred to as "survival stress" training), particularly with regard to use of force (Hickman, 2005; Reaves, 2009). SIT models view stress as the product of the interaction between individual and environment; as such, knowledge of the micro-geography of police stress may assist with the design of survival stress training for individual police departments (as well as individual SIT treatments delivered by clinicians).

Do female officers experience stress differently than male officers? Yes and no. Whereas earlier studies showed distinct differences between male and female officers, recent studies show more similarities than differences. In general, the literature suggests that women and men have different views on what constitutes stress and different methods for coping with the stress (He et al., 2015). Women police officers encounter higher levels of harassment and overt hostility than male officers and this has led to higher levels of workplace stress (Kurtz, 2012). Research has also found that the higher stress levels reported by female officers are often caused, not by work-related experiences, but rather by family and marital issues; specifically the "second shift" of household chores and family responsibilities that await women (more so than men) after their official shift (Kurtz, 2012).

Are there any differences in how officers of different races experience stress? Research found that Latino and Black officers experience greater levels of polarization and discrimination by their fellow officers and fewer opportunities at work which can translate to higher stress levels (Stroshine & Brandl, 2011). There is also evidence that African American males report fewer symptoms of anxiety, stress, and depression than their white male counterparts and that African American male and female officers use more constructive coping strategies than their white counterparts (He, Zhao, & Ren, 2005).

This stress impacts both the officer and the officer's family. Some research has found that officers frequently employ negative coping mechanisms (such as drinking, smoking, and social isolation) and have higher rates of alcoholism, drug addiction, suicide, and health-related problems than the general public. But not all research studies concur, there is a lot of variation and some studies have found lower than average rates of these problems. One study of more than 4000 officers found that, although officers did not drink alcohol more often than the average adult, they did binge drink more frequently (Davey, Obst, & Sheehan, 2000). Further, 30% of the officers drinking behavior placed them in the "at-risk" for harmful alcohol consumption category and another 3% were classified as "alcohol dependent" based on their reported behavior. Surprisingly, 25% of these officers admitted to drinking alcohol while on-duty. Although research studies vary as to the amount, there is consensus that police officers commit suicide at elevated rates when compared to the general public and other government workers (Violanti, 2007); however, some of the precipitating factors (depression, alcoholism, divorce/separation, suffering a negative life event) are similar to the general public. Finally, current research on health-related issues suggests that it is officers' unhealthy lifestyles and diets that lead to health problems, not necessarily their occupational stress (Richmond et al., 1998). Despite the many occupational factors that place strain on officers' marriages and family life, research indicates that divorce rates among officers are similar to, and often lower than, the general population (McCoy & Aamodt, 2010).

Conclusion

In this chapter, we discussed the importance of hiring the right people to become police officers. Individuals who are service-oriented and compassionate guardians who recognize how their actions and responses affect not only citizens' willingness to follow established laws and provide assistance to law enforcement, but also affect the legitimacy of their department as well as their profession. We also examined how the academy format can impact which individuals graduate and how those graduates exercise discretion and perform their job in the field. While representation of women and minorities in policing is growing, neither of these groups is fully represented in policing as yet. There has also been major growth in the proportion of college-educated officers and this has had an effect on how we view policing as a profession and how officers see and experience the police subculture. Finally, we explored some of the realities of policing in the form of police occupational stress.

Review Questions

1. What types of occupational stress do police officer experience and which categories do officers identify as most problematic?
2. What are some of the benefits of a college education for police officers?
3. How does the reality of policing differ from the myth of policing?

References

Boyd, L. (2010). Light blue v. dark blue: Attitudinal differences in quality of life policing. *Journal of Ethnicity in Criminal Justice, 8*(1), 37–48.

Burch, A. (2012, December). *Sheriffs' Departments, 2007—Statistical Tables,* #NCJ 238558, Washington, DC: Bureau of Justice Statistics.

Burriesci, J. J., & Melley, M. (2001, January 19). *OLS research report: State Police educational qualifications and incentives.* Connecticut General Assembly, 2001-R-0092. Retrieved from http://www.cga.ct.gov/2001/rpt/2001-R-0092.htm

Carlan, P. E., & Lewis, J. A. (2009). Dissecting police professionalism: A comparison of predictors within five professionalism subsets. *Police Quarterly, 12*(4), 370–387. doi: 10.1177/1098611109348469

Carter, D. L., & Sapp, A. D. (1989). The effect of higher education on police liability: Implications for police personnel policy. *American Journal of Police, 8*, 153–166.

Carter, D. L., & Sapp, A. D. (1990). The evolution of higher education in law enforcement: Preliminary findings from a national study. *Journal of Criminal Justice Education, 1,* 59–85.

Cascio, W. F. (1977). Formal education and police officer performance. *Journal of Police Science and Administration*, *5*, 89–96.

Chan, J. (2008). Changing police culture. In T. Newburn (Ed.), *Policing: Key readings*. Portland, OR: Willan.

Chapman, C. (2012). Use of force in minority communities is related to police education, age, experience, and ethnicity. *Police Practice and Research, 13*(5), 421–436. doi: 10.1080/15614263.2011.596711

Cohen, B., & Chaiken, J. M. (1972). *Police background characteristics and performance.*
New York, NY: Rand Institute.

Davey, J., Obst, P., & Sheehan, M. (2000). Developing a profile of alcohol consumption patterns of police officers in a large scale sample of an Australian Police Service. *European Addiction Studies, 6*, 205–212.

Fyfe, J. (1988). Police use of deadly force: Research and reform. *Justice Quarterly, 5*(2), 15–205.

Gardiner, C. (2015). College Cops: A study of education and policing in California. *Policing: An International Journal of Policing Strategies and Management*, *38*(4), 1–17.

Gustafson, J. (2013). Diversity in municipal police agencies: A national examination of minority hiring and promotion. *Policing: An International Journal of Policing Strategies and Management*, *36*(4), 719–736.

Harris, R. (1973). *The police academy: An inside view.* New York, NY: Wiley.

He, N., Zhao, J., & Ren, L. (2005). Do race and gender matter in police stress? A preliminary assessment of the interactive effects. *Journal of Criminal Justice, 6*, 535–547.

Hilal, S., & Densley, J. (2013). Higher education and local law enforcement. *FBI Law Enforcement Bulletin*, *82*(5), 1–3.

Kappeler, V. E., Sapp, A. D., & Carter, D. L. (1992). Police officer higher education, citizen complaints and departmental rule violations. *American Journal of Police*, *11*(2), 37–54.

Krimmel, J. T. (1996). The performance of college-educated police: A study of self-rated police performance measures. *American Journal of Police*, *15*(1), 85–96.

Kurtz, D. (2012). Roll call and the second shift: The influences of gender and family on police stress. *Police Practice and Research, 13*(1), 71–86.

Lersch, K. M. (1998). Exploring gender differences in citizen allegations of misconduct: An analysis of a municipal police department. *Women and Criminal Justice, 4*, 69–79.

Lersch, K. M., & Kunzman, L. L. (2001). Misconduct allegations and higher education in a southern sheriff's department. *American Journal of Criminal Justice*, *25*(2), 161–172.

Manis, J., Archbold, C. A., & Hassell, K. D. (2008). Exploring the impact of police officer education level on allegations of police misconduct. *International*

Journal of Police Science and Management, 10(4), 509–523. doi: 10.1350/ijps.2008.10.4.102

McCoy, S., & Aamodt, M. (2010). A comparison of law enforcement divorce rates with those of other occupations. *Journal of Police and Criminal Psychology, 25*, 1–16.

Morash, M., & Greene, J. (1986). Evaluating women on patrol: A critique of contemporary wisdom. *Evaluation Review, 10*, 230–255.

National Center for Women and Policing. (2002, April). *Men, women, and police excessive force: A tale of two genders, a content analysis of civil liability cases, sustained allegations and citizen complaints*. Retrieved from http://womenandpolicing.org/PDF/2002_Excessive_Force.pdf

Paoline, E. A., III, Terrill, W., & Rossier, M. T. (2015). Higher education, college degree major, and police occupational attitudes. *Journal of Criminal Justice Education, 26*(1), 49–73. doi: 10.1080/10511253.2014.923010

President's Commission on Law Enforcement and Administration of Justice. (1967). *The challenge of crime in a free society*. Washington, DC: Government Printing Office.

Rabe-Hemp, C., & Schuck, A. (2007). Violence against police officers: Are female officers at greater risk? *Police Quarterly, 4*, 411–428.

Reaves, B. (2015, May). *Local Police Departments, 2013: Personnel, policies, and practices*. Washington, DC: Bureau of Justice Statistics, Government Printing Office.

Reaves, B. (2010, December). *Local Police Departments, 2007.* Washington, DC: Bureau of Justice Statistics, Government Printing Office.

Reuss-Ianni, E., & Ianni, F. (2008). Street cops and management cops: The two cultures of policing. In T. Newburn (Ed.), *Policing: Key readings*. Portland, OR: Willan.

Richmond, R., Wodak, A., Kehoe, L., & Heather, N. (1998). How healthy are the police? A survey of life-style factors. *Addiction, 93*, 1729–1737.

Roberg, R., & Bonn, S. (2004). Higher education and policing: where are we now? *Policing: An International Journal of Police Strategies & Management*, 27(4), 469–486.

Rydberg, J., & Terrill, W. (2010). The effect of higher education on police behavior. *Police Quarterly, 13*. doi: 10.1177/1098611109357325

Schuck, A. M. (2014). Female representation in law enforcement: The influence of screening, unions, incentives, community policing, CALEA, and size. *Police Quarterly, 17*(1), 54–78. doi: 0.1177/1098611114522467

Schuck, A., & Rabe-Hemp, C. (2005). Women police: The use of force by and against female officers. *Women and Criminal Justice, 4*, 91–117.

Sharp, E. (2014). Minority representation and order maintenance policing: Toward a contingent view. *Social Science Quarterly, 95*(4), 1155–1171.

Sherman, L. W., and The National Advisory Commission on Higher Education for Police Officers. (1978). *The quality of police education: A critical review with recommendations for improving programs in higher education*. San Francisco, CA: Jossey-Bass.

Stalans, L., & Finn, M. (2000). Gender differences in officers' perceptions and decisions about domestic violence cases. *Women and Criminal Justice, 3*, 1–24

Trojanowicz, R. C., & Nicholson, T. (1976). A comparison of behavioral styles of college graduate police officers v. non-college-going police officers. *The Police Chief, 43*, 57–58.

U.S. Census Bureau. (1988). Years of school completed by persons 25 years old and over, by age and sex: Selected years 1940 to 1989. Retrieved from http://www.census.gov/

U.S. Census Bureau. (2006). A half-century of learning: Historical census statistics on educational attainment in the United States, 1940 to 2000: Detailed Tables. Retrieved from http://www.census.gov/

U.S. Census Bureau. (2012). Education attainment in the United States, 2012. Retrieved from http://www.census.gov/

Van Maanen, J. (1973). Observations on the making of policemen. *Human Organizations,* 32, 407–418.

Violanti, J. (2007). *Police Suicide: Epidemic in Blue 2nd edition.* Springfield, IL: Charles C. Thomas.

Waddington, P. A. J. (2008). Police (canteen) sub-culture: An appreciation. In T. Newburn (Ed.), *Policing: Key readings.* Portland, OR: Willan.

Westley, W. (1970). *Violence and the police.* Cambridge, MA: MIT Press (originally a Ph.D. dissertation: University of Chicago).

Whetstone, T. S. (2000). Getting stripes: Educational achievement and study strategy used by sergeant promotional candidates. *American Journal of Criminal Justice, 24*, 247–257.

Wilson, H. (1999). Post-secondary education of the police officer and its effect on the frequency of citizen complaints. *The Journal of California Law Enforcement, 33*, 3–10.

Worden, J. E. (1990). A badge and a baccalaureate: Policies, hypotheses, and further evidence. *Justice Quarterly*, 7, 565–592.

© Billion Photos/Shutterstock.com

CHAPTER 6

The Court System in the United States

KEY TERMS

Appellate brief
Bail
Complaint
Court of last resort
Custodial interrogation
Discovery
Due process
En banc
Fruit of the poisonous tree
Grand jury
Indictment
Initial appearance
Intermediate appellate court
Judicial review
Jurisdiction
Nolo contendere
Plain view
Plea
Probable cause
Reasonable doubt
Recusal
Remand
Speedy Trial Act
Suppression hearing
Trial court
Verdict
Warrant
Writ of certiorari

CHAPTER OBJECTIVES

1 Identify the critical steps in the historical development of state and federal court systems in the United States.

2 Distinguish between the structures of the modern-day state and federal court systems in the United States.

3 Identify the procedural protections the modern U.S. court system provides to criminal defendants.

4 Evaluate the adequacy of court procedures provided to criminal defendants.

5 Examine the importance of juries in the courtroom.

6 Describe the actual structure of a courtroom.

7 Identify the various participants (courtroom workgroup) in a courtroom.

8 Discuss the roles of each of the participants.

9 Evaluate how each role is connected and vital to the others.

Clarence Gideon's 1961 appeal to the U.S. Supreme Court lead the court to rule persons charged in all state cases must have counsel representation.

Case Study: Right to Counsel: Gideon v. Wainwright

In 1961, Florida resident Clarence Earl Gideon was accused of breaking and entering into a pool hall with the intention to commit burglary—a combination of offenses that led to felony charges. At his initial court appearance, Gideon requested that the court appoint an attorney to represent him, as he could not afford to hire one. The judge denied the request, saying that the law in Florida at the time provided appointed attorneys only in capital cases. Gideon was forced to represent himself and conduct his own defense. The jury found him guilty, and he was sentenced to five years in prison.

Gideon made effective use of his time in prison. Using the resources available to him in the prison library, he handwrote an appeal to the U.S. Supreme Court and filed a lawsuit against Louie Wainwright, the Secretary of the Florida Department of Corrections. Gideon argued that, as provided by the Sixth Amendment (as applied to the states in the 14th Amendment), the U.S. Supreme Court guaranteed him the right to be represented by counsel, and, therefore, his rights had been violated by the judge's rule to deny him an attorney. Abe Fortas, a well-known attorney from Washington, D.C., was appointed by the U.S. Supreme Court to represent Gideon on the appeal.

The court handed down its unanimous ruling on March 18, 1963: the denial of Gideon's request for appointed counsel did indeed violate his Sixth Amendment right to counsel. The court specified that by requiring Gideon, who was not an attorney, to defend himself, the judicial system had deprived him of his right to due process, as provided for in the Eighth Amendment. Further, the court ruled that the U.S. Constitution does not specify whether a criminal case must be capital or non-capital for the accused to have the right to be represented by counsel; therefore, qualified legal representation must be provided in all cases.[1]

Gideon's appeal was affirmed, and the case was returned to the Florida Supreme Court, who, in turn, returned the case to the trial court. Gideon was retried on the original charges with a court-appointed attorney and found not guilty.

The impact of *Gideon v. Wainwright* was far-reaching. In Florida alone, several thousand inmates who had been convicted in a like manner were set free after the ruling. The decision also led to the creation and continued development of the public defender system in the United States. The ruling ensured that not only must indigent defendants be afforded legal counsel, but those court-appointed attorneys must be effectively trained in defense to provide their clients with as fair a trial as possible. The case also inspired a book, *Gideon's Trumpet*, published in 1965, which detailed Clarence Earl Gideon's fight for fair representation. The Gideon decision was an important ruling that clarified the rights of criminal defendants as outlined in the U.S. Constitution.[2]

To learn more about *Gideon v. Wainwright:* https://www.youtube.com/watch?v=nrcTqx3t8Gg

Case Study: Presumption of Innocence?

The credibility of North Carolina's criminal justice system was called into question recently by a disturbing revelation. After conducting an audit, the attorney general of the state concluded that the state's Bureau of Investigation had distorted or withheld evidence in the cases of more than 200 potentially innocent men and women.[3] The attorney general's audit uncovered memos indicating that crime lab analysts were trained to help prosecutors; it also indicated that the wrongfully suppressed evidence might have helped absolve certain defendants.[4] Many criminal defendants may have been wrongfully convicted because of the lab's failure to overturn potentially exculpatory evidence.

For a variety of reasons, courts sometimes fail to fulfill one of their primary responsibilities: to safeguard accused individuals from the abuses of overzealous policing and prosecution. Unfortunately, these unprofessional tactics are unlikely to stop unless the courts penalize them—even if it means, in extreme cases, occasionally letting an apparently guilty defendant go free due to these abuses. When courts take these measures, of course, the media and public are unlikely to understand the rationale that can possibly justify them.

Is our court system more error-prone than we can imagine? Perhaps so, and this underscores the continuing need for the procedural and constitutional safeguards that are the hallmark of due process under law. This propensity for error also suggests a much more unsettling problem: that there may be many more innocent people in American prisons than we have long thought. Most people are familiar in some way with the use of DNA evidence to clear persons who were convicted before the technology existed to identify DNA from crime scenes. Several common causes of wrongful conviction include eyewitness misidentification, improper forensics, false or coerced confessions, or informants who provide false testimony.[5]

In the North Carolina cases, the court system failed, for several reasons, to detect professional misconduct by prosecutors and crime labs that led to ill-gotten convictions. Now, the courts will have to fix this, and to revisit many prosecutions that should have concluded long ago. In North Carolina, these errors span many years and include more than 15,000 cases. Why did the court system not detect these problems sooner? At what point does the desire to rapidly convict and punish defendants overwhelm legal safeguards and yield tragic results, falsely incarcerating (or, worse, executing) an innocent person?

Background History of the U.S. Court System

First and foremost, a court is an official venue for resolving disputes. Every day, courts resolve countless conflicts in criminal and civil matters. Under the principle of government known as *federalism*, created in the United States Constitution, the federal government and individual state governments share power. Similarly, the American judicial system exists in two separate but related systems: state and federal, each with its own courts, structure, and functions.[6]

As we discuss the American court system, we must first understand that there is no single, unified apparatus that controls the judiciary at every level. To many people, this is a surprising fact. In fact, there are more than 15,000 courts in the United States, covering a broad spectrum of functions and geographic jurisdictions. Rather than a uniform system, the American judiciary is better understood as 50 individual state court systems and one separate, national system that is part of the federal government.[7]

There are four principal sources of law in the United States: constitutions, statutes, administrative regulations, and common law, also known as case law.[8] Constitutional law is based on a formally adopted document, or constitution, that defines the broad powers of the government. In the

United States, the supreme law of the land is the U.S. Constitution, which defines the powers held by the federal government, establishes the branches of government, and reserves individual rights to all people who are under the jurisdiction of the United States. Each state also has its own constitution, from which its constitutional law is derived. Statutes are ordinances passed by Congress, state legislatures, and governing bodies at the federal, state, or local level. Administrative regulations, in turn, are rules issued by administrative bodies to exercise and interpret the powers given to them by statutes.[9]

Common law is the oldest source of law in the American legal system. The term *common law* refers to the legal rules formed by the accumulated decisions issued by judges in court cases. The American judicial system traces its roots to its colonial heritage and the legacy of English common law. In England, these decisions were made by judges who traveled across the country and rendered decisions based on rules and social norms common to each area. Common law is unique because it is largely shaped by judges, and not simply by applying statutes passed by a legislature.[10] Colonists carried English common law to the New World and incorporated it into the legal structures of colonial governments.

Colonists carried English common law to the New World and incorporated it into the legal structures of colonial governments.

Significantly, common law also forms precedent, which means it can bind future judges to issue similar rulings in future disputes involving similar facts.[11] This essentially establishes a set of procedures designed to ensure fairness. These procedures are known as *due process*, which essentially means "fair play" in legal contexts.[12] The operating principle of due process is that it is unjust to treat similar facts and actions in a different way on different occasions.[13]

State Courts

For the most part, colonial courts adhered to the model they inherited from England, though there were some regional differences.[14] Influences such as religion and geography also led to variations in the structure of colonial courts. No attempt was made to unify the colonial courts until after the American Revolution.[15] Most colonies (and, subsequently, the U.S. states they became), of course, were directly influenced by the common law tradition. A notable exception is Louisiana, which today retains an integrated civil law system based on its French and Spanish traditions.[16]

The common law also led to other hallmarks of the American judicial system. In the minds of British subjects, common law came to represent an unassailable natural law that was higher than the laws of men. This view was reinforced by the English Parliament's use of common law to limit the unchecked power of the monarch. Eventually, this use resulted in the passage of significant provisions in English law, including the Bill of Rights, the right of habeas corpus, and the Petition of Right.[17] Each device would find its way into the American judicial system.

The English Bill of Rights in particular would influence American perceptions of justice and democracy. The 1689 Act of Parliament, which established the Bill of Rights in England, contained specific guarantees that later appeared in the U.S. Constitution. The Bill of Rights protected British subjects against excessive bails and fines and cruel and unusual punishment. It also provided jury trials for the accused, and later yielded protections for free speech and parliamentary debate.[18] These protections were incorporated into American state courts, and subsequently into the U.S. Constitution.

Colonial Judiciary

Before the U.S. Constitution formally established a separation of powers among the three branches of government, judicial power in each colony was vested primarily in the hands of a royal governor. Before the Constitution was ratified, the various state courts existed as colonial judiciaries. By the time of the American Revolution, the colonial judicial system had existed in the same form since the 1720s.[19]

Typically, a justice of the peace, appointed by the royal governor, formed the lowest level of the judiciary. Above him were county courts that adjudicated low-level civil cases and non-capital criminal offenses. The highest-level cases were heard under the jurisdiction of the governor; in some states, the governor appointed a council of judges, while in others, he presided over such a council as a court of appeals.[20] These courts of appeals served as central courts for major offenses, but often traveled only once or twice a year on circuits around the colony.[21] Colonial judiciaries were far more informal than their counterparts in England. Justices of the peace kept few, if any, records. In addition, wealthy members of the community often posted a surety (financial guarantee by one party to assume the debt of another), which would be forfeited if the accused committed another crime.[22]

Colonial courts did not exercise a great deal of power in the colonies. The appeal process from their decisions went to authorities in England, not to the colonial government. Of course, colonial authorities required any laws passed by assemblies or legislatures to accord with English common law. If they did not, they could be overturned by the Privy Council in England, which also could reverse the decisions of colonial judges.[23] Royal governors, the representatives of English control, had the authority to remove judges at their leisure. Additionally, colonial judiciaries were typically less professional and experienced than those in England. Indeed, there were fewer legal experts in the colonies, and judges were often merchants, planters, or wealthy landowners.[24]

Tension between the Judiciary and Legislatures

Tension began to grow between colonial legislatures and the judicial system controlled by a royal governor—and, by extension, the British Crown. During the colonial period, legislative assemblies in the colonies increasingly asserted themselves as law-making bodies. At the same time, the British government in London began to take a much more active and invasive role in colonial affairs.[25] This was because Britain believed the colonies existed only to provide the home country with resources and wealth, and that the colonists did not enjoy the same rights as British subjects at home.

Royal governors, as proxies of the British crown, performed the functions of the executive, legislative, and judicial branches of government.[26] With every ruling that was handed down by courts, colonists believed the British government was infringing on their rights. Not surprisingly, this untenable arrangement led to the relatively weak functioning of the executive and judicial branches under the first national colonial government. Because the executive and judicial branches were so weak, the legislative branch gained increasing power.

Before and immediately after the American Revolution, legislatures were the strongest branch of American government, dominating both the judicial and executive branches. Legislatures had the power to elect and pay judges, and to overrule their decisions or even impeach them. Legislatures could even amend state constitutions without interference from the courts.[27] Adding to the tension was the fact that legislatures and courts had different economic interests in early America. Members of local legislatures, on one hand, were usually interested in protecting the interests of debtors, especially small farmers. Courts, on the other hand, tended to side with the creditors who filed suit against debtors.[28]

Formalization of State Court Systems

Conflict existed not only between the legislature and the judiciary, but also between different levels of the court system. As formalized state court systems developed after the American Revolution, a primary source of tension was the division of power between local and national judicial bodies.

Initially, the federal court system was structured to correspond to state lines. This structure was intended to ensure that federal judges would represent the federal court in their home states, with minimal interference from the federal government.[29] This design was a direct response to the inherent distrust of judicial authority that early American leaders retained from their experiences under British rule. They still saw the judiciary as an arbitrary, coercive, powerful system that interfered with their inalienable rights. Federalists created a basic framework for federal courts that would enforce national law.[30]

Overlap of Civil and Criminal Courts

A second influence on the formalization of the court system was the development of a civil court structure. In the early phases of the American judiciary, the court system was informal enough to allow a great deal of overlap between civil and criminal cases. Justices of the peace met at county courts to hear civil disputes—disputes over contracts, personal injuries, or property—while still holding hearings on petty criminal acts.[31] This overlap of civil and criminal courts continued until the ratification of the U.S. Constitution.

Federal Courts

Initially, the framers of the U.S. Constitution were ambivalent about the need for federal courts and the amount of power they should grant to the courts. This ambivalence is reflected in Article III of the Constitution, which provides for a single supreme court and gives Congress broad powers to establish lower courts at its discretion.[32] Notably, it provides no further detail on the structure of the courts. However, the experience of the relatively weak judiciary underscored the need for a strong, independent federal judiciary, and the founders became concerned with the rights of individual citizens in relation to the government.

Articles of Confederation

In the immediate aftermath of the Revolutionary War, the leaders of the new nation were highly suspicious of strong, centralized executive power as a result of their experiences with the British government. In their writings and actions, they demonstrated an obvious preference for legislative power over executive power.[33]

The first federal courts were created, at least in one sense, by the Articles of Confederation, which were adopted in 1778 and ratified in 1781, as the first constitution of the United States of America. The articles did not create a national judiciary. Congress held almost all power, and there was no true executive or judicial branch. Congress did have the authority to create *ad hoc courts that would settle disputes between states, as well as cases involving events on international waters.*[34] However, the seeds of stronger judicial power were present. During the 1780s, state judiciaries were able to declare several state statutes unconstitutional, presaging a later debate over the extent of judicial authority in American government.[35] This debate would reach a climax with the Supreme Court case of *Marbury v. Madison (1803), which established the doctrine of judicial review.*

U.S. Constitution

For a variety of reasons, the weak and ineffective national government created by the Articles of Confederation lasted only a few years before being replaced. The U.S. Constitution (1787) formally established the federal judiciary as it exists today. Many founders agreed that an independent judiciary was needed to counterbalance potential abuses by the legislative and executive branches. Additionally, they saw a strong judiciary as the most effective way to defend the individual rights guaranteed by the Constitution. The Anti-Federalists (later known as the Jeffersonian-Republicans), who still opposed strong national government, favored a network of self-governing state and local courts instead of a strong, federal "supreme" court that would interpret the Constitution.[36] The Federalists, who advocated strong national government, were successful in arguing that the legislature was the branch most dangerous to the personal freedoms secured by the Constitution. They believed that Congress had been granted a disproportionate amount of power.

The U.S. Constitution instituted the federal judicial system that is in practice today.

The Constitution gave courts the power to prevent the legislature, at both the state and federal levels, from passing bills of attainder (acts of the legislature declaring a person guilty of a crime without a trial) and *ex post facto laws*. In addition, it guaranteed citizens the right to trial by jury, and prohibited the suspension of the right of habeas corpus (the right not to be illegally detained), except in wartime.[37] These basic civil rights and others, collectively known as the "Bill of Rights," compose the first 10 amendments to the Constitution.

The U.S. Constitution also underscored the importance of judicial independence by articulating a clear doctrine of separation of powers. In the English system of government, even today, the legislature retains ultimate authority. American colonists, even before the revolution, began to sharply define the difference between what is considered "legal" and what is considered "constitutional." The British system, by contrast, sees the two concepts as inextricably linked. Americans asserted that the rights and principles outlined by the Constitution take priority over any hasty decisions made by the legislature or the executive.[38]

A crucially important feature of the U.S. Constitution, as compared to the Articles of the Confederation, is the establishment of an independent judiciary. The Constitution is, first and foremost, a "contract" between the people and the government. In the American system, the judiciary is granted the authority and responsibility to guard the freedoms guaranteed by that contract. This authority and responsibility leads directly to the doctrine of judicial review.

The U.S. Constitution authorized two types of federal courts: legislative and constitutional. Legislative courts were established by Congress under

Article I of the Constitution, and serve functions that are both legislative and judicial. They typically have a narrowly defined role and administer a specific statute, such as bankruptcy law. Legislative courts include the Tax Court, the U.S. Court of Appeals for Veterans Claims, the U.S. Court of Appeals for the Armed Forces, and the U.S. Court of Federal Claims. Constitutional courts include the U.S. Supreme Court, circuit courts of appeals, and district courts.

The Road to Judicial Review

The doctrine of judicial review has become the most powerful tool for the judiciary to take an active role in government. The U.S. Constitution tasked federal courts with upholding and supporting the Constitution.[39] Article III provides that "the judicial power of the United States, shall be vested in one supreme Court, and in such inferior Courts as the Congress may from time to time ordain and establish."[40] The scope of those powers was not clearly or comprehensively described in the Constitution itself, but judicial review has become an established—if somewhat controversial—power of the judiciary.

Judicial review The power of the federal judiciary to overturn any legislation or other governmental action ruled inconsistent with the Constitution, Bill of Rights, or federal law.

In the words of David O'Brien, **judicial review** is "the power of the Supreme Court and the federal judiciary to consider and overturn any congressional and state legislation or other official governmental action deemed inconsistent with the Constitution, Bill of Rights, or federal law."[41] This idea was not without controversy. The Jeffersonian-Republicans, the party of Thomas Jefferson, felt the court's power should be limited in regard to the legislature, while the Federalists, the party of John Adams, favored a stronger judiciary.

Since the Constitution did not describe a specific structure for the federal judiciary other than the U.S. Supreme Court, Congress used its authority to establish lower courts by enacting the Judiciary Act of 1789. One clause of that act gave the Supreme Court the power to issue writs of mandamus, which are orders from a higher court compelling a lower court or government officer to perform a specified duty.[42] The act also enabled citizens sued by citizens of another state to transfer the lawsuit to federal circuit court and granted the Supreme Court authority to review the decisions of state courts on appeal.[43]

Nonetheless, there was significant debate about what the U.S. Constitution actually allowed the Supreme Court to do. The Constitution did not explicitly provide the Supreme Court or any of the judiciary the power of judicial review. Article III states that the "judicial Power shall extend to" cases and controversies "arising under this Constitution," implying that the judiciary is empowered to resolve constitutional questions. In addition, Article VI asserts that the Constitution is the "Supreme Law of the Land."[44] But a definitive answer on judicial review would not come until the 1803 U.S. Supreme Court case of *Marbury v. Madison.*

Marbury v. Madison

The pivotal Supreme Court case that established the doctrine of judicial review is *Marbury v. Madison.*[45] In this case, the Supreme Court first asserted its authority to declare an act of Congress unconstitutional.

Exhibit: Excerpt from Marbury v. Madison

"It is emphatically the province and duty of the Judicial Department [the judicial branch] to say what the law is. Those who apply the rule to particular cases must, of necessity, expound and interpret that rule. If two laws conflict with each other, the Courts must decide on the operation of each.

"So, if a law [e.g., a statute or treaty] be in opposition to the Constitution, if both the law and the Constitution apply to a particular case, so that the Court must either decide that case conformably to the law, disregarding the Constitution, or conformably to the Constitution, disregarding the law, the Court must determine which of these conflicting rules governs the case. This is of the very essence of judicial duty. If, then, the Courts are to regard the Constitution, and the Constitution is superior to any ordinary act of the Legislature, the Constitution, and not such ordinary act, must govern the case to which they both apply.

"Those, then, who controvert the principle that the Constitution is to be considered in court as a paramount law are reduced to the necessity of maintaining that courts must close their eyes on the Constitution, and see only the law" [e.g., the statute or treaty].

"This doctrine would subvert the very foundation of all written constitutions."[46]

The dispute arose during the transition between the presidency of John Adams and that of Thomas Jefferson. At the close of Adams' presidency, it became clear that Adams' Federalist party was going to lose power. In a political move designed to frustrate the incoming Jefferson administration, Adams spent his last night as president appointing many fellow Federalists—later called "midnight judges"—to judicial positions in and around Washington, D.C. The next day, the Jefferson administration ordered James Madison, the new secretary of state, not to deliver the commissions to the judges, though they had been approved by the Senate. This order prompted one of the newly appointed justices, William Marbury, to file suit for a writ of mandamus in the Supreme Court that would force Madison to deliver the commissions. Marbury based his claim on the Judiciary Act of 1789, which granted the Supreme Court jurisdiction to issue such writs.

The case reached the Supreme Court, and Chief Justice John Marshall determined that it presented three legal issues: did Marbury have a right to the commission, was there a legal remedy, and was a writ of mandamus from the Supreme Court the correct remedy? Marshall answered the first two in the affirmative, but he determined that the third question involved the jurisdiction of the Supreme Court and was, therefore, a constitutional question.[47] Though he agreed that Marbury was entitled to the commission, he ruled that the Judiciary Act of 1789 conflicted with the Constitution, which did not give the Supreme Court original jurisdiction over writs of mandamus. Essentially, Marshall ruled that Congress did not have the authority to add to the original jurisdiction of the Supreme Court.[48]

The result of Marshall's ruling was that a Supreme Court decision partially invalidated an act of Congress by determining that it conflicted with the U.S. Constitution. The ruling strengthened the power of the judiciary by establishing that the legislature could not add to the jurisdiction of the Supreme Court. This precedent also entrenched the checks and balances system in American government.

In the end, as Justice Marshall put it, "it is emphatically the province and the duty of the judicial department to say what the law is."[49] Judicial review, while controversial at first, has in the past two centuries become a fixture of American constitutionalism. The now-accepted doctrine of judicial review allows the judiciary to adjudicate between two contradictory sources of law.[50]

Court Structure

The American judiciary can best be described as a dual system, including one federal court and 50 state courts. Under this system, federal courts have authority over cases involving an issue of federal law, and state courts have authority over issues of state law.

The separation between the two tiers is not absolute, however. Some cases can be heard in either state or federal court. For example, civil suits in which the parties reside in two different states can be heard in either state or federal court. Narcotics cases and interstate kidnapping charges violate both federal and state statutes. The appeals process can also involve both levels of the judiciary. Those convicted in a state court may appeal to their respective states' appellate courts, to the U.S. Supreme Court, or by petition for a writ of habeas corpus to a federal district court. Detained individuals may petition for a writ of habeas corpus to request their release.

Jurisdiction The power of a court to adjudicate a case, issue orders, and render a decision.

To understand the structure of U.S. courts, both state and federal, it is necessary to understand the concept of **jurisdiction**. There are several different kinds of jurisdiction, but—loosely defined—jurisdiction is the power of a court to adjudicate a case, issue orders, and render a decision. The term also refers to the geographic territory over which a court may exercise its power.

Trial court A court of original jurisdiction that tries a case and renders a judgment.

Original jurisdiction, as the name implies, is the prerogative of a court—typically, a **trial court**—to be the first to hear a case. Appellate jurisdiction refers to the authority of a higher court to consider an appeal from a decision issued by a trial court. Appellate courts do not hear witness testimony in criminal cases or civil cases. Rather, they consider written and oral appeals about the conduct, procedure, and results of a trial, and then determine if the trial court (or trial court jury) committed errors of fact or law.[51]

Jurisdiction can be further broken down into geographic and subject matter jurisdiction. Subject matter jurisdiction applies in cases where a specific legal issue is in controversy, such as the right of contracts or civil rights. Geographic jurisdiction is the authority of a court to try cases that arise within certain geographical areas, such as a county, city, or state. The state of Maryland, for instance, has no jurisdiction to try a person accused of committing a crime in Pennsylvania.

Geographic jurisdiction can become an issue if a defendant flees a state to avoid prosecution, because the state's prosecutor must request extradition to have the defendant brought to the state in which the crime was committed.[52] In addition, issues of geographic jurisdiction become political when a defendant who commits a capital crime in a state with the death penalty flees to a state that does not impose the death penalty.

Structure of State Courts

State courts handle the vast majority of cases that occur in the United States. They derive their authority from state constitutions and statutes, which are far more exhaustive than the U.S. Constitution. The 10th Amendment to the Bill of Rights states that the powers not specifically granted to the federal government by the Constitution are reserved to the states or the people.[53] As such, state courts resolve most disputes between private citizens, prosecute most criminal defendants, handle most family disputes, and adjudicate most disputes between citizens and the government.[54]

State court systems, like their federal counterparts, are divided into trial courts and appellate courts. In criminal cases, trial courts arraign defendants, set bail, consider guilty pleas, conduct trials, and impose criminal sentences. In civil cases, trial courts inform plaintiffs and defendants of the complaint filed, perform pretrial procedures, conduct trials, and award damages. To carry out these steps, trial courts often handle factual disputes and hear testimony from witnesses.

Appellate courts correct erroneous decisions of lower courts. Their role is not to determine factual errors or hear witnesses, but rather to determine if the trial court incorrectly interpreted or applied the relevant statute or law. Most rulings of appellate courts become precedent for trial courts. In addition, appellate courts often reassess the application of legal rules, derive new rules for original situations, and interpret ambiguous language in statutes or court opinions.[55]

© Todd A. Merport/Shutterstock.com

Appellate courts correct erroneous decisions of lower courts.

In general, the lowest level of a state court system consists of county courts, municipal courts, traffic courts, and magistrates, or judicial officers who perform some administrative tasks of a judge without the same level of authority. These are trial courts of limited jurisdiction. *Limited jurisdiction* refers to the authority of courts over a particular subset of cases.

The next highest level consists of specialized courts that consider juvenile, divorce, family, and housing issues. Superior courts handle serious criminal matters; most trials occur at this level. The highest level is the state supreme court, which has the power to hear appeals from lower courts.

Municipal Courts, District Courts, and County Courts

Municipal courts, district courts, and county courts are typically trial courts of limited jurisdiction, and often are referred to as *inferior or lower courts. They constitute almost 77% of all courts in the United States.*[56] Courts in this category frequently use abbreviated procedures due to the commonplace nature of the cases they handle. They sometimes exclude attorneys and do not use juries due to the huge volume of civil and criminal matters they arbitrate, many of which are neither complex nor serious (traffic offenses, moving violations, etc.).[57]

Lower courts of this sort nearly always handle misdemeanor crimes, or crimes for which the penalty does not exceed one year of incarceration, and hear civil suits whose amounts do not exceed $15,000. These courts may also handle the preliminary stages of felony cases, which include preliminary hearings, arraignment, bail, and appointment of counsel. As these courts do not handle serious matters, their proceedings are often not officially recorded. Appeals from trial courts of limited jurisdiction usually go to trial courts of general jurisdiction, instead of directly to an appellate court.

The trial court of general jurisdiction for a state is usually called a district or superior court. Most trial courts have unlimited jurisdiction and are therefore the venue for the majority of serious criminal offenses. Still, there is overlap in some states. Usually, courts are divided into judicial districts or circuits, sometimes along political boundaries, such as counties or boroughs. They are much more formal than lower courts, usually featuring a jury trial and attorneys. Major trial courts often have felony jurisdiction, which gives them the power to issue judgments on cases in which preliminary proceedings have occurred in a lower court of limited jurisdiction. These courts also have incidental appellate jurisdiction, so they can hear appeals from lower-level courts and administrative agencies in certain civil or criminal matters.[58]

The Courtroom Workgroup

Members of the courtroom workgroup collaborate to move cases through the criminal justice system quickly and fairly.

The *courtroom workgroup* plays a hugely important role in criminal justice. This term encompasses the many different players in a courtroom—from the judge to the courtroom staff to the defense and prosecuting attorneys—and the functions of each. The members of the courtroom workgroup perform particular duties to achieve collaborative goals, such as moving cases through the criminal justice system in a timely fashion and ensuring that justice is pursued fairly. Court operation is based not only on the law but also on the judge's decisions as the highest official in the courtroom.[59]

Defendant A person charged with a crime.

Workgroups form in all professions, but the courtroom workgroup is unique in that the person at the center—the **defendant**—has very little power. While the system is designed to protect the rights of the accused, the defendant is not involved in most of the proceedings involving the courtroom workgroup. The other participants work together frequently—usually every day—and include the regular courtroom staff, the judge, and any attorneys. These individuals tend to develop a shared set of norms and values from their contact and work. Eisenstein and Jacob (1970) defined the characteristics of the courtroom workgroup as speed, guilt, cohesion, and secrecy.[60] *Speed* indicates the group's desire to dispose of cases quickly rather than administering and dispensing truly fair justice; guilt implies the group's belief that the defendant is indeed guilty, despite the idea from the U.S. Constitution that a defendant is considered innocent until proven guilty. This philosophy is similar to Herbert Packer's Crime Control Model. *Cohesion* is the unity of the individuals as a group, working together toward the common purpose of punishing the defendant; and *secrecy* describes the group's tendency to keep any discussions or negotiations that do not occur in open court private—sometimes even from the defendant. The dynamic of the courtroom workgroup can strongly affect the outcome of a criminal case, sometimes without the defendant knowing what happened.

The Criminal Trial:

An Overview

There are two types of criminal trials: a bench trial and a jury trial. A *bench* trial is a trial argued directly in front of a judge without a jury, with the judge making the sole decision as to the defendant's guilt or innocence and possible punishment. A *jury trial* is conducted in front of a jury; the jury listens to all evidence presented and makes the decision as to the guilt or innocence, and later any applicable punishment, of the defendant. The defendant has the right to request either a jury trial or a bench trial, and the choice is generally suggested by the defense attorney as a part of trial strategy.[61] While the U.S. Constitution identifies the right to a jury trial, this was not clarified in all states until the 1968 Supreme Court ruling in *Duncan v. Louisiana. In Duncan*, the defendant was charged with a misdemeanor offense that could have resulted in a maximum sentence of two years' imprisonment and a fine of $300. The trial court rejected the defendant's request for a jury trial based on the Louisiana constitution, which allowed jury trials only in cases that could result in a death sentence or hard labor imprisonment. The Supreme Court ruled in favor of Duncan, saying that his right to a jury trial was guaranteed by the Sixth and 14th Amendments.[62]

When the trial begins, the attorneys for each side make opening statements. The **opening statement** is an opportunity for each attorney to provide the jury with a brief summary of what each side intends to show the jury during the trial. The prosecution, which has the burden of proof—the task of demonstrating the guilt of the defendant—makes the first opening statement. The prosecution endeavors to show the jury that it will **prove beyond a reasonable doubt** that the defendant committed the crime of which he or she is accused.[63] The

Opening statement The initial statement of a trial that an attorney makes to the jury, which outlines the argument that will be made during the trial.

Proof Beyond a Reasonal Doubt The burden of proof that is put forward by the prosecution used to determine a person's guilt or innocence. The defendant is always presumed to be innocent unless the burden of proof is undeniable. Black's Law Dictionary.

© wavebreakmedia/Shutterstock.com

Witnesses help describe the series of events that occurred before, during, and after a crime.

defense attorney, on the other hand, will focus the opening statement on the weaknesses of the state's case, arguing that the defendant's guilt cannot be proved beyond a reasonable doubt. The manner in which the defense attorney makes the opening statement may vary according to trial strategy. Sometimes attorneys may withhold details during opening statements, preferring to allow particular information to be revealed during the course of the trial. Another tactic is to use a very detailed opening statement, which may be delivered forcefully or passionately in an attempt to predispose the jury to accept the defense's argument.[64]

Opening statements are broad, and are not intended—or permitted—to be used as a means for the attorneys to testify or offer evidence. The attorneys from both sides are also bound by "good faith" ethical requirements during opening statements. Each lawyer can mention only the evidence that he or she believes will be presented, and that he or she will be allowed to present during the trial. If either attorney gives the idea that he or she will present evidence that in fact he or she has no intention of presenting, this is not only unprofessional, but has been defined by the U.S. Supreme Court as *professional misconduct.*[65]

Case-in-chief The portion of a criminal case presented by the prosecution.

The **case-in-chief** is the argument the state's attorney, who is on the side of the prosecution in criminal proceedings, makes against the defendant. It is the job of the state's attorney to show the jury that the defendant committed, or could have committed, the crime of which he or she has been accused. The case-in-chief is different than the case-as-a-whole, as "the case" includes the entire court case and the arguments for guilt or innocence from both sides, the witnesses, and any experts involved.

Witness Testimony

Witness An individual who gives testimony in court because he or she has information that is pertinent to the case.

Testimony The statement of a witness, given under oath, typically in court.

An important part of any criminal trial is the examination of witnesses. This is the primary means by which evidence is introduced in a trial. **Witnesses** have information that helps put together the series of events that occurred before, during, and after the commission of a crime. The **testimony**, or formal statement, from each witness helps paint a picture of what happened, where it happened, how it happened, who caused it to happen, and why it happened. Since the defendant (who may or may not testify), the victim (who may not be able to testify), and the witnesses are the only individuals involved in the trial process who can answer some of these questions definitively, it is important that the judge and jury learn as much information as possible in order to make fair decisions about the defendant's guilt or innocence and any resultant sentence.

Before a witness will be allowed to testify, the attorney questioning the witness must establish that the person is competent to testify. Competency requires that the witness has personal knowledge of the information that he or she will offer and that the witness understands the duty to tell the truth.[66] The trial process relies on the ability of the witness to give accurate and truthful testimony, so it is important to ensure that the witness is capable of telling the truth. This is a practice that developed primarily in the England and Scotland in the 1600s as the adversarial trial process evolved.[67] A **lay witness** is an everyday citizen, who may or may not personally know the defendant or victims involved in the case, who has some personal knowledge about the facts of the case. A spectator at a sporting event who sees an assault occur several seats away would be considered a lay witness if asked to testify in court. It is important to establish that a lay witness is competent and credible to testify because the witness is relaying what occurred that he or she personally witnessed. Incorrect testimony may harm case procedure or the outcome of the case.

Lay witness An everyday citizen who has some personal knowledge about the facts of a case.

Witness competency is also important when an expert witness testifies. An **expert witness** is considered an expert in his or her field of study or work: for example, a physician would be considered an expert in the medical field, while an auto mechanic would be considered an expert in the internal working of automobiles. One accepted legal definition of *expert witnesses is the following: "Persons who through education or experience have developed skill or knowledge in a particular subject so that he or she may form an opinion that will assist the fact finder."*[68] The expert witness must be knowledgeable in his or her field, as the information explained by the expert witness has potential bearing on the guilt or innocence of the defendant. A forensic pathologist who testifies in a murder trial about the manner in which a victim died must be as factual and accurate as possible; the judge or jury needs to understand the facts presented in the case so that a decision of guilt or innocence can be made. Because juries may not be qualified to evaluate the validity of presented scientific evidence, the U.S. Supreme Court ruled in *Daubert v. Merrill Dow Pharmaceuticals (1993) that judges have the duty to perform preliminary evaluations of the scientific basis of any expert testimony prior to allowing the expert to testify in the presence of the jury.*[69]

Expert witness A person considered to be an expert in his or her profession or field of study who applies that expertise to the facts or circumstances of a case.

When a witness is first called to the stand to testify, this is called **direct examination**. If the witness is called to testify by the state's attorney, the witness is referred to as a witness for the prosecution. If the witness is called to the stand and questioned by the defendant's legal counsel, or **defense attorney**, the witness is referred to as a witness for the defense. When the witness is being questioned directly, he or she may be asked questions that may be answered with a simple "yes" or "no," or the witness may be asked "narrative" questions, which allow the witness to tell a version of events in his or her own words. During direct examination, the judge will not allow the attorneys to ask "leading questions," which are questions that suggest the answer within the question. A basic example of such a question would be, "You called the police immediately after hearing the shots, correct?"

Direct examination The act of a witness being first called to the stand to testify.

Defense attorney The attorney who represents the defendant in a criminal case.

Cross-examination The act of challenging a witness's testimony by asking more questions. Cross-examination is conducted by the other side of the case; the prosecution will cross-examine a defense witness, and the defense will cross-examine a witness for the state.

Prosecutor The attorney, representing the state, who argues the criminal case against the defendant.

Any witness who offers testimony in a criminal trial is subject to being cross-examined. **Cross-examination** is the questioning of a witness by someone other than the direct examiner. After a witness for the defense is questioned directly by the defense attorney, the witness is then available to be cross-examined by the **prosecutor**, or the attorney who represents the state and argues the criminal case against the defendant. Cross-examination tests a witness's credibility and memory by challenging facts that have been entered into evidence by the witness's testimony.[70] The cross-examiner may attempt to discredit the witness by questioning the witness's physical or mental status, criminal record, or prior inconsistencies in the witness's statements. Cross-examination may be followed by redirect examination by the state's attorney, which would attempt to clarify anything to which the witness testified under cross-examination. This procedure continues cycling until all of that side's witnesses have been called and all of their evidence presented.[71]

Several Supreme Court rulings have addressed cross-examination of witnesses. In *Ohio v. Roberts* (1980), the court ruled that a statement made by a witness outside of the courtroom could be introduced during trial as long as there were sufficient "indicia of reliability," even if the witness was not available to testify at trial.[72] In the *Roberts* case, the defendant was accused of forging a check and possession of stolen credit cards, both of which belonged to his daughter. While the daughter was subpoenaed five times to testify at trial, she never appeared. The prosecution offered the transcript of the daughter's testimony to the police at trial, and the defendant was convicted, based partly upon the perceived reliability of his daughter's previous statements.[73] In a later ruling, however, the Supreme Court effectively reversed its position in *Roberts* with the 2004 ruling in *Crawford v. Washington*. In *Crawford*, the prosecution introduced during trial a statement previously made to the police by the defendant's wife. The prosecution used the statement of the wife during trial, particularly during closing arguments, and the defendant was convicted. On appeal, the Supreme Court ruled that the defendant's Sixth Amendment right to confront his accuser had been violated because Mrs. Crawford did not actually testify during the trial, preventing the defense attorney from cross-examining her.[74] The *Crawford* decision effectively means that, when a witness is unavailable to testify at trial, previous testimonial statements made by that witness cannot be admitted into evidence unless the defense had the prior opportunity to cross-examine the witness.

Rebuttal evidence is introduced during trial to oppose or contradict evidence already submitted by the opposing side.

Another way in which an attorney tests the accuracy of the opposing side's case is during the introduction of rebuttal evidence. *Rebuttal evidence* is evidence that is introduced during trial to oppose or contradict evidence already submitted by the opposing side. Rebuttal evidence is submitted during the side's response to the opposing side's presented case. For example, a witness may testify that he witnessed a robbery at a convenience store on a particular date and time, and then an attorney may introduce into evidence a credit card receipt with the witness's signature proving that he was at another location on the same date and time he claimed to witness the robbery. The receipt would be considered rebuttal evidence.

Critical Thinking

If a witness can verify testimony given by a previous witness, is it critical that his or her competency to testify can be demonstrated? Why or why not?

Closing Arguments and Jury Instructions

The **closing arguments** of a trial are the final legal arguments presented by the prosecution and the defense before the case is given to the jury for deliberation. The closing argument can be considered a review and summary of what was argued during the case and whether the arguments demonstrate the defendant's guilt or innocence. Because the burden of proof is on the state, meaning that it is up to the state to demonstrate the guilt of the defendant, the prosecutor is allowed to make a reply to the defense's closing argument. The closing argument does not necessarily have a time limit, although one may be imposed by the judge. The attorneys may avoid lengthy closing arguments for fear of confusing the jurors or losing their attention. In bench trials, it is not uncommon for the sides to waive making closing arguments in the presumption that the judge has already arrived at a decision.[75]

Closing argument The final legal argument of a case presented separately by the prosecution and the defense before the case is given to the jury for deliberation.

After all the evidence has been presented and closing arguments have ended, the judge gives the charge and instructions to the jury. Typically, the judge and attorneys for both sides will discuss the jury instructions outside the presence of the jury so that changes may be discussed, argued, agreed upon, or ruled upon. While the words may vary between jurisdictions, every judge will remind the jury of the duty to objectively consider only evidence that has been presented during trial when deciding the defendant's guilt or innocence; the importance of impartiality will also be stressed.[76] Most judges will remind the jury that the burden of proof rests on the prosecution and the defense is not obligated to show proof of innocence. The judge will also explain the concept of reasonable doubt by stressing that if jury members are to determine that a defendant is guilty, they must hold no reasonable doubts regarding the person's guilt. Additionally, judges may remind the jury of the legal requirements of the alleged charge: that is, if the defendant is accused of murder, the judge may remind the jury members of what, according to the law, constitutes "murder."

Issues have arisen from time to time concerning whether juries actually understood the instructions given to them by the judge. One study by Wiener, Pritchard, and Weston (1995) demonstrated that juror impartiality can be affected by misunderstanding jury instructions; when jurors were given several versions of instructions in a sample capital case, a strong correlation was found between misunderstanding the jury instructions and the willingness of the jurors to impose the death penalty.[77] It is also typical for jurors to confuse the burden of proof in criminal court—"beyond a reasonable doubt"—with the burden of proof in civil court—"preponderance of the evidence."[78] The American Bar Association has addressed this, stating, "All instructions to the jury should be in plain and understandable language."[79] States are making changes to jury instructions to increase juror understanding of the instructions. States such as Florida and Illinois are now creating standard jury instructions that can be altered according to the specific criteria of each case.[80]

Jury instructions have also been clarified by Supreme Court rulings. In *Pope v. Illinois* (1987), the defendant appealed a guilty verdict based on the assertion that the jury was given erroneous instructions. The defendant, who was a clerk at an adult bookstore, was arrested after selling certain magazines to police. The jury was instructed to determine whether the magazines would be considered obscene by determining how the material would be viewed by ordinary adults in the state of Illinois. The Supreme Court ruled that, although the jury was erroneously instructed to use a particular community standard—the state of Illinois—when considering the social value of the magazines, if no rational juror who had been properly instructed could find social value in the magazines, the guilty conviction should stand.[81]

The Verdict

When the jury is done deliberating, the foreman will write the verdict on the court's official verdict form. The bailiff will then be notified that a verdict has been reached, and the court will inform all parties to return to the courtroom to hear the verdict. When the parties, audience, and staff return to the courtroom, the jury will be ushered back into the jury box. The foreman hands the jury form to the bailiff, who then gives the form to the judge. The judge makes sure the verdict is properly written and the paperwork is in proper legal order. In some jurisdictions, such as California, the clerk of the court reads the verdict aloud in court. In other jurisdictions, such as North Dakota, the jury foreperson, referred to as the presiding juror, announces the verdict in court.[82] In cases where unanimous verdicts are required of juries, it is easy to know how each juror voted. However, the prosecuting and defense attorneys do have the right to request of the judge that the jury be polled. If this occurs, each juror must announce individually how he or she voted at the conclusion of deliberations.

Critical Thinking

What possible issues do you believe could arise from polling a jury after they have found a defendant guilty?

Intermediate Appellate Courts

All states have at least one appellate court, but some feature more. In states with large caseloads, there are two levels of appellate courts. The highest is a court of last resort, typically a state supreme court. The lower level consists of **intermediate appellate courts**, which alleviate the burden placed on higher courts in the most populous states. These courts relieve the state's highest court (typically a state supreme court) from having to hear every case that generates an appeal.[83] In 1998, 35 states had at least one intermediate court of appeal.[84] These appeals typically are decided by a three-judge panel, although judges occasionally sit **en banc**, a French term that translates to the phrase "on a bench" and implies that all the judges of the court together will decide a case.

Intermediate appellate court The lower level of state appellate courts.

En banc A French term indicating that all the judges of an appellate court will together consider an appeal.

The losing side in a criminal or civil case has the right of appeal, and the appeal takes place either in a **court of last resort** or an intermediate appellate court. Intermediate appellate courts generally must hear cases that are appealed to them.

Court of last resort The highest court of appeal in a state court system: typically, a state supreme court.

Courts of Last Resort

State supreme courts are the highest level of appellate court and also are referred to as courts of last resort. These courts generally reserve the right to choose which cases they will hear, and they frequently choose cases that carry broad policy and legal implications.[85] Courts of last resort in states without an intermediate level, however, do not get to choose their cases.

All of these courts are composed of five to nine members (most commonly seven) and generally sit *en banc*. Texas and Oklahoma are notable for being the two states to have separate courts of last resort for civil and criminal matters.[86]

State supreme courts are similar to the U.S. Supreme Court in that they interpret state law and have the power to determine whether it violates the state constitution. These courts follow a model similar to the federal model: they require a notice of appeal, require written legal briefs, consider oral arguments by each party's attorneys, and issue a written decision. State supreme courts, like other courts of last resort, do not retry the facts of the case or hear witnesses, but correct errors of law or procedure.[87]

When it is relevant to do so, state supreme courts exercise the authority to interpret the Constitution and, in some instances, federal law. However, if a state court issues an opinion on federal law, its decision is reviewable by the U.S. Supreme Court, whose authority supersedes that of a state court.

The U.S. Supreme Court can review and overrule the state's interpretation of a federal statute or the Constitution.[88]

Specialized State Courts

© Cheryl Casey/Shutterstock.com

Juvenile courts determine cases involving young offenders, generally those less than 18 years old.

The state court system also includes specialized courts that handle specific types of cases. These courts have limited jurisdiction that covers their specialty, and generally have a single judge hear cases without a jury. Probate courts, for instance, consider the administrative concerns of a deceased person's estate. This usually involves making sure the person's will is executed properly or applying relevant state law if there is no will. Family courts consider divorces, custody disputes, annulments, and alimony. Traffic courts adjudicate speeding tickets and other moving violations.[89]

Juvenile courts determine cases involving young offenders, generally those less than 18 years old. Because these offenders are underage, they are not tried in conventional criminal courts. Juvenile courts operate on the premise that sentences should be rehabilitative, rather than punitive, since minors are not as culpable for most criminal acts as an adult would be and can more readily see the error of their ways and remediate their behavior.[90]

Structure of Federal Courts

In their current form, federal courts have three levels. The lowest level is occupied by federal district courts, which function as trial courts. The middle level includes the U.S. Circuit Courts of Appeals, which consider appeals. The top court is the U.S. Supreme Court, which defines and interprets the U.S. Constitution and statutes passed by the legislative branch.[91]

Federal courts have exclusive jurisdiction over "federal questions." These legal issues arise in suits between citizens of different states, or in suits involving foreign ambassadors or public officials, bankruptcy, patent or trademark law, or crimes specifically punishable by federal statutes. Indeed, any crime mentioned in the Constitution (treason, piracy, counterfeiting) or a federal statute qualifies as a federal question, but most statutory crimes are tried in state courts.[92]

Career Connections: Federal Judge

Federal judges sit at the top of the judicial system in the American criminal justice system. They are selected by executive appointment of the president and must be confirmed by at least two-thirds of the U.S. Senate.

This obviously makes the selection process an inherently political one. When a position becomes available, the deputy attorney general of the U.S. Department of Justice conducts a search for qualified lawyers in the state in which the vacancy is located. The initial screening phase involves consulting with local party leaders to ensure that the nominee's political views do not conflict with those of the president.[93]

Federal judges are appointed under Article III of the U.S. Constitution. Judges serve a lifelong term, but can be removed by impeachment. There are no explicit qualifications for a judgeship, but candidates are almost always accomplished attorneys, often working for the government.[94] In addition, it is preferred that judges have a dispassionate demeanor. As arbiters of fairness in the court, judges are expected to be, according to Jackson (1974), "honest, patient, wise, tolerant, compassionate, strong, decisive, articulate, courageous—a list of virtues similar to those in the Boy Scout handbooks."[95]

Some see federal judges as autocratic, but they frequently defer to the advice and opinions of prosecutors and probation officers when it comes to accepting a plea agreement or determining sentencing.[96] In a federal criminal trial, the judge advises the defendant of his or her rights, decides if the defendant should be held in custody until trial, and determines if **probable cause** exists to believe the defendant committed the crime with which he or she is charged. Most defendants (90%) take a plea bargain instead of going to trial, at which point the judge either imposes sentence or waits for a presentence report prepared by a probation officer. If the defendant pleads not guilty, the judge schedules a trial.[97]

Probable cause Reasonable belief that the accused committed the crime with which he or she is charged.

The Judge and Courtroom Staff

The concept of the courtroom workgroup was introduced earlier in the chapter. Each member of the courtroom workgroup has particular duties in the criminal trial process, all of which combine to dispose of cases as smoothly and efficiently as possible. Following is an overview of the members of the courtroom workgroup.

The Judge

Many people view the **judge** as the most important person in the courtroom. While there is an expectation of respect that is bestowed on the person holding a judgeship, the judge makes up only one part of the courtroom workgroup.

Judge A public officer elected or appointed to administer justice and hear cases in a court of law.

There are different levels of judges: lower court judges, such as justices of the peace; major trial court judges, such as those in district courts; intermediate appellate court judges, who serve in state appellate and superior courts; and

© everything possible/Shutterstock.com

The judge has the responsibility of overseeing fairness in the courtroom.

© The Washington Post/Contributor/Getty Images

President Trump announces Neil Gorsuch as his choice for Supreme Court Justice

judges in the courts of last resort, such as the justices in the U.S. Supreme Court. At each level, judges will hear different types of cases. For example, a justice of the peace may preside over charges of traffic violations or school truancy, while the U.S. Supreme Court serves as the final, highest court in the country, hearing appeals that may originate in those local justice of the peace courts. The Supreme Court generally may decide which cases it will review, utilizing the Rule of Four: if four or more justices believe that a case warrants the consideration of the entire court, then the court will review the case.[98]

Selection of Judges

While most judges obtain their positions by election, federal judges hold their offices for life. Judges are selected in different ways. Federal judges are nominated by the president and then confirmed by the U.S. Senate. This process is outlined in the U.S. Constitution for the Supreme Court justices; the Judiciary Act of 1789 adopted the process for all other federal judicial positions.[99] State, county, and municipal or lower court judges are elected to their positions. This means that candidates must gain the nomination from a political party and then campaign with that party.

Campaign Financing

Between 1980 and 1986, campaign contributions to candidates in contested appellate court races increased by 250%. During the same period, there was a 450% increase in the number of contributions in excess of $5,000 to candidates in contested appellate court races. The 1988 supreme court elections were the most expensive in Texas history, with twelve candidates for six seats raising $12 million.

Between 1992 and 1997, the seven winning candidates for the Texas Supreme Court raised nearly $9.2 million dollars. Of this $9.2 million, more than 40% was contributed by parties or lawyers with cases before the court or by contributors linked to those parties. The perceived impropriety of judges soliciting and accepting large campaign contributions from attorneys and parties who appear before them has been the subject of numerous newspaper and magazine articles, as well as television broadcasts. In 1987 and again in 1998, 60 Minutes aired segments that examined whether justice was for sale in Texas, and Frontline explored the same question in 1999.

FIGURE 6.1 THE ROAD TO THE SUPREME COURT.

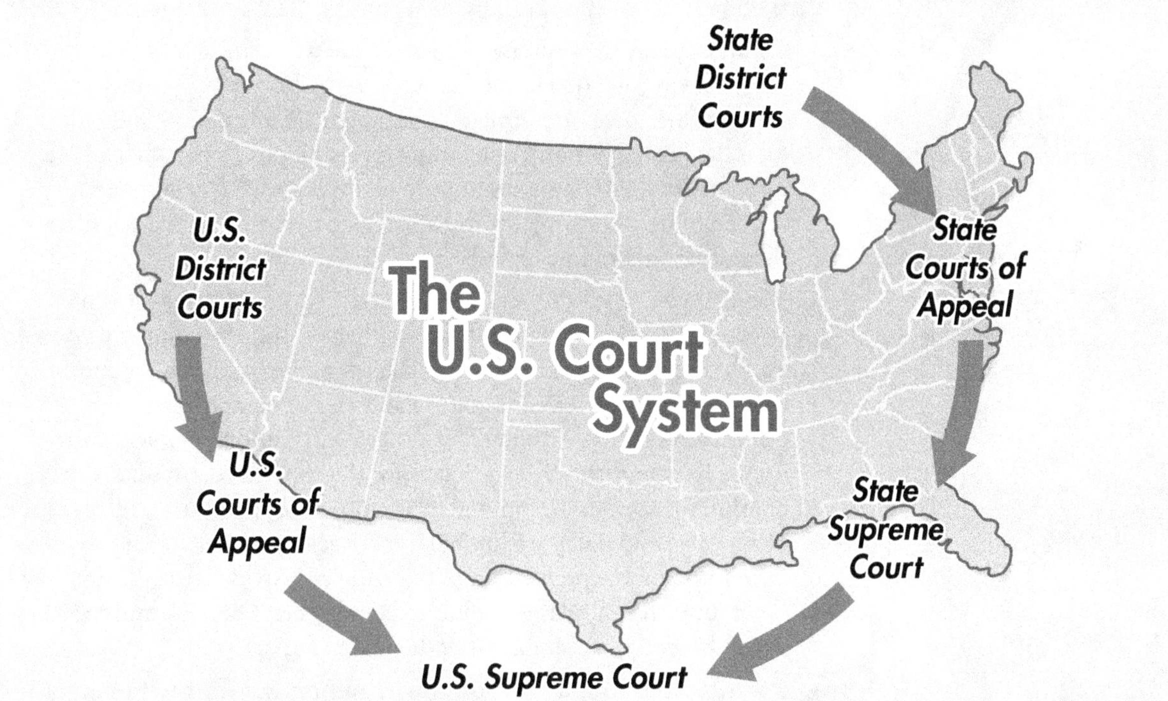

Judicial Campaigns and Elections: Texas

In the early 1980s, plaintiff lawyers were the largest contributors to Texas judicial candidates, but in the late 1980s and 1990s, they were replaced by civil defense attorneys, doctors, insurance companies, and other business interests. In recent years, major contributors to judicial candidates have included the Texas Association of Business and Chambers of Commerce, the Texas Trial Lawyers Association, the Texas Medical Association, Texans for Lawsuit Reform, the insurance industry, energy and natural resources companies, and the Republican and Democratic Parties. Texans for Public Justice, a legal watchdog group founded in 1997, tracks campaign contributions to public officials in Texas, including appellate judges, and has issued a number of reports that examine the relationship between campaign contributions to judges and judicial decisions. Their most recent report, Courtroom Contributions Stain Supreme Court Campaigns, reveals that supreme court candidates receive two thirds of their campaign contributions from lawyers and litigants who appear before them. Other reports include Checks and Imbalances, Payola Justice, and Lowering the Bar.

In 1995, the Judicial Campaign Fairness Act was passed to regulate financing of judicial elections. Under the JCFA:

- Individual contributions to candidates for the supreme court and court of criminal appeals are limited to $5,000. Individual contributions to all other judicial candidates are limited to between $1,000 and $5,000, depending on the population of the judicial district.

- Contributions from law firms and members of law firms are limited to $50 if the aggregate contributions from the firm and its members exceed six times the maximum individual contribution for that judicial office.
- Candidates for the supreme court and court of criminal appeals may accept up to $300,000 in total contributions from PACs. Court of appeals candidates are limited to between $52,500 and $75,000 in total PAC contributions, depending on the population of the judicial district. Total PAC contributions to all other judicial candidates are limited to between $15,000 and $52,500, depending on the population of the judicial district.
- Voluntary expenditure limits are established. Candidates must file a sworn declaration of their intent to either voluntarily comply with or exceed these limits. If a candidate who complies with the expenditure limits is opposed by a candidate who does not comply, the complying candidate is no longer bound by either contribution or expenditure limits. Expenditures by candidates for the supreme court and court of criminal appeals are limited to $2 million. Expenditures by court of appeals candidates are limited to between $350,000 and $500,000, depending on the population of the judicial district. Expenditures by all other judicial candidates are limited to between $100,000 and $350,000, depending on the population of the judicial district.
- Contributions to and expenditures by committees formed to support a judicial candidate, oppose the candidate's opponent, or assist the candidate as an officeholder are considered contributions to and expenditures by the candidate. Contributions to and direct expenditures on behalf of complying candidates from a political party are considered expenditures by the candidate.
- Contribution limits are per candidate, per election. However, the primary election and the general election are considered to be a single election if the candidate is unopposed in the primary *or* if the candidate does not have an opponent on the ballot in the general election. The various contribution limits for that "single election" are increased by 25 percent, but the amount of the increase may only be used for officeholder expenditures. 102

Due to its political nature, the judge selection process can produce controversy. In Texas, for example, elected judges are allowed to preside over cases in which the involved parties and their lawyers have contributed to the judges' election campaigns. In 2000, a public interest group brought this practice to light, claiming it to be unconstitutional.[100] The trial court ruled against the public interest group, saying that the practice should be solved mutually between the citizens and lawmakers of Texas; the Court of Appeals later affirmed this decision.[101]

Critical Thinking

Is it a conflict of interest to permit a judge to preside over a case in which one of the opposing parties is someone who contributed money to the judge's election campaign? Why or why not?

Some state-level judges are appointed by the governor of the state. These positions include the judges for the courts of appeals and sometimes in major district trial courts under certain circumstances. For example, if an elected judge of a district court retires or dies during his or her term, the governor would appoint a replacement. Politics can be involved in this instance as well, as a governor will typically appoint judges who share the same political affiliation.

Qualifications of Judges

Until the 1960s, many states did not require judges to have education, special training, or other qualifications.[102] This meant that anyone who won an election or was appointed to the position—even someone who did not have a law degree—could become a judge. The New York City Criminal Court Act, implemented in 1962, required judges to reside in the city; to have at least 10 years' experience practicing law in the state of New York; and to pass the state bar exam, although it was possible to do so without obtaining a law degree.[103] Now, almost all states require that a judge in general and appellate court have a juris doctor (or Doctor of Law) degree, be a licensed attorney, and be a member of their state's bar association.

It is important that judges receive ongoing legal training to stay current on changes to laws and the application of the laws. Some entities, such as the Texas Justice Court Training Center at Texas State University, hold state-sponsored training sessions for newly elected judges. This training may address such subjects that are foreign to brand-new judges, such as courtroom and evidentiary procedures, dispute resolution, ethics, and other topics.[104] There are also organizations that provide ongoing training for judges, such as the National Judicial College at the University of Nevada, Reno.[105]

Duties of Judges

The judge's primary duty is to oversee the standard procedures of the court system to ensure that justice is fairly served. The American Bar Association has laid out a specific description of the duties of the office: "The trial judge has the responsibility for safeguarding both the rights of the accused and the interests of the public in the administration of criminal justice . . . The purpose of a criminal trial is to determine whether the prosecution has established the guilt of the accused as required by law, and the trial judge should not allow the proceedings to be used for any other purpose."[106]

In the courtroom, the judge must make sure that both the prosecution and the defense are given the chance to state their cases, make their arguments, and question the opposing side's witnesses. In each case, the appointed judge decides whether certain pieces of evidence are admissible or inadmissible and gives support for his or her decisions. While the judge has established laws to follow, the judge does have discretion to decide how to apply the laws in his or her courtroom.[107] In this respect, the judge can wield great power over the progression of a criminal case.

Counsel A title for an attorney presenting a case in court.

Sidebar A discussion conducted during a court hearing between the judge and attorneys outside the hearing of the jury.

During the trial, the judge typically refers to the attorneys of each opposing side as "**counsel**" or "counselor." A counselor is a legal advisor and advocate for one of the sides in a court case. The judge might use this term when addressing the attorneys directly, such as by saying, "Counsel, approach the bench." This is an instruction for each of the attorneys to come to the judge's bench to discuss something with the judge, perhaps out of earshot of the jury and audience. The attorneys may also request to approach the bench by asking the judge for a **sidebar**, which is a discussion held between the judge and the lawyers out of the hearing of the jury.

Probative value Value that is useful in a case.

Limited admissibility Evidence that may be used for one specific purpose but cannot be applied in other ways.

Deciding whether a piece of evidence is admissible in court depends on several criteria and is one of the more important decisions a trial judge will make. The judge will examine whether the evidence is relevant to the case: that is, whether it is important to the argument being presented by either the prosecution or the defense. The judge also has to consider whether the **probative value** of the evidence outweighs any prejudicial or inflammatory qualities it may have.[108] Evidence has probative value when it is useful and relevant to the case.[109] No matter how useful a piece of evidence may be, it can, however, unfairly sway a jury if it is presented in a way that causes particular anger, sadness, or disgust. For example, a graphic photo of a murder victim's body may be considered inadmissible if it serves no purpose other than to produce an emotional reaction from the jury. Sometimes evidence is admitted in only a limited way. **Limited admissibility** means that the evidence may be used for one specific purpose but cannot be applied in other ways.[110] Continuing the previous example, photos of the murder victim's body may only be admissible if they are shown during the questioning of the medical examiner.

In some state jurisdictions, there is a chief judge who serves as a trial judge and also manages the court system in the local jurisdiction. A chief judge will typically assume the position by tenure or seniority.

While the criminal court judge has the duty to follow and enforce the law in his or her courtroom, how those laws are followed and enforced is partly up to the judge. This is known as *judicial discretion*. A judge may disallow certain testimony in a trial because he or she believes it is not relevant to the case; another judge presiding over the same trial may make a different decision. Judges have the discretion to accept or not accept evidence, pleas, and sentencing agreements made between the prosecution and the defense. This discretion can influence the entire courtroom workgroup. As the prosecutor learns the discretionary tendencies of the judge, the prosecutor learns what preliminary evidence to emphasize during the charging process. As the probation officer learns what types of cases the judge may feel most strongly about, the probation officer may suggest additional or alternative conditions of probation for a particular defendant that may coincide with the judge's beliefs.

The Court Clerk

The court clerk has many duties that take place both inside and outside the courtroom, performing many different and important jobs. At minimum, the court clerk calls up cases to be heard before the judge and regularly updates the case files for defendants. Before a trial begins, a court clerk may prepare a jury pool for selection and issue jury summonses. During a trial, the clerk will swear in witnesses who are going to testify and can issue subpoenas for witnesses for the defense and the prosecution. The court clerk, or an assistant clerk, also marks exhibits into evidence and maintains proper custody of that evidence while the case is in court. Additionally, the court clerk performs other duties as requested by the judge. In larger jurisdictions, there may be a court clerk in each courtroom, while in smaller jurisdictions, there may be one or two court clerks for the whole courthouse. Some districts have a chief court clerk, often called a court coordinator, who is in charge of making sure the court clerk staff fulfills these duties properly.[111]

Some jurisdictions assign more power to their court clerks, such as the authority to issue warrants for arrest, prepare formal writs and process court-issued documents, and assist with probate matters (i.e., wills and estates). Sometimes young attorneys will serve as court clerks; this level of responsibility can help them gain valuable hands-on experience with various judicial matters. The court clerk can be a powerful position in the courtroom and may sometimes serve as the gateway to discuss case matters with the judge or prosecutor. In addition, a court clerk may have records or know information about a case, or about the judge's tendencies to rule in certain matters, which would be helpful for defense attorneys to know. This, in turn, may affect how the defense attorney formulates the defense.

Court reporter A person who uses a shorthand typewriter to record everything that occurs or is said during a court hearing.

Court record The official written record of everything that occurs in a court case.

The Court Reporter

A **court reporter** keeps the official record of everything that happens during a trial. This includes accurately recording everything that is said, whether by the witnesses, the attorneys, or the judge. Some verbal interactions may include objections, instructions the judge gives to the jury, and expert testimony. It is common for a court reporter to read back a portion of the record if instructed by the judge; such instructions may be prompted by a request from the prosecution, the defense, or the jury. The reading of **court records** can help remind courtroom officials of statements made in the courtroom or verify that certain information is included in the official record.

The court reporter takes notes of all testimony during trial.

In years past, court reporters were stenographers who used manual shorthand to take detailed notes quickly. Manual shorthand is now largely a thing of the past, and court reporters usually use machine writers to take the transcript of the proceedings. A machine writer looks similar to a small typewriter but has fewer keys, and it is used to type coded letters and combinations of letters rather than entire words and phrases. After the trial has concluded, the court reporter will translate the notes into the official transcript. The notes may be translated visually by the court reporter or scanned by special equipment. In some courts, the court reporter may use computer-aided transcription (CAT) software, which both takes notes and translates those notes into the transcript. Electronic recording equipment, such as audio or video recorders, is used in place of court reporters in some courtrooms, but there are risks to using these machines. Extraneous noises and comments can be recorded and are not easily erased, and the mechanical recorder cannot interrupt proceedings if any testimony is not audible and cannot be recorded properly.

The Probation Officer

A court probation officer serves as the initial liaison from the local probation department to the defendant who has just been sentenced to probation. Part of a probation officer's duty is to explain the conditions of probation to the defendant for a second time—the judge and defense attorney give the initial explanation—to make sure that the defendant understands. A probation officer will also instruct the defendant on when and where to report for the first probation visit and what to bring to the visit. If there are other procedures, such as reporting for a drug screen or attending a workshop, a probation officer will explain to the defendant how those events will be scheduled as well as handle any associated or monitory paperwork.[112]

Additionally, a probation officer usually serves as an intermediary between the probation department and the judge when dealing with special issues with defendants already on probation. For example, a probation officer from a field office will contact the court probation officer when a probationer tests positive for drugs. The court probation officer will advise the court of the violation and make appropriate recommendations to the field probation officer regarding the handling of the defendant. The court probation officer may also work with the district attorney's office when a defendant returns to court for a probation revocation. A court probation officer is also the court's official custodian of records for the probationer's file while any court hearings are pending. The probation officer becomes familiar with the judge and his or her position on certain types of offenses, as well as the judge's typical rulings on certain criminal matters. In this respect, the probation officer can be a valuable person for a defense attorney to know, especially if the defendant violates probation and must appear before the judge.

Bailiff A law enforcement officer, such as a sheriff's deputy, assigned to a particular courtroom to assist the judge and courtroom staff in keeping the peace within the courtroom.

The Bailiff

A **bailiff** is usually an armed law enforcement officer, typically based in the jurisdiction in which the court is located. For example, a state district court based in a particular county usually has a county sheriff's deputy assigned to that court to serve as the bailiff. A bailiff ensures that order is maintained in the courtroom by instructing spectators and participants to keep discussion at a low volume as well as enforcing any orders or instructions given by the judge.[113] When the judge enters the courtroom, the bailiff announces the judge's arrival as he or she takes the seat at the bench. A bailiff sometimes calls witnesses to testify and may even have to prevent the accused from escaping from custody. A bailiff also controls access to the jury while court is in session and during jury deliberations. When a jury is sequestered, or kept from contact with anyone while a trial is in progress, the bailiff supervises contact between the jury and any non-jury members in an attempt to prevent any outside bias from interfering with the case information given to the jury.

The Court Process Server

A court process server is responsible for serving subpoenas to witnesses and other persons who are to appear in court. A **subpoena** is a written document that officially notifies someone that he or she must appear in court. A court process server is typically a sheriff's deputy or local law enforcement officer. While a court process server is able to perform law enforcement duties as the court sees necessary, his or her primary function is to serve process.

Subpoena A written document that officially notifies someone that he or she must appear in court.

The Prosecution and Defense

The attorneys for the prosecution and the defense have several things in common. Each attorney will have a certain level of college education, usually having graduated from law school. Attorneys must also comply with the licensing requirements of the state where they want to practice law; this is typically done by taking and passing a bar examination. The bar is the governing body that licenses and regulates attorneys within a particular jurisdiction.

The attorneys for each side play critical roles in the legal process.

The Prosecution

The prosecution side of judicial proceedings is led by a prosecutor whose primary job is to present a state's case against a defendant. The prosecutor is known by several different names depending on the jurisdiction that he or she represents. The prosecutor may be a district attorney (DA), a county attorney, a state's attorney, or a U.S. attorney. In most states, district attorneys are elected and typically serve four-year terms, although chief federal prosecutors are appointed. In any case, the prosecutor is the lawyer for the government and is the highest law enforcement authority in a particular jurisdiction. When law enforcement officials bring cases to a prosecutor, it is the prosecutor who decides how those cases will be addressed: whether they will be disposed of or dismissed, whether they will be pursued in court, and whether the charges against an accused person may be reduced to a

© Alexander Zavadsky/Shutterstock.com

The state seal is prominently displayed in most state courtrooms.

lesser offense or increased to a more serious charge. In some jurisdictions, prosecutors prepare search and arrest warrants before they are approved and signed by judges.

The role of a prosecutor encompasses many different jobs in one, and each job varies depending on the different stages of the criminal justice process. Prosecutors are involved in various aspects of casework, from investigation, arrest, and trial to sentencing, appeal, and parole, as well as several other additional steps of the judicial process that occur between arrest and trial. Those additional steps may include, but are not limited to, the initial appearance; the preliminary hearing; indictment; arraignment; and pretrial motions. Many prosecutors' offices in the United States have different divisions that handle different types of cases. Each of these divisions may be headed by a chief assistant attorney, who in turn reports to the elected prosecuting attorney. In Franklin County, Ohio, the Criminal Division of the Prosecuting Attorney's Office has 11 different departments, such as the Gang Unit and the Gun Unit, to handle different classifications of criminal offenses.[114]

An initial appearance occurs after a suspect is arrested and becomes a defendant. He or she does not come into contact with a court officer until this appearance. In the initial appearance, the defendant is brought before a magistrate or judge and formally (1) given notice of the charges being brought against him or her, (2) advised of his or her rights, (3) given the opportunity to hire an attorney or request an appointed lawyer, and (4) given the opportunity to request bail. As the agent for the state, a prosecutor is involved in all of these steps, notifying the judge of the charges against the defendant and arguing for a particular bail amount or against bail altogether.

An initial appearance is typically followed by a preliminary hearing, at which the prosecutor for the case must establish probable cause to try the defendant for the crime which he or she is accused of committing. In some instances, a prosecutor will formally notify the court that the case against the defendant will no longer be prosecuted—in other words, charges are dropped. The prosecutor has discretion to decide whether to pursue a case against a defendant. Prosecutorial discretion takes several forms besides the pursuit of charges against a defendant: the prosecutor may offer or accept a plea bargain, may stipulate that the defendant seek counseling or some other treatment before the decision is made to pursue the case, or may dismiss the case entirely.

When judges' discretion, such as on lengths or types of sentences applicable to certain offenses, is limited, discretion often falls by default to the prosecutor. Since the prosecutor is typically voted into office, this can create an ethical conflict. While prosecutors are not supposed to be influenced by political gain or loss that may result from prosecution or non-prosecution of cases, it would be unrealistic to think that this does not occur anywhere in this country. Decisions made by prosecutors are effectively not subject to review by the judicial or administrative processes; this gives prosecutors a great deal of power when deciding whether to proceed with charges against a defendant or in discussion of plea negotiations.[115] Critics argue that the power of the prosecutor's discretion directly contrasts with the ideas of fairness, equity, and accountability upon which the criminal justice system in this country has been based. Still, while plenty of legislation has limited judicial discretion, not much legislation has restrained the discretional power of the American prosecutor.[116]

If a prosecutor decides to proceed with a case, he or she will prepare an information report that demonstrates probable cause to bind over the accused for trial, often called an indictment.[117] In some jurisdictions, such as the state of Texas, the grand jury system is used. In these instances, a prosecutor makes an argument in front of a grand jury to establish probable cause in the hope that the grand jury will return an indictment of the accused. An arraignment may follow.

An *arraignment* has two purposes: to re-inform the defendant of the charges filed against him or her and to give the defendant the chance to enter a plea.[118] According to the Federal Rules of Criminal Procedure, there are three types of pleas allowed: guilty, not guilty, and "no contest," or *nolo contendere.* The phrase *nolo contendere* is Latin and means, "I do not wish to contest." A plea of *nolo contendere* allows for the judge's decision on the defendant's guilt or innocence, while allowing the defendant to refrain from pleading guilty. Defendants in felony charges are arraigned by prosecutors, who bring the accused forward to answer to the indictment or charging instrument. At this stage, a prosecutor may also engage in negotiating a plea with the defendant. This means that the defendant may be allowed to plead guilty to a lesser charge in exchange for a different or reduced sentence.

Before the trial begins, attorneys from both sides may initiate or participate in the arguments of pretrial motions. Pretrial motions may deal with many different issues, such as a request for a trial to be held in a different venue or a motion *in limine*, in which the prosecution seeks to limit the information made available to the defense. A common pretrial motion is a *motion for continuance*, which simply requests that the court postpone the trial to a future date. This motion is generally filed because the requesting side believes there has not been sufficient time to prepare the case for trial.

During a trial, the prosecutor performs his or her primary duty of attempting to prove the defendant's guilt beyond a reasonable doubt. If a defendant is found guilty, sentencing occurs and the prosecutor may recommend a harsher or more lenient sentence, depending on the circumstances of the crime. If a conviction is appealed by the defendant, a prosecutor will typically argue that a conviction was properly obtained and should be upheld. Sometimes, prosecutors may recommend for or against parole for convicted inmates from their jurisdictions when parole reviews arrive. Typically, prosecutors will oppose parole for serious offenders.

Career Connections: Prosecutor

Working as a prosecutor can be a challenging task. Choosing this field as a career can mean committing to a life of short budgets, large caseloads, and long hours. Prosecutors' salaries may lag well behind those of their peers, and the work can be emotionally taxing. Still, life as a prosecutor can be very fulfilling and rewarding.

Prosecution requires a college degree and three years of law school. Most states require an exam at the conclusion of law school that tests students' overall competency in all of the practice areas they might face. Most prospective prosecutors are required to demonstrate a broad knowledge of legal matters in order to be admitted to the legal bar. They can then be sworn in as lawyers and begin to practice law.

Depending on the size of the jurisdiction, a prosecutor may handle all facets of prosecution or may be able to specialize. Prosecution includes two broad phases: the trial phase and the appellate phase. In large jurisdictions, each phase is handled by separate groups of attorneys working as a team. In smaller jurisdictions, one attorney may handle a particular case throughout both phases. The life cycle of a particular case may vary based on the speed of the jurisdiction and the complexities of the litigation, but the typical life cycle of a case is more than a year.

A prosecutor's job consists of being part social worker, part police officer, and part judge. Prosecutors must be able to handle difficult situations. It is not uncommon for prosecutors to be called out to major crime scenes involving violence and death. Attending autopsies and reviewing crime scene photos may be regular parts of a prosecutor's job. Prosecutors need to have good interpersonal skills, as they deal with law enforcement and victims who may or may not be cooperative. They must be able to make sound decisions quickly. Public speaking is a regular part of the job and a critical skill for effective courtroom litigation.

Prosecution is a career that allows an individual to dramatically impact not only individual lives, but also the community at large. Effectively targeting high-crime areas or violent repeat offenders can make dramatic differences in the day-to-day lives of a prosecutor's constituents. Combining aggressive prosecution techniques with effective public relations campaigns can have a significant deterrent effect within a jurisdiction. Partnering with law enforcement, parent-teacher organizations, and local service organizations can foster educational programs for youth that discourage delinquent behavior that leads to adult criminality.

Students who desire a career in law or prosecution should begin their research and participation in the criminal justice community early. They may seek out internships and service programs with local law enforcement agencies or prosecutor offices. Some police agencies have citizen academies that train local citizens to be ambassadors of law enforcement in the general population and respond to emergencies. Because prosecutorial jobs are becoming harder to acquire, a demonstrated interest in criminal law from an early age can be a tremendous asset when pursuing a prosecutorial job.

Prosecution often leads to other careers. Many prosecutors move on to elected offices such as elected district or county attorneys, judges, legislative positions, or local government officials. Many go on to hold advisory or managerial positions in state and federal government. Many take the extensive trial experience they receive and go on to lucrative private practice careers. Often, prosecutors commit to a lifetime of public service in the prosecutorial field. Prosecutors are in demand in both the private and public sectors.

The Defense

A defense attorney is a lawyer who represents the accused during the criminal trial process. A defense attorney is typically a trained and educated attorney who may specialize in criminal law. It is the job of the defense to ensure that the rights of the accused are maintained and upheld during the criminal trial process. Prior to trial, a defense attorney will prepare an appropriate and adequate defense to be presented at trial. To prepare for his or her defense, he or she may use the services of outside parties such as experts, witnesses to the crime, character witnesses, and even private investigators.

The Harper Lee novel *To Kill a Mockingbird,* adapted into a movie starring Gregory Peck, featured the classic defense attorney character of Atticus Finch.

Another pretrial job of the defense attorney is negotiating a plea agreement with the state's attorney. A defense attorney will interact frequently, and often intensely, with the defendant before and during trial. These discussions are called privileged communications and are subject to **attorney-client privilege**, meaning that any information shared between a defense attorney and his or her client (the defendant) is kept confidential and does not need to be shared with other members of the court or the public.

Attorney-client privilege The privilege that any information shared between a defense attorney and his or her client is kept confidential and does not need to be shared with other members of the court or the public.

During the trial, the defense attorney has the chance to place witnesses on the stand—including the defendant, if that is part of the legal strategy—and ask questions of them. The defense attorney will also have the opportunity to clarify previously testified statements by the state's witnesses by cross-examining them. When an attorney from either side wants to interact directly with a witness, the attorney must ask permission from the judge to **approach the witness**. This allows the attorney to interact more closely with the witness on the stand, including showing evidence to the witness and asking the witness to identify the evidence.

Approach the witness An action that occurs when an attorney moves closer to a witness, who is currently on the witness stand, in order to question the witness further or show him or her an exhibit or document. In most jurisdictions, the attorney must request permission from the judge to approach the witness.

If the accused is found guilty, the defense attorney will argue matters at the sentencing trial and will almost assuredly advise the defendant on any civil issues that may arise as a result of the guilty verdict. A defense attorney may be asked to file an appeal on the conviction, although whether the attorney continues to represent the defendant during the appeal process is typically up to the defendant, in the case of a hired attorney, or the judge, in the case of an appointed attorney or public defender.

There are several types of defense attorneys. A *retained attorney* is one that has been hired to represent a defendant: the defendant, or someone on his or her behalf, will pay money to the attorney in exchange for counsel during the criminal process. Retained attorneys may have a world of resources available to them, including investigators, experts, and support staff, which generally correspond with the defendant's ability to pay for such resources.

Sometimes, a court will appoint a local attorney to represent an indigent defendant during the criminal trial, or appeal, process—a process that was affirmed for all criminal causes following *Gideon v. Wainwright.*

Ethics and Professionalism: Defense Attorneys

As officers of the court, judges and prosecutors are held to ethical standards. Judges must remain impartial and not treat either the defense or the prosecution with hostility, nor must they show favoritism toward either side. Prosecutors must disclose all evidence they will use during trial to the defense, and they are not permitted to allow witnesses or complainants to give false testimony. Judges and prosecutors who do not adhere to the ethical standards imposed upon them by their state bar associations or boards of judicial conduct are subject to sanctions. What, however, about defense attorneys? They are also considered officers of the court, but they are not employed by the government as the judges and prosecutors are. Do defense attorneys have ethical standards that they must follow? Are those ethical standards different than those to which the judges and prosecutors are subjected?

Think about a defense attorney who is representing a man for rape. Not only does the prosecution have enough evidence to show that the defendant committed the rape, but the defendant has also admitted to his attorney that he did commit the rape. How is it ethical for an attorney to defend someone who admittedly committed a terrible crime?

Remember that all persons are afforded certain rights in the U.S. Constitution. Each person is presumed innocent until proven guilty. It is the defense attorney's job to make sure that the defendant receives a fair and impartial trial no matter what the circumstances of the crime may be. The defense attorney will do his or her best to ensure that the prosecution conducts the state's case while following the laws set forth by the state and the federal government. The defense attorney is not present to try to help a guilty criminal go free; the defense attorney helps ensure that the state fulfills its burden of demonstrating the defendant's guilt, as well as ensuring that the defendant's civil rights have not been violated. Think about what would happen if we lived in a country where defendants were not allowed to be represented by counsel and the defendant had the burden to show that he or she did not commit the crime. How would our justice system be different?

Court-appointed attorney An attorney typically selected from a list of all criminal attorneys in private practice near the jurisdiction who are willing to accept appointed cases.

A **court-appointed attorney** is typically selected from a list of all criminal attorneys in private practice near the jurisdiction who are willing to accept appointed cases. An appointed attorney performs all the services for the defendant that a retained attorney would, but instead of being paid by the defendant or a representative, the appointed attorney is paid by the jurisdiction of the local court. The attorney may submit a voucher detailing his or her work on the case to the local jurisdiction and may be paid by the hour, by the duty performed, or by the court appearance. Fees for appointed attorney work are normally much lower than the fees earned when retained. For example, in Oakland County, Michigan, a court-appointed attorney is paid between $350 and $460 per day for trial appearances.[119] Retained attorneys around the country routinely charge their clients hundreds of dollars per hour for work performed on their cases.

Public defender An attorney elected in a local jurisdiction to represent indigent defendants in criminal trials.

The ruling in *Gideon v. Wainwright* also helped create the public defender system in the courts, as many defendants cannot afford to hire attorneys to represent them. A **public defender** works much like an appointed attorney, with the exception that a public defender's office is a permanently established office dedicated to represent any indigent defendants in the jurisdiction.

A public defender's office typically employs paralegals, investigators, and other assistants as well as attorneys to conduct the business of defense for the courts. Approximately 64% of counties nationwide now fund public defender programs.[120] Critics of the current public defender system like to demonstrate the inadequate funding the system receives at the state level. The federal public defender system, however, is not experiencing the same problem. The trial defense of Timothy McVeigh, who bombed the Murrah Federal Building in Oklahoma City, cost taxpayers more than $13.8 million. This includes only trial expenses and not appeals.[121]

There are instances in which the court may decide not to appoint an attorney to represent the defendant or refer the case to the local public defender's office. If a defendant claims to be indigent, but is proven to have money or own assets of some amount, such as a car or a home, that can be used to retain an attorney, the judge may deny the request for appointed counsel.

The Jury

The jury is an important part of the criminal trial process; some may say that, besides the judge, the jury is the most important entity in the courtroom. In a jury trial, the jury listens to the evidence presented by both sides and decides whether the defendant is guilty or innocent. In essence, the defendant's life is held in the jury's hands.

Article III of the U.S. Constitution stipulates that "the trial of all crimes . . . shall be by jury." The defendant may choose to waive trial by jury in favor of trial by the judge, as has already been mentioned. In any case where a jury trial is involved, the defendant has been guaranteed by the Supreme Court the right to be judged by a jury of his or her peers.[122]

A jury is empaneled to hear evidence presented by the prosecution and defense attorneys.

During the trial, the judge runs the courtroom, acting as a judicial umpire and responding to the actions and requests of defense attorneys and prosecutors. Judges have discretion to determine how the law applies to the facts of a specific case. They determine which evidence is admissible and which survey questions may be used to select potential jurors, and issue instructions of law to guide the jury in its deliberations.

For many Americans, judges are the most identifiable symbol of justice and fairness in the legal system. As such, judges are invested with a high degree of prestige and respect, as well as a high level of power and responsibility. The Judicial Conference of the United States sets the code of conduct for judges, requiring them to maintain integrity, impartiality, and independence and

Recusal The decision by a judge to remove himself or herself from a case if there is a conflict of interest.

to avoid the appearance of impropriety. To meet these standards, judges must **recuse** themselves from cases in which they have a personal interest or connection. Additionally, federal judges must file regular reports of compensation they receive from extrajudicial activities.[123]

Critical Thinking

Many outcomes in the judicial system (warrants, grand jury indictments, searches, etc.) depend on the definition of probable cause. Is "probable cause" a strong enough basis on which to grant law enforcement and prosecutors such invasive powers? Why or why not?

U.S. District Courts

U.S. district courts are the federal trial courts. They are courts of limited jurisdiction, as the individual state courts have jurisdiction over the majority of cases. District courts have authority over issues of federal law (a "federal question") and issues between citizens of different states ("diversity jurisdiction"). There are 94 U.S. district courts, with each state having at least one. Districts frequently cover large geographic areas and are subdivided into divisions.

District courts employ anywhere between two and 28 judges per court. The judge determines the issue of law, while the jury (if present) determines issues of fact.[124] In addition, district courts employ magistrates, or federal judges who have the authority to hear lesser charges, conduct trials, accept guilty pleas, and impose sentences. Magistrates are appointed by district judges, but serve a fixed term rather than a lifetime one.[125]

EXHIBIT: CASE LOAD

During fiscal year 2013, the United States attorneys' offices received 172,024 criminal matters. This represents an increase of 8,193 criminal matters received from law enforcement agencies during the prior year. After review, the offices declined a total of 25,629 criminal matters during the year. The reasons most commonly reported for the declination of these matters included: (1) weak or insufficient evidence, (2) lack of criminal intent, (3) agency request, (4) suspect to be prosecuted by another authority or on other charges, and (4) no federal offense committed.

At the end of fiscal year 2013, a total of 79,735 criminal matters were pending, a decrease of 358 matters when compared to the end of the prior year; of these, 6,790, or nine percent, were matters where the defendant was a fugitive, was in a pre-trial diversion program, was in a mental institution, or was unknown. Of these pending matters, 49,284, or 62 percent, had been pending for 24 months or less, and 58,218, or 73 percent, had been pending for 36 months or less.

During fiscal year 2013, the United States attorneys' offices filed 61,529 criminal cases against 83,825 defendants in United States district courts. This represents a three percent decrease in the number of cases filed and a two percent decrease in the number of defendants filed when compared to the prior year.

The United States Attorneys' offices handled a total of 41,324 criminal matters during fiscal year 2013, in which grand jury proceedings were conducted, representing a two percent decrease when compared to the previous year.

A total of 61,258 cases against 82,092 defendants were also terminated during 2013, representing a six percent decrease in the number of cases terminated and a six percent decrease in the number of defendants terminated, when compared to the prior year. A total of 2,640, or three percent, of the terminated defendants went to trial. This represents a one percent decrease in the number of defendants tried when compared to the prior year. Of the 82,092 defendants terminated during fiscal year 2013, 75,718, or 92 percent, either pled guilty or were found guilty. The rate of conviction remained over 92 percent, as it has since fiscal year 2010.

During fiscal year 2013, a total of 73,397, or 97 percent, of all convicted defendants pled guilty prior to or during trial. This represents the same percentage of convicted defendants who pled guilty when compared to the prior year.

Source: United States Attorneys' Annual Statistical Report (2013). U.S. Department of Justice Executive Office for United States Attorneys. Retrieved from: https://www.justice.gov/sites/default/files/usao/legacy/2014/09/22/13statrpt.pdf

Circuit Courts of Appeals

The U.S. Circuit Courts of Appeals, created in 1891, are the federal counterparts to the states' intermediate appellate courts; they hear appeals on many cases to ease the burden on the U.S. Supreme Court. The 94 federal districts are subdivided into 12 circuits, with one court of appeals per circuit. Each court hears appeals from district courts and federal administrative agencies. Federal appellate courts also hear appeals involving patent laws, which arise from decisions rendered by the U.S. Court of Federal Claims and the U.S. Court of International Trade.[126]

Federal appellate courts first screen cases to decide whether to dispose of a case or hear it. Cases are heard by panels of three judges, unless the panel is unable to reach a conclusion. In that instance, the court may hear the case *en banc*. After an appellate court decides to hear a case, the attorneys submit written briefs, present their case orally, and answer questions from the judges. The judges then either announce their decision or confer at greater length before rendering a written decision.[127]

Circuit judges are appointed in the same way as district court judges. If a party is dissatisfied with a circuit court of appeals' decision, it may appeal further to the U.S. Supreme Court. However, these requests are rarely granted. Appellate courts also may **remand** cases to a lower court for further proceedings.

Remand An appellate court's process of returning a case to a lower court for further proceedings.

U.S. Supreme Court

The United States Supreme Court is the highest court in the land. It is composed of nine justices who are nominated by the president and confirmed by the U.S. Senate. Like other judges, most U.S. Supreme Court justices are former attorneys (though this is not a prerequisite), and the majority are elevated to the Court from a judgeship in a lower court. The U.S. Supreme Court is a court of discretionary appeal, so it has discretion to decide which cases it will hear. Typically, it selects cases that carry the most profound legal and political ramifications.[128] Also, as an appellate court, it does not hear witness testimony, but instead reviews legal briefs, hears oral arguments by attorneys, and issues written decisions.

FIGURE 6.3 GEOGRAPHIC BOUNDARIES OF UNITED STATES COURTS OF APPEALS AND UNITED STATES DISTRICT COURTS

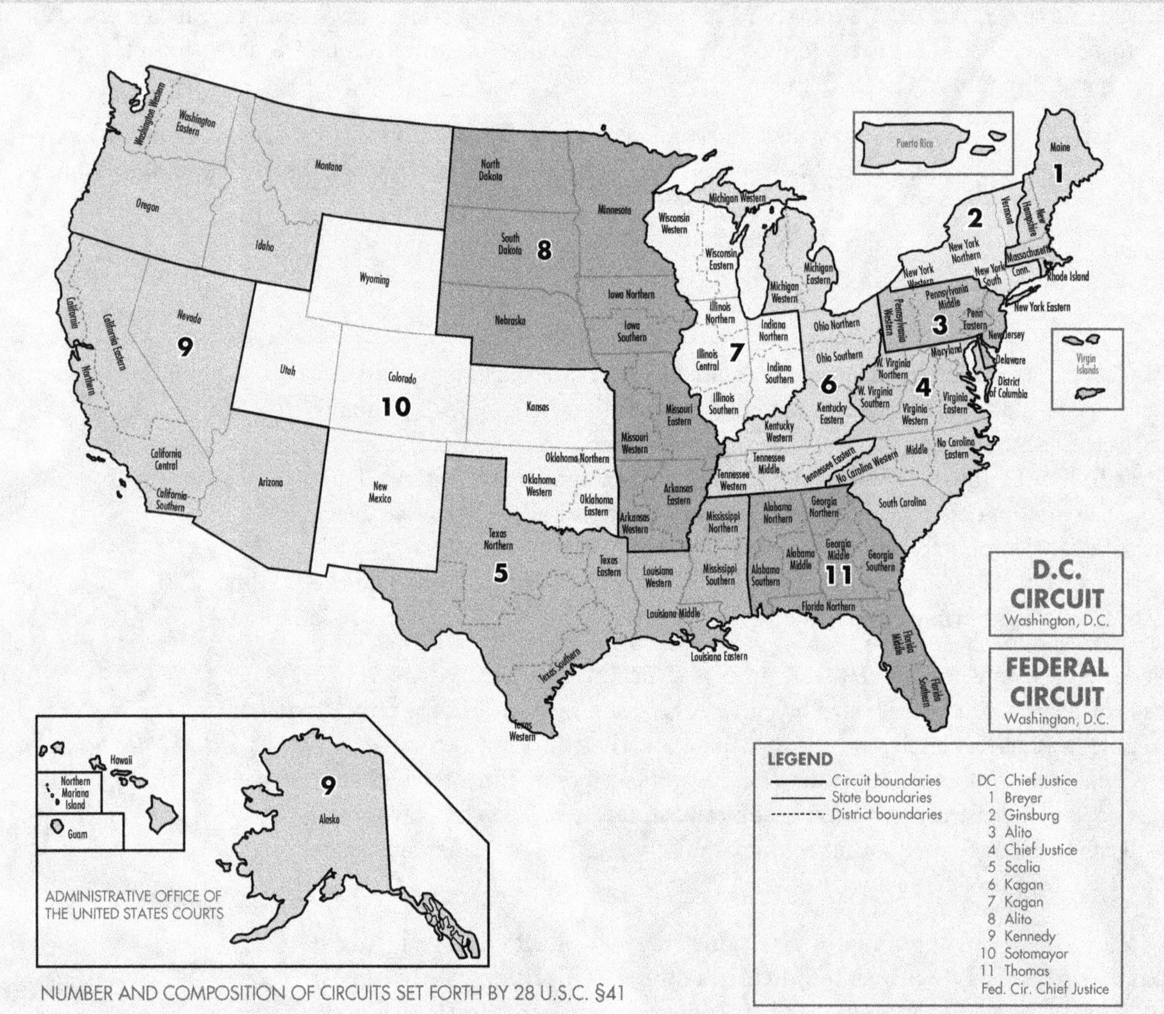

Writ of certiorari
A document issued by the U.S. Supreme Court to confirm that it will review the decision of a federal circuit court of appeals or a state supreme court.

Advancing an appeal to the Supreme Court is not easy; the vast majority of appellants never make it there. The main route to the highest court is through a petition for a **writ of certiorari**, which is a petition filed by a losing party with the Supreme Court, asking it to review the decision of a federal circuit court of appeals or a state supreme court.[129]

The U.S. Supreme Court follows the rule of four: four of the nine justices must vote to hear an appeal, or it will not be heard. Customarily, several criteria must be met in order for an appeal to be heard. First, the plaintiff must have exhausted all other avenues of appeal. Second, the issue must involve a "substantial federal question," as the Supreme Court's jurisdiction is grounded in the U.S. Constitution. Third, the appealed decision must involve an alleged violation of either the Constitution or federal law (the U.S. Code). Finally, the court will not hear cases that ask it to interpret a state's law unless that law violates the U.S. Constitution. This practice rules out most appeals, as they involve either state criminal statutes or personal civil suits. After applying these criteria and others, the Supreme Court hears oral arguments for 75–80 cases per year, out of 10,000 petitions for writs of certiorari.[130]

The U.S. Supreme Court hears between 100 and 200 cases per year.

Judicial review, the power to invalidate acts of Congress, is perhaps the Supreme Court's most significant privilege. It gives the court the authority to interpret authoritatively the supreme law of the land, often to profound social, cultural, and legal effect. The Supreme Court has used this authority about 150 times over acts of Congress, and has invalidated 956 congressional statutes and struck down 1,068 state laws.[131]

Specialized Federal Courts

The federal court system has fewer specialized courts of limited jurisdiction than do the individual states. Article III courts, such as district and circuit courts of appeals, derive their authority from the U.S. Constitution. These courts include the U.S. Court of Federal Claims, which adjudicates suits against the government, and the U.S. Court of International Trade, which entertains cases involving international trade and tariffs.

A second type of specialized federal court is created by Congress. These include magistrate courts, which handle certain civil and criminal cases at the behest of the parties involved; the U.S. Court of Appeals for the Armed Forces, which handles appeals under the Uniform Code of Military Justice; the U.S. Tax Court; and the U.S. Court of Appeals for Veterans Claims. Additionally, bankruptcy courts have sole jurisdiction over cases that fall under the U.S. Bankruptcy Code.[132]

Criminal Procedure and Due Process Overview

Criminal procedure and due process are concepts that describe the rights of individuals accused of crimes. **Due process** is a legal doctrine that requires

Due process The requirement that an accused person receive notice of the charges made against him or her and the right to respond to those charges before being deprived of life, liberty, or property.

equitable treatment of accused individuals. Its purpose is to prevent uncertainty in the justice system, and to ensure that the process does not conflict with the provisions of the Constitution.[133] The term *criminal procedure* refers to the rules of procedure that the government and courts must follow when enforcing substantive criminal law.

The constitutional basis for criminal procedure and due process is the Bill of Rights in the U.S. Constitution. The amendments that compose the Bill of Rights were designed to alleviate fears that the strong federal government would threaten the freedoms of everyday Americans. There are two different but related types of due process. The first is procedural due process. *Procedural due process* refers to the judicial procedures that prosecutors, police, and the courts must adhere to when charging an individual with a criminal offense.[134]

The Bill of Rights was designed to alleviate fears that the strong federal government would threaten the freedoms of everyday Americans.

The second is substantive due process, a concept more far-reaching than the first. *Substantive due process* entails the right to protection against policies and laws that exceed the government's authority, as it is limited by the Constitution.[135] In the context of criminal procedure, this means rights of due process that are not explicitly listed in the Constitution, but are still fundamental liberties. Congress, therefore, cannot pass statutes that violate those rights.[136] Substantive rights are the affirmative rights of citizens to do or say certain things despite the objections of government. These include, in addition to the rights listed above, freedoms of speech and religion.

Number of Felons Convicted in State Courts. In 2006, nearly one million individuals were convicted of felonies in state courts.

These rights are often not enumerated in the Constitution itself. This makes them basic or, in the words of the Supreme Court itself, "fundamental rights implicit in the concept of ordered liberty."[137] Thus, citizens are protected if the legislature enacts a law that violates substantive due process. For the purposes of criminal procedure, substantive due process requires law enforcement officials to inform defendants, at the time of their arrest, of their right to remain silent and to have an attorney present. This right ensures that defendants do not feel compelled to incriminate themselves.

Constitutional Guarantees

Other rights embodied in the Bill of Rights are of critical importance. The Fourth Amendment, for example, protects citizens against unreasonable searches and seizures. These protections extend to searches of persons, homes, and documents. According to the common law decisions derived from the Fourth Amendment, a search warrant may be issued by a judge only if the judge decides there is probable cause to do so. Specifically, the judge must believe an individual has committed an offense or possesses evidence of an offense.

Supreme Court Justification for Jury Trials

© trekandshoot/Shutterstock.com

The U.S. Supreme Court has clarified the right to a speedy trial in Klopfer v. North Carolina and Barker v. Wingo.

The U.S. Constitution guarantees the right to a speedy trial to anyone who is tried in an American courtroom; it is provided in the Sixth Amendment of the Bill of Rights, but it took several rulings from the U.S. Supreme Court to clarify this right. The first ruling to apply the right to speedy trial to the state trial courts was *Klopfer v. North Carolina* in 1967. In this case, the defendant was tried on charges of criminal trespass, but the jury failed to agree on a verdict, resulting in a mistrial. A second trial was supposed to occur, but after one year passed and the second trial did not begin, Klopfer demanded that the trial begin immediately or his case be dismissed. The judge denied Klopfer's request, but granted the state's request to make the case inactive without bringing the defendant to trial, which meant that the case could be made active again at any time the state so chose. Klopfer appealed to the North Carolina Supreme Court, which, in turn, ruled that the right to a speedy trial did not mean the state could be forced to prosecute a defendant. Klopfer's case remained inactive, and Klopfer then appealed to the U.S. Supreme Court. The U.S. Supreme Court ruled in Klopfer's favor, simultaneously striking down the North Carolina law that had allowed the indefinite postponement of Klopfer's trial. This judgment extended the speedy trial provision to the states.[138]

The U.S. Supreme Court heard the case of *Barker v. Wingo* in 1972. Prior to this case, courts assumed that a defendant who did not demand a speedy trial was not opposed to waiting. The U.S. Supreme Court held in *Barker* that passively allowing a case to plod slowly through the system does not equate to the defendant's waiver of his or her Sixth Amendment rights. While this ruling did not specify time frames, it did list a number of factors that trial courts need to take into consideration when determining whether the right to a speedy trial has been denied: how long the delay has lasted, why the delay has taken place, the demand of the defendant to have a speedy trial, and any bias against the defendant.[139]

The next year, 1973, yielded the U.S. Supreme Court's ruling in *Strunk v. United States*. This case determined that if a defendant is denied a speedy trial, the appropriate and "only possible remedy" is dismissal of the charges.[140] Several years later, the U.S. Supreme Court clarified in *United States v. Lovasco* that the Sixth Amendment right applies to delays that occur between a defendant's arrest and the trial—not any delays prior to the initial charges and arrest of a defendant.[141]

Another right provided under the Sixth Amendment is the right to a public trial. This right stemmed from the practice of secret trials in Europe, such as the Spanish Inquisition and the Star Chamber in England. In 1948, the U.S. Supreme Court ruled in *In re Oliver* that the failure to allow a defendant a reasonable opportunity to defend himself against a charge of contempt of court violated due process of law. In this case, a man was subpoenaed to testify as a witness to a crime that was being secretly investigated by a one-man grand jury (i.e., a single judge). The judge believed that the man's testimony was false and evasive and promptly charged him with contempt, found him guilty, and sentenced him to 60 days in jail. This process occurred without the witness's knowledge and did not allow him the opportunity to defend himself. The U.S. Supreme Court ruled that the 14th Amendment prevents an accused from being deprived of his or her rights without due process of law; therefore, an accused person cannot be sentenced to prison in secrecy.[142]

Jury Selection

A defendant has the right to be judged by a jury of his or her peers. The jury must therefore comprise individuals who, in general, reflect the values, rational abilities, and common sense of the average, everyday citizen. A jury of one's peers is supposed to consist of people who are impartial to the case and live in the jurisdiction—typically the county—where the defendant lives. Peer juries are made up of people who represent the community where the alleged crime occurred and where the trial will be held. In 1945, the Supreme Court clarified the meaning of a "jury of one's peers" by stating that while it is unnecessary for each jury to be composed of representatives of every possible economic, racial, religious, gender, and ethnic variable from the community, potential jurors may not be excluded intentionally or systematically due to their social characteristics.[143] The concept of peer juries has origins in the Magna Carta, which guaranteed jury trials for "freemen."[144] This principle was incorporated directly into the U.S. Constitution in Article III, which states: "The trial of all crimes, except in cases of impeachment, shall be by jury."[145] The Sixth Amendment reaffirms Article III by stating, "In all criminal prosecutions, the accused shall enjoy the right to a speedy and public trial by an impartial jury."[146] While federal criminal cases followed suit, some states, such as Louisiana, applied the right to a jury trial selectively. Until 1968, Louisiana granted jury trials only when capital punishment or imprisonment with hard labor were options for sentencing. The Supreme Court ruling in *Duncan v. Louisiana* further applied the jury trial provisions to state-level criminal trials.[147]

Jury members are selected from a master list of all eligible persons in the local jurisdiction of a trial's location. Typically, juries have 12 members, although this is not always the case. State courts are allowed to use as few as six persons in a jury in non-capital cases; federal courts always use 12-member juries. The Supreme Court ruled in *Williams v. Florida* (1970) that states may use juries composed of at least six people in non-capital cases.[39]

There are eligibility requirements for jury service in the United States. In general, jurors must be citizens of the United States and be able to read and write. Jurors must also be older than age 18 and, in most jurisdictions, registered to vote. There are several criteria, which may vary between jurisdictions, that will disqualify someone from being eligible. A serious felony conviction will typically preclude someone from being a juror, for example. Persons such as parents who care for young children during the day, the elderly, or the disabled, who would otherwise be eligible for jury duty, may declare themselves exempt due to physical limitations or personal obligations. This is done on a case-by-case basis and does not permanently exempt the potential juror from service; he or she may be selected again in the future. In the interest of keeping jury panels impartial, as the U.S. Constitution instructs, exemptions are limited at least when preparing the master list.

A *venire*, or *venire facias*, is a writ that summons jurors for service. The potential jurors will report to a designated office or building at a particular date and time. They are interviewed to confirm whether they are eligible and available to serve on a jury. Some are dismissed and sent home, thus fulfilling their jury service. Those who are kept in the jury pool are paid a nominal amount for their service. From the jury pool, several jury panels may be selected and sent to various courtrooms that require juries. A jury panel for a misdemeanor trial will typically be smaller than a jury panel for a felony trial. A felony jury panel could be as many as 36 or more persons. The jury panels are selected at random by the county official, usually a clerk of the court.

A *voir dire* examination is an oath sworn by a potential juror concerning his or her qualifications to serve on a jury. The term *voir dire* means "to speak the truth." During *voir dire*, both the prosecution and the defense will ask potential jurors questions about their personal and professional backgrounds, any prior experience with courts or the legal system, and even personal opinions on current events—which may have relevance for the charge against the defendant. Sometimes the judge will ask jurors questions as well. Any juror who is seen by either side as unacceptable for the jury is typically eliminated by either the challenge for cause or the peremptory challenge. A **challenge for cause** is a specific legal reason to exclude a potential juror. The side that makes the challenge must defend the challenge to the judge, as the challenge typically argues that the juror will be unable to fairly judge the accused for a particular reason. The decision to remove the juror is up to the judge, but there are statutes that specify rules for removing jurors. A **peremptory challenge** is an objection to a potential juror without specifying a reason for the objection. The attorney making the peremptory challenge can make the challenge for any reason, or no reason, and whether a peremptory challenge is made is usually an important part of an attorney's trial strategy. There are limits to the number of jurors who may be eliminated

Challenge for cause
A specific legal reason to exclude a potential juror.

Peremptory challenge
An attorney's objection to the jury service of a potential juror without a particular argument against the juror.

due to peremptory challenges. New York allows three peremptory challenges, except in particularly serious cases, while Texas allows six.[148]

There are also limitations to peremptory challenges. Using challenges to purposely exclude persons of a particular race, particularly African-Americans, was a common occurrence until the late 20th century, and the Supreme Court upheld the practice in its 1965 ruling, *Swain v. Alabama*.[149] However, in 1986, the Court partially overruled *Swain*, proclaiming in *Batson v. Kentucky* that blacks may not be excluded from juries due to concern that they will decide in favor of a black defendant.[150] The *Batson* ruling was later expanded to include challenges that purposely excluded jurors based on gender; however, the ruling was delivered via a paternity case, *J.E.B. v. Alabama ex rel. T.B.*, not a criminal case.[151] The number of challenges allowed varies from state to state and is controlled by statute.

Voir dire continues until the entire jury has been filled, no matter how many challenges occur. Sometimes, alternates are selected. These alternates will sit through the trial with the jury and will take the place of a juror who is forced to leave the trial while it is in progress. Reasons that a juror may leave include illness, family emergency, or disqualification.

Sequester To remove the jury, and any alternate jurors, from all possible influences that may affect their abilities to fairly judge the accused.

As soon as the jury is sworn in, the criminal trial officially begins. The judge must decide whether to **sequester** the jury for the duration of the trial. Sequestering a jury theoretically removes the jury, and any alternate jurors, from all possible influences that may affect their abilities to fairly judge the accused. The sequestered jury is housed in a hotel and not allowed visitors. Any magazines or newspapers they read or television shows they watch are censored. Typically, a judge will sequester a jury only in a high-profile case, when inflammatory news stories or tabloid articles may potentially unduly influence the jury. Sequestering a jury puts a strain on the jury members, as they must remain away from their homes, jobs, and families until the trial is over—regardless of whether the trial lasts three days or three months.

With innovations in technology over the last few decades, including the Internet and mobile phones, it has become increasingly difficult to separate the jury from all outside influences that might affect their ultimate decision-making process. Jurors who are sequestered must be monitored more closely now than in years past, due to the wide availability of cell phones and Internet access.

After the state presents its case, the defense may enter a motion for a directed verdict. This motion asserts that the state failed to present a case proving the defendant's guilt beyond a reasonable doubt and asks the judge to acquit the defendant. If the judge approves this motion, he or she typically will direct the jury to acquit the defendant. Even when this motion is not filed by the defense, a trial judge may still order a directed verdict of not guilty. The judge may also order a directed verdict because the prosecutor behaved improperly in some way, or the testimony from the witnesses for the prosecution was not credible.

Once closing arguments have been made, the judge issues orders directly to the jury. These orders include that the jury retire to the jury room; consider the facts, evidence, and testimony presented in court; and decide on a fair verdict. The judge's order will include instructions about the possible verdicts the jury may decide on and the legal definition of reasonable doubt. In some jurisdictions, judges are allowed to review all of the evidence that has been presented to the jury, such as the testimony of each witness. This can be helpful if the trial has been lengthy, but it may inadvertently influence a jury as well if the judge has suggested an opinion about the defendant's innocence or guilt. It can take some time to deliver the instructions to the jury due to the complexities of the laws that must be followed. It is important that judges deliver the jury instructions in a way that all the jurors can understand them and fulfill their duties. Generally, the final instruction given to the jurors is that they may not discuss the facts of the case with anyone other than their fellow jurors during official deliberations.

Deliberations and Beyond

After the judge's charge has concluded, the jury is removed so that it may begin deliberations. Once the jury retires to the jury room, a foreperson is selected to be the jury's leader. In some courts of law, the first juror selected during *voir dire* is the foreperson. A foreperson typically sits at the head of the table and calls for a vote. Unanimous jury verdicts are required by law in each state except for Oregon and Louisiana. The Oregon Constitution and the Louisiana Codes of Criminal Procedure both allow for non-unanimous jury verdicts in certain non-capital criminal cases. The Supreme Court upheld these state requirements in two 1972 decisions, *Johnson v. Louisiana* and *Apodaca v. Oregon*.[152] There is strength in numbers, however, when it comes to jury deliberation. Twelve unique points of view can expose jury members to different interpretations and opinions about the evidence presented and, thus, discourage them from using only their personal beliefs to select a verdict. Additionally, jurors can work together to refresh improperly or incorrectly recalled memories from the trial.[153]

Jury members are drawn from many different circumstances and situations. They may be schoolteachers, long-haul truck drivers, firefighters, business executives, retired persons, or even students. Because jurors are not always familiar with the legal system, some may not understand legal procedures and complications that arise during the trial process. Even intelligent and well-meaning jurors may not fully understand the judge's charge or some of the jury instructions. Jurors are allowed to ask questions of the court, usually written on paper and delivered to the judge by the bailiff. Communication from the jury is typically read aloud in open court so that it may be entered into the record of the case.

When a jury is unable to generate the required number of votes for a decision, and deliberations have been conducted for some time, the result is a hung jury, which is fairly uncommon. The jury is called into open court and dismissed, and the judge declares a mistrial, allowing the prosecution the choice to drop the case or refile it and attempt to retry the defendant. Juries may be hung due to varying opinions of the significance of a piece of evidence, the meaning of "reasonable doubt," or differing opinions about innocence or guilt.

When a verdict is reached, the jury returns to the courtroom to announce the decision in a formal statement to the court. The jury is then thanked for its service and released by the judge. A prosecutor may request that the court poll the jury members: that is, the judge or bailiff asks each juror whether he or she individually voted for the whole jury's verdict. Polling a jury is typically done to determine whether a juror has been pressured to vote with the remainder of the jurors.

Jury nullification A process that occurs when a jury uses information not provided during a court case to determine the guilt or innocence of a defendant.

One phenomenon in the criminal trial process is **jury nullification**. This occurs when a jury nullifies, or contradicts, the fair and impartial procedure of the trial process in some way. Jury nullification may also occur when a jury does not follow the court's interpretation of the law. A jury may disregard the court's instructions and consider information not presented in court during the trial as evidence in the case. For example, if a defendant claims to have a medical disability that prevented him from being able to commit a murder, and one of the jurors is a medical expert on that disability and subsequently uses personal knowledge to influence the verdict,that is considered jury nullification. A jury may also exercise nullification by refusing to convict the accused because the members believe the penalty is too severe. An example of this would be a case of a young man who shoots his father to prevent the father from committing another incident of spousal abuse on his wife. The jury, feeling that the young man attempted to protect his mother from harm because he knew the beatings would occur again, may find the defendant not guilty.

Judges clearly state in the charge to the jury that jurors are to consider only evidence presented in court, but this does not always occur in a room full of human beings, each with different knowledge and opinions. Attorneys are considered officers of the court with the duty to promote and uphold the law, and many bar associations consider it a breach of ethics for an attorney to make an argument in court that may cause jury nullification. Judges also have the ability to prohibit statements or arguments that request jury nullification. In the *U.S. v. Moylan (*4th Cir. 1969) decision, the right of jury nullification was affirmed, but the Circuit Court also upheld the court's power to disallow statements that informed the jurors of their right of nullification.[154] In a Sixth Circuit Court of Appeals ruling in 1980, the entire panel of judges agreed unanimously that "in criminal cases, a jury is entitled to acquit the defendant because it has no sympathy for the government's position."[155] In contrast, however, the Second Circuit ruled that a juror may be removed, according to Federal Rules of Criminal Procedure 23(b), if there is evidence that he or she intends to nullify the law.[156]

Bifurcated trial A criminal trial that has two separate phases: the first phase determines the defendant's guilt or innocence, and the second phase determines the defendant's potential punishment.

Sometimes, the criminal trial is **bifurcated**, or split into two parts. In the first part, the defendant's guilt or innocence is decided; in the second part, the defendant's punishment is argued. Juries do deliberate on a defendant's punishment, and their "verdict" comes in the form of a recommendation to the judge. A jury may sentence a defendant to a particular punishment, only to be overruled by the judge, who sentences the defendant to a different punishment. This does not happen often, however.

Critical Thinking

A jury believes there is evidence beyond a reasonable doubt to show that a defendant, who is an anti-abortion activist, murdered a doctor who performed abortions in an attempt to prevent further abortions from occurring. The jury assesses a verdict of "not guilty" for the defendant. Do you believe this example of jury nullification is a fair result of the criminal trial system? Why or why not?

The Accused

While the accused person is at the heart of the criminal trial process, the defendant can be largely unaware of many of the legal aspects of his or her criminal case that occur behind the scenes. There are discussions between the attorneys about evidence that may be presented and witnesses that may be called, as well as negotiations for plea bargains. There may be discussions between the state's attorney, the defense attorney, and the judge about procedural matters that can affect the outcome of the defendant's case but have nothing to do with the offense the accused reportedly committed. The defendant's guilt or innocence lies in the public and private aspects of the trial process and will likely affect the rest of his or her life.

Some defendants are allowed to bond out of jail after arrest. This means that they guarantee, with money, that they will appear at all court hearings during the trial process, including any hearings prior to the beginning of the trial. Defendants may post bond by providing the required amount of cash to the jurisdiction or using the services of a bail bondsman. The defendant will pay a small portion of the bond, usually around 10%, to the bondsman, who will in turn provide proof to the jurisdiction that the defendant has paid bond. The bondsman guarantees the jurisdiction that the defendant will appear for all court hearings. If the defendant fails to appear in court, or "jumps" bond, the bond is revoked by the court, and the bail bondsman is responsible for paying the court the amount of the defendant's bond. If the defendant is subsequently found and brought into custody, he or she will appear in court, and the bondsman will receive a refund of the monies paid to the jurisdiction.

© Joe Seer/Shutterstock.com

Actress and celebrity defendant Lindsay Lohan faced felony charges for allegedly taking a necklace from a jewelry store.

Some defendants are unable to post bond due to financial constraints. Bond amounts can range from $500 for some misdemeanors to $1,000,000 for high-profile cases. Some defendants are not approved for bond by the judge because the judge feels that the defendant will run away or because the judge feels it is safer to society if the defendant remains in jail. Bail is not guaranteed by the U.S. Constitution; however, the Eighth Amendment does state that "excessive bail shall not be required." This means that a judge may not prescribe an outrageous bail amount when compared to the alleged crime. In other words, the Eighth

Transport officer A law enforcement officer who transports inmates to and from court and jail.

Amendment prevents judges from assigning a bail amount of $250,000 to a defendant accused of writing a bad check in the amount of $500. Defendants who cannot post bond or do not have an approved bond will remain in jail until trial. **Transport officers** will bring the defendant to court for all court appearances including trial.

© Lisa F. Young/Shutterstock.com

A transport officer brings defendants to and from their court appearances.

During a trial, a defendant will sit next to his or her defense attorney at a table near the front of the courtroom. The U.S. Constitution guarantees an accused person the right to confront his or her accuser, meaning a defendant has the right to be present for all witness testimony. During trial, a defendant will frequently confer with the defense attorney to clarify questions or strategy. Whether or not a defendant testifies is also part of the defense's trial strategy. A defendant has the constitutional right to refrain from testifying in court; this is called the right not to incriminate oneself. If a defendant does testify, he or she is subject to the same process of cross-examination by which any other witness must participate.

If a defendant is in custody during the trial process, he or she will return to a supervised room or area when court is not in session. A defendant is allowed to confer with his or her attorney in private but will not have free access to the building. If a defendant needs to use the restroom, for example, someone will accompany him or her to ensure that there is no escape attempt or harm done to anyone—including the harm of a defendant by another party.

After jury deliberations are over and a verdict is delivered in court, a defendant will be released in the case of a not guilty verdict or remanded to the custody of the local jurisdiction in the case of a guilty verdict. Some judges may, depending on circumstances and arguments from the prosecution and defense, release a defendant who has been found guilty for a temporary time so that he or she can manage personal affairs before punishment is assessed. The defendant may be ordered to turn himself or herself in to the authorities on a particular date and time or may be ordered to return to court for sentencing.

Degradation ceremony The tactic of presenting someone in a negative light so that others may look unfavorably upon that individual. A prosecutor may do this to a defendant, or a defense attorney may do this to a witness for the prosecution.

A defendant in a criminal trial is arguably in a precarious situation. On the one hand, a defendant is technically innocent until proven guilty. Due to human tendencies and public opinion, a defendant may be perceived as guilty even if the jury returns a verdict of not guilty. Such perception of a defendant can affect the defendant's reputation and everyday activities for the rest of his or her life. The prosecuting attorney has the task of proving the defendant's guilt; often, the prosecutor publicly makes the defendant look like a bad person in addition to showing guilt. This process is sometimes known as a **degradation ceremony**.[157] For example, the prosecutor may take on a very negative attitude when speaking to the jury, using body language such as a curled lip or deep frown to demonstrate his or her distaste for the defendant. Presenting the defendant in the worst light possible is part of the prosecutor's job. The defense attorney will attempt to salvage the defendant's appearance during counterargument.

Critical Thinking

Do you believe it is fair for a prosecutor to embellish negative statements about the defendant in an attempt to win the sympathy of the jury? Why or why not?

Exhibit: The Bill of Rights

Amendment I

Congress shall make no law respecting an establishment of religion, or prohibiting the free exercise thereof; or abridging the freedom of speech, or of the press; or the right of the people peaceably to assemble, and to petition the Government for a redress of grievances.

Amendment II

A well regulated Militia, being necessary to the security of a free State, the right of the people to keep and bear Arms, shall not be infringed.

Amendment III

No Soldier shall, in time of peace be quartered in any house, without the consent of the Owner, nor in time of war, but in a manner to be prescribed by law.

Amendment IV

The right of the people to be secure in their persons, houses, papers, and effects, against unreasonable searches and seizures, shall not be violated, and no Warrants shall issue, but upon probable cause, supported by Oath or affirmation, and particularly describing the place to be searched, and the persons or things to be seized.

Amendment V

No person shall be held to answer for a capital, or otherwise infamous crime, unless on a presentment or indictment of a Grand Jury, except in cases arising in the land or naval forces, or in the Militia, when in actual service in time of War or public danger; nor shall any person be subject for the same offence to be twice put in jeopardy of life or limb; nor shall be compelled in any criminal case to be a witness against himself, nor be deprived of life, liberty, or property, without due process of law; nor shall private property be taken for public use, without just compensation.

Amendment VI

In all criminal prosecutions, the accused shall enjoy the right to a speedy and public trial, by an impartial jury of the State and district wherein the crime shall have been committed, which district shall have been previously ascertained by law, and to be informed of the nature and cause of the accusation; to be confronted with the witnesses against him; to have compulsory process for obtaining witnesses in his favor, and to have the Assistance of Counsel for his **defense**.

(Continued)

Exhibit: The Bill of Rights (*Continued*)

Amendment VII

In Suits at common law, where the value in controversy shall exceed twenty dollars, the right of trial by jury shall be preserved, and no fact tried by a jury, shall be otherwise re-examined in any Court of the United States, than according to the rules of the common law.

Amendment VIII

Excessive bail shall not be required, nor excessive fines imposed, nor cruel and unusual punishments inflicted.

Amendment IX

The enumeration in the Constitution, of certain rights, shall not be construed to deny or disparage others retained by the people.

Amendment X

The powers not delegated to the United States by the Constitution, nor prohibited by it to the States, are reserved to the States respectively, or to the people.[158]]

The Fifth Amendment, in turn, protects citizens from being put on trial twice for the same crime, a practice known as double jeopardy. It also protects individuals against self-incrimination. A defendant who "takes the Fifth" during testimony is using this constitutional right. The Fifth Amendment also guarantees due process. Specifically, the Fifth Amendment requires an individual to be notified of the charges against him or her, and affords him or her the right to answer those charges before being deprived of life, liberty, or property.

The Sixth Amendment guarantees the right to a speedy trial and the right to a trial by jury. Additionally, it allows a defendant to confront his or her accuser in court, to force witnesses to provide testimony, and to be represented by an attorney. The Seventh Amendment provides the right to trial by jury in certain types of civil cases. The Eighth Amendment protects defendants against excessive bail and cruel and unusual punishment.

Critical Thinking

Does the Constitution favor the accused at the expense of the victim? If so, what do you think the justifications are for doing so? Explain.

Constitutional Basis for Due Process

The 14th Amendment guarantees due process to every criminal defendant in the United States. Passed in the aftermath of the Civil War, this amendment initially helped protect the civil rights of African-Americans. It contains a due process clause that prevents states from depriving citizens of life, liberty, and property without the due process of law. This clause is similar to the due process clause found in the Fifth Amendment, but the Fifth Amendment version is understood to apply only to the federal government, while the 14th Amendment version also applies to state and local governments.

The judiciary has repeatedly affirmed that the procedural guarantees in the Bill of Rights—specifically the Fifth, Sixth, and Eighth Amendments—limit what the state can do when it charges and prosecutes an individual. If any of these guarantees or rights are violated or denied, then the individual has been denied due process of law, a violation of his or her constitutional rights. The Supreme Court is the ultimate arbiter of remedies for such violations, as it interprets the Constitution. It ruled in *Chapman v. California* (1967) that "we cannot leave to the States the formulation of . . . remedies designed to protect people from infractions by the States of federally guaranteed rights."[159]

The passage of the 14th Amendment allowed the U.S. Supreme Court to enforce the Bill of Rights against state governments. The 14th Amendment contained what has come to be called the "equal protection clause," which prevents a governmental authority from denying an individual equal protection of the laws, such as laws that guarantee civil rights. It was used to force states to provide the same protection under law to individuals of all races.

Amount of Due Process

An accused person is afforded rights even beyond those enumerated in the Constitution and state and federal law. For example, the 14th Amendment's due process clause also prohibits practices that fail to meet a standard of fundamental fairness, even if they do not violate a specific provision.[160] Furthermore, the rights of due process, along with the others enumerated in the U.S. Constitution, can never be repealed by the states. Individual states may add additional rights by amending their own constitutions, but they cannot take away or restrict those guaranteed by the Constitution. Additionally, substantive due process significantly strengthens the power of judicial review. The Supreme Court has retained more extensive discretion in deciding which rights are "substantive" and deserve protection.

Defendants' rights, guaranteed by the U.S. Constitution, are the subject of controversy.

Defendants' Rights

In the American criminal justice system, a defendant is presumed innocent unless and until proven guilty. The burden of proof rests on the prosecution (the state); the prosecution must prove that the defendant is guilty rather than the accused proving they are innocent. In practice, this makes it much more difficult to convict a defendant, as he or she must be proved guilty beyond a **reasonable doubt**. If a judge or jury concludes there is a

Reasonable doubt The standard of proof that the state must meet to convict a criminal defendant; if reasonable doubt exists, the defendant must be acquitted.

reasonable doubt the defendant committed the crime, the defendant must be acquitted.

These defendants' rights, and the guarantees enshrined in the U.S. Constitution, were influenced by the fear of tyrannical government. Under the Constitution, everyone is equal in the eyes of the law. The accused must not be painted as the enemy of the state and must be judged by the rule of law (e.g., due process and criminal procedure). The rule of law is crucial because, according to J.H. Skolnick, "its essential element is the reduction of arbitrariness by officials."[161]

Defendants' rights are the subject of controversy. Critics believe that too many guilty people go free because of these rights, while proponents claim that these rights are necessary to spare the innocent from unjust prosecution. Both sides, of course, are correct, as experience has shown that these rights generally protect innocent persons, and on occasion let an apparently guilty person go free. In the words of Judge Henry Friendly, this is not an unjust result, for most Americans "would allow a considerable number of guilty persons to go free than to convict an appreciable number of innocent men."[162]

Remedies for Violations

While the law provides remedies for violations of judicial procedure or due process, the hope is that these violations never occur. Accordingly, the law provides procedural safeguards to ensure these violations do not occur. For instance, after a suspect is arrested, his or her case must be reviewed by a prosecutor or magistrate. This process ensures that the police follow the rules of due process and have probable cause to believe the arrested person committed the crime with which he or she is being charged.

Another legal tool is the right to petition for a writ of habeas corpus, which allows criminal defendants to compel the government to explain why it has detained them. This writ is a procedural device that protects persons against unjust imprisonment. It does not, however, protect persons against false arrest, so the scope of this power is more limited than commonly imagined.[163]

Another remedy for violations of criminal procedure or due process is the exclusionary rule. This rule holds that evidence is inadmissible in court if it was improperly obtained. The rule rests on the notion that evidence obtained through an unreasonable search and seizure was obtained by violating the civil rights of the suspect. This evidence is called the **fruit of the poisonous tree**, since it is evidence that was tainted from its source.[164]

Fruit of the poisonous tree Evidence obtained by law enforcement as a result of an illegal search or seizure.

As mentioned in the sections dealing with appellate courts, convicted persons may appeal their convictions to a higher court. All states provide appellate review of some sort, and that right cannot be constrained by the appellant's financial limitations. Accordingly, the state must provide an attorney for the defendant, as well as a trial transcript he or she can use during the appeals process. On appeal, an appellant must demonstrate that the trial court made a legal, not factual, error. His or her arguments also must be presented in an **appellate brief**, which is a written legal argument presented to the panel of

Appellate brief A written memorandum filed by the prosecution or defense attorney to explain why the decision of a lower court was erroneous.

judges to persuade them that a legal error was made in the trial court, and the trial court's or trial jury's decision should be reversed.[165]

Ethics and Professionalism: The Disgraced Duke Prosecutor

Law enforcement officers and prosecuting attorneys are held to a high ethical standard. The 2006 rape allegations filed against the Duke University lacrosse team provide a contemporary example of the dangers wrought by the abuse of prosecutorial power. For his actions during that prosecution, former Durham County, North Carolina District Attorney Mike Nifong was removed from his post and disbarred. As prosecutor, Nifong prosecuted several white Duke lacrosse players who were accused of raping an African-American stripper at an off-campus team party. Although initially praised for his willingness to pursue such a case, Nifong ultimately came under fire for his ethical conduct during the investigation and trial.

Nifong first was criticized for making inflammatory and prejudicial statements, including unfounded accusations about the accused, as well as for omitting exculpatory evidence (evidence tending to exonerate the accused) from the DNA report of the victim's rape. In fact, the full report detected the presence of body fluids from several men who were not charged, and it was later revealed that no DNA evidence implicated the men charged. Nifong claimed this omission was an accident, but his claim was later revealed to be inaccurate, showing his serious breach of the rules of ethics and discovery.

Nifong's misconduct, coupled with the witness's continued changing of her story, ultimately resulted in the charges being dropped.[166] But the damage was done. Nifong was hit with ethics charges by the North Carolina State Bar. He was charged with making prejudicial statements and perpetrating a "systematic abuse of prosecutorial discretion" by withholding the DNA evidence.[167] Nifong was subsequently suspended and disbarred. He was later jailed for one day for contempt of court, and recently filed for bankruptcy after being sued by the accused lacrosse players.

Law Enforcement Investigations

Before setting the machinery of the judicial system in motion, the relevant law enforcement agency (usually local or state police) must conduct its investigation. These investigations, like their later prosecutions, must abide by the rules of due process and criminal procedure.

Criminal procedures vary from state to state, but their grounding principles are found in the U.S. Constitution and Bill of Rights. Although the Constitution regulates searches and seizures, as well as interrogations and the right to counsel, law enforcement agencies may conduct investigations free from the interference of the courts. For example, the Constitution does not require police to articulate a reason for focusing their efforts on a certain suspect before investigating him or her.[168]

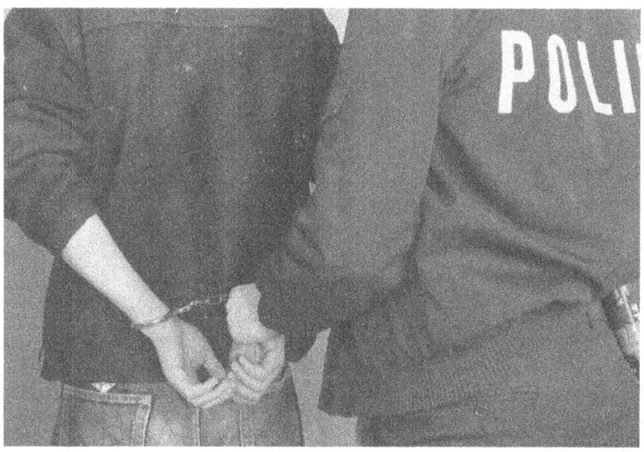

© Corepics VOF/Shutterstock.com

Law enforcement officials must follow specific guidelines when arresting a suspect, including the reading of Miranda rights, to properly protect the suspect's rights.

The Warrant Requirement and Exceptions

Warrant Legal authorization from a judge to make an arrest, conduct a search, or seize evidence.

Police use two types of **warrants** to investigate and apprehend suspected criminals: an arrest warrant and a search warrant. An arrest warrant is issued by a judge or magistrate and authorizes the arrest of a specific person for a specific crime. The majority of arrests occur "in the field," and these arrests do not require an arrest warrant as long as the officer has probable cause to believe the person being arrested has committed a specific crime for which the arrest is authorized. Common law countries allow police officers to take a person into custody if they believe he or she has committed a felony.

The second type of warrant, a search warrant, authorizes police to search and seize premises for items or information listed specifically in the warrant. With few exceptions, police must have a search warrant before conducting a search and seizure. One exception is that police may search for and seize evidence if the evidence is likely to be destroyed before they can obtain a warrant. They also may search for and seize evidence if a crime is currently being committed, or if the owner of the evidence explicitly consents to the search.[169] Officers can enter only the address listed on the warrant, and search only in the areas and for the items listed.[170]

Identification

Before entering a residence, police generally are required to announce their entry and intent to search. However, if the police have reason to believe the evidence will be destroyed or they will be injured, they may enter unannounced. If police identify themselves and request the right to search the premises and the suspect or property owner agrees, they generally do not need to obtain a warrant to search the premises.[171]

Arrest, Search, and Seizure

A person cannot be arrested unless the police have probable cause to believe he or she has committed a crime. Probable cause is determined by the judge who signs the arrest warrant, or by a magistrate after the arrest. In a longer-term investigation in which a grand jury has been convened, the grand jury determines if there is probable cause.[172]

Officers have the right to stop and question individuals if they see or suspect that a crime or violation has been committed.

When a police officer makes an arrest and holds the suspect in custody, he or she must read a suspect his or her Miranda rights before asking the suspect any questions relating to the crime. This procedure derives its name from the case of *Miranda v. Arizona* (1966) and safeguards a suspect's rights against self-incrimination under the Fifth Amendment when he or she is subjected to police interrogation.[173] In brief, the Miranda requirements are satisfied if officers read suspects a warning, which often is written on a "Miranda card," that they have the right to remain silent, as their words may be used against them, and have the right to an attorney, even if they are unable to afford one.[174]

Exhibit: Miranda Rights

"In the absence of other effective measures, the following procedures to safeguard the Fifth Amendment privilege must be observed: the person in custody must, prior to interrogation, be clearly informed that he has the right to remain silent, and that anything he says will be used against him in court; he must be clearly informed that he has the right to consult with a lawyer and to have the lawyer with him during interrogation, and that, if he is indigent, a lawyer will be appointed to represent him" (*Miranda v. Arizona*, 1966).

Before questioning a suspect who is in custody, law enforcement officers must issue a Miranda warning (the exact wording of the text varies slightly from state to state, but essentially conforms to the example shown below adapted from the Kansas City Police Department.[175]).

1. You have the right to remain silent.
2. Anything you say can and will be used against you in a court of law.
3. You have the right to talk to a lawyer and have him present with you while you are being questioned.
4. If you cannot afford to hire a lawyer, one will be appointed to represent you before any questioning, if you wish.
5. You can decide at any time to exercise these rights and not answer any questions or make any statements.

The following questions should be asked after the specific warning has been made, and an affirmative reply is returned to each question. This secures a waiver to legally question the suspect, such that their responses will be admissible in court.

1. Do you understand each of these rights I have explained to you?
2. Having these rights in mind, do you wish to talk to us now?

Custodial Interrogations

The Miranda rights of suspects have expanded over time, reflecting a growing concern during the 1960s with **custodial interrogations**, or the questioning of a suspect in custody. Specifically, several of the U.S. Supreme Court's decisions underscore its desire to control custodial interrogations, such as those that occur in a police station, to ensure the police do not harass or intimidate minority defendants and the impoverished, or others who cannot easily pursue traditional avenues of recourse.[176] Miranda rights now apply to people being questioned by the police as part of a criminal investigation, as well as to those arrested. People may waive these rights before speaking to an officer, but all investigations that occur when a person is in custody require the police to notify him or her of the Miranda rights.[177]

Custodial interrogation The questioning of a witness by law enforcement while he or she is under arrest.

Similarly, the validity of confessions obtained by law enforcement is interpreted through the lens of the Fifth Amendment to the Constitution, which states that "no person shall be compelled in any criminal case to be a witness against himself."[178] This means that confessions must be voluntary and uncoerced (the suspect must not be under threat of torture, for instance). For the purposes of custodial interrogation, the interrogated person must acknowledge his or her Miranda rights for such a statement to be admissible in court.[179]

Pretrial Proceedings

Before trial, a defendant appears in the initial, or bail, appearance, as well as in a preliminary hearing.

In a *preliminary hearing* held before a judge, the defense often presents witness testimony to argue there is insufficient evidence to justify the arrest of the accused. Preliminary hearings are used when a grand jury has not returned an indictment, although a grand jury can also be used after a preliminary hearing to approve the prosecutor's case.

The purpose of a grand jury and a preliminary hearing is to ensure there is probable cause to charge a person with a crime.[180] Preliminary hearings are important because they represent the first time someone other than a law enforcement officer or prosecutor has reviewed the case, thus providing a layer of protection against a baseless charge, as well as the unnecessary humiliation of trial. During these hearings, the burden of proof on the prosecution is far less than it is at trial; it merely must prove it has a *prima facie* (at first sight) case, which requires it to show only that there is probable cause to believe a crime was committed by the accused.[181] This standard of proof, probable cause, is the same used by judges to decide whether to issue an arrest or search warrant. Not all states require preliminary hearings, and such hearings are normally reserved for serious felonies.

The Initial Appearance

Initial appearance The court hearing at which a defendant hears the formal charges levied against him or her.

Complaint A document listing the criminal charges brought against a defendant.

The **initial appearance** in court is the time when a criminal defendant stands in court and hears the formal charges levied against him or her. The defendant enters a plea at this point, most often by declaring himself or herself guilty or not guilty. If the defendant does not yet have an attorney and cannot afford one, the court will appoint one at the public's expense. At this hearing, the official **complaint**, or list of charges brought by the police, is assessed by a magistrate. These first appearances also are known as bail hearings, at which magistrates determine the legality of the arrest and set bail.[182]

Grand Jury and Indictment

Grand jury A group of 16–23 people that hears evidence and decides if probable cause exists to believe a person has committed a crime.

Grand juries are different from trial juries. **Grand juries** consist of 16–23 people who hear evidence about the crime committed. Usually, a prosecutor presents the evidence to the grand jury in a secret session. The grand jury's task is to determine if probable cause exists to believe that the suspect committed a criminal offense.[183] In felony cases, a grand jury returns a formal charge called an **indictment**, which represents its judgment that there is probable cause to believe the defendant committed a crime.[184]

Indictment A written document issued by a grand jury to indicate that there is probable cause to believe a person has committed a crime.

Grand juries do not, however, decide a defendant's ultimate guilt or innocence; that task is left to the trial judge or trial jury. Additionally, grand jury witnesses are not entitled to have their attorneys present, and the suspect's attorney also has no right to be present, since a grand jury is not a criminal court. Historically, grand juries overwhelmingly return the indictment requested by prosecutors.[185]

Critical Thinking

Do you think grand juries are necessary in pretrial proceedings, especially if they generally side with prosecutors? Should they be replaced by preliminary hearings? Why or why not?

Bail

Bail is normally set at the initial appearance or bail hearing stage of the trial. Bail is determined by a judge or magistrate, who considers the seriousness of the crime, the risk the defendant poses to society, and the likelihood that the defendant will flee the court's jurisdiction before trial. If the judge believes the defendant deserves bail, he or she then assigns an amount sufficient to ensure the defendant will appear in court. Bail is usually paid either in cash from the defendant or by bond from a bail bondsman. **Bail** bonds are essentially insurance policies, and the court is the beneficiary if the defendant flees. Excessive bail is prohibited by the Eighth Amendment.

Bail A sum of money that the court receives if a defendant flees from court proceedings.

Discovery The court-ordered process by which attorneys learn about their opponents' cases to prepare for trial.

Discovery

Discovery is the court-ordered process by which attorneys learn about their opponents' cases before trial. The discovery process commonly includes depositions (testimony under oath), exchanges of interrogatories (written questions), requests for admissions (requests to admit the truth or falsity of statements), and requests for production of documents.[186]

Discovery is very limited in criminal cases because information procured by the defense conceivably can be used to harass or intimidate prosecution witnesses.[187] Nonetheless, the prosecution is obligated by law to, at a minimum, provide the defense any materials that appear to show the defendant is not guilty. In addition, the prosecution must provide the defense any materials that tend to impeach, or diminish, the credibility of any witnesses who will testify for the prosecution at trial. Police reports, laboratory results, forensic evidence, medical tests, ballistics reports, and witness statements are other categories of information that prosecutors provide to defense attorneys during discovery.

© Andrey_Kuzmin/Shutterstock.com

During discovery, both testimonial evidence, such as an eyewitness account, and physical evidence, such as fingerprints, are presented.

Prosecutors usually are required to disclose more information in discovery than defense attorneys must disclose. Still, prosecutors often seek to limit the materials they disclose, for fear that disclosing certain categories of evidence (such as witness statements) will lead witnesses to be intimidated and deterred from testifying at trial. Broadly speaking, discovery of physical evidence and confessions made by the defendant is considered a right of the defense, but written and recorded witness statements are more problematic.[188]

Suppression Hearing

Suppression hearing A pretrial hearing where a defendant asks the court to suppress, or disallow, evidence that the police obtained illegally.

A **suppression hearing** is a hearing held if the defense asks the judge to suppress, or disallow, a piece of evidence that it believes the state obtained illegally during the criminal investigation. Usually, motions (requests) to suppress evidence contend that the evidence was obtained only by violating the defendant's Fourth Amendment or Fifth Amendment rights. Defense attorneys may, for example, ask the judge to suppress a confession if the accused was not informed of his or her Miranda rights or was coerced to confess. They also may ask the judge to suppress the evidence gained from a search if the search was conducted without a warrant or otherwise illegally (i.e., fruit of the poisonous tree). If the search was not conducted during an arrest with a warrant or if the evidence was not in **plain view**, then the results of the search may be inadmissible in court.[189]

Plain view A method by which police observe physical evidence that is plainly visible to the human eye, without the need for an intrusive search.

Other motions may challenge the accuracy of the indictment, charge the prosecution with entrapment or delay, or contend that the accused already has been acquitted or convicted of the crime charged (double jeopardy). In addition, the defense may lodge motions about the defendant's physical or mental competency to stand trial.[190] A defendant may also claim that his or her right to a speedy trial has been violated, requiring the judge to dismiss the charge.

Critical Thinking

If evidence obtained through improper procedure turns out to be factually true and is critical to the case, should it be used anyway? Explain.

Speedy Trials

Under the Sixth Amendment, accused individuals have the right to a fair and speedy trial. The goal of this provision is to prevent undue incarceration before trial, reduce anxiety, and ensure that a delay does not hinder the defense. In 1974, Congress passed the **Speedy Trial Act**. With certain exceptions, the act requires district courts to ensure that criminal cases are heard no later than 100 days after the defendant is arrested. Most states have enacted similar statutes, but they have proven difficult to enforce. It is sometimes difficult to prove that a delay is intentional rather than inherent in the system.[191]

Speedy Trial Act A federal law requiring district courts to ensure that a criminal defendant is brought to trial no later than 100 days after his or her arrest, with some exceptions.

Defendants also have the right to a trial by a jury of their peers. The Sixth Amendment enjoins that a speedy trial shall be conducted by an impartial jury in the state where the crime was committed. The phrase "impartial jury" is problematic for due process. Peremptory challenges to a juror's eligibility based on race have been banned,[192] but attorneys still have a great deal of power over who serves on a jury during *voir dire,* when the jury pool is questioned to determine if potential jurors have any specific biases.[193] The jury selection process has been shown by research to be inherently prejudiced against racial minorities, the poor, women, and those of lower educational achievement.[194] This raises a question of fairness in relation to due process: does the makeup of the jury become a right of due process in its own right? Also, whose right is preeminent, that of the victim who has been wronged or the accused on trial?

Pleas

A **plea** is a defendant's formal, in-court assertion that he or she is guilty or not guilty of the criminal charges.[195] At the arraignment or initial appearance, the accused is advised of his or her rights and invited to enter a plea. Aside from pleading guilty or not guilty, a defendant may plead ***nolo contendere***, which means that the defendant does not admit the charges, but will not contest them.[196] A defendant may plead guilty to the charges at any point during the judicial process, as well as negotiate with prosecutors to reach a **plea bargain** agreement, in which the defendant agrees to plead guilty to a lesser charge in exchange for more lenient treatment at the time of sentencing.[197] After a judge accepts a guilty plea, the defendant is sentenced by a judge or jury. Most criminal cases do not result in a finding of guilt or innocence by a judge or jury (**verdict**), but instead are settled by plea bargains.

Plea A defendant's in-court statement that he or she is guilty, is not guilty, or will not contest criminal charges.

Nolo contendere A plea in which the defendant does not admit the charges, but will not contest them.

Verdict Finding of guilt or innocence by a judge or jury.

Chapter Summary

- The American court system was derived from the common law system inherited from England. From this system, the founding fathers derived their basic understanding of fundamental rights, including habeas corpus, the right to trial by jury, the authority of judicial precedent, and due process. Though there were administrative and procedural differences across the colonies, this common legal heritage was the foundation of the American legal system.
- The U.S. court system consists of two parallel judicial structures: state and federal courts. These structures largely mirror each other; both have lower (trial) courts, which hear evidence, try cases, and reach verdicts, in addition to appeals courts, which review the decisions of lower courts. Federal courts handle "federal questions," which deal with explicitly federal law, and legal issues arising between states.

- The United States Supreme Court is the ultimate legal arbiter in the United States on questions of federal law. It has the prerogative of interpreting the Constitution, the highest law in the land. Legislatures, at any level, are bound to abide by the Constitution. If a law or statute contravenes the Constitution, the Supreme Court may declare it unconstitutional. Cases appealed to the Supreme Court from lower courts may be overturned, thus generating case law that becomes binding precedent for the entire American legal system.

  The criminal trial process is an important function of the criminal justice system. Criminal trials determine the guilt or innocence of an accused person. Criminal trials may be conducted in front of a judge—a "bench trial"—or a jury—a "jury trial." The typical criminal trial consists of opening statements from the defense and prosecution, witness testimony (including direct examination and cross-examination), closing arguments, jury instructions, and the verdict.
- Due process and criminal process provide extensive procedures to safeguard criminal defendants against oppression by the state. The guiding principle is that it is better to let many guilty persons go free than to convict one innocent person. Fundamental, or "natural," rights not explicitly enumerated in the Constitution have been incorporated as substantive due process, largely through the 14th Amendment.
- The Bill of Rights determines the boundaries of "fair play," or due process. The rights enumerated, such as the protections against self-incrimination and unreasonable search and seizure, have been updated to keep pace with the electronic and digital age (e.g., wiretaps).

  Gideon v. Wainwright (1963) was an integral Supreme Court decision that not only affirmed that all defendants, even poor ones, are entitled to be represented by counsel, but also spurred the creation of the public defender system.
- The courtroom workgroup includes many important people who are part of the criminal justice process: the judge, the court clerk, the bailiff, the probation officer, the court reporter, and the process server. These individuals ensure that the business of the court runs smoothly.
- The judge, though just one part of the court team, is considered by many the most important person in the courtroom. A judge's primary duty is to oversee the standard procedures of the court system to ensure that justice is fairly served. A judge's responsibilities include making sure that the defense and prosecution both have the opportunity to present their cases, determining the admissibility of evidence, giving instructions to the jury, and using judicial discretion to follow and enforce the law in his or her courtroom.
- The prosecutor is the attorney for the state. The prosecutor makes a criminal case against a defendant and argues that the defendant

is guilty of the charges. A prosecutor has many different duties to fulfill in the criminal trial process. Prosecutors are involved in various aspects of casework, from investigation, arrest, and trial to sentencing, appeal, and parole.

- The defense attorney is the attorney who represents the accused. The defense attorney may be hired by the defendant or appointed by a judge. Some counties have a public defender's office. A public defender is an attorney who represents indigent defendants who cannot afford to hire attorneys.
- In a jury trial, the decision of the defendant's guilt or innocence lies in the hands of a jury of the defendant's peers. The jury listens to arguments made during the trial and then deliberates and renders a verdict. Sometimes after a defendant is found guilty, a sentencing trial will be held in front of a jury. The jury will determine the punishment that they recommend to the court for the defendant.

Critical Thinking?

1. Do the procedural protections afforded to criminal defendants lessen the rights available to other participants in the court system? Explain.
2. Under what circumstances may a law enforcement officer lawfully take the confession of a criminal suspect?
3. Does the requirement of a speedy trial benefit a criminal defendant and the prosecution equally? Discuss.
4. How, if at all, are due process protections affected by the racial, ethnic, and socioeconomic makeup of a trial jury pool?
5. When may a police officer search a person's home without a warrant? Do you think that all searches should require a warrant? Explain.
6. May a person refuse to allow a police officer to enter his or her home if the officer does not have a warrant? Explain.
7. Should victims have a Bill of Rights in the same way that the accused do? Why or why not?
8. Is it fair to allow attorneys to share information during the discovery phase? Explain.
9. Is the right to a speedy trial necessary? Is speed or reaching the truth deliberately more important? Why?
10. Why is the Fifth Amendment important to the accused? How might a person incriminate himself or herself even if he or she did not commit a crime?
11. How do you think trials would be different if our system did not have the presumption of innocence? How might this affect the way trials work?

12. Is it possible for a witness to be competent but not credible? What would be an example of this?
13. Is it important that a judge have experience as an attorney for both the prosecution and the defense? Why or why not?
14. What should be done if a juror lies? What does a "mistrial" really mean for everyone?
15. When might it be in the defendant's best interest to agree, or refuse to agree, to a plea bargain prior to trial? Are the risks in these instances worth it?
16. What is the difference between "not guilty" and "innocent" of a crime? Is there a difference?
17. Do you agree with the concept of limited admissibility of evidence? Why or why not?
18. Legislative efforts to limit judicial discretion shift power from the judge to the prosecutor. How does this affect the intended neutrality of the courtroom process?
19. Is jury nullification an acceptable practice in the criminal trial system? Do you believe it should be allowed? Why or why not?
20. What is the role of the accused in the trial process? Does it matter whether the accused testifies or remains silent?

Media

United States Courts http://www.uscourts.gov/Home.aspx
The website for the federal court system in the United States provides information on federal courts in local areas, as well as educational resources for students and teachers wishing to learn more about the federal judiciary.

Supreme Court of the United States http://www.supremecourt.gov/
The website for the U.S. Supreme Court includes resources related to recent decisions, current justices, court history, and the court's docket.

Rules of Conduct for Lawyers http://www.abanet.org
The website for the American Bar Association, the regulating body for licensed attorneys in the United States, includes information on the ethical standards to which lawyers must adhere, as well as infractions that could lead to disbarment.

***12 Angry Men* (1957):** This movie demonstrates the type of interaction and discussion possible during jury deliberation. There is also an example of jury nullification. For a synopsis of the film and detailed descriptions of the different jurors, visit http://www.filmsite.org/twelve.html.

***To Kill a Mockingbird* (1962):** In this movie, based on the book written by Harper Lee, a defense attorney in the Depression-era American

South defends a black man against undeserved rape charges. While his choice is unpopular with his friends and neighbors, he shows commitment to the integrity of the judicial process and defends his client to the best of his ability. A full description of the story, its characters, and commentary on the racial tensions outlined in the book and movie may be found at http://www.filmsite.org/toki.html.

Lewis, A. (1966). *Gideon's Trumpet.* New York, NY: Vintage Books/ Random House This book chronicles the story behind the *Gideon v. Wainwright* (1963) case, which yielded the U.S. Supreme Court's ruling that criminal case defendants have the right to be represented by an attorney, even if they cannot afford to pay. Commentary on the book is available at http://www.nacdl.org/public.nsf/championarticles/A0301p61?OpenDocument.

Texas Justice Court Training Center: http://www.tjctc.org/ The official website for the Texas Justice Court Training Center provides legal news and updates for judges, bailiffs, constables, and other courtroom personnel.

The National Judicial College: http://www.judges.org/ The agency's official website provides information on continuing education courses, including online offerings, for judges around the country.

Endnotes

1 *Gideon v. Wainwright*, 372 U.S. 335 (1963).

2 McBride, A. (2006). *Supreme Court History: Expanding Civil Rights; Landmark Cases Gideon v. Wainwright.* Retrieved from http://www.pbs.org/wnet/supremecourt/rights/landmark_gideon.html

3 Locke, M., Neff, J., & Curliss, A. (2010, August 7). *Scathing SBI Audit Says 230 Cases Tainted by Shoddy Investigations.* Retrieved May 13, 2011 from http://www.newsobserver.com/2010/08/19/635632/scathing-sbi-audit-says-230-cases.html

4 Waggoner, M. (2010, September 15). "N.C. Lab Scandal Effects Continue in Court System." *The Herald-Sun.*

5 Innocence Project. (n.d.). *The Causes of Wrongful Conviction.* Retrieved May 15, 2011 from http://www.innocenceproject.org/understand/

6 Mecham, L. R. (2011). *Understanding Federal and State Courts.* Retrieved May 2, 2011 from http://www.uscourts.gov/EducationalResources/FederalCourtBasics/CourtStructure/UnderstandingFederalAndStateCourts.aspx

7 Neubauer, D. W. (1979). *America's Courts and the Criminal Justice System.* Belmont, CA: Wadsworth, 23.

8 Bergman, P., & Berman-Barrett, S. J. (2008). *Represent Yourself In Court: How to Prepare & Try a Winning Case* (6th ed.). Berkeley: Nolo, 481.

9 Breyer, S., et al. (2001). *Administrative Law & Regulatory Policy* (5th ed.). New York, NY: Aspen.

10 Garner, B. A. (2001). *A Dictionary of Modern Legal Usage* (revised ed.). New York, NY: Oxford University Press, 177–178.

11 Arnold-Baker, C. (2008). *The Companion to British History.* London, UK: Loncross Denholm Press, 484.

12 Orth, J. V. (2002). "Common Law." In K. L. Hall (Ed.), *The Oxford Companion to American Law.* New York, NY: Oxford University Press.

13 Arnold-Baker, 2008.

14 Curry, J. A., Riley, R. B., & Battistoni, R. M. (2003). *Constitutional Government: The American Experience* (5th ed.). Dubuque, IA: Kendall Hunt, 35.

15 Hoffer, P. (2002). "History of American Law: Colonial Period." In K. L. Hall (Ed.), *The Oxford Companion to American Law.* New York, NY: Oxford University Press, 365.

16 Orth, 2002, 126.

17 Curry et al., 2003, 31.

18 Ibid., 36.

19 Middleton, R. (2002). *Colonial America: A History, 1565–1776* (3rd ed.). Padstow, UK: Blackwell.

20 Elson, H. W. (1904). *History of the United States of America.* New York, NY: MacMillan, 210–216.

21 Hoffer, 2002, 366–367.

22 Ibid., 367.

23 U.S. Department of Justice (1976). *Two Hundred Years of American Criminal Justice.* Washington, DC: Government Printing Office.

24 Glick, H., & Vines, K. (1973). *State Court Systems.* Englewood Cliffs, NJ: Prentice-Hall.

25 Curry et al., 2003.

26 Glick & Vines, 1973.

27 Curry et al., 2003, 53.

28 Neubauer, 1979, 46.

29 Richardson, R., & Vines, K. (1970). *The Politics of the Federal Courts.* Boston, MA: Little, Brown, 20–21.

30 Curry et al., 2003, 81.

31 Hoffer, 2002, 367.

32 U.S. Constitution, Article III.

33 Curry et al., 2003, 36.

34 Ibid., 53.

35 Graber, M. A. (2002). "Court Systems." In K. L. Hall (Ed.), *The Oxford Companion to American Law.* New York, NY: Oxford University Press, 182–183.

36 O'Brien, D. M. (2000). *Constitutional Law and Politics: Struggles for Power and Governmental Accountability* (4th ed., vol. 1). New York, NY: W.W. Norton and Company, 46–47.

37 Curry et al., 2003, 62.

38 Ibid., 46.

39 Pittman, R. C. (1953). "Judicial Supremacy in America: Its Colonial and Constitutional History." *Georgia Bar Journal, 16*, 148.

40 U.S. Constitution, Article III.

41 O'Brien, 2000, 23.

42 Garner, B. A. (2004). *Black's Law Dictionary* (8th ed.). St. Paul, MN: Thomson/West, 980.

43 Adamany, D. (2002). "Judicial Review." In K. L. Hall (Ed.), *The Oxford Companion to American Law.* New York: Oxford University Press, 441.

44 O'Brien, 2000, 31.

45 *Marbury v. Madison*, 5 U.S. (1 Cranch) 137 (1803).

46 5 U.S. (1 Cranch) at 177–178.

47 Ritchie, D. A. (2002). "Government, United States." In K. L. Hall (Ed.), *The Oxford Companion to American Law.* New York, NY: Oxford University Press.

48 O'Brien, 2000.

49 Adamany, 2002, 441.

50 Ibid., 444.

51 Rottman, D. B., Flango, C. R., Cantrell, M. T., & Hansen, R. L. (2000, June). *State Court Organization 1998*. Retrieved May 17, 2011 from http://bjs.ojp.usdoj.gov/content/pub/pdf/sco98.pdf

52 Black, H. C. (1990). *Black's Law Dictionary* (6th ed.). St. Paul, MN: West, 1557.

53 U.S. Constitution, Amendment 10.

54 Hall, M. G. (2002). "Courts, United States: State and Local Courts." In K. L. Hall (Ed.), *The Oxford Companion to American Law.* New York, NY: Oxford University Press, 177.

55 Wheeler, R., & Whitcomb, H. (1974). "The Literature of Court Administration: A Bibliographical Essay." *Arizona State Law Journal,* 689–722.

56 *Advanced Report, State Court Caseload Statistics: Annual Report, 1975.* (1978). Williamsburg, VA: National Center for State Courts.

57 Hall, 2002, 178.

58 Rottman et al., 2000, 315.

59 Ulmer, J. (1994). "Trial Judges in a Rural Court Community." *Journal of Contemporary Ethnography, 23*, 79–108.

60 Eisenstein, J., & Jacob, H. (1970). *Felony Justice: An Organizational Analysis of Criminal Courts.* Boston, MA: Little, Brown.

61 Stuckey, G. B. (1976). *Procedures in the Criminal Justice System. Columbus, OH: Merrill.*

62 *Duncan v. Louisiana* 391 U.S. 145 (1968).

63 *West's Encyclopedia of American Law* (2nd ed.). (2004). Farmington Hills, MI: Gale.

64 Katz, B. S. (1997). *Justice Overruled: Unmasking the Criminal Justice System.* New York, NY: Warner.

65 *U.S. v. Dinitz*, 424 U.S. 600, 612 (1976).

66 Federal Rules of Evidence, Rule 601.

67 Schum, D., & Morris, J. (2007, March). "Assessing the Competence and Credibility of Human Sources of Intelligence Evidence: Contributions from Law and Probability." *Law, Probability, & Risk, 6*(1–4), 247–274.

68 Garner, B. (2004). *Black's Law Dictionary* (8th ed.). St. Paul, MN: Thomson West.

69 *Daubert v. Merrill Dow Pharmaceuticals*, 509 U.S. 579 (1993).

70 Jones, D. (1981). *The Law of Criminal Procedure*. Boston, MA: Little, Brown.

71 Jones, 1981.

72 *Ohio v. Roberts*, 488 U.S. 56 (1980).

73 Ibid.

74 *Crawford v. Washington*, 544 U.S. 36 (2004).

75 Jones, 1981.

76 Inciardi, J. (2010). *Criminal Justice* (9th ed.). Boston, MA: McGraw-Hill.

77 Wiener, R., Pritchard, C., & Weston, M. (1995). "Comprehensibility of Approved Jury Instructions in Capital Murder Cases." *Journal of Applied Psychology, 80*(4).

78 Cronan, J. P. (2002). "Is Any of This Making Sense? Reflecting on Guilty Pleas to Aid Criminal Juror Comprehension." *American Criminal Law Review, 39.*

79 American Jury Project. (2005). *Principles for Juries and Jury Trials*. Chicago, IL: American Bar Association.

80 Florida Supreme Court. (n.d.). *Standard Jury Instructions: Criminal Cases*. Retrieved from http://www.floridasupremecourt.org/jury_instructions/index.shtmlIllinois Courts. (2011). *Recent Criminal Jury Instructions*. Retrieved from http://www.state.il.us/court/circuitcourt/CriminalJuryInstructions/default.asp

81 *Pope v. Illinois*, 481 U.S. 497 (1987).

82 North Dakota Supreme Court. (n.d.). *North Dakota Juror's Handbook*. Retrieved from http://www.ndcourts.gov/court/juror.htm

83 Hall, 2002, 178.

84 Rottman et al., 2000, viii.

85 Ibid., 75.

86 Hall, 2002, 178.

87 Mecham, 2011.

88 Carp, R. (2002). Courts, United States: Federal Courts. In K. L. Hall (Ed.), *The Oxford Companion to American Law*. New York: Oxford University Press, 176–177.

89 Ibid.

90 Gluck, Susan Mezey, D. (2002). United States Courts: Juvenile Courts. In K. L. Hall (Ed.), *The Oxford Companion to American Law*. New York: Oxford University Press, 180–182.

91 Carp, 2002, 174.

92 28 U.S.C. § 1331.

93 Grossman, J. (1965). *Lawyers and Judges: The ABA and the Politics of Judicial Selection.* New York, NY: John Wiley.

94 Ibid, 14.

95 Jackson, D. D. (1974). *Judges.* New York, NY: Atheneum, 7.

96 Office of the Federal Defender, Eastern District of California. (n.d.). *Sentencing.* Retrieved from http://www.cae-fpd.org/Client_Sentencing.pdf

97 Mecham, 2011, 19–20.

98 Judiciary Act of 1925, 43 Stat. 936.

99 Richardson, R. J., & Vines, K. N. (1970). *The Politics of Federal Courts.* Boston, MA: Little, Brown.

100 *Public Citizen, Inc., v. Bomer,* 115 F. Supp. 2d 743 (W.D. Tex 2000).

101 Becker, D., & Reddick, M. (2005). *Judicial Selection Reform: Examples from Six States.* Des Moines, IA: American Judicature Society.

102 Inciardi, 2010.

103 New York City Criminal Court Act, Laws of 1962, chap. 697, sec. 22 (1).

104 Texas Justice Court Training Center. (2011). *New Judges Seminar.* Retrieved from http://www.tjctc.org/New-Justices-of-the-Peace/NewJudges.html

105 National Judicial College. (2011). *About the NJC.* Retrieved from http://www.judges.org/about/index.html

106 American Bar Association. (2000). *ABA Standards for Criminal Justice: Special Functions of the Trial Judge* (3rd ed.). Chicago, IL: Author.

107 *Osborn v. Bank* of the United States, 22 U.S. 738 (1824).

108 Friedman, R. (1986). *A Close Look at Probative Value.* 66 B.U.L. Rev. 733.

109 Hill & Hill, 2009.

110 McLaughlin, J. (1989). *Federal Evidence Practice Guide.* Matthew Bender.

111 Holton, N., & Lamar, L. (1991). *The Criminal Courts: Structures, Personnel, and Processes.* New York, NY: McGraw-Hill.

112 Rabe, G., & Champion, D. (2002). *Criminal Courts: Structures, Process, and Issues.* Upper Saddle River, NJ: Prentice Hall.

113 Holton & Lamar, 1991.

114 Franklin County, Ohio. (n.d.) *Franklin County Prosecutor's Office.* Retrieved from http://www.franklincountyohio.gov/Prosecuting_Attorney/

115 Misner, R. L. (1996). "Recasting Prosecutorial Discretion." *The Journal of Law & Criminology, 86*(3).

116 Ma, Y. (2002). "Prosecutorial Discretion and Plea Bargaining in the United States, France, Germany, and Italy: A Comparative Perspective." *International Criminal Justice Review, 12.*

117 LaFave, W. (1965). *Arrest: The Decision to Take a Suspect Into Custody.* Boston, MA: Little, Brown.

118 Inciardi, 2010.

119 Oakland County, Michigan Circuit Court. (2009). *Appointed Attorney Fee Schedule.* Retrieved from http://www.oakgov.com/circuit/assets/docs/division/atty-fee-sched.pdf

[120] Smith, S., & DeFrances, C. (1996). *Indigent Defense.* Washington, DC: Bureau of Justice Statistics.

[121] "Nationline: McVeigh's Defense Cost Taxpayers $13.8 Million." *USA Today,* July 3, 2001, p. 3A.

[122] *Smith v. Texas,* 311 U.S. 128 (1940).

[123] Ibid., 13–14.

[124] Ibid.

[125] 28 U.S.C. § 631.

[126] Mecham, 2011, 9.

[127] Carp, 2002, 117.

[128] O'Brien, 2002, 771–776.

[129] Ibid., 26.

[130] Supreme Court of the United States. (2011). *Frequently Asked Questions.* Retrieved from http://www.supremecourt.gov/faq.aspx#faqgi9

[131] O'Brien, 2002, 771.

[132] Administrative Office of the U.S. Courts. (2003). *Understanding the Federal Courts.* Retrieved May 8, 2011 from http://www.uscourts.gov/Educational-Resources/FederalCourtBasics/UnderstandingTheFederalCourts.aspx

[133] *Murray v. Hoboken Land,* 59 U.S. 272 (1855).

[134] Brown, R. L. (2002). "Due Process: Procedural." In K. L. Hall (Ed.), *The Oxford Companion to American Law.* New York, NY: Oxford University Press, 232.

[135] Sandefur, T. (2010). *The Right to Earn a Living: Economic Freedom and the Law.* Washington, DC: Cato Institute, 90–100.

[136] White, G. E. (2000). *The Constitution and the New Deal.* Cambridge, MA: Harvard University Press, 244–246.

[137] *Palko v. Connecticut,* 302 U.S. 319 (1937).

[138] *Klopfer v. North Carolina,* 386 U.S. 213 (1967).

[139] *Barker v. Wingo,* 406 U.S. 514 (1972).

[140] *Strunk v. United States,* 412 U.S. 434 (1973).

[141] *United States v. Lovasco,* 421 U.S. 783 (1977).

[142] *In re Oliver,* 333 U.S. 257 (1948).

[143] *Thiel v. Southern PacificCo.,* 328 U.S. 217 (1946).

[144] Magna Carta of 1215.

[145] U.S. Constitution, Article III, Sect. 2, Cl. 2.

[146] U.S. Constitution, Amendment 14, Sect. 1.

[147] *Duncan v. Louisiana,* 391 U.S. 145 (1968).

[148] Federal Rules of Criminal Procedure, Rule 24(6).

[149] *Swain v. Alabama,* 380 U.S. 202 (1965).

[150] *Batson v. Kentucky,* 476 U.S. 79 (1986).

[151] *J.E.B. v. Alabama ex rel. T.B.,* 511 U.S. 127 (1994).

152 Glasser, M. (1997). "Letting the Supermajority Rule: Nonunanimous Jury Verdicts in Criminal Trials." *Florida State University Law Review.* Tallahassee, FL: Florida State University Press.

153 Ellsworth, P. (1989). "Are Twelve Heads Better Than One?" *Law and Contemporary Problems, 52,* 205–224.

154 *U.S. v. Moylan,* 417 F2d 1002 (4th Cir. 1969).

155 *U.S. v. Wilson,* 629 F2d 439 (6th Cir. 1980).

156 *U.S. v. Thomas,* 116 F3d 606 (2nd Cir. 1997).

157 Garfinkel, H. (1956). "Conditions of Successful Degradation Ceremonies." *American Journal of Sociology, 61*(5).

158 U.S. Constitution, Amendments 1–10.

159 *Chapman v. California,* 386 U.S. 18, 22 (1967).

160 *In re Winship,* 397 U.S. 358 (1970).

161 Skolnick, J. H. (1966). *Justice Without Trial: Law Enforcement in Democratic Society.* New York, NY: John Wiley, 8.

162 Friendly, H. J. (1968). *The Fifth Amendment Tomorrow: The Case for Constitutional Change.* 37 U. Cin. L. Rev. 671, 694.

163 Krislov, D. R. (2002). "Habeas Corpus." In K. L. Hall (Ed.), *The Oxford Companion to American Law.* New York, NY: Oxford University Press, 349.

164 Dressler, J. (2002). *Understanding Criminal Procedure* (3rd ed.). Newark, NJ: LexisNexis.

165 Mecham, 2011, 26.

166 Washington Post. (2006, December 31). *Prosecutorial Indiscretion.* Retrieved from http://www.washingtonpost.com/wp-dyn/content/article/2006/12/30/AR2006123000886.html?referrer=emailarticle

167 North Carolina State Bar. (2007, June 16). *State Bar Verdict on Nifong.* Retrieved May 19, 2011 from http://www.ncbar.com/Nifong%20Findings.pdf

168 Meyer, L. R. (2002). "Criminal Procedure." In K. L. Hall (Ed.), *The Oxford Companion to American Law.* New York, NY: Oxford University Press, 651–652.

169 *Groh v. Ramirez,* 540 U.S. 551, 564–65 (2004).

170 American Civil Liberties Union. (2010). *Know Your Rights: What to Do If You're Stopped by Police, Immigration Agents or the FBI.* Retrieved from http://www.aclu.org/drug-law-reform-immigrants-rights-racial-justice/know-your-rights-what-do-if-you

171 Ibid.

172 Ibid.

173 *Miranda v. Arizona,* 384 U.S. 436 (1966).

174 Meyer, 2002.

175 Kansas City, MO Police Department. (2006). *Miranda Warning and Miranda Waiver,* pp. 384 U.S. 467–473. Retrieved from http://www.kcpd.org/masterindex/files/PI/PI0605.pdf

176 Meyer, 2002, 652.

177 Curry et al., 2003, ch. X.

178 *Bram v. United States,* 168 U.S. 532, 542 (1897).

179 *Miranda v. Arizona,* 384 U.S. 436 (1966); *California v. Hodari D.*, 499 U.S. 621, 626 (1991).

180 Meyer, 652.

181 *United States v. Sokolow,* 490 U.S. 1 (1989).

182 Meyer, 2002, 652.

183 Mecham, 2011, 39.

184 Ibid, 40.

185 Spain, J. (1961). "The Grand Jury, Past and Present: A Survey." *American Criminal Law Quarterly, 2,* 126–142.

186 Mecham, 2011, 38.

187 Bishop, J. (1978). *Studies in Comparative Civil and Criminal Procedure* (vol. 2). Sydney: Law Reform Commission.

188 Ibid.

189 *Arizona v. Hicks,* 480 U.S. 321 (1987).

190 Meyer, 653.

191 Downs, D. A., & Ruggiero, C. (2002). "Fair Trial, Criminal." In K. L. Hall (Ed.), *The Oxford Companion to American Law.* New York, NY: Oxford University Press, 292.

192 *Batson v. Kentucky,* 476 U.S. 79 (1986).

193 Duhaime, L. (n.d.). "Voir Dire Definition." *Duhaime's Legal Dictionary.* Retrieved from http://www.duhaime.org/LegalDictionary/V/VoirDire.aspx

194 Alker, H. R. Jr., Hosticka, C., & Mitchell, M. (1976). "Jury Selection as a Biased Social Process." *Law & Society Review, 11*(1), 9–41.

195 Mecham, 2011, 43.

196 Bibas, S. (2003, July). "Harmonizing Substantive Criminal Law Values and Criminal Procedure: The Case of Alford and Nolo contendere Pleas." *Cornell Law Review,* 88(6).

197 Ibid.

198 McBride, A. (2006). *Supreme Court History: Expanding Civil Rights; Landmark Cases Gideon v. Wainwright.* Retrieved from http://www.pbs.org/wnet/supremecourt/rights/landmark_gideon.html

198 Ulmer, J. (1994). "Trial Judges in a Rural Court Community." *Journal of Contemporary Ethnography, 23,* 79–108.

199 Eisenstein, J., & Jacob, H. (1970). *Felony Justice: An Organizational Analysis of Criminal Courts.* Boston, MA: Little, Brown.

200 Stuckey, G. B. (1976). *Procedures in the Criminal Justice System. Columbus, OH: Merrill.*

201 *Duncan v. Louisiana* 391 U.S. 145 (1968).

202 *West's Encyclopedia of American Law* (2nd ed.). (2004). Farmington Hills, MI: Gale.

203 Katz, B. S. (1997). *Justice Overruled: Unmasking the Criminal Justice System.* New York, NY: Warner.

204 *U.S. v. Dinitz*, 424 U.S. 600, 612 (1976).

205 Federal Rules of Evidence, Rule 601.

206 Schum, D., & Morris, J. (2007, March). "Assessing the Competence and Credibility of Human Sources of Intelligence Evidence: Contributions from Law and Probability." *Law, Probability, & Risk, 6*(1–4), 247–274.

207 Garner, B. (2004). *Black's Law Dictionary* (8th ed.). St. Paul, MN: Thomson West.

208 *Daubert v. Merrill Dow Pharmaceuticals*, 509 U.S. 579 (1993).

209 Jones, D. (1981). *The Law of Criminal Procedure.* Boston, MA: Little, Brown.

210 Jones, 1981.

211 *Ohio v. Roberts*, 488 U.S. 56 (1980).

212 Ibid.

213 *Crawford v. Washington*, 544 U.S. 36 (2004).

214 Jones, 1981.

215 Inciardi, J. (2010). *Criminal Justice* (9th ed.). Boston, MA: McGraw-Hill.

216 Wiener, R., Pritchard, C., & Weston, M. (1995). "Comprehensibility of Approved Jury Instructions in Capital Murder Cases." *Journal of Applied Psychology, 80*(4).

217 Cronan, J. P. (2002). "Is Any of This Making Sense? Reflecting on Guilty Pleas to Aid Criminal Juror Comprehension." *American Criminal Law Review, 39.*

218 American Jury Project. (2005). *Principles for Juries and Jury Trials.* Chicago, IL: American Bar Association.

219 Florida Supreme Court. (n.d.). *Standard Jury Instructions: Criminal Cases.* Retrieved from http://www.floridasupremecourt.org/jury_instructions/index.shtmlIllinois Courts. (2011). *Recent Criminal Jury Instructions.* Retrieved from http://www.state.il.us/court/circuitcourt/CriminalJuryInstructions/default.asp

220 *Pope v. Illinois*, 481 U.S. 497 (1987).

221 North Dakota Supreme Court. (n.d.). *North Dakota Juror's Handbook.* Retrieved from http://www.ndcourts.gov/court/juror.htm

222 Judiciary Act of 1925, 43 Stat. 936.

223 Richardson, R. J., & Vines, K. N. (1970). *The Politics of Federal Courts.* Boston, MA: Little, Brown.

224 *Public Citizen, Inc., v. Bomer*, 115 F. Supp. 2d 743 (W.D. Tex 2000).

225 Becker, D., & Reddick, M. (2005). *Judicial Selection Reform: Examples from Six States.* Des Moines, IA: American Judicature Society.

226 Tex El. Code Ann. 253.151.

227 Inciardi, 2010.

228 New York City Criminal Court Act, Laws of 1962, chap. 697, sec. 22 (1).

229 Texas Justice Court Training Center. (2011). *New Judges Seminar.* Retrieved from http://www.tjctc.org/New-Justices-of-the-Peace/NewJudges.html

230 National Judicial College. (2011). *About the NJC.* Retrieved from http://www.judges.org/about/index.html

231 American Bar Association. (2000). *ABA Standards for Criminal Justice: Special Functions of the Trial Judge* (3rd ed.). Chicago, IL: Author.

232 *Osborn v. Bank* of the United States, 22 U.S. 738 (1824).

233 Friedman, R. (1986). *A Close Look at Probative Value.* 66 B.U.L. Rev. 733.

234 Hill & Hill, 2009.

235 McLaughlin, J. (1989). *Federal Evidence Practice Guide.* Matthew Bender.

236 Holton, N., & Lamar, L. (1991). *The Criminal Courts: Structures, Personnel, and Processes.* New York, NY: McGraw-Hill.

237 Rabe, G., & Champion, D. (2002). *Criminal Courts: Structures, Process, and Issues.* Upper Saddle River, NJ: Prentice Hall.

238 Holton & Lamar, 1991.

239 Franklin County, Ohio. (n.d.) *Franklin County Prosecutor's Office.* Retrieved from http://www.franklincountyohio.gov/Prosecuting_Attorney/

240 Misner, R. L. (1996). "Recasting Prosecutorial Discretion." *The Journal of Law & Criminology, 86*(3).

241 Ma, Y. (2002). "Prosecutorial Discretion and Plea Bargaining in the United States, France, Germany, and Italy: A Comparative Perspective." *International Criminal Justice Review, 12.*

242 LaFave, W. (1965). *Arrest: The Decision to Take a Suspect Into Custody.* Boston, MA: Little, Brown.

243 Inciardi, 2010.

244 Oakland County, Michigan Circuit Court. (2009). *Appointed Attorney Fee Schedule.* Retrieved from http://www.oakgov.com/circuit/assets/docs/division/atty-fee-sched.pdf

245 Smith, S., & DeFrances, C. (1996). *Indigent Defense.* Washington, DC: Bureau of Justice Statistics.

246 "Nationline: McVeigh's Defense Cost Taxpayers $13.8 Million." *USA Today,* July 3, 2001, p. 3A.

247 *Smith v. Texas*, 311 U.S. 128 (1940).

248 *Klopfer v. North Carolina*, 386 U.S. 213 (1967).

249 *Barker v. Wingo*, 406 U.S. 514 (1972).

250 *Strunk v. United States*, 412 U.S. 434 (1973).

251 *United States v. Lovasco*, 421 U.S. 783 (1977).

252 *In re Oliver*, 333 U.S. 257 (1948).

253 *Thiel v. Southern PacificCo.*, 328 U.S. 217 (1946).

254 Magna Carta of 1215.

255 U.S. Constitution, Article III, Sect. 2, Cl. 2.

256 U.S. Constitution, Amendment 14, Sect. 1.

257 *Duncan v. Louisiana*, 391 U.S. 145 (1968).

258 Federal Rules of Criminal Procedure, Rule 24(6).

259 *Swain v. Alabama*, 380 U.S. 202 (1965).

260 *Batson v. Kentucky*, 476 U.S. 79 (1986).

261 *J.E.B. v. Alabama ex rel. T.B.*, 511 U.S. 127 (1994).

262 Glasser, M. (1997). "Letting the Supermajority Rule: Nonunanimous Jury Verdicts in Criminal Trials." *Florida State University Law Review.* Tallahassee, FL: Florida State University Press.

263 Ellsworth, P. (1989). "Are Twelve Heads Better Than One?" *Law and Contemporary Problems, 52*, 205–224.

264 *U.S. v. Moylan*, 417 F2d 1002 (4th Cir. 1969).

265 *U.S. v. Wilson*, 629 F2d 439 (6th Cir. 1980).

266 *U.S. v. Thomas,* 116 F3d 606 (2nd Cir. 1997).

267 Garfinkel, H. (1956). "Conditions of Successful Degradation Ceremonies." *American Journal of Sociology, 61*(5).

© sakhorn/Shutterstock.com

CHAPTER 7

Sentencing and Judgment

KEY TERMS

Aggravating circumstances
Community service
Deferred adjudication
Determinate sentence
Electronic monitoring
Good time credit
House arrest, Incapacitation
Incarceration, Indeterminate sentence
Intensive supervision probation
Just deserts
Law violation, Mandatory minimum
Mitigating circumstances
Mitigation specialist
Parole board
Pre-sentence investigation
Pretrial diversion
Rehabilitation, Restitution
Retribution
Sentence
Shock probation
Technical violation
Three-strikes law
Vengeance

CHAPTER OBJECTIVES

1. Understand the philosophy and goals of criminal sentencing.
2. Describe determinate and indeterminate sentencing.
3. Identify the range of sentencing options.
4. Describe "truth in sentencing" and the motivation for truth-in-sentencing laws.
5. Discuss the role of presentence investigations.

Case Study: *State of Texas v. Robert Coulson*

On November 13, 1992, the Houston Fire Department discovered five bodies while extinguishing a house fire. The bodies were those of the adoptive parents, two sisters, and brother-in-law (a county sheriff's deputy) of Robert Coulson. Coulson, in an attempt to collect an inheritance from his parents, had subdued each victim with a stun gun, tied their hands and feet, and placed plastic bags over their heads, which caused all the victims to suffocate. Coulson then poured gasoline on the bodies in an attempt to set the house on fire. While the home did catch on fire, the blaze did not entirely engulf the house as planned. It is speculated that while Coulson poured gasoline around the house to destroy evidence, the pilot light from the water heater ignited the gas fumes earlier than Coulson had expected.

An accomplice, Jared Althaus, later confessed to the Harris County District Attorney that he had helped Coulson plan the murders. Althaus described in great detail how he and Coulson left the murder scene and drove to the Althaus family lake house, discarding various pieces of evidence along the way by throwing them out of the car's windows. Coulson maintained that he was at a shopping mall when his family was murdered. Althaus took investigators to the locations along the highway where the tools from the murder scene had been discarded, and each piece of evidence was recovered in the corresponding areas. During the trial, eight witnesses testified against Coulson, who denied their allegations and accused them of lying under oath, but he was subsequently convicted of the murders of his family. At his sentencing, Coulson maintained that he was innocent of the murders. The State argued that Coulson was a manipulative sociopath and only wanted his inheritance. In jail, Coulson reportedly admitted that he did not harbor any resentment toward his family, but felt that the murders were the only way out of his dire financial situation.[1]

Robert Coulson was sentenced to death for the slayings of two of his family members. To avoid a lengthy prison sentence or possibly a sentence of death, Althaus testified against Coulson and received 10 years in prison, a relatively minor sentence considering his alleged involvement with a series of pre-planned murders, in exchange for his cooperation with the district attorney's office. On June 25, 2002, Coulson was executed for the murders of his family members.

Althaus repeatedly denied to investigators that he was inside the Coulson home while the murders were being committed, and said he was sitting in a car outside. Like Coulson, Althaus denied committing the murders. Is it probable, however, that Robert Coulson could have singlehandedly subdued, bound, and killed five adults, one of whom was a trained law enforcement officer?

In this case, two men accused of the same crime received very different sentences. This chapter will explain and discuss sentencing theories and guidelines, disparity in sentencing, plea bargaining, and other issues in sentencing.

Goals of Sentencing

In the early days of the criminal justice system in the United States, punishments generally followed the philosophy that a person must suffer for committing a crime against society. Historically, the goal of punishing criminals was to cause them to suffer and therefore learn never to commit the offense again. Punishments were generally imposed by taking offenders out of society and placing them in jail cells for the purpose of having them repent to God for their sins. In fact, the word "penitentiary" is based upon this ideal. This is a practice that was introduced to the United States by the Puritans and Quakers, but this philosophy still influences our modern-day criminal justice system. The goals of punishment in the modern criminal justice system in America are to protect society and to rehabilitate the offender. These goals will be covered in detail in the next few pages.

In a criminal proceeding, a defendant who has either pleaded guilty or been found guilty by a judge or jury must have a punishment imposed. These punishments can range from a simple fine to death. For example, in the Robert Coulson case, Coulson was found guilty of murdering his family and sentenced to death, while Coulson's accomplice testified against him and received 10 years in prison. Sentencing is one of the biggest responsibilities of a judge or jury. A **sentence** is a punishment given to an offender by a judge or jury for the crime committed by the offender. Sentencing is the process by which this punishment is determined. All sentences are governed by statutory provisions and vary from state to state and even among local jurisdictions. The states are given the authority to punish criminal defendants; however, the federal government can also punish individuals who are convicted of federal crimes.

Sentence A punishment imposed by a judicial body on an offender who has committed a crime.

Deterrence

Early philosophers such as Cesare Beccaria believed that the only purpose for punishment was the deterrence of crime.[2] Deterrence is a philosophy of punishment that presumes that the punishment inflicted will have the effect of causing criminals to refrain from committing crimes.[3] Deterrence works by influencing the perceptions of potential offenders and, by consequence, their behavior. Punishment can only deter criminals from committing crimes if it is made public. There are two forms of deterrence: general deterrence and special or specific deterrence. *General deterrence* means that by punishing one defendant for a crime, the legal system makes an example of the individual so that other persons will be deterred from committing crimes. Special or *specific deterrence* means that after a defendant is punished for committing a particular crime, that individual will refrain from committing further crimes. Gibbs (1975) further established a difference between absolute and restrictive deterrence. When a person refrains from committing a crime out of fear of being punished for the crime, that individual has been deterred absolutely. When a person limits his or her involvement in committing a crime to reduce the risk of punishment—such as a drug dealer selling smaller amounts of drugs, rather than refraining from the sale of drugs—that person has been deterred restrictively. The individual is still committing the crime, but perhaps on a more limited scale.[4]

Beccaria also asserted that, to be effective, punishment must be swift, certain, and appropriately severe. He believed that punishment for a crime committed must be enacted within a reasonable amount of time after the crime has occurred; if the punishment is delayed for too long, the criminal may not make the connection between the punishment and the crime.[5] For example, if a woman who is arrested on a charge of Driving While Intoxicated (DWI) does not make her first court appearance for six months, will she truly make the connection that her involvement in the justice system is due to her actions? Certainty of punishment means that punishment will be applied, and the potential scope of the punishment is clear to all involved in the process, including the defendant.[6] In the example of the woman arrested for the DWI charge, she should be made to understand the possible range of punishments that she may be subjected to as a result of her crime. Beccaria suggested limitations on the severity of punishments applied: he asserted that the punishment should be proportionate to its corresponding crime, and it should not go beyond the point of severity where it deters others from committing the same crime or prevents the defendant from further harming others.[7] In other words, while the woman charged with DWI did put other individuals at risk by driving drunk, is it appropriate to sentence her, and other persons charged with DWI, to life in prison for the offense?

A complication of general deterrence as a punishment philosophy is that, while it may make sense in theory, its effects cannot be measured by social scientists. This means that whether deterrence works cannot be accurately determined, especially in the cases of people who have been tempted to commit crimes but have refrained from doing so. One cannot easily measure the number of people who have not committed crimes. Only persons who have not been deterred from committing further crimes can be measured, as their repeated crimes are documented by the criminal justice system.[8]

For example, a burglar who commits one burglary and then commits no further crimes was successfully deterred from committing further crimes, while an auto thief who repeatedly commits auto thefts keeps re-entering the criminal justice system.

Specific deterrence, however, does seem to have some impact on the behavior of first-time misdemeanor and white-collar offenders whose arrests and entrances into the criminal justice system cause them embarrassment. The threats of public disgrace and negative effects upon professional and family matters appear to have positive effects on these "small-time" criminals, leading to reductions in further crimes committed by these offenders.[9]

Critical Thinking

Think about Beccaria's points that punishment should be swift, certain, and appropriately severe. What would sentencing be like if only two of those three ideas were applied, such as swift and appropriately severe punishment without certainty? Would criminals know what punishments they faced for their crimes? What if punishment was swift but not certain or appropriately severe? Could that lead, for example, to murderers being executed by police shortly after their arrests?

Retribution

Societies from the ancient Middle East to the American Quakers primarily justified punishment of criminals based on the principle of **retribution**. Some of the oldest examples of retributive punishment are in the Code of Hammurabi, a series of nearly 300 laws and punishments detailed thoroughly under the order of the sixth Babylonian king, Hammurabi, around 1700 B.C. The Code of Hammurabi relies heavily on the concept of "an eye for an eye," as shown by a few examples:

©jsp/Shutterstock.com

The Code of Hammurabi is one of the oldest known examples of law systems that incorporate retribution.

> If a man puts out the eye of a patrician, his eye shall be put out.
>
> If a man knocks the teeth out of another man, his own teeth will be knocked out.
>
> If a son strikes his father, his hands shall be hewn off.[10]

Retribution The idea that a criminal should be punished in a manner that is commensurate, or as equal as possible, to the crime committed.

Retribution suggests that a person who commits a crime should suffer punishment for that crime, and the punishment must be commensurate with the crime. In other words, offenders who commit more heinous crimes receive harsher punishments, while lesser criminals receive more lenient punishments. Someone who commits murder would be put to death under the practice of retribution, and someone who steals money from a store may pay back the money and perhaps any legal costs incurred by the store.

Vengeance The idea, based on the biblical philosophy of "an eye for an eye," of seeing that a criminal is punished, and that some satisfaction is taken from the fact that the criminal is punished.

Just deserts A philosophy of punishment that states that a person who commits a crime should suffer for that crime; the amount of time incarcerated or type of punishment for a particular offender is generally proportionate to the type of offense that was committed.

Rehabilitation A philosophy of punishment that is based on the idea that the offender's behavior can and will change through treatment programs by professionals. Rehabilitation can involve treating offenders for drug and alcohol issues, anger problems, mental health counseling, and other services.

Incarceration The act of confining a person in a jail or prison facility.

Incapacitation A theory of punishment that imprisons offenders to prevent them from committing other crimes while incarcerated.

Vengeance is the justification for punishment that draws on the biblical idea of "an eye for an eye." Proponents of vengeance want offenders to pay for what they have done by suffering punishment; a measure of satisfaction is gained from knowing that the criminal has been punished. "**Just deserts**" is a concept that further suggests that the criminal's punishment should be comparable to the crime that was committed. In other words, if a man burns down his neighbor's home, the concept of "just deserts" may force him to lose his home and possessions as well. This justification is based partly on ideas suggested by the German philosopher Immanuel Kant (1724–1804), who stated that offenders should be automatically punished; they have committed crimes, so they "deserve" the punishment.[11] Retribution is the only justification for criminal punishment that focuses on what has happened in the past. All other rationales for punishment hope to influence the future by preventing an offender from committing future crimes.

Rehabilitation

Rehabilitation is a corrections philosophy stating that the offender's behavior and personality can be changed by participation in treatment programs provided by qualified professionals. Offenders are typically put through assessments to determine what issues may be challenging for them, but may also participate in particular types of treatment depending on the nature of the offense and the length of the offender's sentence.[12] Treatment may address more than one issue depending on the offender's identified needs. Examples of rehabilitative treatment may include inpatient substance abuse treatment, participation in 12-step groups, individual psychotherapy, anger management classes, educational or vocational training, and other services.[13] Educational services could include preparation to take a high school equivalency examination, but many prison systems offer inmates the opportunity to complete high school diplomas and even college degrees. Vocational training could include on-the-job training in the prison unit, such as working as a cook in the kitchen or as a mechanic in the garage.

Rehabilitation was the primary rationale for punishing criminals from the 1870s to the 1970s. The goal of rehabilitation was to return offenders to society after **incarceration** as productive, law-abiding citizens. Rehabilitation was de-emphasized in the 1970s in favor of the goals of retribution and incapacitation because the appropriate methods to correct the behavior of offenders are unclear and we do not fully understand what causes crime. This country also experienced a shift away from rehabilitation due to more emphasis on "get tough" policies on crime. While critics suggest that rehabilitation and punishment are not mutually compatible ways to control crime, and that prisons are inappropriate settings to achieve rehabilitation, judges still send offenders to prison for rehabilitation.[14]

Incapacitation

The removal from society or restriction of the freedom of criminal offenders is called **incapacitation**. In some historical societies, banishment or exile was used to achieve incapacitation. Banishment was utilized in ancient Greece and Rome. When banished, offenders were forced out of a civilized area, leaving them to wander the wilderness, significantly reducing their chances of survival and removing any potential future harm they might cause to their home society. In modern times, foreign nationals may be deported out of the United States if they are convicted of particular crimes. For example, a foreign national who has repeated convictions for drug possession may be deported from the United States to his home country and prevented from returning. The purpose of incapacitation is to make conditions all but impossible for offenders to commit crimes during the period of incapacitation. Prisons are used to incapacitate criminals; incarcerated offenders cannot commit crimes in society outside the prison.

At this time, life imprisonment without parole and execution are the only forms of incapacitation guaranteeing that the offender will no longer commit crimes against the community. The foremost issue concerning incapacitation is that incapacitation by perpetual imprisonment is costly. Additional prisons would need to be built and more employees would need to be hired. Temporary incapacitation—that is, imprisonment until the offender will no longer commit crimes—is unreasonable, as criminality cannot always be predicted. Another issue to consider is the humanity, as well as the practicality, of permanent incapacitation. A criminal permanently ensconced in a prison cell would cause no further harm to society, but permanently imprisoning an offender can be considered cruel and unusual punishment, especially in comparison to the crime. Taking Cesare Beccaria's idea of swift, certain, and appropriately severe punishment into account, is it reasonable to incapacitate all criminals by permanently removing them from society, whether their crimes are small thefts or murders? Permanent incapacitation of offenders also violates their civil rights, which are afforded to all citizens in the U.S. Constitution and its amendments.

Restorative Justice

Some jurisdictions are making efforts to restore victims of crime as much as possible to their states before the crimes occurred, making them "whole." John Braithwaite, an Australian criminologist, has encouraged the enabling of both the offender and the victim to repair the social damage caused by the crime. This is the concept of restorative justice. Braithwaite stresses that the focus of the mainstream criminal justice system on punishment irreversibly shames the offender and thereby perpetuates criminal association and activity: "When individuals are shamed so remorselessly and unforgivingly that they become outcasts, or even begin to think of themselves as outcasts it becomes more rewarding to associate with others who are perceived in some limited or total way as also at odds with mainstream standards."[15] Sullivan and Tifft (2005) have written that in situations where people have experienced harm, they as victims hope that the one who has caused the harm will accept responsibility for his or her actions, and perhaps offer an apology; acknowledgement of victims' worsened state and subsequent repair of that state—to the extent that it can be repaired—allows the victims to move on.[16] Restorative justice is, essentially, a means for the offender to "make things right" with society by addressing the needs and rights of the victims of the crime.

In the early 1980s, only four states had laws protecting the basic rights of victims in the criminal justice system. Today, every state has some laws protecting victims' rights, thanks largely to the victims' rights movement and increased research in the area. Over 30,000 statutes related to crime victims have been enacted, and federal legislation has been passed to provide basic rights and services to crime victims within the last 25 years.[17]

Critical Thinking

What are some of the laws in your state to protect victims' rights? Do you believe those laws serve their purpose?

Career Connections: Pre-Sentence Investigator

A pre-sentence investigator compiles a report for the court prior to the sentencing of a defendant. The report, also known as a **pre-sentence investigation**, details the defendant's background and any extenuating circumstances that may have contributed to the criminal behavior, then recommends an appropriate sentence. Some information that may be included in the pre-sentence investigation report includes family history, educational history, economic data, military record, health history, and prior criminal history.

A pre-sentence investigator will interview the defendant, the victim, and any other persons who may contribute relevant information, such as employers, mental health professionals, or even neighbors. Review and compilation of the defendant's records are common to ensure a thorough report. Effective interview skills, critical analysis, and attention to detail are highly desirable qualities for a pre-sentence investigator. A pre-sentence investigator typically has a bachelor's degree in criminal justice or a social or human science, and almost all pre-sentence investigators work for probation departments or the courts. There are, however, persons who conduct pre-sentence investigations for the defense. These individuals are usually known as **mitigation specialists**.

Pre-sentence investigation A report to the court which outlines the defendant's prior alcohol and drug history, medical history, criminal history, education, and other factors that is given to the judge to assist with determination of sentence. Pre-sentence investigations are generally written by local probation departments.

Mitigation specialist A person educated in the social sciences who assists the defendant in obtaining evidence to minimize the impact of punishment. Mitigation specialists are generally social workers or criminologists who compile past history of the defendant's life to assist with the defense.

Types of Sentences

A sentence is the sanction or sanctions imposed upon a convicted criminal by a judicial body such as a jury or a judge. Once the conviction occurs, the court's purpose shifts from impartial case litigation to imposition of sanctions. Different goals of sentencing exist but can intertwine and overlap depending on multiple considerations. The primary goal is to protect the public from the offender; other goals may be to make an example of the offender in an attempt to prevent others from committing the crime, to rehabilitate the offender, or the most obvious and well-known purpose, to punish the offender. In light of the different goals in sentencing, there are also different types of sentences. Some of these sentences may include fines, probation (of which there are different types), and community service, among others.

Fines

Offenders may be forced to pay fines in place of or in tandem with probation or incarceration. Most traffic offenses and many misdemeanors are traditionally addressed by assessing fines on the offenders. Felony offenders may also be assigned fines, although felony fines are much higher amounts than misdemeanor fines. Sometimes fines are twice the amount of what the offender gained from committing the crime. In New York State, for example, a typical fine imposed for a felony drug conviction is $10,000, even if the offender was in possession of drugs with a street value of far less than $10,000.[18] The imposition of fines has declined somewhat due to two Supreme Court rulings: *Williams v. Illinois* (1970) and *Bearden v. Georgia* (1983). The ruling in *Williams* pronounced that a person cannot be incarcerated longer than the length of the maximum sentence needed to work off a fine the individual was unable to pay. At the time of the ruling, 47 states frequently held defendants beyond the maximum sentence.[19] The *Bearden* decision stated that a sentencing court could not revoke a defendant's probation if a defendant had completed every condition of probation but the payment of fines due to the defendant's inability to pay.[20] This keeps offenders who are on probation from having their probation revoked and going to jail, possibly losing their jobs in the process.

Probation

Probation, or community supervision, returns an offender to the community under the supervision of an agent of the court or a probation agency. The word "probation" comes from the Latin word *probare*, which means "to test or prove." Probation offers the offender a chance to prove that, if given a second chance, he or she can engage in socially acceptable behavior.

Probationers have been found guilty by the court or have pleaded guilty. The offender who has been placed on probation is not confined in jail or prison and must fulfill conditions of a sentence imposed by the court. When a court sentences a criminal to probation, the judge will set the conditions of probation. The conditions are, in effect, a contract between the court and the probationer. The probation agreement usually comes in the form of general and specific conditions. General conditions are set by law and stipulate the behavior and rules that must be followed by all probationers under the court's jurisdiction. Specific conditions are those additional stipulations that a judge may impose in an effort to customize the probation sentence to fit the individual and crime. General and specific conditions of probation for all states and the federal government may be found online in state and federal government statutes. Probation can include a multitude of conditions, such as community service, participation in therapeutic intervention, and fines.

The concept of probation in the United States was first discussed by John Augustus, a Boston shoemaker, in the early 1840s. The "father of probation" volunteered to pay bail and assume responsibility for certain less serious offenders in exchange for the judge deferring their sentences. Augustus provided the offenders with friendship, support with family and personal issues, and even employment assistance for the period of their release. The offenders later returned to court for sentencing. Augustus would report on their progress toward rehabilitation and request that they be required to pay a fine and court costs rather than being imprisoned. If the judge was satisfied with an offender's performance in the community, the charges were dropped; otherwise, the judge proceeded with the sentence.[21] Augustus worked with the Boston courts for 18 years, never receiving any salary for his efforts. He used his own money and donations from others to support his work.[22] The state of Massachusetts used his basic ideas to pass the country's first official probation law in 1878. Most states allowed probation by 1920, but not until 1957 did all states have probation laws.[23]

Probation is not typically given for dangerous or more serious offenders. In the best situations, probation provides a therapeutic alternative to incarceration, where the offender would be surrounded by more hardcore criminals and hostile situations, making prison a more unlikely place for rehabilitation to take place than the everyday free community. Offenders who are placed on probation and do not successfully complete the court-ordered requirements are violating their probation and are in danger of having their probation revoked. Having probation revoked means the offender typically has to go to jail to complete his or her sentence.

At yearend 2015, an estimated 4,650,900 adults were under community supervision—a decrease of 62,300 offenders from yearend 2014 (Figure 7.1 below). About 1 in 53 adults in the United States was under community supervision at yearend 2015. This population includes adults on probation, parole, or any other post-prison supervision, with probationers accounting for the majority (81%) of adults under community supervision.

Law violation A new criminal charge against an offender on probation.

Technical violation A parole violation that is less serious than a law violation and could include failure to report to the probation officer, failure to make child support payments, or failure to complete other stipulations of probation such as community service hours.

There are two general types of probation violations: law and technical. A **law violation** occurs when an offender on probation receives a new criminal charge. For most jurisdictions, the probation officer will be notified when this occurs and will then contact the court to notify the judge of the violation, possibly resulting in the offender being brought in front of the judge to address the violation. A **technical violation** is usually noticed only by the supervising probation officer. Technical violations are less serious than law violations and could include failure to report to the probation officer, failure to make child support payments, or failure to complete other stipulations of probation such as community service hours.[24] The probation

FIGURE 7.1 ADULTS UNDER COMMUNITY SUPERVISION ON DECEMBER 31 AND ANNUAL PERCENT CHANGE, 2005–2015

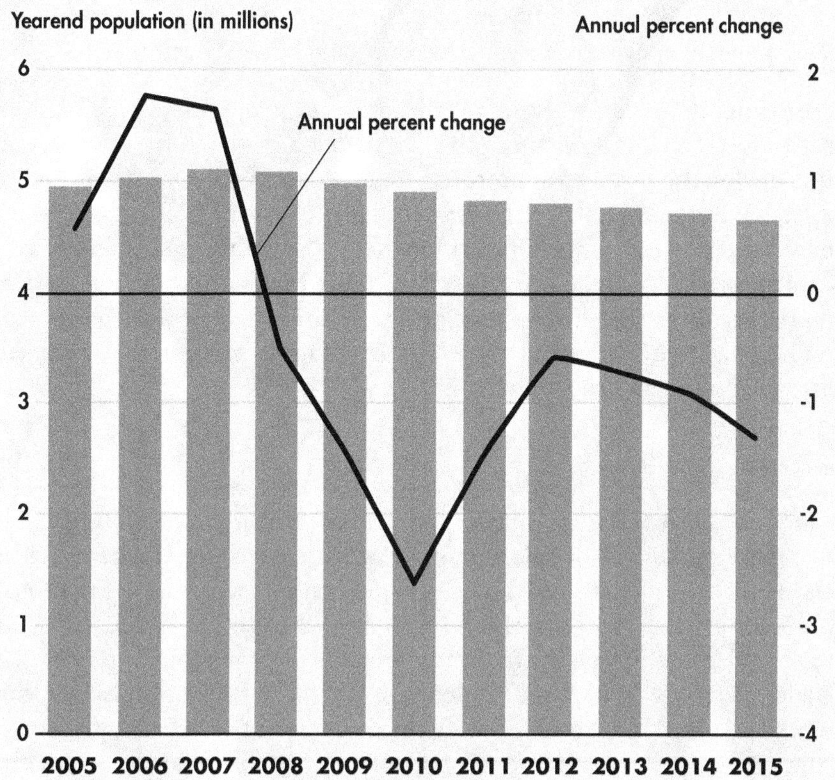

Note: Estimates are based on most recent data and may differ from previously published statistice. See *Methodology*.
Source: Burea of Justic Staistics, Annual Probation Survey and Annual Parole Survey, 2005–2015.
Source: Kaeble, D. & Bonczar, T. (2016). "Probation and Parole in the United States, 2015." Bureau of Justice Statistics. https://www.bjs.gov/content/pub/pdf/ppus15.pdf.

officer typically then has the discretion to cite the probationer for the violation, involve the probationer in more intensive supervision and counseling, or overlook the violation. Technical violation proceedings are started by the supervising officer and typically begin only when the officer has made the decision to approach the court to request that the offender's probation be revoked. Only the court has the final authority to revoke probation, no matter what violations have been committed by the offender.

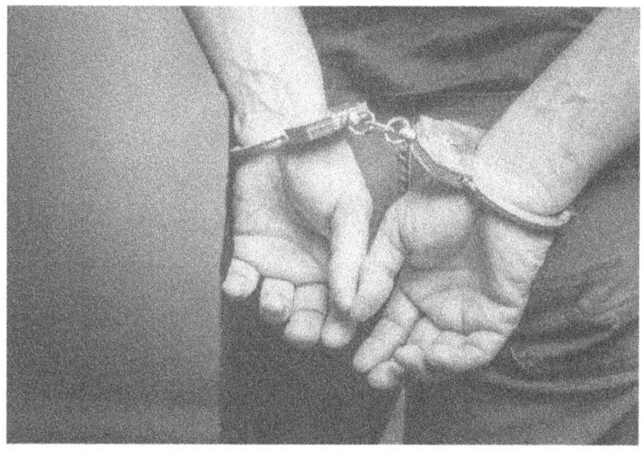

© BortN66/Shutterstock.com

Jail time is one type of sentence a guilty defendant may receive.

Probationers are not incarcerated but are also not free citizens. Probationers do not enjoy the full range of protections under the U.S. Constitution that the rest of society enjoys. As part of the probation agreement, probationers agree that the probation officer may enter their homes or places of business unannounced and conduct contraband and weapons searches. They must also submit to drug and alcohol tests. If a probationer is found to be in violation of the probation agreement, he or she may be ordered to jail or prison by the court.

A probationer has not given up all constitutional protections, though. Probationers have a constitutional right to have an attorney represent them during the revocation process.[25] In *Morrissey v. Brewer* (1972) and in *Gagnon v. Scapelli* (1973),[26] the United States Supreme Court recognized limited due process rights of probationers. As part of the rulings, the court established a three-stage procedure that must be followed during revocation proceedings. These stages include a preliminary hearing, the revocation hearing, and sentencing. Often, in lieu of incarceration, the judge will reimpose probation but with stricter terms.

Deferred Adjudication Probation

Deferred adjudication
A type of probation in which the court's decision of the case disposition is delayed while the defendant completes certain requirements of probation.

Deferred adjudication is a special type of probation. Adjudication is the court's process of decision making; when something is deferred, it is delayed for a period of time. Deferred adjudication, then, is a type of probation in which the court's decision of the case disposition is delayed while the defendant completes certain requirements of probation. Typically, the defendant pleads "guilty" or "no contest" at the disposition hearing, but no final disposition is recorded with the court until the defendant successfully completes the requirements of probation, or fails to do so and has the probation revoked. If the defendant successfully completes the probation requirements, there may be no formal conviction documented on the defendant's record, as the case is typically dismissed altogether.

Critical Thinking
Are there advantages to deferred adjudication probation for the defendant and the prosecution? Are there disadvantages for each? What are they?

Community Service

Community service
Unpaid labor or service to the community as an intermediate sanction ordered by the court.

Community service is typically not used as a correctional sentence by itself, but may be a condition of probation for offenders found guilty of lesser offenses, such as shoplifting, first or second drunk driving charges, or minor drug possession. Community service is unpaid work performed for public tax-supported or nonprofit agencies. This form of punishment is consistent with the idea that while each crime has a specific victim, communities as a whole are also victimized by crime. Since crime is an offense against the person as well as the community, service is a good way to offer restitution to the community while reminding the offender of the importance of following rules agreed on by residents of the community. As such, community service is a more restorative process than other forms of punishment. Examples of community service jobs could include picking up trash on state highways, shelving books for the local library, or collecting and organizing canned goods for a food pantry. Community service may be integrated into a probation sentence with the purpose of teaching offenders a specific lesson or exposing them to the possible harm their actions may have caused. For example, a person convicted of cruelty to animals may be sentenced to clean stalls at an animal shelter, or an offender convicted of selling drugs may be ordered to perform community service at a drug abuse treatment program.

Picking up trash in the community is an example of community service.

Ethics and Professionalism: Innocent of the Crime

As a probation officer for your county, you are ordered by a court to complete a pre-sentence investigative (PSI) report for the court. The defendant pleads guilty to the charge. When you interview the defendant to get his side of the story, he informs you that he is innocent of the charge and he suspects his brother actually committed the crime. The defendant's brother is a parolee who will probably return to prison if he is implicated in another crime. The district attorney's office in your county has enough circumstantial evidence to successfully argue that your defendant committed the crime, and if he is found guilty, there is a good chance that he will go to jail, subsequently losing his job and his home. The defendant has elected to plead guilty to the charge in the hope that he will be placed on probation, allowing him to keep his job and his apartment and potentially preventing his brother from returning to prison.

What do you do? Can the defendant dispute the PSI report while stating he is innocent of the charges? Do you include the defendant's disclosure in your report?

Offenders who have community service as a condition of probation will receive a sentence of a particular amount of hours of community service to complete, such as 50 or 100. The maximum number of community service hours an offender can be ordered to complete varies from state to state; in Texas, for example, an offender can be sentenced to a maximum of 1500 hours of community service for a felony charge.[27] In Illinois, an offender convicted of his first charge of Driving Under the Influence (DUI) without proof of driver's license or insurance is automatically sentenced to 480 hours of community service.[28]

Community service is not currently viewed as an alternative to imprisonment. While community service itself is generally looked upon as positive, the general public does not consider the substitution of a community service sentence for a prison sentence to be punitive enough for most offenders,[29] even though one of the benefits of community service is its value to the public. The state of Georgia reported that in 2007, offenders provided $4.5 million worth of work to the state in the form of community service hours.[30] Another benefit of community service is that it is not costly to implement and monitor. Some proponents, such as Petersilia (2002), argue that community service is beneficial to all parties, as the probation department develops and maintains positive relationships with local agencies by sending them workers, the local agencies benefit from the unpaid work, and the offenders are personally inconvenienced, paying back some of their debts to society.[31]

Shock Probation

Shock probation A type of probation in which the court sends offenders to prison for a short period of time to "shock" them by exposing them to the limits of prison life, then returns them to the original jurisdiction to be placed on probation.

Shock probation—technically a misnomer, since probation is designed to be used as an alternative to incarceration—is allowed by some statutes and involves the court sending offenders to prison for a short period of time, usually less than 180 days.[32] This is designed to "shock" offenders by exposing them to the limits of prison life before returning them to the original jurisdiction to be placed on probation. Incarcerating the offenders for a shorter period of time prevents them from absorbing too much of the "hard-core" inmate culture while allowing them to experience the harsh realities of daily prison existence. The first shock probation law in the United States was passed in the state of Ohio in 1965.[33]

There are several pros and cons to shock probation. Offenders who are sentenced to shock probation are made to understand the seriousness of their offenses without being subjected to the effects—as well as the taxpayers' cost—of a lengthy prison sentence. Shock probation also allows offenders who have positive rehabilitation potential to participate in community-based treatment and services, while the court still acknowledges the responsibility for imposing harsher, deterrent sentences in certain circumstances. Economically speaking, the short prison sentences of shock probation are less costly to society than lengthy sentences. On the negative side, shock probation has cost many offenders their jobs and interfered with their family and community support systems. There is also the possibility that even when offenders spend short periods of time in prison, they are exposed to serious offenders and hardened criminals, who generally have deteriorated social skills and hatred of prison life and other prisoners. Offenders may also be stigmatized by being incarcerated, causing confusion of their self-esteem and self-concepts. Whatever the arguments for or against shock probation, as yet, there is no evidence that shock probation reduces recidivism; the research findings on the subject remain inconclusive.

Intensive supervision probation A type of probation with a higher level of offender supervision, plus a stricter regimen of other services, including such stipulations as treatment programs and community service.

Intensive Supervision Probation

Some offenders who require additional supervision but may not need outright incarceration may be placed on **intensive supervision probation** (ISP), which includes a higher level of offender supervision, plus a stricter regimen of other services, including such stipulations as treatment programs and community service. Usually the offender is placed on intensive supervision because the probation department has determined that the offender's level of risk and needs require it; however, the court may order the offender directly to an intensive supervision program if the offense warrants, or if the offender was on a less intensive probation regimen but failed to successfully complete its requirements.

Probation officers who supervise intensive offenders typically have much smaller caseloads than other officers, and they may be trained in additional therapeutic interventions. Some of the stricter requirements of ISP may include:

- Multiple office, home, or work visits each week with an officer.
- Mandatory curfews.
- Participation in treatment programs.
- Employment or education requirements.
- Frequent testing for drug and alcohol use.[34]

While intensive supervision probation can help relieve overcrowding in prisons, it is not utilized frequently due to budget constraints and resource limitations. Every additional active intensive supervision officer occupies a spot that could be held by a routine probation officer with a much higher number of clients. Studies of the effectiveness of ISP show mixed results. A study by social scientists Billie Erwin and Lawrence Bennett (1987) examined the intensive supervision probation program in Georgia and found that recidivism rates for probationers on intensive supervision were better than for those on regular probation. The state also saved nearly $7,000 for each defendant assigned to intensive supervision probation rather than prison.[35] Petersilia and Turner (1993) found no clear relationship between more intensive supervision and recidivism. In other words, probationers on intensive supervision were as likely as offenders on regular probation to commit further crimes. Additionally, probationers on ISP had a substantially higher rate of technical violations than those on regular probation. Those offenders in intensive programs, however, came to believe that their chances of getting caught for committing additional crimes while on ISP were high, and they believed that if caught, they would be treated more severely than those on regular probation.[36] Perhaps this secondary effect of ISP led some offenders to refrain from further criminal activity, but this is not known.

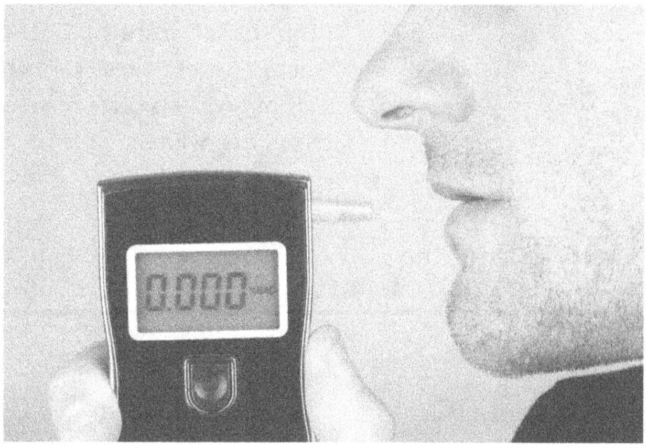

Frequent alcohol and drug testing may be a requirement of intensive supervision probation.

Restitution

Restitution is an aspect of probation or punishment that requires the offender to repay the victim, or the victim's family, for the harm that was caused.

Restitution Punishment that requires the offender to repay the victim for the harm that was caused, generally through monetary remuneration or community service.

The idea of restitution is to attempt to make the victim or the family of the victim whole again, theoretically restoring things to their original state. Restitution is generally provided by monetary remuneration (paying money to the family) or performing community work service, such as working in nursing homes, alcohol and drug treatment centers, or juvenile counseling or mentoring programs. Restitution not only compensates the crime victims for injuries and other losses, but also forces the offender to take responsibility for the crime committed. Restitution also allows the victim to be included in the process of administering justice.

Critics of restitution programs believe that these programs are punitive rather than rehabilitative because offenders may be subjected to additional sanctions that they cannot fulfill. Some feel that restitution negates any deterrent effects of the offender's sentence because it allows the offender to "pay off" the offense like a traffic ticket or late fee. White-collar criminals are usually sentenced to restitution payments with high dollar amounts to compensate for the large amount of monetary damage their crimes cause victims. The media attention given to white-collar crime also suggests that white-collar restitution amounts compensate for the shorter prison sentences given to these criminals. In other words, the general public seems to feel that white-collar restitution amounts "hit them where it hurts"—in the criminals' wallets.

Critical Thinking

Do you believe restitution as it is practiced today serves the purpose of making the victim, or the victim's family, whole again? Why or why not?

House Arrest and Electronic Monitoring

House arrest—also known as home detention, home confinement, and several other names—is a program in which the offender is required to remain in the home except at prearranged and preapproved times, such as to attend work, school, or treatment services. **House arrest** is stricter and seemingly more punitive than ISP, but they may be used in combination. House arrest may also be used as an alternative to pretrial incarceration in jail. While house arrest of some form has probably been implemented by parents since ancient times, it was not used in the United States as an official sanction for criminal activity until the mid-1980s.[37] It became a popular punishment idea due to prison overcrowding. House arrest was not readily considered a reasonable alternative to incarceration because without 24-hour surveillance by law enforcement or court officers, there was no perceived way to ensure that a defendant would comply with the stipulations of home confinement.

House arrest A method of punishment in which the defendant is kept under close supervision in his or her own home rather than in prison.

Electronic monitoring A form of technology used with house arrests to track and limit an offender's movement outside the home with telephone or radio signals.

House arrest became more common with the advent of widely available **electronic monitoring** equipment, which enabled the needed 24-hour surveillance. Electronic monitoring is not a form of detention, but rather a form of technology that tracks and limits an offender's movement outside the home using telephone or radio signals. There are two primary types of electronic monitoring systems used today: continuous monitoring and programmed contact. With the continuous monitoring system, the offender wears a device—typically a type of anklet—programmed to emit continuous signals to a nearby receiver at certain intervals. The receiver communicates with the monitoring agency's computer and cross-checks the offender's location with his or her schedule, which is programmed into the computer, to determine if the offender is in the right place at the required time. With the programmed contact system, the agency's computer makes telephone calls to the offender's approved locations at either random or preprogrammed times, and the offender must respond promptly to those calls to verify his or her location.[38] The type of device utilized governs the offender's response. Some devices require the offender to speak, using voice verification to complete the response. Others require the offender to insert a wrist-worn monitor into a verifier device attached to the telephone. Whatever type of monitoring system is used, each device worn by the offender is usually programmed to detect if it has been tampered with. If an offender tries to remove the device, a signal is sent to the monitoring computer reporting the attempted removal. Offenders who try to remove their monitoring devices may be subjected to more restrictions or incarcerated, as removing the device constitutes failure to comply with the monitoring stipulations.

Supporters state that house arrest and electronic monitoring are more cost-effective than incarceration while allowing the offenders to have more individual supervision than traditional probation. Offenders on electronic monitoring, by not being sent to prison, are spared from the potentially harmful effects of exposure to hardened criminals, some of which were discussed in the section on shock probation. Participants in combined house arrest and electronic monitoring programs are five times more likely to successfully complete their programs and are 50% less likely to abscond from their sentences.[39]

Critics of house arrest and monitoring think that these methods interfere with the offenders' rights to privacy and protection from unreasonable search and seizure as afforded by the U.S. Constitution. This interference, critics say, is also thrust upon those who live in the residence with the offender. Criminologists Rolando del Carmen and Joseph Vaughn (1992) commented, "A review of decided cases in probation and parole indicates that while the use of electronic devices raises constitutional issues, its constitutionality will most likely be upheld by the courts, primarily based on the concept of diminished rights [for offenders]."[40] An offender who is on electronic monitoring experiences a decrease in freedoms, namely the freedom to come and go as one pleases, because he or she is potentially being "watched" at all hours of the day. Other opponents believe that house arrest and electronic monitoring are unfair to economically disadvantaged offenders, who are not as apt to have homes and telephones where the monitoring devices must be installed. Offenders being monitored must also pay costly fees for the monitoring devices and services, which is more difficult for disadvantaged offenders. Another problem with house arrest and electronic monitoring is that while offenders are not allowed to abscond from the program, many still do and may commit more crimes. An examination of Florida's house arrest program revealed that between 1983 and 2008, offenders in the program killed approximately 462 people and committed over 720 sex crimes; approximately 32% of the murderers and 17% of the sex offenders had absconded from their monitoring programs at the time their crimes were committed.[41]

Pretrial Diversion

Pretrial diversion An informal arrangement that involves referring the defendant to rehabilitative programs prior to arraignment in an attempt to address the offense reasonably while offering the defendant the opportunity to keep the offense off his or her criminal record.

Some jurisdictions offer judges the option to sentence offenders to a **pretrial diversion**, which operates much like a probation sentence. The defendant makes at least one court appearance and, depending on the defendant's personal situation and the crime itself, could be recommended by the district attorney to participate in a pretrial diversion. There is no trial and no plea by the defendant. The defendant sees a pretrial officer—who is a probation officer—and performs whatever tasks are assigned by the court. If the offender completes the tasks satisfactorily, the case is typically dismissed without ever going to trial. Pretrial diversions can last for various periods of time depending on judicial preference and local or state laws.

One example of how a pretrial diversion works might be in the instance of an 18-year-old who has been charged with possession of marijuana but has never previously been in trouble. The offender might be sentenced to complete a substance abuse evaluation, urine drug screens, monthly visits with a pretrial officer, and community service hours, all to be done within six months. If the offender completes all of these tasks within the allotted amount of time and does not test positive for substances, the district attorney would then drop the charges.

Capital Punishment: The Death Penalty

Perhaps the most controversial, hotly debated topic in sentencing for several decades has been capital punishment, also known as the death penalty. A capital crime is a crime that is punishable, according to legislation, by putting the guilty offender to death. Capital crimes, such as the murders committed by Robert Coulson described at the beginning of this chapter, are the most heinous of crimes. Capital punishment is different from any other criminal sanctions not just in its nature but also in its legal process.

History of Capital Punishment in the United States

When Europeans settled America, they brought the legal systems and processes from their homelands. The English Penal Code was adopted by the British colonies on America's Atlantic coast and included over

50 capital offenses. The adaptation of the rules varied between colonies, so not every colony executed offenders for the same crimes. As an example, the Massachusetts Bay colony observed 12 crimes that were punishable by death. One of these 12 crimes, murder, is still punishable by death in many states today, but several other current-day lesser crimes were capital offenses in colonial days, including witchcraft, rebellion, and sodomy. In the Massachusetts Bay statute, capital punishment was justified for each crime by a supporting quote from the Bible, and the colony later added arson and grand larceny to the approved list of capital offenses. On the less deadly side of the spectrum, the Great Act of 1682 in Pennsylvania listed only treason and murder as crimes punishable by death.[42]

The death penalty is one of the most controversial topics in sentencing.

In colonial America, capital punishment was neither rare nor considered cruel and unusual. It was widely accepted as an effective and efficient way to handle criminals; an executed criminal does not live to commit further crimes. The earliest documented lawful execution in the American colonies happened in Virginia in 1608. Captain George Kendall, a prominent citizen in the colony, was found guilty of spying for Spain and executed. Even execution of juveniles was permitted in colonial days.[43]

When the Eighth Amendment of the Constitution was created to ban cruel and unusual punishment, banning the death penalty was apparently not an issue under consideration. The creators of the Constitution were probably thinking of ghastly forms of execution such as boiling in hot oil or impaling with spikes as cruel and unusual.

As time progressed, capital punishment changed. After approximately 1890, the death penalty became an increasingly popular sentence. The 1930s was the peak period for the death penalty: over 1,500 executions occurred in the United States during that decade. After that, use of the death penalty steadily declined, with less than 200 executions carried out in the 1960s.[44] In the southern states, African-Americans were far more likely to be sentenced to death than whites. In mid-1830s Virginia, there were five legislated capital crimes for whites and over 70 for African-Americans. The number of death sentences can be partially explained by the sheer number of states with capital statutes in their penal codes and the offenses listed by state that are punishable by death. In 1961, 48 states had capital offense statutes. Of those [48, 47] considered homicide to be a capital offense; 16 considered rape to be capital; four considered train robbery to be capital; and two considered espionage to be capital.[45]

Critical Thinking

Do you believe the death penalty in the Coulson case was cruel and unusual punishment, just deserts, wholly justified, or something else?

The Supreme Court Weighs In

The first argument before the Supreme Court which presented the idea that punishment of offenders could be cruel and unusual was in the case of *O'Neil v. Vermont* (1892). The petitioner faced a sentence of a total of 19,915 days—nearly 55 years—in jail for over 300 separate illegal sales of liquor. The sentence imposed by the court in Vermont was upheld because the Supreme Court found that there was no federal dilemma involved in the case, as the Eighth Amendment did not limit state sentences. Three justices strongly dissented with the opinion, and one, Justice Stephen J. Field, stated that punishment more severe than the crime it was intended to punish was cruel and unusual.[46] The Supreme Court did not hear another cruel and unusual punishment case until 1910, when *Weems v. United States* was decided. The court reversed a sentence imposed upon an offender who made false entries into official government records: 15 years of hard labor, ankle chains, the permanent loss of certain civil rights, and other stipulations. The court determined that the sentence was severely disproportionate to the offense, and *Weems* became the first case in which the court negated a criminal sentence on Eighth Amendment grounds.[47]

© Sean Pavone/Shutterstock.com

Justices of the U.S. Supreme Court have made important case decisions affecting the death penalty.

A barrage of court battles over certain parts of capital punishment, as well as the capital sentence itself, occurred between 1968 and 1972. The initial case decision indicating that the death penalty might be in jeopardy was Witherspoon v. Illinois (1968). In this case, a court in Illinois had allowed a guilty verdict and subsequent death sentence to be handed down by a jury after the state's attorney had methodically excluded all members from the jury pool who were against, or possibly against, capital punishment. The Supreme Court agreed with Witherspoon, ruling that the "death-qualified jury"—meaning that every single jury member was ready, willing, and able to sentence the defendant to die—was not a proper representation of the community as a whole, and therefore violated the Eighth Amendment.[48]

More death penalty challenges made their way to the Supreme Court. States observed an informal moratorium on executions while awaiting the court rulings: in other words, no executions were carried out during this time. The landmark decision finally came on June 29, 1972, when for the first time in history, the Supreme Court set aside death sentences. Three cases, *Furman v. Georgia, Jackson v. Georgia, and Branch v. Texas*, led the court to decide that the capital punishment statutes in those cases were indeed unconstitutional. In those cases, the juries had been given full discretion to decide between imposing the death penalty or a lesser punishment in those capital cases. The majority ruling was five justices to four, and every single justice wrote an opinion—an extremely rare occurrence. The majority justices ruled that those statutes constituted "cruel and unusual punishment" under the Eighth and 14th Amendments because the death penalty was arbitrarily and unfairly imposed against non-whites. This ruling did not declare the death penalty unconstitutional, but rather the methods by which it was administered.[49] The decision in these cases (known collectively as the *Furman* decision) negated the death penalty laws of approximately 35 states, and over 600 inmates had their death sentences set aside and commuted to prison terms. By late 1974, however, 30 states had enacted new death penalty laws that conformed to the *Furman* ruling. Some states mandated capital punishment upon conviction for certain crimes, while others listed specific rules that judges and juries had to follow when deciding whether execution was the appropriate sentence for a specific case.

Another Supreme Court ruling affecting the death penalty was, like the *Furman* decision, a collection of court cases. In *Gregg v. Georgia*, the court addressed the new bifurcated trial structure in the state of Georgia: after defendants were convicted in first-degree murder cases, the punishment was determined in a separate court process. The law at the time in Georgia mandated the judge or jury to take into account any additional aggravating circumstances or mitigating circumstances, such as a murder occurring while the defendant was attempting to avoid being arrested; a murder of a corrections officer, an on-duty law enforcement officer, or a firefighter; a murder committed in exchange for money; or a murder committed while a rape, armed robbery, burglary, kidnapping, or act of arson occurred. The Supreme Court upheld the Georgia law, saying that because juries had to consider another circumstance in addition to the guilty finding, they were prevented from assessing death sentences with their previous wild abandon. In two companion cases, *Proffitt v. Florida* and *Jurek v. Texas*, the court upheld procedures in those states similar to Georgia's. By handing down these three rulings, the Supreme Court restated that capital punishment laws were indeed constitutional as long as those state laws provided clear and unbiased criteria for judges and juries to follow when determining whether to sentence the guilty party to death.[50]

Aggravating circumstances
Circumstances that go above and beyond the basic requirements for a crime to be considered serious; the facts or situations that increase the seriousness of a criminal act.

Mitigating circumstances
Circumstances that do not justify a criminal act, but make the crime less reprehensible and may be used to reduce the sentence in a criminal trial.

After the collective *Furman* and *Gregg* decisions, state-sponsored executions resumed. The first state to complete an execution was Utah, on January 17, 1977. Gary Gilmore, convicted of the robbery and murder of a hotel manager, was executed by firing squad. At the time of his sentencing, Utah had two methods of execution—firing squad or hanging—and the judge allowed Gilmore his choice.[51] Since Gilmore's execution, more than half of the executions completed in the United States have occurred in only three states: Texas, Virginia, and Oklahoma.[52]

Methods of Execution

In 1977, several states legally retired hanging, electrocution, and lethal gas as methods of execution and replaced them with death by lethal injection. Supporters of this method argued that it would be a far more humane mode of execution, as the prisoner would fall asleep, and death would be virtually instantaneous. The American Medical Association argued against lethal injection and issued instructions to its member doctors to refrain from taking part in the act, pointing out that the role of a doctor is to protect and save life, not end it.[53] The first inmate to die in the United States by state-supported lethal injection was Charles Brooks, Jr. He was put to death in Huntsville, Texas, on December 7, 1982, for committing capital murder in 1976.[54]

In 1994, a federal court ruled that execution by lethal gas was in violation of the Eighth Amendment clause on cruel and unusual punishment. The presiding judge cited as evidence doctor reports and eyewitness accounts of many past executions, all of which stated that the dying inmates were still conscious for a minute or more once the gas was administered. Consequently, the inmates could be suffering intense physical pain, including the deprivation of air akin to the experience of being strangled or drowning. This ruling stipulated that all future executions in California would be done by lethal injection.[55] The Supreme Court has declared death by electrocution to be constitutional, but due to the gruesomeness of the act, most states do not allow it. As of November 2016, only Washington and New Hampshire still offer hanging for executions; seven states offer electrocution; five states allow lethal gas; and one allows death by firing squad. Nineteen states and the District of Columbia have no death penalty.[56] However, most states use lethal injection.

Death sentences, executions, and public support for capital punishment all continued historic declines in 2016. American juries imposed the fewest death sentences in the modern era of U.S. capital punishment, since the Supreme Court declared existing death penalty statutes unconstitutional in 1972. The 30 new death sentences imposed in 2016 represent a 39 percent decline from 2015's already 40-year low of 49. The 20 executions in 2016 marked the lowest number in a quarter century, according to a report released by the Death Penalty Information Center (DPIC). National public opinion polls also showed support for capital punishment at a 40-year low. 66

"America is in the midst of a major climate change concerning capital punishment. While there may be fits and starts and occasional steps backward, the long-term trend remains clear," according to Robert Dunham, DPIC's Executive Director. "Whether it's concerns about innocence, costs, and discrimination, availability of life without parole as a safe alternative, or the questionable way in which states are attempting to carry out executions, the public grows increasingly uncomfortable with the death penalty each year." 66

For the first time in more than 40 years, no state imposed ten or more death sentences. Only five states imposed more than one death sentence. California imposed the most (9) followed by Ohio (4), Texas (4), Alabama (3), and Florida (2). Death sentences continued to be clustered in *two percent* of counties nationwide, with Los Angeles County imposing four death sentences, the most of any county. But death sentences were down 39 percent, even in those two-percent counties. 66

The 20 executions conducted in 2016 marked a decline of more than 25 percent since the previous year, when there were 28 executions. Only five states conducted executions in 2016, the fewest number of states to do so since 1983. Two states—Georgia, which had the most executions (9), and Texas, which had the second highest number (7)—accounted for 80 percent of all executions in the U.S. Although Georgia carried out more executions than at any other time since the 1950s, juries in that state have not imposed any new death sentences in the past two years. 66

Limits to the Death Penalty

Subsequent Supreme Court rulings have imposed limits on which crimes may appropriately generate death sentences and have further clarified capital punishment as a whole. Figure 7.2 is a list of many of these rulings.

FIGURE 7.2 SUPREME COURT RULINGS ON THE DEATH PENALTY

Coker v. Georgia (1977)	Rape without murder does not warrant a death sentence.[59]
Eberheart v. Georgia (1977)	Kidnapping when the victim does not die does not warrant a death sentence.[60]
Ford v. Wainwright (1986)	States are prevented from executing death row inmates who have developed diagnosed mental illnesses while they are on death row.[61]
McCleskey v. Kemp (1987)	State death penalty laws are constitutional even when research shows that they may have been applied in a racially biased or prejudicial manner. While racial discrimination exists, it must be demonstrated in individual and separate cases.[62]
Thompson v. Oklahoma (1988)	States may not execute persons who were under the age of 16 when they committed their offenses unless the states in which the offenses occurred had established a clear, set minimum age for the death penalty.[63]
Stanford v. Kentucky (1989)	It is not a violation of the Eighth Amendment to impose the death penalty upon a defendant who committed his or her crime at the age of 16 or 17 years.[64]
Atkins v. Virginia (2002)	It is considered cruel and unusual punishment to execute the mentally retarded, since it cannot be determined that they understood their crimes, much less their sentences.[65]
Roper v. Simmons (2005)	The *Stanford* ruling was overturned. It is now unconstitutional to sentence a juvenile (person under the age of 18 years) to death.[66]
Kennedy v. Louisiana (2008)	Child rape in which the child victim does not die does not warrant a death sentence.[67]

The Debate: To Execute or Not to Execute?

Proponents of the death penalty argue that it is, practically speaking, cheaper to execute offenders than to house them in prison for life, which could be many years. Due to state and federal laws, however, all defendants sentenced to death enter a mandatory appeal process, which has several steps and can take quite a few years. There are multiple sets of documents filed in multiple levels of courts, which must be reviewed by judges and attorneys in those courts, and verbal arguments are taken in some of those courts. The appellate courts are usually in wholly different cities or states than the attorneys' offices and the defendant's prison unit. The entire process is costly, from filing court documents, to traveling to and appearing in the courts, to corresponding with the defendant and his or her legal team. Since a judge appoints the defendant's legal team, the costs fall to the taxpayers. The average amount of time a prisoner spends on death row before being executed is long: 10.6 years in Texas (TDCJ) and at least 12 years in Florida (Florida Dept. of Corrections) and Arizona (Arizona Dept. of Corrections).[57] Most quantitative studies of the economic argument for the death penalty have shown that the death penalty exerts a much higher cost to taxpayers than life imprisonment, due to the costs of the appeals process. The state can spend up to $5 million per appeal.[58]

Probably the most hotly argued reason to discontinue the death penalty is the justifiability of punishing someone who has killed by killing that individual. Murder is against the law, yet many opponents of the death penalty consider capital punishment to be state-sanctioned murder. Cesare Beccaria advocated against capital punishment, writing, "The death penalty cannot be useful because of the example of barbarity it gives to men . . . it seems absurd to me that the laws . . . which punish homicide should themselves commit it."[68] Supporters of capital punishment might argue that by killing another individual, the offender has stolen the victim's right to live, and has thereby forfeited his or her own right to live.[69]

There is also the argument that since the death penalty is irreversible, innocent persons may be executed. Research by Radelet and Bedau determined that between 1972 and 1996, 86 death row inmates were released prior to their executions due to doubts about their guilt.[70] These inmates were tried, found guilty, sentenced to death, and later released due to their erroneous convictions. The number of convicted death row inmates receiving exonerations has increased as well, from three per year from 1973 to 1999, to five per year from 2000 through 2007.[71] Opponents of the death penalty argue that one innocent person executed is too many.

Another issue regarding the death penalty is whether it is applied fairly to all races in this country. Since 1976, approximately 35% of executed offenders have been black, despite the black population in the United States being approximately 15% of the total population. Of the current death row offenders in this country, nearly four times as many offenders were convicted in cases involving white victims as were convicted in cases involving non-white victims.[72] Research published in 1989 by Radelet revealed the startling statistic that less than 0.2% of known, sanctioned executions in the United States were of a white individual for committing a crime against a black individual.[73] Updated statistics show that compared to 16 white offenders in the United States who were executed for killing black victims, there have been 253 black offenders executed for killing white victims.[74]

© Andrey_Popov/Shutterstock.com

While a jury may recommend a sentence, the judge may overrule the recommendation and pronounce a different sentence.

Public support in the U.S. for the death penalty reached its lowest point in 1966, during the height of the Vietnam War and American political activism; the highest was in 1984.[75] Several issues have arisen over time that have led an increasing number of people to question the validity and appropriateness of the death penalty. The fact that putting an offender to death is absolutely irreversible raises huge concerns for many death penalty abolitionists. Some offenders who were on death row have been released after new DNA testing technology proved their innocence of the crimes for which they were convicted. One study showed that out of over 4,500 death penalty cases examined, more than two-thirds contained serious legal discrepancies, such as incompetent defense counsel or corrupt prosecution.[76] Many death penalty states now offer sentences of "life without parole" for offenders who are convicted of capital offenses but are not sentenced to death. Life without parole effectively imparts the benefits of the death penalty—deterrence from committing future murders and no re-release into society—without taking the life of the accused.[77] Since 1998, the number of death sentences pronounced per year has dropped by more than half: 294 offenders were sentenced to death in 1998, while 112 were sentenced to death in 2009. [78] In 2016, 30 people were sentenced to death in America, and 20 people were executed. [57]

Special Issues in Sentencing

The **indeterminate sentence** is the most common type of sentence. It has fixed minimum and maximum terms for imprisonment. The paroling authority determines the amount of time the inmate serves. When a defendant is sentenced to, for example, one to five years' imprisonment or 20 years to life, those are indeterminate sentences.

Indeterminate sentence A prison sentence that consists of a range of years (such as "five to ten years"). The state parole board holds hearings that determine when, during that range, the convicted person will be eligible for parole.

The indeterminate sentence is based on the idea of teaching offenders to learn to refrain from criminal behavior so they can be returned to society as productive, law-abiding citizens. Theoretically, the indeterminate sentence should meet each defendant's rehabilitative needs. After the inmate is incarcerated, the rehabilitation begins, and the inmate is imprisoned until he or she can demonstrate signs of rehabilitation. The paroling authority, or **parole board**, has the duty to assess the extent to which the offender has

Parole board The governmental board that will determine if an offender receives parole and under what conditions.

been rehabilitated or not rehabilitated and orders the offender's release or return to prison. The readiness of the offender for his or her release theoretically lies with the individual and varies according to the individual's participation in rehabilitation and improvement while incarcerated.[79]

While indeterminate sentencing became popular in the 1950s and 1960s, it lost steam in the 1970s and 1980s. Many offenders who had been deemed to be rehabilitated recidivated, causing politicians and the general public to lose faith in the justice system.[80] Many inmates learned how to "play the game" and behave like they were rehabilitated in order to convince parole officials that they could be released into society. They participated in available treatment programs and learned how to use the appropriate verbiage to obtain their release.[81] As justice system reforms occurred, the decision-making authority regarding the length of an inmate's sentence moved from the parole board and prison staff to the prosecutors and lawmakers when the determinate sentence was introduced.

Determinate sentence
A sentence for a specific criminal act that is determined by the state legislature; a sentence that requires a specific amount of time, as ordered by the trial judge, for a person to serve in prison.

Offenders sanctioned with **determinate sentences** have fixed spans of incarceration and know precisely when they will be released, which eliminates the need for parole boards. The federal government and some states have established guidelines for determinate sentencing, while other states have sentencing commissions. The purpose of determinate sentencing is not so much rehabilitation as it is incapacitation: its main purpose is to keep criminals out of society. Stories about lenient judges and liberal parole boards releasing offenders back into society when they were not successfully rehabilitated caused legislators to create sentencing laws that controlled criminal justice professionals' discretion in any particular case. Many of these laws stated that the length of an inmate's sentence would not be determined by any person, such as the judge or the parole board, but by the actual crime committed.[82] In Texas, the parole board is appointed by the governor.

While it appears that determinate sentencing is advantageous because it creates uniformity in sentencing, removing any focus from factors such as race, gender, and social class, unintended consequences have been created. With the removal of discretion and decision-making power from those professionals closely involved with the case, the potential to apply the most appropriate sentence for an offender with extenuating or mitigating circumstances is also removed. This means the welfare of society and the offender's punishment cannot be balanced effectively, as in the case of a young man who kills his father to prevent him from repeatedly beating his wife. Legislators also presumably did not take into account the effect that determinate sentencing would have on correctional resources. Prison overcrowding has grown rampant in this country, with limits to even the number of beds in prisons. While many legislators assume a "get tough on crime" agenda in order to get elected or remain in office, the same legislators are loath to increase resource allocation in order to appropriately address overcrowding in jails and prisons. As a result, the civil and human rights of prisoners are violated.[83]

Another effect of determinate sentencing is that it has caused a power shift from the judge to the prosecutor. With determinate sentencing laws limiting the judge's discretion in sentence imposition, the power of the prosecutor to decide what charges can be filed against the defendant has increased. This has unintentionally caused a ripple effect, as defendants who are unwilling to accept longer determinate sentences for some crimes may be pressured into accepting plea bargains for lesser crimes. This gives the prosecutor a huge amount of leverage in coercing defendants and their attorneys to accept plea bargains, particularly in cases involving sex or drug offenses.[84]

Mandatory Minimums

The concept of the mandatory minimum sentence came about during the "war on drugs," which took hold particularly during the 1980s. A **mandatory minimum** sentence is governed by the lawmakers in each state and prescribes a set span of imprisonment for drug offenses such as possession or distribution. Other crimes can have punishments dictated by mandatory minimums, such as armed robbery with a gun. All 50 states and the federal government now have at least one mandatory minimum sentencing law. Mandatory minimums do not always work, however, because judges and other officials have the authority to alter those sentences. Mandatory minimum sentencing also does not take into account any special circumstances particular to one crime, forcing defendants who may be small-time or first-time offenders into the hardened culture of prison life with hardcore, repeat offenders.

Mandatory minimum
A sentence that is imposed by the state legislature with no discretion given by the trial judge. The defendant is required by law to serve a certain amount of time in the state penitentiary.

Three-strikes law
A specific legislative mandate that requires offenders, after their third conviction for any offense, to serve a minimum amount of time in incarceration.

Three-Strikes Law

In the legal systems of some states, if an offender commits three felonies, he or she earns a sentence of life in prison. These "three-strikes" laws earn their collective name from the game of baseball, in which the at-bat is over if the batter earns three strikes. Washington was the first state to pass a **three-strikes law**, in 1993. Washington's Persistent Offender Accountability Act allows for offenders who have committed three felonies to be sent to prison for life without parole. California followed suit in 1994 with what has been deemed one of the most encompassing three-strikes laws. Under California law, some of the felonies considered "strikes" are sexual abuse of a child, kidnapping, murder, or rape. The first two felonies must be in the serious felony category; any third felony committed dooms the offender to a mandatory

© Paul Hippauf/Shutterstock.com

In the legal systems of some states, if an offender commits three felonies, he or she earns a sentence of life in prison.

life sentence.[85] Over half of the states, as well as the federal government, have three-strikes provisions in their laws. Opponents of three-strikes laws believe they constitute cruel and unusual punishment. One example is the Supreme Court ruling in *Ewing v. California*, in which Gary Ewing's third felony was the theft of three golf clubs. While it was argued that the life sentence was severely disproportionate to the crime, the court upheld the law, and Ewing is currently serving a sentence of 25 years to life.[86]

On November 6, 2012 California voters approved Proposition 36, which substantially amended the law with two primary provisions:

1. The requirements for sentencing a defendant as a third-strike offender were changed by requiring the new felony to be a serious *or violent felony* with two or more prior strikes to qualify for the 25-year-to-life sentence as a third-strike offender; and
2. The addition of a means by which designated defendants *currently serving* a third-strike sentence may petition the court for reduction of their term to a second-strike sentence, if they would have been eligible for second strike sentencing under the new law. * Source: *California's Three Strikes Sentencing Law* (2016). California Courts. The Judicial Branch of California. http://www.courts.ca.gov/20142.htm.

Truth in Sentencing

Truth-in-sentencing laws mandate that offenders serve a substantial, or even a majority, of their sentences. These laws were enacted because prisoners typically serve less time in prison than their original sentences stipulated due to time off for good behavior or parole. Inmates are also released early due to prison overcrowding, and in some states, inmates who learn a trade or complete school could get time taken off their sentences. The truth-in-sentencing laws restrict **good time credits**, which in turn increases the percentage of a sentence an inmate serves. Most states have adopted truth-in-sentencing laws, and three states require that 100% of a minimum sentence must be served prior to an inmate becoming eligible to be released.[87]

Good time credit The amount of time that a state penitentiary gives the offender for maintaining good behavior while incarcerated; time that is taken off the sentence.

Federal Sentencing Guidelines

Sentencing guidelines may be developed by sentencing commissions made up of criminal justice professionals and private citizens. Sentencing guidelines are a way to restrict judges' discretion. Both state and federal jurisdictions have guidelines in place that serve as general rules on which judges may base sentences. While the guidelines used to be considered mandatory, after the Supreme Court ruling in *United States v. Booker*, the guidelines are considered advisory only.[88] This means that judges may use the sentencing guidelines when determining a defendant's sentence, but this is no longer required.

The United States Congress created the U.S. Sentencing Commission in 1985. This commission creates, maintains, and changes federal sentencing guidelines to prevent sentencing disparities at the federal level. The guidelines are suggestions based on the defendant's conduct during the commission of the offense and the defendant's criminal history. There are 43 offense levels, six criminal history categories based on points, and four sentencing zones: A, B, C, and D. The offense levels rank different types of offenses by severity. Sentencing zones group the lengths of sentences into types and lengths of sentences, from least severe to most severe. Zone A includes sentences ranging from zero to six months; Zone B includes sentences ranging from one to seven months up to six to 12 months, with the possibility of using alternate methods of confinement, split sentences, or incarceration only; Zone C sentences range from eight to 14 months up to 10 to 16 months, with the possibility of a split sentence only if at least one half of the minimum sentence is served while incarcerated; and Zone D includes all sentences ranging from 12 to 18 months up to life in prison, with all time required to be served in prison.[89] New sentencing guidelines implemented resulted in increased similarity of sentences between offenders and sent more federal defendants to prison for shorter periods of time. Figure 7.3 is a table of sentencing guidelines.

FIGURE 7.3 2016 FEDERAL SENTENCING GUIDELINES (IN MONTHS OF IMPRISONMENT).[90]

		Criminal History Category (Criminal History Points)					
	Offense Level	**I (0 or 1)**	**II (2 or 3)**	**III (4, 5, 6)**	**IV (7, 8, 9)**	**V (10, 11, 12)**	**VI (13 or more)**
Zone A	1	0–6	0–6	0–6	0–6	0–6	0–6
	2	0–6	0–6	0–6	0–6	0–6	1–7
	3	0–6	0–6	0–6	0–6	2–8	3–9
	4	0–6	0–6	0–6	2–8	4–10	6–12
	5	0–6	0–6	1–7	4–10	6–12	9–15
	6	0–6	1–7	2–8	6–12	9–15	12–18
	7	0–6	2–8	4–10	8–14	12–18	15–21
	8	0–6	4–10	6–12	10–16	15–21	18–24
Zone B	9	4–10	6–12	8–14	12–18	18–24	21–27
	10	6–12	8–14	10–16	15–21	21–27	24–30
	11	8–14	10–16	12–18	18–24	24–30	27–33
Zone C	12	10–16	12–18	15–21	21–27	27–33	30–37
Zone D	13	12–18	15–21	18–24	24–30	30–37	33–41
	14	15–21	18–24	21–27	27–33	33–41	37–46
	15	18–24	21–27	24–30	30–37	37–46	41–51
	16	21–27	24–30	27–33	33–41	41–51	46–57
	17	24–30	27–33	30–37	37–46	46–57	51–63

18	27-33	30-37	33-41	41-51	51-63	57-71
19	30-37	33-41	37-46	46-57	57-71	63-78
20	33-41	37-46	41-51	51-63	63-78	70-87
21	37-46	41-51	46-57	57-71	70-87	77-96
22	41-51	46-57	51-63	63-78	77-96	84-105
23	46-57	51-63	57-71	70-87	84-105	92-115
24	51-63	57-71	63-78	77-96	92-115	100-125
25	57-71	63-78	70-87	84-105	100-125	110-137
26	63-78	70-87	78-97	92-115	110-137	120-150
27	70-87	78-97	87-108	100-125	120-150	130-162
28	78-97	87-108	97-121	110-137	130-162	140-175
29	87-108	97-121	108-135	121-151	140-175	151-188
30	97-121	108-135	121-151	135-168	151-188	168-210
31	108-135	121-151	135-168	151-188	168-210	188-235
32	121-151	135-168	151-188	168-210	188-235	210-262
33	135-168	151-188	168-210	188-235	210-262	235-293
34	151-188	168-210	188-235	210-262	235-293	262-327
35	168-210	188-235	210-262	235-293	262-327	292-365
36	188-235	210-262	235-293	262-327	292-365	324-405
37	210-262	235-293	262-327	292-365	324-405	360-life
38	235-293	262-327	292-365	324-405	360-life	360-life
39	262-327	292-365	324-405	360-life	360-life	360-life
40	292-365	324-405	360-life	360-life	360-life	360-life
41	324-405	360-life	360-life	360-life	360-life	360-life
42	360-life	360-life	360-life	360-life	360-life	360-life
43	life	life	life	life	life	life

Commentary to Sentencing Table

Application Notes:

1. The Offense Level (1-43) forms the vertical axis of the Sentencing Table. The Criminal History Category (I-VI) forms the horizontal axis of the Table. The intersection of the Offense Level and Criminal History Category displays the Guideline Range in months of imprisonment. "Life" means life imprisonment. For example, the guideline range applicable to a defendant with an Offense Level of 15 and a Criminal History Category of III is 24-30 months of imprisonment.
2. In rare cases, a total offense level of less than 1 or more than 43 may result from application of the guidelines. A total offense level of less than 1 is to be treated as an offense level of 1. An offense level of more than 43 is to be treated as an offense level of 43.
3. The Criminal History Category is determined by the total criminal history points from Chapter Four, Part A, except as provided in §§4B1.1 (Career Offender) and 4B1.4 (Armed Career Criminal). The total criminal history points associated with each Criminal History Category are shown under each Criminal History Category in the Sentencing Table.

Victim Characteristics That Affect Punishment

Some crimes are determined to be more heinous than others depending on the circumstances of the crime or even the characteristics of the victims. For example, the difference between murder and capital murder in some states

Critical Thinking

Is there a difference between the murder of a six-month-old infant girl and the murder of her 60-year-old grandmother? What about the murder of 11-year-old twin boys, one of whom has been diagnosed with Down Syndrome? Should some conditions be taken into consideration when pronouncing sentence on the defendants who committed those crimes, or should the defendants be sentenced equally?

can be the age or mental capacity of the victim. In Texas, the murder of a peace officer is considered a capital offense, as is a murder committed during the commission of abuse of a minor under the age of 16 years in Wyoming.

Plea Bargaining

Plea bargaining is a process involving the prosecutor and the accused or the defense counsel. During this process, the parties discuss the stipulations under which the defendant will plead guilty to a charge in exchange for some kind of concession, or trade-off, from the prosecutor or the judge.[91] One or more of several things may happen as the result of plea bargaining. The charges the defendant is facing may be reduced, which leads to a reduction in the defendant's sentence. If the defendant is charged with multiple crimes, the number of crimes may be reduced, also leading by default to a reduction in the defendant's sentence. The prosecutor can choose to recommend that the judge be lenient on the defendant, which could reduce the defendant's sentence from jail or prison time to probation. And finally, in cases involving crimes with negative or inflammatory labels—such as sex crimes—the charge may be reduced to a less incendiary one, thus sparing the defendant from several hardships that may arise due to the label.

Plea bargaining has advantages for both the state and the accused. The financial costs of prosecuting the defendant are reduced. Cases that are taken to plea bargain do not go to trial, which not only saves the government money but also increases the efficiency of the courts.[92] The prosecution is also able to dedicate its time and resources to more involved and serious cases. For the defendant, the possibility of jail time during the pretrial and trial periods is reduced, as are the costs of legal representation. The defendant also increases his or her chances of receiving a reduced sentence.

There are issues with plea bargaining, the foremost being the possibility that an innocent person who faces a harsh sentence if found guilty agrees to plead guilty and accept a lighter punishment rather than risk going to prison or worse. When a defendant accepts a plea bargain, he or she also waives the constitutional rights to trial and appeal. Opponents of plea bargaining argue that by accepting a less severe charge or punishment, the defendant has defeated the system.[93]

The Supreme Court formally upheld the practice of plea bargaining, saying that it served the interests of both the court and the defendant, in *Brady v.*

© CartoonResource/Shutterstock.com

"Let's take some of the pleading out of your plea bargain."

United States in 1970.[94] The Supreme Court has also supported the position of the prosecution in the plea bargaining process with its ruling in *North Carolina v. Alford.* In this ruling, the court announced that a judge can accept a guilty plea from a defendant who declares his or her innocence if the defendant makes the plea both voluntarily and with understanding of the plea, and if there is enough factual evidence to demonstrate that the defendant is guilty.[95]

The only state without plea bargaining is the state of Alaska.

> In 1975, Alaska Attorney General Avrum Gross banned plea bargaining in Alaska. The Judicial Council's initial evaluation of the ban found that plea bargaining, both charge and sentence bargaining, was substantially curtailed, and that despite the dire predictions of unmanageable caseloads and backlogged trials, disposition times for criminal cases actually improved. Although few thought that the policy still would be in effect fifteen years later, the Alaska Judicial Council's most recent evaluation of the ban, completed in 1990, shows that the ban continues to affect virtually every important aspect of Alaska's criminal justice system. The ban as it exists today in Alaska differs in several important respects from its original form. The changes in the ban can be linked to two major historical developments. In 1980,

a new criminal code and presumptive sentencing went into effect in Alaska, both reflecting societal changes in thinking about crime and punishment. In 1985 and 1986, changes in personnel and declines in state revenues combined to create new opportunities and impetus for charge bargaining. Thus, by 1990, the written guidelines for the policy prohibiting plea bargaining remained unchanged from their 1986 version, but attorneys and judges throughout the state agreed that charge bargaining had become fairly common in most courts.[96]

Race and Gender

Race and gender are examples of extralegal factors that can affect sentencing. Extralegal factors are aspects concerning the defendant, the victim, or the crime that may not be clearly defined by law and, thus, are not supposed to be taken into consideration when assessing a sentence; however, this is sometimes not the case. Examples of extralegal factors include race, gender, socioeconomic status, and class status. The two perhaps most controversial of these factors, race and gender, will be addressed in this section.

In the United States, there is a disproportionate percentage of non-whites in prison. As of June 30, 2010, the U.S. incarceration rate was 732 per 100,000 residents. But when you break down the statistics, as shown in Figure 7.4, you see that incarceration has a disproportionate share of non-whites and is not an equal opportunity punishment.

FIGURE 7.4 U.S. INCARCERATION RATES BY RACE AND ETHNICITY, 2010.

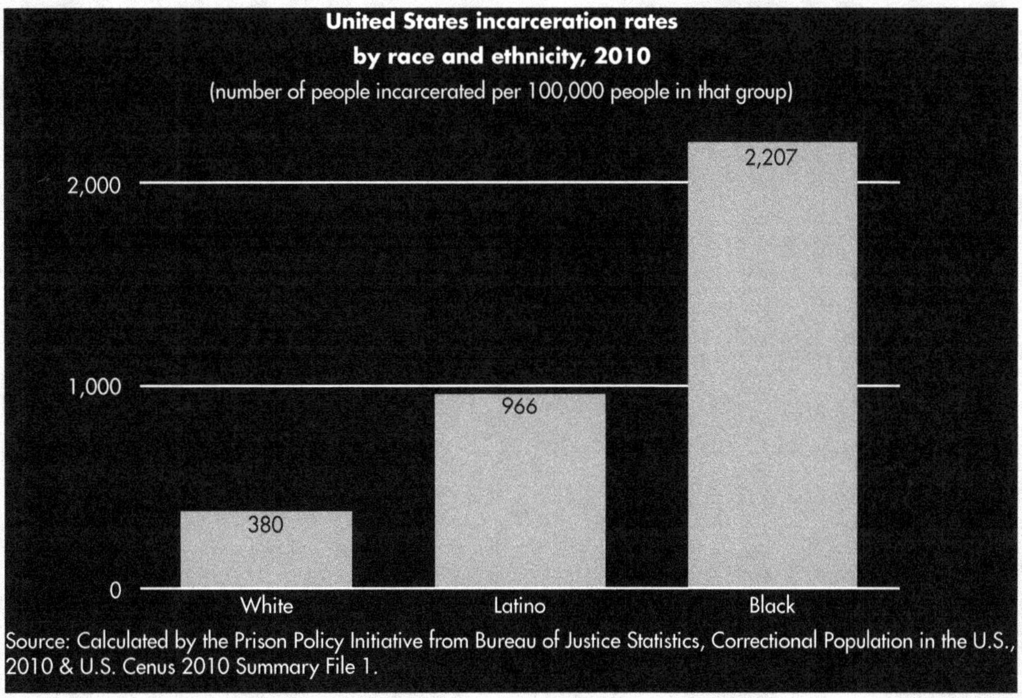

At the end of 2010, there were 2,266,800 people in U.S. prisons and jails. For the second year in a row, the total prison population fell slightly, although some states and the federal system continued to increase the number of people incarcerated. [97]

As of June 30, 2010, the U.S. incarceration rate was 732 per 100,000 residents. But when you break down the statistics you see that incarceration is not an equal opportunity punishment. The graph above illustrates the young Black and Latino male are disproportionately incarcerated. Put those factors together and you have almost 9% of Black men in their late 20s behind bars and almost 4% of Latino men of that age are incarcerated.[97]

Gender is another important consideration in sentencing, especially since the fastest-growing population in prisons is women. There has been a tremendous increase in female prisoners since 1995. Two-thirds of women in prison are non-white, only one-third of women sentenced to prison have graduated from high school or gotten a GED prior to entering prison, and many of them suffer from major depression or other serious psychological disorders. Being sentenced to prison does not seem to act as a deterrent: 65% of women in prison have been found guilty of prior criminal charges. One of the reasons for the increase of women in prisons may be the changes in sentencing laws relating especially to drug offenses. Nearly one-third of female inmates in state prison facilities and over one-half of women sentenced to federal prisons are incarcerated for drug-related and nonviolent crimes.[97] Figures 7.5 and 7.6 show numbers from the Bureau of Justice Statistics demonstrating the overall growth of the female prison population for the years 2006, 2013, and 2014.

FIGURE 7.5 FEMALE PRISONERS UNDER THE JURISDICTION OF STATE OR FEDERAL CORRECTIONAL AUTHORITIES, BY JURISDICTION, DECEMBER 31, 2006, 2013, AND 2014

Jurisdiction		2006	2013	2014	% Change 2006-2014	% Change 2013-2014
U.S. Total		103,337	104,301	106,232	2.8%	1.9%
Federal/b		11,116	12,720	12,560	13.0%	-1.3%
State		92,221	91,581	93,672	1.6%	2.3%
	Alabama	1,960	2,567	2,442	24.6%	-4.9%
	Alaska/c	242	256	263	8.7%	2.7%
	Arizona/d	2,783	3,387	3,550	27.6%	4.8%
	Arkansas	1,041	1,319	1,393	33.8%	5.6%
	California	11,581	6,297	6,382	-44.9%	1.3%
	Colorado/e	2,302	1,815	1,908	-17.1%	5.1%

Connecticut/c	799	668	637	-20.3%	-4.6%
Delaware/c,d	229	233	214	-6.6%	-8.2%
District of Columbia	--	--	--	--	--
Florida	6,485	7,271	7,303	12.6%	0.4%
Georgia	3,557	3,525	3,475	-2.3%	-1.4%
Hawaii/c,f	499	347	309	-38.1%	-11.0%
Idaho	777	1,066	1,026	32.0%	-3.8%
Illinois/g	2,720	2,916	2,888	6.2%	-1.0%
Indiana	2,161	2,835	2,875	33.0%	1.4%
Iowa	789	703	740	-6.2%	5.3%
Kansas	638	691	721	13.0%	4.3%
Kentucky	1,989	2,183	2,420	21.7%	10.9%
Louisiana	2,377	2,228	2,075	-12.7%	-6.9%
Maine	133	136	142	6.8%	4.4%
Maryland	1,020	887	890	-12.7%	0.3%
Massachusetts/h	422	443	426	0.9%	-3.8%
Michigan	2,170	2,059	2,123	-2.2%	3.1%
Minnesota	562	723	736	31.0%	1.8%
Mississippi	1,558	1,405	1,197	-23.2%	-14.8%
Missouri	2,579	2,782	3,106	20.4%	11.6%
Mantuan	354	412	388	9.6%	-5.8%
Nebraska	378	360	428	13.2%	18.9%
Nevada	1,128	1,085	1,085	-3.8%	0.0%
New Hampshire	153	212	244	59.5%	15.1%
New Jersey/g	1,428	1,025	1,019	-28.6%	-0.6%
New Mexico	627	640	659	5.1%	3.0%
New York	2,810	2,337	2,308	-17.9%	-1.2%
North Carolina	1,883	2,239	2,444	29.8%	9.2%
North Dakota	157	149	187	19.1%	25.5%
Ohio/e	3,701	4,150	4,208	13.7%	1.4%
Oklahoma	2,351	2,742	2,801	19.1%	2.2%
Oregon	1,012	1,285	1,276	26.1%	-0.7%
Pennsylvania	2,200	2,655	2,693	22.4%	1.4%
Rhode Island/c,f	70	79	68	-2.9%	-13.9%
South Carolina	1,480	1,296	1,285	-13.2%	-0.8%
South Dakota	348	441	408	17.2%	-7.5%

Tennessee	1,958	2,452	2,609	33.2%	6.4%
Texas	11,569	12,001	12,690	9.7%	5.7%
Utah	602	662	662	10.0%	0.0%
Vermont/c	105	96	105	0.0%	9.4%
Virginia/g	2,893	2,849	3,015	4.2%	5.8%
Washington/e	1,472	1,442	1,439	-2.2%	-0.2%
West Virginia	569	801	828	45.5%	3.4%
Wisconsin	1,357	1,169	1,305	-3.8%	11.6%
Wyoming	243	260	277	14.0%	6.5%

Note: Jurisdiction refers to the legal authority of state or federal correctional officials over a prisoner regardless of where the prisoner is held. State methods of enumeration may change over time. Consult the state notes for particular years to ensure parity between years and jurisdictions. As of December 31, 2001, sentenced felons from the District of Columbia are the responsibility of the Federal Bureau of Prisons.
a/Counts based on prisoners with sentences of more than 1 year under the jurisdiction of state or federal correctional officials.
b/Includes inmates held in nonsecure privately operated community corrections facilities and juveniles held in contract facilities.
c/Prisons and jails form one integrated system. Data include total jail and prison populations.
d/Prison jurisdiction population based on custody counts.
e/Includes some prisoners sentenced to 1 year or less.
f/Counts include dual jurisdiction cases where the inmate is currently housed in another jurisdiction's facilities.
g/Includes some prisoners sentence to 1 year.
h/Counts exclude prisoners sentenced to more than 1 year but held in local jails or houses of correction in the Commonwealth of Massachusetts; please see individual years' Prisoners in YYYY for an accounting of these people.

Source: Bureau of Justice Statistic, National Prisoners Statistic Program, 1978-2014.

FIGURE 7.6 PRISONERS UNDER THE JURISDICTION OF STATE OR FEDERAL CORRECTIONAL AUTHORITIES, DECEMBER 31, 2003-2013.

Year	Total	Federal[a]	State	Male	Female
2003	1,468,601	173,059	1,295,542	1,367,755	100,846
2004	1,497,100	180,328	1,316,772	1,392,278	104,822
2005	1,525,910	187,618	1,338,292	1,418,392	107,518
2006	1,568,674	193,046	1,375,628	1,456,366	112,308
2007	1,596,835	199,618	1,397,217	1,482,524	114,311
2008	1,608,282	201,280	1,407,002	1,493,670	114,612
2009	1,615,487	208,118	1,407,369	1,502,002	113,485
2010	1,613,803	209,771	1,404,032	1,500,936	112,867
2011	1,598,968	216,362	1,382,606	1,487,561	111,407
2012	1,570,397	217,815	1,352,582	1,461,625	108,772
2013[b]	1,574,741	215,866	1,358,875	1,463,454	111,287

Percent change					
Average annual, 2003-2012	0.7%	2.2%	0.5%	0.7%	1.0
2012-2013	0.3	-0.9	0.5	0.1	2.3

Note: Jurisdiction refers to the legal authority of state of federal correctional officials over a prisoner, regardless of where the prisoner is held.
a Includes inmates held innonsecure privately operated community corrections facilities and juveniles held in contract facilities.
b Total and state estimates include imputed counts for Nevada. In addition, Alaska did not submit sex-specific jurisdiction counts to NPS in 2013. See Methodology for Imputation strategy.

Source: Bureau of Justice Statistics, National Prisoner Statistics Program, 2003-2013.

Chapter Summary

- There is no single primary guiding principle for sentencing, so most practices tend to blend multiple schools of thought. Common theories behind sentencing in the United States are deterrence, incapacitation, rehabilitation, and retribution. Alternatives or partners to sentencing include fines, probation, rehabilitative programs, and community service. Additional options for sentencing, depending on the circumstances of the offense, include imprisonment and the death penalty.
- Deterrence attempts to prevent crime by making examples of offenders in the hope of deterring others from committing crime, or by inflicting punishment on a person with the intent to impart the lesson that crime is not worth committing. Rehabilitation attempts to change the behavior and thinking of offenders by providing them with services that will help change their behavior. Restorative justice seeks to return the crime victims as closely as possible to their original states before the crime was committed. Incapacitation attempts to control crime by removing the offender from the community.
- Retribution refers to the idea that individuals who commit crimes should be punished to a degree commensurate with the seriousness of the crime. Vengeance and "just deserts" fall under retribution: vengeance suggests that satisfaction will be gained simply by punishing the criminal, while "just deserts" intends for the punishment to be comparably equal to the crime.
- The death penalty has been under review for many years to determine whether aspects of it constitute cruel and unusual punishment. The Supreme Court has further clarified stipulations of the death penalty with numerous rulings, but the two most groundbreaking rulings were *Furman v. Georgia* (1972) and *Gregg v. Georgia* (1976). Furman negated the enforcement of state death

penalty laws on Eighth Amendment grounds, causing a halt to executions and the commutations of many death sentences to life in prison. *Gregg* upheld the revised laws, which required a multiple-step process in order for judges or juries to assess a death sentence on an inmate.
- Other issues to consider in sentencing are truth in sentencing, mandatory minimum sentences, characteristics of the victim, three-strikes laws, race, and gender. Whether each aspect has measurable effects on sentencing is being studied on a regular basis. Available data is typically a minimum of two to three years old due to reporting and measurement limitations.

Critical Thinking?

1. Should offense type influence a probation officer's recommendation in the pre-sentence investigation report? Explain why or why not.
2. If deterrence does not work on capital offenders, why do states still utilize the death penalty?
3. How does the law apply rehabilitation and retribution at the same time?
4. Compare and contrast the various sentencing theories. Would the same theory that applies to a large metropolitan city also apply to a rural village in Alaska?
5. What is the purpose of a jury that is death penalty qualified?
6. Who should sentence, the judge or the jury?
7. The concept of jury nullification was introduced in Chapter 6. How might jury nullification affect the sentencing process?
8. In many cases, offenders are offered plea bargains by the prosecuting attorneys. Do you feel that the plea bargain process is fair to all parties involved in the case? The accused? The victim(s)? Why or why not?
9. Do gender and race play a role in sentencing procedures and, if so, how much?
10. Why do you think sentencing disparities still exist?

Media

Free Sentencing Guidelines Calculator: http://www.sentencing.us/ Based on 2010 guidelines, this website allows users to get an idea of the length of a federal prison sentence based on the crime committed and special circumstances that may apply.

The Death Penalty Information Center: http://www.deathpenaltyinfo.org/ The Death Penalty Information Center is a nonprofit organization that provides the media and the general public with facts and information relating to capital punishment.

Texas Department of Criminal Justice: http://www.tdcj.state.tx.us/ and Florida Department of Corrections: http://www.dc.state.fl.us/ The official websites for some state correctional systems offer a wealth of information, including statistics, about their prison systems.

Death Penalty Blog: http://www.deathpenaltyblog.com Written by attorneys from Florida and Texas, the Death Penalty Blog shares news articles about legislation and other current events relating to capital punishment.

The Growth of Incarceration in the U.S. https://www.youtube.com/watch?v=I-kFNDlzL9k. This video illustrates the findings of the NRC report The Growth of Incarceration in the United States: Exploring Causes and Consequences. The nation's reliance on imprisonment has not clearly improved public safety and may have had large unwanted consequences for society. A change in course is needed. The report urges policymakers to reconsider sentencing policies and to seek crime-control strategies that are more effective, with better public safety benefits and fewer unwanted consequences.

Endnotes

1 Riddle, L. (1997). *Ashes to Ashes. New York, NY: Pinnacle Books.*

2 Beccaria, C. (1764). *Dei Delitti e delle Pene. (Of Crimes and Punishment)*

3 Ibid., 32–24.

4 Gibbs, J. (1975). *Crime, Punishment, and Deterrence. New York, NY: Elsevier.*

5 Beccaria, 1764.

6 Ibid.

7 Ibid.

8 Zimring, F., & Hawkins, G. (1973). *Deterrence.* Chicago, IL: University of Chicago Press.

9 Pontell, H. (1994). *A Capacity to Punish: The Ecology of Crime and Punishment.* Bloomington, IN: Indiana University Press.

10 King, L. W. (2005). *The Code of Hammurabi: Translated by L.W. King.* New Haven, CT: Yale University Press.

11 Kant, I. (1790). *The Science of Right.*

12 Texas Department of Corrections. (2004). *Offender Orientation Handbook.* Mississippi Department of Corrections. *(2009). Inmate Handbook,* State of Washington Department of Corrections. (2008). *Reception, Initial Classification, and Custody Facility Plan.*

13 Inciardi, 2010.

14 Bohm & Haley, 2010.

15 Braithwaite, J. (1989). *Crime, Shame, and Reintegration.* New York, NY: Cambridge University Press.

16 Sullivan, D., & Tifft, L. (2005). *Restorative Justice: Healing the Foundations of Our Everyday Lives* (2nd ed.). Boulder, CO: Lynne Reiner Publishing.

17 U.S. Department of Justice, Office for Victims of Crime. (2004, December). "New Directions from the Field: Victims' Rights and Services for the 21st Century." *OVC Bulletin.* Washington, D.C.

18 New York State Unified Court System. (2010). *Statistics.*

19 *Williams v. Illinois,* 399 U.S. 235 (1970).

20 *Bearden v. Georgia,* 33 CrL 3103 (1983).

21 Petersilia, J. (1998). "Probation and Parole." In M. Tonry (Ed.), *The Handbook of Crime and Punishment.* New York, NY: Oxford University Press. New York City Department of Probation. (n.d.). History of Probation. Retrieved from http://www.nyc.gov/html/prob/html/about/history.shtml

22 Center on Juvenile and Criminal Justice. (n.d.). *The History of the Presentence Report.* Retrieved from http://www.cjcj.org/files/the_history.pdf

23 National Probation Association. (1939). *John Augustus, First Probation Officer.* New York.

24 Inciardi, 2010.

25 *Mempa v. Rhay,* 389 U.S. 128 (1967).

26 *Morrissey v. Brewer,* 389 U.S. 128 (1972). *Gagnon v. Scarpelli,* 411 U.S. 778 (1973).

27 *Texas Code of Criminal Procedure,* Art. 42.12.

28 Illinois General Assembly. (2011). 625 ILCS 5/11-501.

29 Inciardi, 2010.

30 Georgia Department of Corrections, Probation Division. *FY 2007 Annual Report.* Atlanta, GA.

31 Petersilia, J. (2002). *Reforming Probation & Parole in the 21st Century.* Lanham, MD: American Correctional Association.

32 Waldron, J., & Angelino, H. (1977). "Shock Probation: A Natural Experiment on the Effect of a Short Period of Incarceration." *Prison Journal, 57.*

33 Ohio Department of Rehabilitation and Correction. (2005). *Ohio Adult Parole Authority: 1965–2005.*

34 The Judicial Branch of Arizona. (2011). *Intensive Probation Supervision.*

35 Erwin, B., & Bennett, L. (1987). *New Dimensions in Probation: Georgia's Experience with Intensive Probation Supervision.* National Institute of Justice Research in Brief.

36 Petersilia, J., & Turner, S. (1993). *Evaluating Intensive Supervision Probation/Parole: Results of a Nationwide Experiment.* National Institute of Justice Research in Brief.

37 Ball, R., & Lilly, J. (1986). "A Theoretical Examination of Home Incarceration." *Federal Probation, 50,* 17–24.

38 Gowen, D. (2001). "Remote Location Monitoring—A Supervision Strategy to Enhance Risk Control." *Federal Probation, 65*(2).

39 Florida Department of Corrections. (2007). *Annual Statistics for Fiscal Year 2005–2006.*

40 Del Carmen, R., & Vaughn, J. (1992). "Legal Issues in the Use of Electronic Surveillance in Probation." In T. Ellsworth (Ed.), *Contemporary Community Corrections.* Prospect Heights, IL: Waveland Press.

41 Bureau of Probation & Parole Field Services, Florida Department of Corrections. (2008).

42 Bohm, R. (2007). *Deathquest III: An Introduction to the Theory and Practice of Capital Punishment in the United States* (3rd ed.). Cincinnati, OH: Anderson.

43 The Death Penalty Information Center.

44 Teeters, N., & Zibulka, C. (1974). "Executions Under State Authority: 1864–1967." In W. Bowers (Ed.), *Executions in America. Lexington, MA: Heath.*

45 Bedau, H. (1964). *The Death Penalty in America.* Chicago, IL: Aldine.

46 *O'Neil v. Vermont,* 144 U.S. 323 (1892).

47 *Weems v. United States,* 217 U.S. 349 (1910).

48 *Witherspoon v. Illinois,* 391 U.S. 510 (1960).

49 *Furman v. Georgia, Jackson v. Georgia, Branch v. Texas,* 408 U.S. 238 (1972).

50 *Gregg v. Georgia,* Proffitt v. Florida, Jurek v. Texas, 428 U.S. 153.

51 Katz, L. (1980). *The Justice Imperative.* Cincinnati, OH: Anderson.

52 The Death Penalty Information Center.

53 Ibid.

54 Reinhold, R. (1982, December 7). "Technician Executes Murderer in Texas by Lethal Injection." *The New York Times.*

55 *Fierro v. Gomez,* 56 CrL 1085 (1994)

56 The Death Penalty Information Center.

57 The Death Penalty Information Center.

58 Ibid.

59 *Coker v. Georgia*, 433 U.S. 584 (1977).

60 *Eberheart v. Georgia*, 433 U.S. 917 (1977).

61 *Ford v. Wainwright*, 477 U.S. 399 (1986).

62 *McCleskey v. Kemp*, 481 U.S. 279 (1987).

63 *Thompson v. Oklahoma*, 487 U.S. 815 (1987-1988).

64 *Stanford v. Kentucky*, 492 U.S. 361 (1989).

65 *Atkins v. Virginia*, 536 U.S. 304 (2002).

66 *Roper v. Simmons*, 543 U.S. 551 (2005).

67 *Kennedy v. Louisiana*, 554 U.S. 407 (2008).

68 Beccaria, 1764.

69 Pojman, L., & Reiman, J. (1998). *The Death Penalty: For and Against.* Lanham, MD: Rowman & Littlefield.

70 Radelet, M., Lofquist, W., & Bedau, H. (1996). "Prisoners Released from Death Rows Since 1970 Because of Doubts About Their Guilt." *T.M. Cooley Law Review, 13 (907).*

71 The Death Penalty Information Center.

72 Stull, B. (2009). *Race and Death Penalty Links Run Deep and Wide.* New York, NY: American Civil Liberties Union.

73 Radelet, M. (1989). "Executions of Whites for Crimes Against Blacks." *Sociological Quarterly, 30, 529–44.*

74 The Death Penalty Information Center.

75 Ibid.

76 Liebmann, J., Fagan, J., & West, V. (n.d.). "A Broken System: Error Rates in Capital Cases, 1973–1995." *The Justice Project.* Retrieved April 12, 2011, from http://www.thejusticeproject.org

77 Bedau, H., Radelet, M., & Putnam, C. (2004). "Convicting the Innocent in Capital Cases: Criteria, Evidence, and Interference." *Drake Law Review, 52,* 587–603.

78 Bureau of Justice Statistics. (2010). *Capital Punishment 2009.* Washington, D.C.

79 Tonry, M. (1999). "Fragmentation of Sentencing and Corrections in the United States." *Research in Brief—Sentencing & Corrections: Issues for the 21st Century.* Washington, D.C.: National Institute of Justice.

80 Lab, S., & Whitehead, J. (1990). "From 'Nothing Works' to 'The Appropriate Works': The Latest Stop in the Search for the Secular Grail." *Criminology, 28,* 405–418.

81 Jacobs, J. (1977). *Statesville: The Penitentiary in Mass Society.* Chicago, IL: University of Chicago Press.

82 Ulner, J. (1997). *Social Worlds of Sentencing: Court Communities Under Sentencing Guidelines.* Albany, NY: State University of New York Press.

83 Austin, J., & Irwin, J. (1997). *It's About Time: America's Imprisonment Binge* (3rd ed.). Belmont, CA: Wadsworth.

84 Harris, J., & Jesilow, P. (2000). "It's Not the Old Ball Game: Three Strikes and the Courtroom Workgroup." *Justice Quarterly, 17,* 185–204.

85 Fischer, C. (2003). "Supreme Court Allows Penalties Under California 3-Strikes Law." *Corrections Journal, 1*(3).

86 *Ewing v. California, 538 U.S. 11 (2003).*

87 *California's Three Strikes Sentencing Law* (2016). California Courts. The Judicial Branch of California. Retrieved fhttp://www.courts.ca.gov/20142.htm.

87 Durose, M., & Langan, P. (2004). "Felony Sentences in State Courts, 2002." *Bureau of Justice Statistics Bulletin. Washington, D.C.*

88 *United States v. Booker,* 543 U.S. 200 (2005).

89 Kitchens, C. (2010, August). "Federal Sentencing Data and Analysis Issues." *United States Sentencing Commission Research Notes.*

90 United States Sentencing Commission. (2016). *2016 Federal Sentencing Guidelines Manual.*

[91] Bibas, S. (2004). "Plea Bargaining Outside the Shadow of Trial." *Harvard Law Review, 117*(8), 2463–2547.

[92] Ibid.

[93] Nagel, I., & Schulhofer, S. (1992). "A Tale of Three Cities: An Empirical Study of Charging and Bargaining Practices Under the Federal Sentencing Guidelines." *Southern California Law Review, 66,* 501–530.

[94] *Brady v. United States,* 397 U.S. 742 (1970).

[95] *North Carolina v. Alford,* 40 U.S. 25 (1970).

[96] Carns, T. & Kruse, J. (1991). *Alaska's Plea Bargaining Ban: Re-Evaluated.* Retrieved from http://www.ajc.state.ak.us/reports/plea91Exec.pdf.

[97] Wagner, P. (2012). *Incarceration is not an equal opportunity punishment.* Prison Policy Initiative. Retrieved from https://www.prisonpolicy.org/articles/notequal.html.

[97] Schmalleger & Smykla, 2011.

CHAPTER

8

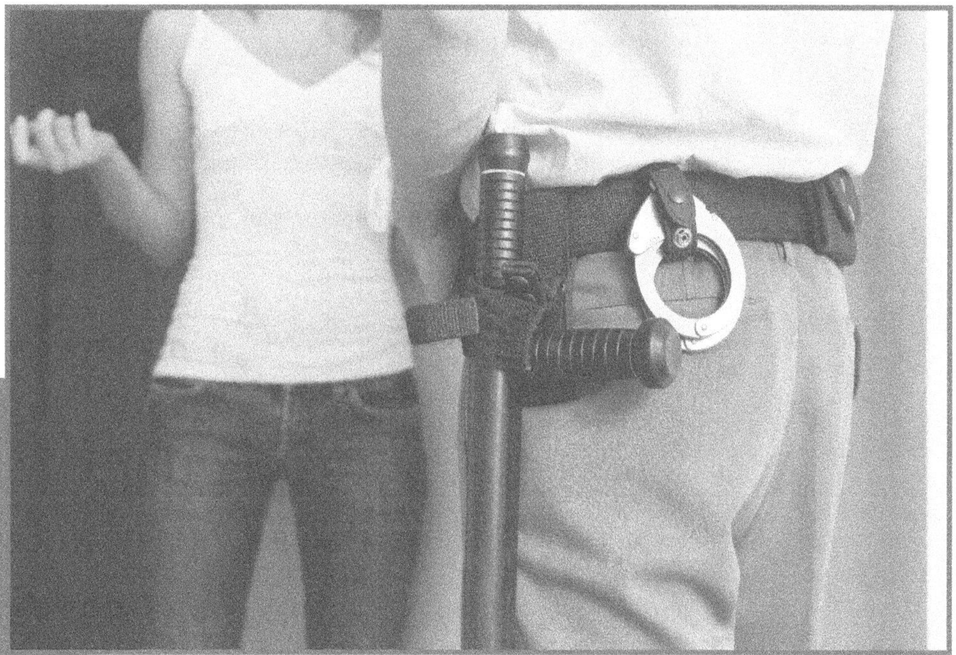

© Kzenon/Shutterstock.com

Probation and Parole

KEY TERMS

Community-Based Probation
Executive Privilege
Formal Probation
Furlough
Halfway House
Informal or Summary Probation
Restorative Justice
Shock Probation

CHAPTER OBJECTIVES

After studying this chapter, you should be able to do the following:

1. Explain the purpose and functions of probation and parole.
2. Explain the differences between parole and probation.
3. List and discuss the roles of probation and parole officers.
4. List the qualifications for probation.
5. Outline and explain the several conditions of probation and parole.
6. Explain the process of revocation of parole or probation.
7. List and explain the three types of executive clemency.

Introduction

Probation is the first sanction of choice for the first-time nonviolent offender. In many cases, probation is not punishment at all but a second, or third, or fourth chance for the offender to mend his or her ways and avoid any further involvement with the criminal justice system.

Probation is a conditional release from custody and avoidance of jail or prison for a specified period of time. The conditions vary, such as the simple requirement that the individual not commit any violation of the law for a specified period of time with no other strings attached. That is *informal,* or *summary,* probation.

© JupiterImages, Inc

Other forms of probation carry more conditions and restrictions, such as to refrain from using alcohol or illegal drugs, submitting to search by any peace officer at any time of the day or night, regularly reporting to a probation officer, staying employed or in school, and various other conditions.

At the end of 2007 there were 4,293,163 men and women on probation in the United States.[1] Of that number, 51% had been convicted of a misdemeanor, 47% for a felony, and 3% for other infractions. Women comprised 23% of the probationers; 55% of adults on probation were white, 29% were black, and 13% were Hispanic.

Parole is similar to probation in many respects, with the major difference being that parole is a conditional release after serving a substantial period of time in prison with considerably more stringent requirements of good behavior in order to avoid return to prison to serve out the remainder of the sentence.

Another difference between probation and parole is that in most jurisdictions probation agencies and their officers operate under the aegis of the state or county courts, while parole is an extension of the government's department of corrections.

In this chapter we cover the similarities and the dissimilarities of the two processes and their goals and objectives.

Probation

It all started when a shoemaker named John Augustus secured the release of a drunk from jail in Boston by posting bail for him in 1841 and helping him restore his life to a productive one. Eighteen years later when Augustus died, in 1859, he had helped salvage the lives of more than 1,800 men. Thus was the beginning of probation.[2] In 1878 Massachusetts became the first state to adopt juvenile probation, and other states had followed by 1938. By 1956 all states had adult probation.[3]

Probation Timeline

1841	John Augustus started probation in Boston.
1848	Massachusetts had probation statewide.
1925	President Calvin Coolidge signed the Probation Act, establishing probation as a federal court sentence, and assigned probation officers.
1940	Federal probation was transferred to the administrative office of the federal courts from the Bureau of Prisons.
1954	All states had juvenile probation.
1956	All states had adult probation.
1973	*Gagnon v. Scarpelli*, 411 U.S. 778. The Supreme Court held that probationers are entitled to hearing before probations are revoked.
1987	*Griffin v. Wisconsin*, 483 U.S. 868. The Court ruled that warrantless searches of probationers' homes are reasonable.
1994	The Violent Crime Control and Law Enforcement Act (VCCLEA) required a drug testing program for federal offenders on probation and toughened laws on address change requirements for probationers.

Advantages of Probation

1. Probation gives the offender a chance to avoid incarceration or postpone it until a later conviction, which can be reinstated if the offender commits another crime.
2. Allows the individual to prove to himself or herself and to the court that the threat of imprisonment and the period of probation were sufficient to keep him or her from repeating any criminal behavior.
3. The probation allows the individual offender to continue his or her gainful employment and employability. Once the offender acquires the label of "jailbird" or "ex-con," many employers will shy away from candidates with criminal histories.
4. Saves money for the government. Once an individual enters the jail or prison, the government must not only pay for room and board, training, medical and psychological services for the inmate but also support spouses and families, who become dependent on the government because the breadwinner is no longer making money to support them.
5. Saves personnel costs of supervision. Many probationers can be supervised while outside prison much cheaper than in prison.

> Probation is not only far less costly than jail or prison, but it keeps the naive offender away from the more evil influences of more experienced offenders in custody.

Qualification for Probation

The nonviolent violator of a property crime with no prior arrest record is usually the best candidate as opposed to the violent repeat offender who apparently did not benefit from previous lenient treatment.

The individual who has a relatively stable family and private life and a steady job with a good attendance record is also a more likely candidate for probation than the unemployed or unemployable person who has a volatile and unstable lifestyle and constant association with others with similar records. The active gang member is more likely to go to jail or prison as a preventative measure in an effort to separate him or her from the negative influences on the street. Of course, the influences and associations in jail or prison are going to be negative, sometimes even more intense and influential. The judge must weigh the alternatives and decide which is best for the public's safety.

Types of Probation

Summary, or Informal, Probation

A common type of probation for the circumstantial or infrequent violator, which may include those convicted of driving under the influence of alcohol or prescription medications, or a first-time nonviolent offender.

When one is placed on informal probation, his or her name is entered into the probation department's database with no conditions except that he or she shall not get arrested again during a specified period of time, such as three years. If there is a rearrest, the judge may revoke the original probation and send the offender to jail for the full term for that offense, in addition to the sentence for the second conviction.

Informal or Summary Probation A sentence where a person is shown as on probation but may have no or little conditions imposed and does not have to see a probation officer during the term of probation.

Based on your own reading and research, what is your opinion of the value of boot camps for rehabilitation?

Shock Probation

The shock is affected by a relatively brief imprisonment—perhaps three to six months maximum—as part of a term of probation for three years or more. The objective of shock probation is to shock the offender with the stark reality of being locked up in a caged environment like an animal and totally isolated from every aspect of a normal life. The effect of such a shock is more than enough to cause the offender to fervently hope to avoid such humiliation and deprivation again.

Shock Probation A process of sentencing an individual to a short jail or prison stay then placed on probation in an attempt to influence the individual away from committing additional crimes

Formal Probation

The probationer is assigned a specific list of conditions and must sign on to them in order to be granted probation. Conditions of a formal probation will include many of following:

- Keep regular hours and constant attendance at work, school, or counseling sessions.
- Stay alcohol and drug free. Submit to random drug and sobriety tests.
- Regular attendance at alcohol and drug abuse rehabilitation meetings.
- Frequent scheduled and unscheduled meetings with a probation officer.
- Anger management counseling.
- Restitution and personal apologies to victims.
- Attend church.

Formal Probation A sentence where a set of conditions is imposed by a judge and monitored by a probation officer for compliance.

- Carry signs in public admitting guilt, put a sticker on vehicle, or post a sign in front of the residence.
- Perform specific public service tasks, such as cleaning animal cages at the zoo, sweeping streets, making public service announcements on radio or television, or counseling juvenile offenders against the evils of using drugs or alcohol.
- Home confinement and GPS monitoring.
- Change jobs or living conditions only with consent of probation officer or the judge.
- Other conditions imposed by judges with creative ideas.

Community-Based Probation

Community-Based Probation A flexible system locally designed to deal with crime that provides alternatives to standard probation, jail or prison.

This is a variation of a formal probation, which involves the community. The probationer may have special talents and be required to participate with nonprofit organizations such as Big Brothers and Sisters, or Child Advocacy for the Department of Child Protective Services. An attorney may be required to perform services for the courts, or a doctor may be required to contribute his or her services to a county health program.

Functions of Probation Officers

The probation officer (PO) has often been called a "change agent" for good reason. Since the objective of probation is for the offender to change behavior and divert his or her activities and proclivities away from criminal ventures, the PO's goal is to facilitate and encourage those changes. Among other activities, the PO's functions include the following:

1. Conduct presentence investigations and make recommendations to the court for sanctions to be imposed on the offenders.
2. Serve as intake officers at juvenile detention facilities to evaluate status and delinquent offenders, and petition them to the court or counsel and release.
3. Administer diagnostic tests, interview, evaluate, and recommend treatment to the courts.
4. Classify offenders and assist corrections personnel in determining offenders' risk levels.
5. Recommend and supervise community treatment probationers.
6. Counsel and supervise probationers.
7. Collect restitution and nonsupport payments.

One of the most important functions of the PO is preparing the presentence report.

Restorative Justice

The purpose for this type of probation is to repair relationships of offenders with their families and their victims. This type of probation would include the following:

- Victim—offender mediation.
- Family group counseling; the offender is only one part of the total family unit.
- Intervention in disputes between offender and employer, teacher, or others.

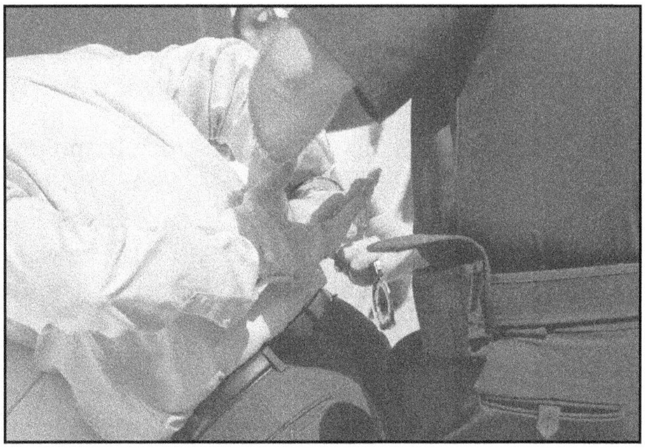

Work and Academic Furlough

While serving time in jail or prison, the inmate may be allowed to go to work or attend school off the premises as part of his or her rehabilitation. Furloughs also reduce the cost of incarceration as well as allow the individual to continue an occupation or profession that will continue after he or she completes the sentence. The inmate will also be able to support his or her dependents and lessen the state's cost of supporting them during the inmate's imprisonment.

Halfway Houses

The halfway house concept can actually work two ways: (1) as a diversion from jail or prison, allowing the individual to continue work and school and avoid association with a more sophisticated and negative influence on the novice; and (2) as a way station after a long term in prison, easing the parolee back into free society. Moving from the caged and severely restricted existence in prison into the free world again can be a traumatic experience. The longer the time in prison, the longer and more difficult the transition back into society.

Restorative Justice A system that focuses on the rehabilitation of the offender through reconciliation and the victim, victims family and the community at large

Furlough A leave or absence from jail or prison for a specific reason before the term of incarceration has expired.

Halfway House A structure used for those who are leaving prison so that they can adjust to life outside of prison giving them a better chance to succeed.

Origin of Parole

In early colonial days, wealthy landowners in Virginia paid the debts of inmates serving time in debtors' prison in England and brought them to the colonies, where they would work as indentured servants until they worked off their debts. They would then be released and given a small plot of land to start their lives as free men and women in the less fertile fields of West Virginia. This was a form of parole, which followed several years of forced servitude.

The principal reason for the creation of parole was prison overcrowding. In the early 1800s, when the prisons were full to the breaking point, governors were required to commute the sentences of many inmates who had demonstrated good behavior and let them serve the balance of their time in the community to make room for new arrivals. By the 1930s parole programs became more formalized and a regular practice of the courts to prescribe the terms of sentences to include parole following release.

In 1840 in Norfolk Island, Australia, where prisoners were transported from England, Alexander Macanochie, known as the father of parole, introduced the concept of awarding marks to inmates for good behavior and early release. Although he was not allowed to grant such releases, his principles were published in a book he wrote in 1844.[4]

Purpose of Parole

For all practical purposes, parole is an extension of the prison sentence. The parolee serves the balance of his or her sentence in relative freedom, but under close supervision and specific conditions that must be met or be returned to prison for the balance of the sentence. The prisoner's good conduct while in prison allows him or her to build up credits worth time off, with the built-up credits amounting to one half or one third of the sentence to be spent on parole.

> One key to ingratiating oneself with the parole board is to convince them that the prison experience has been a rehabilitative experience, and the applicant must accept full responsibility for the crime that led to the conviction.

The Parole Board

An inmate must serve at least one third to one half of his or her sentence before being eligible to apply for parole. This provision does not apply in states where mandatory release times are set by the judge or legislature. The board invites prosecution and defense attorneys who were involved in the trial of the convicted offender, the victim's family members, and the inmate's friends and relatives.to testify and present their recommendations as to the fate of the applicant.

If they do not appear, all of those invited may send written statement to the board expressing their appeals for the board's action.

The board meets with the petitioner for parole, who may make a personal presentation and plea for the parole. The board takes into consideration all of the following when it votes *yes* or *no* for the parole:

- Nature and circumstances of the crime.
- Aggravating and mitigating circumstances.
- The sentencing court's statements at time of sentencing.

- Nature and seriousness of prior offenses the applicant has committed.
- The inmate's conduct while serving time in the institution.
- The inmate's attitude and general outlook on life.
- Inmate's openness and acceptance of responsibility for his or her crimes.
- Participation in educational rehabilitation programs.
- Plans for employment and place of residence.

Parole Officer

The parole officer has complete authority to supervise the parolee and to ensure that he or she is following the rules. For example, if there is any reasonable cause to believe that the parolee is dealing or in possession of illegal drugs or other contraband, the officer may conduct a search of the individual at his or her place of residence or employment or anywhere on the streets without having to go through the formality of going to a judge and seeking a warrant.

Parole Revocation

The parolee may be brought before a revocation hearing upon petition by the parole officer who presents evidence of technical violations. If the parolee commits a new crime, then that matter is handled through the prosecuting attorneys and the courts as any other criminal prosecution. At the revocation hearing to determine whether the parolee should be returned to prison for technical violations, he or she is given a written notice with the charges specifying the purpose(s) for the revocation and is given a hearing accompanied by an attorney with a provision for pleading that the revocation not take place. The hearing is similar to a criminal trial.

If the parolee commits a criminal offense, there will be a separate indictment and trial, and sentencing will be independent in addition to the revocation hearing. If the parolee gets arrested for a new offense, it is possible that there will be no revocation proceeding. For example, the parolee who has served time for robbery may get caught for a misdemeanor, such as petty theft or assault. He or she may be convicted for that crime and be sent to jail instead of prison, and released without a revocation hearing. It is possible that the parolee will be on probation simultaneous with the parole.

A parolee is a felon and has lost certain privileges of citizenship, such as holding a public office, getting a government job, and voting. These privileges are not restored at the conclusion of parole.

At the end of 2007 there were 824, 385 adult men and women on parole in the U.S.[5] Over 96% of parolees had been sentenced to one year or more, and the most common type of offense for which they were on parole was a drug offense (37%). Women comprised 12% of the nation's parolees, and 42% of parolees were white, 37% were black, and 19% were Hispanic.

Conditions of Parole

A parolee's contract is more generally restrictive than that of a probationer, principally because of the more serious nature of felony convictions. Following are some parole restrictions:

1. Change residence and living arrangements (roommates, etc.) only with consent of the parole officer.
2. Forbidden to associate with other parolees in any type of social milieu.
3. Forbidden to use nonprescription drugs or alcohol with random tests.
4. Active participation in rehabilitation programs.
5. Cannot operate any motor vehicle.
6. Not allowed to leave the jurisdiction.
7. Strict curfew hours and home confinement in some cases.
8. Regularly scheduled meetings with parole officers.
9. Unannounced visits by parole officers on the job, in school, or at place of residence.
10. Must stay out of bars, nightclubs, and certain types of sporting events.
11. No gambling.
12. Search at any time or place by parole or peace officers.

> What is the reason for a parolee to get permission for changing his or her place of residence?

Executive Privilege

Executive Privilege The authority and power given to the chief executive of a nation or state. In the context of criminal justice it is the power to pardon, commute or provide amnesty to an individual for a crime that they committed.

There are three types of intervention by a president or governor known as executive privilege that are sometimes available to the individual who has been convicted and carries the label "criminal" for life. The president, in federal cases, and the governor, in state cases, may forgive the offender and restore his or her good record by commutation, pardon, or amnesty.

> Executive grants of commutation, pardon, and amnesty are awarded in greatest numbers around Christmas time.

Upon petition by an inmate or someone on his or her behalf or the initiative of the chief executive, the governor or president decrees the sentence cut short or canceled at a specific time. With a commuted sentence, the inmate is summarily freed with no further encumbrance of a parole. This sort of clemency may be granted for an individual or a class of people, for example, all inmates on death row in all states had their death sentences commuted to life in prison following the *Furman v. Georgia* decision that the death penalty laws were unconstitutional.[6]

A pardon not only forgives and releases the convicted person but also wipes his or her criminal record completely off the books. A pardon may accompany a commutation, but may also be granted to a person long since released from prison but who still carries the felony record. For example, a young man or woman may have been convicted for felony assault in a bar fight twenty-five years ago and served time and parole, followed by a period of nearly twenty years with absolutely no negative contact with the police. Now the individual would like to vote and seek a government job. He or she files an appeal to the governor or president for a pardon accompanied by petitions by friends, relatives, and employers attesting to the subject's clean record. The chief executive signs the pardon and the record is expunged, restoring the petitioner to full citizenship status.

The third form of clemency is amnesty. The chief executive declares the individual free from indictment for past or future crimes. For example, an individual might have been indicted for a federal crime, but the president or governor grants amnesty, ordering all criminal proceedings to be canceled.

Summary

In this chapter we examined the principles and practices of probation and parole, one that precedes or replaces incarceration and the other that follows a long term of imprisonment. The goals of both are to attempt to dissuade the offender from repeating his or her crimes. The probation and parole officers, in their roles as change agents, strive to supervise the offenders and steer them back on course as law-abiding citizens.

We also briefly covered three types of executive clemency by presidents and governors designed to give the reformed offender to resume his or her respected place in society as a law-abiding citizen.

Suggested Semester Project

Create an imaginary criminal offender who went to prison for a serious felony, such as armed robbery with aggravated assault by a habitual drug user. Write a list of conditions for the offender to abide by in acceptance of parole.

Critical Thinking

1. When was probation created in the United States?
2. Where and when was parole started?

3. What are the academic requirements for entry-level probation and parole officers?
4. What type of offender would be a good candidate for probation?
5. Which branch of government manages most probation systems?
6. Which branch of government manages most parole systems?
7. How is parole revoked?
8. How does restorative justice work?
9. What restrictions are there on the individual on summary, or informal, probation?
10. List at least six conditions of a formal probation.
11. How is parole different than probation?
12. Give an example of shock probation.
13. Who was John Augustus?
14. What are three financial advantages of putting a person on probation instead of in jail or prison?
15. Is a parolee required to seek permission from the court or parole officer to marry?
16. Under what conditions would a parolee be forbidden to associate with family members?
17. What does a probation officer do at juvenile intake?
18. Does a probationer or parolee have a right to legal representation at a revocation hearing?
19. When does an offender go to a halfway house?
20. What is the effect of an amnesty order?

Endnotes

1 Bureau of Justice Statistics website. For the most recent statistics, go to this website and others cited throughout this text.

2 J. Petersilia, "Probation in the U.S." *Crime and Justice* 22, 2002, pp.149–200.

3 Ibid.

4 Wikipedia.

5 Bureau of Justice Statistics website.

6 *Furman v. Georgia* 408 U.S. 238, 92 S. Ct. 2726 (1972).

CHAPTER 9

© Ana Aguirre Perez/Shutterstock.com

Prisons and Jails

KEY TERMS

Absconder
Auburn System
Bridewells
Classification officer
Conditional release
Correctional officer
Correctional institution
Deterrence
Disciplinary report
Early release
Escape
Inmate
Institutional capacity
Jail
Juvenile
Offender
Panopticon
Pardon
Pennsylvania System
Prison
Recidivism
Sanctuary
Special Housing Unit (SHU)
Supervised release
Youthful offender

CHAPTER OBJECTIVES

1. Understand the historical events preceding the modern prison system.
2. Identify the Eighth Amendment and its prohibition on cruel and unusual punishment.
3. Differentiate between prisons and jails.
4. Differentiate between minimum, medium, maximum, and supermax prisons.
5. Discuss the privatization of correctional facilities.

Case Study: Guantánamo Bay Naval Base

The terrorist attacks of September 11, 2001 and the wars in Afghanistan and Iraq have populated arguably the most notorious prison of modern times. The detention center at Guantánamo Bay Naval Base, presumably outside of U.S. legal jurisdiction, has been accused of violating the human rights of its detainees. This special-purpose prison does not hold criminals. It holds terrorists and others who have waged war against the United States. In 2009, President Barack Obama signed an order to close the Guantánamo Bay detention facility within one year. Eight years later, the facility remains in operation, with 41 prisoners currently being held there.

In a 2002 Department of Defense news briefing, Vice Admiral John Stufflebeem stated in reference to those imprisoned at Guantánamo Bay, "These are the worst of the worst, and if let out on the street, they will go back to the proclivity of trying to kill Americans and others." The detainees were captured fighting for Al-Qaeda or the Taliban, and were not recognized as lawful warriors under international law.[1] By February 10, 2009, 581 tribunals had been held, and it was determined that the 539 current detainees were properly classified as enemy combatants.[2]

Unlike criminals, prisoners of war are not detained as punishment. They are held for security and for strategic and tactical necessity. Though their purposes may be different, the role of detention remains comparable for both criminal prisons and prisoner of war facilities. Most countries recognize that the detention of enemy forces is a legitimate wartime function that serves to prevent detainees from returning to the battlefield.

The Department of Defense is committed to a safe, secure, and humane detention experience for its detainees. Detainees receive three meals per day, comfortable sleeping implements, running water, full uniform and hygiene products, mail privileges, a library, recreation, and religious supplies and opportunity.[3] These amenities are similar to those afforded inmates in U.S. jails and prisons.

The Guantánamo Bay detention center has gained notoriety in part because some Americans and their congressional representatives believe that the detainees are not receiving full constitutional protections.[4] Some have proposed that the detainees be transferred to federal prisons and tried in criminal courts. Here, the detainees would receive the full protection of the U.S. Constitution. These protections are so important to Americans that many feel these rights should be extended even to those considered enemies of the United States. Others, though, do not believe that constitutional protections should apply to these prisoners or other terrorist suspects.

The top-security detention facility at Guantánamo Bay has been compared to America's supermax prisons. Many of the security measures are similar, especially those that subject some inmates to long-term restrictions on social interaction and meaningful activity. Experts studying the supermax and Guantánamo inmates assert that even inmates with no prior mental health issues may become considerably ill from long-term isolation. Comparisons of inmates in isolation with inmates who are allowed regular social interaction demonstrate higher rates of psychiatric and psychological health problems among those in isolation.[5]

Experts note that Guantánamo Bay and the nation's supermax prisons share many of the same practices and procedures, and therefore, cause similar injuries to the inmates' mental health.[6] The wisdom of inflicting psychological trauma on the Guantánamo Bay detainees and in America's supermax prisons is in question, especially since most of those supermax inmates are expected to one day return to open society in America.

The detention center at Guantánamo Bay is introduced here as an extreme example of an American top-security detention facility. While it serves a different purpose than criminal prisons, and its detainees are classified as terrorists and not as prisoners, it demonstrates how difficult and harsh the living conditions may be for extreme and difficult populations.

> Over the eight years of the Obama administration, President Obama attempted to honor his original campaign promise to close Guantánamo Bay down. A total of 779 prisoners have been held by the U.S. military at Guantánamo since the prison opened on January 11, 2002. Of those, 729 have been released or transferred, including one who was transferred to the U.S. to be tried, and nine have died, the most recent being Adnan Latif, in September 2012. As of May 2017, 41 men are still held in the detention center, and five of these men have been recommended for release by high-level governmental review processes. Ten men were released to Oman on January 16, 2017, and four more men were released on Jan. 19, 2017, Obama's last day in office."[7]

The History of Prisons and Jails

Throughout history, societies have found ways to punish individuals who break laws and commit crimes. Individuals and governments both have employed a variety of methods to prevent and to punish the transgressions of these **offenders**. Within the last few hundred years, detention has been an acceptable method of punishment.

Offender One who breaks a rule or commits a crime.

Incarceration is now one of the most widespread criminal punishments throughout the world. Though the details differ widely among countries of the world, most use incarceration for punishment or pretrial detention. As detention methods have advanced, the types of facilities used to detain individuals have evolved as well. The most common of these detention facilities are known as **prisons** and **jails**.

Prison A correctional facility that confines those convicted of felonies; may hold both misdemeanants and felons convicted of federal crimes.

Jail A correctional facility that holds people accused of or convicted of crimes.

In early American history, jails were used primarily to hold for trial those who could not make bail or those who were unable to pay debts.[7] The living conditions in these primitive houses of detention bred most every form of immorality one can imagine. Men, women, and children of all ages were thrown together in undisciplined and poorly supervised micro-communities where the strong overpowered the weak. There was little medical treatment and most were poorly fed. More often than not, those who did manage to eat did so because family or other benefactors delivered food to the jail. Those lacking outside support often suffered significantly.[8]

A pillory device, which secured the head and hands in an uncomfortable position, was used to inflict physical punishment and public humiliation.

At trial, those convicted were regularly sentenced to public humiliation such as the stocks and pillories. Other punishments included whippings, transportation, banishment, branding, amputation, or even death. The offenders would rarely see the jail again after conviction. The jail was used as detention for trial; then the real punishment would be imposed.

Eventually, society began to recognize the cruelty they were inflicting on others in the name of justice. The public began to demand punishments that were more sophisticated and more effective in reducing **recidivism**, or repeat crime by offenders. Forcing offenders to repent or to offer penitence eventually became the new method of punishment. Thus, the inspiration for the penitentiary was born.

Recidivism The rate of repeat crime by offenders; the rate of relapse back into criminal activity or behavior.

This fresh and novel plan for a house of penitence spread throughout the early American colonies. The Constitution of Pennsylvania in 1776 decreed that "houses ought to be provided for punishing by hard labour, those who shall be convicted of crimes."[9] The "House of Hard Labour" requirement led to the development of the Walnut Street Jail, which is widely recognized as the first jail or prison where one would be incarcerated as punishment for crimes.

Early Punishments

History is rife with imaginative techniques to punish criminals. Codified punishment of criminals goes back to ancient Sumerian (1860 B.C.) and Babylonian (1750 B.C.) codes. Both codes contained descriptions of crimes and the punishment meted out to those who committed them. These penalties included whipping, servitude, mutilation, and death.[10]

The Codex Justinianus, or Code of Justinian, in sixth-century Rome was an attempt to codify all possible crimes with an appropriate balance of punishment. The "scales of justice" metaphor is assumed to have developed in this period, as they are depicted in art of the time. The Code of Justinian vanished with the fall of the Roman Empire.

Several decades after the Codex Justinianus, Greece enacted the Code of Draco. This harsh form of criminal law provided the same criminal penalties for citizens and slaves alike. It also allowed any citizen to prosecute an offender. Equal enforcement among citizens was an important advancement in the treatment of criminals. Public interest and public order were now recognized as superior to individual revenge and harm.[11] The Code of Draco has found its way into the modern lexicon through the eponymous term *draconian,* meaning markedly harsh or cruel.

The Inquisition, an invention of the Catholic Church in the Middle Ages, established a tribunal to seek out offenders and heretics and then to determine their innocence or guilt. The Inquisition, which lasted about 500 years, expected those charged to demonstrate their innocence rather than to have guilt proven by evidence at trial. The Inquisition also officially recognized the concept of free will. The concept of free will means that individuals choose their actions and are responsible for them; this concept can be found in our modern system of justice.

At least since the Code of Hammurabi (18th century B.C.) and the Sumerians a thousand years earlier, forms of criminal punishment included death, torture, mutilation, branding, fines, and the loss of property.[12] Ancient Mediterranean societies in the first century B.C. practiced banishment and slavery.[13] These criminal punishments existed in many forms throughout much of human history. In the 17th and 18th centuries in America, creative punishments such as the stocks and pillories were used. Often, the public was invited to watch and even to participate in the punishment of an offender.

The death penalty has long been imposed as a punishment against offenders. Trials, sometimes nothing more than a summary judgment from a group of interested citizens, would merely take offenders straight to their punishment. Punishment of death was accomplished by both crude and sophisticated methods. Impaling, beating, drowning, hanging, crucifixion, and burning at the stake have all been used as methods of execution.[14]

As technology advanced, instruments of death such as the guillotine were invented. Many of these executions were performed in public.

© Adwo/Shutterstock.com

The guillotine is an instrument of capital punishment by beheading. French physician Joseph-Ignace Guillotin proposed the mechanism as a more humane form of capital punishment in 1789. The guillotine was subsequently invented by Antoine Louis in 1792 during the French Revolution.[16]

Often, there would be a festival of sorts with public executions as the main attraction, especially if there were several condemned prisoners. In some cases, the public would be invited to participate in the execution process. Stoning is one of those participatory punishments and is still used in some parts of the world. Though the details may vary among eras and cultures, the condemned would be prepared for stoning by tightly binding their limbs and then burying them halfway or more in the ground. The public would then hurl rocks at the fated individuals until they died.[15]

Lesser punishments also involved the public. In colonial America, the pillory and the stocks were used for minor offenses, and they were often staged as community entertainment. Stocks, which held the offender's wrists and ankles while he or she sat on a stool, and the pillory, which locked around a standing offender's neck and wrists, were forms of public humiliation. After an offender was placed in the device, a flogging was often administered. The public would take part by yelling, spitting, and throwing garbage at the offender. At times, the offender might even have his or her ears nailed to the wooden pillory.[17] Those in the crowd were encouraged to get creative in their efforts at destroying the dignity of the offender. Young boys were especially creative with this form of amusement.

Critical Thinking

Historical punishments for minor crimes involved state-sponsored humiliation. Though practices such as stocks and pillories are now prohibited, some argue that state-sponsored humiliation remains through online arrest records, prisoners working on roadsides, DUI offenders placing stickers on their cars to alert others, and even some offenders being sentenced to carry placards or post signs in public areas identifying them by their crime. Do you think that these public notices and actions should be allowed? Are these just "modern" forms of the pillory?

Mutilation was another method of criminal punishment. Often, the type of mutilation was determined by the crime. A thief's hand might be cut off; liars or people who talked too much might have their tongues cut out; a rapist might also receive a targeted amputation. Branding, a form of mutilation, would burn a word or a letter onto the offender's body so that she or he could always be recognized. A burglar might have a "B" branded on one hand and possibly another letter on the opposite hand for a subsequent offense. Adulterers, gossips, debtors, and others might all have received similar fates, as creative and even unusual punishments were typical for all levels of crime. Many of these punishments were used in early colonial

America, and some, such as the removal of a thief's hand, are still used in a few parts of the world.

Critical Thinking

Could mutilation and branding be considered a form of life punishment? In some states, convicted felons often never regain all of their civil rights. Is this a modern form of life punishment even after the sentence has been served?

Such early punishments seem barbaric by today's standards. It is important to note that many of the punishments were not designed to kill, yet nonetheless, they often resulted in death. The ducking stool is a good example of unintended execution. The ducking stool was a contraption whereby the offender, strapped to a seat, would be submerged in a pond or lake. Every so often, a person would be held underwater beyond their capacity to hold their breath and would drown. In some early societies, offenders would even be put to a test of death to prove or disprove guilt. For instance, if someone were deliberately held underwater beyond what was thought survivable and lived, that person would be determined to be innocent.

Not all criminals were mutilated or tortured: some were simply forced to leave their homes. In some ancient societies, when an individual was determined to have committed an egregious offense against the group, the group would force the offender from the tribe. This was a simple yet effective way to keep order within small societies.

Later civilizations, most notably the British Empire, continued this practice and banished criminals in bulk to lands far away. From 1718 to 1775, the British criminal system transported nearly 50,000 convicts to colonial America. With the exception of African slaves, this group of convicted criminals was the largest immigration population to America during the period.[18] The practice was halted when the American colonies asserted their independence from English rule in 1776. However, Captain Cook had discovered the Australian continent in 1770, and it became the new destination for criminal transportation. It is estimated that more than 135,000 people were transported to Australia before this system was abandoned in 1875.[19]

Those early methods were part of the evolution of how criminals are treated in modern society. The U.S. founding fathers who framed the Constitution had a different vision for how people should be treated. They established the Bill of Rights so that those living under the new Constitution would be protected from governmental abuses. One of these rights, a prohibition against cruel and unusual punishment, was formed from the desire to treat convicted criminals humanely and professionalize the criminal justice system. The founding fathers were well aware of the past abuses of offenders, and they therefore sought to prohibit the government from inflicting cruel and unusual treatment on the criminally accused and those convicted of crimes.

The Eighth Amendment states, "Excessive bail shall not be required, nor excessive fines imposed, nor cruel and unusual punishments inflicted."

In spite of our efforts to treat criminals humanely, we still struggle to define *cruel and unusual*. The death penalty is a good example. Many consider the death penalty to be cruel, and others do not. There is also controversy over the methods used to deliver the death penalty. Some even consider the death penalty to be a practice that should be prohibited.

Major Figures

The practice of punishing criminals has evolved over the course of human civilization. The evolution of the modern prison and jail system is a result of the collective thoughts and efforts of many, but there have been a few key individuals who have revolutionized or made a lasting impact on the global detainment framework.

Montesquieu (1689–1755)

Charles-Louis de Secondat, Baron de Montesquieu, or simply Montesquieu, a French nobleman, wrote on the political thought of the day and published it in his work *The Spirit of Laws* in 1748. Montesquieu believed in liberty for every man; however, he also believed in classes and a hierarchy of people, which classified people into three descending categories: monarchy, aristocracy, and commoner. Still, he asserted that no man of any class should be in fear of another.[20]

Montesquieu wrote about the separation of powers in government affairs. His philosophy, taken for granted today, maintained that the legislative, executive, and judicial branches of a government should not unduly be influenced by one another. If any of these were to combine, there could be no liberty.[21]

Much of Montesquieu's writing concerned the structure of governments and the protection of liberty. This was the age of the Enlightenment, which

Critical Thinking

The U.S. Constitution's Eighth Amendment prohibits cruel and unusual punishment. This means a punishment must be declared both unusual *and* cruel in order for it to be prohibited. Some states have tightened this requirement in their own constitutions and state that cruel or unusual punishment is prohibited. Examine your own state's constitution. Does it prohibit cruel and unusual punishment? If the issue is not addressed, what do you suppose the default prohibition would be?

took place during the 17th and 18th centuries, and man's yearning to be free was a changing force for governments around the world. These philosophies were especially influential on the British colonies as they moved closer and closer to a revolution. James Madison, considered the father of the U.S. Constitution, was heavily influenced by Montesquieu, and much of the Constitution reflects the philosophy of this French nobleman.

John Howard (1726-1790)

John Howard was an early English prison reformer. Having inherited wealth, Howard traveled throughout Europe. He was captured by French privateers during a voyage to Portugal and was imprisoned. Eventually, he was freed in a prisoner exchange, and it is assumed that this experience was the catalyst for Howard's interest in prison reform.[22]

Appointed as High Sheriff of Bedfordshire, Howard witnessed the appalling conditions of prisons throughout England. He published his findings in his work *The State of Prisons of England and Wales* in 1777, which described, in detail, the conditions he had witnessed. He particularly abhorred the practice of the jailer's fee, which demanded payment for one's detention before release.[23]

Howard proposed many improvements in the prison system. His plans included physical reforms such as improved locations, construction, and furnishings of the prisons. He also insisted on proper diets, fresh water and air, exercise, hygiene, and general health. Moreover, he believed that prison personnel should be of a high quality and prisons should be subjected to independent inspections.[24]

Howard contracted typhus on a prison visit and died in 1790. His legacy remains today in the John Howard Society, a Canadian group that seeks effective solutions to the causes of crime, as well as other groups around the world that invoke his philosophies and remember him as one of the original reformers of modern systems of criminal justice.

Cesare Beccaria (1738-1794)

Like his contemporaries, Cesare Beccaria was a social reformer who believed in criminal justice transformation. Born to a wealthy family in Milan, Italy, Beccaria anonymously published his work On *Crimes and Punishment* in 1764. Only after this work was widely approved did he claim authorship. Many influential people approved of his treatise: Catherine the Great of Russia, Voltaire, Thomas Jefferson, and Adam Smith all praised his work.

Beccaria believed that a government is right to have laws and punishments so that all obey the social contract, and that those laws should be created by dispassionate, educated, and enlightened males who would create such rational laws to benefit the greatest number in the community. Furthermore, the government has the right and the duty to punish those who violate the law, but punishments should have limits and should fit the degree of the offense. His thoughts on improvements in government, crime, punishment, and human rights influenced methods of punishment and the design of **correctional institutions** around the world.

Correctional institution A jail or a prison where offenders are confined.

Beccaria wrote on criminal theory and on how the system should work. He stated that laws should be simply written so that the people and judges do not need to interpret their meaning. He also championed that judges be impartial, suspects be judged by their peers, questions and proceedings at trial be fair, punishment be swift and certain, torture not be used to gain confessions, harsh crimes be punished with longer periods in prison than less harsh crimes, attempting crime be punished, accomplices to crime be punished, and lesser crimes be punished by fines. Moreover, Beccaria was against the death penalty. He asserted that a public murder does nothing to deter a private one.[25]

Panopticon A circular prison designed with a central observation area so that officers can view all parts of the facility, originally designed by Jeremy Bentham. Variations of this concept are still used in modern correctional facilities so that correctional officers have an unobstructed view of most inmate areas.

Much of Beccaria's influence is found in the U.S. Bill of Rights. In the document one will find conventions such as the right to a trial by a jury of one's peers, the right to be informed of accusations, the right to bail, the right to have representation, the right to a speedy trial, the right to confront witnesses, the prohibition on cruel and unusual punishment, and even the right to bear arms, all of which parallel many of Beccaria's reform recommendations. America's forefathers supported the thoughts of the classical criminologists and insisted these principles be codified into the law of the land.

Inmate An offender or an arrestee in a correctional institution.

After Beccaria's death, his work lived on and his reputation expanded. He is called the father of classical criminal theory, and many criminologists and other criminal justice experts consider Beccaria's work *On Crimes and Punishment* to be the foundation on which all modern criminology theory is based.[26]

Modern prisons with a rotunda structure and central guard post are reminiscent of Jeremy Bentham's Panopticon.

Jeremy Bentham (1748–1832)

Jeremy Bentham is considered one of the first and most significant reformers of criminal punishment and social thought. Schooled as a lawyer, Bentham never practiced law but instead chose to influence social and legal reform. He was a strong supporter of utilitarianism, a form of social thought that—while stated many different ways—essentially means the greatest good for the greatest number.[27] Here, the term *utility* means usefulness or satisfaction.

Bentham also was a reformer in prison design. In order to maximize observation of inmates, he conceived the idea of the **Panopticon**, or all-seeing prison. Designed as a circular building with a watchtower in the middle, the Panopticon afforded the prison guards the ability to see every cell and to observe the **inmates** within. Many contemporary prisons utilize this concept in various forms to maximize the observation of inmates.

Alexis de Tocqueville (1805-1859)

Alexis de Tocqueville was a French aristocrat, historian, and philosopher in the early nineteenth century. In 1831, de Tocqueville was granted a commission by King Louis Philippe of France to travel to America and study penitentiaries. The French and other European governments were interested in the new approach in America called rehabilitation, which was the restoration of offenders to a lawful and useful place in society. He traveled with his friend Gustave de Beaumont. Together, they toured the American landscape and wrote about American politics, social systems, and prisons. Though de Beaumont was instrumental in this project and wrote his own books on prison systems, he did not achieve the acclaim of de Tocqueville. The results of their observations were published as *On the Penitentiary System in the United States and its Application in France* and *Democracy in America*. The work *Democracy in America* continues to be printed and is still studied widely, often as assigned reading for those majoring in the political and social sciences, including the study of criminal justice.[28]

Tocqueville and Beaumont focused their work on the Auburn State Prison in New York and the Eastern State Prison in Pennsylvania. In Pennsylvania, inmates were isolated 24 hours a day. The idea was that they would have ample time to read their Bibles and reflect on their lives. At Auburn, the inmates were isolated only at night, and they performed simple labor and ate with other inmates during the day. Though strict silence was enforced at Auburn, there was human contact, unlike at Eastern State. By the middle of the 19th century, the Auburn system was the model for U.S. prisons and the Pennsylvania system became the standard for other countries.[29]

Not content only to observe, de Tocqueville offered his philosophies on most issues. He believed that prisons should rehabilitate and not simply punish. He opposed the death penalty and corporal punishment. He connected poverty with crime, suggesting that those with fewer opportunities would resort to criminal acts. He opposed the constant solitude found at Eastern State and approved of the partial isolation at Auburn. He observed that constant isolation destroyed inmates' spirits and that the interludes of social contact were productive. Additionally, de Tocqueville lamented that though the criminals might be rehabilitated, they would likely return to the conditions that encouraged their criminal activity in the first place.[30]

Early Forms of Imprisonment

Thanks to advancements in criminal thought, led by de Tocqueville and other reformers, the value of human dignity and life has greatly increased. In most of the industrialized world, prisoners are treated immensely better than in the past. Though prisons are oppressive places and provide for an onerous existence, most countries at least provide prisoners a survivable diet, some medical care, human contact, and some form of classification that separates **juveniles** from adults and men from women.

Juvenile A young person, usually a minor.

Incarceration as punishment is a recent development in human history and its treatment of criminals. Early jails were used primarily for the temporary detention of a prisoner before trial. In the early 18th century, England had the gaol (pronounced *jail,* and the source of the modern word *jail*). Upon trial, if an offender were found guilty, he or she would not be returned to the gaol, but instead be subjected to demeaning or abusive forms of punishment as discussed earlier. The concept of "locking up" criminals did not exist until the late 18th century in early America.

Though there may be anecdotal events during which detention was used as a form of punishment, it was most often a byproduct of the intended punishment. In some societies, people of high standing, such as the English nobility, were sentenced to house arrest. In other punishments, detention was only incidental. Consider those sentenced to servitude or to the galleys. These offenders had to be detained somewhere during their sentence or they would simply be able to escape. Some early prison administrators used abandoned mines and quarries to hold inmates, or prisoners.

The Mamertine Prison

The Mamertine prison, one of the oldest known prisons, was constructed in Rome around 640–618 B.C. Mamertine, also known as the "Prison of Kings," still exists beneath the church of S. Giuseppe dei Falegnami in Rome. It is said to have held St. Peter, who baptized his jailers while imprisoned there.[31]

Mamertine was originally a cistern for water from a nearby spring. Later, it was used for the temporary detention of prisoners of some importance. These higher-level prisoners would eventually be paraded through the streets of Rome and then publicly executed. Others would simply be put to death inside the prison.[32]

Sanctuaries, Fortresses, Hulks, and Bridewells

Sanctuary A sacred place of worship where one can take refuge.

Throughout human history, many other forms of detention have been used. **Sanctuaries** were mentioned in the Old Testament, and this form of safe haven was common through the 12th century. A person accused of a crime could seek sanctuary at a church, and he or she would often be protected from the authorities. Early Christians formalized a policy that if any part of a criminal's body touched the church, then he or she would be given protection from prosecution.[33]

Another historical place of detention and imprisonment is the fortress. Fortresses were simply fortified structures for defense. Though designed to keep enemies out, they were often used to keep criminals in. The criminals would be held until their punishment was decided. Often, they were publicly executed. The Tower of London is an example of a fortress being used as a prison, though that was not its primary purpose.[34]

A *hulk* is a non-functional ship. Ships that were no longer seaworthy were ready-made facilities that were easily used for criminal detention purposes. These opportune facilities have long been used by governments to hold prisoners. As recently as 1997, England used the *Weare*, a decommissioned ship, to relieve prison overcrowding. The ship was never intended to be a permanent facility, and it closed as a prison in 2005.[35]

© Amy Laughinghouse/Shutterstock.com

The Tower of London imprisoned infamous historical figures such as William Hastings, Anne Boleyn, and Lady Jane Grey before their ultimate death by beheading.[36]

Bridewells were jails in England and Ireland in the 16th century that typically housed petty criminals. The name came from Bridewell Palace, which was originally a home to King Henry VIII; it ultimately became a poorhouse and a correctional facility for prostitutes with the intent of rehabilitation. Soon, *Bridewell* became a common term for any jail or police station in England or Ireland. These poorhouses were at first considered successful, but eventually their conditions and the treatment of prisoners became deplorable. There was no classification of prisoners based on crime, sex, age, or other criteria. Corruption became rampant among staff and inmates alike, and disease and death were common. After public outcry over the conditions, Bridewells were no longer used.

Bridewells Jails and police stations in England and Ireland in the 16th century that typically housed petty criminals.

The Walnut Street Jail

The Walnut Street Jail was named after the Philadelphia street on which it was located. It was originally constructed in the 18th century to alleviate the overcrowding of another Philadelphia jail, the Old Stone Jail, where men, women, and boys were all housed together. The Walnut Street Jail instituted reforms that are still in use today.

The reforms at the Walnut Street Jail included the classification of inmates according to gender, type of crime, and violent tendencies. It also separated juveniles from adults. In addition, they began attempts at rehabilitation by providing work and trade skills to the inmates. Even with these reforms, the Walnut Street Jail, too, eventually became overcrowded. The Walnut Street Jail continued its service for a number of years as a confinement facility for the more difficult prisoners at the newer Eastern State Prison.

© Iryna Liveoak/Shutterstock.com

Walnut Street in Philadelphia was home to an overcrowded prison. By 1795, each of the Walnut Street Jail's 18-square-foot cells held 30 to 40 inmates at one time.[38]

The Walnut Street Jail was still being used as a prison during the Constitutional Convention in Philadelphia after the Revolutionary War. Benjamin Franklin, now an old and frail man in poor health, could barely walk, and prisoners from the Walnut Street Jail would carry Franklin on a sedan chair to the convention meetings.[37]

The Pennsylvania System

The Walnut Street Jail had actually originated before the American Revolution. After the United States gained its independence, this jail on Walnut Street in Philadelphia was expanded to abide by the new Pennsylvania Constitution requiring that "houses ought to be provided for punishing by hard labour."[39] This expansion of the Walnut Street Jail included a cellular construction for housing prisoners, with some cells reserved for the isolation of some of the inmates.

The Philadelphia legislature, having heard the protests of Quakers who rejected the shedding of blood, had created a substitution for corporal punishment. Here, prisoners were classified based on their crimes. Solitary cells were used for those sentenced to absolute isolation by the courts and for those who refused to work. Those inmates in isolation did not perform any labor.

This new method of dealing with criminals was a great leap from past methods used to punish offenders. Offenders who previously would have been sentenced to death were now sentenced to isolation in one of the individual cells at the Walnut Street Jail. Since belligerent inmates and those who refused to work were also forced into isolation, the jail grew quite large by period standards. This became quite expensive.

This system of cellular isolation was soon copied by other states. Maryland, Massachusetts, Maine, New York, New Jersey, and Virginia adopted the Philadelphia form of isolation for certain classes of criminal.[40] These reforms, though well intentioned, did not have the desired results. The prisons found that many of the same individuals kept returning after their release and the expense of housing all of the criminals was "ruinous to the public treasury."[41] It was believed that the solution was simply to add more cells. This, however, involved an even greater expense to the states that chose this method.

Roughly two decades after the advent of the Walnut Street Jail, the Western Penitentiary in Pittsburgh opened. This penitentiary, somewhat modeled after Jeremy Bentham's Panopticon, at first was designed only for the isolation of inmates. Later, inmates were forced to perform some labor within their isolation. Exercise areas were also constructed. Western Penitentiary was considered superior to previous systems, and soon yet another Pennsylvania prison, the Eastern State Penitentiary in Philadelphia, was built not far from the Walnut Street Jail.

Pennsylvania System A penal system advocated by Quakers that used solitary confinement and penitence to reform offenders. Eventually, work such as shoemaking and weaving was allowed to be done in the cells.

The Eastern State Penitentiary was the model for what became known as the **Pennsylvania System**. Here, the Quaker belief that man is inherently good and can be reformed was a foundation for rehabilitation. Proponents of the Pennsylvania System believed that solitary confinement and penitence could reform people into productive and honest citizens.[42]

The Eastern State Penitentiary was constructed similar to Jeremy Bentham's Panopticon, but it was square. Additionally, individual cells had an adjoining outside cell that was used as an exercise yard. This system advocated individual isolation combined with labor. The labor consisted of making crafts in one's cell that were sold to help support the institution. It was assumed that this isolation would prevent corruption through association with other inmates and that prisoners would concentrate more on redemption. Thus, in theory, isolation should require shorter sentences, and it would be less expensive per inmate to run the prison.

The Auburn System

In 1816, sometime after the Eastern State Penitentiary opened, a new prison was constructed in Auburn, New York. With this new prison came a new prison system. The **Auburn System** was different in many respects from the Pennsylvania System. The cells at Auburn Prison were smaller than those at Eastern State Penitentiary, and they were all enclosed with no individual exercise yard. These cells were for sleeping only, and the inmates worked in a large room with one another. Though silence was strictly enforced, it was thought that the human contact would be good for the inmates and for their rehabilitation.

© Mopic/Shutterstock.com

Both the Pennsylvania and Auburn Systems focused on inmate isolation, a practice that philosophers believed could devastate the human mind.

The discipline at Auburn was harsh by today's standards. Silence was enforced by the whip and with isolation cells. Inmates marched in step when being moved, and they sat facing away from one another during meals. Though this was considered an improvement over Eastern State Penitentiary, the forced silence even when seated next to one another took its toll on the inmates, and by some accounts, on the jailers as well.

Auburn System A prison system, also known as the New York System, in which silence is enforced at all times. Inmates work during the day and spend nights in solitary confinement.

These two new prison systems competed somewhat for recognition of superiority.[43] The Pennsylvania System boasted a solitary existence and solitary work, while the Auburn System boasted group work in silence. Nineteenth-century philosophers debated the two systems. Though they disagreed on much, they did agree that isolation without work would devastate the human mind. Total isolation was attempted at various institutions of the time. Inmates often went mad and suicide rates went up. The jailers, it was found, often developed psychological issues as well.[44]

Notorious Contemporary Prisons

Nothing today can compare with the prisons of the past. The squalid living conditions and the brutality imposed cannot be matched. This does not mean that the modern world is without prisons and jails that have achieved notoriety for their conditions and their contents. Alcatraz Prison, though closed since 1963, is famous for its legendary inmates, and the Maricopa County Jail, still in operation, is known for its tough sheriff, Joe Arpaio.

Alcatraz

In the early 20th century, the federal prison system included specialized institutions. Some were less restrictive, "easy" prisons that housed the less dangerous inmates, and some were very grim, dungeon-type, supermaximum prisons. These supermaximum prisons held the most notorious and hated criminals of the country. One such prison was built on Alcatraz Island in San Francisco Bay. Alcatraz, also known as "The Rock," was surrounded by swift currents of cold water that, presumably, would kill any prisoner trying to traverse the path to freedom. Thus, the location alone provided its greatest resource; that of being able to contain all of its prisoners and prevent escape.

With one guard to every three prisoners, the inmates at Alcatraz were strictly monitored. At 6:30 A.M., the wake-up call was sounded, and by 7:00 A.M., the prisoners, having dressed, cleaned their cells, and been counted, would march off to the mess hall for the morning meal. Then, it was off to their individual jobs.

The routine at Alcatraz was sternly enforced and rarely varied. The most brutal aspect, at least in Alcatraz's early years, was the forced silence. Many inmates considered this the most unbearable punishment. The silence policy was relaxed in the prison's later years, but it was one of the few rule changes to occur.

Most know Alcatraz Island only for its infamous federal prison. However, Alcatraz was also a civil war fortress, a bird sanctuary, the home of the first lighthouse on the West Coast, and the site of an American Indian occupation in the 1960s.[45] The 1979 movie *Escape from Alcatraz*, which was loosely based on the only known successful escape from the maximum-security prison, further sealed the prison's notoriety. Alcatraz is now a tourist attraction that is visited by hundreds every day.

Maricopa County's Tent City

Joseph "Joe" Arpaio, the popular yet widely criticized sheriff of Maricopa County, Arizona, has become known as America's toughest sheriff. Sheriff Arpaio runs a jail that has gained notoriety because of his unconventional methods. From forcing inmates to wear pink underwear to housing some of them in tents to endure sweltering heat, the sheriff has earned an extreme reputation among both critics and supporters.

The Maricopa County Jail in Phoenix, Arizona includes a modern, state-of-the-art facility with more than 2,000 beds and seven smaller facilities, including the infamous tent city. According to the Maricopa County Sheriff's Office website, in 1993 Sheriff Arpaio began housing inmates in surplus army tents, due in part to his promises that there would be no early releases because of overcrowding.[46] He houses less dangerous inmates in the tents because of the lower level of security. He was able to create this tent city jail with minimal expense. Currently, it can hold up to 2,000 prisoners. Other jail administrators have considered using Arpaio's methods when their own facilities begin to exceed institutional capacity, resulting in overcrowding.

© Chris Curtis/Shutterstock.com

Sheriff Joseph Arpaio brands himself as "America's toughest sheriff."

The sheriff made a number of other changes to the prison system, such as eliminating coffee to save money, and even bragged that it cost him less per day to feed an inmate than a police dog. He brought back several long-abandoned features from decades past, such as chain gangs and the iconic, stigmatized black-and-white striped jumpsuits. In an attempt to humiliate inmates, Sheriff Arpaio requires them to wear pink underwear and other pink clothing. Additionally, cigarettes, adult magazines, regular television programming, and many other comfort items have been forbidden. The conditions of tent living in the hot and arid Arizona elements can be brutal, and the sheriff considers this a consequence of going to jail. These harsh conditions of detention are expected to have a deterrent effect on offenders. Even though the sheriff has saved the taxpayers much money, critics claim the high legal costs incurred from lawsuits because of his methods negate any savings.[47]

Early release Release from a correctional institution prior to the expiration of an offender's sentence.

Institutional capacity The maximum number of inmates an institution can hold.

Deterrence The threat of punishment that will result from criminal activity. Deterrence is further categorized into general deterrence, which threatens everyone with criminal sanctions, and specific deterrence, which is a threat to a specific individual who may offend or reoffend.

Sheriffs are publicly elected officials, and thus, Sheriff Arpaio must gain support from sufficient numbers of voters to win elections. Arpaio's methods have won him some eager supporters, but also vociferous opponents. Some claim that Arpaio's main objective is publicity. Organizations have developed with the objective of getting rid of Joe Arpaio at the ballot box. These organizations present evidence that the sheriff wastes public funds in his "publicity stunts." They also claim that deputies on county time are assigned as his personal bodyguards, that Arpaio will not debate political opponents, that he is vindictive and abuses his authority, and that he has lied to the public about his biographical information, the costs of lawsuits, and the money he claims to save taxpayers. As evidence, critics tell of Arpaio's claim that an $8.25 million settlement over a dead inmate cost the county nothing because of the jail's liability insurance. What he neglected to say, though, was that the jail had a $1 million deductible.[48]

In 2010, the U.S. Department of Justice sued Arpaio for civil rights violations.[49] There have been other lawsuits as well. The *New York Times* states that according to Maricopa County Risk Management, the sheriff has had over 6,000 claims and lawsuits filed against him since he was first elected, at a cost to taxpayers of over $50 million.[50]

The case study at the beginning of this chapter noted that the detention center at Guantánamo Bay and supermax facilities can be considered extreme examples of prisons. The human suffering at these prisons has generated and maintained their notorious reputations. The Maricopa County Jail is similar in that it may be considered an extreme example of an American jail. The jail receives incredible publicity because of the atypical methods used on the inmates and the unreserved behavior of the sheriff.

Role and Structure of Prisons and Jails

The history of jails and prisons, discussed in the previous section, has brought us to the modern system of corrections. Modern correctional facilities have evolved from past successes and mistakes. Currently, in the United States, there are more than 7 million people incarcerated or under correctional supervision.[51] This is larger than the populations of many states. Since there are so many American citizens incarcerated, the issue of corrections has become a significant issue for all levels of government and the public as well.

Modern correctional facilities exist at the local, state, and federal levels. All have their own missions and roles in criminal justice. Some are old and outdated, and others are modern and very secure. Many have inmate amenities for recreation, education, and training. All have access to medical care. There are also different levels of security, ranging from minimum security to supermaximum prisons. None of the facilities and systems exists without controversy.

Prisoners in America have gained many constitutional rights in the past 50 or so years. Of course, some may argue that these rights were already present, but simply not recognized until the U.S. Supreme Court asserted their existence. Among these rights is access to reasonable medical care. In 1976, the U.S. Supreme Court presented the "deliberate indifference" standard pertaining to correctional facilities and the medical care afforded inmates. The court held that deliberate indifference of correctional staff to an inmate's serious medical illness or injury constitutes cruel and unusual punishment.[52]

In the late 1970s, the American Medical Association addressed this issue by creating a program to assist correctional facilities in establishing proper levels of inmate medical care. This program evolved into what is now known as the National Commission on Correctional Health Care (NCCHC). The not-for-profit NCCHC sets standards and offers education, accreditation, and assistance to correctional facilities. Participation is voluntary, but the program is well established, recognized, and respected; many correctional facilities have adopted the standards of the NCCHC and sought their accreditation.[53]

The U.S. Supreme Court has also ordered that correctional facilities must provide law libraries. An inmate's right to access to a law library and to those skilled in providing legal assistance was established in *Bounds v. Smith*[54]

(1977) and in *Younger v. Gilmore*[55] (1971). The decisions were based on an inmate's widely accepted constitutional right to court access.[56] Subsequent U.S. Supreme Court cases have ruled on this issue even further. *Lewis v. Casey*[57] (1996), for example, may have relaxed some of the privileges gained from the 1971 and 1977 cases. *Lewis* limits access to the types of legal proceedings an inmate may pursue and tightens the rules for an inmate's legal standing in order to file a lawsuit.[58]

Critical Thinking

Correctional administrators tell us that television is a good way for inmates to pass the time and to keep them occupied. Is television for inmates a good idea in prisons and/or jails? What about cable television? Expand some on this concept. What about Internet access, weightlifting, gyms, pool tables, and basketball courts? What about entertainment venues such as comedians and musicians? Are any or all of these a good idea or not? Why?

The Historical Role of Incarceration

Throughout human history, prisoners have been confined for a variety of reasons. Mostly, confinement was used for the temporary detention of individuals until they could be brought to judgment by the governing authority and either released or punished accordingly. If the offender was found guilty, he or she would receive a punishment. As discussed earlier in the chapter, these punishments often included methods that by contemporary standards would be considered cruel and unusual, such as stoning or boiling.

When the American colonies declared themselves independent from English rule, the colonists also insisted that this independence included rules concerning criminal justice. Whereas the British legal system recognized that the monarch was the ultimate source of law, many colonists felt that the ultimate source of law should originate in the people and that leaders should also be bound to laws. British law was, at the time, so merciless that even a petty thief could be put to death. Some higher-class criminals, however, were able to escape justice through a system of patronage. This system allowed offenders to appeal to the crown or others in local authority who would either issue a **pardon**—an exemption from penalty—or otherwise suspend or delay the offender's sentence. The colonists demanded a justice system that treated suspects the same without consideration of their social status.

Pardon To forgive, release, or exempt a person from a penalty.

Having won independence in the Revolutionary War, the United States created its own system of laws. Issues of criminal justice are addressed in several sections of the U.S. Constitution. Some of these sections include laws against counterfeiting, treason, and piracy. In addition, there are laws that prohibit federal and state governments from enacting *bills of attainder*, which are edicts that proclaim a person or group guilty without the benefit of a trial, and *ex post facto laws*, which are laws retroactively applied to previous events.

Criminal law was addressed more specifically in the Bill of Rights. The Bill of Rights recognizes the right of people to be free from governmental abuse and codifies this natural human rights acknowledgment into law. Among other things, the Bill of Rights prohibits the government from unreasonably searching or seizing persons or property, from trying someone repeatedly for the same crime, from holding someone "for a capital [death penalty eligible], or otherwise infamous [felony] crime," and from demanding confessions in that a person is not compelled to "be a witness against himself." It also prohibits the government from bringing charges except upon indictment or presentment. Additionally, the Bill of Rights states that an individual has a right to a speedy trial by an impartial jury and punishments deemed cruel and unusual are prohibited.

The provisions in the Bill of Rights were not based on hypothetical situations: they were responses to known abuses from tyrannical governments that the framers of this document intended to prohibit. The text of the Declaration of Independence includes a long list of these "abuses and usurpations." The Bill of Rights was created to protect all citizens from unchecked power and to prevent the government from tyrannical abuses. The Eighth Amendment outlawed cruel and unusual forms of punishment and permitted the modern philosophies of penitence to replace them. Thus, penitentiaries became the new method of punishment.

With the goal of establishing a system based on fair adjudication and punishment, the U.S. founding fathers created the Eighth Amendment to protect the basic human rights of the innocent and the guilty.

At first, the Bill of Rights applied only to federal laws. The states had their own bills of rights, but most were fashioned from those in the U.S. Constitution. It was not until the mid-19th century with the enactment of the 14th Amendment that many of the U.S. Constitutional rights were applied to the states.

The Role of Incarceration in Contemporary Society

It is a commonly held tenet of criminal justice that people are sent to prison *as* punishment, not *for* punishment. This is a fine distinction, but an important one. In other words, the loss of freedom and many rights is the punishment. Inmates are not to receive punishment in excess of what was ordered by the court.

There have been many correctional ideologies proposed and tried over the centuries. Most of them fall into the categories of punishment, rehabilitation, or prevention. Of course, there is no defined position where one ideology ends before another one begins. They often overlap. For instance, one could easily make a reasonable argument that the goal of both punishment and rehabilitation is prevention.

Punishment of criminals falls into three general categories. The first of these categories is retribution. Retribution has come in many forms through the ages, and is viewed by some as the basest of human qualities. It means getting even, such as in the maxim "an eye for an eye." Banishment, death, and humiliation are all forms of retribution.[59]

The next form of punishment is deterrence. This simple term means a person is deterred from doing wrong because he or she fears the punishment. Deterrence is further broken down into the categories of general and specific deterrence. General deterrence is what all members of society feel that prevents them from doing wrong. This feeling can come from a moral or a religious view, or it can come simply from a fear of being caught. Specific deterrence is a sanction imposed upon a specific person in hopes that the punishment will deter that specific individual from reoffending, or recidivating.[60]

A third reason for punishment is incapacitation. To incapacitate an offender means to remove him or her from the opportunity and availability to commit further criminal acts. This usually means that an offender is locked up, preventing further criminal opportunity and actions.[61]

Rehabilitation, discussed earlier in the chapter, means to restore an offender to a lawful and useful place in society. This, in theory, is accomplished through treatment and education. The treatment model is often referred to as the medical model. In the *medical model*, an offender is viewed as "ill" and in need of treatment. The *educational model* recognizes the offender as disadvantaged and in need of education, training, and discipline. Rehabilitation seems easier in theory than in practice. High rates of recidivism tend to challenge the success of rehabilitation efforts.[62]

The *prevention ideology* is often recognized as something that must begin in early life. Prevention programs attempt to identify early signs of behavior that are statistically tied to criminal behavior. Truancy, dropping out of school, and poor school performance are often viewed as precursors to criminal behavior later in life. Prevention programs attempt to break the path to crime by developing specialized classes, counseling, vocational training, and even alternate schools.[63]

Countless state, federal, appeals, and U.S. Supreme Court cases address issues of prisoner rights. In *Wolff v. McDonnell*, a 1974 case involving prison

Critical Thinking

Incarcerated individuals lose many of their civil rights, such as the right of liberty, the right to assemble, and in most states, the right to vote. What rights do you believe inmates should be allowed to keep?

inmate rights, Supreme Court Justice Byron White asserted in the majority opinion, "But though [the prisoner's] rights may be diminished by the needs and exigencies of the institutional environment, a prisoner is not wholly stripped of constitutional protections when he is imprisoned for crime. There is no iron curtain drawn between the Constitution and the prisons of this country."[64]

Exhibit: *Wolff v. McDonnell*

"Petitioners assert that the procedure for disciplining prison inmates for serious misconduct is a matter of policy raising no constitutional issue. If the position implies that prisoners in state institutions are wholly without the protections of the Constitution and the Due Process Clause, it is plainly untenable. Lawful imprisonment necessarily makes unavailable many rights and privileges of the ordinary citizen . . . But though his rights may be diminished by the needs and exigencies of the institutional environment, a prisoner is not wholly stripped of constitutional protections when he is imprisoned for crime. There is no iron curtain drawn between the Constitution and the prisons of this country. Prisoners have been held to enjoy substantial religious freedom under the First and Fourteenth Amendments. They retain right of access to the courts. Prisoners are protected under the Equal Protection Clause of the Fourteenth Amendment from invidious discrimination based on race. Prisoners may also claim the protections of the Due Process Clause. They may not be deprived of life, liberty, or property without due process of law."

A drop in the number of probationers accounted for most of the decrease in the correctional population during 2015.

After a peak in 2007, the U.S. correctional population declined annually through 2015. However, the composition of the population remained stable despite the decreasing size of the population during that time. Between 2007 (58%) and 2015 (56%), probationers accounted for the majority of offenders under correctional supervision (Figure 9.1). Prisoners represented slightly less than a quarter of the U.S. correctional population in 2007 (22%) and 2015 (23%). Parolees (11% in 2007 and 13% in 2015) and jail inmates (11% in both 2007 and 2015) remained the smallest shares of the correctional population during the 8-year period.

Is It a Prison or a Jail?

In the United States and in many other countries, there are distinct differences between prisons and jails. Jails and prisons are both **correctional institutions**, but have different missions and therefore serve

FIGURE 9.1 U.S. ADULT CORRECTIONAL POPULATION 2007 AND 2015. THIS FIGURE DEMONSTRATES THAT THE TOTAL NUMBER OF ADULTS UNDER CORRECTIONAL SUPERVISION AS OF 2015 WAS MORE THAN 6.7 MILLION.

Number of persons supervised by U.S. adult correctional systems, by correctional status, 2007 and 2015

	2007		2015	
Correctional populations	**Population**	**Percent of total population**	**Population**	**Percent of total population**
Total[a]	7,339,600	100%	6,741,400	100%
Probation[b]	4,293,000	58.5	3,789,800	56.2
Prison[b]	1,596,800	21.8	1,526,800	22.6
Parole[b]	826,100	11.3	870,500	12.9
Local jail[c]	780,200	10.6	728,200	10.8
Offenders with multiple correctional statuses[d]	156,400	:	174,000	:

Note: Counts were rounded to the nearest 100 and include estimates for nonresponding jurisdictions. Detail may not sum to total due to rounding and because offenders with multiple correctional statuses were excluded from the total correctional population.

:Not calculated.

[a]Total was adjusted to exclude offenders with multiple correctional statuses to avoid double counting.

[b]Population as of December 31.

[c]Population as of the last weekday in June.

[d]Some probationers and parolees on December 31 were held in a prison or jail but still remained under the jurisdiction of a probation or parole agency and some parolees were also on probation. In addition, some prisoners were being held in jail. They were excluded from the total correctional population to avoid double counting.

Sources: Bureau of Justice Statistics, Annual Probation Survey, Annual Parole Survey, Annual Survey of Jails, and National Prisoner Statistics Program, 2007 and 2015.

different purposes. *Jails* are usually run by local governments or a county sheriff's office. This is most often determined by the local government or individual state laws. *Prisons* are run by the states and the federal government and are often sprawling complexes with varying degrees of security. Some prisons are run by private organizations, but they are usually under contract with the state. The status of the offender and his or her crime are normally what determines whether the person is in a jail or a prison. In addition, youthful offenders—typically offenders under the age of 18—may be tried and sentenced as adults to jail or prison, but most often, juveniles are adjudicated as delinquent and not as criminals. They may then be sent to a juvenile detention facility.

Youthful offender
Typically, an offender under 18 years old, though the age requirement can differ among states.

Jails and prisons have evolved significantly over the centuries. In early human history, confinement areas were built from whatever could be used. This often was a natural formation such as a cave. As humankind progressed, cages, special rooms in castles, and even specially built structures would hold prisoners. While some jails today may still be old and poorly built, most jails and prisons are technological wonders with modern security built into the structure. They are designed for maximum observation of inmates by correctional staff. **Escapes** from inside the secure area are very rare. Many of the escapes mentioned in the media are inmates who have simply absconded. **Absconders** are walk-offs from work crews, work release centers, halfway houses, and other inmate areas not inside the main secure facility itself. Typically, the inmates in these other areas are considered less dangerous to society or are nearing the ends of their sentences.[65]

Escape The illegal departure of an offender from legal custody.

Absconder One who leaves without authorization. This term is usually used in reference to walk-offs from work crews, work release centers, halfway houses, and other inmate areas not inside the main secure facility.

Jails and prisons are now often designed in sections called pods. The goal of the pod system is to maximize observation while sectioning off areas for security reasons. These pods may be used to separate inmates based on gender, classification of their crimes, medical reasons, etc. Additionally, should a disturbance erupt, the officers can secure the area and prevent the spread of violence and therefore maintain control of the facility while addressing the disorder.

Jails

Jails are multipurpose facilities operated by local governments or sheriffs. Almost all offenders begin their experience with the correctional system in a local jail. Many minor offenders will go no further. For major offenders, jail may be only the first stop in their progression through the correctional system. Most of a jail's population includes those recently arrested, those awaiting trial, and those serving sentences of one year or less. Others found in jail include mentally ill inmates for whom no other facility is available, parolees and probationers awaiting violation hearings, federal prisoners awaiting pickup by marshals, and bail jumpers held overnight by traveling bounty hunters.

Jails are usually the first contact an offender has with the correctional system. When an individual is first arrested, he or she is taken to a jail and is "booked," or has personal information placed in the facility's books. Here, an inmate may be held until trial, known as pretrial detention, or may be given a **conditional release**, which allows the inmate to be released under specific conditions such as an order to enter a treatment program. Others may be released on bail, also known as a bond. Sometimes, charges may be dropped very quickly. Those who are convicted of their offense may be sentenced to jail or prison. Often, sentencing involves probation, which is a form of **supervised release**. Offenders convicted of misdemeanors and sentenced to one year or less of detention usually serve their time in jail. Those convicted of felonies and sentenced to more than one year (at least 366 days) of detention usually go to prison.[66] These situations do have exceptions, as there are few absolutes in criminal justice. Moreover, these procedures are

Conditional release The release of a defendant under specific conditions such as an order to enter a treatment program.

Supervised release Court-ordered supervision of someone who is awaiting trial or serving probation or parole.

determined by state law, and not all states follow the same practice. For instance, in some states, a misdemeanor sentence can carry a punishment of up to two years of imprisonment, which may be served in a jail. Moreover, some states have indeterminate sentencing laws that mandate a penalty, such as six months to a year or five to 10 years, instead of a determinate amount of time. An inmate may gain an earlier release date based on his or her behavior and efforts to rehabilitate.

Staffing at the jail includes correctional officers, classification officers, medical professionals, and administrative workers. **Correctional officers** are usually academy-trained individuals who meet strict criteria for physical condition, mental condition, and a noncriminal history. **Classification officers** are those who determine the inmate's placement and level of dangerousness. They also calculate sentences as mandated by the courts.

Correctional officer An officer, also called a prison guard, jail guard, or corrections officer, who oversees and supervises all inmate activity.

Classification officer The officer assigned to determine individual inmate needs and assign them to appropriate custody levels, institutions, and programs.

Depending on the size of the jail, there may be a staff of administrative professionals. These individuals perform the back-office functions such as managing funds or ordering supplies. All jails have access to medical care, and jails of significant size often have their own staff for routine medical needs and emergencies. The Eighth Amendment's prohibition on cruel and unusual punishment provides that inmates receive a minimum standard of living, which includes access to medical services.

Prisons

Prisons are run by the states and the federal government. In some cases, the government oversees a private facility contracted to perform correctional services. Usually, state prisons hold those convicted of felonies who are sentenced to more than one year of imprisonment. States enact their own laws concerning sentencing and correctional facilities, so there is some variation throughout the country. Federal prisons house those convicted of federal crimes, both misdemeanants and felons. Whether the inmate was convicted of a state or a federal crime determines whether he or she goes to a state or a federal prison.

Sometimes, a person is accused of a crime that is prohibited by both state and federal law. Weapons and drug offenses commonly involve both jurisdictions. Since there are state and federal laws against illegal drugs and weapons, offenders may find themselves prosecuted in both state and federal courts. The offender may even be convicted and sentenced in both

Critical Thinking

Higher-custody prisons not only keep inmates from escaping, but also prevent inmates from committing crimes while in prison. What kinds of crimes are committed inside of prison? How does prison design help deter or prevent crime from occurring?

jurisdictions. If that occurs, the offender may serve a segmented sentence in both state and federal prison. In practice, however, the jurisdictions often work together to bring a resolution to the case. Sometimes, jurisdictions may defer to the prosecution with the strongest case or the longest sentence. In other cases, one jurisdiction may delay completion of the investigation to see what happens in the other jurisdiction's court before deciding whether to proceed. There may even be a cross-jurisdictional agreement in exchange for a guilty plea.

It is important to note that the Fifth Amendment's prohibition on double jeopardy allows an individual to be convicted in two jurisdictions for the same crime. This is because there are two separate jurisdictions that prohibit the offense. The Fifth Amendment states that no person can be tried twice for "the same offense," but if there are separate offense statutes for a crime on the state and federal levels, then they are not considered the same offense. Thus, an offender may be tried and convicted under both jurisdictions. This is known as the dual sovereignty exception. In *United States v. Lanza,* Chief Justice Howard Taft in delivering the opinion of the court stated, "It follows that an act denounced as a crime by both national and state sovereignties is an offense against the peace and dignity of both, and may be punished by each."[67]

When an inmate is received into most state prison systems, he or she is processed through a classification system. The classification of inmates simply is a means to fit an inmate into a specific category of custody level, medical needs, predisposition to violence or escape, training and educational needs, and other categories as determined by state statute. This classification procedure will determine primarily which security level the inmate requires. Then, after considering the other criteria, the inmate will be assigned to a state prison facility that fits his or her characteristics. The classification procedure usually continues at the receiving facility, and decisions will be made concerning the inmate's abilities, training, counseling, and efforts regarding the inmate's reentry to open society.

Accurate classification of inmates is an admirable goal, and the objectives are achieved to a significant degree. However, institutional needs are the primary forces that determine classification efforts. Often, classification decisions are made based on availability of programs and space at the institution where the inmate's needs would best be served.

Custody Levels

Inmates are classified to a custody level in jails and in prisons. In jail, the inmate may bond out for pretrial release or may be serving a relatively short sentence of one year or less. In prison, proper classification becomes a continuous process that involves constant reclassification for many inmates based on their behavior and history. These levels of custody usually include minimum, medium, and maximum security. There are others such as community custody, typically for those on parole or probation; death row

FIGURE 9.2 U.S. ADULT CORRECTIONAL SYSTEMS, BY CORRECTIONAL STATUS, 2000 AND 2005-2015.

Number of persons supervised by U.S. adult correctional systems, by correctional status, 2000 and 2005-2015

		Community supervision				Incarcerated[b]	
Year	**Total correctional population[a]**	**Total[a,c]**	**Probation**	**Parole**	**Total[a]**	**Local jail**	**Prison**
2000	6,467,800	4,564,900	3,839,400	725,500	1,945,400	621,100	1,394,200
2005	7,055,600	4,946,600	4,162,300	784,400	2,200,400	747,500	1,525,900
2006	7,199,600	5,035,000	4,236,800	798,200	2,256,600	765,800	1,568,700
2007	7,339,600	5,119,000	4,293,000	826,100	2,296,400	780,200	1,596,800
2008	7,312,600	5,093,400	4,271,200	826,100	2,310,300	785,500	1,608,300
2009	7,239,100	5,019,900	4,199,800	824,600	2,297,700	767,400	1,615,500
2010	7,089,000	4,888,500	4,055,900	840,800	2,279,100	748,700	1,613,800
2011	6,994,500	4,818,300	3,973,800	855,500	2,252,500	735,600	1,599,000
2012	6,949,800	4,790,700	3,944,900	858,400	2,231,300	744,500	1,570,400
2013	6,899,700	4,749,800	3,912,000	849,500	2,222,500	731,200	1,577,000
2014	6,856,900	4,713,200	3,868,400	857,700	2,225,100	744,600	1,562,300
2015	6,741,400	4,650,900	3,789,800	870,500	2,173,800	728,200	1,526,800
Average annual percent change, 2007-2015	−1.1%	−1.2%	−1.6%	0.7%	−0.7%	−0.9%	−0.6%
Percent change, 2014-2015	−1.7%	−1.3%	−2.0%	1.5%	−2.3%	−2.2%	−2.3%

Note: Estimates were rounded to the nearest 100 and may not be comparable to previously published BJS reports due to updated information or rounding. Counts include estimates for nonresponding jurisdictions. All probation, parole, and prison counts are not December 31; jail counts are for the last weekday in June. Detail may not sum to total due to rounding and adjustments made to account for offenders with multiple correctional statuses. See Methodology. See the Key Statistics page on the BJS website for correctional population statistics prior to 2000 or other years not included in this table.

[a]Total was adjusted to account for offenders with multiple correctional statuses. See Methodology.

[b]Includes offenders held in local jails or under the jurisdiction of state or federal prisons.

[c]Includes some offenders held in a prison or jail but who remained under the jurisdiction of a probation or parole agency.

Source: Bureau of Justice Statistics, Annual Probation Survey, Annual Parole Survey, Annual Survey of Jails, Census of Jail Inmates, and National Prisoner Statistics Program. 2000 and 2005-2015.

custody; and supermax custody. The various states determine their own categories and criteria for custody levels. For instance, in Florida prisons, most inmates are classified as minimum, medium, or close custody. Maximum custody refers to death row inmates and a few other categories of especially dangerous individuals.

At yearend 2015, an estimated 6,741,400 persons were under the supervision of U.S. adult correctional systems, about 115,600 fewer persons than yearend 2014 (Figure 9.2). This was the first time since 2002 (6,730,900) that the correctional population fell below 6.8 million. The population declined by 1.7% during 2015, which was the largest decline since 2010 (down 2.1%). Additionally, the decrease was a change from a 3-year trend of stable annual rate declines of about 0.6% between 2012 and 2014. About 1 in 37 adults in the United States was under some form of correctional supervision at the end of 2015. This was the lowest rate observed since 1994, when about 1 in 38 adults (1.6 million fewer persons) were under correctional supervision in the nation (not shown).

Minimum and medium custody levels are usually assigned to the least dangerous inmates. Inmates at higher levels may also be reclassified to a lower level if they are nearing the end of their sentence. The theory is that they are less of a trouble and escape risk because they want to complete their time easily and get out. Unfortunately, this theory does not always prove true because many criminals are unable to process this kind of logic. They may be impulsive and unable to understand the consequences of current actions and the result on their future. However, most do finish the end of a sentence quietly. The Bureau of Justice Statistics once estimated that 25% of inmates lost good time credits for good behavior, which means that a full sentence was served without an early release.[68]

Lower-custody institutions are less expensive to operate. Not only is the architecture designed with fewer security barriers, there is usually a lower staff-to-inmate ratio. Since fewer escape attempts and disturbances are expected, fewer security staff are required to supervise the population. When a prison is deemed a close- or maximum-custody institution, there will be more security staff per inmate and the prison design is such that disturbances can be contained in a small area. Escape is nearly impossible. The secure perimeter will often have more than one high fence with razor wire coiled at the bottom and up the side of the fence and topped off as well. The fences are frequently electrified and will contain detection devices to alert control room staff of any movement. In addition, the outside perimeter is patrolled by armed security staff that is in constant contact with the control room, and they will respond to all detected perimeter alerts.

Inmates at most levels of security have jobs that keep them busy on the prison grounds. Most labor in a prison is performed by inmates. Simple jobs such as mowing the grass, picking up trash, cleaning tables at the dining hall, or washing dishes are part of prisoners' daily routines. Skilled inmates may also paint, maintain plumbing and air conditioning, repair structural issues, and maintain prison vehicles. All jobs are supervised by security staff.

The Supermax

Most prisons have special housing units for disruptive inmates who pose disciplinary problems. Inmates will be placed in one of these units usually after an officer writes a **disciplinary report** describing the offense committed by the inmate. Often, these segregated areas are referred to as the **Special Housing Unit**, or the **SHU**, which is pronounced *shoe.* Inmates needing special housing due to assaultive behavior, escapes, escape attempts, inciting others, gang activity, and other categories of prohibited behavior may be reclassified to a higher custody level. In some states, such inmates will be reclassified to a supermaximum status. This is a management decision in response to an inmate's dangerous and disruptive behavior. The supermax facility may be special housing on the institutional grounds. The supermax that most have heard of is a separate facility designed and staffed exclusively for supermax inmates.

Disciplinary report
A written report describing the inappropriate behavior or the breaking of institutional rules by an inmate.

Special Housing Unit (SHU) Usually an area of confinement within a correctional facility designed to hold the more dangerous or violent inmates, those who are discipline problems, or those who need supervised protection from others.

The first supermax prison in this country was Alcatraz. Currently, the only freestanding federal supermax facility is the Administrative Maximum facility in Florence, Colorado, called by some "the Alcatraz of the Rockies." Better known as ADMAX, the prison opened in 1994 and has never incurred a successful escape. Here, the most dangerous and escape-prone long-term inmates live a strict lifestyle that is controlled by officers who operate the prison remotely so that staff/inmate contact is kept to a minimum. As of early 2011, ADMAX houses notorious prisoners such as terrorist Zacarias Moussaoui, Unabomber Theodore Kaczynski, Oklahoma bombing accomplice Terry Nichols, shoe bomber Richard Reid, and FBI agent turned Soviet spy Robert Hanssen.[69]

Many states have supermax facilities constructed on the grounds of existing facilities. There, those deemed the worst of the worst reside. These special housing units are closely monitored and movement is restricted. Inmates in these units are often kept in isolation and are escorted in chains whenever they leave their cells. The supermax inmate is often granted a few hours a week out of the cell for fresh air and exercise in a monitored cage. Even this privilege may be revoked based on the inmate's behavior. Because of the extreme restrictions, the supermax prison is considered by some to be a violation of the Eighth Amendment's prohibition on cruel and unusual punishment. Numerous lawsuits have been filed by inmates and human rights groups. The United Nations has even weighed in on the controversy surrounding supermax prisons, calling for guidelines concerning torture and cruel, inhuman, and degrading treatment and punishment. Specifically, practices such as solitary confinement, excessive use of restraints, and forced psychiatric interventions are viewed as violations by the United Nations.[70]

Current Notorious Prisons

Many prisons throughout history have achieved notoriety for one reason or another. Some have become famous for alleged human rights violations. The ADMAX prison in Colorado and its extreme conditions is an example of such infamy. Across the nation, other prisons have their own unique characteristics.

In California's Marin County, on 275 acres of valuable waterfront property, sits San Quentin Prison. Home to California's only gas chamber and death row, San Quentin is one of the nation's best-known prisons. It was constructed in 1852 by inmate labor, and inmates slept on a ship while the prison was built. With more than 5,000 inmates, San Quentin is one of the largest prisons in the nation. San Quentin's notoriety comes mostly from its legendary depictions in movies and in song. San Quentin has been home to many infamous criminals, such as Richard Ramirez, known as the Night Stalker; Charles Bolles, known as Black Bart; Eldridge Cleaver of the Black Panthers; Charles Manson; and Sirhan Sirhan, who assassinated Robert Kennedy.[71]

Sing Sing Prison in Ossining, New York, is where the phrases "the big house" and "up the river" originated in the American lexicon.[72] Over Sing Sing's nearly two-century existence, it gained notoriety for its historic brutal discipline such as beatings, extended solitary confinement, and withholding of food for even minor violations. Though it is now a fully modern and accredited facility, Sing Sing is legendary in American criminal lore. Famous inmates include Ethel and Julius Rosenberg and bank robber Willie Sutton.

New York is also home to Attica Correctional Facility. Attica gained notoriety in 1971 when a riot erupted in which 29 inmates and 10 correctional officers were killed.[73] By many accounts, among the many grievances that inmates suffered, racial issues seemed to be the touch point that sparked the riots. New York eventually settled with the families of those killed. Nearly $12 million went to the families of the inmates killed, and another $12 million went to the families of those officers who died.[74]

France is home to an especially notorious prison. In 2000, the *New York Times* published an expose about the La Santé prison in Paris. Dr. Veronique Vasseur began working at La Santé in the 1990s and was so shocked by the conditions that she began recording her experiences. Among the atrocities, she found high suicide rates, brutal guards, rapes, bug and rodent infestations, regular beatings, poor medical care, disease, and even the intentional placement of younger inmates in cells knowing they would be raped by men with AIDS.[75] Though conditions may have improved, La Santé can still be found on lists of the most brutal and deadly prisons of the world.

Tibet's Drapchi Prison easily ranks as one of the most notorious prisons on earth. At Drapchi, there are special units for male prisoners, female prisoners, criminals, and political prisoners. The official methods of controlling inmates include torture and other inhumane treatment. Some punishments include standing in the sun for extended periods without moving, running for lengthy times without stopping, and beatings. There are few medical services, especially for the political prisoners. The inmates' diet is poor and barely sustains life, and suicide rates are high. Human rights groups, protest groups, and even international organizations have tried to influence the conditions at Drapchi. However, the Communist regime in China prevents any serious outside investigation or interference. Most information about the prison is gained from former inmates and guards. Conditions are so atrocious that the United Nations Commission on Human Rights has tried, without success, to intervene.[76]

The Privatization of Prisons

Prisons are very expensive and labor-intensive operations. State governments dedicate tremendous amounts of taxpayer money to correctional systems, both publicly and privately owned. The costs of staffing and running a prison are unlikely to come down anytime soon, if ever. With constant court challenges and demands from the citizenry to improve conditions for prisoners, costs will only increase.[77]

A current movement to reduce costs is to contract out correctional responsibilities to private organizations. Private correctional organizations have contracted with governments at the federal, state, and local levels to assume responsibility for criminal custody and detention functions. There are many successful private correctional organizations operating profitably in the United States. Often, the private facility is paid on a per-inmate basis.

The incentive for governments to turn over correctional functions to private organizations usually involves cost savings for taxpayers. In 2001, the cost for operating state prisons, excluding the cost of the land and the infrastructure, was $100 per U.S. resident.[78] This was up more than 10% from only five years earlier. This trend for increasing expenditures on prisons, operating costs, and inmate expenses will likely continue.

These private companies often promise to deliver reduced costs per inmate and better conditions through cost-efficient construction, cost-efficient operations, and competitive incentives to provide high-quality services while keeping expenses low. This efficiency and competitiveness is expected to leave room for the organization to make a profit. The state governments also expect that the funds paid to the private organizations will be less than the costs of state-run correctional facilities. Some local governments hire private correctional organizations to operate jails as well.[79]

Opponents of privatization point to the many indirect costs for the taxpayer. These costs include contract administration, contract monitoring, and the additional government regulation required. The government also retains legal liability for contractor actions. This alone has the potential for tremendous amounts of taxpayer money to be paid out in legal expenses and for lost or settled lawsuits. Research indicates that these tangential expenses negate any savings expected from the privatization of correctional systems.[80]

On August 18, 2016, Deputy Attorney General Sally Yates, announced that she has instructed the Justice Department to end its use of private prisons. The Justice Department plans to end its use of private prisons after officials concluded the facilities are both less safe and less effective at providing correctional services than those run by the government. Yates stated that prison prisons do not provide the same level of correctional resources, programs, and services. Additionally, they do not save substantially on costs.[81]

While experts said the directive is significant, privately run federal prisons house only a fraction of the overall population of inmates. The vast majority of the incarcerated in America are housed in state prisons rather than federal ones and Yates' memo does not apply to any of those, even the ones that are privately run. Nor does it apply to Immigration and Customs Enforcement and U.S. Marshals Service detainees, who are technically in the federal system but not under the purview of the federal Bureau of Prisons.[81]

In 2013, Yates stated, the prison population began to decline because of efforts to adjust sentencing guidelines, sometimes retroactively, and to change the way low-level drug offenders are charged. She said the drop in federal inmates gave officials the opportunity to reevaluate the use of private prisons.

Yates wrote that private prisons "served an important role during a difficult time period," but they had proven less effective than facilities run by the government The Bureau of Prisons spent $639 million on private prisons in fiscal year 2014, according to the inspectors general's report. [81]

On February 23, 2017, President Donald Trump's administration reinstated the use of private prisons for federal inmates, saying commercial prison operators are needed for the correctional system's "future needs." Trump's new attorney general, Jeff Sessions, officially rescinded the Barack Obama administration's move last August to phase out the management of prisons by private companies, which Obama's justice department had said proved to be inadequate, more dangerous and not cheaper than government-run prisons. Sessions said in an order that the move last year had reversed a longstanding policy at the Federal Bureau of Prisons to have private companies involved, "and impaired the bureau's ability to meet the future needs of the federal correctional system."[82]

The Obama move had only affected a small portion of the US prison system: 13 privately run prisons housing just over 22,000 people, or about 11 percent of the federal prison population. Most are foreign nationals, mainly Mexicans incarcerated for immigration violations. The Trump government has promised a crackdown on crime and illegal immigration, suggesting the prisons bureau could require greater holding capacity in a short time. The 13 prisons are run by three companies: CoreCivic (known until recently as Corrections Corporation of America), GEO Group and Management, and Training Corporation. [82]

The criminal justice system consists of the police, the courts, and corrections. This system is an established government obligation, and some believe that no part of it can be severed from its foundation. Correctional systems traditionally are a government responsibility. The duty of the government to punish lawbreakers is confused when private organizations fulfill the correctional functions. Harvard political scientist John Dilulio is vocal with this view. He says, "It is precisely because corrections involves the deprivation of liberty, precisely because it involves the legally sanctioned exercise of coercion by some citizens over others, that it must remain wholly within public hands."[81]

A Brief History of Private Correctional Facilities

Modern private prisons appear to have originated from the convergence of two separate events. In the 1970s, the U.S. prison population began to expand somewhat rapidly. A decade later, under the leadership of President Ronald Reagan, the government began to look to the private sector for government solutions. These private-sector solutions were applied to the problem of rising prison populations.

The first known private prison in the United States was San Quentin Prison in California in the 1850s.[82] Even then, the basis for privatization was reduced costs. It was also assumed that there would be less corruption.[83] The first government award for local correctional services occurred in Hamilton County, Tennessee.[84] As of 2009, there were more than 25,000 federal prisoners in private facilities and more than 95,000 in privately operated state facilities.[85]

Correctional Corporations

Some of the largest private correctional corporations build, manage, and operate prisons with strict government oversight. The CCA claims the title of "America's Leader in Partnership Corrections." The corporation, established in the early 1980s, operates federal, state, and local correctional facilities around the nation. The CCA is a publicly traded corporation that operates about 50% of the private correctional facilities in the nation. This makes CCA the largest private correctional provider, with more than 17,000 employees. The organization also owns and operates TransCor America. TransCor provides inmate transportation services to correctional facilities that need to move inmates from one location to another.[86]

Private prisons have become a very profitable part of the prison-industrial complex. However, saving money for states and the federal government is still in question. A study by Vanderbilt University claims that states can save $13 million to $15 million by contracting out correctional services,[87] while a study by Cornell University demonstrates that the savings are accounting shifts.[88] Many states have taken notice, and those who do not yet use private correctional services are examining the possibility.

Privatization is often criticized because these private organizations may assume custody of healthy populations of inmates and lower-custody inmates. This reduces the costs to the private companies because there are fewer medical expenses and they need less secure facilities and fewer security staff to supervise the inmates. This leaves the more expensive populations, such as the violent, dangerous, elderly, and those with special medical needs, for the government facilities.

Major criticisms of prison privatization often come from criminologists who are convinced that privatization does not result in the promised savings. Comparing the actual costs of private prisons with those of state and federally operated institutions is complex and is often illusory. Cost analysis studies frequently return different results depending on what organization is conducting the study. In addition, the accounting methods and populations can be very different. Since there is no private prison that is exactly like a corresponding government prison, precise cost comparisons are nearly impossible.

To study this issue, in 2007, the National Institute of Justice brought together researchers, private service providers, government prison officials, and proponents and opponents of prison privatization. The study focused on two separate analyses of the same four prisons that produced different results.[89] The privatization study concluded that overhead costs and inmate population sizes were being measured differently between private and government prisons. It found that private prisons were only measuring direct costs—such as staffing, food, medical care, and other services—while government prisons were measuring both direct costs and indirect costs associated with planning, automation, computer services, and budget development. It was assumed that the government would continue to absorb the indirect costs even for those prisons operated by private organizations, thereby eliminating promised savings. The study concluded that, in order to obtain a more accurate measurement of the costs of privatization, these indirect costs should be included in the estimates for private prisons.[90]

The Hiring and Training of Correctional Officers

Correctional officers provide security and maintain accountability of inmates for detention centers, jails, and prisons. In detention centers, they may be known as detention officers, though *correctional officer* is the generally accepted universal term. The officer must always diligently work to prevent disturbances, assaults, and escapes.

In 2008, correctional officers and jailors accounted for approximately 454,500 jobs in the United States. Employment in this career is expected to increase 9% by 2018. However, cash-strapped prisons are also using technology to eliminate the staffed towers so prominent at many prisons.

In order to become a correctional officer, one must meet stringent standards. Federal and state requirements mandate that officers have a high school diploma or GED, and some governments require at least a bachelor's degree. Certain states and local governments will also accept military service in lieu of college credit. Others will also accept combinations of college, military, counseling, and supervisory experience.[91]

Recruit officers receive academy training that varies by state. The Federal Bureau of Prisons has its own recruit and training requirements.[92] The American Correctional Association and the American Jail

Career Connections: Correctional Officer

Correctional officers provide security, maintain order, and prevent escapes in detention facilities, jails, and prisons. Employers are state and local governments and private correctional services providers. All officers must be certified by their respective federal and state governments, and recruits must be trained by government-approved training facilities. Most require applicants to have at least a high school diploma, be at least 18 years old and of good character, and have a stable job history. In addition, the correctional officer candidate must not have an extensive or significant criminal history. Some agencies will accept minor violations such as a childhood minor theft incident or misdemeanor drug charges. However, they generally will not tolerate recent charges or allow current officers who commit crimes to remain employed.

The working conditions are sometimes harsh. A correctional officer must be able to perform all job functions in all weather conditions and in sometimes dirty or cramped environments. This occupation can be hazardous and stressful. Correctional officers have one of the highest non-fatal on-the-job occupational injury rates and face the risk of assault daily. Because correctional facilities operate around the clock, officers work at all times, including holidays and weekends. Correctional officers are often required to work overtime. Typically, because of the diverse populations, jails tend to be more dangerous facilities than are prisons. Prisons generally have populations that have been segregated based upon violent tendencies of inmates and have higher staff-to-inmate ratios. Therefore, in general, prisons are safer places to work than are jails.[95]

Association provide accrediting and certification services as well as guidelines for correctional officer training.[93] Officers also receive ongoing education and inservice training provided by their own organizations. Advanced training is also made available to those officers performing specialized functions such as K-9, emergency response teams, special weapons and munitions, and others.

The national occupational outlook for correctional officers is expected to increase by 48,000 between 2008 and 2018.[94] This means that the growth of this field is favorable to those seeking such careers. Mandatory sentencing in many states has increased the correctional inmate populations and, in turn, has increased the need for additional correctional officers. Should the trend for mandatory sentencing reverse, as is being considered in some states for budgetary reasons, the need for correctional officers may decline.

According to the Bureau of Labor Statistics (BLS), the outlook for correctional officers is favorable and is expected to increase by about 9% of current numbers by 2018. This means that an additional 48,000 officers will be needed based on 2008 figures. In 2010, the median salary of correctional officers was $39,040. Supervisors and managers can earn significantly more. The turnover for correctional officers appears to be about average for all occupations.

FIGURE 9.3 NATIONAL ESTIMATES FOR CORRECTIONAL OFFICERS

Percentile wage estimates for this occupation: May (2015)

Percentile	10%	25%	50% (Median)	75%	90%
Hourly Wage	$13.38	$15.84	$19.49	$26.79	$35.12
Annual Wage	$27,830	$32,960	$40,530	$55,720	$73,060

Source: Bureau of Labor Statistics. (2016). Correctional Officers and Jailers. Washington, D.C.: Author.

All officers in the United States are required to have at least a high school diploma. Some states may require some college or military experience. Local governments may have requirements in addition to what is required for an officer to be certified by the state. Federal prison officers are required to have at least a bachelor's degree or other acceptable work experience in lieu of the degree.

New officers receive academy training in subjects ranging from basic report writing to defensive tactics and weapons training. Federal officers receive training at the Federal Law Enforcement Training Center (FLETC) in Glynco, Georgia. Officers also receive ongoing inservice training and specialized training for those on special teams such as K-9 and emergency response. Both female and male officers receive the same training and must meet the same standards. It has been found that female correctional officers may be especially well suited to defuse potentially violent situations in the early stages.[96]

FIGURE 9.4 NATIONAL ESTIMATES FOR CORRECTIONAL OFFICERS: AS OF MAY 2015

States with the highest employment level in this occupation:

State	Employment	Employment per thousand jobs	Hourly mean wage	Annual mean wage
Texas	48,280	4.17	$18.37	$38,210
California	34,640	2.24	$33.19	$69,040
New York	34,140	3.80	$29.41	$61,160
Florida	34,470	4.35	$20.83	$43,330
Georgia	16,710	4.07	$14.26	$29,650

Source: Bureau of Labor Statistics. (2016). Correctional Officers and Jailers. Washington, D.C.: Author.

Most states have public service unions, and correctional officers are often represented by collective bargaining organizations. There are arguments both for and against correctional officer unions. However, unions have a very strong presence, and they negotiate with governments and private correctional organizations for higher wages and increased benefits for members. Contracts also define working conditions and promotional guidelines. In states that do not require union membership as a condition of employment, officers who are not members will still be recipients of most negotiated benefits, just like those officers who are members and who pay union dues.[97]

Career Connections: Correctional Officer

Should correctional officers be considered professionals or simply skilled workers?

Ethics and Professionalism

The warden at a major corrections institution has several correctional officer positions he needs to fill. He has more than enough applications because the poor economy has left many people looking for work. As he peruses the applications, he ponders what kind of applicant would best serve the mission of the department.

He has many tools at his disposal, including the usual background checks, psychological exams, and truth detection technologies. However, the warden wants to upgrade the professionalism in his ranks. He contemplates tests such as career aptitude inventories, aggressiveness profiles, and ethical assessments. He also wishes to narrow his selection to those with at least some college experience.

Do you believe that he would get a better-quality officer using these recruitment tools? If the warden uses these new tests, how might the hiring decisions he makes differ from his hiring decisions of the past? Why are ethics important for new officers? Are college-educated officers necessarily better officers?

Chapter Summary

- Detention has been an acceptable method of punishment for criminal offenders for only a few hundred years. In early American history, jails were used primarily to hold for trial those who could not make bail or those who were unable to pay debts. The living conditions in these early jails were cruel and immoral. Men, women, and children of all ages were thrown together in undisciplined and poorly supervised micro-communities where the strong overpowered the weak. There was little medical treatment and most were poorly fed. Early prisons around the world included the Mamertine Prison as well as fortresses, hulks, workhouses, and Bridewells.

- Early techniques to punish criminals date back to the ancient Sumerians and Babylonians and included whipping, servitude, mutilation, and death. Over the centuries, thanks to reformers such as Montesquieu, John Howard, Cesare Beccaria, Jeremy Bentham, Alexis de Tocqueville, and Gustave de Beaumont, human dignity and life became increasingly valued. In most of the industrialized world, prisoners are treated immensely better than in the past. Though prisons are oppressive places and provide for an onerous existence, most countries at least provide prisoners a survivable diet, some medical care, human contact, and some form of classification that separates juveniles from adults and men from women. The Walnut Street Jail in Philadelphia was one of the first to institute reforms.
- Modern correctional facilities exist at the local, state, and federal levels. Jails are multipurpose facilities operated by local governments or sheriffs and are usually the offender's first contact with the criminal justice system. Prisons are operated by the states and the federal government and usually house offenders who are serving a sentence of more than one year. All correctional facilities have their own missions and roles in criminal justice. Some are old and outdated, and others are modern and very secure. Many have inmate amenities for recreation, education, and training. All have access to medical care. There are also different levels of security, ranging from minimum security to the supermaximum prisons.
- When an inmate is received into most state prison systems, he or she will be processed through a classification system. Classification of inmates simply is a means to fit an inmate into a specific category of custody level, medical needs, predisposition to violence or escape, training and educational needs, and other categories as determined by state statute. This classification procedure will determine primarily which security level the inmate requires. The inmate will be assigned to a state prison facility that fits his or her characteristics.
- Most prisons have special housing units for disruptive inmates who pose disciplinary problems. Inmates needing special housing for assaultive behavior, escapes, escape attempts, inciting others, gang activity, and other categories of prohibited behavior may be reclassified to a higher custody level. In some states, such inmates will be reclassified to a supermaximum status. The supermax facility may be special housing on the institutional grounds or a separate facility for particularly dangerous offenders.
- A current movement to reduce costs is to contract out correctional responsibilities to private organizations. These private companies often promise and may deliver reduced costs per inmate and better conditions through cost-efficient construction, cost-efficient

operations, and competitive incentives to provide high-quality services while keeping expenses low. This efficiency and competitiveness is expected to leave room for the organization to make a profit. Privatization is a topic of controversy; while some studies indicate that private prisons save money for states and the federal government, critics believes privatization has not led to the anticipated savings. Studies have noted irregularities in measurements of costs between private prisons and government prisons.

- In order to become a correctional officer, one must meet stringent standards. Federal and state requirements mandate that one have a high school diploma or GED, and some require at least a bachelor's degree. Some state and local governments will also accept military service in lieu of college credit. Others will also accept combinations of college, military, counseling, and supervisory experience.

Critical Thinking?

1. Why was the Eighth Amendment's prohibition on cruel and unusual punishment incorporated into the Bill of Rights?
2. Is there a difference between the U.S. Constitution's prohibition on cruel and unusual punishment and several state constitutional prohibitions on cruel or unusual punishment?
3. Could supermax prisons be considered cruel and unusual? Could they be considered cruel but not unusual? Or unusual but not cruel?
4. Some people are sent to prison for very long periods, even for life. Do you feel this is a good public expenditure of taxes, or is there a better way to deal with those who violate laws?
5. In 1986, Congress enacted legislation that sentenced offenders differently for possessing different forms of cocaine. Possession of five grams of crack cocaine results in a minimum sentence of five years in federal prison. It takes nearly 100 times that amount in powdered cocaine to receive a comparable sentence. Crack cocaine is found heavily in African-American communities, while powdered cocaine is found primarily in white areas. Is there an issue with disparity in sentencing or is this fair?
6. Civil rights restoration for inmates returning to open society is becoming increasingly popular. What civil rights should be restored and which, if any, should not?
7. With all of the security measures in place, how is it possible that drugs, weapons, and other contraband manage to get into prisons and into prisoners' possession?
8. Since many inmates are able to function well in work release centers and halfway houses, is it a good idea to simply release these inmates to cut down on costs?

9. Do privately owned correctional facilities provide the same services as government-run facilities? Is there any difference as far as criminal justice is concerned?
10. Is the money spent on jails and prisons justified? Is there a better way to punish criminals than by imprisoning them?

Media

Federal Bureau of Prisons: http://www.bop.gov/ This website contains much information about the correctional system, its history, and references for further reading.

Bureau of Justice Statistics: http://www.bjs.gov/ This government website contains official statistics for all areas of law enforcement.

National Institute of Justice Multimedia: http://www.ojp.usdoj.gov/nij/journals/media.htm This website contains multimedia from the National Institute of Justice.

Occupational Employment Statistics, Correctional Officer: http://www.bls.gov/oes/current/oes333012.htm. This is the official government website for statistics that may be of interest to those wishing to become correctional officers.

Endnotes

1 JTF-GTMO. (2011). *Overview: Joint Task Force Guantanamo.* Retrieved from http://www.jtfgtmo.southcom.mil/index/Fact%20Sheets/GTMO%20Overview.pdf

2 U.S. Department of Defense (DOD). (2011). *Combatant Status Review Tribunal Summary.* Retrieved from http://www.defense.gov/news/csrtsummary.pdf

3 JTF-GTMO, 2011.

4 Congressional Research Service. (2009). *Closing the Guantanamo Detention Center: Legal Issues.* Retrieved from http://www.henrywaxman.house.gov/UploadedFiles/R40139.pdf

5 Human Rights Watch. (2008). *Locked Up Alone: Detention Conditions and Mental Health at Guantanamo.* Retrieved from http://www.defense.gov/pubs/pdfs/App7.pdf

6 Ibid.

7 Wilner, T, & Worthington, A. Close Guantanamo. *Prisoners.* Retrieved from http://www.closeguantanamo.org/Prisoners

7 Friedman, L. (1993). *Crime and Punishment in American History.* New York, NY: Basic Books.

8 Ibid., 50.

9 American Archives. (1776). *Constitution of Pennsylvania*. Retrieved from http://lincoln.lib.niu.edu/cgi-bin/ amarch/getdoc.pl?/var/lib/philologic/databases/amarch/.22309

10 King, L. W. (1997). *Hammurabi's Code*. Retrieved from http://eawc.evansville.edu/index.htm

11 International World History Project. (n.d.). *A History of Ancient Greece: Draco and Solon Laws*. Retrieved from http://history-world.org/draco_and_solon_laws.htm

12 Halsall, P. (1998). "Ancient History Sourcebook: Code of Hammurabi, c. 1780 BCE." *Fordham University*. Retrieved from http://www.fordham.edu/halsall/ancient/hamcode.html

13 Roman Colosseum. (2008). *Roman Punishment*. Retrieved from http://www.roman-colosseum.info/roman-life/ roman-punishment.htm

14 *Capital Punishment*. (2000). Retrieved from http://autocww.colorado.edu/~toldy2/E64ContentFiles/Law AndCourts/CapitalPunishment.html

15 Alasti, S. (2007). *Comparative Study of Stoning Punishment in the Religions of Islam and Judaism*. Retrieved from http://ggu.academia.edu/SanazAlasti/Papers/195679/Comparative_Study_of_Stoning_Punishments_In_the_Religions_of_Islam_and_Judaism

16 "Guillotine." (2011). *Britannica Online Encyclopedia*. Retrieved from http://www.britannica.com/EBchecked/topic/248765/guillotine

17 Friedman, 1993, 42.

18 Ekirch, R. (1987). *Bound for America: The Transportation of British Convicts to the Colonies*. New York, NY: Oxford University Press.

19 Montgomery, R. (1998). *A History of Correctional Violence*. American Correctional Association.

20 Halsall, P. (1997). "Modern History Sourcebook: Montesquieu: The Spirit of the Laws, 1748." *Fordham University*. Retrieved from http://www.fordham.edu/halsall/mod/montesquieu-spirit.html

21 Ibid.

22 Hay, G. (2011). "Biography of John Howard." *The John Howard Society of Canada*. Retrieved from http://www.johnhoward.ca/about/biography

23 Ibid.

24 Ibid.

25 Beccaria, C. (1764). *Of Crimes and Punishments*. Retrieved from http://www.constitution.org/cb/crim_pun.htm

26 Ibid.

27 Bentham, J. (1789). "An Introduction to the Principles of Morals and Legislation." *Library of Economics and Liberty*. Retrieved from http://www.econlib.org/library/Bentham/bnthPML1.html#Chapter%20I,%20Of%20the%20 Principle%20of%20Utility

28 De Tocqueville, A. (n.d.). *Democracy in America*. Retrieved from http://xroads.virginia.edu/~HYPER/DETOC/home.html

29 Ibid.

30 Ibid.

31 Hassett, M. (1910). "Mamertine Prison." *The Catholic Encyclopedia*. Retrieved from http://www.newadvent.org/cathen/09579a.htm

32 *The Carcer—Mamertine Prison*. (n.d.). Retrieved from http://www.mmdtkw.org/VCarcer.html

33 Salvi, S. (2011). *The Original List of Sanctuary Cities, USA*. Retrieved from http://www.ojjpac.org/sanctuary.asp

34 Historic Royal Palaces. (2011). *Tower of London*. Retrieved from http://www.hrp.org.uk/TowerOfLondon/stories.aspx

35 Morris, S. (2005). "Britain's Only Prison Ship Ends Up on the Beach." *The Guardian*. Retrieved from http://www.guardian.co.uk/uk/2005/aug/12/ukcrime.prisonsandprobation

36 Ibid.

37 Independence National Historical Park. (2007). *Following in Franklin's Footsteps*. Retrieved from http://www. independenceparkinstitute.com/FranklinDropInPacket6-26-07.pdf

38 Johnston, N. (2000). "Prison Reform in Pennsylvania." *The Pennsylvania Prison Society*. Retrieved from http://www.prisonsociety.org/about/history.shtml

39 Ibid.

40 Stohr, M., Walsh, A., & Hemmens, C. (2009). *Corrections, a Text Reader*. Thousand Oaks, CA: Sage.

41 Ibid.

42 Northstar Gallery. (n.d.). *Eastern State Penitentiary*. http://northstargallery.com/esp/easternstatehistory01.htm

43 Friedman, 1993, 79.

44 Ibid., 79–80.

45 National Park Service. (2011). "Alcatraz Island: History & Culture." *NPS.gov*. Retrieved from http://www.nps.gov/alca/historyculture/index.htm

46 Ibid.

47 Overthrow Arpaio. (2009). *Top Ten Reasons to Recall Joe*. Retrieved from http://www.arpaio.com/top-ten/index.php#9 *Maricopa County Sheriff's Office*. (2011). Retrieved from http://www.mcso.org

48 *Overthrow Arpaio*. (2009). Retrieved from http://www.arpaio.com

49 Lacy, M. (2010, September 2). "Justice Dept. Sues Sheriff Over Bias Investigation." *New York Times*. http://www.nytimes.com/2010/09/03/us/03sheriff.html Wingett, Y., Hensley, J. J., & Kiefer, M. (2010, September 3). "Sheriff Joe Arpaio Sued by Justice Department in Civil-Rights Probe." *AZCentral.com*. Retrieved from http://www.azcentral.com/news/election/azelections/articles/2010/09/02/20100902joe-arpaio-sued-by-justice-department-brk-02-ON.html

50 Rangel, C. (2011, May 13). "YOUR Tax Dollars: How Much Does It Cost to Defend the Maricopa County Sheriff's Office?" *ABC15.com*. Retrieved from http://www.abc15.com/dpp/news/local_news/investigations/your-tax-dollars-being-spent-to-fight-sheriff-joe-arpaio%E2%80%99s-lawsuits

51 Bureau of Justice Statistics. (2011). *Key Facts at a Glance: Correctional Populations*. Retrieved from http://bjs.ojp.usdoj.gov/content/glance/tables/corr2tab.cfm

52 *Estelle v. Gamble*, 429 U.S. 97 (1976).

53 National Commission on Correctional Health Care. http://www.ncchc.org/index.html

54 *Bounds v. Smith*, 430 U.S. 817 (1977).

55 *Younger v. Gilmore*, 404 U.S. 15 (1971).

56 *Bounds v. Smith*, 1977.

57 *Lewis v. Casey*, 518 U.S. 343 (1996).

58 Ibid.

59 Stanford Encyclopedia of Philosophy. (2008). *Legal Punishment.* Retrieved from http://plato.stanford.edu/entries/legal-punishment/

60 Ibid.

61 Ibid.

62 Ibid.

63 Ibid.

64 *Wolff v. McDonnell*, 418 U.S. 539 (1974).

65 Council of State Governments Justice Center. (2011). *Reentry Policy Council.* Retrieved from http://reentrypolicy.org

66 United States Attorney's Office, District of Minnesota. (2009). *Federal Criminal Prosecution.* Retrieved from http://www.justice.gov/usao/mn/downloads/federal%20criminal%20brochure.2009.final.pdf

67 *U.S. v. Lanza*, 260 U.S. 377 (1922).

68 Tibbs, D. (2006). "Peeking Behind the Iron Curtain: How Law 'Works' Behind Prison Walls." *Southern California Interdisciplinary Law Journal, 16*, 137-182. Retrieved from http://www-bcf.usc.edu/~idjlaw/PDF/16-1/16-1%20Tibbs.pdf
Bureau of Justice Statistics. (n.d.). *Prison Rule Violators.* Retrieved from http://bjs.ojp.usdoj.gov/index.cfm?ty=gsearch

69 Federal Bureau of Prisons. (2011). *Inmate Locator.* Retrieved from http://www.bop.gov/iloc2/LocateInmate.jsp

70 U.S. Department of Justice, National Institute of Corrections. (1999). *Supermax Prisons: Overview and General Considerations.* Retrieved from http://static.nicic.gov/Library/014937.pdf
United Nations. (2008). *Torture and other Cruel, Inhuman or Degrading Treatment or Punishment.* Retrieved from http://www.un.org/disabilities/images/A.63.175.doc
For a cost analysis, see Lawrence, S., & Mears, D. (2004). *Benefit-Cost Analysis of Supermax Prisons.* Retrieved from http://www.hawaii.edu/hivandaids/Benefit-Cost_Analysis_of_Supermax_Prisons.pdf

71 California Department of Corrections and Rehabilitation. (2011). *Adult Facilities Locator: San Quentin State Prison.* Retrieved from http://www.cdcr.ca.gov/Facilities_Locator/SQ-Institution_Stats.html

72 Investigation Discovery. (2011). *Notorious Prisons: Sing Sing Correctional Facility.* Retrieved from http://investigation. discovery.com/investigation/notorious-prisons/sing-sing/sing-sing.html

New York Correction History Society. (n.d.). *Images of America: Sing Sing Prison*. Retrieved from http://www. correctionhistory.org/html/chronicl/state/singsing/cheliindex.html
For further reading and a firsthand account by a Sing Sing correctional officer, see Conover, T. (2000). *Newjack: Guarding Sing Sing*. New York, NY: Random House.

73 Jackson, B. (1999). "Attica: An Anniversary of Death." *Artvoice*. Retrieved from http://www.acsu.buffalo.edu/~bjackson/attica.htm
Libcom.org. (2006). *1971: The Attica Prison Uprising*. Retrieved from http://libcom.org/history/1971-the-attica-prison-uprising
National Geographic. (n.d.). *The Final Report: Attica* [Video]. Retrieved from http://channel.nationalgeographic.com/series/final-report/3418/Videos#tab-Videos/05524_00

74 Ibid.

75 Daley, S. (2000, January 28). "Expose of Brutal Prison Jolts France's Self-Image." *New York Times*. Retrieved from http://www.nytimes.com/2000/01/28/world/expose-of-brutal-prison-jolts-france-s-self-image.html

76 Tibetan Center for Human Rights and Democracy. (n.d.). *Drapchi Prison: Tibet's Most Dreaded Prison*. Retrieved from http://www.tchrd.org/publications/topical_reports/drapchi_prison-2001/
News Blaze. (2011, January 5). *Tibetan Political Prisoner Tortured After Speaking To UN*. Retrieved from http:// newsblaze.com/story/20110105080436zzzz.nb/topstory.html

77 Bureau of Justice Statistics. (2004). *State Prison Expenditures, 2001* (NCJ 2020949). Retrieved from http://bjs.ojp.usdoj.gov/content/pub/ascii/spe01.txt

78 Ibid.

79 Austin, J., & Coventry, G. (2001). *Emerging Issues on Privatized Prisons* (NCJ 181249). Retrieved from https://www.ncjrs.gov/pdffiles1/bja/181249.pdf

80 Ibid.

81 Zapotosky, M. & Harlan, C. (2016). *Justice Department says it will end use of private prisons*. The Washington Post. Retrieved from https://www.washingtonpost.com/news/post-nation/wp/2016/08/18/justice-department-says-it-will-end-use-of-private-prisons/?utm_term=.3f800e3ce23f

82 **NDTV.** (2017, February 23). *Donald Trump Reverses Barack Obama Ban On Private Prisons*. Retrieved from http://www.ndtv.com/world-news/donald-trump-reverses-barack-obama-ban-on-private-prisons-1662943.

81 Dilulio, J. J. (1986). "Prisons, Profits, and the Public Good: The Privatization of Corrections." *Research Bulletin No. 1*. Huntsville, TX: Sam Houston State University Criminal Justice Center.

82 Austin & Coventry, 2001.

83 Ibid.

84 *Privatization of Prisons*. (2008). Retrieved from http://privatizationofprisons.com

85 Bureau of Justice Statistics. (2009). *Correctional Populations in the United States, 2009*. Retrieved from http://bjs.ojp.usdoj.gov/content/pub/pdf/cpus09.pdf

86 Corrections Corporation of America. (2011). *CCA*. Retrieved from http://www.cca.com/

87 Blumstein, J., Cohen, M. A., & Seth, S. (2007). "Do Government Agencies Respond to Market Pressures? Evidence from Private Prisons." *Social Science Research Network*. Retrieved from http://papers.ssrn.com/sol3/papers.cfm?abstract_id=441007

88 McFarland, S., McGowan, C., & O'Toole, T. (2002). *Prisons, Privatization, and Public Values*. Retrieved from http://government.cce.cornell.edu/doc/html/PrisonsPrivatization.htm#_Opponents_of_Privatization:

89 Gaes, G. (2008). "Cost, Performance Studies Look at Prison Privatization." *NJJ Journal, 259*. Retrieved from http://www.nij.gov/journals/259/prison-privatization.htm

90 Ibid.

91 Bureau of Labor Statistics. (2010). *Occupational Outlook Handbook, 2010–2011 Edition: Correctional Officers*. Retrieved from http://www.bls.gov/oco/ocos156.htm

92 Ibid.

93 Ibid.

94 Ibid.

95 Cheeseman, K. A., & Worley, R. (2006). "Women on the Wing: Inmate Perceptions about Female Correctional Officer Job Competency in a Southern Prison System." *Southwest Journal of Criminal Justice, 3*(2), 86–102. Retrieved from http://www.utsa.edu/swjcj/archives/3.2/CheesemanWorley.pdf

96 Ibid.

97 Greenhouse, S. (2011, January 3). "Strained States Turning to Laws to Curb Labor Unions." *New York Times*. Retrieved from http://www.nytimes.com/2011/01/04/business/04labor.html
*Worthington, A. Close Guantanamo. Retrieved from http://www.closeguantanamo.org/Prisoners

© Normana Karia/Shutterstock.com

CHAPTER 10

Prison Life

KEY TERMS

Day fine
Day reporting center
Deprivation
Doing time
Halfway house
Importation
Indigenous model
Inmate code
Outlaw motorcycle gangs
Pains of imprisonment
Principle of least eligibility
Prison gangs
Prisonization
Street gangs
Total institution

CHAPTER OBJECTIVES

1. Discuss correctional facilities as total institutions.
2. Understand the roles of both inmate and officer subcultures behind institutional walls.
3. Discuss the implications of relying on incarceration and other corrections-based responses to crime.
4. Discuss the economic realities of incarcerating persons in the United States.
5. Define the various forms of community-based alternatives available.

Case Study: Richard Speck

On July 13, 1966, the city of Chicago was shaken by the methodical torture, rape, and murder of eight nurses from the South Chicago Community Hospital. One victim survived the attack, and she was later able to provide a detailed description of her assailant. A few days later, 24-year-old Richard Speck saw his likeness and description in a local newspaper. Speck then attempted suicide by slashing his wrists.[1] Apparently, his desire to die was overcome by his will to live, because he called authorities for help.

The police did not realize whom they were assisting as Speck was taken to the hospital. It was not until a doctor noticed the identifying tattoos and compared him to photographs in the newspaper that his identity was known. He was then arrested. Speck was eventually tried and convicted of all eight murders and was sentenced to death.[2] Fortunately for Speck, the United States Supreme Court abolished the death penalty in 1972.[3] His death sentence was subsequently set at consecutive life sentences.

Speck had a lurid history of abuse toward women along with accusations of murder. His abhorrent behavior continued behind the institutional walls at Statesville (Illinois) Correctional Center; his escapades in prison were infamous. While incarcerated, he was included in a study by the Federal Bureau of Investigation Behavioral Science Unit (BSU), which was collecting information to develop a profile of mass murderers.[4]

A homemade video Speck made while in prison that leaked following his death in 1991 from a heart attack showed him having sex with another inmate, waving around $100 bills, and ingesting cocaine. He further bragged about the "good" time he was having while incarcerated. The leaking of this video launched an investigation into the Illinois Department of Corrections.[5] Because the tape had been made years earlier, it was too late to bring any criminal charges; however, the Illinois prison system was prompted to make changes in their operations as a result.

The Richard Speck case is an extraordinary example of life inside prison. Though certainly not a typical representation, it is not particularly shocking to those who have studied and worked in high-security facilities. The appalling aspects of the Speck video are the lack of security and the apparent cooperation of the security staff that allowed the taping session to take place. This experience and countless others worldwide have contributed to the development of modern correctional principles. This chapter examines the prison existence and the way of life for those who reside in prison.

Prison Culture

Charles Dickens, in *A Walk in a Workhouse*, wrote, "We have come to this absurd, this dangerous, this monstrous pass, that the dishonest felon is, in respect of cleanliness, order, diet, and accommodation, better provided for, and taken care of, than the honest pauper."[6] This is understood to mean that the living conditions of the criminal in the workhouse should be no better than that of the poorest laborer outside of the workhouse.

Early English law attempted to uphold this rule. An early English statute, the Poor Law Amendment Act of 1834 (PLAA)[7], first codified the **principle of least eligibility**. The principle simply means that the conditions provided (in this case, for the poor) by the government should not be better than the existence of the poorest member of society. Only the truly destitute would qualify for aid under the PLAA. This limitation was meant to discourage those who would simply take advantage of the public generosity.

Principle of least eligibility The view that those who commit crimes, particularly those in prison, are the least deserving members of society to benefit from government-provided assistance and support, such as education, vocational training, and other forms of support.

The principle of least eligibility has long been society's attitude for those who have been duly incarcerated. Edward Sieh suggests that if imprisonment is to act as a deterrent, then those in the lowest socioeconomic class should lead a better existence than those imprisoned.[8] The attitude that prison should present a harsh existence clashes with many who feel that the imprisoned are treated inhumanely at worst and indifferently at best. Some further believe that the treatment of America's prison and jail populations is unconstitutional.

Indeed, the federal government, along with most state and countless local authorities, has been under court order to improve conditions in prisons and jails.[9] Numerous cases brought before the Supreme Court have challenged the conditions of incarceration, arguing that deprivation of certain liberties constitutes cruel and unusual punishment. One notable case, *Pell v. Procunier* (1974), outlined a benchmark for prisoners' rights, establishing that each inmate "retains those First Amendment rights that are not inconsistent with his status as a prisoner."[10] Two years later, *Estelle v. Gamble* (1976) clarified that prison officials have a responsibility to provide medical care to prisoners because "deliberate indifference" to prisoners' medical needs was a violation of constitutional rights.[11] The concept of "deliberate indifference" has become something of a baseline in determining which prison conditions are deemed unconstitutional and which are legal forms of punishment.

The Supreme Court has ruled on countless issues related to prison policies and prisoners' rights, further delineating which practices are considered acceptable. Some of these rulings have sided with prison policies, such as *Procunier v. Martinez* (1974), which affirmed that prison staff can monitor inmates' mail for security purposes,[12] and *Block v. Rutherford* (1984), which upheld a Los Angeles prison's policy of denying prisoners any outside visitors.[13] Additionally, cases such as *Hudson v. Palmer* (1984) ruled that prisoners do not have a right to privacy and can be subjected to searches.[14] By contrast, other Supreme Court rulings have established prisoners' freedoms, such as *Cruz v. Beto* (1972), which gave inmates the opportunity to pursue their religious faith,[15] and *Wolf v. McDonnell* (1974), which stated that appropriate due process must be followed before sanctions can be levied on a prisoner.[16]

Critical Thinking

Should prisoners have a living standard while incarcerated that exceeds that of the poorest in our society? Should they have better medical care? Should they have better recreation? Should they have better food? Stated differently, should the poorest of the honest citizens have better living conditions than convicted felons in prison?

Exhibit: *Estelle v. Gamble*

"An inmate must rely on prison authorities to treat his medical needs; if the authorities fail to do so, those needs will not be met. In the worst cases, such a failure may actually produce physical 'torture or a lingering death,' ... In less serious cases, denial of medical care may result in pain and suffering which no one suggests would serve any penological purpose. . . .

"We therefore conclude that deliberate indifference to serious medical needs of prisoners constitutes the 'unnecessary and wanton infliction of pain,' . . . This is true whether the indifference is manifested by prison doctors in their response to the prisoner's needs or by prison guards in intentionally denying or delaying access to medical care or intentionally interfering with the treatment once prescribed."

Adjusting to Prison Life

When a convicted criminal is first incarcerated, he or she often undergoes a painful adjustment to prison. These experiences were dubbed the "pains of imprisonment" by sociologist Gresham Sykes, who in 1958 published *The Society of Captives*, his study of prison life at the New Jersey State Prison. His work is still considered one of the most important criminological studies conducted, and it laid the foundation for subsequent studies on the effects that prisons have on both inmates and staff.

Sykes explains that the **pains of imprisonment** on a person's personality, though less obvious than physical injuries, are "no less fearful."[17] These pains develop from those deprivations and frustrations that are felt by those who must suffer this threat to self-esteem and personal security. Sykes further notes that this loss of freedom, a scarcity of goods and services, the loss of domestic relationships, and so on, may be acceptable and unavoidable for those imprisoned, but the effects on the inmate must be recognized as serious, just as are physical punishments.[18]

Pains of imprisonment Described by Gresham Sykes as the pains that develop from the deprivations and frustrations of those who are incarcerated.

The **deprivation** of liberty, or loss of freedom, is the most obvious of the painful conditions of imprisonment.[19] In a prison, inmates are restricted to their assigned living space, most likely a cell. Sociologist Erving Goffman described prisons as **total institutions**.[20] The prison as a total institution defines the inmate and his or her entire life. Interaction with the world outside of the institution is tightly controlled, and perhaps nonexistent. For the incarcerated, other people have arranged their lives and the inmate must follow the same general routine that the other inmates are required to follow. The inmate's freedom to make choices is limited to what the institution allows.[21] Here, a new cultural and social world develops. Discipline is tightly controlled and rules are abundant. Punishment for infractions is usually swift and more severe than it is for similar violations in open society. Every aspect of the inmate's life is closely monitored, and privacy is minimal. Movement throughout the institution is tightly regulated by a system of permissions, passes, and standardized orderliness. In a total institution, human needs for the entire group are controlled by a bureaucracy.[22]

Deprivation Described in Sykes's "pains of imprisonment" as loss of freedom, a scarcity of goods and services, and the loss of domestic relationships for inmates.

Total institution An institution that provides everything a person needs for survival, usually at a lower level than what is enjoyed in an open society.

Additionally, the act of imprisonment represents the rejection of the individual from the free society. The inmate (and eventually, the former inmate) has sacrificed his or her status as a trusted member of society. There are certain rights that the inmate will find it difficult or impossible to regain, such as the right to vote, to hold political office, and to obtain certain employment. Sykes suggests that, in order for convicts to endure psychologically, they must find some method of "rejecting [their] rejectors."[23]

© Aerovista Luchtfotografie/ Shutterstock.com

The total institution is a fully self-contained community that provides all required needs and services to its residents.

The deprivation of goods and services, too, is outlined by Sykes as a pain of imprisonment.[24] Attempts to compare the free world with prison are difficult. In prison, the inmate exists in a threadbare environment. Even the floor is usually only bare concrete. The inmate has very few possessions; Bruce Hood, director of the Bristol Cognitive Development

Center in Bristol, England, maintains that prisons remove all belongings deliberately in order to eradicate inmates' sense of self.[25] Goffman describes what happens to an inmate when first introduced to the total institution as a stripping process. This process is one that mortifies, humiliates, degrades, and crushes the self-identity of the new inhabitant. The inmate is stripped of personal physical property that is placed in an area of inaccessible storage. The new inmate will then receive replacement property, such as a prison uniform, that defines his or her new self as an inmate. The effects of this experience are further compounded as the inmate witnesses the mortification process of fellow inmates.[26]

Though basic needs such as food, medical care, and dry living areas are provided, all these resources are strictly supervised and scheduled. An established square footage of living space, defined amounts of calories per day, and scheduled opportunities for exercise and recreation must be considered deprivations from what one is accustomed to in the free world. Though some may claim that the inmate is provided all that is necessary, inmates will define their "material impoverishment" as a painful loss.[27]

Another of Sykes's pains of imprisonment is the deprivation of autonomy. Autonomy, which means one's self-government or self-directing freedom and moral independence,[28] is effectively removed from the inmate through rules and orders that control the inmate's every movement.[29] Every aspect of an inmate's life is regulated. Even the inmate's personal mail may be read by prison staff looking for statements of which the organization does not approve. Moreover, sleeping hours, eating times, and the exact routes taken to different areas of the institution are strictly controlled.

Inmates often express frustration with certain rules, viewing them as nonsensical authoritarian acts on the part of the prison. Inmates may be prohibited from removing anything from the dining hall, even an item such as a packet of sugar that may simply have gone in the trash. Many prisons require that inmates walk down a small painted-off section of the sidewalk while the larger part is reserved for officers and staff. Inmates may also be required to maintain uniform short haircuts and to shave every day. Rules are often enforced without explanation. An inmate may be denied parole one day and told that mail has been delayed another, but rarely given reasons. Moreover, an inmate who demands justification is viewed as a troublemaker and will be treated as such.

This indifference and lack of concern are often institutional policy. The worry is that if prison staff explains the enforcement of the rules to inmates, the inmates may find the explanations unsatisfactory and will begin challenging the situation and arguing with captors. This could then disrupt the power relationship that prison staff must maintain over inmates.[30] This denial of their ability to make choices and the denial of rule and order explanations have profound effects on inmates' psyches. They are rendered helpless, weak, and dependent. The normal self-determining individual has lost his or her autonomy and must somehow develop a method to cope.[31]

Indeed, under Goffman's total institution concept, facilities such as prisons and jails, which protect society from those who are deliberate dangers, present a major division between those who live there and those who work there. This partitioning between staff and inmate is of necessary intent, as they share common sociological worlds with one another. The two sides must spend considerable time together, and each views the other with a great deal of disdain and distrust.[32]

John Irwin, a noted criminologist who himself was incarcerated for an armed robbery in the 1950s, states, "The human density and total lack of privacy expose them to one another in ways that can occur only in total institutions."[33] Everyone witnesses each other's most private activities and habits because the prisoner in a total institution no longer has the privacy once taken for granted.[34]

Irwin notes that the "functionaries" of the criminal justice system, officers and others, contribute to the degradation felt by prisoners because they openly express contempt and hostility toward them.[35] Inmates may view staff as mean and condescending. Staff often views inmates as untrustworthy and secretive. This divide is usually quite wide by design, and even the tones of voice used for communication between the groups are different. Security staff tends to speak to inmates in a firm and commanding tone, while inmates speak to staff in a tone of deference and respect, even if not genuine. Staff members tend to feel superior and inmates, in some ways, feel inferior.[36]

In the total institution, sociological roles are somewhat different from such roles in open society. In an open society, and in the case of the prison staff, people usually work for a particular reward, most often to be paid for their contributions. In a prison, inmates will work not for reward, but from threat of severe punishment if they do not. Another confusion of roles is that of family. The inmate cannot sustain a family existence in the customary sense. Of course, a staff member leaves at the end of a shift and returns to his or her family.[37] This widens the divide even further between the actors in this total institution.

The last of Sykes's pains of imprisonment is the deprivation of security that an inmate must endure. Sykes believes it is strange that society chooses to reduce criminal behavior in offenders by placing them in the company of so many other offenders.[38] Though an individual inmate may not prey on other inmates, it is reasonable for one to believe that others will take advantage of weaker and less resourceful inmates. Therefore, there are those within the criminal population who are considered criminal even to the average inmate. Since the inmate is living with and associating with outlaws of all sorts, it is rational for the inmate to experience, on some level, a lack of personal security.[39]

In prison, the inmate is aware that he or she will likely be faced with another aggressive inmate. The inmate believes that he or she must be prepared to defend person and property. If he or she loses this battle for dominance, the inmate will be considered weak and defenseless. Conversely, should the inmate win this battle, other inmates may seek to gain greater standing by defeating the one who has already earned a reputation for toughness. Since both success and failure in personal battles may bring additional attacks, the inmate never fully gains a sense of security.[40]

Prisonization The taking on in greater or lesser degree of the customs and general culture of the penitentiary.

Despite these many deprivations, over time, many inmates begin to acclimate themselves to prison life. The term **prisonization** was coined in 1940 by Donald Clemmer, who defined it as "The taking on in greater or lesser degree of the folkways, mores, customs, and general culture of the penitentiary."[41] This refers to the socialization process into the culture and life of a prison inmate. Prisonization also describes those whose prison socialization has become so psychologically ingrained into their personalities that they would have difficulty readjusting to life outside of the prison. Prisonization may be thought of as a subcategory of institutionalization, which describes an excessive dependency on the institution.[42]

Inmate code Rules and roles that inmates adopt while incarcerated.

Doing time Jargon used by inmates to describe their good behavior.

Prisonization is a process that does not happen to all incarcerated individuals at the same rate. However, most prisoners do learn a few simple rules, roles, and **inmate codes** very quickly. Inmates learn to behave as good cons **doing time**, meaning they are on their best behavior and are not causing trouble. They learn many informal codes of conduct for being an inmate, such as not getting involved in other inmates' personal affairs, refusing to report another inmate who is breaking rules, never crying or backing down from a fight, never associating with officers, and warning other inmates when an officer is approaching. These informal rules blend into the inmate subculture and allow them to coexist in very cramped and close living arrangements. These learned behaviors aid the progression of the prisonization process.

Prisonization has been identified as one of the variables that frustrate a former inmate's reintegration into open society. Many ex-inmates can never completely regain the social position they held before entering the institution. The stigmatization of being an ex-prisoner creates an individual who is secretive about his or her past and who wishes to conceal particular characteristics of his or her identity.[43] The effects of prisonization often lead inmates to internalize their emotions, which later interferes with their ability to form intimate interpersonal relationships, to find employment, or to gain a sufficient economic level. These frustrations of reintegration have been identified as possible contributing factors in recidivism.[44]

Inmate Subcultures

The inmate culture and subcultures are defining factors in the prisonization of inmates. There are many subcultures to be found in correctional institutions. These sociological divisions may be positive or negative in nature. It appears that each institution has its own dominant culture and subcultures. The cultures deemed positive are those where inmates offer encouragement and support to other inmates for engaging in programs that reinforce successful reentry and institutional behavior. Other cultures and subcultures are negative and create barriers to successful rehabilitative and reentry efforts. High-security institutions tend to have more negative cultures than do those of lesser security, though this is partly because these high-security institutions tend to have more inmates with strong criminal and anti-authority personalities. The negative cultures create a paradox of sorts. The more difficult the inmates become, the more staff will assert their control. This, in turn, will create a cycle of conflict with little chance of resolution.[45]

The indigenous model evolves from the isolation and loss of freedom an inmate suffers while incarcerated.

According to Kelly Cheeseman of Sam Houston State University, there are two predominant theories regarding inmate subcultures. One is the **importation** model, which simply means that the criminal culture one participates in outside of prison is often how the person will continue to behave inside the prison. Those inmates who were violent on the outside are likely to be violent on the inside. The inmate subcultures are therefore influenced by characteristics and experiences obtained before and outside of prison.[46]

Importation The tendency for inmates to bring into the prison the criminal culture they participated in outside of prison.

The second of Cheeseman's major subculture theories is the **indigenous model**, also known as the deprivation model.[47] This model holds that those preexisting conditions of deprivation in a prison have a great effect on how the inmate will adjust to prison life. The indigenous model evolves from the isolation, constant monitoring, loss of possessions, and the loss of freedom an inmate experiences.[48] This is consistent with Sykes's pains of imprisonment and the other models discussed in this section. This model refers to the scarcity of all that was known socially and materially to the inmate. The deprivation of human wants and desires and the pains of imprisonment will be the primary factors in the individual's response to incarceration.[49]

Indigenous model A model that refers to the scarcity of all that was previously known socially and materially to the inmate. This model evolves from the isolation, constant monitoring, loss of possessions, and loss of freedom an inmate experiences.

According to Dr. Mandeep Dhami, et al., indigenous and importation models both explain how inmates adapt to prison. It has been found that each model may have a greater effect than the other on certain behaviors. Even different characteristics within each model may elicit certain manners of conduct. For instance, when trying to predict which inmates are more likely to violate institutional rules, the importation model—considering age, gender, and marital status—is a better predictor than the indigenous model. However, the importation model characteristics of education, mental illness, and substance abuse are not significant predictors of rule violations. Conversely, some researchers have found that indigenous characteristics, such as security, explain the incidence of violence against staff and other inmates.[50]

Gangs

One ever-present subculture in America's jails, prisons, and juvenile facilities, both public and private, is that of gangs. The importation model helps explain this culture. Inmates who belonged to a gang before coming to prison often continue their gang involvement behind bars. In fact, in early 2011, U.S. District Attorney Paul J. Fishman remarked in reference to a gang in New Jersey, "The presence of this gang is unacceptable, whether its leaders are on the streets or behind bars. Prison sentences must mean more than a change of a gang's base of operations."[51] This is a typical challenge that correctional authorities must address when setting gang policy in their institutions.

Inmates typically come from a wide geographic area and they represent all races and socioeconomic groups. Therefore, competing gangs are often imported into prison simply by chance. In addition, it should be noted that not all gangs are first formed on the street. Some gangs originate in prison; they are frequently referred to as "prison gangs." Gangs such as the Black Guerrilla Family and the Aryan Brotherhood are examples of pure prison gangs.[52]

The designation of a gang belongs to the greater category of "Security Threat Group." A *Security Threat Group*, or STG, is defined by the National Gang Crime Research Center as "any group of three or more persons with recurring threatening or disruptive behavior." Some definitions of an STG or a gang require that there be only two participants.[53] On the other hand, federal law defines a gang as numbering at least five participants.[54] However, in the sociological sense, a true social group must have three or more members,[55] so that will be the working definition in this chapter. Regardless of size, the overarching characteristic of an STG is that it poses a threat to the security of the institution.

Defining a gang is even more problematic than agreeing on the minimum number of its members. According to the United States Department of Justice, there is no nationally accepted standard definition of a gang. Therefore, different jurisdictions may have diverse definitions that may even disagree with one another. One measure that is standard in most gang definitions is that the group is involved in ongoing criminal activity.[56]

Gangs comprise all races and ethnicities, and include groups representing immigrants, youths, neighborhoods, motorcycles, drugs, and prisons.[57] Again, the importation theory of prison subcultures explains that many gang members bring their gang activity with them when they are admitted into prison. Therefore, gangs are found at almost all prisons, though statistics show there is more gang activity in state prisons than at their federal counterparts.[58]

Critical Thinking

How might correctional officers protect weaker inmates? What alternatives for protection exist in a correctional institution?

Gang membership in the U.S. as of September 2008 was estimated at around 1 million. This is an increase of about 20% over 2005. It was estimated that about 90% of those gang members resided in local communities, with the rest being incarcerated in local, state, and federal correctional facilities. The FBI believes that some of the increase in gang membership is attributable to better reporting and identification methods by law enforcement. However, most of the increase is due to gang recruitment efforts and the release of incarcerated gang members. The three basic types of gangs identified by law enforcement are street gangs, prison gangs, and outlaw motorcycle gangs.[59]

Street Gangs

Street gangs are those gangs that originate at the street level. These gangs are a significant security threat group because of the large geographic areas where they proliferate. National and regional-level street gangs have expanded their membership outside the United States to Mexico, Central America, and Canada. Currently, 11 national street gangs have been identified in one or more of these three areas.[60] Street gangs are imported into correctional facilities and are often found in jails and prisons; they will often continue running outside business from inside the prisons.

Street gangs Organized criminal networks that originate at the street level.

The Bloods street gang consists of large structured and smaller unstructured gangs that have joined together, forming a single culture. Most Blood members are African-American males, and membership may be as high as 20,000.[61] The Bloods were formed in the 1970s for protection against the Crips.[62]

The Crips street gang is estimated to have up to 35,000 members, mostly African-American males. Their main source of income is drug distribution. Secondary sources come from all manner of felony crime.[63]

Another significant street gang is the Latin Kings, a Chicago-based gang with an estimated membership of 20,000 to 35,000 nationwide. Most of the members are Mexican-American or Puerto Rican males. Again, the gang's main source of income is drug distribution, though the Latin Kings are also known for money laundering activities.[64]

Prison Gangs

Prison gangs are organized criminal networks within the federal and state prison systems. These gangs also operate in communities, where they usually consist of members who belonged to the gang while incarcerated. Prison gangs frequently maintain alliances with other gangs both inside and outside prison, and remain highly influential even while behind bars. When a prison gang member is released from prison, he will often become a representative in his home community and will recruit members to perform criminal activity on behalf of the gang.[65]

Prison gangs Organized criminal networks within the federal and state prison systems.

One infamous prison gang, the Aryan Brotherhood, is composed mostly of Caucasian males. It is strongest in the Southwest and Pacific regions of the

United States. The Aryan Brotherhood is extremely violent and is known to commit murder-for-hire. Some of the Aryan Brotherhood membership is aligned with Mexican gangs to smuggle drugs into the Southwest from Mexico.[66]

The Black Guerrilla Family (BGF) prison gang was founded at California's San Quentin State Prison. Its organization is similar to that of a paramilitary organization. It is highly structured with a national charter, code of ethics, and oath of allegiance. The BGF operates mainly in California, Maryland, Missouri, and Georgia. The membership is relatively small, with around 300 members, all African-American males. Their main source of income is drug distribution.[67]

Many gangs use drug distribution and violence as sources of income.

One of the largest and most violent prison gangs is Neta, which began in Puerto Rico and spread to the mainland United States. Neta members in Puerto Rico exist only in prison rather than on the streets. Once a member is released from prison, he is no longer considered a member. Mainland Neta members, however, usually maintain membership after prison release. The main source of income for Neta is drug distribution.[68]

Outlaw Motorcycle Gangs

Outlaw motorcycle gangs Organized criminal networks with a motorcycle lifestyle.

Outlaw motorcycle gangs are a serious threat to local public safety because of their extensive criminal activities. They are characteristically quick to use violence. Members engage in drug trafficking, weapons trafficking, and violent crime. They usually have a strong centralized leadership that implements rules, regulates membership, and coordinates criminal activity. It is estimated that there are between 280 and 520 outlaw motorcycle gangs in the United States that have a total membership of around 20,000.

The Hells Angels Motorcycle Club (HAMC) is one of the most well-known of the outlaw motorcycle gangs. This gang comprises about 2,500 members and has chapters in 26 foreign countries. The HAMC indulges in drug distribution, money laundering, extortion, homicide, assault, and motorcycle theft.[69]

Another outlaw motorcycle gang is the Mongols Motorcycle Club (MMC). The MMC is established mostly in the Southwest and Pacific regions. The gang numbers about 300 and consists mostly of Hispanics residing in the Los Angeles area. Many members of the Mongols formerly belonged to street gangs and have a long history of violence. The MMC is allied with several other gangs in opposition to the Hells Angels.[70]

The Outlaws Motorcycle Club consists of more than 1,700 members. Their main source of revenue is drug distribution. They are also involved in such crimes as assault, robbery, kidnapping, money laundering, extortion, fraud, arson, explosives, prostitution, and theft.[71]

Critical Thinking

Most gangs earn income primarily from the distribution of drugs. The United States expends tremendous resources on the "war on drugs." Do you think that the current methods authorities use in this "war" are effective? How would you do things differently?

Correctional Officer Subcultures

Within any organization or group of people, cultures and subcultures will ultimately develop. All cultures and subcultures share certain values, beliefs, and norms of behavior, influenced by their leaders, their followers, the national culture, the geographical environment, and the industry.[72] The industry of corrections has developed its own unique culture.

Just as prison inmates have developed their own subcultures, prison staff—particularly correctional officers—have done the same. Correctional officers have an occupation that offers danger every time they go to work. They are surrounded by hostile individuals who have already demonstrated their propensity for breaking laws and not conforming to society's prevailing culture. Officers also face long hours, shift work, and overtime that may or may not be desired.[73] Because prisons and jails never close, this 24-hour industry can make family life challenging. The working schedules are especially challenging for families with young children and even more challenging for single parents.[74]

There are norms of correctional officer behavior that are a part of the officers' code. Correctional officers expect each other to adhere to certain guidelines—some of which are "unwritten" rules. Among these rules: Officers are expected to show positive concern for fellow officers and always come to the aid of another officer in dangerous situations. Officers should always support each other in disputes with inmates and in punishments of inmates, and should never make another officer look bad in front of inmates. Officers are expected to maintain solidarity with each other against outside groups.[75]

Exhibit: Florida State Correctional Officers' Code of Conduct.

I. I will never forget that I am a public official sworn to uphold the Constitutions of the United States and the State of Florida.

II. I am a professional committed to the public safety, the support and protection of my fellow officers, and co-workers, and the supervision and care of those in my charge. I am prepared to go in harm's way in fulfillment of these missions.

III. As a professional, I am skilled in the performance of my duties and governed by a code of ethics that demands integrity in word and deed, fidelity to the lawful orders of those appointed over me, and, above all, allegiance to my oath of office and the laws that govern our nation.

IV. I will seek neither personal favor nor advantage in the performance of my duties. I will treat all with whom I come in contact with civility and respect. I will lead by example and conduct myself in a disciplined manner at all times.

V. I am proud to selflessly serve my fellow citizens as a member of the Florida Department of Corrections.

Source: Florida Department of Corrections Website. http://www.dc.state.fl.us/vision.html

Correctional officers are trained to look for and address any signs of trouble.

The officers' code becomes a part of the correctional officers' subculture. This subculture is distinct from the larger culture of the organization that includes civilian staff and the administration. The behaviors of officers are observed and imitated by new recruits, and the culture of the correctional officer passes to newer generations. The new officers develop beliefs and thoughts that are similar to those of officers before them. Sometimes, this can lead to further conflict between officers and inmates. Officers develop a perception that inmates view them as the enemy. Officers typically strongly dislike inmates, and some may look for opportunities to make an inmate's life especially difficult. Moreover, they believe that inmates cannot be trusted.

Still, the subculture also develops positive traits in officers. Officers learn to anticipate trouble at any time. They learn what signs to look for to identify trouble, such as unusual quietness or loudness. An officer who does not develop the proper skills for detecting what is unusual or usual may be excluded from the subculture. Officers will also learn inmate management, though the officer subculture encourages as little interaction with inmates as possible.[76] The correctional officer subculture, like subcultures in other industries, can help the officers handle stress in an occupation that constantly puts them at risk.

There are many studies demonstrating that correctional officers experience higher levels of stress than most other occupations. Often, the correctional officer is required to perform the role of treatment counselor and custody officer at the same time. These seemingly opposite functions can lead to stress and eventually burnout among officers.[77]

Correctional officer role conflict occurs when an officer has conflicting orders. Role conflict also occurs when there is disagreement about how a task should be handled. An additional stressor on correctional officers is role ambiguity, which occurs when an officer does not have enough information about how to perform a particular job function, especially when responsibilities are vague and poorly defined. In some cases, policies are contradictory. These issues seem to afflict correctional officers more than many other occupations and are a significant cause of officer burnout.[78]

Ethics and Professionalism

Smuggling in prisons is an ongoing concern. Heroin, marijuana, tobacco, other drugs, and weapons can all make their way into prisons throughout the country. Over a five-year stretch, the Bureau of Prisons recorded more than 2,800 positive drug tests for each of those years in federal prisons.[79] The same report recognizes that weapons smuggling is also a serious threat to the security of the institutions. Though there are several mechanisms in place to prevent the entry of contraband into prisons, the found weapons, drugs, and overdoses demonstrate a serious problem.

When officers are caught smuggling drugs, weapons, or other contraband into a jail or a prison, they are usually prosecuted. This general form of deterrence, however, has not stopped the problem. Why would an officer risk his or her occupation, reputation, and personal way of life by trying to introduce contraband into a correctional institution?

Correctional officers face many ethical dilemmas, and they generally receive training on how to handle such situations. The temptation, though, must be too great for some officers to resist.

Consider the following situation. A young officer, already struggling to meet monthly expenses, is soon expecting his first child. Correctional officer pay is not enough to support a growing family and to service the debts already accumulated. A friend of a friend offers him a few thousand dollars a month to take cell phones and drugs to a contact in the prison. Because he knows how the prison security system works, he knows he would likely be able to do so without being caught. It would be easy and profitable. What would you do?

Consider another situation. You are an experienced correctional officer approaching your 20th year. You have known some of your coworkers for most of that time, and many are considered good friends. One day, you see a fellow correctional officer and close friend drop what appears to be a small bag of marijuana while he is adjusting his clothing. What do you do? Do you ignore it? Do you demand to see it? Do you report it? What circumstances would you need to take into account?

Growth of Corrections

When 2015 ended, the United States held more than 2.1 million people in jails and in prisons throughout the country. In addition, more than 4.6 million were on probation or parole.[80] Both the prison population and the imprisonment rate in the United States are the highest in the world.[81] One will find differences in statistical numbers depending upon the source. The figures above are the official United States government statistics and are more conservative than many others are. Therefore, depending on the source, one may find a much higher prison population and rate of incarceration than what has been quoted here.

In 2000, the United States had 3060 supervised adults per 100,000 in the adult correctional system. In 2015, the number had decreased to 2,710 supervised adults per 100,000 with 1 in 37 adult residents under United States supervision. It may help to think of other countries where, by American standards, people are oppressed and imprisoned without the cherished rights that we enjoy under our laws and customs. Rwanda, Cuba, Russia, and countries known for human rights violations have lower incarceration rates than does the United States.[82] Overall, including probation and parole, one in every 31 adults in this country is under some sort of correctional supervision.[83] Some feel this is a shameful indictment of our system of justice.

The dramatic increase in the prison population has affected the economy. As the rate of incarceration increases, the demand for correctional workers increases as well. Over 470,000 people in the United States were employed in corrections in 2014 according to the Bureau of Labor Statistics. Some rural areas have entire communities with local economies tied to correctional facilities.[84] The U.S. Labor Department projects about a 4% growth for the field of corrections through 2024.[85]

The growth of corrections is tied to several factors. One factor is mandatory sentencing laws, which put criminals behind bars for longer periods than in recent history. Another significant factor is the proliferation of "tough on crime" laws. Current laws that take a hard-line stance on crime have been legislated throughout the country in an effort to reduce crime. Whereas previously an individual might have served a fraction of an imposed sentence, the get-tough laws have created mandatory minimums that are closer to the imposed sentence. Some states now require an inmate to serve at least 85% of a sentence in prison before becoming eligible for probation or parole. Moreover, life sentences, true to their meaning, may mean that the person will never be allowed to go free.[86]

FIGURE 10.1 COMPARISON OF IMPRISONMENT RATES (SELECTED COUNTRIES).

Country	Prison Population Rate per/100,000
Seychelles	799
USA	666
El Salvador	574
Cuba	510
Russian Federation	436

Source: http://www.prisonstudies.org/highest-to-lowest/prison_population_rate?field_region_taxonomy_tid=All&=Apply

Critical Thinking

The crime rate has been decreasing and the prison population has been increasing. Many argue that it does not make sense to lock up so many people when the crime rate is down. Others argue that the reason crime rates are down is because those who would normally be committing crimes are now in prison for longer periods. Are both or either of these arguments credible? Discuss.

Some criminologists suggest that the trend to incarcerate more people for longer periods has reached a position where it is no longer effective. One prominent criminologist, James Q. Wilson, states that we have reached a point of diminishing returns on our correctional efforts and investment.[87] Wilson says that judges have always sentenced violent offenders to long sentences, but that we now are "dipping deeper into the bucket of person's eligibility for prison, dredging up offenders with shorter and shorter criminal records."[88] He explains that if we continue to lengthen prison sentences and increase the numbers of people sent to prison, a diminishing marginal return on crime rate reductions will occur. In other words, at some point, imposing longer sentences will have no more effect on the crime rate. Some would argue that this point has already passed.

Special Populations

All manner of people are represented within the prison population—men, women, the young, the elderly, those with mental illnesses, those with physical illnesses, and those with physical disabilities. Every one of these subsets is represented by all races as well. Many of these special populations are segregated from other populations for security reasons as well as for medical and program functions.

Female Inmates

Female inmates have special needs that are not typically required by the male population. They require the same generalists and specialists for health needs that any woman outside of prison requires. Moreover, as many as 10% of women are pregnant when they are incarcerated.[89]

The typical female prisoner has been sentenced for a nonviolent crime and is a recidivist, which means she has previously been incarcerated or on probation. Of all female inmates, one-third report that they were under the influence of drugs or alcohol when they were arrested. More than 80% had been drug users at some time in their lives, which is slightly higher than the rate for men, and about 40% had been in drug treatment at some point in their lives. Further, many have a history of sexual abuse.[90]

Youthful Inmates

While there is a separate system for juvenile justice, some juveniles are tried and convicted in adult courts and sentenced as adults. Many states

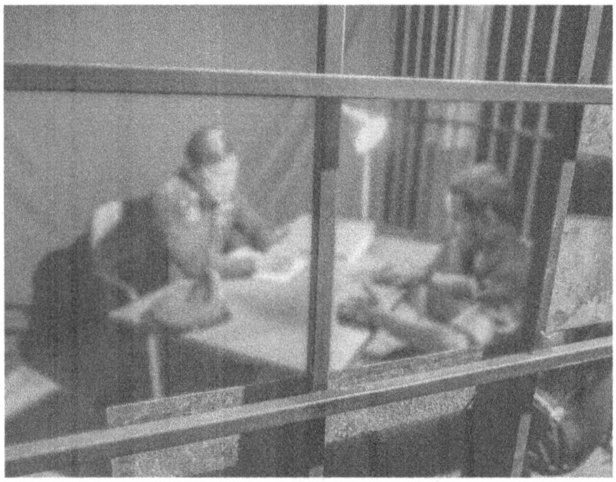

© Kasinpoj Wiriyakajornitham/Shutterstock.com

Many facilities have special facilities for youthful offenders to separate them from adult inmates.

have special facilities for youthful offenders. Where this is not practical, the young and weak are typically segregated from the adult population. For example, in Florida, the Youthful Offender Act was passed in 1978. It was designed to improve youth corrections with the goal of successful reentry to open society. Since the act was first passed, it has expanded to provide vocational education and training, counseling, and public service opportunities to young inmates, and requires that the youthful offender attend substance abuse programs.[91]

The Florida Youthful Offender Act applies to those offenders who are under the age of 21 when sentenced. The act also includes those juveniles who have been tried and sentenced as an adult. Moreover, even if a court does not sentence an offender as youthful, the correctional authorities may designate those less than 25 years old as youthful offenders if they are deemed vulnerable in the adult prison population.[92]

Elderly Inmates

Some researchers, such as Rikard and Rosenberg (2007), estimate that by the year 2020, 21% to 33% of prison residents will be elderly.[93] This increase is partially attributable to medical advances that extend life. However, substance abuse, lack of adequate diet, and poor medical care are found disproportionately in elderly criminals when compared to law-abiding seniors. This lifestyle places elderly offenders' health at about 11.5 years older physically and mentally than their non-incarcerated peers.[94]

An inmate typically is designated elderly at 50 years old. This reflects the physiological age averages discussed in the previous paragraph. Moreover, their elderly status is a reflection of poorer health, including chronic conditions, substance abuse issues, and the fact that they suffer psychological problems more than younger inmates do. An elderly inmate costs roughly three times as much to incarcerate as a younger inmate. They are also more likely to have committed violent acts. Seventy-five percent of elderly inmates are still serving time for their first offense.[95]

Mentally Ill Inmates

The rate of mental illness among prison inmates is considerable. It is estimated that between 200,000 and 300,000 inmates suffer from mental illnesses, including bipolar disorder, schizophrenia, and major depression.[96] This makes the mentally ill percentage of the prison population two to four times higher than that of the general population.[97]

Mentally ill inmates often find it difficult to comply with the many rules and regulations that control prison populations. Mentally ill inmates tend to break rules at a higher rate than do other inmates. Often, rule breaking is the illness showing itself through aggression and disruptive behavior. These rule violators are regularly punished as discipline problems and without a diagnosis of mental health issues.[98]

Prison authorities have responsibility for the safety and security of staff and inmates. This often does not help the mentally ill inmate who is "acting out" and may be viewed as a discipline problem. Some prison systems have taken measures to diagnose and treat more discipline problems as psychological problems; however, some experts, such as Abramsky and Fellner (2003), maintain that there is an urgent need to reassess the disciplinary procedures as possible mental health issues.[99]

Chronically Ill Inmates

Another important category of special needs inmates is those with chronic infectious illnesses such as hepatitis B and C, HIV, and AIDS. Much chronic infectious disease is imported into prisons and jails, but other illnesses arise from the sexual activity and drug use that take place in correctional facilities. Therefore, the spread of disease is of significant concern to correctional administrators.[100]

Since many diseases are spread through sexual and drug activity, some researchers have suggested that needle exchanges and condoms should be provided in prisons. Though there are no needle exchange efforts in the United States, some European countries have reported success with these programs. Those countries that have adopted needle exchanges have reported no increase in security issues.[101]

Only a few correctional facilities in the United States provide condoms, but the practice is standard in many other countries, including Canada. There is one such condom distribution program in Washington, D.C. A survey of 100 correctional officers and 300 inmates who participated in the program showed that condom distribution was largely supported and caused no additional security problems. Such prevention measures provide significant protection not only to the inmate population but to the general population as well, because most inmates will return to a life outside of prison.[102]

Economic Realities

Government at all levels spent about $265 billion on police, courts, and corrections in 2012. Of this, $126 billion went for police protection, $57 billion went for the courts, and $80 billion went for corrections. Breaking it down further reveals that over half of all criminal justice spending came from local governments.[103] These expenses are quite heavy considering

FIGURE 10.2 CRIMINAL JUSTICE EXPENDITURES BY LEVEL OF GOVERNMENT.

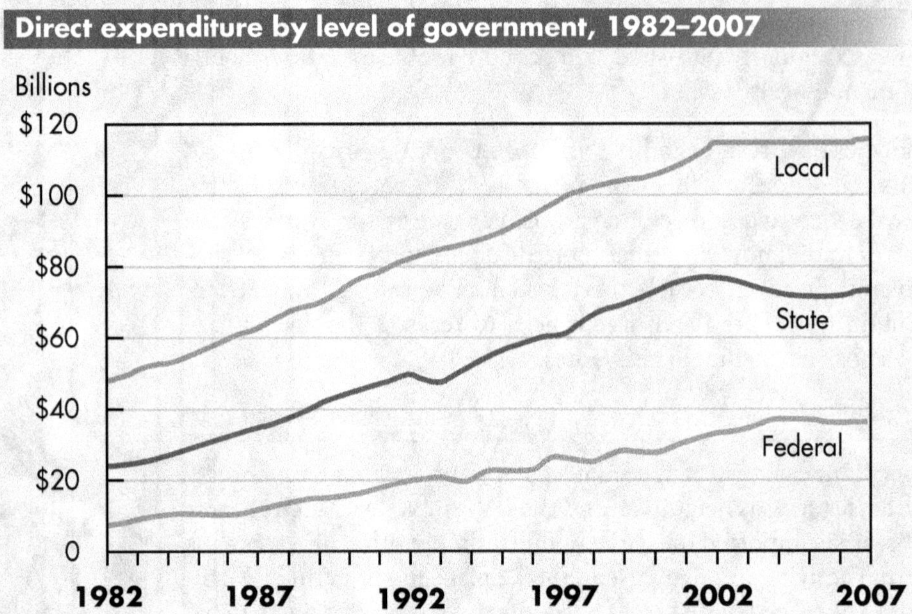

Source: Bureau of Justice Statistics. http://bjs.ojp.usdoj.gov/index.cfm?ty=tp&tid=5

FIGURE 10.3 EXPENDITURES BY CRIMINAL JUSTICE FUNCTION.

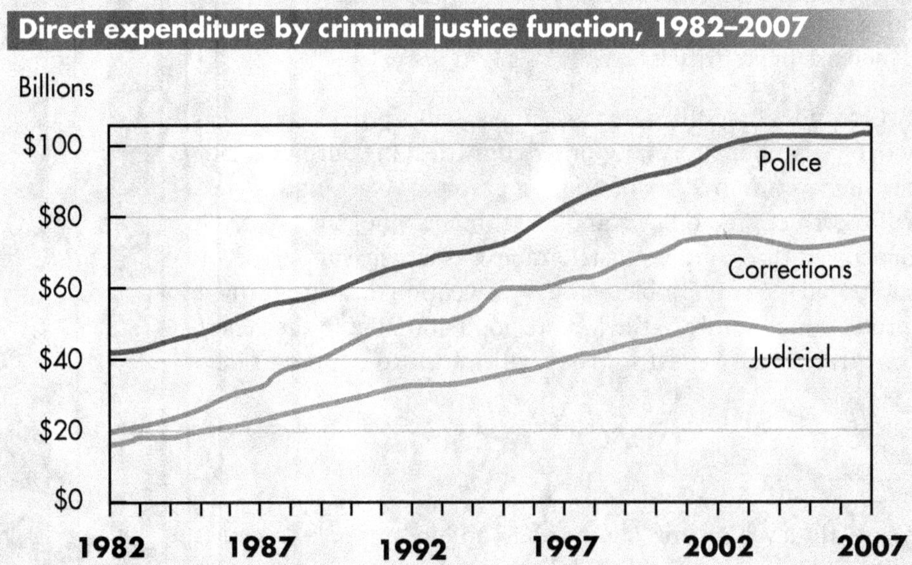

Source: Bureau of Justice Statistics. http://bjs.ojp.usdoj.gov/index.cfm?ty=tp&tid=5

that government budgets at all levels are facing difficult decisions regarding spending and resource allocation in the corrections system.

In 1982, $20 billion was spent on corrections at all levels of government. In 2012, this expense had increased 4 times to $80 billion. The realities of correctional expenses have caused the nation's elected leaders at all levels of government to reconsider how money is spent. Americans want prisons that will hold people accountable for their crimes and keep communities safe. However, citizens also deserve to have their tax money used in appropriate and intelligent ways.

One major reason for the escalating expenditures in corrections is the high rate of recidivism in the United States, which ultimately requires incarcerating the same individuals for multiple stints. A 2009 Pew study demonstrated that more than 40% of inmates will ultimately return to prison for new crimes.[104] For prison systems, reducing these high rates of recidivism is essential in order to help the incarcerated, protect the safety of American communities, and reduce state spending on corrections.

Many prison systems have established programs designed to aid inmates' rehabilitation and produce a positive prison culture that can demonstrably reduce recidivism. These programs include faith-based prisons, GED and college credit opportunities, vocational training, and substance abuse training. These reentry programs implemented at the state and federal levels show great promise for changing offenders' lives.

Many states are already demonstrating success with lowering recidivism through these prison programs. A study for the Florida Department of Corrections found that inmates who complete the programs designed to reduce recidivism are more successful than those who do not. Specifically, the study found that inmates who earned a GED are 8.7% less likely to recidivate, inmates who earn a vocational certificate are 14.6% less likely to recidivate, and inmates who complete substance abuse programs are 6.2% less likely to recidivate.[105]

The federal government, recognizing this pressing need for correctional transformation, has enacted legislation to aid the successful return to society for adults and juveniles leaving prison. In 2008, the Second Chance Act was enacted. The act allows for government agencies and nonprofits to receive grants that will aid in reducing recidivism. Programs such as substance abuse treatment, assistance in finding employment and housing, mentoring, and victim support are made available through these grants.[106] In 2009, $28 million was awarded to grant recipients. The following year saw an even larger allocation of grant money. In October 2010, more than $82 million was awarded to 187 grant recipients to reduce adult and juvenile recidivism, for reentry courts to monitor and provide treatment services, to establish and enhance existing substance abuse treatment programs, to improve education and vocational training at adult and juvenile facilities, to train inmates for technology jobs, and to provide mentors to adult and juvenile offenders.[107]

Alternatives to Prison

As prison populations continue to expand, governments at all levels look for more ways to control costs. While doing this, they must also attempt to live up to the implied promise of returning repentant former criminals back to the streets as law-abiding citizens. The unfortunate truth, though, evidenced by alarming recidivism rates, is that many former prisoners return to criminal activity.

There are a number of objectives for imprisonment. One is that the convicted criminal is punished through deprivation of liberty. Another is that the criminal is incapacitated from committing further crimes while incarcerated. Presumably, rehabilitation efforts are attempted with the expectation that the individual will leave prison better able to live and work in a law-abiding manner.

Many of those sentenced to jail or prison come from disadvantaged socioeconomic backgrounds. Many are in prison for violent crimes, while others are in prison for nonviolent offenses. Some are incarcerated for traffic offenses or simple possession of illicit substances. Their crimes range from the most horrible imaginable to the relatively mundane and victimless, yet

FIGURE 10.4 FY2010 SECOND CHANCE ACT GRANT PROGRAM APPLICATION RESULTS

FY2010 SCA Grant Program Application Results

FY10 Grant Program	Total applications received	Total grants awarded	Total amount awarded
Adult Demonstration (101)	145	52	$27,324,543
Juvenile Demonstration (101)	39	14	$7,955,996
Reentry Courts (111)	9	9	$2,651,703
Family-Based Substance Abuse Treatment (113)	36	23	$6,645,611
Evaluate and Improve Education in Prisons, Jails, and Juvenile Facilities (114)	12	1	$2,463,635
Technology Career Training Demonstration (115)	44	7	$4,679,466
Substance Abuse & Criminal Justice Collaboration (201)	77	22	$11,705,855
Adult Mentoring (211)	613	50	$13,968,672
Juvenile Mentoring (211)	214	9	$5,018,909
Total	1189	187	$82,414,390

Source: National Reentry Resource Center.http://www.nationalreentryresourcecenter.org/about/second-chance-act

are still eligible for sentences that may involve incarceration. This can easily compound already difficult issues in many lives. Incarceration interferes with an inmate's employment and family life. It also decreases the inmate's employment prospects after release and limits his or her access to other opportunities, such as an education financed with federal student loans.

Overcrowding of prisons is associated with the spread of infectious diseases such as tuberculosis and HIV. In addition, violence is always a possibility. These fears alone can create health problems associated with stress. Moreover, overcrowding generates the demand for more prison space, meaning more money must again be allocated to build, operate, and maintain these human warehouses.

For these and many other reasons, the criminal justice system utilizes a number of alternatives to prison. The goal of these alternatives, in addition to relieving overcrowding in prisons and giving less severe punishments to offenders who commit less severe crimes, is to move from a punishment model to one of restorative justice and to help reintegrate former criminals back into society.

Probation and Parole: Effectiveness and Statistics

Probation is the most common form of modern court-imposed punishment. *Probation* is still a sentence, but unlike jail or prison, a sentence of probation is court-ordered supervision that is served while living in the community.[108] Probation may also be a part of a combined sentence in which the community supervision follows incarceration. Probation has three primary goals: rehabilitation, protection of society, and protection of victim rights.[109]

At yearend 2015, an estimated 4,650,900 adults were under community supervision—a decrease of 62,300 offenders from yearend 2014. About 1 in 53 adults in the United States was under community supervision at yearend 2015. This population includes adults on probation, parole, or any other post-prison supervision, with probationers accounting for the majority (81%) of adults under community supervision. The 1.3% decline observed in the adult community corrections population was due to the drop in the probation population. The probation population declined from an estimated 3,868,400 offenders at yearend 2014 to 3,789,800 at yearend 2015. The parole population continued to rise with a 1.5% increase, from 857,700 offenders at yearend 2014 to 870,500 at yearend 2015.[110]

Unlike probation, which is an actual sentence but is served in the community, *parole* is the early supervised release of someone already incarcerated. Often, probationers and parolees are supervised by the same state agencies. Many states and the federal government, however, have abolished parole.[111]

The federal government and many states have shifted away from indeterminate sentences, which establish a range rather than an exact length of a prison term, and now use determinate sentencing, which places mandatory, specifically set sentences on offenders and no longer offers parole. However, some states have defined mandatory sentencing as a percentage of time served. For instance, by statute, some states require that an offender serve at least 85% of a sentence in prison. The other 15% may be served on probation or parole depending on the offender's behavior while in prison. These statutes are known as truth-in-sentencing laws. In 1994, the federal government passed a law that provided funding to states that enacted truth-in-sentencing laws. As of 2008, 35 states qualified to receive the federal funding for truth-in sentencing.[112]

Economically speaking, the probation system is cheaper than incarceration. For example, for the fiscal year of 2012–2013 in the state of Florida, it cost an average of $47.50 per day to house an offender in prison,[113] while monitoring an offender on pretrial release. The cost of supervising a defendant in the community in Broward County is $1.48 per defendant per day, compared to a daily cost of $107.71 for housing a defendant in the Broward County Jail.[114]

Critical Thinking

Should states continue to use indeterminate sentencing structures and parole boards to release offenders early? Explain.

Other Community-Based Alternatives

Community-based alternatives are used effectively for less serious crimes, so-called victimless crimes, and public order crimes. This is also cost-effective in that it does not cost as much to supervise someone in the community as it does to house them in a prison or in a jail. In 2010, at least 26 states have cut the budgets of their corrections departments.[115]

Many of the states that have cut corrections budgets have already increased efficiencies and are now looking to cut costs in other areas.[116] States have reduced inmate healthcare expenses, frozen officer hiring, reduced staff salaries, reduced staff benefits, and eliminated pay increases. Some are considering the consolidation of facilities and forgoing planned expansions.[117]

The largest savings in correctional budgets come from reducing the number of people who come to prison and the length of stay for those who do. Staffing accounts for up to 80% of a prison's budget. In order to reduce staffing, the number of inmates must be reduced. Therefore, states look for ways to close prisons, or at least parts of them, in order to achieve savings. In 2010, states found that they could identify offender populations that could be safely released from prison after serving reduced sentences. Much of these savings can be realized through community-based alternatives to incarceration.[118]

A variety of community-based alternatives are currently in use throughout the United States. House arrest allows an offender to live at his or her residence. The offender is restricted from activity outside the home. Usually, the individual is only allowed to leave for work, school, church, or court-approved activities. The offender is under close scrutiny and there is often electronic monitoring equipment in use to ensure compliance.

Electronic monitoring is often an active system whereby an ankle bracelet transmits a continuous signal to a landline telephone to verify the offender's location. Any deviation or attempts to tamper with the equipment will send a signal to the monitoring station to be reported to the proper authorities.[119] Many agencies are now using more advanced GPS devices, especially for high-risk sex offenders.[120]

House arrest allows an offender to live at his or her residence, but he or she is restricted from activity outside of the home.

Halfway houses are group homes that often house newly released offenders with nowhere else to go. They may not have family, friends, or anyone willing to give them a place to live, at least temporarily. Many halfway houses, however, are specifically for sex offenders; they provide a supervised residence and resources specifically designed for this population.

Halfway house A group home often used by newly released offenders who have nowhere else to go. Many halfway houses are specifically designed for sex offenders, providing a supervised residence and resources specifically designed for this population.

Day reporting centers are locations for offenders to receive services such as counseling, life skills education, drug abuse treatment, and substance abuse testing. The offender only reports according to a specified schedule and does not live there. These centers also offer access to community services for employment, housing, health services, proper identification, legal support, and wellness.

Day reporting center A location for offenders to receive services such as counseling, life skills education, drug abuse treatment, and substance abuse testing. The offender only reports according to a specified schedule and does not live there.

Community service is often an intermediate sanction imposed by a court. Community service is an unpaid service to the community, often at a nonprofit organization that provides a service to society. Sometimes a judge will impose community service that is related to an offender's skill. For instance, a person skilled with animals may work at a pet adoption center or a person with legal skills may work at a community legal aid center.

Day fines are popular in some European countries. A day fine is a fine that is based on a person's daily income. The amount of the fine is progressive in relation to the money the offender earns. The more income one has, the higher the fine.

Day fine A fine based on a person's daily income; the amount of the fine is progressive in relation to the money the offender earns.

Critical Thinking

What factors do you think would or should influence a judge's decision to sentence an offender to confinement or to community supervision?

Career Connections: Correctional Treatment Specialist

The United States Department of Labor publishes statistics and general information for a large number of occupations. Within these pages, the occupation outlook sections offer current and projected future needs. The highest rating outlook for employment in any given occupation is excellent. One of those occupations expected to have excellent growth and opportunity is that of correctional treatment specialist.[121]

© gpointstudio/Shutterstock.com

Correctional treatment specialists plan educational and occupational programs to improve inmates' likelihood of a successful transition to open society.

Correctional treatment specialists may work from probation offices, jails, or prisons. They evaluate inmate progress, administer psychological tests, and work with probation and parole offices to coordinate inmate releases to community supervision. They also plan educational and occupational programs to improve inmates' likelihood of a successful transition to open society. In addition, they may provide anger management skills, drug and alcohol abuse education, and counseling related to crimes such as sexual offenses.[122]

Daily duties of the correctional treatment specialist may include referring offenders to social services agencies, determining specific needs for rehabilitation, consulting with attorneys and judges, and following up on offender progress. Further, the correctional treatment specialist will confer with the offender's family members to help tend to family business that may impede the inmate's transition or help the offender's family group. The correctional treatment specialist may also be required to testify in court.[123]

The correctional treatment specialist must have specific knowledge and skills. Some of the most important knowledge is that of counseling. The person in this occupation must understand how to use rehabilitative techniques for a population that may not be receptive to treatment and may have other mental ailments. They must also be able to evaluate the effects of treatment. Knowledge of psychology, law, public safety, sociology, computers, and other subjects is considered important.[124]

A bachelor's degree is often a requirement, as is a clean criminal record. Entry into this field may require extensive testing for psychological fitness, physical fitness, and drug use, as well as written exams. One must have good interpersonal skills and good report writing skills. Advancement in this field is often dependent upon experience, performance, and education. A graduate degree may be helpful or required for advancement into the senior ranks.[125]

Chapter Summary

- Early English law first applied the "principle of least eligibility," meant to discourage anyone from intentionally having themselves completely cared for by the government by making such care no better than the most destitute of society. The principle of least eligibility has long been society's attitude for those who have been duly incarcerated.
- In 1958, sociologist Gresham Sykes presented a study on the effects that prisons have on both inmates and staff. Sykes explains that the pains of imprisonment on a person's personality, though less obvious than are physical injuries, are "no less fearful." Sykes explains that this loss of freedom, a scarcity of goods and services, the loss of domestic relationships, and so on, may be acceptable and unavoidable for those imprisoned, but the effects on the inmate must be recognized as serious, just as are physical punishments.
- Erving Goffman described prisons as total institutions. In the total institution, everything is provided for those who reside there. All aspects of life are conducted within the total institution. Rules are abundant and punishment is swift.
- The term prisonization was first used in 1940 by Donald Clemmer, who defined it as "the taking on in greater or lesser degree of the folkways, mores, customs, and general culture of the penitentiary." This refers to the socialization process into the culture and life of a prison inmate. Prisonization also describes those whose prison socialization has become so psychologically ingrained into their personalities that they would have difficulty readjusting to life outside of the prison.
- There are many subcultures in correctional institutions. The importation model means that the criminal culture one participates in outside of prison is often how the person will continue to behave inside the prison. The indigenous model holds that the preexisting conditions of deprivation in a prison have a great effect on how the inmate adjusts to prison life.
- Gangs present an ongoing problem for correctional facilities. Gangs originate from the street and in prison. The designation of a gang belongs to the greater category of "Security Threat Group," defined by the National Gang Crime Research Center as "any group of three or more persons with recurring threatening or disruptive behavior." The three basic types of gangs identified by law enforcement are street gangs, prison gangs, and outlaw motorcycle gangs.
- The industry of corrections has developed its own unique cultures and subcultures among both inmates and correctional officers. Inmates and officers each adhere to certain unwritten rules to help them adapt to the daily routines of the prison culture.

- When 2015 ended, roughly 2.1 million people were incarcerated in the United States and more than 4.6 million were on probation or parole. Both the prison population and the imprisonment rate in the United States are the highest in the world. Government at all levels spent about $265 billion on police, courts, and corrections in 2012.
- Because of the high cost of incarcerating inmates, states look for alternative methods to punish offenders in order to achieve savings. Such alternatives include probation, parole, and community-based alternatives such as house arrest, halfway houses, day reporting centers, community service, and day fines.

Critical Thinking?

1. Why is it less expensive to supervise offenders using methods other than incarceration? Should these alternatives be expanded? Why? Is money the only concern?
2. Are those who are incarcerated entitled to free medical care? If so, to what level? Should there be a limit on medical procedures that inmates are allowed to receive?
3. What categories of offender should be subjected to electronic monitoring? What categories of offender should not be candidates for electronic monitoring?
4. How might inmates lessen the pains of imprisonment? How would you attempt to lessen these pains should you be imprisoned?
5. How would you explain the rising prison population?
6. What effects might prison overcrowding have on treatment programs?
7. Do you believe the failure rate of recidivism is too high? What can be done to correct the problem?
8. Gang members in prisons are sometimes separated. What might be an undesirable result of gang member separation?
9. Should a correctional treatment specialist have correctional officer training as well? Should they receive training in defensive tactics?
10. What types of rights should inmates lose? Should there be any loss of rights for those who have completed their sentences? Why or why not?

Media

National Institute of Corrections: http://nicic.gov/
The National Institute of Corrections helps to shape and advance effective correctional practice and public policy.

American Probation and Parole Association: http://www.appa-net.org/eweb/

The American Probation and Parole Association is actively involved with probation, parole, and community-based corrections, in both adult and juvenile sectors.

Bureau of Justice Statistics: http://www.bjs.gov
This is a premier website for law enforcement and correctional statistics.

Endnotes

1 Secter, B. (1966, July 13). "The Richard Speck Case." *Chicago Tribune.* Retrieved from http://www.chicagotribune.com/news/politics/chi-chicagodays-richardspeck-story,0,4911196.story

2 Ibid.

3 *Furman v. Georgia,* 408 U.S. 238 (1972). The death penalty was reinstated in *Gregg v. Georgia,* 428 U.S. 153 (1976).

4 Olson, J. *Historical Dictionary of the 1960s.*

5 Ibid.

6 Dickens, C. (1850). *A Walk in a Workhouse.* Retrieved from http://www2.hn.psu.edu/faculty/jmanis/dickens/pieces.pdf

7 The Poor Law Amendment Act of 1834." (1834). *The Workhouse.* Retrieved from http://www.workhouses.org.uk/poorlaws/1834act.shtml

8 Sieh, E. W. (1989). "Less Eligibility: The Upper Limits of Penal Policy." *Criminal Justice Policy Review, 3*(2), 159–183.

9 Rubin, E. L., & Feeley, M. M. (2003, April). "Judicial Policy Making and Litigation against the Government." *University of Pennsylvania Journal of Constitutional Law,* 617.

10 *Pell v. Procunier,* 417 U.S. 817, 822 (1974).

11 *Estelle v. Gamble,* 429 U.S. 97 (1976).

12 *Procunier v. Martinez,* 416 U.S. 396 (1974).

13 *Block v. Rutherford,* 486 U.S. 576 (1984).

14 *Hudson v. Palmer,* 468 U.S. 517 (1984).

15 *Cruz v. Beto,* 405 U.S. 319 (1972).

16 *Wolff v. McDonnell,* 94 S.Ct. 2963 (1974).

17 Sykes, G. (1958). *The Society of Captives: A Study of a Maximum Security Prison.* Princeton, NJ: Princeton University Press.

18 Ibid.

19 Ibid.

20 Goffman, E. (1961). *Total Institutions.* Retrieved from http://www.markfoster.net/neurelitism/totalinstitutions.pdf

21 Ibid.

22 Ibid.

23 Sykes, 1958.

24 Ibid.

25 "Mine!" *Scientific American Mind, 22*(4), 59.

26 Goffman, 1961.

27 Sykes, 1958.

28 "Autonomy." (2011). *Merriam-Webster Dictionary.* Retrieved from http://www.merriam-webster.com/dictionary/autonomy

29 Sykes, 1958.

30 Ibid.

31 Ibid.

32 Goffman, 1961.

33 Irwin, J. (1992). *The Jail.* Berkeley, CA: University of California Press, 73.

34 Ibid.

35 Ibid., 74.

36 Goffman, 1961.

37 Ibid.

38 Sykes, 1958.

39 Ibid.

40 Ibid.

41 Clemmer, D. (1940). *The Prison Community. Boston, MA:* Christopher Publishing House, 279.

42 O'Toole, M. (Ed.). (2003). "Institutionalization." In *Miller-Keane Encyclopedia and Dictionary of Medicine, Nursing, and Allied Health* (7th ed.). Philadelphia, PA: W.B. Saunders.

43 Goffman, 1961.

44 Harrison, B., & Schehr, R. C. (2004). "Offenders and Post-Release Jobs: Variables Influencing Success and Failure." *Journal of Offender Rehabilitation, 39*(3), 35–68.

45 *Report of the Task Force on Security, Respect.* (2008). Correctional Service Canada.

46 Cheeseman, K. (2003). "Importing Aggression: An Examination and Application of Subculture Theories to Prison Violence." *The Southwest Journal of Criminal Justice,* 1(1), 24–38. Retrieved from http://www.utsa.edu/swjcj/archives/1.1/Cheeseman.pdf

47 Goffman, 1961; Sykes, 1958; Sykes & Messinger, 1960.

48 National Council on Crime and Delinquency. (1994). *Understanding why Inmates are Misclassified.* Retrieved from http://static.nicic.gov/Library/011994.pdf

49 Dhami, M. K., Ayton, P., & Loewenstein, G. (2007). "Adaptation to Imprisonment: Indigenous or Imported?" *Criminal Justice and Behavior.* Retrieved from http://sds.hss.cmu.edu/media/pdfs/loewenstein/AdaptPrisonment-Indigenous.pdf

50 Ibid.

51 United States Attorney District of New Jersey. (2011, January). *Sweeping Racketeering Indictment Charges 15 Members of the Fruit Town and*

Brick City Brims Bloods Set. Retrieved from http://www.atf.gov/press/releases/2011/01/012411-new-sweeping-racketeering-indictment-charges-15-members-of-the-fruittown-and-brick-city-brims-bloods-set.pdf

52 Knox, G. W. (2005). *The Problem of Gangs and Security Threat Groups (STG's) in American Prisons Today: Recent Research Findings from the 2004 Prison Gang Survey.* Retrieved from http://www.ngcrc.com/corr2006.html

53 Ibid.

54 18 U.S.C. § 521.

55 Knox, 2005.

56 "Gangs." (2006). *United States Department of Justice Attorney's Bulletin, 54*(3).

57 Ibid.

58 Ibid.

59 FBI National Gang Intelligence Center. (2009). *National Gang Threat Assessment 2009.* Retrieved from http://www.fbi.gov/stats-services/publications/national-gang-threat-assessment-2009-pdf

60 Ibid.

61 United States Department of Justice. (2008). *National Drug Intelligence Center, Attorney General's Report to Congress on the Growth of Violent Street Gangs in Suburban Areas.* Retrieved from http://www.justice.gov/ndic/pubs27/27612/appendb.htm

62 Ibid.

63 Ibid.

64 Ibid.

65 FBI National Gang Intelligence Center, 2009.

66 Ibid.

67 United States Department of Justice. (2008). "Appendix B. National-Level Street, Prison, and Outlaw Motorcycle Gang Profiles." *Attorney General's Report to Congress on the Growth of Violent Street Gangs in Suburban Areas.* Retrieved from http://www.justice.gov/ndic/pubs27/27612/appendb.htm

68 Ibid.

69 Ibid.

70 Ibid.

71 Ibid.

72 Smircich, L. (1983). "Concepts of Culture and Organizational Analysis." *Administrative Science Quarterly,* 342.

73 Bureau of Labor Statistics. (2011). "Correctional Officers." *Occupational Outlook Handbook, 2010–11 Edition.* Retrieved from http://www.bls.gov/oco/ocos156.htm

74 Dial, K. C., & Johnson, W. W. (2008). "Working Within the Walls: The Effect of Care From Coworkers on Correctional Employees." *Professional Issues in Criminal Justice,* 3(2), 17–31. Retrieved from https://kucampus.kaplan.edu/documentstore/docs09/pdf/picj/vol3/issue2/PICJ_Volume3_2_dial.pdf

75 Kauffman, K. (1988). *Prison Officers and Their World.* Cambridge, MA: Harvard University Press, 86.

76 Marquart, J. W., & Crouch, B. M. (1984). "Coopting the Kept: Using Inmates for Social Control in a Southern Prison." *Justice Quarterly, 1,* 491–509.

77 Lambert, E. G., Cluse-Tolar, T., & Hogan, N. L. (2007). "This Job is Killing Me: The Impact of Job Characteristics on Correctional Staff Job Stress." *Applied Psychology in Criminal Justice,* 3(2). Retrieved from http://www.apcj.org/documents/3_2_correctionalstaff.pdf

78 Ibid.

79 Federal Bureau of Prisons. (2003). *The Federal Bureau of Prisons' Drug Interdiction Activities.* Retrieved from http://www.justice.gov/oig/reports/BOP/e0302/final.pdf

80 Bureau of Justice Statistics. (2016). *Correctional Populations in the United States, 2016.* Retrieved from https://www.bjs.gov/content/pub/pdf/cpus15.pdf

81 Walmsley, R. (2008). *World Prison Population List* (8th ed.). Retrieved from http://www.kcl.ac.uk/depsta/law/research/icps/downloads/wppl-8th_41.pdf

82 Ibid.

83 Kirchhoff, S. M. (2010). "Economic Impacts of Prison Growth." *Congressional Research Service.* Retrieved from http://www.fas.org/sgp/crs/misc/R41177.pdf

84 Ibid.

85 Bureau of Labor Statistics, 2011.

86 Ditton, P. M., & Wilson, D. J. (1999). *Truth in Sentencing in State Prisons* (NCJ 170032). Retrieved from http://bjs.ojp.usdoj.gov/content/pub/pdf/tssp.pdf

Mauer, M., King, R. S., & Young, M. C. (2004). "The Meaning of 'Life': Long Prison Sentences in Context." *The Sentencing Project.* Retrieved from http://www.hawaii.edu/hivandaids/The_Meaning_Life__Long_Prison_Sentences_in_Context.pdf

87 Wilson, J. Q. (1995). "Crime and Public Policy." In J. Q. Wilson & J. Petersilia (Eds.), *Crime* (pp. 489–507). San Francisco, CA: Institute for Contemporary Studies Press.

88 Ibid., 501.

89 Maruschak, L. M. (2011). "Medical Problems of Prisoners." *Bureau of Justice Statistics.* Retrieved from http://www.bjs.gov/content/pub/html/mpp/mpp.cfm

Law Students for Reproductive Justice. (2008). *Women in Prison.* Retrieved from http://lsrj.org/documents/factsheets/08-09_Women_in_Prison.pdf

90 U. S. Department of Justice. (1999). *Substance Abuse and Treatment, State and Federal Prisoners.*

91 Florida Senate. (2010, October). *Youthful Offender Designation in the Department of Corrections, Interim Report 2011-114.*

92 Ibid.

93 Rikard, R. V., & Rosenberg, E. (2007). "Aging Inmates: A Convergence of Trends in the American Criminal Justice System." *Journal of Correctional Health Care, 13*(3), 150–162.

94 Doughty, P. (1999). *A Concern in Corrections: Special Health Needs.* Oklahoma City, OK: Oklahoma Department of Corrections.

95 Sheppard, R. (2001, April 9). "Growing Old Inside." *Maclean's,* 30–33.

96 Abramsky, S., & Fellner, J. (2003). "Ill Equipped: U.S. Prisons and Offenders with Mental Illness." *Human Rights Watch.* Retrieved from http://www.hrw.org/reports/2003/usa1003/usa1003.pdf

97 Fellner, J. (2006). "A Corrections Quandary: Mental Illness and Prison Rules." *Harvard Civil Rights-Civil Liberties Law Review, 41*(2), 391–412. Retrieved from http://www.law.harvard.edu/students/orgs/crcl/vol41_2/fellner.pdf

98 Abramsky & Fellner, 2003.

99 Ibid.

100 Hammett, T. M. (2006, June). "HIV/AIDS and Other Infectious Diseases Among Correctional Inmates: Transmission, Burden, and an Appropriate Response." *American Journal of Public Health, 96*(6), 974–978.

101 Ibid.

102 Ibid.

103 Bureau of Justice Statistics. (2015) Justice Expenditure and Employment Extracts, 2012 - Preliminary Justice Expenditure and Employment Extracts, 2012 – Preliminary. Retrieved from https://www.bjs.gov/index.cfm?ty=pbdetail&iid=5239

104 Pew Center on the States. (2010, April). *Prison Count 201.* Washington, D.C.

105 Florida Department of Corrections. (2001). *Analysis of the Impact of Inmate Programsupon Recidivism.*

106 Council of State Governments Justice Center. (n.d.). "Second Chance Act." *National Reentry Resource Center.* Retrieved from http://www.nationalreentryresourcecenter.org/about/second-chance-act

107 Ibid.

108 Glaze, L. E., & Bonczar, T. P. (2010). *Probation and Parole in the United States, 2009* (NCJ 231674). Retrieved from http://bjs.ojp.usdoj.gov/content/pub/pdf/ppus09.pdf

109 "Probation." (2011). *FindLaw.* Retrieved from http://criminal.findlaw.com/crimes/criminal_stages/stages-alternative-sentences/probation.html

110 Bureau of Justice Statistics. (2016). *Correctional Populations in the United States, 2015.* Retrieved from https://www.bjs.gov/content/pub/pdf/cpus15.pdf

111 Federal Bureau of Prisons. (2011). *Brief History of the Bureau of Prisons.* Retrieved from http://www.bop.gov/about/history.jsp

112 Ditton & Wilson, 1999.

113 Florida Department of Corrections. (2010). *Annual Statistics for Fiscal Year 2009–2010.*

114 Piquero, A. (2010). *Cost-Benefit Analysis for Jail and Alternatives to Jail.* Florida State University.

115 Scott-Hayward, C. S. (2009). "The Fiscal Crisis in Corrections: Rethinking Policies and Practices." *Center on Sentencing and Corrections.* Retrieved from http://www.pewcenteronthestates.org/uploadedFiles/Vera_state_budgets.pdf

116 Ibid.

117 Ibid.

118 Ibid.

119 Bottos, S. (2008). "An Overview of Electronic Monitoring in Corrections: The Issues and Implications." *Correctional Service Canada.* Retrieved from http://www.csc-scc.gc.ca/text/rsrch/reports/r182/r182-eng.pdf

120 DeMichele, M., & Payne, B. (2009). "Using Technology to Monitor Offenders: A Community Corrections Perspective." *American Correctional Association.* Retrieved from https://aca.org/fileupload/177/ahaidar/DeMichele_Payne.pdf

121 U.S. Department of Labor. (2011). Retrieved from http://bls.gov

122 Ibid.

123 Occupational Information Network. (n.d.). *Probation and Correctional Treatment Specialists.* Retrieved from http://www.occupationalinfo.org/onet/27305c.html

124 Ibid.

125 Ibid.

© GERARD BOTTINO/Shutterstock.com

CHAPTER 11

Juvenile Justice

KEY TERMS

- Adjudication hearing
- Age of majority
- Amenability hearing
- Boot camp
- Child Savers movement
- Cottage reformatories
- Deinstitutionalization
- Diminished culpability
- Disposition
- Drug Abuse Resistance Education (D.A.R.E.)
- Houses of refuge
- Juvenile delinquency
- Juvenile waiver hearing
- Monitoring the Future
- Moral panic
- National Youth Survey
- *Parens patriae*
- Reform schools
- Scared-straight programs
- Status offenses

CHAPTER OBJECTIVES

1. Describe the differences between juvenile courts and criminal courts.
2. Discuss the history of the juvenile justice system in the United States.
3. Analyze contemporary debates regarding the treatment and punishment of juvenile offenders.
4. Differentiate between types of juvenile corrections.
5. Explain theories of juvenile delinquency.
6. Examine patterns in juvenile victimization and offending.

Case Study: Kent v. United States

Prior to the Supreme Court's 1966 ruling in *Kent v. United States*, juveniles had few, if any, rights recognized within the legal system. This changed when the Supreme Court recognized that under the 14th Amendment to the Constitution, a juvenile had due process rights. In *Kent*, the court held that a juvenile has the right to counsel, the right to a hearing, and the right to be informed of what he or she is being charged with.

On September 2, 1961, an intruder entered a woman's apartment in Washington, D.C., stole her wallet, and raped her. Police discovered fingerprints at the scene and matched them to fingerprints taken from Morris A. Kent, a 16-year-old who had been on juvenile probation when he was 14 for house-breaking and an attempted purse-snatching. Kent was taken into custody by police on September 5, 1961. Rather than release Kent to a parent or take him to a juvenile court designee, as required by D.C. law, Kent was taken to police headquarters and interrogated for seven hours. That evening, he was taken to a local children's home, then picked up the next morning for further interrogation by the police. During his interrogations, Kent confessed to the incidents on September 2 and several other offenses. The day after his arrest, Kent's mother retained counsel for her son.

Under the D.C. Juvenile Court Act, Kent was legally a minor and therefore under the jurisdiction of the local juvenile court. The District of Columbia defines a minor as a person under the age of 18. Similar to other jurisdictions, however, Washington, D.C.'s juvenile code allowed for transfer (or waiver) of jurisdiction of a juvenile case to the adult criminal court on a case-by-case basis. To transfer a juvenile, a juvenile court judge was required to conduct a "full investigation" into the child's background and into the circumstances surrounding the offense. The court did not conduct an investigation and neither Kent, Kent's attorney, nor his mother were able to participate in a transfer decision hearing. Further, the court offered no written statement justifying Kent's transfer.

Kent was indicted on eight counts in the District Court and the case went to trial. A jury found Kent guilty on six of the eight counts and he received a total sentence of 30 to 90 years to serve.

After he was found guilty, Kent appealed his conviction and his case was eventually brought before the Supreme Court of the United States. There, the court ruled that the juvenile court's waiver of jurisdiction was procedurally invalid. The court ruled that the juvenile court, by not holding a hearing where Kent, his counsel, and his parents could have participated, violated Kent's fundamental due process rights. This violation made the waiver invalid, and the Supreme Court ordered that the case be remanded back to the juvenile court for a waiver hearing. A waiver can only be valid if the juvenile made it knowingly, intelligently, and voluntarily. The court found that Kent could not have made a knowing, intelligent, and voluntary waiver because he had been denied his due process rights.

Kent was one of the first times that the United States Supreme Court stepped in with regards to a juvenile case, and the ruling was significant. The court said that juvenile defendants were afforded rights under the 14th Amendment, including the right to counsel, the right to a hearing, and the right to know what they are being charged with.[1]

Delinquency

Delinquency can refer to many different things. Delinquency can refer to an account that has not been paid or a failure to do something that the law or duty requires. Within the context of this textbook, delinquency will refer to **juvenile delinquency**.

Juvenile delinquency A finding of criminal behavior in the juvenile system.

Juvenile delinquency can include any offense that would be a criminal offense if committed by an adult. Juvenile delinquency also includes status offenses—offenses that are criminal because of the defendant's age. Juvenile courts do not find juvenile defendants guilty or not guilty: instead, they find them either delinquent or not delinquent. In the United States in 2014, just over three out of every 100 youths from ages 10 through 17 were arrested.[2] In 1996, the juvenile arrest rate reached its highest levels in two decades, but by 2014, it had declined 65%.[3]

In order for a juvenile to be found delinquent, the burden of proof is on the state to demonstrate that the juvenile has committed a crime beyond

Adjudication hearing A hearing in which the juvenile offender is found to either be delinquent or not delinquent.

Status offenses Offenses that can only be committed by a juvenile, not an adult.

a reasonable doubt. This occurs during the **adjudication hearing**, which is the juvenile equivalent to a trial.

A juvenile defendant can be found delinquent by committing either a crime or a status offense. Crimes are illegal acts committed by a person of any age, whereas a **status offense** is an offense that is only illegal or forbidden to a limited number of people—in this case, juveniles. A status offense describes any behavior that is illegal for children yet legal for adults.[4] Examples of status offenses include truancy, consumption of alcohol by a minor, running away from home, incorrigibility, and violating curfew ordinances.[6] In the late 1960s and early 1970s there was a movement, discussed later in this chapter, aimed at removing status offenses from the jurisdiction of the juvenile courts.

Juvenile courts handled 46% of delinquency cases without the filing of a petition, more than half of these non-petitioned cases received some sort of sanction. Juveniles may have agreed to informal probation, restitution, or community service, or the court may have referred them to another agency for services. Although probation staff monitor the juvenile's compliance with the informal agreement, such dispositions generally involve little or no continuing supervision by probation staff.[96]

In 41% of all petitioned delinquency cases, the youth was not adjudicated delinquent. The court dismissed 60% of these cases. The cases dismissed by the court, together with the cases that were dismissed at intake, accounted for 448,200 cases (or 328 of 1,000 cases handled).[96]

In 59% of all petitioned cases, the courts imposed a formal sanction or waived the case to criminal court. Thus, of every 1,000 delinquency cases handled in 2010, 317 resulted in a court-ordered sanction or waiver.[96]

In 2010, 58% (428,200) of the cases that were handled formally (with the filing of a petition) resulted in a delinquency adjudication. In 61% (260,300) of cases adjudicated delinquent in 2010, formal probation was the most severe sanction ordered by the court. In contrast, 26% (112,600) of cases adjudicated delinquent resulted in placement outside the home in a residential facility.[96]

Like crime in general, much of juvenile crime is unreported. In order to better understand how much delinquent or criminal behavior juveniles are engaging in, academics, researchers, and politicians rely upon different methods for gathering information. The most common methods include the use of official records and self-report surveys.

One way that delinquency is measured is with the Uniform Crime Report (UCR). The UCR is an FBI compilation of information from law enforcement agencies from across the country. The UCR relies upon different agencies within each state to submit information about crimes that occur. Additionally, it compiles information from court records and police reports from across the country, and the information is further broken down by state and by major cities within each state.

FIGURE 11.1 HOW WERE DELINQUENCY CASES PROCESSED IN JUVENILE COURTS IN 2010?

The most severe sanction ordered in more than 55,000 adjudicated deliquency cases (13%) in 2010 was something other than residential placement or probation, such as restitution or community service

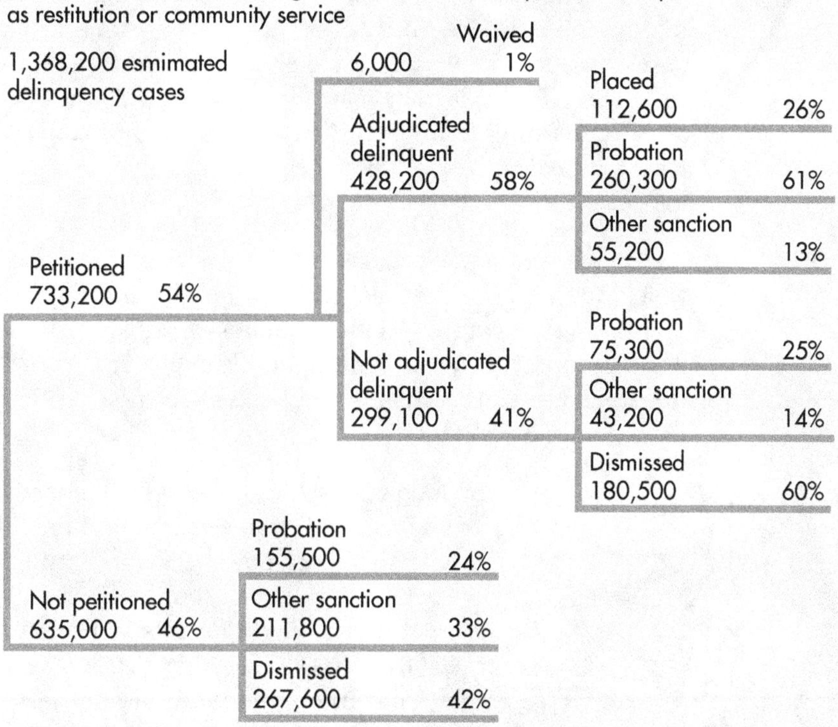

Adjudicated cases receiving sanctions other than residential placement or probation accounted for 40 out of 1,000 delinquency cases processed during the year

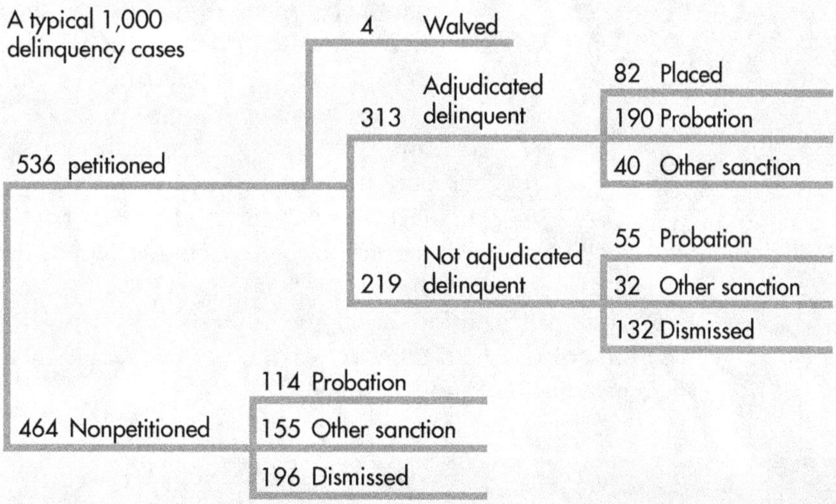

Notes: Cases are categorized by their most seververe or restrictive sanction. Detail may not add to totals because of rounding. Annual case processing flow diagrams for 1985 through 2010 are available online at ojjdp.gov/ojstatbb/court/laqs.asp

Source: Authors' adaptation of Puzzanchera et al.'s Juvenlo Court Statiscs 2010.

Delinquency reporting is also done through self-reporting. Self-reporting allows juveniles, and others involved in criminal activity, to report their own criminal activity through anonymous questionnaires. Most commonly, self-reporting questionnaires are handed out at schools and local detention centers. Social scientists then use the answers to track trends. Social scientists like using self-reporting questionnaires because they think that juveniles are less likely to lie about their criminal activity when the answers are anonymous. If juveniles are required to answer out loud and in front of their friends, they may not be as truthful. They could be boasting and exaggerating to impress their friends, or they could be lying to hide their criminal activity. Without peer pressure, their answers are more likely to be truthful.

Monitoring the Future A program that collects data on juveniles and is used by many social scientists.

Another program that collects data on juveniles is **Monitoring the Future**, which annually surveys about 50,000 middle and high school students.[7] Monitoring the Future specifically monitors smoking, drinking, and illegal drug use among students from eighth through 12th grade. The survey asks the same questions each year and looks to see how responses to the questions change over time.

© Sabphoto/Shutterstock.com

Monitoring the Future surveys juveniles regarding smoking, drinking, and illegal drug use.

By following some of the same students year after year and by asking the same questions, Monitoring the Future is able to reflect how behaviors, attitudes, and values change across all age groups, especially as the students leave different environments and transition into new roles. The survey reflects the developmental changes that show up consistently, and shows the inherent differences within class cohorts that remain through all stages of life.

National Youth Survey A compilation of many different surveys measuring gang participation and drug use.

The final way that delinquency is commonly reported is through the **National Youth Survey**. The National Youth Survey is sponsored by the National Institute of Mental Health and contains a multitude of different surveys. Each survey is designed to look at specific issues ranging from gang participation to drug use to families. The questions are designed to find out participants' age, race, languages spoken, extracurricular participation, family income, family background, relationships with parents or guardians, and feelings about drugs, smoking, and alcohol. Researchers look at all of this information and try to understand why some juveniles commit crimes and if there are any factors that would make it more likely for a juvenile to commit a crime.

The Nature and History of Juvenile Justice

Over the last few decades, the judicial system has dramatically changed the way that it treats children. Historically, in the American legal system children were treated either as property or as adults. The idea that a system should be created to deal with juveniles, and juveniles alone, did not develop until the 20th century.[8] Children under the age of five or six were considered to be the property of their parents: when they were delinquent, they were released to their parents to be dealt with as their parents saw fit. Depending upon the state, as soon as the child turned either five or six, he or she was considered to be an adult in the eyes of the law. It was assumed that a child of that age could form the requisite mens rea, or criminal intent, to be held responsible for their crimes.

Since the 1920s, the Supreme Court has continually recognized the rights of parents and guardians to raise and discipline their children. In 1923, the Supreme Court stated that it was "the natural duty of the parent to give his children education suitable to his station in life."[9] In *Prince v. Commonwealth of Massachusetts*, the Supreme Court reiterated its stance and said, "It is cardinal with us that the custody, care and nurture of the child reside first in the parents, whose primary function and freedom include preparation for obligations the state can neither supply nor hinder. . . . It is in recognition of this that these decisions have respected the private realm of family life which the state cannot enter."[10]

Dating back to the 1500s and 1600s, when children got into trouble that could not simply be disciplined by their parents or families, they could be punished in one of three ways. The first was the apprenticeship system, mostly used for middle- and upper-class children, who would serve as assistants to a skilled craftsman. A second form of punishment, used mainly for poor children, was the binding-out system, in which children could be bound out to any responsible adult for whatever purpose needed. A third form of punishment was church discipline, in which children were flogged, whipped, or branded by church officials. Punishments for children were not significantly different than those for adults.

Early social reformers pushed for changes within the judicial system. Initially, these changes took place outside the confines of the state-run legal system and were funded privately. Social reformers were the champions for change, and in 1825 the first house of refuge was founded. It later was followed by cottage reformatories and reform schools. Houses of refuge were precursors to modern-day juvenile facilities. These houses sought to help juveniles by rehabilitating them, educating them, and teaching them life skills. Cottage reformatories had goals similar to those of the houses of refuge. The main difference between the two was location: a house of refuge was located in the city and a cottage reformatory was located in the country. Juveniles housed in cottage reformatories were taught more agricultural life skills than industrial life skills. Reform schools were juvenile correctional institutes.

In 1899, Cook County in Illinois established the first American juvenile court. In doing so, Illinois was the first state to officially recognize that a child should not be treated the same way as an adult. The early juvenile court was influenced by the British legal doctrine of *parens patriae*.

Parens patriae A legal theory, most often associated with juveniles and the mentally ill, that allows the state to step in and protect those who legally cannot protect themselves. Latin for "the state as a parent."

Parens patriae, Latin for "the state as parent," is the idea that the state has a duty to serve as a guardian of juveniles when parents are unable or unwilling to do so.[11] The state assumes the role of the parent and takes responsibility for punishing, guiding, teaching, and educating juveniles. Under the legal doctrine of *parens patriae*, the court is responsible for acting in the best interest of the child. By 1925, juvenile court systems had been established in 48 states.

Prior to 1904, the concept of adolescence had no distinct and formal legal meaning. In 1904, five years after the first juvenile court was established, psychologist Stanley G. Hall published *Adolescence*, an influential book in which he attempted to define adolescence. Hall described adolescence as a "turbulent period of physical, emotional, and sexual development during which youths needed to be shielded from adult duties and expectations."[12] Beginning to understand that juveniles and adults were different led to further development of the juvenile system. Psychology, a growing field at the time, helped bring attention to the differences between children and adults.

In recognizing the inherent differences between adults and children, the juvenile court sought to treat juvenile offenders differently. The juvenile court's mission was fundamentally different from that of the adult criminal court, which was designed to be punitive. Proceedings in adult courts could result in the loss of liberty, or in some cases, life. To ensure that the state does not overstep its authority in causing the loss of liberty or life, defendants within the adult system are protected by due process. In contrast, the juvenile system was designed to rehabilitate. The juvenile court's job was to fashion a **disposition**, or sentence, that would fit that particular juvenile's social and emotional needs.

Disposition The sentencing of a defendant.

The Child Savers Movement

Child Savers movement A movement by a group of reformers in the early 19th century that sought to change the way juveniles were treated by the justice system.

Many of the changes and reforms that came about during the late 19th and early 20th centuries were the result of the **Child Savers movement**. Members of the Child Savers movement were concerned that children were being treated the same as adults. They were outraged that children could receive long prison sentences and be placed in jails with adult criminals, with no distinction between the two. Klein (1998) wrote that the Child Savers movement "believed society's role was not to ascertain whether the child was 'guilty' or 'innocent,' but 'What is he, how has he become what he is, and what had best be done in his interest and in the interest of the state to save him from a downward career.'" In their view, children should not be made to feel that they were under arrest or on trial, but rather that they were the object of the state's care.[13]

Child Savers wanted the state to step in to care for and rehabilitate wayward juveniles. They did not want to see juveniles punished as harshly as their adult counterparts, and believed that intervention and rehabilitation would "save" troubled juveniles. The Child Savers were biased in their efforts, and the majority of their efforts were directed at the poor or children of immigrants. Though middle- and upper-class white children misbehaved, they were shielded from state intervention or control.

Child Savers not only advocated for changes within the legal system, but also developed their own programs to rehabilitate juveniles, to educate them, and to teach them a craft. Many of the programs that were developed by the Child Savers, including orphan trains, houses of refuge, cottage reformatories, and reform schools, will be discussed further in the next section.

Critical Thinking
At what age should a child be considered criminally responsible?

Orphan Trains

Charles Loring Brace and other New York social reformers founded the Children's Aid Society, one of the major proponents of the orphan trains, in 1853. For the following 75 years, the Children's Aid Society helped to transport over 200,000 abandoned, orphaned, and homeless children from New York City to the Midwest.[14]

Brace's devotion to helping poor children was considered radical at the time. His goal was to transform New York's orphans into productive and contributing members of society by providing them with work opportunities, education, and a welcoming family atmosphere.[15]

Brace wanted to send New York's abandoned, orphaned, and homeless children to live with what he considered moral farm families in the Midwest. This idea was sometimes called "placing out." In placing out, a child was removed from an urban area and placed with a family in the Midwest. Brace believed the best way to help orphans improve their lives was to remove them from the poverty and debauchery of New York City streets.[16] Each orphan, upon being placed on an "orphan train," was given a small suitcase to carry his or her possessions. Often, this was just a change of clothes and nothing else.

The trains, carrying children as young as five and as old as 16, would travel from New York across the country and into Canada and Mexico. Upon arriving in each town, the children would be cleaned up, marched from the train, and taken to the meeting place. The meeting place could be anywhere—from the town square to a barn, a courthouse, or even a church. Usually, the meeting place had a platform where the children all stood. The townspeople were able to examine the children prior to agreeing to adopt them. Some were looking for children to help on the farm and would examine a child's teeth and muscles before selecting them. Still others were looking for young children, some were looking for only girls, and some were looking for boys. Once selected, children went home with their new families. If a child was not selected, he or she re-boarded the train and headed to the next town.

© A3pfamily/Shutterstock.com

Over 200,000 homeless children were transported from New York City to the Midwest on Orphan Trains.

After settling with their new families, the orphans were encouraged to forget about their old lives in New York. They were asked to forget about their parents, brothers, sisters, grandparents, aunts, uncles, and cousins—most never saw their New York families again.

Orphan Trains were the precursor to state intervention in juveniles' lives and reflective of the middle- and upper-class bias of Child Savers. Poor, urban, and largely immigrant children were taken from big cities and given to farming families. It is questionable whether these children were indeed "homeless" or "abandoned." Brace's beliefs were founded in the idea of *parens patriae*. He and the others in the Children's Aid Society substituted their judgment for the judgment of the parents.

Houses of Refuge

The New York House of Refuge was the first juvenile reformatory in the country.[17] From the very beginning, the state of New York helped to organize, fund, establish daily procedures, and develop treatment programs. The New York House of Refuge officially opened in 1825 with six boys and three girls, and within a decade it had close to 1,700 inmates.[18] The New York House of Refuge did not close its doors until 1935—110 years after it first began to house inmates.

Within a few years of the New York House of Refuge opening its doors, other houses of refuge opened across the country. All followed similar models and had similar goals. Price (2009) writes: "These houses were created for juveniles who lived in an environment that produced bad habits. These habits were considered a setback for juveniles trying to escape the pressures of committing serious offenses."[19] **Houses of refuge** sought to rehabilitate, educate, and provide vocational training and religion to wayward youth. Children could be committed to the houses for vagrancy or because they had committed petty crimes. They could be committed indefinitely or sentenced for a period of time.

Houses of refuge Houses that sought to rehabilitate, educate, and provide vocational training and religion to juvenile offenders and vagrants.

The houses were privately run, but accepted juveniles by court order. The Pennsylvania Supreme Court, in discussing a house of refuge's goal and why a house of refuge was the proper place for wayward youth, stated:

> "The House of Refuge is not a prison, but a school. . . . The object of charity is reformation by training of inmates: by imbuing their minds with principles of morality and religion; by furnishing them with a means to earn a living, and above all, by separating them from the corrupting influences of improper associates. To this end,

> may not the natural parents when unequal to the task of education, or unworthy of it, be superseded by the *parens patriae* or common community."[20]

The concept of *parens patriae* has developed into a legal theory, most often associated with juveniles and the mentally ill, that allows the state to step in and protect those who legally cannot protect themselves. Again, the state used this theory to substitute its own decision-making abilities for those of the natural parents.

While houses of refuge fell out of favor almost 110 years after the first one opened, the doctrine of *parens patriae* is still seen today within the modern judicial system in Child In Need of Assistance (CINA) or Child In Need of Supervision cases (CHINS), as well as foster care.

CINA or CHINS cases are generally emergency cases where the state seeks to remove a child or children from the home of their natural parent or guardian. The state seeks to prove that the parent is not the proper person to have custody of the child, and that the child would be safer and better off in the care and custody of the state.

Cottage Reformatories and Reform Schools

In the mid-to-late 1880s, houses of refuge were facing harsh criticism. Critics focused on the fact that the houses were overcrowded, conditions were harsh, children were abused, and there was little rehabilitation. From these criticisms, the idea for the cottage reformatory was born. The cottage reformatory had many of the same goals as a house of refuge, but operated in a different manner.

Cottage reformatories, unlike houses of refuge, were located in rural areas and tried to simulate family. A juvenile sent to a cottage reformatory would find himself or herself in a rural area with approximately 20 to 40 other juveniles. This process of moving a juvenile from the city to the country was commonly referred to as "placing out." The juveniles would then be broken up into smaller groups, and from there, they would go live in "cottages" with cottage parents. Cottage parents were adults that lived in the cottages with a small group of juveniles, helping simulate the family experience for the juveniles. These "parents" would teach them skills—mainly farming and manual labor—and be in charge of educating them. This was different from a house of refuge, which was located in the city and housed hundreds of juveniles in one location.

Cottage reformatories Reformatories that taught juveniles farm skills; designed to house 20 to 40 offenders in a cottage with cottage parents.

Following on the heels of the houses of refuge and cottage reformatories, states began to build and fund state-run **reform schools**. In 1847, Massachusetts opened its first reform school. It was followed closely by New York in 1849, and Maine in 1853. Price writes:

Reform schools The first state-run schools designed to reform juvenile offenders.

> "These schools were founded on strong principles: (1) Young offenders must be segregated from the corrupting influences of

> adult criminals, (2) Delinquents need to be removed from their environment and imprisoned for their own good and protection; reformatories should be guarded sanctuaries, (3) Delinquents should be assigned to reformatories without trial and with minimal legal requirements . . . (4) Sentences should be indeterminate, so that inmates are encouraged to cooperate in their own reform and recalcitrant delinquents are not allowed to resume their criminal careers, and (5) Reformation should not be confused with sentimentality."[21]

Reform schools remained in effect until the emergence of the modern-day juvenile justice system. Today, reform schools are referred to as juvenile detention centers. Reform schools are different from alternative schools, which will be discussed in more detail later in the chapter.

Emergence of the Juvenile Courts

In 1899, with the passage of *An Act for the Treatment and Control of Dependent, Neglected, and Delinquent Children*, Cook County, Illinois, established the first juvenile justice system. Within 25 years, 48 states had created a juvenile justice system based on the model started in Cook County.

The newly developed juvenile courts focused less on punishment and more on rehabilitation and socialization. Brink (2004) writes: "Separate juvenile correctional facilities were created that stressed educational and vocational training, sentences were often shorter, courts made greater use of probationary and other diversionary alternatives to incarceration, and the criminal records of juvenile offenders were not made a matter of public record in order to prevent stigmatization that might interfere with successful rehabilitation."[22]

For any criminal acts committed by juveniles, juvenile court holds jurisdiction.[23] In some cases, though, a juvenile court will transfer a juvenile matter to criminal court. A juvenile court may waive jurisdiction over a case, or in some instances, the legislature may mandate juveniles accused of certain crimes to be transferred to criminal court. In some jurisdictions, prosecutors have the power to choose whether to file a case in juvenile or criminal court.[24] These waiver hearings are sometimes called **amenability hearings** because the court must decide whether the juvenile will be amenable to treatment within the juvenile system or needs to be dealt with in the adult system.

Amenability hearing
A hearing to determine how well a juvenile offender will respond to treatment within the juvenile system or if the juvenile is better suited to be in the adult system.

Juvenile waiver hearing
A hearing held before a judge to determine whether a juvenile will remain in the juvenile system or be transferred to adult criminal court.

Often, the prosecutor and the defense attorney are at odds over which court should have jurisdiction over a case where a juvenile defendant is involved. As discussed earlier, under *Kent v. United States*, a juvenile has the right to a **juvenile waiver hearing**.

Prior to a juvenile waiver hearing, a report is prepared for the judge. The report usually contains information regarding the juvenile defendant's background, including family, education, medical history, and past (if any) criminal record. The report also discusses the age of the defendant at the time the alleged crime occurred, the severity of the crime, and the defendant's amenability to treatment. The judge weighs each factor and decides whether the factor weighs in favor of the prosecution or the defense, or is neutral to both parties. Once the judge has finished weighing each factor, he or she decides whether to retain the case in the adult court or to remand the case back to the juvenile courts.

Juvenile Court vs. Adult Criminal Court

© Africa Studio/Shutterstock.com

Prior to a juvenile waiver hearing, the judge receives a report containing information about the crime and the juvenile defendant's background.

Most people have some familiarity with the adult criminal court system through firsthand experience or television. They know that a defendant charged with a crime in the adult criminal system has certain trial rights—the right to confront witnesses; the right to a jury or bench trial; the right to remain silent; and the right to counsel. They know that a defendant can be found guilty or not guilty, and that the courtroom is open to the public.

The public's knowledge about the juvenile court system is much more limited. There are significant differences between the two systems. The first difference is the offenders themselves. The adult criminal system has exclusive jurisdiction over any defendant who committed a crime while over the age of majority (which varies depending on the state) and concurrent jurisdiction with the juvenile court system with a defendant who committed a crime while under the age of majority. Concurrent jurisdiction occurs when a defendant can be charged in the juvenile system, but, because of age, the severity of the crime, and the offender's prior criminal history, the prosecutor has charged the defendant within the adult criminal system. The defendant can only be tried in the juvenile system or the adult criminal system—not both. In *Breed v. Jones* (1975), the Supreme Court held that once a juvenile had been adjudicated in juvenile court, the juvenile could not be transferred to adult criminal court.[25] This would constitute double jeopardy.

When the adult criminal court and the juvenile court share concurrent jurisdiction over a defendant, a waiver hearing is held. In that hearing, a judge determines whether or not the defendant will be under the jurisdiction of the adult or juvenile system.

If a defendant is to be tried within the adult criminal system, all court proceedings are open to the public and the public has the right to examine the files, unless sealed by court order. If the defendant is placed under the jurisdiction of the juvenile system, the public's right to know is severely limited. Juvenile proceedings can be open or closed to the public, but juvenile records—including information about charges and sentences—are closed.

Accessibility to the public is one of the biggest differences between the juvenile and adult system. The public's accessibility to information regarding proceedings is limited because the goals of the two systems are drastically different. The adult criminal system is looking to punish those who break the law and deter them from doing it again, while the juvenile justice system is looking to rehabilitate. By limiting the public's access to juveniles' records, the juvenile justice system is hoping to allow juveniles to begin their adult lives without any of the baggage or limitations that attach to an adult criminal conviction.

Critical Thinking

Why do you think that juvenile waiver hearings are so important in the juvenile justice system?

The juvenile justice system offers many offenders access to psychiatric and drug treatment and job training.

Another major difference between the two systems is the programs that are available within the juvenile justice system. The juvenile system has many more programs available to it than the adult system, because the juvenile system is looking to rehabilitate offenders while the adult system is seeking to punish. Within the juvenile system, the offenders have access to psychiatric and drug treatment, job training, and other classes. These programs are designed to give the offenders the best chance of joining society as productive members.

With the emergence of the juvenile courts and the programs associated with them, the hope was that the juvenile system would be able to prevent juvenile offenders from re-offending once they became adults.

Critical Thinking

Assess the current differences between juvenile and adult courts. Do you believe further changes are needed to juvenile courts? What changes do you think would be appropriate?

Major U.S. Supreme Court Decisions

Kent v. United States was not the only major juvenile justice decision that came from the United States Supreme Court. The 1960s and 1970s saw the Supreme Court issue opinions that directly affected juvenile offenders. During this time, the Supreme Court was especially concerned because it felt that juveniles were receiving the worst of both worlds. In the juvenile system, they were being denied due process rights including the right to counsel, the right to cross-examine and confront witnesses, the right to a hearing, and so forth. *Kent*, and the cases that followed, sought to protect juveniles by guaranteeing them their due process rights.

In re Gault

In 1967, the United States Supreme Court heard arguments in *In re Gault.*[26] On June 8, 1964, Gerald Francis Gault and his friend Ronald Lewis were taken into custody in Arizona because a complaint had been filed against the two by their neighbor, Mrs. Cook. Mrs. Cook alleged that the boys had telephoned her and made lewd, offensive, and sexually suggestive remarks.[27]

Gerald's parents were at work when he was taken into custody, and they did not learn that he was in custody until his older brother was sent to look for him at the Lewis home. On June 9, a hearing was held in front of a juvenile judge. No record of the hearing was made, and neither of Gerald's parents saw a notice of the hearing. A subsequent hearing was held on June 15, and again no record of the hearing was made.

Mrs. Cook, the complainant against Gerald and Ronald, was not present at the June 9 or the June 15 hearings. At the June 15 hearing, the probation officers filed a "referral report" with the juvenile judge, but the report was not given or disclosed to the Gaults. At the hearing, Gerald was committed as a juvenile delinquent to the State Industrial School until he reached the age of 21. At the time of his commitment, Gerald was 15 years old.

The Gaults appealed the case to the U.S. Supreme Court alleging that Gerald's due process rights were denied. Specifically, they alleged that Gerald, and they, had been denied notice of the charges, their right to counsel, their right to dispute evidence and to cross-examine witnesses, protection against self-incrimination, and a right to a transcript of the proceedings.

The Supreme Court reaffirmed its holding in *Kent v. United States* in *Gault* and addressed each of the Gaults' allegations. First, the court found that the Gaults did not receive adequate notice in the case. "Notice, to comply with due process requirements, must be given sufficiently in advance of scheduled court proceedings so that reasonable opportunity to prepare will be afforded, and it must set for the alleged misconduct with particularity."[28] If the juvenile offender or the offender's parents does not receive notice of a hearing, then the juvenile offender's due process rights have been violated.

Next, the court looked at the Gaults' allegation that they were denied the right to counsel. The court concluded that under the due process clause of the 14th Amendment, "the child and his parents must be notified of the child's right to be represented by counsel retained by them, or if they are unable to afford counsel, that counsel will be appointed to represent the child."[29]

The court then looked to see if Gerald's statements were lawfully obtained. The court found that neither Gerald nor his parents were informed of his right to not make a statement, and they were not informed that Gerald could be committed as a delinquent if he made an incriminating statement. The court found, after a careful examination of the language of the Fifth Amendment and looking at case law from other states, that the "constitutional privilege against self-incrimination is applicable in the case of juveniles as it is with respect to adults."[30] Because it was not made in the presence of counsel or his parents, and he was not made aware of his right to remain silent and to not make incriminating statements, Gerald's confession could not be used against him.

After the court addressed the validity of Gerald's confession, it addressed Gerald's right to confrontation and cross-examination. Mrs. Cook, the complainant, was not present at any of the hearings, and Gerald could not confront her about her complaint or cross-examine her about anything that she said. Both were violations of his due process rights guaranteed under the 14th Amendment.

This case was important to the evolution of juvenile proceedings because the Supreme Court specifically held that juvenile defendants were to be afforded due process rights under the 14th Amendment.

Exhibit: Excerpt from *In re Gault*

"I think the Constitution requires that he be tried in accordance with the guarantees of all the provisions of the Bill of Rights made applicable to the States by the Fourteenth Amendment. Undoubtedly this would be true of an adult defendant, and it would be a plain denial of equal protection of the laws—an invidious discrimination—to hold that others subject to heavier punishments could because they are children, be denied these same constitutional safeguards. I consequently agree with the Court that the Arizona law as applied here denied to the parents and their son the right of notice, right to counsel, right against self-incrimination, and right to confront the witnesses against young Gault. Appellants are entitled to these rights, not because 'fairness, impartiality and orderliness—in short, the essentials of due process'—require them and not because they are 'the procedural rules which have been fashioned from the generality of due process,' but because they are specifically and unequivocally granted by provisions of the Fifth and Sixth Amendments which the Fourteenth Amendment makes applicable to the States."

In re Winship

Following *In re Gault*, the Supreme Court's next major decision involving juveniles was decided in 1970, in *In re Winship*.[31] In *Winship*, the court decided the question of "whether proof beyond a reasonable doubt is among the 'essentials of due process and fair treatment' required during the adjudicatory stage when a juvenile is charged with an act which would constitute a crime if committed by an adult."[32] The court decided that under the due process clause, the state was required to prove every element beyond a reasonable doubt in order to find the juvenile delinquent.

Samuel Winship, then 12 years old, was first found delinquent at a 1967 adjudicatory hearing. A judge in New York Family Court found that Winship had stolen $112 from a wallet in a locker. Winship's counsel asserted that the state needed to prove that he was guilty beyond a reasonable doubt, as required in adult criminal court. The judge disagreed and found that he only needed to find Winship delinquent by a preponderance of the evidence as required by New York statutes.

Later, at a disposition hearing, Winship was ordered to be placed in a training school for 18 months, with possible yearly extensions of his commitment until he reached the age of 18—six years later.

The case was appealed to the U.S. Supreme Court, which found that Winship was entitled to be found delinquent by the same standard, beyond a reasonable doubt, as an adult criminal charged with the same offense would.

This case further solidified the juvenile defendant's rights under the 14th Amendment and the due process clause. Most importantly, the decision held that a juvenile defendant could not be found delinquent of a crime unless the state had proved every element of the crime beyond a reasonable doubt. This changed the standard of proof in juvenile proceedings and made a juvenile proceeding more similar to an adult criminal proceeding.

The Supreme Court case of In re Gault held that juveniles were to be afforded due process rights under the 14th Amendment.

Recent Changes in the Juvenile System

In 1974, Congress brought about changes within the juvenile system by enacting the Juvenile Justice and Delinquency Prevention Act (JJDPA).[33] The original act established the Office of Juvenile Justice and Delinquency Prevention to oversee programs established under the act. It was later updated in 2002. The Act is now expired, but the Coalition for Juvenile Justice Organization is working with Congress to get the Juvenile Justice and Delinquency Prevention Act reauthorized.

This act provided funding for many community-based programs.[34] The JJDPA also set up requirements to assure that status offenders were not housed with delinquents in juvenile correctional facilities. In order for state juvenile justice facilities to receive federal grants, they needed to adhere to the requirements of the JJDPA.[35]

Today, the juvenile justice system does not seek to just rehabilitate and institutionalize. It seeks to rehabilitate through community-based programs to provide juveniles with the skills and tools to operate in the world.

Deinstitutionalization Movement

Deinstitutionalization The process of removing status offenders from the juvenile court system and removing juvenile offenders from adult detention centers.

The **deinstitutionalization** movement developed in the 1970s, seeking to remove many of the nonviolent juvenile offenders and status offenders from being housed in juvenile detention centers, and to remove juvenile offenders from adult detention centers. Proponents of deinstitutionalization were fearful that status offenders and nonviolent offenders would learn violent behaviors while in custody. In 1980, Congress passed legislation prohibiting the United States from detaining juveniles in jails and correctional facilities, and specified that status offenders and nonviolent offenders should be removed from these institutions.[36]

Exhibit: Excerpt from *In re Winship*

"We turn to the question whether juveniles, like adults, are constitutionally entitled to proof beyond a reasonable doubt when they are charged with violation of a criminal law. The same considerations that demand extreme caution in fact finding to protect the innocent adult apply as well to the innocent child. . . . In sum, the constitutional safeguard of proof beyond a reasonable doubt is as much required during the adjudicatory stage of a delinquency proceeding as are those constitutional safeguards applied in Gault—notice of charges, right to counsel, the rights of confrontation and examination, and the privilege against self-incrimination. We therefore hold, in agreement with Chief Judge Fuld in dissent in the Court of Appeals, 'that, where a 12-year-old child is charged with an act of stealing which renders him liable to confinement for as long as six years, then, as a matter of due process . . . the case against him must be proved beyond a reasonable doubt.'"

Critical Thinking

Should juveniles ever be housed in adult prisons? If yes, in what situations?

Contemporary Juvenile Corrections

The first goal of the juvenile justice system is to rehabilitate. The juvenile justice system hopes that rehabilitation will prevent juvenile offenders from entering the adult criminal justice system. The juvenile justice system has many tools that it employs to first try to rehabilitate and then to punish.

Juvenile Probation

As with adult offenders, juveniles can be placed on probation. Probation allows the juvenile justice system to keep tabs on offenders while at the same time keeping the offenders out of the more formal institutions like juvenile correction institutes.[37] Probation has ranges of supervision intensity. It can be anywhere from highly intensive to essentially unsupervised.

Probation can follow a period of confinement, but when judges sentence juvenile offenders, they have many options when crafting a sentence. They can give the offender a straight period of confinement; a period of confinement followed by probation; a period of confinement, where either part or all has been suspended, followed by probation; or, finally, a period of straight probation.

While on probation, juvenile offenders are monitored by and have a probation agent who is specifically assigned to their case. While the duties of juvenile probation officers can vary by state or jurisdiction, these responsibilities typically include screening juvenile or family court cases, conducting a pre-sentence investigation of juveniles, and supervising juvenile offenders.[38] An offender who is on an intensive period of supervision may have to contact his or her probation agent a few times per week or every day either by phone or in person. An offender who is under less intensive supervision may only have to see the probation agent once a month.

The juvenile probation agent monitors offenders and makes sure that they are following their probation—if not, the agent will report the violations of probation to the court. Violating probation can lead to serious consequences for juvenile offenders. Periodically, probation agents will send the courts "violation of probation" reports. These reports are designed to keep the courts informed if an offender has violated any of the terms of his or her probation. Upon receiving a violation of probation report, the court will hold an evidentiary hearing in order to decide whether the offender is guilty or not guilty of violating his or her probation.

One of the most common and most serious ways a juvenile offender can violate his or her probation is to be found guilty of another charge. Other ways include not following a certain condition of probation. If the court finds the juvenile offender guilty of violating his or her probation, there are a number of recourses available to the judge. The judge can do one of several things: impose the balance of the offender's suspended sentence if the offender received a split sentence; impose up to the remainder of the suspended sentence if the judge suspended all of the time; continue probation; or terminate probation.

How a judge handles a violation of probation can differ from judge to judge, offender to offender, and case to case. Some judges prefer to continue offenders on probation and give them second chances, especially for minor

FIGURE 11.2 JUVENILES IN RESIDENTIAL PLACEMENT, PLACEMENT STATUS BY STATE, 2013 98

In 2013, 173 Juvenile offenders were in placement for every 100,000 juveniles in the U.S. population

In 2013, the national commitment rate was twice the detention rate, but rates varied by state

State of offense	Juveniles in placement	Placement rate per 100,000 Total	Detained	Committed	State of offense	Juveniles in placement	Placement rate per 100,000 Total	Detained	Committed
U.S. total	54,148	173	57	114	**Upper age 17 (continued)**				
Upper age 17					North Dakota	171	253	22	231
Alabama	933	184	72	99	Ohio	2,283	186	77	109
Alaska	195	241	96	145	Oklahoma	519	125	57	68
Arizona	882	122	46	73	Oregon	1,086	281	35	245
Arkansas	681	215	70	142	Pennsylvania	2,781	222	35	186
California	8,094	197	88	108	Rhode Island	159	158	27	131
Colorado	1,077	197	61	134	South Dakota	333	376	71	302
Connecticut	279	74	32	41	Tennessee	666	99	33	66
Delaware	159	176	86	90	Utah	612	160	53	108
Dist. of Columbia	228	560	258	302	Vermont	27	46	25	20
Florida	2,802	152	45	106	Virginia	1,563	188	65	122
Hawaii	78	60	25	34	Washington	1,014	144	39	105
Idaho	450	236	64	170	West Virginia	510	294	112	178
Indiana	1,581	219	89	126	Wyoming	165	279	15*	264
Iowa	735	227	53	168	**Upper age 16**				
Kansas	885	278	89	186	Georgia	1,557	159	79	79
Kentucky	774	170	48	120	Illinois	1,617	134	61	72
Maine	162	130	31	99	Louisiana	774	180	51	128
Maryland	771	127	50	78	Michigan	1,683	183	47	133
Massachusetts	393	60	24	36	Missouri	1,053	191	38	146
Minnesota	939	165	38	119	New Hampshire	78	68	13	52
Mississippi	243	74	30	44	South Carolina	672	159	24	134
Montana	150	151	60	84	Texas	4,383	161	65	95
Nebraska	411	204	67	136	Wisconsin	816	156	47	107
Nevada	591	201	33	134	**Upper age 15**				
New Jersy	888	95	41	54	New York	1,650	116	28	87
New Mexico	402	179	52	127	North Carolina	543	70	19	41

Detention rate

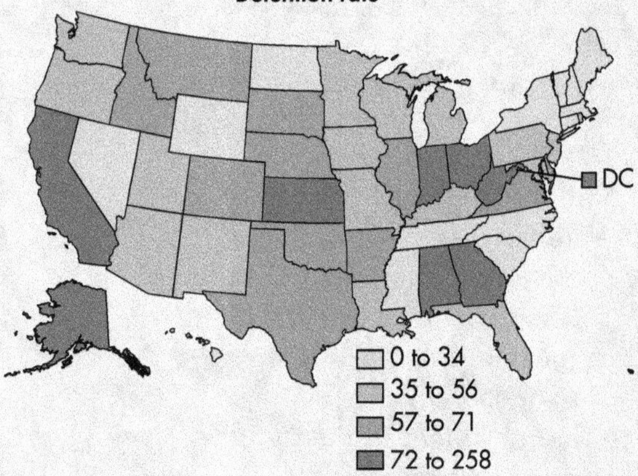

Commitment rate

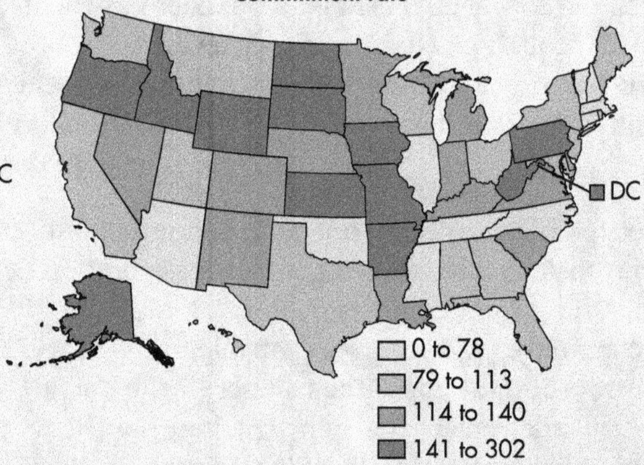

* Rate is based on fewer than 10 juveniles.

Notes: Placement rate is the count of juvenile offenders in placement on the census data per 100,000 youth ages 10 throughs the upper age of original juvenile court jurisdiction in each state. U.S. total includes 2,648 youth in private facilities for whom state of offense was not reported and 5 youth who committed their offense in a U.S. territory.

Data source: Author's analysis of OJJDP's Census of Juveniles inResidential placement for 2013 [machine-readable data files].

infractions. Still others believe that by placing offenders on probation instead of strictly committing them, they have already given the offenders their second chance, and so if they violate probation, the only way to teach and reform them is to commit them.

In an effort to keep nonviolent juveniles out of juvenile detention centers as part of the deinstitutionalization movement, judges have put juvenile defendants into diversionary programs. The idea of diversionary programs was to divert a portion of the juveniles from the system. As the state created more ways to deal with offenders, it expanded the number of people it supervised, even though these programs were intended to replace or reduce more punitive options. This phenomenon is known as "net-widening," and it is an ongoing issue throughout the criminal justice system, not just the juvenile system.[39]

Career Connections: Juvenile Probation Officer

A juvenile probation officer supervises juvenile offenders who have been put on probation by a judge in the juvenile court. The juvenile probation officer's responsibilities include supervising juveniles, maintaining communications with judges and law enforcement agencies, and connecting juveniles with needed resources in the community. Juvenile probation officers prepare and maintain case records and various reports, forms, and court documents regarding the juveniles they oversee.

A juvenile probation agent may be required to make inquiries into probationers' problems, antecedents, character, family history, and environment. Further, he or she may make recommendations to the courts through written reports and oral testimony to be used during disposition. Juvenile probation officers also testify at hearings and transport clients between residential and correctional facilities.

A juvenile probation officer must have a bachelor's degree in criminal justice, social work, psychology, or a related field. The median salary for a probation officer in the United States earns approximately $47,149 per year. The most influential factor affecting pay for this group is location, though years of experience and the individual firm have a (lesser) impact as well. Male probation officers are just a bit more common among those who completed the questionnaire than female ones, with male workers composing 52 percent of the field. A large number report receiving medical coverage from their employers and a fair number collect dental insurance. Most probation officers like their work and job satisfaction is high.[40]

Community-Based Corrections

In the 1980s, the idea of community-based corrections began to take hold. Community-based correctional facilities provide nonviolent offenders with the rehabilitative programs that they need. Funding for community-based corrections was provided by the Juvenile Justice and Delinquency Prevention Act of 1974. The act defined a community-based facility to be a "small, open group home or other suitable place located near the juvenile's home or family and programs of community supervision and service which maintain community and consumer participation in the planning operation, and evaluation of their programs which may include, but are not limited to, medical, educational, vocational, social, and psychological guidance, training, special education, counseling, alcoholism treatment, drug treatment, and other rehabilitative services."[41] Examples of community-based correction centers include residential and group homes.

The goal of the community-based correction facility was to take nonviolent offenders out of the jails and prisons and place them into the community under strict scrutiny. Offenders can enter a community-based correctional program in one of two ways. The first is after they have served all or part of their sentence. Upon release, the offender is released to the custody of the community-based correction program, where that program will monitor the offender and help the offender adjust to life outside of jail or prison walls.

An offender can also enter a community-based correctional program without being incarcerated. The judge, instead of sentencing the offender to jail, can sentence the offender to report directly to the program that has been ordered.

Community-based correctional programs gained popularity for a number of reasons. One of the biggest reasons that judges began sentencing defendants to these programs was because the programs provided for greater supervision than normal probation. Defendants subject to the rules of the community-based programs are usually drug tested, or on house arrest, or living in halfway houses. The programs were designed to help juveniles better adapt to the world that they were going to be released into and to help their families cope with the problems they would soon be facing.

Additionally, community-based correctional programs are much cheaper than housing an inmate in a normal correctional facility. They also help to alleviate overcrowding issues that are prevalent in many of today's correctional facilities.

Juvenile Detention Centers

Juvenile detention centers (JDCs), sometimes called youth detention centers, house and detain juvenile offenders awaiting their hearing dates and those who have already been adjudicated. Anyone who has committed a crime while under the age of majority can be housed in a juvenile detention center.

The **age of majority** is when a person is legally recognized as an adult. This can vary from state to state. For the majority of states, an individual reaches the age of majority at 18, but in other states this age can span from 19 to 21.

Age of majority The age at which a person reaches adulthood in the eyes of the law. This age is generally 18, but can vary from state to state.

Juvenile detention centers were created to separate adult inmates from juvenile offenders. The prevailing thought was that a juvenile offender was not physically or emotionally mature enough to handle the day-to-day trials that being housed in an adult facility would bring. JDCs were originally thought to be safer and easier places for juveniles to be placed.

FIGURE 11.3 AGE OF MAJORITY BY STATE AND UNITED STATES POSSESSION

State	Age	State	Age
Alabama	19	Nebraska	19
Alaska	18	Nevada	18
Arizona	18	New Hampshire	18
Arkansas	18	New Jersey	18
California	18	New Mexico	18
Colorado	18	New York	18
Connecticut	18	North Carolina	18
Delaware	18	North Dakota	18
District of Columbia	18	Ohio	18
Florida	18	Oklahoma	18
Georgia	18	Oregon	18
Hawaii	18	Pennsylvania	21
Idaho	18	Puerto Rico	21
Illinois	18	Rhode Island	18
Indiana	18	South Carolina	18
Iowa	18	South Dakota	18
Kansas	18	Tennessee	18
Kentucky	18	Texas	18
Louisiana	18	Utah	18
Maine	18	Vermont	18
Maryland	18	Virginia	18
Massachusetts	18	Virgin Islands	18
Michigan	18	Washington	18
Minnesota	18	West Virginia	18
Mississippi	21	Wisconsin	18
Missouri	18	Wyoming	18
Montana	18		

Recent studies have shown that JDCs are facing many of the same problems that the adult facilities are facing. Juvenile delinquents are coming in with serious health problems and mental illnesses that the facilities are not capable of handling. Research has found that most juvenile delinquents qualify for at least one diagnosable mental health disorder.[42] High rates of mental health issues have turned the juvenile detention centers from institutions meant to rehabilitate offenders into surrogate mental health facilities.[43] Thus, juvenile detention centers need to develop more programs to help deal with the mental health needs of juveniles.

JDCs are also facing increased scrutiny as they move from being state-run centers to being run by the private sector. In 2009, two judges in Pennsylvania were accused of receiving financial kickbacks from a privately run juvenile detention center for each juvenile that was sent to them. The scheme is alleged to have run from 2004 to 2009, and involved over 5,000 juveniles. The judges are alleged to have made over \$2 million in the scheme. In August 2011, one of the judges was sentenced to 28 years in prison for his role. Many of the juveniles who appeared before the judges appeared without counsel, despite the 1976 ruling in *In re Gault* that guaranteed juvenile offenders the right to counsel. Many were first-time offenders, and many had probation agents that recommended they not be sent to detention centers.[44] Despite this, the judges sent the offenders to the privately run facilities.[45] As a result of this scandal, more attention is being paid to who is running JDCs and how many juveniles are being sent to them.

Juvenile detention centers face many of the same problems as adult facilities.

Trends

Rates of juveniles in residential placement have fallen for more than a decade. In 2013, 173 juveniles per 100,000 population (54,000 total) were in residential placements, compared with 356 per 100,000 in 1997. The rate per 100,000 fell among whites, blacks, and Hispanics about equally (between 50 and 65 percent). (Figure 11.4) In that period, rates of residential placement for Asian youth fell the most (86 percent), while rates for American Indians fell the least (32 percent).97

FIGURE 11.4

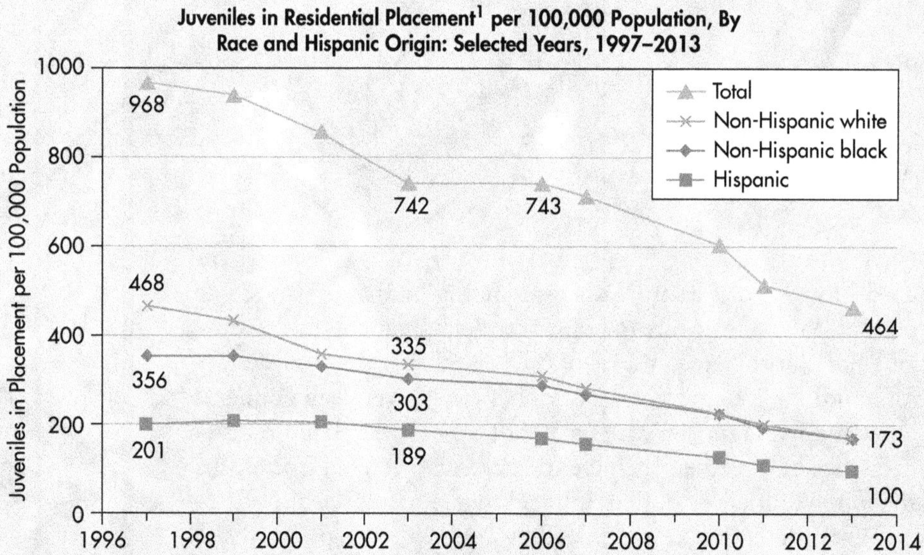

[1]The Census of Juveniles in Resudential Placement collects data from all juvenile residential custody facilities in the U.S., asking for information on each youth assigned a bed in the facility on the last Wednesday in October.
Rates are calculated per 100,000 juveniles ages 10 through the upper agre of each state's juvenile court jurisdiction.

Source: National Center for Juvenile Justice (2013). Easy access to the census of juveniles in residential placement 1997–2011, (online tool). Available at: http://www.ojjdp.gov/ojstatbb/ exacjrp/asp/selection.asp

Boot Camps and Scared-Straight Programs

During the "get tough" movement, crime deterrent programs such as boot camps and scared-straight programs gained popularity with the public. These programs were designed to "scare" juvenile offenders into behaving correctly.

Boot camp An alternative to juvenile correctional facilities that follows the model of a military basic-training program and is focused on disciplining juvenile offenders.

Boot camps are among the most well known of the alternative programs within the juvenile system. These camps follow the model of a military basic-training program and are focused on disciplining juvenile offenders.[46]

Boot camps pride themselves on their military structure. The goal is to "break" troubled juveniles and return them to their parents or guardians as obedient children. While attending boot camps, juvenile offenders are placed within small groups usually composed of other juvenile offenders. One suggested change to the boot camp model is that the boot camp population not be selected by judges, but instead by correctional officials who would select participants based on juveniles who have been sentenced to or already confined in a facility.[47] During his or her time in the program, the juvenile offender focuses on one or two skills instead of a wide range of skills more commonly seen in other programs like community-based programs.[48]

Boot camps do not look to coddle their participants. They believe that participants will benefit from hard work. Boot camps, unlike other programs, do not provide their participants with therapy or other rehabilitative programs.

Some evidence suggests that boot camps may be doing more harm than good. According to a report by the Surgeon General's Office, "Compared to traditional forms of incarceration, boot camps produced no significant effects on recidivism in three out of four evaluations and trends toward increased recidivism in two. The fourth evaluation showed significant harmful effects on youths, with a significant increase in recidivism."[49]

Scared-straight programs Programs designed to scare juveniles into behaving correctly, including boot camps and juveniles visiting inmates in prisons.

Scared-straight programs involve taking juvenile delinquents, or children who may be at risk of becoming delinquent, to adult prison facilities. Scared-straight programs are designed to give participants a firsthand view of prison life and allow them to interact with adult inmates, in the hope that it will deter them from future offending.[50] Scared-straight programs began in the 1970s in New Jersey.[51] The first scared-straight programs featured inmates who were serving life sentences telling juveniles about life in adult prison. The prisoners spared no details, and the juveniles were told stories of rape and murder.[52] These stories aimed to scare juveniles away from a life that would lead them to prison.

Despite reports of early success rates, questions have arisen as to the effectiveness of scared-straight programs. The University of Maryland published an evaluation of over 500 crime prevention programs and found evidence that scared-straight programs were not an effective crime deterrent.[53]

The study showed that juveniles' success in reentering the outside world depends more heavily upon their families, communities, and the labor market. Still, these programs remain in popular use all over the country and the world, in the hope of discouraging juveniles from continuing a downward spiral that will eventually land them in adult jails or prisons.

Death Penalty for Juveniles

Prior to 2005, seven states—Georgia, Louisiana, Missouri, Oklahoma, South Carolina, Texas, and Virginia—allowed for juveniles to be sentenced to death if they committed their crime prior to the age of majority. Most states did not. In 2005, the Supreme Court case of *Roper v. Simmons*[54] established a clear judgment on this issue.

The defendant, Christopher Simmons, was 17 years and three months old when he planned and committed a murder. On September 8, 1993, Simmons and one other friend entered the home of Mrs. Shirley Crook, bound her in duct tape, and drove her to a state park. Once there, Simmons and his co-defendant threw Mrs. Crook from a bridge and watched her drown.[55]

Simmons, who had begun bragging about the murder, was quickly found and taken into police custody. Upon confessing, Simmons was charged with burglary, kidnapping, stealing, and murder in the first degree. Simmons was charged as an adult, as under Missouri law a juvenile who has turned 17 must be charged as an adult.[56]

At trial, the jury found Simmons guilty of first-degree murder. At the sentencing stage, the state sought to prove three mitigating factors in order to sentence Simmons to death. First, that Simmons committed the murder for the purpose of receiving money. Next, that Simmons committed the murder to avoid or interfere with his lawful arrest. Finally, that the murder was the act of a depraved mind and was outrageously vile, horrible, and inhuman.[57] The jury found that the state had proved its aggravating factors and recommended a sentence of death. Upon their recommendation, the trial judge sentenced Simmons to death.

After his trial concluded and he was sentenced, Simmons appealed to the Missouri Supreme Court and cited the U.S. Supreme Court's decision in *Atkins v. Virginia,*[58] which held that it was a violation of the Eighth Amendment to sentence a mentally retarded person to death.[59] Simmons argued that the reasoning in *Atkins* applied to his case. The Missouri Supreme Court agreed and amended Simmons' sentence to life imprisonment without eligibility for parole, probation, or release unless by an act of the governor.[60]

The modified decision was appealed to the United States Supreme Court, which affirmed the new sentence. It held that no one who committed an offense under the age of 18 shall be put to death for that offense, because it violates the Eighth Amendment that prohibits cruel and unusual punishment.[61] The court focused on three important differences between juveniles and adults. The first was that juveniles tend to lack maturity and do not have a fully developed sense of responsibility, which leads to more poor decisions than in adults. Secondly, juveniles tend to have less control over their environments because they can be easily influenced by peer pressure and other negative influences. Finally, the court recognized that the character of a juvenile is not as well developed as it is in an adult.

The Supreme Court considered all of these factors and concluded that juveniles have **diminished culpability**, or the inability to fully understand the consequences of their actions. The court considered a juvenile's limited culpability to be similar to that of a mentally handicapped defendant. Using the same reasoning as in the *Atkins* decision, the court held that it would violate the cruel and unusual punishment clause to execute a juvenile who was under the age of 18 when the crime was committed.

Diminished culpability The inability to fully understand the consequences of an action because of age or cognitive abilities.

This ruling raises new questions for the death-penalty states. If a defendant who is found guilty of committing a murder or any other death-penalty-eligible offense was under the age of 18 at the time of the offense, what is the maximum punishment he or she should be eligible for? Many states have settled on the term of life without the possibility of parole, which means that a defendant will never have the opportunity to be eligible for a parole hearing.[62] A "life without parole" sentence, or LWOP, is different from a sentence of life with the possibility of parole. A "life with" sentence means that a defendant is eligible for parole, after serving a statutory number of years, and may petition the parole board for a parole hearing.

Critical Thinking

Do you believe that life without possibility of parole is an appropriate sentence for juveniles convicted of violent crimes?

Exhibit: *Roper v. Simmons*

"Three general differences between juveniles under 18 and adults demonstrate that juvenile offenders cannot with reliability be classified among the worst offenders. First, as any parent knows and as the scientific and sociological studies respondent and his *amici* cite tend to confirm, '[a] lack of maturity and an underdeveloped sense of responsibility are found in youth more often than in adults and are more understandable among the young. These qualities often result in impetuous and ill-considered actions and decisions.' . . .

The second area of difference is that juveniles are more vulnerable or susceptible to negative influences and outside pressures, including peer pressure. . . . This is explained in part by the prevailing circumstance that juveniles have less control, or less experience with control, over their own environment. . . .

The third broad difference is that the character of a juvenile is not as well formed as that of an adult. The personality traits of juveniles are more transitory, less fixed. . . .

These differences render suspect any conclusion that a juvenile falls among the worst offenders. The susceptibility of juveniles to immature and irresponsible behavior means 'their irresponsible conduct is not as morally reprehensible as that of an adult.' Their own vulnerability and comparative lack of control over their immediate surroundings mean juveniles have a greater claim than adults to be forgiven for failing to escape negative influences in their whole environment. The reality that juveniles still struggle to define their identity means it is less supportable to conclude that even a heinous crime committed by a juvenile is evidence of irretrievably depraved character. From a moral standpoint it would be misguided to equate the failings of a minor with those of an adult, for a greater possibility exists that a minor's character deficiencies will be reformed."

Problematic Issues in Juvenile Justice

In recent years, the public has grown increasingly concerned that the juvenile justice system is not working effectively enough.[63] The media constantly covers violent juvenile crime, and the public is calling for tougher punishment for juvenile offenders. The focus on the rise of gangs and drug and alcohol abuse has contributed to the public's panic, which is sometimes referred to as a **moral panic**.

Moral panic A term coined by Stanley Cohen describing the public's irrational fear and concern over a particular issue.

Stanley Cohen, a leading sociologist, coined the phrase "moral panic" in 1972 in his book *Folk Devils and Moral Panics*.[64] He focused on the media's help in causing a moral panic by portraying a group of people—in this instance, juveniles—as a threat to society's values. The media's portrayal of juvenile crime has led the public to believe that troubled youths are the downfall of society. One of the largest contributors to the moral panic is the media's coverage of extreme cases that include children killing children. Although these cases are very rare, the sensationalist way in which the media covers these crimes captures the nation's attention and often leads the public to believe that youth-on-youth violence and murder are more common than they actually are.

But while the public is calling for the juvenile justice system to crack down on violent juvenile offenders, many fail to realize or understand the complexities of the juvenile system. The juvenile system is currently experiencing many of the same problems as adult correctional facilities. Like adult correctional facilities, juvenile correctional facilities are struggling to provide mental health care so desperately needed by inmates. Juvenile correctional facilities have reported high levels of drug abuse. A survey conducted in 2000 found that nearly 56% of boys and 40% of the girls tested positive for drugs at the time of their arrest.[65] Some juvenile offenders are either a member of a gang prior to entering the juvenile system or are a member of a gang by the time they leave.[66]

Gangs

The Bloods, the Crips, and the Aryan Brotherhood are three of the most well-known gangs, but hundreds of others exist within jails, prisons, juvenile detention centers, and out on the street. An FBI investigation concluded, "Some 20,000 violent street gangs, motorcycle gangs, and prison gangs with nearly one million members are criminally active in the U.S. today. Many are sophisticated and well organized; all use violence to control neighborhoods and boost their illegal money-making activities, which include robbery, drug and gun trafficking, fraud, extortion, and prostitution rings."[67]

Gang members do not just commit violent crimes. Howell (1993) noted that "violent behavior is not the only behavior in which gang members partake. For the most part, gang members 'hang out' and are involved in other normal adolescent social activities, but drinking, drug use, and drug trafficking are also common."[68]

Gang presence, in addition to the streets, jails, prisons, and juvenile detention centers, is also active in schools. According to an August 2010 survey by the National Center on Addiction and Substance Abuse, 45% of high school students say that their school has gangs or students who consider themselves to be part of a gang. For middle school students, this number is 35%.[69]

As the presence of gangs in schools continues to grow, schools must adjust in order to reduce and prevent gang violence within the school. Two different approaches to preventing gangs from having a large presence in schools prevail.

One is the *whole-school approach*. Under the whole-school approach, schools set strict standards of behavior to ensure that gang-related activity is not present in schools. Staff members are trained to identify gang trends and to closely monitor known gang members. Students also must adhere to dress-code policies that forbid gang identifiers or paraphernalia.[70]

Another approach is the *individual gang intervention approach*. The individual gang intervention approach has many of the same aspects of the whole-school approach, but gives extra support to particular students known to be involved in gangs. Under this approach, staff members provide gang-involved students with specific skills and support to help them pull themselves away from gang life.[71]

State legislatures have also passed legislation in hopes of reducing gangs. Many have passed "anti-loitering" laws, which are primarily targeted at juveniles. *Anti-loitering laws* allow for police to break up or arrest groups of people, particularly teenagers, who are hanging out in front of storefronts and on street corners. The fear is that these teenagers are members of gangs and will somehow harm businesses.

Gang crime can include robbery and trafficking as well as violent crime.

Anti-loitering laws have come under scrutiny and some, like in Chicago, have been struck down as unconstitutional because they violate citizens' rights to gather on the streets. The right to peaceably assemble is guaranteed by the Constitution under the First Amendment.

Anti-loitering laws are not the only laws that are aimed at juveniles. Both Illinois and New Mexico enacted anti-sagging laws because the public associated low-slung pants with rap music, gangs, and other parts of society it disapproved of.[72] Other states have enacted laws that ban skateboarding because there is a perception that kids on skateboards will destroy property and cause trouble.

Many of these "tough on youth" policies and laws are fueled by moral panics and by the public's perception that certain juveniles are dangerous to society. The public's perception is in some cases shaped by sensationalist media stories on juvenile crime, which do not always provide an accurate portrait of what is actually happening. As a result, many citizens and lawmakers have developed a fear of youth that overestimates the prevalence and frequency of juvenile crime.

Searches in Schools

The rights of juveniles in schools is an important issue that has been heavily debated in the criminal justice system. What rights does a student have in school that protect him or her against a Fourth Amendment search or seizure? Do schools have to follow the same standards as police when conducting a search? The U.S. Supreme Court has attempted to answer these questions through a series of rulings.

In 1985, in *N.J. v. T.L.O.*, the Supreme Court held that, "under ordinary circumstances, a search of a student by a teacher or other school official will be 'justified at its inception' when there are reasonable grounds for suspecting that the search will turn up evidence that the student has violated or is violating either the law or the rules of the school."[73] This decision affirmed that schools can conduct searches based on reasonable suspicion because of the nature of the location. This is a different standard than the one that police must abide by. Police must have probable cause in order to conduct a search or a seizure.

The Supreme Court further clarified its position on searches within the school in 1995, in *Vernonia School District 47J v. Acton*, a case that dealt with urinalysis of student-athletes.[74] The court determined that conducting urinalysis on student-athletes was reasonable and not an invasion of privacy because student-athletes had been found to be the leaders of drug culture within the schools. The court found that this was reasonable and did not declare these urinalysis tests unconstitutional. However, in 2009, the court did find that a student's rights guaranteed under the Fourth Amendment were violated when she was subjected to a strip search because there was no reasonable suspicion to believe that she was hiding drugs in her underwear.[75]

Ethics and Professionalism: Searches in Schools

Consider this scenario. A school principal hears from a student that members of the school's lacrosse team are using drugs. What should the principal do? Does the information from one student qualify as reasonable suspicion sufficient enough to conduct a search of the lacrosse players' bags? Should she gather more information before conducting a search?

Consider a scenario in which the principal decides to search the lacrosse players' bags when they return to the school after playing an away game. As the players exit the team bus, the principal pulls each student aside and asks him to open his bag so that she may search it. After the search is complete, the principal has not found any drugs, but she has discovered that several members of the team are carrying Swiss Army knives. The boys claim that they have the Swiss Army knives because they are tools they use to fix their lacrosse sticks.

Swiss Army knives are classified as weapons under the school's policy, and the policy states that the principal must report all students who have weapons in their possession on school policy. Should the principal report the boys to the police? Should she be legally compelled to do so? What would you do?

Drugs and Alcohol

Drug use is an ever-present problem in today's society, and juveniles are no exception. Law enforcement agencies have increased their focus on drug crimes, launching undercover investigations to identify drug dealers who sell to minors. Legislatures have passed punitive laws against the use, possession, and sale of illegal drugs.[76]

In the 1970s, President Richard Nixon began America's "War on Drugs." The War on Drugs focuses on reducing the foreign and illegal drug trade with the hope of decreasing the use and production of drugs in America. Forty years after President Nixon began the U.S. government's War on Drugs and 50 years after the United Nations had its first conference on narcotics, the Global Commission on Drug Policy issued a report examining drug policies both nationally and internationally. In the report, the United Nations estimates that consumption of drugs from 1998 to 2008 has steadily increased and that the United States' War on Drugs has had little impact.[77] In 1998, 12.9 million people used opiates; this number grew to 17.35 million people in 2008, an increase of nearly 34.5%.[78] In that same time frame, cocaine use rose 27% and cannabis use rose 8.5%.[79]

Further, the commission compared the Dutch city of Amsterdam, famous for its cannabis cafes, to the U.S. city of San Francisco to see if different regulatory environments affected cannabis use.[80] The commission's report concluded, "Our findings do not support claims that criminalization reduces cannabis use and that decriminalization increases cannabis use . . . With the exception of higher drug use in San Francisco, we found strong similarities across both cities."[81]

Finally, the study concluded that "countries that continue to invest mostly in a law enforcement approach (despite the evidence) should focus their repressive actions on violent organized crime and drug traffickers, in order to reduce the harms associated with the illegal drug market."[82]

Drug Abuse Resistance Education (D.A.R.E.)
A program designed to keep kids off drugs by teaching children how to resist peer pressure and avoid drugs and violence.

Los Angeles, California, started the first **Drug Abuse Resistance Education (D.A.R.E.)** program in 1983 to help keep kids off of drugs. The D.A.R.E. program consists of police-officer-led classroom lessons that teach children how to avoid drugs and violence and resist peer pressure. Shortly after the D.A.R.E. program began in 1983, First Lady Nancy Reagan released the "Just Say No" slogan. The slogan was designed to encourage juveniles to just say no to drugs and peer pressure.

Nearly 75% of schools in America have a D.A.R.E. program, but despite its popularity, D.A.R.E. has proven to be counterproductive. Many studies have shown that D.A.R.E. has little lasting impact. Some have even shown higher drug use among suburban youths who had graduated from a D.A.R.E. program. A report by the U.S. Government Accountability Office stated, "In brief, the six long-term evaluations of the D.A.R.E. elementary school curriculum that we reviewed found no significant differences in illicit drug use between students who received D.A.R.E. in the fifth or sixth grade (the intervention group) and students who did not (the control group.)"[83] The report looked at six major evaluations done on the effectiveness of D.A.R.E. Two of the evaluations showed that "D.A.R.E. students showed stronger negative attitudes about illicit drug use and improved peer pressure resistance skills and self-esteem about illicit drug use about 1 year after the intervention. These positive effects diminish over time."[84]

A 2009 National Youth Risk Behavior Survey Overview measured the drug and alcohol use of both male and female juveniles and reported that "72% of students had at least one drink of alcohol on at least 1 day during their life and 41.8% of students had at least one drink of alcohol on at least 1 day during the 30 days before the survey," and "24.2% of students had had five or more drinks of alcohol in a row (i.e., within a couple of hours) on at least 1 day during the 30 days before the survey."[85] Further, it reported that in the 30 days before the survey, 4.5% of students had drunk alcohol on school property.[86]

The same survey, in reporting on drug use, showed that more students used marijuana than any other drug, as "36.8% of students had used marijuana one or more times in their life" and "20.8% of students had used marijuana one or more times during the 30 days before the survey."[87]

Still, despite these somewhat alarming numbers, drug use among juveniles has gone down. In 2009, the national Youth Risk Behavior Survey released a study entitled *Trends in the Prevalence of Marijuana, Cocaine, and Other Illegal Drug Use (1991–2009)*. The survey showed that from 1999–2009, marijuana use among high school students decreased, as did the use of cocaine and other methamphetamines.[88]

School Violence and Bullying

On April 20, 1999, in Columbine, Colorado, high school students Eric Harris and Dylan Kelbold shot and killed 12 students and one teacher and injured 24 other students before committing suicide at Columbine High School. This incident rocked the nation and made parents across the country question whether schools were really the safest place for children. In 2007, the nation was rocked again when a Virginia Tech student, Seung-Hui Cho, killed 32 people and injured 25 more.

These incidents have led to a greater focus on school violence and school bullying. It is important to note that these extreme examples of school violence are incredibly rare, and that schools in general are safe places for children to be. However, nonviolent examples of bullying can be a problem. Bullying exists at every level of life, from a kid on the playground to a boss in the workplace. One survey showed that approximately 160,000 students leave school early every day because they are afraid of being bullied.[89] Nearly 15% of all students who miss school on any given day do so because they fear being bullied.[90]

With the prominence of Facebook, text messaging, and YouTube, a new form of bullying called "cyberbullying" has emerged. Cyberbullying occurs outside of the classroom and can be done from behind closed doors and not face to face. Cyberbullying occurs when a disparaging remark about someone is spread through electronic means. It can occur through text messages, blogs, personal web pages, emails, cyberstalking, etc.

Regulation and punishment of cyberbullying can be a difficult task. For the most part, cyberbullying takes place outside of the traditional school setting, and it becomes very hard for schools to intervene.[91] Schools that attempt to discipline a student for cyberbullying actions that take place outside of school property and school hours can be sued for exceeding their authority and violating the student's right to free speech.[92] When schools are unable to address the issue, the criminal justice system can step in if the level of harassment rises to a criminal level.

For instance, in September 2010, a Rutgers University freshman, Tyler Clementi, committed suicide after his roommate and his roommate's friend secretly filmed him and a partner having sex and broadcast it on the Internet. The roommate, Dharun Ravi, and friend Molly Wei both faced criminal charges for invasion of privacy for secretly filming Clementi without his or his partner's permission. In May 2011, Wei entered into a plea deal with the prosecution. In exchange for charges against her to be dropped, she had to enter into a pretrial intervention program, perform 300 hours of community service, testify at any proceeding, participate in counseling to deter cyberbullying, and cooperate with authorities.[93] In March 2012, Ravi was tried and convicted for his role. He was sentenced to 30 days in jail, 3 years probation, 300 hours of community service, a $10,000 fine, and counseling on bullying and alternative lifestyles.[94]

Phoebe Prince, an Irish immigrant to the United States, committed suicide in January 2010 after enduring cyberbullying and bullying from classmates. After her death, nine students were charged with a range of felony crimes and have since pleaded to misdemeanors.[95]

Chapter Summary

- Beginning in 1966 with *Kent v. United States*, and continuing with *Roper v. Simmons*, the United States Supreme Court has issued opinions that change and mold the juvenile system and how juveniles are treated within both the juvenile and adult systems. *Kent*, the first of the decisions, gave juveniles some rights under the due process clause. *In re Gault* and *In re Winship* further solidified juveniles' due process rights, while *Simmons* established that juveniles who committed death-penalty-eligible offenses while under the age of 18 could not be executed for their crimes.
- The concept of what a child is has evolved over time. Children have evolved from being treated as little adults or as the property of their parents to being treated as a distinct class that has its own understandings and limitations. The emergence of adolescence as a distinct time period within a human life helped lead to the formation of the juvenile court system.
- The juvenile court system was first implemented in 1899, in Cook County, Illinois. The juvenile court system first sought to rehabilitate juveniles, but as time went on, the emergence of a "get tough" movement and deinstitutionalization movement moved the juvenile courts away from rehabilitation and into punishment.
- Juvenile courts and adult criminal courts have some similarities and differences. Juvenile courts deal with all juveniles under the state's mandatory age, but these offenders can, after a juvenile waiver hearing, be waived into the adult criminal court. Juvenile courts do not find defendants guilty or not guilty, but rather delinquent or not delinquent. Defendants in adult criminal courts are found guilty or not guilty. In both courts, the state has the burden to prove the defendant's guilt or delinquency beyond a reasonable doubt.
- Probation is a tool used by both juvenile and adult criminal courts as a way to monitor the defendant's behavior. Juvenile defendants can be placed on probation prior to adjudication; after they have gone through the adjudication process and been given a suspended sentence; or after serving part of their sentence.
- The late 19th and early 20th century Child Savers movement can be directly linked to many of the changes that occurred to form a juvenile system. The Child Savers movement was an early form of state intervention and represented an early form of *parens patrie.* Houses of refuge and cottage reformatories were the early versions of juvenile detention facilities.

- Problematic issues still face the juvenile justice system today. The media's focus on crimes committed by juveniles has caused a moral panic in society despite the fact that juveniles commit just a small percentage of all crimes. Providing further issues for the juvenile justice system is the strong presence of gangs within schools and the community.

Critical Thinking?

1. What differences do you see between a finding of guilt and a finding of delinquency?
2. Should the juvenile court systems rid themselves of status offenses so that they can spend more time focusing on violent offenders?
3. What are some of the major differences between the juvenile courts and the adult criminal courts?
4. Do you think that placing juvenile offenders on probation is a good way to monitor defendants?
5. Do you think that community-based corrections produce results or are a waste?
6. Should there be a minimum age before the court can consider housing a juvenile defendant within an adult correctional facility? Should a juvenile ever be housed in an adult correctional facility?
7. Do you believe boot camps and scared-straight programs are effective? Why or why not?
8. Do you think that the Supreme Court was right, in *Simmons*, when it decided that anyone who committed a death-penalty-eligible offense under the age of 18 could not be subject to the death penalty?
9. What are the major problems you see facing the juvenile justice system today?
10. Should the juvenile justice system focus on rehabilitation or retribution/punishment?

Media

Office of Juvenile Justice and Delinquency Prevention: http://www.ojjdp.gov
The Office of Juvenile Justice and Delinquency Prevention is tasked with trying to improve juvenile justice policies and practices.

U.S. Department of Education, Office of Safe and Drug-Free Schools: http://www2.ed.gov/about/offices/list/osdfs/index.html
The Office of Safe and Drug-Free Schools helps to implement programs within the school system that relate to drug and violence prevention and promote the general well-being of students.

Additionally, this organization provides the financial assistance needed for these programs.

The Coalition for Juvenile Justice: http://www.juvjustice.org
The Coalition for Juvenile Justice is a group of volunteers devoted to helping juveniles who have been accused within the juvenile justice system. The coalition makes sure that juveniles are treated with care.

National Council on Crime and Delinquency: http://www.nccdglobal.org/
By applying research to policy and practice, the National Council on Crime and Delinquency has helped to advise on and design reforms within the juvenile justice system.

Centers for Disease Control and Prevention's (CDC) Striving to Reduce Youth Violence Everywhere (STRYVE): http://www.safeyouth.gov/pages/home.aspx
This group takes a public health approach to preventing youth violence.

Annie E. Casey Foundation: http://www.aecf.org
This is a private organization founded by Jim Casey, the founder of UPS, to provide grants to organizations that help to meet the needs of vulnerable children and their families.

National Youth Court Center: http://www.youthcourt.net
The National Youth Court Center is a central location for information about all youth courts. In youth courts, juveniles who are charged with minor delinquencies and status offenses are sentenced by their peers, who serve as judges, bailiffs, and attorneys.

Endnotes

1 *Kent v. United States*, 383 U.S. 541 (1966).

2 Office of Juvenile Justice and Delinquency Prevention. (2011). "Juvenile Arrest Rate Trends." *Statistical Briefing Book.* Retrieved from http://www.ojjdp.gov/ojstatbb/crime/JAR_Display.asp?ID=qa05200

3 Ibid.

4 Steinhart, D. J. (1996). "Status Offenses, The Future of Children." *The Juvenile Court, 6*(3). Retrieved from http://futureofchildren.org/futureofchildren/publications/journals/article/index.xml?journalid=55&articleid=316

6 Ibid.

7 *Monitoring the Future.* (2011). Retrieved from http://monitoringthefuture.org/

8 ABA, Division for Public Education, Part 1: The History of Juvenile Justice.

9 *Meyers v. State of Nebraska*, 262 U.S. 390 (1923).

10 *Prince v. Commonwealth of Massachusetts*, 321 U.S. 158 (1944).

11 Frontline. (2011). *Child or Adult? A Century Long View.* Retrieved from http://www.pbs.org/wgbh/pages/frontline/shows/juvenile/stats/childadult.html

12 Ehrlich, J. S. (2003). "Shifting Boundaries: Abortion, Criminal Culpability and the Indeterminate Legal Status of Adolescents." *Wisconsin Women's Law Journal, 18*, 77–116.

13 Klein, E. K. (1998). "Dennis the Menace or Billy the Kid: An Analysis of the Role of Transfer to Criminal Court in Juvenile Justice." *American Criminal Law Review, 35*, 371–410.

14 *National Orphan Train Complex.* (2011). Retrieved from http://www.orphantraindepot.com

15 The Children's Aid Society. (n.d.). *History.* Retrieved from http://www.childrensaidsociety.org/about/history

16 Ibid.

17 New York State Archives. (n.d.). *New York House of Refuge.* http://www.archives.nysed.gov/a/research/res_topics_ed_reform_history.shtml

18 Ibid.

19 Price, J. R. (2009, Spring). "Birthing Out Delinquents: Alternative Treatment Options for Juvenile Delinquents." *Criminal Law Brief*, 51–57.

20 Ibid.

21 Ibid.

22 Brink, D. O. (2004). "Immaturity, Normative Competence, and Juvenile Transfer: How (Not) to Punish Minors for Major Crimes." *Texas Law Review, 82*, 1555–1585.

23 Klein, 1998, 373.

24 Ibid., 374.

25 *Breed v. Jones*, 421 U.S. 519 (1975).

26 *In re Gault*, 387 U.S. 1 (1967).

27 Ibid., 4.

28 Ibid., 33.

29 Ibid., 41.

30 Ibid., 55.

31 *In re Winship*, 397 US 358 (1970).

32 Ibid.

33 Juvenile Justice and Delinquency Prevention Act of 1974, Pub. L. No. 93-415.

34 42 U.S.C. 5601.

35 Weithorn, L. A. (2005, Summer). "Envisioning Second-Order Change in America's Responses to Troubled and Troublesome Youth." *Hofstra Law Review, 33*, 1305–1506.

36 Holden, G. A., & Kapler, R. A. (1995). "Deinstitutionalizing Status Offenders: A Record of Progress." *Juvenile Justice, 2*(2), 3–10.

37 *Black's Law Dictionary* (4th ed.).

38 Torbet, P. M. (1996). *Juvenile Probation: The Workhorse of the Juvenile Justice System*. Washington, D.C.: U.S. Department of Justice.

39 *Diversionary Programs: An Overview.* (1999). Retrieved from https://www.ncjrs.gov/html/ojjdp/9909-3/div.html

40 http://www.bls.gov/oes/current/oes211092.htm#ind PayScale, Human Capital. Retrieved from http://www.payscale.com/research/US/Job=Probation_Officer_or_Correctional_Treatment_Specialist/Salary

41 42 U.S.C. 5603 §103(1).

42 *Prevalence of Mental Health Disorders Among Youth: Youth With Mental Health Disorders: Issues and Emerging Responses.* (2000). Retrieved from https://www.ncjrs.gov/html/ojjdp/jjjnl_2000_4/youth_2.html

43. Ibid.

44 Associated Press. (2009). "Pa. Judges Accused of Jailing Kids for Cash." *MSNBC.* Retrieved from http://www.msnbcmsn.com/id/29142654/ns/us_news-crime_and_courts/t/pa-judges-accused-jailing-kids-cash/#.TkiWhr_gVys

45 Ibid.

46 Mental Health America. (2011). *Juvenile Boot Camps.* Retrieved from http://www.nmha.org/go/boot-camps

47 Office of Juvenile Justice and Delinquency Prevention. (1997). *Boot Camps for Juvenile Offenders*, 4.

48 Ibid., 8.

49 Surgeon General's Office. (n.d.). "Chapter 5: Ineffective Tertiary Programs and Strategies." *Youth Violence: A Report of the Surgeon General.* Retrieved from http://www.surgeongeneral.gov/library/youthviolence/chapter5/sec6.html

50 Petrosino, A., Turpin-Petrosino, C., & Buehler, J. (2003, November). "'Scared Straight' and Other Juvenile Awareness Programs for Preventing Juvenile Delinquency." In *The Campbell Collaboration Reviews of Intervention and Policy Evaluations (C2-RIPE).* Philadelphia, PA: Campbell Collaboration.

51 Ibid., 4.

52 Ibid.

53 Sherman, L. W., Gottfredson, D., MacKenzie, D. L., Eck, J., Reuter, P., & Bushway, S. (1997). *Preventing Crime: What Works, What Doesn't, What's Promising. A Report to the United States Congress.* College Park, MD: University of Maryland.

54 *Roper v. Simmons*, 543 U.S. 551 (2005).

55 Ibid.

56 *Miranda v. Arizona*, 384 U.S. 436 (1966).

57 *Roper v. Simmons*, 2005.

58 *Atkins v. Virginia*, 536 U.S. 304 (2002).

59 *Roper v. Simmons*, 2005.

60 Ibid.

61 Ibid.

62 *Death Penalty Information Center.* (2011). Retrieved from http://www.deathpenaltyinfo.org

63 McLatchey, S. F. (1999). "Media Access to Juvenile Records: In Search of a Solution." *Georgia State University Law Review, 16*(2), 337–359.

64 Cohen, S. (2002). *Folk Devils and Moral Panics: The Creation of the Mods and Rockers.* New York, NY: Routledge.

65 *Principles of Drug Abuse Treatment for Criminal Justice Populations: A Research-Based Guide*, 13.

66 Howell, J. C. (1998, August). *Youth Gangs: An Overview.* Washington, D.C.: U.S. Department of Justice.

67 Federal Bureau of Investigation. (2011). *Gangs.* Retrieved from http://www.fbi.gov/about-us/investigate/vc_majorthefts/gangs/gangs

68 Howell, 1998, 8.

69 Howell, J. C., & Moore, J. P. (2010). *National Gang Center Bulletin: History of Street Gangs.* 1–25.

70 Ibid., 4.

71 Ibid.

72 Garrison, C. (2011, July 12). "Collinsville Mayor Apologizes for City's New Anti-Sagging Law, Calls It a 'Step Backward.'" *Riverfront Times.* Retrieved from http://blogs.riverfronttimes.com/dailyrft/2011/07/collinsville_sagging_law_mayor_apology.php

73 *New Jersey v. T.L.O.*, 469 U.S. 325, 341-342 (1985).

74 *Vernonia School District 47J v. Acton, et ux., etc.*, 515 U.S. 646 (1995).

75 *Safford Unified School District #1 v. Redding*, 557 U.S. ___ (2009).

76 Belenko, S. (2000). "The Challenges of Integrating Drug Treatment into the Criminal Justice Process." *Albany Law Review, 3*(3), 833–876.

77 Global Commission on Drug Policy. (2011). *War on Drugs: Report of the Global Commission on Drug Policy.*

78 Ibid.

79 Ibid.

80 Ibid., 10.

81 Ibid.

82 Ibid., 14.

83 U.S. General Accounting Office. (2003, January 15). *Letter to Senator Richard Durbin.* Retrieved from http://www.gao.gov/new.items/d03172r.pdf

84 Ibid.

85 Centers for Disease Control and Prevention. (2011). *YRBSS in Brief.* Retrieved from http://www.cdc.gov/healthyyouth/yrbs/brief.htm

86 Ibid.

87 Ibid.

88 Centers for Disease Control and Prevention. (2010). "Alcohol & Drug Use." *Healthy Youth!* Retrieved from http://www.cdc.gov/healthyyouth/alcoholdrug/index.htm

89 Bullying Statistics. (n.d.). *Bullying Statistics 2010.* Retrieved from http://www.bullyingstatistics.org/content/bullying-statistics-2010.html

90 Ibid.

91 *Stop Cyberbullying.* (n.d.). Retrieved from http://www.stopcyberbullying.org/prevention/schools_role.html

92 Ibid.

93 Schweber, N. (2011, May 7). "In Fallout of Suicide by Student, a Plea Deal." *The New York Times.* Retrieved from http://www.nytimes.com/2011/05/07/nyregion/in-rutgers-suicide-case-ex-student-gets-plea-deal.html

94 DeMarco, M. and Friedman, A. (2012, May 21). "Dharun Ravi Sentenced to 30 Days in Jail." *The Star-Ledger.* Retrieved from http://www.nj.com/news/index.ssf/2012/05/dharun_ravi_sentenced_for_bias.html

95 Lavoie, D. (2011, April 27). "5 Teens Strike Plea Deal in Phoebe Prince Bullying Case." *The Huffington Post.* Retrieved from http://www.huffingtonpost.com/2011/04/27/phoebe-prince-bullying-case_n_854446.html

96 Sickmund, M. & Puzzanchera, C. (2014). *Juvenile Offenders and Victims:* 2014 National Report. National Center for Juvenile Justice. December 2014.

97 Child Trends, Data Bank. *Juvenile Detention: Indicators on Children and Youth.* December 2015. Retrieved from https://www.childtrends.org/wp-content/uploads/2012/05/88_Juvenile_Detention.pdf.

98 Hockenberry, S. (2016). *Juveniles in Residential Placement, 2013.* Juvenile Justice Statistics. National Report Series Bulletin. Office of Juvenile Justice and Delinquency Prevention.

www.ingramcontent.com/pod-product-compliance
Lightning Source LLC
LaVergne TN
LVHW082053230525
811723LV00013B/6